The Life of the

Virgin Mary,

the Theotokos

THE LIFE OF THE VIRGIN MARY, THE THEOTOKOS

viewed and treated within the framework of
Sacred Scriptures,
Holy Tradition,
Patristics and other ancient writings,
together with the Liturgical and Iconographic Traditions
of the Holy Orthodox Church

Written and Compiled

by

HOLY APOSTLES CONVENT
16975 Highway 306
Buena Vista, Colorado 81211

O Theotokos, thou hope of all Christians,
protect, watch over, and guard all them
that put their hope in thee.

Matins Canon of Meeting (2 Feb),
Ode Nine, Tone Three by
St. Cosmas the Poet, Bishop of Maiouma

THE LIFE OF THE

VIRGIN MARY,

THE THEOTOKOS

Published by

HOLY APOSTLES CONVENT
and
DORMITION SKETE
Buena Vista, Colorado 81211

1989

Printed in the United States of America

Printed with the blessing of
His Grace, ALYPY,
Bishop of Chicago and Detroit and Middle America
RUSSIAN ORTHODOX CHURCH
OUTSIDE OF RUSSIA

Library of Congress Catalog Number:
89-081686

ISBN 0-944359-03-5

First printed, February 1990
Reprinted, August 1990

Iconography and Art Design, Courtesy of Dormition Skete

PREFACE

*In the Name of the Father, and of the Son,
and of the Holy Spirit. Amen.*

ABOUT THIS BOOK

Saint Ambrose (339-397), Bishop of Milan, wrote that "Mary's life, is a rule of life for all."[1] Mary Theotokos was to become an icon of the renewed Church. The following accounts narrated in this book will include all the important events in the life and times of the Virgin-Mother, from her Conception to her Dormition and bodily translation. Each chapter of her dedicated and sublime life will be viewed and treated within the framework of Sacred Scriptures and Holy Tradition; patristics and ancient writings; and the liturgical and iconographic traditions of the Holy Orthodox Church.

We shall read about the Virgin Mary as an infant, a toddler, a young girl growing into early womanhood, and her betrothal and motherhood as an adolescent. We shall delve into her family and background and those people and places that shaped her life. We shall peer into her thoughts, pastimes and activities that were wholly dedicated to God. We shall contemplate her eminent place in the incarnation of the God-Man, Jesus. Then we shall follow her perilous and uncomfortable flight into Egypt with the infant Christ, the aged Joseph and the young James. A map of Egypt has been included, designed to help the reader visualize the geographic setting of the cities and places mentioned. After that, we shall look over the life and routine of a Hebrew mother and her family. At middle age, the concerns and the role of the Theotokos during her Son's ministry will be investigated. Then a close study will be made of her thoughts, conversations and actions during the betrayal, scourging, mocking, death and resurrection of her Son and God.

We shall examine her position and labors in the early Church and her relationship to her Son's disciples and close associates, both male and female. We shall explore where she traveled and the extent of her participation in the spreading of the Gospel. On the other hand, we shall also discover how certain of the Jews attempted to slander her fair reputation with clumsy fabrications and even sought to slay her. We shall then touch upon her latter days and then devote our attention to her august repose and bodily translation. After this a comparative study will follow wherein we shall discuss Mary Theotokos and the Church. Finally, we shall comment on the Theotokos as our Mediatress, all within the context of Holy Orthodox Tradition.

It is important that as Orthodox Christians we know and examine the life of the Theotokos who, after Christ Jesus, so influenced every creature, both the bodiless ones and the earthborn, before, during and after her earthly sojourn.

SCRIPTURES AND ANCIENT WRITINGS

With the exception of St. Paul, all the writers of the New Testament were eyewitnesses to the words and deeds of Christ. Until the Gospels, Epistles, *Acts of the Apostles* and the *Apocalypse* were written, the early Christian community abided by "oral tradition." Saint John Chrysostom (354-407) writes that this tradition of the Church is passed on not only in written documents, but in unwritten form.[2] After the holy Apostles were directly instructed by the Lord, they, in turn, appointed others to perpetuate these traditions.

It would not be until the fourth century that the twenty-seven canonical books of the New Testament were officially compiled and distributed in one collection. Thus for many generations the Christians lived by the authority of oral tradition and the writings of the early Fathers. Although the complete theme of the Theotokos has not been left to us in writing as part of the apostolic preaching, yet the mystery of Christ's Mother was always revealed to the children of the Church. The mystery then gradually blossomed in Orthodox Tradition, sacred arts and the hymnography of the Church. Some of the earliest holy men whom we have quoted herein are St. Ignatios of Antioch (c.110), St. Justin Martyr (c.100-c.165), St. Irenaeus of Lyons (+c.193) and St. Hippolytos (c.170-236), and we have continued to present extracts of other righteous ones, up to these latter times.

This book will present extracts of writings of the great Orthodox hierarchs, confessors, ascetics and hymnographers concerning the Theotokos and Ever-Virgin Mary. Their teachings, purity of doctrine and holiness of life have been lauded by the Church. Thus these "Doctors" of the Church are in a sense teachers, who open up the mysteries of Faith. They did not compose the Scriptures, but dedicated themselves to their interpretation in homilies, treatises and hymns to promote and defend the Orthodox veneration of the Mother of God.

Although patristic literature is considered the basis for explaining and commenting on the Holy Bible, yet other ancient writings will contain some sources of Christian truths. Orthodox patristic literature, hymnography and iconography are the indispensable depositories and custodians of the truths and traditions concerning the teaching on the Virgin-Mother. Thus one may learn the Christian truths recorded in the Bible, by the interpretation and expositions of the patristic writings, and through the sacred arts of hymnography and iconography.

Saint Paul writes: "Stand fast, and hold the traditions which ye have been taught" [2 Thess. 2:15]. The growth of tradition occurs not in the teachings of the Church, but in their form; that is, it is expressed in different ways through the course of ecclesiastical history in different places. This tradition comprises the experience of the saints. It is an experience that has grown rich during the past two millennia. It is a rich and immense storehouse of wisdom and proofs of every truth in Holy Scripture. We must not cast aside or consider as a secondary source all the wisdom, proofs and experience of the saints.

We shall also review many inspired writings and learn how the influence of the Holy Spirit came upon the saints of the Old and New Testaments. These God-bearers sought to serve God as special vessels of grace. They were constant in prayer and became dwelling-places of God. Thus, they were enlightened and anointed by God to prophesy, to teach, to compose hymns and to paint holy icons for the edification of the Church.

In the Gospels, details are often scanty or even absent from Christ's early life. But the purpose of the Evangelists was not to furnish a detailed biography of Jesus Christ, much less that of the Virgin-Mother. This was their object: that those who read them might believe that Jesus is the Christ, the Son of God, and that believing they might have life through His name.

A venerable monastic historian, Bede (c.673-735), makes the following valuable comment: "Luke omits that which he knew was already sufficiently recorded by Matthew.

Individually the Evangelists were wont to omit certain things, which they knew to be recorded by others, or which they foresaw in the Spirit would be recorded by others, so that in the continuous thread of their narration nothing seems omitted. What has thus been passed over in one Gospel, the diligent reader will discover by carefully going through the other Gospels in turn."[3]

As we shall see in the present volume, faith in Christ cannot exclude His Mother, for she was the summit of Old Testament sanctity. Passages referring to the Virgin Mary occur in the literature of apologetics from the second century, as in the works of Saints Justin and Irenaeus. She was the mirror of the prophecies and the happy outcome of them all. As St. John of Damascus wrote: "the whole mystery of the divine economy is personified in her."[4]

Apart from two or three exceptions, so noted, we have used the *Septuagint*, or Greek version of the Old Testament which was the work of seventy or seventy-two scholars, many of whom were Alexandrian Jews. With few exceptions, the books of the New Testament abound in references to the Old Testament and in quotations from the *Septuagint*.[5]

THE PURPOSE OF HYMNOGRAPHY

Theological testimony finds great expression in the hymns of the Church. The soul of the Orthodox hymnographer must possess real piety, humility, inner wakefulness and understanding. God-inspired, the hymnographer is flooded with boundless love of God, exultation and gratefulness. Ecclesiastical poetry is a great gift of God to the Church. Saint Symeon the New Theologian says, "Every prayer and psalmody is a conversation with God in which we entreat Him to give us those things which are proper for God to give men, or we thank Him for His gifts, or we glorify Him for all the creatures which He has made, or we narrate His wonderful and timely deeds for the salvation of men and the punishment of the unrighteous, or we narrate the great mystery of the incarnation of the Son and Logos of God, and the like." Some hymns unequivocally declare the great dogmatic truths, others the love of God, and others place our pain, problems and aspirations before God and His saints. They have survived because they express Truth, therefore, their messages are always timely and eternal. They are also messages of victory and the resurrection.[6]

Some of Orthodoxy's Hymnographers

Among our elect list of hymnographers from whom we have cited, we will make use of the works are St. Andrew of Jerusalem and Bishop of Crete (c.660-740), St. Cosmas the Poet and Bishop of Maiouma (6th-7th c.), St. John the Damascene (c.675-c.750), St. Stephen of the Holy City (8th c.), and St. Theophanes the Poet and Bishop of Nicaea (+1381). The lives, beliefs and hopes of many of these saints are to be found in our Volume 3, *The Lives of the Saints of the Holy Land and the Sinai Desert.*

Other ancient hymn writers that were outside the area of Palestine, whom we have enrolled to enhance and amplify our narratives, will include St. Cassiane the Nun (9th c.), St. George the Bishop of Nicomedia (+c.880), St. Germanos the Patriarch of Constantinople (c.653-733), St. John Mavropous the Metropolitan of Euchaites (+1079), St. Joseph the Hymnographer (+883), St. Theodore the Studite (c.759-826), Anatolios, Andrew of Pyros (9th c.), Basil the Monk (10th c.), Byzas and Leo the Master.

We owe a special debt of gratitude to the two Syrian masters of chant: St. Ephraim the Syrian (Syros) (c.306-373) and St. Romanos the Melodist (c.490-c.556). To understand more about the development of certain forms of hymnography, we will briefly explain the role that each of these inspired deacons played.

Saint Ephraim the Syrian

The poet, St. Ephraim the Syrian, combined an astonishing technical artistry with a richness of imagery. Throughout his homilies he displays that characteristic Semitic love of parallelism and antithesis which, in his hands, proves an admirable tool for expressing the various paradoxes of the Christian mystery. His attitude and treatment of the Bible are grace-filled, creative and inspired.

It is generally believed that the Syrian *soughitha* (dramatic verses) was the precursor of Byzantine dramatic and semi-dramatic homilies. The *soughitha*, part of the religious literature developed in Syria, also effected the writings of St. Romanos. They were sung antiphonically into which biblical episodes were introduced in the form of dialogues. They were sometimes written in strophes and attached to homilies; during religious festivals they were sung by choirs and often contained dialogue and an acrostic.

The *madrascha* (metrical sermon) were performed by a chorus. The complicated system of strophes found in the *madrascha* represent the highest development of St. Ephraim Syros' technique. These always had a refrain, but not always an acrostic, which revealed a wider variety of meter, a refrain, an acrostic and rhyme.[7]

Saint Romanos the Melodist

Saint Romanos, one of the greatest of the Byzantine melodists and Christian poets, authored about one thousand kontakia. He belonged to the sixth century and exceeds all others in poetical genius and justly deserves the title "orator of God" *(theo-rhetor)*. Much literature of that time has been neglected and scorned because of the long compendia and overly contrived verbosity that characterized the works of later centuries. However, St. Romanos combines the solemnity and dignity of the sermon with the delicacy and liveliness of lyric and dramatic poetry. English literature contains no equivalent of the kontakion (sing.) It is religious drama set in a poetic sermon that was sung.

It contained highly dramatic features with dialogue passing from strophe to strophe. Saint Romanos, interestingly enough, did not call his compositions of rhythmical poetry kontakia (pl.), but poems, odes, or hymns. The word kontakion, probably

derived from *kontos* (which was the shaft on which the parchment of a scroll was stretched), came into use in the ninth century.[8]

Hymns that Amplify the Gospel Narratives

Thus, we shall see that there was a widespread tradition in Byzantine literature that cast certain feasts in semi-dramatic form; a technique which many God-inspired hymnographers would employ. Those familiar with Orthodox hymnography are aware of the poetical hymns related to the Theotokos at the Cross, known as the *Stavrotheotokia*. Within these hymns, we may hear a dialogue between the Virgin and her crucified Son. The various Matins *Lamentations* that we use on Great and Holy Saturday, still in ecclesiastical usage today, also contain purely rhetorical dialogues.

It was St. Romanos, in particular, who attempted to add to his religious dramatizations the qualities of intuitive sympathy and imaginative perception. This might especially be seen in the Feast of the Annunciation when, not only St. Romanos, but other holy Fathers, such as St. Germanos and St. John of Damascus, employ this same literary technique of creating dialogues which are purely rhetorical in character, yet dogmatical. Throughout our book we present examples from both the sermons of the Fathers and the philological monuments to be found in our Orthodox service books. Thus, our readers will experience the rich poetic prose that serves to amplify Gospel narratives, all within the tradition of Orthodoxy.

Unless otherwise specified, hymns will be presented *italicized* in the present volume.

USE OF APOCRYPHAL CHRISTIAN LITERATURE

Little is known of the background of the most important woman in the New Testament and of all time--the *Theotokos* (God-birthgiver), the *Panagia* (All-holy one), *Meeter Theou* (Mother of God) and *A-ee Parthenos* (Ever-Virgin) Mary, who is more honorable than the Cherubim and incomparably more glorious than the Seraphim. She was deemed to be the gateway through whom the eternal Logos, the Word of God, entered the age of man: "The Word was made flesh, and dwelt among us..." [Jn. 1:14]. We hope to portray the profound attractiveness of her personality that was endowed with all the virtues, so that all may be inspired by its radiant loveliness, and that with pure minds we may honor the pure Lady, the beauty and excellency of Jacob. What is known about her background is to be found in the

Holy Gospels, the *Acts of the Apostles*, and only those portions of various apocryphal accounts which have, in part, been accepted by the Church.

Apocryphal manuscripts describe her as an innocent child, making her role awesome and wondrous. Their very delicate treatment of the figure of Mary contributes to her warm and mysterious presence.

The apocryphal books are a group of disparate writings on biblical subjects that had appeared in the age of the New Testament or within memory of it, yet they have been excluded from the canonical writings. The character of most of the material is such that its historical reliability cannot be substantiated. Popular curiosity does much to account for their existence. The oldest and most famous of the infancy Gospels is the *Protoevangelium of James*, which clearly glorifies Mary. It was to have a significant influence on later developments in the history of Mariology.

Many of the apocryphal stories are fantastic legends that went against the simplicity of the Gospels. Most of these stories have been rejected by the Church as having been corrupted and distorted by the Gnostics, Manicheans and other heretical sects.

However, in several instances the holy Fathers of the Church, together with the hymnographers and the iconographers--with great spiritual discernment--borrowed from and expanded certain episodes within the *Apocrypha*. They believed that these accounts, like buried pearls, were valid and edifying, and, having incorporated them into their writings, these accounts have become part of the ancient Tradition.

There is above all, the *Protoevangelium of James* of Judeo-Christian origin, a composite work, in which the part concerning the Virgin Mary goes back to the date 130-140. The venerable antiquity of this source allows the acceptance of the veracity of certain particulars that it gives about her family. Later modifications of this primitive account gave rise to discordant traditions.[9] These books have been adjudged unfit for public use, not only because of certain errors, but because of the depth and difficulty of their contents. Therefore, only those accounts that have received the approbation of the conscience of the Church and have proved constructive, have we chosen to narrate herein.[10]

Apocryphal Sources in Marian Theology

It should be understood that all that is good and edifying in the *Apocrypha* has already been absorbed by the Church. These true accounts have been presented to the faithful through the hymns, iconography and writings of the holy Fathers, and there is no need for the Orthodox Christian to search these writings.

Another important factor is the role in which the *Apocrypha* plays in Marian theology. The origin of four major feasts of the Theotokos: her Conception (December 9th), her Nativity (September 9th), her Entrance into the Temple (November 21st), and her Dormition (August 15th) are taken from the *Protoevangelium of James, Pseudo-Matthew, The Gospel of the Nativity of Mary, The Falling Asleep of Mary* and *The Passing of Mary*, respectively. The influence of apocryphal writings in these services and, especially, in the sacred art of iconography, has often been more marked than that of the canonical Gospels. Admittedly, some of the little stories within these narratives have proved demonstrably unreliable, but others have influenced the development of doctrine, notably in the Conception, Entrance, Annunciation and Dormition of the Theotokos. Where apocryphal and secondary sources are used, they will be so indicated within the present text.

The influence in both art and literature of the *Protoevangelium* has been considerable and great is the family of texts which borrowed from it. As we indicated, four major feasts of the Virgin and the feasts of her parents, are derived from the *apocryphon*. *Pseudo-Matthew*, an adaptation of the *Protoevangelium*, appeared in the West between the fourth and sixth centuries. *The Gospel of Thomas* is avoided completely because invention is unbridled and often bizarre and distasteful. Saint Cyril of Jerusalem (318-c.386) asserts that this *Gospel of Thomas* was written by the Manicheans and is especially harmful and corrupts simple folk.[11] The *Gospel of the Birth of Mary* is a Latin account of the Virgin's birth and childhood. It is included among the works attributed to blessed Jerome (347-420);[12] but it is actually an improved version of the first part of the *Gospel of Pseudo-Matthew*, which in turn is based on the *Protoevangelium of James*. Another apocryphal account, *The History of Joseph the Carpenter*, may have been originally written in Greek. It is now extant only in Coptic and the Arabic translation made from the Coptic. The translations which have been utilized have been made from the critical edition of Tichendorf, who is of the opinion that the text dates to the fourth century.[13] This document is the oldest one extant intended to glorify the Elder Joseph and foster his cult.

The Fathers Use Apocryphal Sources

As we will soon learn, apocryphal details, drawn from the *Protoevangelium of James* and other sources, are particularly plentiful in sermons from the holy Fathers. Some examples are: St. Andrew of Crete (c.660-740) in his *Homily on the Annunciation*;[14] works attributed to the St. Germanos (c.635-733), Patriarch of Constantinople;[15] and St. Gregory the Wonder-worker.[16] A contemporary of St. Photios, St. George (d. after 880), Bishop of Nicomedia, also makes extensive use of the apocryphal details in his homilies.[17]

Also we shall read how St. Photios (+c.897), in his homilies, used the semi-dramatic form which does nothing more than follow a tradition which had become firmly entrenched by the ninth century. This particular form had been established in Byzantine literature by the fifth century, as demonstrated by the short dialogue found in the Annunciation homily by the priest-monk, St. Hesychios of Jerusalem (c.451) [PG 93, cols. 1453 sq.].[18]

Apocrypha dealing with the Theotokos' Dormition and eventual assumption can be based on Syriac manuscripts from the second century. There are many versions in about nine different languages. Several Greek homilies, drawing from these apocryphal sources, dealt with her Dormition and bodily translation. Some were authored by St. Gregory Palamas (+1391), St. Andrew of Crete, St. Germanos of Constantinople and St. Gregory of Tours (538-594). The emphasis on the Apostles as eyewitnesses would suggest that it was of apostolic origin.

ICONS: PASSAGES INTO A GREATER REALITY

Orthodox Byzantine iconography is a religious art that is theological. The Seventh Ecumenical Council (787 A.D.) declared firmly that we preach the Gospel in two ways, by words and by images. Its themes do not simply relate to religious history, but consist of the theology of the Church. Whatever is taught by the Divine Liturgy, by the hymns of the Church, by her Fathers, is excellently commented upon by the silence of iconography, theology in color.   Saint Gregory of Nyssa (c.335-394) comments, "While silent on the wall, painting speaks many and more useful things."[19]   Thus icons are not simply illustrations of biblical themes and stories; rather, they are an embodiment of the validity of these themes and events.   Just as the theologians who developed the allegorical interpretation of the Scriptures saw in the written text many different levels of truth which they would interpret or transmit, so we who approach icons must be aware of the possibly several levels of truth and their significance.   We need to be aware of the range of scriptural interpretation that forms part of the theological and religious background of the icon painters.[20]

Many icons depicting episodes taken from apocryphal gospels have become an integral part of the mainstream Orthodox Tradition, theology and spirituality.   Full iconographic schemes have translated the New Testament into visual language.   Some, however, have viewed icons taken from apocryphal sources with great suspicion since they belong to the "fringe" world of spirituality.[21]   Nevertheless, in many instances certain iconographic traditions depicting apocryphal scenes must be recognized together with the hymns accompanying the icons, for they detail the earthly life of the holy Virgin and have become the source of four of her major feasts in the Church liturgical cycle.   In Orthodoxy, theology and art, word and image, are seen as two aspects of the one Revelation.[22]   The language of sacred art is thus a language that corresponds to that of the sacred writings.   It is not simply a matter of art illustrating the words of Scripture.[23]   The iconographer's work is bound up closely with the Church's worship; they are servants of a liturgical tradition.[24]   Thus, liturgical poetry can also form the basis for certain iconographic sequences, such as those scenes taken from the twenty-four verses of the *Akathist Hymn* to the Theotokos.

Though many Orthodox Byzantine iconographers introduced certain scenes in their icons that are not found in the canonical Gospels, they were not always appreciated. Nevertheless, apocryphal episodes may be viewed in such renowned Orthodox churches as those at Constantinople, Mystra and on Athos.   Indeed, the poetic and gentle narrative of Mary's birth, childhood and betrothal to Joseph was the source of much of the iconographic tradition of Christian artists. The human interest of these stories did much to ensure their popularity. After an early vogue in sixth century iconography (e.g. the frescos at Perustica in Thrace), their popularity waned, and it was only from the thirteenth century on, under the Paleologi, that they returned to favor.[25]

An example in point is the scene of the Nativity of Christ when the child is seen being bathed by the midwives. Orthodox Tradition accepted the scene of the bathing from the beginning, absorbing it and sanctifying it as it absorbed and sanctified other subjects from the *Apocrypha*.[26] Another example in point is the Church of Kariye Djami in Constantinople. Thanks to the enlightened munificence of a cultured Byzantine court dignitary, Theodore Metochite (+1332), this church, originally the church of the Monastery of Christ of Chora, depicts the life of the Virgin-Mother in mosaics. Although most of the narratives illustrated therein are derived from apocryphal sources, the Church has always permitted their use.[27]

IN CLOSING

The tool of language is often limited and inadequate in its expressions to describe the exalted and revered position of the Mother of God. However, being mindful of the words of St. Theodore the Studite, "It is better to contribute what one can than to leave the whole task undone," we undertook this work of compiling the life of our most holy, most pure, most blessed, glorious Lady Theotokos and Ever-Virgin Mary.

In closing, we bring forward the most excellent of hymnographers, St. John of Damascus, who endeavored also with language to express his profound love for the Theotokos in the famous hymn chanted during one of the most solemn moments of the Divine Liturgy of St. Basil: *"In thee, O full of grace, all creation, both the company of angels and the race of men doth rejoice. O hallowed temple and spiritual paradise, boast of virgins: from thee God was incarnate and became a child, He, our God Who existed before the ages; for He made thy womb a throne, and He made thee more spacious than the heavens. In thee, of full of grace, all creation doth rejoice; glory be to thee!"*[28]

We, too, offer this volume on the life of Mary Theotokos to her in whom all creation rejoices. We pray that the all-immaculate one accepts our words of praise, as her Son, our Lord and God, accepted the widow's two mites. We also hope that our pious readers, upon learning of her wondrous life, may continue to rejoice with all creation in glorifying her, the Theotokos and Mother of Light.

By the intercessions of the Theotokos, O Saviour save us.

Date: October 1/14, 1989, Holy Protection of the Theotokos

TABLE OF CONTENTS

My soul doth magnify the Lord,
and my spirit hath rejoiced in God my Saviour.
[Luke 1:46-47]

Chapter I.
The Conception by Righteous ANNA
of the VIRGIN MARY

the Memory of which the Holy Church
Celebrates on the
9th of December

+ + +

The Orthodox Church accepts the validity of the information supplied in the first five chapters of the *Protoevangelium of James* concerning the conception by the righteous foremother of Christ, Anna. Many Fathers quote the *Protoevangelium* regarding this event; included in this catalogue are St. John of Damascus,[1] St. Germanos,[2] St. Leo the Wise,[3] and St. Gregory Palamas,[4] to mention a few.

THE PARENTAGE OF THE VIRGIN MARY

The blessed and ever-glorious Virgin Mary, sprung from the royal stock and family of David. Her father's name was Joachim, and her mother's name was Anna. Her father's family, of the tribe of Judah, was from Nazareth of Galilee, but her mother's family was from Bethlehem of Judea.[5] Her mother, Anna, was the daughter of Matthan the priest, of the tribe of Levi.

Their lives were plain and righteous before the Lord, and irreproachable and pious before men. Joachim was the shepherd of his own sheep. He feared the Lord in integrity and singleness of heart. Apart from his herds, he had no other occupation.[6] Joachim was an exceedingly rich man and was wont to bring double offerings of what the law required, saying, "The superabundance of my substance shall be for the benefit of all the people, but the offering I make for myself is so that I might find mercy and forgiveness from the Lord for my sins."[7]

In fact, Joachim supplied the poor and all that feared God with food. His lambs, sheep, and their wool, and whatsoever things he possessed, he would divide into three portions: one he gave to the orphans, widows, strangers and the poor; the second to the temple and its servants, and those that worshipped God; and the third he kept for himself

1

and all his house and family. Thus doing, the Lord multiplied Joachim's herds, so that there was no man like him
among the sons of Israel. He had this custom since he was
fifteen years old. Thus Joachim was dear to God and kind to
men.[8]

At the age of twenty, he took to wife Anna. They had
lived many years together, some say fifty, but had neither a
son nor daughter.[9] This fact saddened the righteous ones,
because they could not hope that any progeny of theirs
would see the Messiah.[10] Nevertheless, they vowed that,
should the Lord grant them offspring, they would dedicate it
to the service of the Lord. On account of this the pious
couple were wont to go up to Jerusalem, to the temple of
the Lord, at each of the yearly festivals.[11]

In the East, to be a wife without motherhood was not
only regarded as a matter of regret, but also a matter of
reproach and humiliation, that could even lead to divorce. If
a woman could not have children, it was viewed as a curse
from God, for it meant extinction. It was thought that she
must have in some way displeased the Lord. Society then
usually considered the wife as the problem. It was also a
constant source of embarrassment to both the wife and her
husband, for the welfare of the children is a never-omitted
subject of inquiry in all courteous Oriental salutations.

Even those who loved her treated her as an object of
pity. Aggravating the family misfortune of barrenness was
the loss of hope of mothering the Messiah or, as they
believed, having seed that would behold the Messiah.
Moreover, to have had children and to have lost them was
the strongest possible claim upon receiving sympathy.

Jewish parents believed that a part of them lived on in
their children and, therefore, looked upon children as a
blessing. It followed that to be without offspring was to
exist in name only. Children were also hoped for so as to
keep inheritances in the family. If a woman did have
children, it greatly increased her prestige in the family. For
example, to avoid disgrace, we know that the wives of the
patriarchs, Sarah [Gen. 16:2] and Rachel [Gen. 30:3], gave
their handmaids to their husbands; other methods were
adoption or polygamy. Polygamy first appeared in the
reprobate line of Cain, when Lamech took two wives [Gen.
4:19].

THE FEAST OF THE DEDICATION

Now the great day of the Lord was at hand, the Feast of the Dedication (Hanukkah) and the Feast of Lights, commencing on the 25th of Chislev or Kislev (the ninth month; November-December), which was celebrated for eight days, when the sons of Israel would bring their offerings [1 Macc. 4:52-59; 2 Macc. 10:5]. At this time, Joachim, too, was preparing his gifts to offer to the Lord. When the high priest Reuben beheld Joachim, he despised him and spurned his gifts, saying, "It is not lawful for thee to stand among them that are offering sacrifice to God, because God has not blessed thee, so as to give thee seed in Israel. Cursed is every one who has not begot a male or a female in Israel!"[12]

Thus, a hymn for this feast says, *The holy Joachim and Anna brought their gift to the sanctuary, but it was not received on account of their childlessness.*[13]

Reuben then said that Joachim ought first to be freed from this curse by begetting some issue; and then only should he come into the presence of the Lord with his offerings.[14]

A kontakion of St. Romanos (c.490-c.556) speaks of the holy man's rejection: *He (Joachim) brought gifts to the temple but they were not received; the priests did not wish to accept them, since they were from a childless man who had no seed. And Joachim was scorned by the sons of Israel. But at the proper time, along with Anna, he brought in the Virgin with gifts of thanksgiving.*[15]

Publicly disdained for childlessness, the confounded Joachim, covered with shame from this reproach that was thrown in his teeth, retreated weeping from the Court of Men in the temple of the Lord. Exceedingly grieved, he went away to the registers of the twelve tribes of the people, and said, "I shall see the registers of the twelve tribes of Israel, to see if I alone have not made seed in Israel." Thus Joachim searched the records only to find that all the righteous had raised up seed in Israel. Saddened by this, he, nevertheless, comforted himself when he called to

3

mind the Patriarch Abraham whom God gave a son in his latter days.[16]

JOACHIM RETIRES INTO THE WILDERNESS

At that time, Joachim was not inclined to return home, lest his neighbors and those of his tribe, who were present and heard the rebuke of the high priest, should publicly reproach and brand him in the same manner.[17] Therefore, not returning to his house, Joachim went to his shepherds and flocks, and took them to a far place into the mountains.[18] There, in the hill country, Joachim retired. He pitched his tent and fasted, saying, "I will not go down either for food or drink until the Lord my God shall look upon me; prayer shall be my food and drink."[19]

Again, St. Romanos chants, *Joachim on the mountain prayed to receive fruit from the womb of Anna; and the prayer of the holy man was accepted.*[20]

ANNA MOURNS

Anna, meanwhile, departed the Court of Women in the temple, and went home weeping bitterly. Indeed, Anna mourned doubly, saying, "I shall bewail my widowhood; I shall bewail my childlessness."

Now the great day of the Lord was at hand and Anna put off her garments of mourning. At about the ninth hour she went down to the garden to walk. She saw a laurel tree, and sat under it, and prayed to the Lord, saying, "O God of our fathers, bless me and hear my prayer, as thou didst open the womb of Sarah and gave her a son Isaac" [Gen. 21:2-3].[21]

4

Then gazing towards heaven, she noticed a sparrow's nest in the laurel, and bemoaned her barrenness within herself, saying, "Alas, who begot me? And what womb did bear me, that I should be thus accursed before the children of Israel, and that they should reproach and deride me in the temple of my God? Woe is me, to what can I be compared? I am not like the fowls of the heaven, because even the fowls of the heaven are productive before Thee, O Lord. Alas! to what can I be compared? I am not like the beasts of the earth, because even the beasts of the earth are fruitful before Thee, O Lord. Alas! to what can I be likened? I am not like these waters, because even the waters are productive before Thee, O Lord. Woe is me, to what can I be compared? I am not comparable to the waves of the sea; for these, whether they are calm, or in motion, with the fishes which are in them, praise thee, O Lord. Alas! to what have I been likened? I am not like this earth, because even the earth bringeth forth its fruit in season and blesseth Thee, O Lord."[22]

On this occasion St. Romanos chants, *The prayer and groaning of Joachim and Anna at their barrenness and childlessness have proved acceptable, and have come unto the ears of the Lord; and they have put forth a fruit that brings life to the world. The one offered his prayer in the mountain, the other bore her reproach in the garden. But with joy the barren woman bears the Theotokos who sustains our life.*[23]

In comparing the mother Anna with her future daughter Mary, St. Ephraim the Syrian (c.306-373) chants, *The wife (Anna) proved barren, and withheld her fruit; but the bosom of Mary, bodily conceived (the Christ). To wonder at fields, and to admire plants she (Mary) needed not who received, and rendered what she borrowed not. Nature confessed its defeat; the womb was aware of it, and restored what nature gave not.*[24]

AN ANGEL APPEARS TO JOACHIM

When Joachim had been in the mountains for some time, on a certain day when he was alone, the Archangel Gabriel stood by him. Joachim was disturbed at his appearance, but the angel endeavored to restrain his fear, saying, "Fear not, Joachim, nor be disturbed by my appearance. I am the angel of the Lord and have been sent by Him to tell thee that thy prayers have been heard and that thy charitable deeds have gone up into His presence. God has seen thy shame and has heard the reproach of unfruitfulness which has been unjustly brought against thee; for God is the avenger of sin, not of nature.

"Therefore, when He shuts up the womb of anyone, He does so that He may in a more wonderful manner open it, so that which is born may be acknowledged to be the gift of God and not the product of lust. Was this not the case of the mother of thy nation, Sarah, who was barren? [Gen. 17:17]. Nevertheless, in extreme old age she brought forth Isaac, in whom the promise was made a blessing to all nations [Gen. 16:2]. Rachel also, so much in favor with the Lord and beloved by the holy Jacob, was a long time barren; yet she brought forth Joseph [Gen. 30:23-24], who was not only the lord of Egypt [Gen. 41:40-41], but the deliverer of many nations that were ready to perish with hunger [Gen. 41:56-57]. Who among the judges was stronger than Samson or more holy than Samuel? And yet both their mothers were barren [Judg. 13:2; 1 Sam. 1:20].[25]

"If, therefore, the reasonableness of my words does not persuade thee, believe in fact that conceptions very late in life, and births in the case of women that have been barren, are usually attended with something wonderful. Accordingly,

Anna, thy wife, will bring forth a daughter to thee and thou shalt call her name **MARY**. According to thy vow, she shall be devoted to the Lord from her infancy, and she shall be filled with the Holy Spirit, even from her mother's womb. Mary shall not eat or drink anything unclean, nor shall her conversation or life be among the crowds of the people, but in the temple of the Lord, that it may not be possible to say, or so much as to suspect, any evil concerning her."[26]

The account of the *Nativity of Mary* portrays the Archangel Gabriel as knowledgeable of the great destiny of Mary when he utters the following sentence: "So in the

6

process of her years, as she shall be in a miraculous manner born of one that was barren, so she shall, while yet a virgin, in an incomparable manner, bring forth the Son of the Most High, the Saviour of all nations.[27]

"And this shall be a sign to thee of the things which I announce: When thou shalt come to the Golden Gate in Jerusalem, thou shalt meet there thy wife Anna who, lately, has been anxious from the delay of thy return, and will rejoice to see thee." Having thus spoken, the angel departed from Joachim.[28]

Joachim then went down and called his shepherds, saying, "Bring me hither ten she-lambs without spot or blemish, and they shall be for the Lord my God; and bring me twelve tender calves, and they shall be for the priests and elders; and a hundred goats for all the people."[29]

THE ANGEL APPEARS TO ANNA

While the holy Anna was in the garden, behold, the same angel of the Lord then appeared to her, saying, "Anna, Anna, the Lord hath heard thy prayer, and thou shalt conceive and bring forth; and thy seed shall be spoken of in all the world." And Anna said, "As the Lord my God liveth, if I beget either male or female, I will bring it as a gift to the Lord my God; and it shall minister unto Him all the days of its life [1 Sam. 1:11]."[30]

Wise Anna prayed faithfully and God hearkened. And she heard the angel's confirmation of her many entreaties....[31]

"I am the angel who has presented thy prayers and alms before God; and now I have been sent to thee to announce to thee that thou shalt bring forth a daughter, who shall be

7

called Mary, and who shall be blessed above all women. She shall be full of the favor of the Lord, even from her birth. She shall remain in her father's house until she is weaned and, thereafter, she shall be delivered to the service of the Lord. She shall serve God, day and night, in fasting and prayers. She shall abstain from every unclean thing and shall not depart from the temple until she shall reach the years of discretion."

Again, the same apocryphal account portrays the archangel as knowing of the future incarnation of the Word, when he says, "She shall never know man, but alone and without precedent, as an immaculate and undefiled virgin, without intercourse with man, she shall bring forth a Son. She, His handmaiden, shall bring forth the Lord, both in grace, and in name, and in work, the Saviour of the world."[32]

Saint John of Damascus (c.676-c.750), in a hymn, offers the following response of Anna: *To the angel that was sent, Anna cried out in amazement, "O divine announcement! O strange utterance! I, too, shall conceive."*[33]

Gabriel then said, "Arise, therefore, and go up to Jerusalem; and when thou shalt come to the gate which, because it is plated with gold, is called 'Golden', there, for a sign, thou shalt meet thy husband, for whose safety thou hast been anxious. When, therefore, thou shalt find these things accomplished, believe that all the rest which I have told thee shall also undoubtedly be accomplished."[34]

Today the world celebrates Anna's conception which was effected by God; for she conceived her who conceived the Word that is beyond word.[35]

JOACHIM AND ANNA MEET AND REJOICE

Therefore, as the angel had commanded, both Joachim and Anna had set out from their respective places and went up to the Beautiful Gate of the temple. Anna hastened with her maidens and, praying to the Lord, she stood a long time in the gate waiting for him. When she was wearied with long waiting, she lifted up her eyes and saw Joachim afar off, coming with his flocks. She ran to him and hung on his neck, giving thanks to God, saying, "Now I know that the Lord hath blessed me exceedingly; for, behold I was a widow and now I am not so; I, the childless one, shall conceive!"[36]

Then, rejoicing at seeing each other, and secure in the certainty of the promised offspring, they gave the thanks due to the Lord who exalts the humble. And Joachim rested that day.[37]

Today the bonds of barrenness are loosed; for God hearkened to Joachim and Anna. And though it was beyond hope, He clearly promised them that they would bear a divine child, from whom would be born the uncircumscribable Himself, Who became mortal.[38]

THE CONCEPTION BY ANNA

On the following day, Joachim brought his offerings into the temple. And, having worshipped the Lord, they returned home, and Anna conceived by Joachim's seed, and they awaited the divine promise in certainty and in gladness.[39] When it was heard that Anna had conceived, there was great joy among all their neighbors and acquaintances, so that the whole land of Israel congratulated them.[40]

Saint George (d. after 880), Bishop of Nicomedia, chants, *He Who supports all things with His word, in His mercy has hearkened unto the prayer of righteous Joachim and Anna. He has loosed them from the anguish of barrenness and given them her that is the cause of our joy.*[41]

Saint Epiphanios of Cyprus (c.315-403) writes that Mary "was a woman by nature, not to be distinguished at all from others. She was conceived by marital union and the seed of man...."[42] And, "Mary is not God, and did not receive a body from heaven, but from the joining of man and woman; and according to the promise, like Isaac, she was prepared to take part in the divine economy."[43]

Thus, the pre-eternal Word has now made a throne for Himself on earth, so the Church chants, *Today God Who rests upon the spiritual thrones has made ready for Himself a holy throne upon earth. He Who made firm the heavens in His wisdom has prepared a living heaven in His love for man. For from a barren root He has made a life-giving branch spring up for us, even His Mother. God of wonders and hope of the hopeless, glory be to Thee, O Lord.*[44]

THE HETERODOX TEACHING OF "IMMACULATE CONCEPTION" AND "ORIGINAL SIN"

Saint Ambrose (339-397), Bishop of Milan, comments that "Of all those born of women, there is not a single one who is perfectly holy, apart from the Lord Jesus Christ...."[45]

The Orthodox Church teaches that the Virgin Mary was conceived by Joachim's seed and the period of gestation was nine months. None of the ancient holy Fathers say that God in miraculous fashion purified the Virgin Mary while yet in Anna's womb. Only Jesus Christ is completely pure of every sin, while all men, being born of Adam, have borne a flesh subject to the law of sin. Many have correctly indicated that the Virgin Mary, just as all men, endured a battle with sinfulness, but was victorious over temptations and was saved by her divine Son.

Blessed John Maximovitch (+1966) affirms that the Church teaches that through the fall of Adam and Eve, all of the human race inherited death, becoming enslaved to the devil through the passions. The progeny of Adam and Eve are not guilty of their first parents' tasting of the fruit; we are not being punished for this first sin or "original sin". If, for the sake of argument, we maintain the invalid heterodox teaching that the Theotokos was preserved from this "original sin", that would make God unmerciful and unjust. If God preserved her, why then does He not purify all men? But then that would have meant saving men before their birth, apart from their will. This teaching would then deny all her virtues. After all, if Mary, even in the womb of Anna, when she could not even desire anything either good or evil, was preserved by God's grace from every impurity, and then by that grace was preserved from sin even after her birth, then in what does her virtue consist? She would have been placed in the state of being unable to sin.[46]

The Virgin, as a true daughter of Adam and Eve, also inherited death. She was not in a state of never being able to die. Thus, St. John of Damascus writes on the occasion of her Dormition, *O pure Virgin, sprung from mortal loins, thine end was conformable to nature.*[47]

Blessed Archbishop John continues to comment that the Virgin was not placed in the state of being unable to sin,

but continued to take care for her salvation and overcame all temptations.[48] The righteousness and sanctity of the Virgin Mary was manifested in the fact that she, being "human with passions like us," so loved God and gave herself over to Him, that by her purity she was exalted above all other creatures.[49] Mary was to become the Mother of God, the Theotokos, not because she was to give birth to divinity, but that through her the Word became true man, God-Man.

Chapter II.
The Nativity of the
VIRGIN MARY

the Memory of which the Holy Church
Celebrates on the
8th of September

+ + +

Saint Andrew of Crete (c.660-740) chants, *O Bride of the Father, immaculate Mother of the Son, and holy and resplendent temple of the Holy Spirit; O most chaste of all creation, most suitable to His ultimate purpose, on this account the universe was created and, by thy birth, was the eternal will of the Creator fulfilled.*[1]

What was God's ultimate purpose for us and how did her birth fulfill the eternal will? It is our unification with God and deification. Suffice it to add these thoughtful words of St. Ambrose (339-397), Bishop of Milan: "Unless man were redeemed, it would avail him nothing to be born."[2]

Saint Andrew of Crete also comments, "This day is for us the beginning of all holy days. It is the door to kindness and truth." He then goes on to write: *Let both the barren and mothers dance for joy; make bold and leap up in gladness, O ye childless: for the barren and childless woman brings forth the Theotokos, who is to deliver Eve from her pains in travail and Adam from the curse* [Gen. 3:16-19].[3]

Saint Gregory Palamas (+1359) comments that "for her sake, the God-possessed prophets pronounced prophesies, and miracles are wrought to foretell that future great miracle of the world, the Ever-Virgin Mother of God. Generation after generation of vicissitudes and historical events, make a path to their ultimate destination, to the new mystery that will be wrought in her. The rites and laws had provided beforehand a type of the future truth of the Spirit. The end, or rather the beginning and root of those earlier events and wonders of God is the annunciation to Joachim and Anna, who were accomplished in the virtues, of what was to be accomplished (in their daughter)."[4] In another homily, he comments, "all divinely-inspired Scripture was written for the sake of the Virgin who begat God."[5]

Saint Photios (+c.897) also writes that "the present feast honoring the birth of the Virgin Mother of God easily carries off the glittering prize of seniority against every competitor...for without the Virgin's feast none of those that sprang out would appear....The Virgin's feast, in fulfilling the function of the root, the source, the foundation...takes on with good reason the ornament of all those other feasts, and it is conspicuous with many great boons, and is recognized as the day of universal salvation."[6]

Israel as a community was not to give birth to the Messiah by means of natural generation, that is, by man's seed. By natural means they would produce the Virgin-Mother, who is the beauty and excellency of Israel. The prophets prophesied of her, yet, most Israelites were unaware that they were awaiting the birth of a virgin daughter from their stock who, virginally, without father, would bring forth the Messiah, the incarnate Son of God and Only-Begotten of His Father without mother.

Saint Photios clearly believes that the birth of the Virgin happened by a natural union, though the mother was barren and aged. "Dost thou accept Adam to have been molded out of clay and produced without a natural birth? Dost thou accept Eve to be the offspring not of intercourse but of his rib? Yet these things cannot be ascribed to natural law. Shall not grace which formed nature not be able to repair her? Cannot the Creator warm and irrigate that which has grown old? Shall not the Creator easily at His will restore her to the state in which He set her at first? Grace is not subservient to nature, but the Mistress of nature."[7]

Saint Andrew of Crete chants, *Anna, the barren and sterile, was not childless before God: for she was fore-ordained from many generations to become the mother of the pure Virgin, from whom the Maker of all creation sprang forth in the form of a servant.*[8]

Saint Neophytos of Cyprus (1134-1220), styled the "Chrysostom of Cyprus", treats our Lady in many passages of his writings. "Anna, delivered by the Creator of nature from the bonds of sterility conceives, by her spouse, Mary a daughter of God. Anna, today, gave birth to Mary, the first-fruits of our salvation, the immaculate Mother of God the Word, and the first-fruits of the renewal of our nature that had been aged and tarnished by transgression of the divine precept."[9]

Saint John of Damascus (c.676-c.750) also writes: "On the birth of the Mother of God, the sorrow of our first mother Eve is turned to joy. While one heard, 'in sorrow thou shalt bring forth children' [Gen. 3:16], the other heard, 'Rejoice, thou who art full of grace' [Lk. 1:28]; one heard, 'thy turning shall be to thy husband', and the other heard, 'the Lord is with thee.'"[10]

THE PATRIARCHS AND PROPHETS PROPHESY

In the hymns of this feast, St. Stephen of the Holy City chants that Eve *declares her daughter and descendant blessed,* "for unto me is born deliverance, through which I shall be set free from the bonds of hell."[11]

14

Old Testament types clearly manifest the Virgin Mary; for, *She is the fountain of life that gushes forth from the flinty rock* [Ex. 17:6]; *she is the Bush* [Ex. 3:2] *springing from barren ground and burning with the immaterial fire that cleanses and enlightens our souls.*[12] Saint John of Damascus adds to this, chanting, *Inspired by God, the divine choir (the patriarchs and prophets of the Old Testament) spoke of thee in prophecy as the Mountain* [Dan. 2:45], *the Gate of Heaven* [Ez. 44:2], *and the spiritual Ladder* [Gen. 28:12-17]: *for out of thee was hewn a stone, not cut by the hand of man; and thou art the gate through which passed the Lord of wonders, the God of our fathers.*[13] And, *The East gate* [Ez. 44:1-3], *newly born, awaits the entrance of the Great Priest.*[14]

The righteous David and Jesse exult and Judah is filled with pride, for from their root a blossom has sprung. *Cry out, O David: what has God sworn to thee? "What God swore to me He has now fulfilled," said he, "from the fruit of my body He has given the Virgin. From her the Creator, Christ the New Adam, is born, a King to sit upon my throne. Today He reigns, whose rule cannot be shaken"* [Ps. 88:3-4].[15]

The ninth century hymnographer, Sergios of the Holy City, chants, *She is the treasure of virginity, the rod of Aaron* [Num. 17:23] *springing from the root of Jesse, the preaching of the prophets, offshoot of the righteous Joachim and Anna. She is born, and with her is the world become*

15

new again. She is born, and the Church clothes herself in majesty. She is the holy temple, the receiver of the Godhead: the instrument of virginity, the bridal chamber of the King, wherein was accomplished the marvelous mystery of the ineffable union of the natures which come together in Christ.[16]

THE BARREN WOMAN BEARS THE THEOTOKOS WHO SUSTAINS OUR LIFE[17]

Saint Andrew of Crete then compares the holy Anna to the righteous foremother Sarah, saying, *O Lord, Thou hast opened the womb of Sarah, giving her Isaac as fruit in her old age* [Gen. 21:1-3]. *Today, O Saviour, Thou hast likewise given to godly Anna a fruit born from her womb, even Thine own Mother without spot.*[18]

Nevertheless, as the following hymn affirms: *Although by the will of God other women who were barren have brought forth famous offspring, yet among all such children Mary has shone most brightly with divine glory.*[19]

After nine months, Anna brought forth. She said to the midwife, "What have I brought forth?" And she told her, "A girl."

Then Anna said, "My soul has been magnified this day." And she laid her down. When the days of her purification had been fulfilled, and Anna was purified, she called her name **MARY** *(Miriam* in  Hebrew, *Mariam* in Greek), in accordance with the prophecy uttered by the Archangel.[20]

A NAME DESTINED FOR GREATNESS

What is the etymology of the name and what is its significance? There have been numerous explanations put forward as to the meaning of the Virgin's name, in contrast to her parents. It is nearly unanimous that her parents' names Joachim (in Hebrew *Jehoiakim*) was understood to mean "the Lord's restoration" or "may the Lord raise up"; whereas

Anna's name means "grace". Their names are indicative of their characteristics and qualities. But the name *Miriam* has been translated as "Lordless", "Hope", "Myrrh of the Seas", "Star of the Seas" (Jerome), "Illuminated", "Beloved one", "Lady", "Lady of the Sea", "Drop of the Sea", "Exalted", "Highness", "Excellency", "Lady", "One who surpasses" or "One who dominates." Some translators give the meaning "bitter sea", but this explanation has met with certain obstacles in Hebrew grammar, for it places the adjective after the noun, and the meaning seems to go against the positive attributes which are ascribed to the Virgin Mary.[21] The interpretation preferred by St. John of Damascus is "Lady"; thus he writes, "Accordingly it was grace (for this is the interpretation of Anna) that bore the Lady and Mistress (in Greek, *Despina*), for that is the meaning of the name Mary: for she became truly the Mistress of all creation, since she was vouchsafed to be the Mother of the Creator."[22]

THE INDIGNITY OF OUR FIRST PARENTS
IS PURGED THROUGH THEE

The *common salvation and glory of all generations* is the appellation given by St. John of Damascus to her who bore our Creator and God.[23] Saint Germanos (c.635-733), Patriarch of Constantinople chants, *As foretold by the angel, today hast thou come forth, O Virgin, the all-holy offspring of righteous Joachim and Anna...thou dost destroy the curse and givest blessing in its place.*[24]

Saint Romanos the Melodist (c.490-c.556] chants, *O mystery brought about on earth! After the birth, Anna prayed to our God and Maker Who knows all things in advance: "Thou hast heard me, O Lord, as Thou hast heard Hannah who was accused before Eli of being drunk [1 Sam. 1:14]. She promised Samuel, after his birth, to the Lord to become a priest. Just as formerly, thou hast given me too, a gift, the barren woman gives birth to the Mother of God and the nurse of our life."*[25]

Saint Andrew of Crete, adds these words to Anna's lips: *Thou hast granted me today the fruit of the promise, her that among all generations and women was foreordained to be Thy pure and undefiled Mother.*[26]

In the kontakion of this Feast, St. Romanos declares that Adam and Eve are now set free from the corruption of death.[27] Thus, St. Andrew continues speaking of Anna's exultation: *Now Anna makes glad and cries aloud exulting, saying, "Though barren, I have given birth to the Mother of God, through whom the condemnation of Eve has been remitted, and all her pains in travail."*[28]

Mary is born of a barren mother, thus renewing our nature that had grown barren. *Through her cruel hell has been trampled underfoot, and Eve with all her line is established secure in life.*[29]

Set free from the reproach of childlessness, *The barren woman gives suck to her child Mary, and Joachim rejoices at this birth, saying, "A rod is born unto me, and from it the flower that is Christ shall blossom from the root of David* [Is. 11:1]. *Marvelous in truth is this wonder!"*[30] For from her, in a manner past understanding, will be born the Maker of all, Who in His goodness shall purge all the indignity of our first parents.

AS A LILY AMONG THORNS, SO IS MY COMPANION AMONG DAUGHTERS[31]

Saint Joseph the Hymnographer (c.816-886) writes that the spiritual Spouse found her alone, a lily among thorns and a flower of the valleys.

THE VIRGIN'S BIRTHPLACE

A discrepancy exists as to the place of her birth. Some apocryphal accounts speak of Nazareth as the home of her parents; others claim that the house of Joachim was located near the Sheep Gate in Jerusalem. This latter point is confirmed by St. Sophronios and further certified by St. John of Damascus. Thus, her Jerusalem home might have been very convenient to the temple. We read in the latter's

18

Sermon on the Birth of the Theotokos, "The Mother of God was born to us in the holy Sheep Gate. Rejoice, O Sheep Gate, the most holy temple of God's Mother. Rejoice, O Sheep Gate, the wall of Joachim's sheep."[32] It is also quite possible, that a man as wealthy as Joachim had residences in both Judea and Galilee.

In icons depicting the Virgin being caressed by her parents, it was intended to show the infant before the incident of her first steps. She is usually shown inclining towards her mother for the parental kiss, though in the mosaic at Kariye Djami, the child is about to be kissed by Joachim, while she places her hand on the face of her mother.[33]

THE INFANT MARY

According to the *Protoevangelium*, a charming incident relating Mary's first steps is recounted, where she displays miraculous precocity.

The child grew and increased in strength daily. When Mary was about nine months old, Anna set her on the ground to see whether her daughter could stand. Mary indeed walked seven steps and came again to her mother. Anna then picked her up.[34]

Anna had made her daughter's bed-chamber into a holy place, a sanctuary, permitting nothing common or unclean to pass through Mary. Anna then invited certain undefiled maidens of the daughters of Israel and they attended to Mary also, by carrying her about hither and thither.[35]

JOACHIM MAKES A FEAST

Mary's first anniversary of her nativity, according to the *Protoevangelium*, was celebrated by Joachim with a feast to which he invited the priests, scribes, elders and all the people of Israel.[36]

Also the Church chants, *What is this sound of feasting that we hear? Joachim and Anna mystically keep festival. "O Adam and Eve," they cry, "rejoice with us today: for if by your transgression ye closed the gate of Paradise to those of old, we have now been given a glorious fruit, Mary the child of God, who opens its entrance to us all."*[37]

The hymnographer, St. Romanos, also chants, *Consequently, the tribes of Israel heard that Anna had given birth to the pure Virgin, and they all rejoiced with great gladness. Joachim held a great feast and celebrated splendidly the miraculous birth. And when he had summoned to prayer the priests and the Levites, he placed Mary in the midst of all, in order that she be magnified.*[38]

During the festivities, Joachim brought his daughter before the priests; and they blessed her, and said, "O God of our fathers, bless this child, and give her an everlasting name throughout all generations." And all the people replied, "So be it, Amen."[39]

Patriarch Germanos (c.635-733) adds, *No more are the gifts of Joachim turned away: for the lament of Anna is changed to joy. "Let all the chosen Israel rejoice with me," she says, "for behold, the Lord has given me the living Pavilion of His divine glory, unto the joy and gladness of us all and the salvation of our souls."*[40]

Joachim then brought his daughter before the chief priests, and they too blessed her, saying, "O God Most High, look upon this child, and bless her with the utmost blessing, which shall be an everlasting blessing."[41]

In this incident, Mary's divinely appointed role is being manifested to all people. An exceptional religious rite is also being performed, whereby, Mary, though a female, is sanctified by the invited priests. According to Jewish religious practice, birthdays were not celebrated. Also, only firstborn males, on the fortieth day after birth, received the priestly blessing in the temple. In this case, however, for a married couple after fifty years of marriage to produce a much desired offspring, became the cause of communal joy. Moreover, the elderly couple fully intended to dedicate their offspring, male or female, to the temple and service of God.

In the icons of the famous Monastery of Chora (Kariye Djami) Joachim is seen presenting his infant daughter, but Anna is excluded from the rite. Joachim advances to receive the benediction from the three high priests sitting on a long bench behind a table. The all-holy one (*Panagia*) is nestled in drapery that completely covers her father's hands, thus symbolizing her sacredness and likens her to a holy vessel being borne toward the altar.[42]

THE BARREN WOMAN HAS GIVEN BIRTH
TO THE NURSE OF OUR LIFE[43]

Anna then snatched her up and took her into the sanctuary of her bed-chamber, and then gave her the breast. Anna then uttered a song to the Lord, saying, "I will sing a song to the Lord my God, for He hath looked upon me, and hath taken away the reproach of my enemies. The Lord hath given me the fruit of His righteousness, singular in its kind and richly endowed before Him. Who will tell the sons of Reuben that Anna gives suck? Hear ye, O twelve tribes of Israel, Anna gives suck!"[44]

She then laid Mary down to rest in the room which she had consecrated and went out and ministered to her guests. When the feast concluded, all went away rejoicing and praising the God of Israel.[45]

JACOB'S LADDER

Many objects have been regarded as types of the Virgin and have been depicted in the iconography of Orthodox churches. Analogies and interpretations of this kind abound also in the liturgy, hymnography and homilies of the Church. Within the literary authority of the Church, iconography developed a typology of the Virgin. One such "type" is described in Jacob's vision, which is read in the service of Great Vespers of three of the Virgin's feasts: the Nativity of the Virgin, the Annunciation and her Dormition. We read that Jacob's vision of the ladder reached to heaven, upon which angels ascended and descended, and above the Lord stood [Gen. 28:10-17].[46] Saint Photios writes that Mary, "The ladder leading up to heaven is being built, and earthly nature, leaping over her proper boundaries, comes to dwell in the heavenly tabernacles."[47]

THE OVERTHROW OF THE ANCESTRAL DEFEAT

Saint Photios, in a homily on the present feast, explains that "After God had bestowed on man the enjoyment and mastery over everything in the Garden, it was meet for him who was entrusted with so great authority to be disciplined and trained with some command. However, after transgressing this command, the Creator did not overlook His creatures though they had plunged themselves into such great error. It was needful, therefore, that one Person of the Trinity become man, to make it manifest that the re-creation too, like the creation, was Its own work. Incarnation entailed a pregnancy and a mother. So it was needful that a mother should be prepared down below for the Creator, for the re-creation of shattered humanity. She was to be a virgin, just as the first man had been formed of virgin earth, so the re-creation, too, should be carried out through a virgin womb, and that no transitory pleasure, even lawful,

22

should be as much as imagined in the Creator's birth; for the Lord suffered to be born for the deliverance of him who was a captive of pleasure.[48]

"Who then was worthy? Clearly it was she who this day strangely issued from Joachim and Anna, the barren root. It was needful, yea needful, that she who from the very cradle had by a superior reason preserved her body pure, her soul pure, her thoughts pure, should be marked out to be the Creator's Mother.

"It was needful that she who had been brought to the temple as an infant, who had trodden the untrodden places, should appear as a living temple for Him Who gave her life. It was needful that she who had been born in a wondrous manner from a sterile womb, and had removed her parents' reproach, should also make good the failure of her fore-fathers; for she, the descendant, was able to repair the ancestral defeat, who brought forth the Saviour of our race by a husbandless birth, and molded His body."[49]

Saint Photios also comments that, "The Lord's throne (Mary) is being prepared on earth, earthly things are sanctified, the heavenly hosts are mingled with us, and the wicked one, who first deceived us and was the contriver of the plot against us, has his power crushed, as his wiles and devices rot away."[50]

Thus, we chant with St. John of Damascus: *The holy parents of the Mother of God received from heaven a gift worthy of God, a throne higher than the very cherubim* [Is. 6:1; Ez. 1:4]--*she who in childbirth would bear the Word and the Creator.*[51]

Chapter III.
The Entrance of the
VIRGIN MARY
Into the Temple,

the Memory of which the Holy Church
Celebrates on the
21st of November

+ + +

"Behold, the days come, saith the Lord, when I will make a new covenant with the house of Israel, and with the house of Judah" [Jer. 38:31-32].

In the hymns at Vespers of the Feast, we chant: *Thou, O Virgin Mother of God, art she whom the prophets proclaimed. Thou art the glory of the apostles and the pride of martyrs, the restoration of all who dwell on earth: for through thee we are reconciled to God.*[1]

ABOUT THE FESTIVAL

The Feast of the Entrance of the Virgin in the Temple is not among the most ancient festivals of the Church. Nonetheless, it must have been earlier than the seventh century, since St. Andrew of Crete (c.660-740) had known about it. Saint Tarasios (+806), the Patriarch, introduced it at Constantinople a century later. The festival blossomed forth from the Tradition of the Church, which made use of the apocryphal source, the *Protoevangelium*, in order to emphasize the fulfillment of the economy of the Creator and the self-consecration of the chosen Virgin to a life in the service of God. The Church breaks the silence of the canonical Gospels that we may behold the incomprehensible

24

ways of providence which prepare Mary, the receptacle of the Word and the Mother predetermined before the ages. She who was preached by the prophets is now introduced into the Holy of Holies, like a hidden treasure of the glory of God.[2]

God has sanctified all things by her entry and has made godlike the fallen nature of mortal men.[3]

THE VIRGIN'S PARENTS

The child grew and when she reached two years old, Joachim said to Anna, "Let us take her up to the temple of the Lord, that we may pay the vow that we have vowed, lest the Lord depart from us or, perchance, the Lord send us someone to warn us that we have been too long in paying our vow because our 'offering' hath not yet been received." But Anna said, "Let us wait for her third year, so that our daughter might not be at a loss to know her father and also that she might not look for us."   Therefore, Joachim conceded and said, "So let us wait."[4]

Much of both the poetic imagery and iconography of this Feast, which are used liturgically, are derived from the following passage of the *Protoevangelium*: "When the child reached her third birthday, Joachim said, 'Let us invite the daughters of the Hebrews that are virgins. Let each maiden take a lamp and stand with the lamps burning, that the child might not turn back and then her mind would be set against the temple of the Lord.'"[5]

When all hope was gone, Joachim and Anna gave birth to the undefiled Virgin and, in piety, they promised to offer her to God. Today they fulfil their promise, giving their child as a sacrifice in the house of God.[6]

Before thou wast conceived, O pure Virgin, thou wast consecrated to God: and now after thy birth thou art offered as a gift to Him, in fulfillment of thy parents' promise.[7]

Saint Gregory Palamas (+1359) aptly comments that "in a strange manner the Mother of God changed her dwelling from the house of her father to the house of God while still an infant."[8]

THE ENTRY

Thus, her parents departed their home and went up to the temple with an escort of young maidens. Upon arriving, they then put off Mary's traveling clothes and arrayed her with garments that were neater and cleaner; indeed, clothes befitting a queen. Now there were fifteen steps at the temple that led from the Court of the Women to that of the men. The significance of the number fifteen, to the Jews, was that it corresponded to the fifteen Psalms of Degrees [Ps. 119-133, LXX]. The temple had been built on a mountain, thus the altar of burnt offering could not be reached except by steps. On one of these steps, they placed the little maiden Mary. Then the whole company ascended into the temple of the Lord; the maidens bearing lamps and singing psalms. And Mary, without anyone leading her or lifting her, ascended the steps one after the other.[9]

The Virgin's father, Joachim, was *bright with joy and kept feast with Anna.*[10] Now *Anna, truly blessed by God's grace, led with gladness, into the temple of the Lord, the pure and Ever-Virgin who is full of grace. And Anna called the young maidens to go before her, lamps in hand. "Go, child," she said, "to Him Who gave thee unto me; be unto Him an offering and a sweet smelling incense. Go into the place that none may enter: learn its mysteries and prepare thyself to become the pleasing and beautiful dwelling-place of Jesus Who grants the world great mercy."*[11]

HOLY IS THY TEMPLE,
WONDERFUL IN RIGHTEOUSNESS

Entering the temple with virginal glory, she is compared to that area of the temple known as the Holy of Holies. Thus, in hymns we can hear St. Andrew of Crete chant, *Thy wise parents, O undefiled one, brought thee, who art the 'holy of holies', as an offering to the house of the Lord, there to be reared in holiness and made ready to become His Mother.*[12] In a Vespers hymn of this Entrance service, we chant that *it was fitting that she be brought to dwell in the Holy of Holies, as a sacrifice acceptable to God.*[13]

The young girls rejoice today and, with their lamps in hand, they go in reverence before the spiritual "lamp", as she enters into the Holy of Holies.[14]

As the Bride of the King of all, *Into the divine temple thou art brought, thyself a temple truly divine, innocent from the time thou wast a babe; thou hast appeared in the sanctuary accompanied by brightly burning lamps, thou who art the receiver of the Divine Light that no man can approach. Magnificent in truth is thy entry, O only Bride of God and Ever-Virgin.*[15]

As the icon of the Feast portrays, the righteous Joachim and Anna, rejoicing in spirit, offer their daughter in the temple of the law that she might make her dwelling therein. "The virgins that follow after her shall be brought unto the King; those near her shall be brought unto Thee. They shall be brought with gladness and rejoicing, they shall be brought into the temple of the King" [Ps. 44:14-15]. Thus we chant that the *choirs of virgins sing to the Lord, chanting psalms and honoring His Mother who alone among women is pure and blessed.*[16]

THE WORDS OF THE PROPHETS ARE FULFILLED

When St. Anna came up to the high priest, she uttered, *I stand here as the suppliant of God, calling upon Him with faith and prayer to receive the fruit of my travail. For I promised that after childbirth I would present my child to Him Who gave her to me.*[17]

The High Priest Zacharias, the husband of Anna's niece Elisabeth, is the future father of St. John the Baptist. When he beheld the Virgin's approach, he rejoiced in Spirit, and said, "Mary, the Lord God hath magnified thy name to all generations and, by thee, to the very end of time, the Lord will show His redemption to the children of Israel."[18]

The High Priest Zacharias unites in his person two traditions--priestly and prophetic. Thus, "Zacharias, the archpriest," writes Theophylactos (765-840), Patriarch of Bulgaria, "was amazed and, being divinely-inspired, he saw the divine gifts within this young maiden and he gave her

the temple as her habitation..."[19] Then the priest of God, filled with the spirit, exclaimed:

"Rejoice, Queen of the universe! Rejoice, all-holy Mother of God, Mother of the great King Christ!

"Rejoice, preaching of the prophets and the fulfillment of their words! The prophets prophesied of thee and have thee as their boast. All that they prophesied of thee, hath been accomplished this day! Today the souls of the prophets rejoice, for they beheld thee in the temple.

"Jacob foresaw thee as the 'ladder': 'Behold a ladder fixed on the earth whose top reached to heaven, and the angels of God ascended and descended on it' [Gen. 28:12]. Thus will the Lord desire to descend upon thee and become incarnate and, thereby, men will be able to ascend to heaven.

"The golden urn of manna, that Moses gave command to be laid up so that future generations might see the bread with which the Hebrews were fed in the wilderness [Ex. 16: 32-33], also prefigured thee. Thus thou wilt give flesh to the heavenly Bread that will nourish the race of the anointed ones.

"The dry rod of Aaron was a sign of thee, in that, without water, it budded [Num. 17:8]. In like manner, wilt thou, without seed from man, virginally, give birth to God, for this is His will.

"The fleece of Gideon prefigured thee, for as rain came down upon the fleece, without anyone's knowledge [Judg. 6:37-38], thus does God desire to condescend to put on flesh of thee--and not even the angels will understand how He would become incarnate."

Let us all magnify the radiant cloud, in which the Master of all descended, as dew from heaven upon the fleece, and for our sake took flesh and was made man, He Who is without beginning: for she is the pure Mother of our God.[20]

"The Prophet David wrote: 'He shall come down like rain upon a fleece, and like rain-drops that fall upon the earth' [Ps. 71:6].

The same prophet and king called thee 'Queen', and uttered:

'At Thy right hand stood the Queen, arrayed in a vesture of inwoven gold, adorned in varied colors'" [Ps. 44:8].

A hymnographer, to whom we refer repeatedly, St. George (d. after 880), Bishop of Nicomedia, chants of the appearance of the Queen: *David sang in honor of thee, calling thee the daughter of the King, for he saw thee in the beauty of the virtues, in raiment of many-colored needle-work, at the right hand of God* [Ps. 44].[21]

"David the prophet, who is of thine own tribe, O Lady and Queen, Mother of God, clearly foresaw and uttered: 'Hearken, O daughter, and see, and incline thine ear; and forget thine own people and thy father's house, and the King shall greatly desire thy beauty' [Ps. 44:9-10]. And, again, the prophet-king goes on to say: 'The virgins that follow after her shall be brought unto the King, those near her shall be brought unto Thee. They shall be brought with gladness and rejoicing, they shall be brought into the temple of the King' [Ps. 44:14-15]. All those who are devoted to virginity are close to thee and will desire to enter rejoicing into the kingdom of the heavens."

The Church in the following hymn confirms that David spoke in the preceding verses of Mary: *It is for her of whom thou hast sung in the "Book of Psalms", calling her Daughter, Child of God and Virgin.*[22]

Continuing with the high priest's exaltation of Mary, he said, "Solomon remarked that thou art more precious and honorable above all women, saying: 'Many daughters have obtained wealth, many have wrought valiantly; but thou hast exceeded, thou hast surpassed all'" [Prov. 29:29].

Saint George here chants, *Solomon, foreseeing how thou wast to receive God, spoke of thee in dark sayings as the "gate" of the King and the living "fountain" sealed* [Song of Songs 4:12], *from which came forth untroubled waters unto us.*[23]

The High-Priest Zacharias continued, saying, "Isaiah called thee 'virgin' and uttered: 'Behold, a virgin shall conceive in the womb, and shall bring forth a son, and thou shalt call his name Emmanuel' [Is. 7:14].

"Ezekiel forecalled thee 'gate' and said: 'This gate shall be shut, it shall not be opened, and no one shall pass through it' [Ez. 44:4]. The gate spoken of by Ezekiel also foretells that just as the great King enters and exits, He will again close the gate. Thus the great King desires to be born. He will leave thee virgin, just as thou art now."

On this account does St. George of Nicomedia chant, *Today the house of God receives the "gate" through which none may pass* [Ez. 44:1-2]*; so it has brought an end to the worship commanded by the shadow of the law, and it cries*

aloud, "Verily the truth has appeared to those on earth."[24]

Bringing forward yet another prophet, Zacharias says, "Daniel called thee 'mountain' when he said: '...a Stone was cut out of a mountain without hands' [Dan. 2:34].

"The mountain beheld by Nebuchadrezzar and interpreted by Daniel also foreshadowed thee. The Stone cut out of the mountain without human hands smote the image to powder. In like manner, without the will of man, the King of heaven and earth, of His own will, shall take flesh, that He might shatter all the kingdoms of the world and proclaim the everlasting kingdom of heaven."

Other types in the Old Testament of the Virgin-Mother may be heard in the hymn of St. George the hymnographer: *The mountain overshadowed, that Habakkum foresaw of old and announced* [Hab. 3:3]*, has come to dwell within the inaccessible sanctuary of the temple; there she doth flourish with virtue and she doth cover the ends of the earth therewith.*[25]

30

"The Prophet Zacharias, in a vision, beheld the Virgin as a gold seven-branched lampstand [Zach. 4:2], with its spiritual light shining in the world.

"The Prophet Jeremias pointed to thee, saying, "I beheld thee, O Israel, as a young maiden, newly led forth along the paths of life."

Saint Zacharias continues speaking, in spirit, thus: "Blessed are thy parents, O Mistress, and the breasts which thou hast sucked. The angels venerate thee, the archangels honor thee, the demons tremble, the patriarchs laud thee, the righteous praise thee, kings hymns thee, rulers supplicate thee, the rich entreat thee, and the anointed of God proclaim thee. Thy parents boast in thee and thy people rejoice. The souls of the condemned rejoice and the patriarchs exult. Our forefathers hoped in thee that they might be delivered from the hands of the devil."

The high priest then finishes, saying, "Enter into the Holy of Holies, for thou art much purer than myself. I, O Mistress, once a year enter therein, but thou, sit and abide forever. For thou art the Temple of God, therefore, remain in the temple. Thou art the vessel of the Holy Spirit, enter thou into the elect place. Wait therein until thou art vouchsafed to be the worthy vessel of the All-Holy Spirit. Rejoice and dance, for angels desire to minister unto thee!"[26]

THE VIRGIN, THE OFFERING
WITHOUT BLEMISH, IS LED UP

The ewe-lamb of God without spot [Num. 6:14, Lev. 14:10], the dove without blemish [Lev. 14:22], the tabernacle that is to hold God, the sanctuary of the glory, has chosen to dwell in the holy temple.[27]

Then Zacharias turned to Mary's parents and said: "O blessed and grace-filled couple, rejoice and be glad, for thou hast been vouchsafed to become the parents of such a daughter. Ye have surpassed our forefathers and fathers, in that ye have given birth to the Queen of the universe, and ye will receive glory from both God and men!"

This and many other things were uttered by Zacharias before both parents and their daughter. Then Anna spoke: "Receive, our daughter, O high priest or, much rather, God. Accept her who is pure and blameless and higher than heaven. Take her into the temple for that is where she, the temple of God, must be and dwell. She is holy, and in a pure place she is to abide. Therefore, into the hands of God is she surrendered. Indeed, to a holy place is she to be placed and to be sanctified. O Zacharias, take my daughter and dedicate her to the temple, for this is what I vowed."[28]

The hymnographer and bishop, St. George of Nicomedia, provides this dialogue between mother and priest. It is noteworthy that during the hymns of Vespers and Matins of this Feast, that one is given the impression that the venerable Anna clearly knew of her daughter's place in the history of redemption. Thus we hear her say, *Take the child given to me by God and lead her into the temple of thy Creator.*[29]

The priest answers her, saying, *Truly this work has been accomplished in full measure. I perceive that this is a thing wholly strange: for I see led into the house of God she who wondrously surpasses the sanctuary in grace!*[30]

Anna, answering, said, *Take her whom the prophets of God proclaimed in the Spirit, and lead her into the holy temple, there to be brought up in reverence, that she may become the divine "throne" of the Master of all, His "palace", His resting place, and His dwelling filled with light.*[31]

The response to this utterance may be found in this hymn of St. George: *Zacharias said to her in spirit, "Thou dost lead here the true Mother of life, whom the prophets of God heralded from afar as God's birthgiver: and how shall the temple contain her? Therefore in wonder I cry: O all ye works of the Lord, bless ye the Lord."*[32]

Within the same Matinal canon, St. George continues the dialogue thus: *"Hearing thy words," said Anna to him, "I am filled with new strength. For thou dost understand these things by the Spirit of God, and hast clearly announced what shall come to pass in the Virgin. Take, then, the undefiled one into the temple of thy Creator."*[33]

THE SON OF BARACHIAS
RECEIVES HER AS THE
DWELLING-PLACE OF GOD

The son of Barachias, Zacharias, [Mt. 23:35], *beholding Mary, gave her his blessing and cried out in joy, "Rejoice! Thou wonder of all the world."*[34]

After Zacharias heard the words of offering from Anna, he received the child and kissed her. He then uttered, "The Lord has magnified thy name in all generations. In thee, in

the latter days, shall the Lord make manifest His redemption unto the children of Israel."[35]

Saint George then has the high priest speak to the young maiden, saying, *Seeing the beauty of thy soul, O undefiled Virgin, thou art our deliverance; thou art the joy of all. Thou art our restoration, through whom the incomprehensible appears comprehensible to me.*[36] And, *O "gate" of the Lord! Unto thee I open the gates of the temple: rejoice and go round it in gladness. For I know and believe that the deliverance of Israel shall now come to dwell openly in our midst and that from thee shall be born God the Word Who grants the world great mercy.*[37]

ALL THE HOUSE OF ISRAEL LOVED HER

Zacharias then set her down upon the third step of the altar, and the Lord God sent grace upon her; and she danced with her feet, and all the house of Israel loved her.

The Virgin of the Lord then went up all the steps one after another, without the help of any to lead or lift her. It was evident from henceforth that she was of perfect age because she walked with a step so mature and she spoke so perfectly.[38]

Three years old in the flesh and many years old in spirit.[39] Therefore, *Let us praise in hymns the child by nature who was shown forth as a mother beyond nature.*[40]

The parents then, after offering up their sacrifice (according to the custom of the law), left the Virgin with other maidens in the apartments of the temple to be brought up therein. Mary's parents then went down marveling and

33

praising the Lord God, because the child did not turn back. They then returned to their home. And Mary was in the temple of the Lord, as if she were a dove that dwelt there.

For the next seven years, the parents of the little Virgin visited her often until they reposed, leaving her an orphan. Bishop Nikolai Velimirovic (+1956) records that the righteous Joachim was eighty years old and the venerable Anna was seventy-nine years old when they reposed in peace.[41] The dormition of St. Anna is commemorated by the Holy Church on the 25th of July. Both of the Virgin's parents are commemorated together on the 9th of September.

THE TEMPLE AT JERUSALEM

In the words of St. Gregory Palamas: "The Temple of Jerusalem was the 'type' of Mary, for she is the 'true place of God.'"[42] The temple was to be the dwelling-place of the divine glory, for "the glory of the Lord came into the house, by the way of the gate looking eastward...and, behold, the house of the Lord was full of glory" [Ez. 43:4,5]. And then the prophet was told, "thou hast seen the place of My throne, and the place of the soles of My feet, in which My name shall dwell in the midst of the house of Israel forever..." [Ez. 43:7].

In the hymns of the Feast we also see the analogy of the Virgin and the temple with its holy vessels, as in the hymn of St. George the hymnographer: *The law prefigured thee most gloriously as the tabernacle* [Ex. 26:1], *the divine jar of manna* [Ex. 16:33] *the wondrous ark* [Ex. 25:10], *the veil of the temple* [Mt. 27:51; Heb. 10:20], *the rod of Aaron* [Num. 17:8], *the temple never to be destroyed* [Jn. 2:19], *and the gate of God* [Ex. 44:1-3]; *and so all these teach us to cry to thee: "O pure Virgin, thou art truly highly exalted above all."*[43]

Saint Cosmas (7th-8th century) the Poet takes up this theme, comparing her to liturgical vessels, and chants, *Thy Son, O Virgin, has truly made thee dwell in the Holy of Holies as a bright candlestick, flaming with immaterial fire, as a golden censer burning with divine coal, as the vessel of*

34

manna, the rod of Aaron, and the tablet written by God, as a holy ark and table of the bread of life.[44]

On this Feast of the Entrance of the Virgin into the Temple, one of the lessons read during Vespers is 3 Kings 8:1-11, which describes the dedication of Solomon's temple (c.960 B.C.).

In icons of the Church, as those seen in the Stavronikita Monastery or the Monastery at Chora (Kariye Djami), it is evident that the actions of bringing the Ark of the Covenant and the holy vessels into the temple are illustrated as prefigurations of Mary's presentation and life in the temple.

As can be seen in this icon from Stavronikita Monastery, the priests are carrying the ark into the temple. Note how the iconographer, Theophanes the Cretan (16th c.), has placed a depiction of the Mother of God upon it. She was an anti-type of the ark, the abode of God, through her role in the incarnation. Thus, this vessel, borne aloft by the priests, will figure prominently among her epithets in Byzantine hymnography and exegesis.[45]

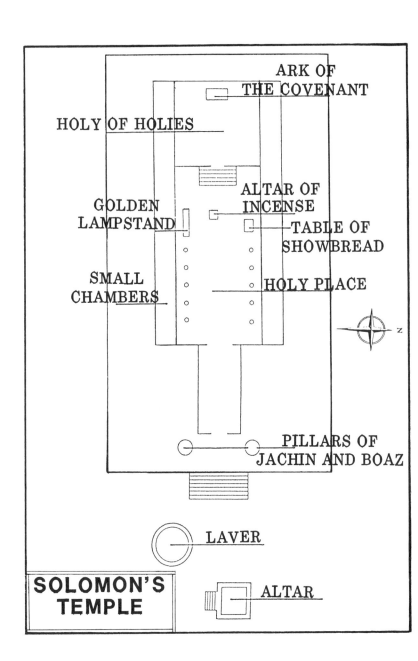

ARK OF
THE COVENANT

HOLY OF HOLIES

GOLDEN
LAMPSTAND

ALTAR OF
INCENSE

TABLE OF
SHOWBREAD

SMALL
CHAMBERS

HOLY PLACE

z

PILLARS OF
JACHIN AND BOAZ

LAVER

SOLOMON'S
TEMPLE

ALTAR

36

An icon that is to be found in Constantinopolitan Church of Pammakaristos (Fethiye Camii), the Virgin is depicted, in the sanctuary, above the High Priest Aaron and his sons.

In this icon we recall the prophecy of Ezekiel, who had seen the Virgin-Mother as the shut outer gate of the sanctuary that looks eastward [Ez. 44:1].

Rejoice, Mary Theotokos, temple of holiness and temple that shall never be destroyed, as the prophet cried, "Holy is Thy temple, wonderful in righteousness!" [Ps. 64:5-6].[46]

In the canon of the *Akathist to the Theotokos*, we chant this verse: *Rejoice, O pure Maiden, the spacious "tabernacle" of the Logos.*[47]

THE TEMPLE OF HEROD

Herod the Great had attacked Jerusalem in 37 B.C. He was a prolific builder and decided to dismantle the old structure of the temple and rebuild it in the prevailing Hellenistic-Roman style. This was probably a political gesture to reconcile the Jews. Work began c. 20-19 B.C.[48] Herod, taking pains to respect the sacred area, trained one thousand priests as masons to build the shrine, since only priests could enter the house and the inner court. Although the central part was completed within a year and a half, some of the subsidiary buildings were still under construction half a century later.[49]

At the age of three years and two and one-half months, the young Virgin Mary in all likelihood entered some time shortly after the completion of the central part of the building, that is, some time between 17 and 16 B.C.

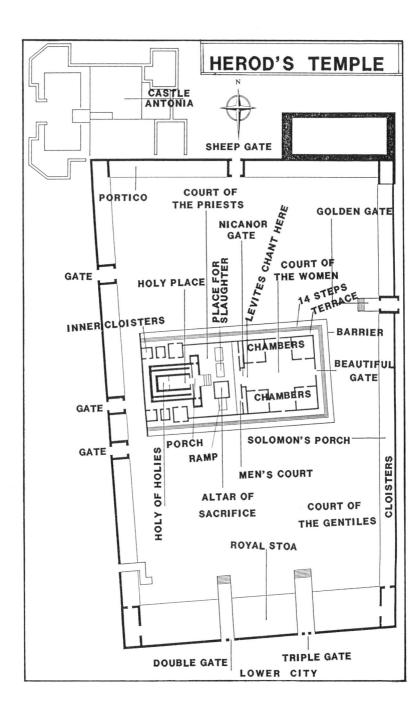

HEROD'S TEMPLE

N

CASTLE ANTONIA

SHEEP GATE

PORTICO

COURT OF THE PRIESTS

NICANOR GATE

GOLDEN GATE

LEVITES CHANT HERE

GATE

HOLY PLACE

PLACE FOR SLAUGHTER

COURT OF THE WOMEN

14 STEPS

TERRACE

INNER CLOISTERS

BARRIER

CHAMBERS

BEAUTIFUL GATE

GATE

CHAMBERS

GATE

PORCH

SOLOMON'S PORCH

RAMP

HOLY OF HOLIES

MEN'S COURT

CLOISTERS

ALTAR OF SACRIFICE

COURT OF THE GENTILES

ROYAL STOA

DOUBLE GATE

TRIPLE GATE

LOWER CITY

38

The temple building is spoken of as exceedingly impressive in its grandeur of gleaming white marble, which became one of the wonders of the ancient world.[50] Passing out of the colonnade, or eastern porch, known as Solomon's Porch, it was pierced by the Golden Gate, which was an exit from the city. The area known as the Court of the Gentiles, or what the rabbis call the "Mount of the House" was a place to which Gentiles had access. Here, too, more than likely was the market for the sale of sacrificial animals, the tables of the money changers, and places for the sale of other needful articles. The roofs were carved cedar. On the south side there were the royal porticoes which had 162 columns with Corinthian capitals, that formed three aisles. Advancing within this court, you reached a place where no Gentile, nor Levitically unclean person, might proceed. There were tablets, bearing inscriptions to that effect, to warn people. Thirteen openings admitted into the inner part of the court and then fourteen steps led up to the terrace. Then a flight of steps led up to massive splendid gates. There were four gates, but the most splendid gate was that to the east, termed "the Beautiful".

Entering by the Beautiful Gate, you came into the Court of Women, so called because the women occupied in it two elevated and separated galleries, which, however, filled only part of the court. Then fifteen steps led up to the upper court, which was bounded by a wall, and where was to be found the celebrated Nicanor Gate. Here the Levites, who conducted the musical part of the service, placed their instruments. In the Court of the Women was the Beautiful Gate where the treasury and the thirteen trumpet-shaped receptacles for monetary offerings were located, while at each corner there were chambers and halls, destined for various purposes. The four chambers in the courtyard were for storing wood for sacrifice, for storing oil, wine, and salt that was to be spread on the slippery marble courtyards in case of wet weather, a room for quietness and separation for those performing vows (named Nazarite), and one where instruction could be received and questions asked.[51]

Men could ascend through the Nicanor Gate to a narrow courtyard where they could look over a low wall into the Court of the Priests. There the priests sacrificed at the altar of sacrifice, which, with the laver, was placed before the temple porch. The laver was huge (about 7.5 feet high with about a 10,000 gallon capacity) and was supported on the backs of twelve bronze bulls, in groups of three facing the four directions. The round bronze basin stood in the court between the altar and the porch. It is unclear whether the brazen sea was to be found in Herod's Temple, since it is last mentioned being part of Solomon's Temple, because the Chaldeans broke the sea into pieces and carried them away to Babylon [2 Kings 25:13; Jer. 52:17, 20].[52]

From the porch a descent of twelve steps led to the priests' court. At the porch-way could be seen the two pillars named Jacin and Boaz. A pair of cypress doors separated the entrance porch from the holy place, but it was possible to see through the porch-way to the darkened interior that was lit by a lampstand and the altar of incense, which, like the table of shewbread, were there as it had been in earlier times. At the lighting of the incense, musical instruments sounded.[53] Music was an important part of worship and, as earlier indicated, the Levites led in the singing of the Psalms.[54]

Now there was a thick curtain that separated the holy place from the Holy of Holies. Beyond it was empty space. The Ark of the Covenant stood there, overshadowed by two olive-wood carved cherubim whose wings touched each other and the side walls.[55] Another feature was the rock of Moriah, which pierced the floor.[56] In Genesis 22:2 [KJV], God had instructed Abraham to offer up Isaac on one of the mountains in the land of Moriah. This Moriah was also the same location where Solomon built his temple [2 Ch. 3:1].[57] Both the holy place and the Holy of Holies were panelled with cedar-wood and the floor was planked with cypress. Walls and double-doors were decorated with carvings of flowers, palm trees and cherubim overlaid with gold. There was no visible stonework inside.[58]

Apart from these there were many other side rooms in the temple precincts. The Sanhedrin would meet in the "Hall of Hewn Stones". There was a room where the priests who were on duty would meet to see who would be chosen by lot to enter the holy place for the day.[59] On all sides except the east, where the porch was, there were thirty-eight chambers (inner cloisters), arranged in three stories, which were used to store utensils and where the priests resided.[60]

The upper court was divided into two parts by a boundary--the narrow part forming the "Court of Israel", and the wider that of the priests, in which were the great altar and laver.

The sanctuary itself was on a higher terrace than the Court of the Priests. Twelve steps led up to its porch, which extended beyond it on either side (north and south). Here, in separate chambers, all that was necessary for the sacrificial service was kept. On a gold overlaid table, near the entrance, the old shewbread which was taken out, and the new that was brought in, were respectively placed. The shewbread consisted of twelve loaves of unleavened bread which were placed one above the other in two columns. They remained on the table for one week and then were removed and eaten by the priests in the precincts of the sanctuary [Lev. 24:5-9]. The porch was adorned by votive offerings, and conspicuous among them was a massive golden vine. A two-leaved gate opened into the sanctuary itself, which was divided into two parts. The holy place (in Hebrew, *hekal*) had the golden candlestick (south), the table of shewbread (north), and the golden altar of incense between them. A heavy double veil concealed the entrance to the Holy of Holies. All around the sanctuary and each of the courts were various chambers and outer buildings, which served different purposes with the services of the temple.[61] The most holy place (in Hebrew, *debir*) was entered by the high priest once a year, viz. on the Day of Atonement. Only the officiating priests were permitted to enter the larger room, the *hekal*, to bring in the incense morning and evening, to trim the lamp, which was done once a day and, as we said, to replace the table with fresh shewbread, which was done every Sabbath.

Rejoice, O living Table, holding the Bread of Life.[62]

THE ARK OF THE COVENANT

The Ark of the Covenant was the most important object of peculiar sanctity. In the history of the ark, it is expressly recognized as the leader of the Hebrew host in their exodus and march through the desert, in virtue of its being, in some sense, the dwelling-place of God. More so than any other object, the ark is used to typify the Theotokos. In patristic times, the text, "Arise, O Lord, into Thy rest, Thou and the ark of Thy holiness" [Ps. 131:8] inspired much homiletic treatment. It is therefore fitting that the Virgin Mary, as was in the case of the ark when it was borne aloft by the Levites, should be borne by Anna, one of the daughters of Aaron. And, as in the time of David [2 Sam. 6:13-17] and, even more so, Solomon, of the kingly tribe of Judah, who escorted the ark to the Temple [1 Kings 8:1-11], just as Joachim of David's house escorts his daughter to the temple, as the animate ark.

In the present 14th century Serbian icon, the brothers, Prophet Moses and the High Priest Aaron, are shown standing in the Tabernacle of Witness. Depictions of the Theotokos may be seen on the altar (in a medallion) and on the upper lid of the Ark of the Covenant.

We learn, however, from 1 Kings 8:9 that by the time of Solomon (10th c. B.C.), only the two tablets were to be found in the ark, not Aaron's rod. At that time, Solomon moved the ark from its modest tent to the inner sanctuary of the temple, under the wings of the cherubim.

From the time that the ark took up residence in the Temple of Solomon, there has been no other mention of the Ark of the Covenant in the older historical books, apart from the Prophet Jeremias. In c.627 B.C., the Prophet Jeremias wrote: "In those days they shall no more say, 'The Ark of the Covenant of the Holy One of Israel: it shall not come to mind; it shall not be named; neither shall it be visited...'" [Jer. 3:16]. It is unknown if perhaps this treasure was carried off by the King of Egypt, Shishak or Susakim (c.950-929 B.C.) [1 Kings 14:26] or if it perished in the destruction of the city and temple by Nebuchadrezzar (c.597 B.C.). According to the Jewish historian Josephus (c.37 A.D.-c.100 A.D.), there was no ark in the second temple (Herod's temple).[63] Thus, historical evidence seems to point that when the Virgin entered the Temple of Herod, the Ark of the Covenant was not present. But it did not matter, because there was no need for the "type" when the living "ark", Mary, was present in the Holy of Holies.

Saint Irenaeus (d. after 193) writes: "The ark is shown to be a type of the body of Christ, pure and undefiled...."[64] It was actually the noted Father of the Church, Hippolytos of Rome (c.170-c.236], who would identify the Virgin-Mother with the ark when he wrote: "Now the Lord was without sin, being in His human nature from incorruptible wood, that is from the Virgin, and being sheathed, as it were, in the pure gold of the Word within and of the Spirit without."[65] Saint Hesychios of Jerusalem (d. after 451) writes: "The ark of Thy sanctification is the Virgin Theotokos surely. If Thou art the Pearl, then she must be the ark."[66] Chrysippos of Jerusalem (399-479), who we read about in the Life of St. Euthymios (celebrated on the 20th of January) writes: "The truly royal ark, the most precious ark, was the Ever-Virgin Theotokos; the ark which received the treasure of all sanctification...."[67] Chrysippos hints here that the incorruptible wood of the ark would eventually signify the Virgin-Mother's immunity from corruption in the grave. Many other Fathers will speak of Mary as the ark: St. Proclos of Constantinople;[68] in the hymns of St. Romanos;[69] St. Andrew of Crete;[70] and St. John of Damascus.[71]

The ark is described in Ex. 25:10-22 as a box surmounted by two figures of cherubim. Provisions were made for gold-plated acacia wood staves permanently inserted and fixed through golden rings so that it could be carried. The acacia wood box measured about 4 ft. by 2 ft. by 2 ft. and was gold-plated inside and out, with a gold molding. The initial purpose of the chest was to hold the "testimony" to God's salvation. The ark was a throne for the invisible God Who was seated on the wings of the cherubim. Now within the chest were the two stone tablets of the "covenant of the Lord" (the Ten Commandments) [1 Kings 8:21]; a *homer* (c. two quarts) of manna in a golden pot [Ex. 16:33-34], as a memorial to God's provision; and the rod of Aaron which bloomed blossoms and produced almonds as "a testimony...against murmurings" [Num. 17:10] to the exclusive priesthood of the sons of Aaron and the authority of Moses and Aaron.[72]

The Rod Of Aaron Budded,
Thus Showing Who Would Be Priest

How did the budding of the rod of Aaron come about and what did it testify unto? We learn from the *Book of Numbers* that three men from the tribe of Reuben, Dathan, Abiram and Aun rose up with Korah the Levite, and led 250 leaders of the Israelites in rebellion against Moses, declaring that Moses and Aaron had exalted themselves above the assembly of the Lord [Num. 16:1-3]. Korah, Dathan and Abiram, and all their households were swallowed up alive into the earth as a punishment of God [Num. 16:25-33]. After this, the Lord commanded Moses saying that rods should be taken according to the houses. The rod of Aaron was also in the midst of the twelve rods. Moses then took them before the Lord in the tabernacle of witness [Num. 6-7]. On the following day, Moses and Aaron went into the tabernacle of witness and the rod of Aaron, of the house of Levi, had blossomed and put forth a bud, and bloomed blossoms and produced almonds [Num. 17:8].

It was from this that God then said, "Lay up the rod of Aaron before the testimonies to be kept as a sign for the children of the disobedient; and let their murmuring cease from Me, and they shall not die" [Num. 17:10]. Thus, the

Levites were to be taken out of the midst of the children of Israel; that tribe was to be a present given unto the Lord, to minister in the services of the tabernacle of witness. Thus upon Aaron and his sons was bestowed the honor of keeping up the priestly ministration of the altar and of that within the veil. The tribe of Levi was to minister before the Lord exclusively, but the stranger that came near shall die [Num. 18: 6-7].

Though the Christ is from David's line, of the tribe of Judah, Christ's Mother was from both tribes: Judah on her father's side and Levi on her mother's side. Though only the levitical line served and offered in the temple, nevertheless, she embodied both the royal and priestly lines. It is meet and right that she should offer her Fruit upon the immac-

44

ulate and virginal altar of her womb, as a propitiation for us, acceptable to God.

But why were almonds produced? Saint Paulinus (353-431), in speaking of the rod of Jacob, taken from the almond[73] tree [Gen. 25:37], comments upon the mystical significance of the almond. "The rod of the almond tree is Christ, for there is food within that tree, which has an outer casing consisting of bitter bark over its green skin. Here you must recognize the divine Christ clothed in our human body. In that flesh He can be broken; the food lies in the Word, the bitterness in the Cross. His hard covering consists of the tidings of the Cross and the food of that Cross, and it encloses within the divine remedy in the flesh of Christ. Yet in His Cross He is also sweet, because God our life brought forth life from the Tree."[74]

Furthermore, the almond was the emblem of the divine "forwardness" in bringing God's promises to pass. The Hebrew word for almond is *shaqed*, and it signifies the 'waker' or 'be wakeful'. This is an allusion to its being the first tree to wake to life in the winter. The flowers of the almond appear long before the leaves.[75] Thus Christ would be the "firstborn among many brethren" [Rom. 8:29] and the "firstborn among the dead" [Col. 1:18]. Indeed, He was the first to "wake" and overcome the long winter of death.

THE SACRED VESSELS

Brief mention here now will be made of the sacred objects of the Jews. Liturgical vessels from the Old Testa-

ment are shown as prefigurative types of the Virgin-Mother in both iconography and hymnology.

In this icon, the iconographer sought to establish the altar of Moses as the type of the Virgin.

Saint Gregory Palamas will comment that she is "the true throne of the Lord, for where the King sits, there is His Throne."[76] She is the receptacle of the Treasure which God granted to men,"[77] and "the tongs which the seraphim

45

used to take up the live coal which touched the mouth of the Prophet Isaias, prefiguring the incarnation."[78] All these epithets that are applied to Mary do not infringe on the worship due to God alone; all refer to her part in the incarnation.

In describing the Virgin with such temple vessels as "candlestick" and "lampstand", we offer three examples out of many. Saint George chants, *Thou "candlestick" with many lights* [Ex. 25:31], *O Bride of God, thou hast shone forth today in the house of the Lord, and thou dost illuminate us with the august gifts of thy grace and wonders, O pure and all-hymned Theotokos.*[79]

The hymnographer, St. Joseph (c.816-886), chants, *All of us honor thee, O Virgin undefiled, as the shining "lamp" and "candlestick" in which the fire of the Godhead came to dwell, bringing light to them held fast in the dark night of corruption; and we bless thy child-bearing, O blessed among women.*[80]

In the *Canon of the Akathist*, we also say, *Rejoice, O "lampstand" and "urn of Manna" from on high. Rejoice, O "lamp" and "jar" containing the "Manna" which sweetens the senses of the faithful.*[81]

The prophets proclaimed thee in ages past, speaking of thee as the ark of His holiness [Ps. 131:8], *the golden censer* [Heb. 9:4; 3 Kings 7:50], *the candlestick* [Ex. 25:31], *and the table* [Ex. 25: 23]; *and we sing thy praises as the tabernacle that held God.*[82]

The mercy seat, literally "place of propitiary atonement" (in Greek, *ilasteerion)* was a covering plate of pure gold that corresponded to the dimensions of the ark.[83]

Saint Theodore the Studite (c.759-826) also calls her a "mercy seat." *O Mary, called by God, truly thou art the "mercy seat" of the faithful: for through thee forgiveness is freely bestowed upon all. Cease not to intercede before thy*

46

Son and Lord, gaining His gracious favor for us who sing thy praises.[84]   Also in the *Canon of the Akathist*, we hear, *Rejoice, most gracious "mercy seat" and "throne" of Christ, the King of all.*[85]

At the ends of the mercy seat and facing each other were two hammered gold cherubim with wings outspread and overshadowing the plate and with their faces toward it.[86] Once every year, in the Day of Atonement service [Lev. 16:2; Heb. 9:7], Aaron or the high priest would sprinkle the ark's cover, or mercy seat, seven times: first with the blood of a bull, slain as a sin offering for himself, and then with that of a goat for the people, so as to cleanse Israel [Lev. 16: 14,15,30].[87] Although Moses appointed the Kohathite Levites, under Aaron's son Eleazar to be responsible for the ark, they could not touch it on pain of death [Num. 4:15].[88]

The Israelites were not permitted to make a material representation of the presence of God.   The mercy seat seems to be the nearest approximation of His presence.   The pillar of cloud by day and the pillar of fire by night [Ex. 13:21], which represented God's presence among them, hovered over the mercy seat. Apparently, it was not the lid or the cherubim, but the space between the cherubim that represented God's presence among them.   This space could not be confined or controlled by man, thus it conveyed to the Israelites the idea that God was in their midst without a material representation.[89]

Saint Ambrose (339-397) comments in *Letter 19* that "...the Ark of the Testament is all covered with gold. This gold covering means the teaching of Christ, the teaching of the Wisdom of God.   There is the golden vessel containing manna, the vessel of spiritual nourishment, the storehouse of divine knowledge.   There is the rod of Aaron, symbol of the grace of the priesthood.   In the past it withered, but it has budded anew in Christ.   There are the cherubim above the tablets of the Testament, the latter which are the knowledge of holy Scripture.   There is the propitiary (the mercy seat), and high aloft is God the Word, the image of the invisible God, who says to you, '...I will speak to thee above the propitiary between the two cherubs, which are upon the Ark of Testimony....'[Ex. 25:22].   He speaks to us in such a way that we may understand His speech.   Thus, because He speaks not of worldly matters but of those of the soul, He says, 'I will open my mouth in parables'" [Ps. 77:2].[90]

In the holy place there were three objects: a table, a lampstand, and an altar. The table was known as the table of shewbread. It is described in Ex. 25:23-30. It measured about 3 ft. by 1.5 ft. and on it were placed twelve baked cakes. The shewbread was actually called "bread of the presence" because it was in the presence of God [1 Sam. 21:6]. It was renewed every Sabbath by one of the priests, and the old shewbread was then removed to be eaten by the priests [Lev. 24:5-9; 1 Sam. 21:6]. The holy place was illuminated by a golden lampstand which had three branches ending in flower-shaped holders projecting from each side of a main stem, which also supported a lamp-holder [Ex. 25:31-36]. In between the table of shewbread and the lampstand was an altar on which incense was burned. It measured only 1 ft. by 6 in., and was made of acacia and overlaid with gold [Ex. 30:1-10]. The incense itself was also sacred and could not be made for any other purpose than for worship.[91]

The Jews also used sacred lots, known as Urim and Thummin, that is, 'Manifestation' and the 'Truth' [Lev. 8:8], by which the will of God was sometimes divined by the high priest. The high priest wore a close-fitting, armless outer vest of varying length called an ephod. It was fastened around the waist with a beautifully woven girdle, and held together at the top by shoulder pieces set with onyx stones engraved with the names of the twelve tribes. The ceremonial golden breastplate contained twelve gem stones also inscribed with the names of the twelve tribes; that is, four rows of three stones. It was an elaborately decorated square of linen worn on the breast as part of the robes of Israel's high priest. It was made of gold, blue, purple, scarlet, and fine linen folded double into a square of about 9 in. by 9 in. It was fastened with gold cords to a set of rings on the ephod. This breastplate contained the Urim and Thummin, which refer to an oracular function. There is no consistent rendering of just how divine messages would be interpreted. Some authorities have suggested that there were two lots or discs, one white the other black. When the stones were cast from the bag, two whites meant "yes"; two black meant "no"; and a black and white meant "wait". Some suggest that Thummin was "yes" and Urim "no". However, it must be remembered that there is no valid tradition that has survived to explain their meaning.[92]

THE VIRGIN ENTERS THE HOLY OF HOLIES

Then   Zacharias, the   priest   of   God, received   her   into   the temple   with   rejoicing and   established   her there.[93]

He then took Mary to the bema. Thus she abode in the Holy of Holies for more than nine years, though some apocryphal manuscripts record her stay for as long as twelve years. The Holy of Holies, a place that none dared enter, except the high priest--and, then again, only at his appointed time and this happened but once a year.

The Holy of Holies was that place in the temple, the dwelling-place of God, in which God came into contact with man through the intermediary of the high priest. Now God, Who will condescend to become man, foreordained the holy Virgin to become the supreme 'holy of holies' through which He would come into permanent contact with man in the Holy Church, becoming man Himself, Christ Jesus, the great High-Priest and intermediary. As the Holy of Holies was filled with the glory of God's presence--so much that the priests could not bear the glory of it--so the womb of the all-holy Virgin was to be filled with the glory of God's presence.[94]

THE VIRGIN RECEIVES BREAD
FROM THE ARCHANGEL

In a mosaic at the Monastery of Chora, Mary is seated on a golden throne beneath a ciborium, her feet resting on a three-stepped podium. An angel in flight appears from the left and offers her bread. Seated on a footstool on the lower left is one of the company of daughters of the

Hebrews who had, from her early infancy, served as guardians and attendants to the Virgin.[95]

Saint George writes that the angels were astonished to see the Virgin enter the Holy of Holies, as we hear in the festal hymn: *Beholding the entry of the all-pure one, the angels were struck with amazement, seeing how the Virgin entered into the Holy of Holies.*[96]

Saint Andrew of Crete writes that Mary, *the "holy of holies", is placed as an infant in the holy sanctuary, to be reared by the hands of an angel.*[97] In the hymns, we learn that the angel is the Archangel Gabriel: *And Gabriel was then sent to thee, O Virgin all-undefiled, to bring thee food. All the powers of heaven stood amazed, seeing the Holy Spirit dwell in thee."*[98]

The manifold wisdom of God, according to the eternal purpose which the Father purposed in Christ Jesus [Eph. 3:10-11], had been hid in God. The principalities and powers in heavenly places knew it only in part. It was by and through the Church that all came to know the mystery which, from the beginning of the world, had been hid in God [Eph. 3:9-10]. It is the secret preparation of the humanity of Christ. In the temple at Jerusalem, the elect Virgin would prepare herself for her future role as the "temple" of His Body--a Body that would be destroyed but that He would raise up in three days [Jn. 2:19] and, then, with that same Body, He would be received up into heaven, and sit at the right hand of God [Mk. 16:19].

Moreover, she did not venture to leave this place, but remained therein and conversed with the angels. Her attitude is described by the hymnographer thus: *O venerable "holy of holies," thou dost love to dwell in the holy temple; and thou abidest, O Virgin, in converse with angels, receiving bread most marvelously from heaven, O thou who dost sustain our life.*[99] Her behavior as a young infant is brought out in the following Vespers hymn: *She, the all-pure one, with rejoicing, goes round the divine habitations.*[100]

THE LIVING BRIDAL CHAMBER
OF GOD THE WORD

Saint Romanos states in his kontakion that he believed that *she was given over to the temple to be reared; and she received nourishment from the angels. She became a saint among saints, and just as she was dedicated, she became the "temple" and the "tabernacle" of the Lord.*[101]

Saint Germanos of Constantinople (c. 635-733) in a sermon, presents a rich eulogy of Mary: "Fed by angels...the child grew and became strong, and the whole force of the curse by which we were struck in Eden was foiled."[102]

Saint George chants, *From Eve of old the transgression came upon mankind and, now, from Eve's stock has flowered forth our restoration and incorruption, even the Theotokos, who is brought today into the house of God.*[103]

Saint Gregory Palamas in *Homily 37* writes: "She passed not a few years in the Holy of Holies itself, wherein under the care of an angel she enjoyed ineffable nourishment such as even Adam did not succeed in tasting; for indeed if he had, like this immaculate one, he would not have fallen away from life,...and so that she might prove to be his daughter, she yielded a little to nature, as would her Son...." He also comments that "while yet three years of age and not yet possessing the super-celestial in-dwelling (Christ), she seemed not to bear our flesh as she dwelt in the Holy of Holies. Here, she became most perfect as regards her body by such great marvels."[104]

Other hymns of the Feast describe her as *indeed more holy than the heavenly powers;*[105] and that even *God's angels sing in praise that she is indeed the heavenly "tabernacle."*[106]

Again, the Virgin's role is emphasized when she is called the living "bridal chamber".[107] Her "bridal role" and mystical betrothal is brought to mind in this matinal Laud of the present Feast: *O Virgin, fed in faith by heavenly bread in the temple of the Lord, thou hast brought forth unto the world the Bread of life, that is, the Word; and as His chosen temple without spot, thou wast betrothed mystically through the Spirit, to be the Bride of God the Father.*[108]

Saint George describes Mary Theotokos as the living "bridal chamber" when he chants, *Today has the temple become a wedding adornment and a fair chamber for the Virgin, as it receives the living "bridal chamber" of God, pure and without spot, she who shines more brightly than all the creation.*[109]

Supernatural sustenance has occurred in other times and places to the saints of God. In the Old Testament, the Israelite nation was fed in the wilderness [Ex. 16:14-18] with "the bread of angels" [Ps. 77:29]. Prophet Elias the Thesbite [3 Kings 17:6] and the Prophet Daniel [Bel and the Dragon 1:33-39] were sustained by God's grace and fed by His messengers. After the coming of Christ, other recipients of this grace were the infant Forerunner John, St. Paisios the Great,[110] St. Mary Golinduc[111] and other many ascetics, both men and women throughout the centuries.

THE PREORDAINED QUEEN OF ALL
HAS OPENED THE KINGDOM OF HEAVEN
UNTO US[112]

Let us, with all the earth, look upon these marvelous, strange and wonderful events, for *she was forechosen from all generations to be the dwelling-place of Christ, the Master and God of all.*[113]

Saint Ildefonsus (+667), Archbishop of Toledo, writes that Mary's destiny was theocentric. She was "chosen by God, assumed by God, called by God, near to God, adhering to God, and united with God."[114]

In closing, the Theotokos, who is described as the glorious fruit of a sacred promise, who is truly revealed unto the world as higher than all creation, was piously led into the house of God, where she fulfilled the vow of her parents and was preserved by the Holy Spirit.[115] Thus, St. George of Nicomedia comments, *Strange is the manner of thy birth: strange is the manner of thy growing. Strange and most marvelous are all things concerning thee, O Bride of God, and they are beyond the telling of mortal man!*[116]

Chapter IV.
The VIRGIN Growing Up In The Temple

+ + +

Mary was held in admiration by all the people of Israel. She spent her time so assiduously in the praises of God that all were astonished and wondered at her. She was not reckoned a young infant but, as it were, a grown-up person of thirty years old.[1] Indeed, according to the psalmist, when her father and mother forsook her, the Lord took care of her [Ps. 26:12].

Blessed John Maximovitch (1896-1966) writes that Mary was settled in the quarters for virgins which existed in the temple. She spent so much time in prayer in the Holy of Holies that one might say that she lived in it.[2] She desired to fulfil the commandment of God, "Ye shall be holy; for I the Lord your God am holy" [Lev. 19:2].

Bishop Ignatius Brianchaninov (1807-1867), in his *Exposition*, comments, "Despite the righteousness and the purity of life which the Mother of God led, sin and eternal death manifested their presence in her. They could not but be manifested: such is the precise and faithful teaching of the Orthodox Church concerning the Virgin with relation to fallen nature and death."[3] Verily, the more pure and perfect one is, the more one notices one's own imperfections and considers oneself all the more unworthy.

Saint Ambrose (339-397), in his *Commentary on the 118th Psalm*, comments, "She was a stranger to any fall into sin, but not a stranger to sinful temptations. God alone is without sin."[4]

Apocryphal sources record that she was constant in prayer and her appearance was beautiful and glorious; hardly any one could look into her face. She occupied herself with wool-work, so that even in her tender years she achieved such skill as to surpass old women.[5]

These sources present the following schedule that she followed, that is, the hours of prayer that she set for herself. From the morning until 9:00 a.m., she remained in prayer; from 9:00 a.m. until 3:00 p.m., she was occupied with her weaving; and from 3:00 p.m., she again applied herself to prayer. She did not retire from praying until the appearance of the angel of the Lord after the ninth hour or after 3:00 p.m., from whose hand she received food. Thus, she refreshed herself only once daily with that food brought by the Archangel. The food that she received from the priests was distributed among the poor.[6] Apocryphal sources describe Mary's precocity as being so great, and her life so fully ordered by divine rather than by human means, that instruction, it would seem, was also given to her by the angels of God.[7]

Therefore, Mary continued in the temple as a dove and was educated there. Everyday she had converse with angels who preserved her from all sorts of evil and caused her to abound with all good things.

Thus, she became more and more perfect in the work of God. Thus, far from the turmoil of every day life, the all-holy one meditated and nourished her soul on scripture day and night. When the older virgins rested from the praises of God, she did not rest. None exceeded her in the praises and vigils of God, and no one was more learned in the wisdom of the law of God. No one was more lowly in humility, more elegant in singing and more perfect in all virtue.[8]

Saint Ambrose comments, in *Concerning the Ever-Virginity of the Virgin Mary,* that she was adorned with all virtue and manifested an example of an extraordinarily pure life. Being submissive and obedient to all, she offended no one and was friendly to all. She never said a crude word to anyone and did not allow any unclean thought.[9]

She was steadfast, immoveable, unchangeable and daily advanced to perfection. None saw Mary ever angry nor heard her speak evil. All of her conversations were full of grace. She was ever occupied in prayer or in searching the law. She was anxious also about her companions, lest any should sin even in one word or raise her voice in senseless laughter or should be in the wrong, or proud before their parents. Moreover, she herself feared to even inadvertently offend or appear proud before her peers.[10]

Mary blessed God without interruption and, lest perchance, even in greeting others she might cease from her praises to the Lord, she even answered then, praising God, in her salutation, by saying: "Thanks be to God" or "Glory be to God". (From the Virgin began the custom of this expression when people greet one another.)

The sojourn of the Virgin Mary in the temple is described by St. Gregory Palamas (+1359) in terms that make  Mary the model of the hesychastic life. Extolling constant prayer, the saint indicates that the Virgin was the first to take it upon herself to pray unceasingly. According to St. Gregory, her asceticism therein did not lead her to come to an understanding of the grace received from the time of her conception, but to learn more of the nature of the sins of Adam. It was there that she perceived and realized that "no one could halt the murderous rush which was bearing away the human race."[11]

Thus she was filled with pity for people who were brought to ruin and condemnation through disobedience. Therefore, she resolved to have her heart, mind and soul dwell on God, and endeavored to remain attentive and struggle in prayer. She would pray for the human race and God's great mercy. She understood the most excellent way to converse with God was through holy silence and silence of the mind. Hence, she withdrew from the world and put away all earthly things. Through this, by God's grace, she ascended to contemplation of Him. Thus, the Virgin pioneered a new path to God, by the path of silencing the thoughts. Abiding in prayer day and night, and maintaining silence, she cleansed her heart and was inexpressibly united with Him. Rising above all creation and creatures, the all-holy Virgin contemplated God's glory more fully than did Moses, and communed of divine grace in such a way that defies words and even reason. She became a luminous cloud of living water, the dawn of the unspeakable day, and the fiery chariot of the Word. There, in the Holy of Holies, through prayer of the heart, she ascended to the summit of contemplation. Renouncing the world for the world's sake, by holy silence, and attentive inner prayer, she would serve as a model for those future monastics of her Son and God.

MARY'S ASCENT INTO THE TEMPLE, A REFLECTION OF THE INTERIOR LIFE

Many have used the symbolism which likens the three sections of the temple to the three stages of the spiritual life, that is, purification, illumination and union. They will also compare this to the three books of Solomon--Proverbs, Ecclesiastes and the Song of Songs. But as regards the temple, the court corresponds to the active life, where the aim is freedom from passions *(apathia)*. The holy place with its veil, that is, the second part of the temple, opens the way of natural contemplation *(physike theoria)*--knowledge of God in the creation. The Holy of Holies corresponds to contemplation, which is *theologia*, or knowledge of God in His Word, the Logos.[12]

In iconography, we, too, may see the three parts of the temple in the scene of her entrance, presentation and installation. The scene opens in the inner court of the temple, near the entrance to the holy place, marked off by the veil. The priest Zacharias, clothed in his priestly robes, stands before the entrance of the holy place. To be more precise, he is usually seen standing on the first step of the staircase (the fifteen steps of the temple correspond to the fifteen "Psalms of degrees"). The Virgin may be seen with outstretched hands towards Zacharias, moving in the direction of the steps that lead to the Holy of Holies. In some icons, she may be seen sitting on the highest step, near the entrance of the Holy of Holies, where an angel comes to assist her and nourish her with heavenly bread. This symbolizes that degree of contemplation, the pre-engagement with God, which is the beginning of the way toward union with divinity.[13]

A VIRGIN SHALL CONCEIVE IN THE WOMB

As we mentioned earlier, the young Virgin Mary gave herself up entirely to God and repulsed from herself every impulse to sin, yet still she felt the weakness of human nature more powerfully than others. Therefore, she greatly desired the coming of the Saviour.

Saint Ephraim the Syrian (c.306-373) chants that *Women heard that a virgin would conceive and bring forth a Son: honorable women hoped that Thou would rise from them; yea, noble ladies hoped that Thou might spring up from them! Blessed be Thy majesty, that humbled itself, and rose from the poor!*[14]

Though Jewish women in each successive age had been hoping to be the Mother of the Messiah, Mary alone, in her great humility, had put aside the desire and the thought of so great a dignity, that is, to be the *Gebirah, Ghebireh* or *G'vee-rah*, whose meaning in Hebrew denotes "the mighty one" or the eldest and most respected female, referring to the King's Mother or Queen-Mother. The Hebrew understanding of the roots and prominence of this title, Queen-Mother, though it has various translations, basically means "mighty one." It can be better understood after a study of the Old Testament and the role of the king's mother.[15]

The Queen-Mother was usually the widow of the former king and the mother of the reigning one. She had certain obligations and received much respect. She was then the most important and influential woman in the household. A man might have many wives, but only one mother. He had been trained in deference and obedience to his mother, while his wives were subject to his authority. In a polygamous family, each wife, when she became a mother, began a kind of sub-family, which made her much more important to her children than their father. Management of the household was mostly in the mother's hands, as was education and training. Domestic friction was not uncommon due to the many clashes among the sub-families. We have as witness several examples given in Scriptures: Sarah and Hagar, Leah and Rachel, Hannah and Peninnah.[16] In fact, it was necessary that the sisters Leah and Rachel live in separate tents.

In the histories of the royal house of Judah and Israel, there are numerous indications of the exalted position of the mother of the reigning king. Her name is regularly recorded in the paragraph describing an accession, while nothing is said about the wives. See the Queen-Mother's name recorded in 1 Kings 14:21; 15:10; 22:42; 2 Kings 12:1; 14:2; 15:2,33; 18:2; 21:1,19; 23:36; 24:8;]. Maacah, Jezebel, Athaliah and Nestha appear as exercising great influence, though not always commendable, in the reigns of their sons [2 Kings 24:8, 12, 14; Jer. 22:26].[17] When the Queen-Mother Bathsheba came in to speak to her son, Solomon, "the king rose up to meet her, and bowed (in Hebrew, *shah-ghah*) himself unto her, and sat down on his throne, and caused a seat to be set for the king's mother; and she sat at his right hand (in Hebrew, *yahmeen*)" [1 Kings 2:19 KJV].

To the Hebrew mentality, the Mother of the Messiah was to occupy a special place. In their history, Solomon was the first of Israel's kings to include a "Queen-Mother" in his administration. We read that Bathsheba received great honor and sat at his right hand [1 Kings 2:19]. Her power was not simply that of a mother over her son, but she was considered an important advisor.[18]

The Prophet-King David foresaw his daughter Mary's day, too, when he wrote: "At Thy right hand stood the Queen, arrayed in a vesture of inwoven gold, adorned in varied colors" [Ps. 44:8].

Saint John of Damascus wrote that "In becoming the Mother of the Creator, she became the Mistress of all creation."

In her humility, which showed her great spiritual height, Mary considered herself unworthy to even be the servant girl of the Queen-Mother or Virgin, prophesied by Isaias, who was to give birth to the Messiah.[19] Nevertheless, Mary alone, being God-inspired, dedicated her virginity to the Lord, not consciously aware that what was meant in the prophecy was that a consecrated virgin would give birth, not a virgin who would conceive after marriage by her husband's seed.

Saint Ephraim again speaks: *In Mary, as in the eye, the Light came to dwell and it cleansed her spirit, refined her thoughts, sanctified her mind and purified her virginity.*[20]

Saint John of Damascus (c.676-c.750), agreeing with this account of her formative years, wrote that when "she grew up in the house of God, nourished by the Spirit, like a fruitful olive tree [Ps. 51:9], she became an abode of every virtue, turning her mind away from every worldly and carnal desire. This was fitting for her who was to conceive God within herself. She kept her soul and body virginal, for He is Holy and finds rest among the holy. Therefore, she sought and strove after holiness and was shown to be holy and a wondrous temple for the most high God."[21]

Saint Gregory of Palamas praises Mary in superlative terms, writing: "Today a new world and a wonderful paradise have appeared. In it and from it a new Adam is born to reform the old Adam and renew the whole world....God has kept this Virgin for Himself before all ages. He chose her from among all generations and bestowed on her grace higher than that given to all others, making her, before her wondrous childbirth, the saint of saints, giving her the honor of His own house in the Holy of Holies....Wishing to create an image of absolute beauty and to manifest clearly, to angels and to men, the power of His art, God made Mary truly all beautiful....He made of her a blend of all divine, angelic and human perfection, a sublime beauty embellishing the two worlds, rising from earth to heaven and surpassing even this latter."[22]

Saint Joseph the Hymnographer (c.816-886) writes: "The Holy Spirit wholly sanctified thee in the temple, wherefore thou hast become the fair spouse of the Father and Mother of the Son.[23]

Chapter V.
The VIRGIN Comes of Age

+ + +

When Mary was about thirteen, it was an occasion for the Pharisees to remark that it was not the custom to allow a woman of that age to abide in the temple of God. Therefore, at that time, the high priest made a public order: all virgins who had public settlements in the temple and had come of age were to return home. Furthermore, since they attained a proper age of maturity, in accordance with Hebrew custom, they should endeavor to be married.[1]

Saint Romanos the Melodist (c.490-c.556) made the following observation: *Mary did not leave the temple of the saints. Now, at the proper time, Mary had become radiant, and Zacharias observed that she was past the bloom of girlhood.*[2]

The accommodations provided by the temple for young female virgins is not clear scripturally or historically. Evidently, they were dedicated to God and were brought up according to the Scriptures. The young ladies received a proper education in the doctrines, commandments and sacred rites of their religion. Although consecrating the firstborn, the first produced, whatever opens the womb generally spoke of dedicating male infants, it is entirely possible that some pious parents could have consecrated the firstborn female child to the Lord, especially if the child were the product of prayers and supplications, as in the case of the Virgin Mary.[3]

THE VOW OF VIRGINITY

All the virgins of the temple readily yielded obedience to the high priest's order, except Mary who alone answered that she could not comply. She said, "It cannot be that I should know a man or that a man should know me." She assigned the following reasons for her resolve to remain a virgin: that both she and her parents had devoted her to the service of the Lord and that she herself had vowed never to lie with a man.

Although both of Mary's parents had reposed about three years earlier, the priests and her relations kept saying to her, "God is worshipped in children and adored in posterity, as has always been the custom among the sons of Israel."[4]

Nevertheless, Mary answered them saying, "God is worshipped in chastity as can be seen from the beginning, that is, before Abel there was none righteous among men. By his offerings he pleased God but was mercilessly slain by him who displeased God. Therefore, Abel received two crowns, that of oblation and of virginity. Also, Elias, when he was in the flesh was taken up in the flesh, having kept his flesh unsullied. Now I, from my infancy, in this temple, have learned that virginity can be sufficiently dear to God. Wherefore, because I can offer what is dear to God, I have resolved in my heart not to know a man."[5]

Mary, evidently, did not believe that marriage was an end in itself, nor essential to the wholeness of her person. Later, the divine Paul would write that one can find full freedom and completeness attending "upon the Lord without distraction" [1 Cor. 7:35]. It is not incredible to suppose that the Apostle might have been thinking of the Virgin as a model when he wrote to the Romans, saying, "present your bodies as a living sacrifice, holy and well-pleasing to God, which is your rational worship; not being conformed to this age, but be ye transformed by the renewing of your mind, that ye may test what is the good, and well-pleasing, and perfect will of God [Rom. 12:1-2].

Saint Gregory of Nyssa (c.335-394) implied that Moses' and Aaron's sister, Miriam, was the first to perfect virginity. He believed that Miriam was a type of Mary (Miriam) the Mother of God. Miriam the prophetess had taken a timbrel in her hand, and all the women went forth after her with

timbrels and dances [Ex. 15:20]. Just as the timbrel is a dead thing, so is virginity a deadening of bodily passions. And just as the timbrel emits a loud sound because it is devoid of all moisture and reduced to the highest degree of dryness, so has virginity a clear and ringing report among men. He asserts Miriam's virginity, because history makes no mention of her marriage or being a mother.

On the other hand, certain Jewish traditions and Josephus remark that Miriam did in fact have a husband and his name was Hur.[6] It was he who, with Aaron, stood at either side of Moses and held up his arms that Israel might prevail over Amalek [Ex. 17:12]. While Moses was absent and on Mt. Sinai, this Hur assisted in the ruling of the tribes [Ex. 24:14]. If Hur were Miriam's husband, she would also be the grandmother of Bezalel. Bezalel was the chief artisan and foundry man of the tabernacle, being given the gift of technological insight by the Holy Spirit to perform the work [Ex. 31:2-5; 36:1]. Moreover, if Miriam did in fact marry Hur, it means that she married outside of her tribe of Levi, because Hur was of Judah and a descendent of Phares [1 Chron. 2:5; 18-20; cf. 2 Chron. 1:5].

Yet, St. Gregory maintains that she is described as "Aaron's sister", and would not have thus been named and known if she had a husband. The grace of virginity came to be regarded as a precious thing, though among a people with whom motherhood was sought after and considered a blessing--and even regarded as a public duty.[7]

Though we recognize that in the situation of both the Virgin's mother Anna and the Virgin's cousin Elisabeth that childlessness was a "reproach among men", yet there are Old and New Testament examples of women without children who were honored--Judith, Esther, Anna the daughter of Phanuel and Mary of Magdala. Nevertheless, assuming that the general pattern of the social milieu at that time was marriage with a view to children, Mary had the pioneering personality and determination to transcend the thinking of her environment, being thus inspired by God.

Wherefore, the high priest was brought into a difficulty. He did not wish to dissolve the maiden's vow and disobey the sacred Scriptures which declare, "Make your vows and pay them to the Lord our God" [Ps. 75:10; Eccl. 5:4-6]. On the other hand, he did not wish to introduce a new custom among the people.[8]

Saint Gregory of Nyssa comments that Mary had bound herself to virginity and that "it would be akin to sacrilege if a man were to become master of a gift sacred to God." The priests then thought to espouse Mary to someone who would ensure the custody of her virginity;[9] for Mary felt obliged "to remain untouched and to entirely dedicate her flesh as a sacred offering to God."[10]

THE RESOLUTION OF MARY'S CASE

At that time, in September, the feast was approaching when many of the principal persons of Jerusalem and the neighboring areas would meet at the temple. The priest resolved to seek their advice how he might best proceed in such a difficult case.[11]

Then, when they met in council, the other priests said, "Behold, Mary is of age; what shall we do with her?; for fear lest the holy place of the Lord our God be defiled." Then the priests replied unanimously that the Lord's counsel should be sought concerning the matter, and they said to Zacharias, "Do thou stand before the altar of the Lord and enter into the holy place. Petition the Lord concerning her and whatsoever the Lord shall make manifest to thee, that thou must perform."[12]

Saint Germanos (c.635–733), Patriarch of Constantinople, confirms this story, writing, that "through the inspiration of God and the will of the priests, lots were cast for her...."[13]

While they were all engaged in prayer, the high priest entered into the holy place. Wearing the breastplate of judgment that was used in determining God's will [Ex. 28:15–29], he made prayers concerning Mary. Then, behold, an angel of the Lord stood by Zacharias, and said unto him, "Zacharias, Zacharias, go forth and call together all the widowers among the people and have each man bring his rod. And he by whom the Lord shall show a sign, shall be the husband of Mary. For the matter concerning to whom the Virgin should be given and be betrothed would be resolved in accordance with the prophecy of Isaias, where he says, 'there shall come forth a rod out of the root of Jesse, and a blossom shall come up from his root' [Is. 11:1].[14] The spirit of the God shall rest upon Him, the spirit of wisdom and understanding, the spirit of counsel and might, the spirit of knowledge and piety shall fill Him, and the spirit of the fear of God shall fill Him [Is. 11:2]."[15] Therefore, God put it into the mind of Zacharias to betroth the Virgin, that the devil might overlook her as the possible virgin of Isaias' prophecy.[16]

Then Abiathar, one of the priests, stood up and said, "Hear me, O sons of Israel, and receive my words into your ears. Since the time when this temple was built by Solomon, there have been in it virgins, the daughters of kings and the daughters of prophets, and of high priests and priests. They were great and worthy of admiration. But when the maidens came to the proper age they were given in marriage and followed the path that their mothers had before them; and they were pleasing to God. However, Mary has found a new order of life, for she has vowed to remain a virgin to God. Wherefore, it seems to me, that by the answer we received as a result of our inquiry, we should try to ascertain to whom Mary should be entrusted."[17]

These words found favor with all the synagogue. The lot was then cast by the priests upon the twelve tribes, and the lot fell upon the tribe of Judah. Then the priest announced that all eligible widowers of Judah be summoned, saying: "Let every man who has no wife come and bring his rod in his hand." Thus the criers went out through all of Israel and when the trumpet of the Lord sounded, all the people ran and met together.[18]

There was at that time, the aged Joseph of Nazareth, then eighty years old, of the tribe of Judah and of the royal house of David. After forty years of marriage, he was a recent widower of about one year. Not wishing to slight the order of the high priest, he put down his axe, for he was a carpenter by profession and lived honorably by the labor of his hands. He came forward bearing his rod in his hand with the other widowers of his tribe.

His first wife, a pious and God-fearing woman, Salome, had borne him seven children: James, Jude, Simon and Joses; and three daughters. The names of the daughters are Salome (she being the future mother of the Apostles James and John the Theologian), Esther, and a third girl whose name has been recorded with several appellations.[19]

Supporting the apocryphal account, as did other Eastern Fathers, St. Epiphanios of Cyprus (c.315-403) gave the opinion that Joseph had been formerly married and had children, both sons and daughters.[20] Saint Cyril of Alexandria (+444) considered the "brothers of the Lord" to be children of an earlier marriage of the elder Joseph.[21] In the West, St. Hilary of Poitiers (c.315-367) defended the opinion of Joseph being formerly married.

The rods were then handed over to the high priest who offered a sacrifice to the Lord God, and inquired of the Lord. The angel of the Lord then revealed to the high priest that all the rods were to be placed into the Holy of Holies of God. They were to remain there and, the following day, the men were to return to receive back their rods. The sign that was to be shown was that out of whomever's rod a flower should bud forth...he was the man to whom the Virgin would be given and betrothed.[22]

This incident of Zacharias praying before the rods is illustrated in a mosaic at the Kariye Djami (Monastery of Chora, in Constantinople).

Mary is standing in prayer behind the altar in the Holy of Holies. Neatly arrayed on the altar before her are the rods. Before the gate, the high priest Zacharias is depicted kneeling as he prays that a sign might be given by the Lord in designation of Mary's future husband. In the following icon, Joseph's rod is seen to have sprouted three small leaves from the knob at the upper end of his walking stick.

The analogy of the budding of Aaron's rod [Num. 17:8] and the blossoming of Joseph's rod is explicitly brought out in the mosaic at Kariye Djami. In the icon we may see the high priest holding the rod in one hand and firmly placing his other hand upon the head of the Virgin. The "budding rod" is also associated with the prophecy that "...there shall come forth a rod out of the root of Jesse, and a blossom shall come up from his root: and the Spirit of God shall rest upon Him..." [Is. 11:1-2], which has been universally interpreted as a prefiguration of the advent of Christ.[23]

65

Returning to the apocryphal account, the following day all assembled early. The high priest went into the Holy of Holies and brought forth their rods. However, when the rods had been distributed, no sign had appeared. The priest then put on the twelve bells and the sacerdotal robe. Having entered the Holy of Holies, he made a burnt offering and poured forth prayers. The angel of the Lord then appeared to him, saying, "There is here the shortest rod, of which thou hast made no account. Thou didst bring it in with the rest, but neglected to take it out with the others. When thou hast taken it out and hast given it to him whose it is, then the sign will appear of which I had spoken to thee." Indeed, the rod in question was Joseph's. The elderly widower, acknowledging his great age and feeling that he presented a pitiful appearance, did not volunteer to request his rod back, lest perchance he might be enjoined to receive the young maiden.[24]

When he was standing last of all, the high priest cried out to him with a great voice, "Joseph, come and receive thy rod; for we are waiting for thee." Trembling, because the high priest had called him with a very loud voice, Joseph came forward. As soon as he laid hold of his rod, straightway, from the top of it there blossomed forth a bud and it flowered.[25]

Saint Romanos speaks of this, chanting, *Zacharias submitted to lot the choice of bridegroom for her; and Joseph was betrothed to her from God. For she was given to him when it was revealed in the rod from the Holy Spirit.*[26]

Then all the people congratulated the elderly man, remarking, "Thou hast been made blessed in thine old age, O father Joseph, seeing that God hath shown thee worthy to receive Mary." The priests then said, "Take her, because of all the tribe of Judah thou alone hast been chosen by God. Take the Virgin of the Lord and keep her for Him." But Joseph began bashfully to address them, saying, "I am an old man and have children. Why do ye hand over to me this infant, who is younger than my grandsons? She is quite young, and I fear lest I should appear ridiculous in Israel."[27]

Then Abiathar said to him, "Remember, Joseph, how Dathan, Abiram and Korah perished when the earth opened and swallowed them up, because they contradicted and despised the will of God [Num. 16:25-33].[28] So will it happen to thee and thy family, if thou choose to despise this which is commanded of thee by God." Joseph, fearing, answered him, "I do not despise the will of God. I shall be her guardian until I can ascertain the will of God as to which of my sons can have her to wife. Therefore, let some virgins, her companions, with whom she might spend her time, be given as a solace to her." Abiathar then answered and said, "Five virgins indeed shall be given to her for consolation, until the appointed day shall come when thou may receive her; for to none other may she be married."[29]

THE VIRGIN IS DELIVERED TO THE ELDER JOSEPH

Saint Evodos (1st c.), a disciple of St. Peter and one of the Apostles of the Seventy, wrote in his work on the Mother of God how the Virgin was taken to the temple at the age of three and remained there for almost eleven years. She was then given into Joseph's keeping and gave birth to the Lord in her fifteenth year.[30]

Saint Epiphanios merely notes that "the Virgin was delivered to Joseph...and was compelled to do so."[31] Nicephoros Callistos (+c.1335) writes: "The priests, through divine inspiration, came to understand their duty concerning her and betrothed the child to one from the temple. None was found to be more fitting than Joseph. He was of the same tribe, elderly, and had led an irreproachable, trustworthy and honorable life."[32] Saint Germanos also adds that "The righteous Joseph drew the lot and by this means did the Virgin leave God's temple."[33] Thus, Mary was given to the fatherly care of a proper guardian. Actually, in the case of Mary, as being the sole heiress of her father's property, regardless of its value, the law insisted that she be betrothed only to a man from her own city and tribe to prevent the transfer of property to another tribe [Num. 27:8], since landed property was carefully guarded. Thus Mary fulfilled this obligation of the law.

Saint John of Damascus (c.676-c.750) comments that "The enemy of our salvation was keeping an eye on virgins, according to the prophecy of Isaias who spoke of a virgin conceiving. Thus the maiden is given in marriage to Joseph by the priests, thereby deceiving the enemy who always glories in his wisdom. Hence the marriage was both a protection and deception to him who was keeping a watchful eye on virgins."[34]

Accordingly, the usual ceremonies of betrothing being over, Joseph returned to his own city of Bethlehem, to set his house in order and make the needful provisions for the marriage. However, the Virgin, in the company of five other temple virgins, Rebecca, Sepphora, Susanna, Abigail and Jael was to remain in Joseph's house at Nazareth. These other virgins, about the same age as Mary, had been appointed by the priest to accompany her.[35]

THE BETROTHAL

Few are the depictions in Orthodox iconography of the event of the Virgin's betrothal to the elderly Joseph. Some examples may be found in the frescoes of the Monastery of Perivleptou of Mystra. Moreover, the event was not elevated to a separate feast on the Orthodox Church calendar. The Church has set aside only the Sunday after the Nativity of Christ as the feast day to commemorate St. Joseph the Betrothed.

According to Hebrew custom, a special formality, that of the betrothal, preceded the actual marriage by a period varying in length, but not exceeding a twelvemonth in the case of a maiden. In the east, courtship with the prospective bride was unknown. At the betrothal, the bridegroom, personally or by deputy, handed to the bride a piece of money or a letter, it being expressly stated in each case that the man thereby espoused the woman. At the time of their betrothal, Joseph and Mary were poor. Accordingly their betrothal must have been the simplest, and the dowry settled as the smallest possible.

In the presence of witnesses, one of two modes of betrothal may have been applied: either by solemn word of mouth, in due prescribed formality, with the added pledge of a piece of money, however small; or else by writing, but there would be no sumptuous feast to follow. The official words pronounced to the maiden were: "By this, thou art set apart for me, according to the laws of Moses and of Israel."[30] The ceremony would conclude with some benediction over the statutory cup of wine, which was tasted in turn by the betrothed. From that moment, Mary was the betrothed wife of Joseph. Their relationship was sacred. From the moment of betrothal both parties were regarded, and treated in law (as to inheritance, adultery, need of formal divorce), as if they had been actually married, except as regarded their physically consummating the marriage. Any breach of it would be treated as adultery. The band of it could not be dissolved except, as in marriage, by regular divorce. Further, a legal document fixed the dowry which each brought, the mutual obligations, and all other legal points. Generally a festive meal closed the ceremony of the betrothal--but not in this case. Indeed, most from Galilee did not do thus, because habits were more simple and pure.[37]

Furthermore, as soon as the dower was paid in full, the bride then belonged solely to the husband.[38]

Of further interest, it should be known that the "bride price" was not always obtained with money. Jacob offered to labor seven years under his prospective father-in-law Laban for his youngest daughter, Rachel [Gen. 29:18]. The dowry could also be in the form of clothing [Judg. 14:8-20] or some other valuable item. The young David was asked to take one hundred foreskins of the Philistines for Michal, Saul's youngest daughter [1 Sam. 18:25]. This dowry was definitely beyond the ordinary, but Saul had insidious motives. The giving of a bride price did not indicate that the wife had been sold to the husband as though she were his property; it was an acknowledgment and realization of the loss of the economic worth of the daughter to her parents' house. And as we know, the custom in Israel was that the bride usually went to her husband's home, and became a part of his family. Thus her father's house was compensated for the loss. However, a portion was appropriated to ensure the comfort and security of the bride. A part was usually diverted in the event of the husband's death or an arbitrary divorce.

The iconographic scene of Joseph and one of his sons escorting Mary to his house may be seen in the Kariye Djami. This subject is rarely depicted, but it portrays Joseph striding forward and, curiously, and almost unsatisfactorily, turns around to catch a glimpse of Mary. The rapid pace of their movements is shown by the fluttering drapery around their feet.[39]

One apocryphal source mentions that James, the youngest son of Joseph, was still broken-hearted and sad on account of the loss of his mother, Salome. But when Mary entered Joseph's home, she brought up James. Henceforward, she was called the "mother of James" [Lk. 24:10].[40] Another tradition remarks that she became close with Joseph's daughters, especially Salome the future myrrh-bearer.

JOSEPH TAKES LEAVE OF THE VIRGIN

Joseph then said to her, "Behold, I have taken thee from the temple of the Lord and now I will leave thee in my house. I must now depart to tend to my trade of building. I will come again unto thee. The Lord be with thee."

Joseph then departed for many months to build houses abroad, for this was his trade.

In the lunette at Kariye Djami, Joseph is seen departing with one of his sons. The youth, with a basket of carpenter's tools on his back, looks back toward Mary and Joseph as he strides away. In the background are depicted two large buildings connected by a wall.[41] We present here a detail of that icon.

A NEW VEIL FOR THE TEMPLE

It came to pass that a council of the priests decided to have a new veil made for the temple. The high priest then said, "Call together five of the undefiled virgins of the tribe of David." Then the priest remembered the child Mary, for it was not long after that she departed. Therefore, the temple servants went and brought Mary and her companions into the temple of the Lord. Since the Priest Zacharias became mute [Lk. 1:22], Samuel replaced him as the high priest; and he said unto the maidens, "Cast lots before me now, so we might ascertain which of ye shall spin the golden thread, the blue (hyacinth), the scarlet, the fine spun linen, and the true purple." They then cast lots among themselves what each virgin would do. And the purple for the veil of the temple fell to the lot of Mary.[42] Apocryphal sources are in discrepancy if there were five colors or as many as seven;

nonetheless, all are in agreement that the Virgin received the purple thread.

Mary by now had departed the temple to live in the house of Joseph. By this incident the *Protoevangelium* demonstrates that Mary was still pure and undefiled. Alone among the virgins of the tribe of David, she receives the purple skein as a sign that the long-prophesied Messiah, who was to be King and Saviour of His people, was about to spring from the body of David.[43]

The veil, as described in Ex. 26:31, also had cherubs inwoven. The veil was heavy and of a great size. It was hung with golden hooks upon four pillars of acacia wood overlaid with gold which were set in sockets or bases of silver [Ex. 26:32].

We know that the way into the holiest was through this curtain of cherubs. Similarly, this is expressed in Gen. 3:24-25, where we read: "He [Lord God] cast out Adam and caused him to dwell over against the garden of Delight, and stationed the cherubs and the fiery sword that turns about to keep the way of the tree of life." At the Crucifixion of Christ, it was precisely this veil of the temple that was torn in two, from top to bottom, exposing the Holy of Holies [Mt. 27:51; Mk. 15:38; Lk. 23:34]. With the victory of Christ over death by the "tree" of the Cross, Paradise was once again opened, "for He is our peace, Who hath made both one, and hath broken down the middle wall of partition between us" [Eph. 2:14].

The account of *Pseudo-Matthew* mentions the following episode: The priest then gave the maidens the silk to spin. When Mary received the true purple, her companions remarked, "Since thou art the last and humble--and younger than all--thou hast deserved to receive the purple." Then they called her, with voices betraying a trace of annoyance, "Queen of virgins." While, however, they were so doing, an angel of the Lord appeared in the midst of them, saying, "The words that ye utter have not been uttered by way of annoyance, but prophesied as a prophecy most true!" The maidens trembled at the sight of the angel and, on account of his words, they asked Mary's pardon and that she pray for them.[44]

Mary then took the true purple and spun it in Nazareth. The linen was spun by feeding the threads on to a wooden spindle which was turned in order to twist the threads into yarn. Sometimes the spindle was rotated in one hand and the thread fed to it from the mass of wool or flax with the other hand. But the spindle could also hang loose, leaving the spinner's hands free to draw out the threads and wind them on to the spindle.[45]

This account of receiving the purple may be seen in the iconography of the Church. In Constantinople, in the Kariye Djami, there is a wonderful mosaic of the fourteenth century which has survived to this day. It was composed according to this narrative of the *Protoevangelium* and *Pseudo-Matthew*. The priest is seen giving the threads to the virgins, beginning with the modest and most noble Mary, who stands next to him.

Chapter VI.
The Annunciation of the
MOTHER OF GOD and
EVER-VIRGIN MARY,

**Which the Holy Church
Celebrates on the
25th of March**

+ + +

The narrative we are about to read tells of one of the most important events in world history, the incarnation of the eternal Son of God. Saint Photios remarks that "This festival is the beginning of all the other festivals, in that it gives us the contract for heavenly commerce, enriches the world with the inviolate wealth of the Lord's advent, and both effects the cleansing of our human frame and offers us the enjoyment of the undefiled goods...for today, the Virgin, on behalf of our whole race, is being betrothed to the common Lord."

"Verily, the betrothal of the Ever-Virgin is the foundation and groundwork of our salvation....With good reason does humanity bear itself proudly and rejoice; for upon receiving the news of a marriage contract with the Lord, it casts off the shameful yoke of slavery."[1]

TODAY IS REVEALED THE MYSTERY
FROM ALL ETERNITY

On the day of the Annunciation, the Word of God entered mankind in a way hitherto unexampled: the Father sent the Son; the Son was made flesh by the power and operation of the Spirit *(Ruah)*.

The coeternal Word of the Father without beginning, not being parted from the things on high, has now descended here below, in His infinite compassion taking pity upon fallen men; and assuming the poverty of Adam, He has put on a form that is alien to Him.[2]

In the Dismissal Hymn *(Apolytikion)* of this Feast, we chant, *Today is the crown of our salvation and the manifestation of the mystery that is from all eternity. The Son of God becomes the Son of the Virgin, and Gabriel announces the good tidings of grace. Therefore, let us also join him and cry aloud to the Theotokos: "Rejoice, thou who art full of grace: the Lord is with thee."*[3]

Saint Irenaeus of Lyons (d. after 193) comments that "Just as Adam had been created by the Word of God from the unworked and virgin earth, so also the Word of God created flesh for Himself from a virgin womb when the Son of God became the new Adam, so as to correct the fall into sin of the first Adam."[4]

Saint Theophanes the "Branded" and Poet (+1381), in a hymn from the Feast, chants, *Today is revealed the mystery that is from all eternity. The Son of God becomes the Son of man, that, sharing in what is worse, He may make me share in what is better. In times of old Adam was once deceived: he sought to become God* [Gen. 3:5], *but received not his desire. Now God becomes man, that He may make Adam god. Let creation rejoice, let nature exult: for the Archangel stands in fear before the Virgin and, saying to her "Rejoice," he brings the joyful greeting whereby our sorrow is assuaged. O Thou Who in Thy merciful compassion wast made man, our God, glory to Thee!*[5]

REJOICE, O VESSEL OF REJOICING, THROUGH WHOM OUR FIRST MOTHER'S CURSE IS UTTERLY DISPELLED[6]

Saint Cyril of Jerusalem (318-c.386) continues the Eve-Mary parallel: "Through Eve, yet a virgin, came death, there was need that through a virgin, or rather from a virgin, life should appear; that as the serpent deceived the one, so Gabriel should bring the good news to the other."[7]

Saint Ambrose (339-397) makes this comment: "By a man and a woman flesh was driven from Paradise; by a Virgin it was joined with God."[8] He also comments about the overthrow of satan's power, writing: "Mary, who gave birth to the Victor, conquered you, without her virginity being lessened. She brought forth Him Who, when crucified, would defeat you and, when dead, would bring you into subjection. You will be conquered today so that the woman should defeat your attacks."[9]

Saint John Chrysostom (354-407) put the Eve-Mary parallel pithily when he writes that Christ had triumphed by the very weapons that the devil had used. "A virgin, the wood, and death were the symbols of our defeat. The virgin was Eve, for she had not yet known her husband; the wood was the tree....And behold, a second time, a virgin, the wood and death; the symbols of defeat have become the symbols of victory. For Mary is in the place of Eve."[10]

Saint Proclos of Constantinople (+446), one of the great Byzantine sacred orators, continues the parallel and contrast, rooted in patristic tradition: "Thou alone hast remedied the sorrow of Eve; thou alone has wiped away the tears of the one that groaned...thou wilt bear the price of the world's redemption."[11]

Mary's obedience repairs the disobedience of Eve, by her obedience to God's plan."[12] Through her all women are blessed and have a title to glory of incomparable excellence.

In the works of St. Sophronios (569-638), Patriarch of Jerusalem, Byzantine exaltation of the Theotokos finds expression. In his *Homily on the Annunciation*, he puts his inspired words on the lips of Gabriel speaking to Mary, thus expanding the dialogue given by the Evangelist Luke. "Truly, thou art blessed among women for thou hast changed the curse of Eve into a blessing, since, through thee, Adam who was first stricken by the malediction, has received a blessing. Truly thou art blessed among women since, through thee, the blessing of the Father has shone on men and freed them from the ancient curse. Truly thou art blessed among women because, through thee, thy ancestors found salvation; for thou hast brought forth a Saviour Who made divine salvation available to them."[13]

Saint Photios comments, "Today Adam's daughter, having retrieved the transgression of the first mother Eve and cleansed herself of the stain that emanated thence, fair and beautiful in the eyes of the Creator, pledges salvation to the human race. Through her all creation is enriched in joy."[14]

THE PROPHETS SPEAK

Let us now hear the renowned hymnographers St. John of Damascus, St. Theophanes and Basil the monk bring forward the prophets of the Old Testament, who spoke of the Virgin.

In the *Book of Exodus* [3:2], *The bush and the fire showed a strange marvel to Moses, the initiate in sacred things* [Ex. 3:2]. *Seeking its fulfillment in the course of time, he said, "I shall observe it brought to pass in the pure Virgin."*[15]

The rod of Aaron once put forth shoots [Num. 17:8], *prefiguring, O undefiled Virgin, thy divine childbirth. For without seed thou shalt conceive and not suffer corruption; and after bearing child shalt thou remain virgin, giving suck to a babe Who is God of all.*[16]

The forefathers also beheld mystically the virgin daughter they would beget. *The Holy Scriptures speak of thee mystically, O Mother of the Most High. For Jacob* [Gen. 28:12] *saw in days of old the ladder that prefigured thee,*[17] and said, "The Lord is in this place, and I knew it not....How fearful is this place! This is none other than the house of God, and this is the gate of heaven" [Gen. 28:16-17].

Let thy forefather David sing to thee, O Lady, striking upon the harp of the Spirit, "Hearken, O Daughter [Ps. 44:9], *to the glad voice of the angel, for he discloses to thee joy past telling."*[18]

O Prophet Isaias, prophesy to us: who is the Virgin that shall conceive? [Is. 7:14] *"It is she who has come forth from the root of Judah and who was born of David the king, glorious fruit of a holy seed."*[19]

The Prophet (Ezekiel) spoke of the holy Virgin as the gate through which none might pass, save our God alone [Ez. 44:1-3]. *Through her did the Lord go, from her did the Most High come forth, yet left her still sealed, delivering our life from corruption.*[20]

The Chaldean furnace that brought refreshment as the dew plainly prefigured thee, O Bride of God; for in a material womb, unconsumed thou hast received the divine and immaterial fire.[21]

Daniel called thee a spiritual mountain [Dan. 2:34]; *Isaias, the Mother of God* [Is. 7:14]; *Gideon saw thee as a fleece* [Judg. 6:38]; *and David called thee sanctuary* [Ps. 95:6]; *another called thee gate* [Ez. 44:2]. *And Gabriel, in his turn, cries out to thee: "Rejoice, thou who art full of grace, the Lord is with thee"* [Lk. 1:28].[22]

THE LIFESTYLE OF THE VIRGIN

Saint Ambrose describes the Virgin Mary's lifestyle in the home of her betrothed, the elderly Joseph, in these terms: "The Virgin bore a body without contact with another body. She was a virgin not only in body but also in mind, who never stained the genuine disposition of her virginity with guile. She was always humble in heart, grave in speech, prudent in mind, sparing of words, studious in reading, resting her hope not on uncertain riches, but on requests of the poor, intent on work, and modest in discourse. She sought God as the judge of her thoughts and not men [1 Cor. 4:4]. She never sought to injure anyone but to have goodwill towards all. She never thought to rise up before her elders nor to envy her equals. She avoided boasting, loved virtue and to follow reason. Never a word passed her lips that was not with grace. She never disagreed with her neighbors nor despised the lowly. She never avoided those in need and never despised anyone though they were poor. She never laughed at anyone but covered all that she saw with her love.

"There was nothing gloomy in her eyes, nothing forward in her words and nothing unseemly in her acts. She never made silly movements, nor took unrestrained steps. Her voice was never petulant. Simply put, her very outward appearance was a reflection of her inner perfection, goodness and meekness.

"Who can describe the spareness of her diet and the abundant services--the one insufficient for nature, the other abounding beyond nature? There were no seasons of slackness, but days of fasting, one after the other. If the desire for refreshment came upon her, she took what food was generally at hand, but never to cater to comfort, just so as not to destroy her life. Only necessity caused her to sleep, and yet while her body was resting her soul was awake. Often in sleep, she would go through what she had been reading, for she read sacred Scripture almost unceasingly, or she went on with what sleep had previously interrupted, or she would carry out what she purposed or foresaw what was to be carried out.

"She was unaccustomed to go out of the house, except for divine services, and this was always in the company of kinsfolk. She was always busy at home. Though the Virgin had other persons who were protectors of her body, yet she alone guarded her character. She inspired respect by her gait and address, not so much the progress of her feet as by step upon step of virtue. She possessed all the virtues, for whatever she did is a lesson in itself. Mary attended to everything as though she were warned by many, and fulfilled every obligation of virtue as though she were teaching rather than learning.

"Indeed, when the Archangel Gabriel enters, she was found at home in privacy, without a companion. She desired no one to interrupt her attention or disturb her. She did not desire any women as companions, for she had as her companions good thoughts. Moreover, she seemed to herself to be less alone when she was alone. For how could she be alone, who had with her so many writings, so many archangels, so many prophets?"[23]

Saint Athanasios (296-373) adds that "Mary was then a pure virgin, serene in her state of soul, doubly enriched. In fact she liked good works while fulfilling her duties, and upholding right thoughts on faith and purity. She did not like to be seen by men but prayed to God to be her Judge. She was in no haste to leave her home, had no acquaintance with public places, preferring to remain constantly indoors living a withdrawn life, like the honey bee. She gave generously to the poor whatever in her household was left over....Her words were discreet and her voice measured; she did not shout and was watchful in her heart to speak no wrong of another, nor to even willingly listen to wrongs spoken of...."[24]

Saint Athanasios, in his *Letter to the Virgins*, writes: "You have the conduct of Mary, who is the example and image of the heavenly life."[25]

Saint Ambrose adds: "This is the image of virginity. For such was Mary that her life alone is an example to all."[26]

In another place, he writes that "she is the rod which brings forth a flower. For she is pure, and her virginity is directed to God with a free heart and is not deflected by the dissipation of worldly cares."[27] And, "She was not less than what becometh one who was to be the Mother of Christ."[28]

Saint Ephraim the Syrian (c.306-373) writes: "Mary, who conceived Him, abhorred the marriage bed; let not that soul, in which He dwelleth, commit whoredom in the which He dwelleth. He dwelleth in chaste virgins, if they perceive Him."[29]

Saint Gregory of Nyssa (c.335-394) expressed this idea, as follows: "What was achieved in the body of Mary, the inviolate Virgin, by the perfect divinity of Christ, which shone forth in that Virgin, the same will happen in the soul of everyone who is adorned with chastity and in a virginal way follows reason as a guide."[30]

Saint Leo the Great (+461) writes thus of Mary's pure conception of her Son: "A royal virgin, of the stem of David is chosen, who would become pregnant with a sacred Offspring and would conceive her divine and human Offspring in her mind before doing so in her body."[31] He speaks of the importance of Mary's participation in the incarnation saying, "Nothing can impair God's truth. Truth only saves us in our flesh; for as the prophet said, 'truth is sprung up out of the earth' [Ps. 84:11]. Thus the Virgin Mary conceived the Word that she should provide, of her substance, flesh to be united with Him, without the addition of a second person, and without the disappearance of her nature."[32]

The great monastic historian Bede (c.673-735) comments that Mary was the first woman to take the vow of virginity: "Since she was the first who surrendered herself to such great virtue, she deserved by special right to surpass other women in happiness."[33]

Saint Theodore the Studite (c.759-826) writes: "God sovereign and all immaculate light, found in her so many gifts that He united Himself to her substantially by the descent of the Holy Spirit."[34]

Saint Photios writes here that "It was needful that she who had formed herself beautifully with spiritual comeliness should appear as a chosen bride, fit for the heavenly Bridegroom. It was needful that she, who with her virtuous ways, as with stars, had likened herself to the heavens, should be revealed to all the faithful as giving rise to the 'Sun of righteousness'. It was needful that she who had dyed herself once with the dye of her virginal blood should serve as the purple of the universal Emperor. From the barren and fruitless womb (Anna) comes forth the holy mountain (Mary), from which has been cut without hands a precious Cornerstone [Is. 28:16; Eph. 2:20; 1 Pet. 2:6], Christ our God...."[35]

Saint Photios adds that "Today the commander of the incorporeal beings comes flying down from the arches of heaven to Mary...that fragrant and never-fading flower of the Davidic race; that admirable, great and God-garbed ornament of humanity. For this virgin had been steeped in the virtues from the very swaddling clothes. She grew in the virtues and devoted herself to leading a life of the spirit on earth. Mary, having opened the gates of the road to virtue, made entrance possible by her example to them that have an unquenchable desire for the heavenly bridal chamber. For who, from childhood up, was ever so self-controlled towards pleasures, not only those that are within nature's limits and those practised without infringing on laws, but even those which have their seat in the mind and indulge their raptures no further? Nay, the blessed Virgin did not permit even her thoughts to incline towards any of these, but was entirely possessed by divine law, showing and proclaiming in these and all other respects that she had been truly set apart as a bride for the Creator of all, even before her birth. Moreover, having also fettered anger, with her impassive mind, she made her whole soul a holy shrine of meekness, having with steady judgment at no time appeared to weaken the strength of her fortitude.

"Even at the Lord's Passion in the future, no word of blasphemy or indignation fell from her lips, which distressed mothers are wont to do at such great suffering of their children. Her unequalled gift of sagacity and clear understanding bloomed out in deeds and words, by means of which she prudently and on all sides composed and trimmed herself against all the storms of life's temptations, even them that were roused by the violent hurricane of evil spirits, never allowing any of her wares (deeds and words) as much as to touch for a moment the brine of evil."[36]

Saint Gregory Palamas (+1359) writes: "It was necessary that she, who was to bear the fairest among the children of men [Ps. 44:2], should herself be incomparable in all things and prepared to receive that beauty; a wondrous beauty since it came from her child Who in all things resembled her exactly."[37]

Saint Andrew of Crete (c.660-740) praises Mary in these terms: "Beauty outstanding, she was a statue carved by God, the image of the divine archetype superbly expressed."[38]

Elsewhere, St. Gregory Palamas writes: "The one thing that would be impossible for God to do is to unite Himself to something impure, before it had been purified in anticipation of that union; so it was necessary that it would be a virgin, free from all blemish and perfectly pure, who should bear and engender Him Who loves and bestows purity."[39]

Finally, let us listen to this laudation of St. John of Kronstadt (1829-1908), who writes this of the Virgin: "He Who has adorned the heavens with stars, could He not still more beautifully adorn His mental heaven, the most pure Virgin, His Mother? He Who has adorned the earth with various and many-colored flowers, and poured fragrance upon it, could He not adorn His earthly Mother with all the various flowers of virtues, making her fragrant with all spiritual perfumes? Truly He could. Our Lady has become the heaven and the temple of the Godhead, adorned with all beauties, and more fragrant than all earthly perfumes."[40]

In another place, he writes: "Imagine how resplendently adorned, what a pure and perfect palace of the Almighty must have been the most holy soul and the most pure body of the Mother of God, in whose womb God the Word--Godhead, soul and body--came to dwell!....Imagine of what reverence she is worthy, how we should glorify her!"[41]

THE VIRGIN'S OUTWARD APPEARANCE

A description of the sanctity of soul and her outward appearance is given to us by Saints Epiphanios and Nicephoros:

"In any case she preserved a virginity worthy of honor, as well as constancy. She spoke very little--only about what was necessary and good. Her words were sweet to the ear. She treated everyone with due respect. With each person she carried on a corresponding conversation without laughing, without being upset, still more without getting angry.

"She was of medium size. The color of her complexion was as the color of a grain of wheat. Her hair was long, lovely and somewhat dark. Her glance was quick and penetrating. Her eyes reminiscent of the color of olives. Her eyebrows were slightly curved and dark. Her nose was medium. Her lips were the color of roses and sweet-worded. Her face was not quite round, and her fingers were long.

"There was no pride in her whatever, but simplicity in everything, without the least pretence. She was a stranger to all indulgence and, at the same time, showed an example of sublime humility.

"Her clothes were simple, without any artificial adornment (as her head-covering exhibits which has been preserved till the time of this writing). In a word, in everything, she showed forth the divine grace that had penetrated her."[42]

THE HOLY VIRGIN IN ICONS

Countless icons depict the Virgin. At times she may be painted alone, but on the iconostasis *(iconostasion)* she is always shown holding the Christ child in her lap. We see that her head is modestly covered and that she is wearing a deep red-wine *maphorion*, which is a broad and hieratic dress that drapes over her shoulders. Partially visible under this veil is a headband that bind her hair and falls across her forehead, leaving only the tips of her ears exposed. Her beautiful face is usually oval. Her brows are slightly arched, lively, long and narrow. Her brown eyes are almost almond-shaped and serious, yet very sweet.[43]

Her gaze can be seen as simple, straight, quiet, sympathetic, lovable, sorrowful but at the same time gladdening. She can appear both stern but at the same time compassionate and benevolent. She is depicted at times innocent, blameless, most modest, chaste and sisterly; at other times saintly, spiritual or meditative. Sometimes her gaze inspires hope. At times her expression is searching or entreating. Her countenance scorches all who have evil thoughts; it can appear piercing, reproving, immovable, but at the same time patient and meek. She is also seen as motherly, elegant, noble and unfeigned.[44]

Her nose is Judaic, long and narrow, with thin nostrils. She has a small mouth that betrays shyness but prudence.

Her pure lips are shown always closed. Her cheeks are pale with a very light rosy hew. Her delicate swan-like neck is inclined humbly and joins the chin in a soft shadow. Her whole face is hieratic and religious, and testifies that she is of an ancient race. Her hands are delicate and graceful, and the fingers are long with short narrow nails.[45]

She is almost always seen wearing the usual long blue tunic *(chiton)*, with long sleeves that end with cuffs. The dark red or reddish-purple outer garment *(maphorion)* is bordered with gold trim. Upon her *maphorion* we may also see three stars: one is depicted on her forehead and one on each of her shoulders. This signifies her perpetual virginity, before, during and after birth. At times she is depicted wearing the *clavus*, that material which is draped over her shoulders and gracefully reaching the center of her upper arm; it also has a gold fringe with the three stars. The presence of this gold fringe and trim was seen, in spirit, by the Prophet David when he wrote: "At Thy right hand stood the Queen, arrayed in a vesture of inwoven gold..." [Ps. 44:8] and "All the glory of the daughter is within, with gold-fringed garments is she arrayed..." [Ps. 44:12].

Icons depicting the Virgin will also bear her monogram. Reading left to right, we see the Greek capital letters of Mee-Ro (MP), the first and last letters of the word *Meeteer*, meaning "Mother"; then the three Greek letters, capital Theeta, then lower case Omicron with a lower case Ipsilon above it or just two capital letters Theeta-Ipsilon (ΘY), for *Theou*, meaning "of God". Hence, her title, "Mother of God".

GABRIEL SENT BY GOD ALMIGHTY

Mary, now living in Nazareth, began spinning the true purple for the veil of the temple of the Lord. Joseph was occupied with his work, house building, in the districts by the seashore.[46]

Let us hearken to the hymns of the Feast which characterize the Archangel Gabriel as *the greatest and most godlike of the spiritual powers, shining with heavenly brightness, who, with the hosts on high gazes upon the light of the Threefold Sun, comes to the Virgin to announce to her the glad tidings.*[47]

The Archangel himself *is ever filled with light and does the will and fulfills the decrees of the Almighty.*[48] As one of the chief leaders, to him alone, *was entrusted the great mystery, till then unknown to the angels and hid from all eternity. Coming to Nazareth, thou (Gabriel) hast not dared to impart thy message to any except the pure Virgin alone.*[49]

The Archangel heard the command from God, Who said, "Go Gabriel, genuine minister, to Nazareth, a city of Galilee, to where the Virgin Mary dwells. She is the daughter of Joachim and Anna and prepare her to be a worthy dwelling-place of the Son and Word of God. Proceed carefully and do not trouble her soul, for she is a pure and blameless virgin."[50]

When the Lord wishes to reveal a mystery, the Arch-angel Gabriel is dispatched, as he was to Daniel [Dan. 8:16; 9:21], to Anna and Joachim, and to the Zacharias [Lk. 1:19], the father of the Baptist John.[51]

Saint Romanos (c.490-c.550) writes: *Gabriel considered how the Most High associated in love with the humble: "The entire Heaven and the throne of fire cannot contain my Master; and this poor maiden, how can she receive Him? On high, He is awesome; how can He be visible on earth? In any event, be it as He wills. Why do I remain here and not fly to address the maiden, 'Rejoice, O Bride unwedded!'"*[52]

Saint John of Damascus also voices the thoughts of the mighty captain of the companies of angels, chanting, *Coming to Nazareth he pondered in amazement on this wonder. "O how shall He Who dwelleth in the heights, whom none can comprehend, be born of a virgin? How shall He Whose throne is heaven and Whose footstool is the earth* [Is. 66:1] *be held in the womb of a woman? He upon Whom the six-winged seraphim and the many-eyed cherubim cannot gaze has been pleased at a single word to be made flesh of this His creature. It is the Word of God Who will dwell within her. Why then do I stand here, and not say to the maiden: 'Rejoice, thou who art full of grace: the Lord is with thee. Rejoice, O pure Virgin; Rejoice, Bride unwedded. Rejoice, Mother of Life: blessed is the fruit of thy womb.'"*[53]

"And in the sixth month the angel Gabriel was sent from God unto a city of Galilee, named Nazareth, to a virgin espoused to a man whose name was Joseph, of the house of David; and the virgin's name was Mary" [Lk. 1:26-27].

Tradition has it that the Virgin conceived on a Friday. In Hippolytos' (+235) newly-recovered *Fourth Book of Daniel*, he chronicles not only the conception of Christ on March

85

25th, but that it would also be the day upon which He was crucified.[54]

Saint John Chrysostom comments that it was the way of the ancients, for the most part, to keep their espoused wives in their house. Mary then likewise was in the house of Joseph.[55]

It is evident that a virgin without a protector and defender places herself in a precarious position. Therefore, formally, according to the law, she was considered as the "wife" of Joseph. This arrangement protected her from all attempts against the purity of her virginity. In those times, when Mary was taken out of the temple by Joseph, betrothal was legally considered equal to marriage. However, the betrothal was not consummated in that it did not grant the man who was betrothed the privilege to enter entirely into the rights of a husband.

St. Cyril, Patriarch of Alexandria (+444) comments that "The sacred Evangelist Matthew says that Mary was betrothed to Joseph, to show that the conception had taken place upon her betrothal solely, and that the birth of Emmanuel was miraculous, and not in accordance with the laws of nature. For the holy Virgin did not conceive as a result of man's seed. What, therefore, was the reason for this? Christ, Who is the first-fruits of all, the second Adam according to the Scriptures, was born of the Spirit, that He might transmit the grace of the spiritual birth to us also; for we too were intended no longer to bear the name of sons of men, but of God rather, having obtained the new birth of the Spirit in Christ first, that He might be foremost among all, as the most wise Paul declares" [Col. 1:15].[56]

Saint Athanasios the Great points out that Gabriel was sent not simply to a virgin, but to a virgin betrothed to a man, in order that by means of the betrothed man he might show that Mary was really a human being.[57]

THE VIRGIN AT THE WELL

Mary then went out of the house, taking a pot, that she might draw water from the well. She then heard a voice saying, "Rejoice, thou who art full of grace, the Lord is with thee: thou art blessed among women." Looking about, Mary wished to see whence that voice came. Trembling, she took the water pot into the house. She then took up the purple thread and sat down in her seat to work it with her fingers.[58]

This "pre-annunciation" image is based also in apocryphal literature and commented upon by the Fathers. Blessed Jerome makes reference to this occurrence in his writing to Eustochium in 400 A.D. The angel first addressed the Virgin invisibly. Frightened, she returns to the house where he appears to her in his more familiar human form. We rarely see this icon but it can be found mostly with icons depicting, in detail, her life story.[59]

THE SALUTATION OF GABRIEL

"And the angel came in unto her, and said, 'Rejoice, thou that art highly favored, the Lord is with thee: blessed art thou among women'" [Lk. 1:28].

In Eden, the virgin Eve hears "in pain thou shalt bring forth children" [Gen. 3:17], but the Virgin Theotokos, "Rejoice, thou who art full of grace."

After abiding in Joseph's home for about six months, from September to March, *In the sixth month (March), the chief of the angelic hosts was sent to thee, pure Virgin, to declare unto thee the word of salvation and to greet thee, saying,*[60] *"Rejoice, thou pure chariot of the divinity: God has loved thee from eternity, and He has chosen thee to be His dwelling. As servant of thy Master am I come to proclaim His coming. Thou shalt bring forth the Lord, yet still remain inviolate."*[61] For, *Thou shalt hold in thy womb God made flesh and, through thee, in His compassion, He shall call back mankind to its ancient state. Blessed is the divine and immortal fruit of thy womb, that through thee grants the world great mercy.*[62]

Referring to Old Testament types, the Church hymnographers have the Archangel say, *Rejoice, thou earth that has not been sown; Rejoice, thou burning bush that remains unconsumed* [Ex. 3:2]; *Rejoice, thou unsearchable depth; Rejoice, thou bridge that leads to heaven, and ladder raised on high that Jacob saw* [Gen. 28:12]; *Rejoice, thou divine jar of manna* [Ex. 16:33]; *Rejoice, thou deliverance from the curse; Rejoice, thou restoration of Adam, the Lord is with thee.*[63]

Rejoice, for thou shalt conceive a Son, more ancient than Adam, the Maker of all things.[64]

Rejoice, fiery throne, more glorious by far than the living creatures with four faces [Ez. 1:5-6]. *Rejoice, thou seat of the King of Heaven; Rejoice, uncut mountain* [Dan. 2:34-35] *and precious vessel. For in thee the whole fullness of the Godhead has come to dwell bodily* [Col. 2:9], *by the good pleasure of the everlasting Father, and by the joint cooperation of the Holy Spirit.*[65]

Rejoice, lamp [Ex. 25:31]. *Rejoice, swift cloud* [Is. 19:1]. *Rejoice, tabernacle* [Ex. 26:1] *and table* [Ex. 25:23].[66]

The majority of the icons of this joyous feast depict Gabriel in swift motion. He has just descended from heaven and his look is that of a diligent servant intent on carrying out the task assigned by his Master. We may even see his legs in a position as though he were running. In his left

hand he bears a staff, the symbol of a messenger. His right hand, with strong movement, is stretched towards the Virgin Mary, in a gesture of blessing. The configuration of his fingers, almost like a sign language, spells out *IC XC*, that is "Jesus Christ". Iconographers will present the Virgin in one of two positions: she is either standing erect, listening to the King's command, or she is sitting, thus emphasizing her superiority over the angel. As a rule she usually is holding the purple yarn in her hands. The latter detail came from Holy Tradition, but can be traced to the apocryphal *Proto-evangelium of James.*[67]

Saint Photios remarks: "Thus, the Virgin, by surpassing human standards, showed herself worthy of the heavenly bridal chambers, and brightened with her own beauty our unsightly aspect--that beauty which the pollution of our ancestors stained. For this reason David, the ancestor of God, as he holds his spiritual lyre, appears to dance in his soul at his daughter's betrothal...'Hearken, O daughter, and see, and incline thine ear; and forget thine own people and thy father's house. And the King shall greatly desire thy beauty, for He Himself is thy Lord, and thou shalt worship Him' [Ps. 44:9-10]...that is: Hear, O daughter, and incline thine ear to Gabriel's message, for it is through that, through the pure tidings given thee, that we have washed off the poison of disobedience which the serpent's advice instilled into Eve's ears and so made all mankind to share of that venomous drop, and that we are enabled to submit and hearken only to the commands of our Creator. Hear, O daughter, and receive obediently the tidings of conception...for the co-eternal Word of the Father, not departing from His own essence, nor turning into mere flesh, but keeping each of the components unmingled in an indissoluble unity, has in a manner befitting God chosen to inhabit thee for our renovation, and mercifully opens wide the heavenly tabernacles for us to dwell in."[68]

Saint Gregory the Theologian (c.329-c.391) writes: "The Word of God became a complete man, with the exception of sin, born of a Virgin who was first purified *(proto-kathar-theises)* by the Spirit in her soul and in her body."[69] The fourteenth century Byzantine theologian, Nicholas Cabasilas, writes: "If certain holy doctors have said that the Virgin had been purified beforehand by the Spirit, we must believe that they understood this purification in the sense of an increase of grace."[70]

Therefore, St. Gregory Palamas likewise writes: "'Thou art already holy and full of grace, O Virgin,' says the angel to Mary. 'But the Holy Spirit will come upon thee again, preparing thee, by an increase of grace for the divine mystery.'"[71] He also proclaimed that "the pre-eternal God chose her for Himself and thought her worthy of a grace more abundant than that granted to other humans. He made her holy of the holy even before her wondrous child-bearing."[72]

In *Homily 37*, St. Gregory Palamas writes that "after that indescribable nourishment, a most mystical economy of betrothal came to pass in regards to the Virgin. From above, the Archangel descends to address her with a strange and sublime greeting that overturns the sentence of Eve and Adam, surgically treating the curse and implanting a blessing in its place. As David foretold [Ps. 44:10], the King of all greatly desired the mystical beauty of the Ever-Virgin and 'bowed the heavens and came down'" [Ps. 17:9].[73]

THOU ART A LILY DYED WITH THE ROYAL PURPLE OF THE DIVINE SPIRIT[74]

St. Andrew of Crete, in his *Great Canon*, kept before him this apocryphal account of Mary preparing the purple for the veil. He interpreted it symbolically when he chanted, *As from purple silk, O undefiled Virgin, the spiritual robe of Emmanuel, His flesh, was woven in thy womb. Therefore, we honor thee as Theotokos in very truth.*[75]

This latter detail of the purple thread for the temple veil and the Virgin holding a weaver's spindle was a notion very popular among the Byzantines. It is always included in icons of this feast. Often there is the portrayal of the thread falling away. The significance of this is that Mary will now turn from the external work with the thread for a veil in the Jerusalem Temple, to attend to the vocation to become herself the temple and dwelling-place of the incarnate Lord.[76]

Saint Proclos (+446), Patriarch of Constantinople, also enhances this theme and proclaims, "O Virgin! From where didst thou obtain the wool to fashion a garment to clothe the Master of Creation? How in the web of thy womb didst thou weave the pure and sinless cloak? Adam was naked, and with the leaves of a fig tree covered his shame. But to restore that which was corrupted, Wisdom in the workshop of virginity, has, by divine operation, woven a new covering!"[77] And the same writes that the Theotokos is the "web of the dispensation on which the incomprehensible cloak of union was woven. The weaver was the Holy Spirit. And the wool was the divine power descending from above, and also that wool of the ancient world, Adam's flesh, from the immaculate flesh of the Virgin, would encompass the immeasurable grace of Him Who clothes all flesh."[78]

THE VIRGIN'S REACTION TO THE ARCHANGEL

"And when she saw him, she was troubled at his saying, and cast in her mind what manner of salutation this should be" [Lk. 1:29].

The Archangel Gabriel, entering as a young man of ineffable beauty, filled the chamber with light, and courteously saluted her. Now Mary, who was already well acquainted with angelic faces and not unfamiliar with the light from heaven, was neither terrified by the vision of the angel, nor astonished at the greatness of the light, but only

91

perplexed by his words. She began to consider what the nature of such an unusual salutation might portend.[79]

There is a difference between the appearance of the Archangel Gabriel to the Priest Zacharias and to the Virgin Mary. The Archangel gave his name to the priest, "I am Gabriel, who stands in the presence of God" [Lk. 1:19]; he does not identify himself to Mary, which means that Mary identified him herself.

Saint Photios says, "The maiden is troubled, but she does not reject. She is troubled by his words, but does not turn away; she cast in her mind the manner of this salutation, yet perceived that its cause escaped understanding. She thought within herself, 'I see the messenger standing reverently and I am moved to receive his message joyfully; but he addresses me with bridal words, and changes the joy to fear, and troubles my soul with his message. I see his face restrained by modesty, but he announces to me the coming of a Bridegroom. I see him conversing wisely, but he utters words of conception; and the love of virginity forces me to suspect his saying as a wile. I am troubled. I see the messenger's rank and manner, and his seemly aspect indicate that the message comes from God. His words, however, which give the impression of being those of a suitor, prompt me to refuse assent.' She beheld the angel to look upon her with chaste eyes, yet he brought the tidings of a suitor. Seeing him attending with a seemly gaze, yet he spoke of a marriage contract. Having heard these bridal words, and seeing the manner of the conversation to be untouched by the passions, the holy Virgin was troubled by her conflicting thoughts and, seized by prudent fear, was amazed by the strangeness of the salutation."[80]

Saint Photios continues explaining that "Gabriel, commander of the host, the Virgin's initiator, the messenger and spokesman of our salvation,[81]...does not leave her to be tossed by the waves of perplexity. If he did, would that not have proved him to be a worthless minister of the command? Would the angel not have rightly paid a penalty because he had left the Virgin to be disturbed? What then does he say? 'Fear not, Mary, I have not come to speak to thee in deceit, but to introduce the abolition of deceit. I have not arrived to lead thee into error, but to pledge deliverance from error. I have not visited thee to violate thy inviolate virginity, but to bring the good tidings of the inhabitation of the Creator and Guardian of virginity. Fear not, Mary, I am not the servant of the serpent's wickedness, but the delegate of Him Who suppresses the serpent. The former, by means of his words, instilled the poison into human nature, and having mixed death into the potion, poured out the plague on everyone. The former, by deceit, pushed Adam into disobedience, and made him exchange his painless existence for a toilsome life. I bring thee the good tidings that the universal Creator shall truly make man divine in thy virginal and stainless womb, and dispel the spurious divinisation. I have come as a bridal escort, not as a plotter; an instigator

of joy, not of sorrow; as a herald of salvation, not a counsellor of perdition. Fear not, Mary, I will heal thy thoughts with the Lord's commands; I will undo the bonds of thy perplexity. Thou hast found favor with God. The salutation is of divine favor, of godly favor, not a human plot and not of bodily intercourse. It is a favor which overleaps human understanding.'"[82]

THE NEW EVE

Saint Photios comments: "When thou hearest of favor, O man, think not that this gift was granted to the Virgin in vain, nor consider the present as an empty honor. For the Virgin found favor with God because she had made herself worthy before her Creator, because, having adorned her soul with the fairness of purity, she had prepared herself as an agreeable habitation of Him Who by His Word had established the heavens [Ps. 32:6]. She found favor with Him not only because she had kept her virginity inviolate, but also because she had maintained her desires unsullied; because since she was a babe she had been sanctified to God as a living and unquarried temple, built for the King of glory, for the stainlessness of her body, the exceeding splendor of her virginity, her undefiled chastity, the great purity of her disposition, her soul unwavering to sin and clinging to the best."[83]

Saint Gregory of Nyssa comments: "Mary was always a virgin, undefiled, pious and dutiful, the honor of our nature, the gate of our life, the one who won salvation for us."[84] Saint Gregory also takes up the Eve-Mary theme: "Woman was defended by woman; the first opened the way to sin; the present one served to open the way to justice. The former followed the advice of the serpent, the latter brought forth the Slayer of the serpent and brought to light the Author of light. The former introduced sin through the tree, the latter brings in grace through the tree"--that is, the tree of the Cross.[85]

Saint Hesychios of Jerusalem (c.451) contrasts Mary-- the "second virgin"--with Eve, the first virgin. Mary reversed all the misery of the female sex, all the sadness in child-bearing; she "dispelled the cloud of anxiousness which hangs over all women in childbirth."[86] He further praises her saying, "Conspicuous among women, chosen from virgins, outstanding ornament of our nature, pride of our clay, who freed Eve from her disgrace, Adam from the penalty threatening him, cut down the dragon's insolence, she whom the smoke of our desire never reached, whom the worm of sensual pleasure has not spoiled either."[87]

Many Church Fathers and hymnographers enhanced the Lucan account by introducing in their writings and sermons a type of religious drama. The development of this liturgical style is discussed in the *Preface* of this volume. Let us examine by hearing the divinely inspired hymns of St. Theophanes, St. John of Damascus and St. Romanos. The Archangel, in the following hymns, attempts to answer the thoughts of Mary:

Archangel: "Thou, O most pure one, hast found grace before the Lord such as no other woman ever found."[88]

Virgin: "O angel, help me to understand the meaning of thy words. How shalt what thou sayest come to pass? Tell me clearly, how shall I conceive, who am a virgin maiden? And how shall I become the Mother of my Maker?"[89]

Archangel: "Thou dost think, so it seems, that I utter words deceitfully; but I rejoice to see thy prudence. But take courage, O Lady: for where God wills, strange wonders are easily accomplished."[90]

Virgin: "What shall I call thee? A man? But thy words are of things divine. An angel? But thou dost appear as a man. I fear that thou might be telling me lies. I hear that Eve hearkened to the words of the serpent and she fell. I fear, too, that thou might deceive me, for thou dost speak of things that are impossible. And God, how shall He take flesh in my womb? Uncircumscribed, yet how will He be circumscribed from a virgin? The King, how shall He rest in a place so small? I wonder and am amazed at whence cometh thy words."[91]

The name Gabriel means "man of God." Saint Paulinus of Nola (353-431), remarks that Gabriel's "person, distinguished with heavenly beauty, stood before her eyes, and she dropped her chaste gaze, and her ruddy cheeks colored as the blood welled up, and he said:

'Maiden,...thou hast been chosen by the great God to be called the Mother of Him Whose Father is God Himself. Come, then, and in thy blessedness conceive this Burden, for thou art unstained by a husband and unprofaned by any intercourse, but pregnant by the Word of

God. Let thy womb provide a body for Him Who made heaven and earth, sea and stars, Who always was, is now, and ever shall be in all time the Lord of the world and the Creator of light. He Himself, the Light of heaven, will put on mortal limbs by thy aid, and appear before the eyes and assemblies of men....God will give thee strength and faith, for He has decided to be thy Son, though He is the Son of God, and He rules and guides all things by His nod."[92]

Archangel: "Thou hast well said that this matter is hard to grasp. Doubt not as though it were deceitful, but believe in this thing as very true."[93]

Virgin: "My mother Eve, accepting the suggestion of the serpent, was banished from divine delight: and therefore I fear thy strange salutation, for I take heed lest I slip."[94]

"Why does thy figure blaze with fire?....Thou dost announce to me that I shall bring forth a child, yet I have no experience of man. Lead me not astray, O man, with crafty words, as the crafty serpent once led astray Eve our mother (far from God).[95]

"Thou dost appear unto me in the form of a man....How then dost thou speak to me of things that pass man's power? For thou hast said that God shall be with me, and that He shall take up His dwelling in my womb; and how, tell me, shall I become the spacious habitation and the holy place of Him that rides upon the cherubim? [Ps. 17:10].[96]

"Strange is thy speech and strange thine appearance, strange thy sayings and thy disclosures....Thou sayest that I shall conceive Him Who remains uncircumscribed: and how shall my womb contain Him Whom the wide spaces of the heavens cannot contain?[97]

"It is true that the Prophet Isaias foresaw into the future that a virgin would bring forth. But tell me, how shall this be?"[98]

Archangel: "O Virgin, let the tent of Abraham that once contained God teach thee [Gen. 18:1-16]: for it prefigured thy womb, which now receives the Godhead.[99]

"Do not be amazed, O Mary, that a virgin will give birth. How did the rod of Aaron blossom forth? How did water gush forth from the rock in the wilderness that Moses tapped with his rod? How were the tablets of the law written without a man's hand? How did the bush burn, yet was not consumed? How did the aged and barren Sarah give birth to Isaac? Furthermore, how did thine own mother, who was barren, bring thee forth? Therefore, do not be amazed at what I tell thee.[100]

"Thou shalt conceive in thy womb Him Whom the world cannot contain, yet He shall be contained in thee; and thou shalt be the bearer of Him Who hath shone forth from the Father before the morning star" [Ps. 109:4].[101]

Saint Photios also employs this type of religious dialogue. He has the Archangel speaking to the Virgin thus: "...Thou shalt conceive in thy womb and bring forth a Son, Whom the cherubim praise in fear and Whom the ranks of the angels tremble to see, and the entire creation is unable to contain. Thou shalt conceive in thy womb and bring forth a Son, the Creator of thine inviolate womb, not corrupting thy virginity, but sealing the bolts of virginity; not destroying the purity of thy pregnancy, but showing it uncorrupted by fornication. Thou shalt conceive in thy womb Him Who is present everywhere, but is contained by nothing. Thou shalt conceive in thy womb the Creator of thy first ancestor. For it was about thee that the prophet also cried out, saying, 'Behold, a virgin shall conceive in the womb, and bring forth a son, and they shall call His name Emmanuel, which being interpreted is, God with us' [Is. 7:14, Mt. 1:23]. He is the mighty God and the Prince of peace. The prophecies made concerning thee I, too, announce to thee today. I am not come to offer my own words, but to bring the commands of Him Who has sent me. It is He that inspired the Prophet Isaias to prophesy concerning thee; it is He, again, Who entrusted me also to announce today the outcome of that prophecy which is soon to be fulfilled."[102]

"THOU HAST
FOUND FAVOR WITH GOD"

"And the angel said unto her, 'Fear not, Mary: for thou hast found favor with God'" [Lk. 1:30]

Saint Sophronios, Patriarch of Jerusalem, extols the Virgin's primacy over all the choirs of angels, writing:

"In a word thou far outdistanced every creature, for thou hast shone beyond every creature in purity and received within thyself the Creator of all creatures; thou hast bore Him in thy womb and brought Him forth, and alone of all creatures became the Mother of God."[103] Expounding upon the divine motherhood, the saint concludes: "For from thee joy was not only given to men, but is also bestowed on the heavenly powers."

Let us listen to the dialogue between the Virgin and the Archangel, as composed by the leading hymnographers St. Theophanes and St. Romanos.

Archangel: "I stand before thee in fear, as a servant before his mistress, and in awe I am afraid to look at thee now.[104]

"I am sent as the envoy of God to disclose to thee the divine will. O undefiled maiden, why art thou afraid of me, who rather am afraid of thee? Why, O Lady, dost thou stand in awe of me, who stand in reverent awe of thee?[105]

"Be not struck with dismay by my strange form, nor be afraid: I am an Archangel. Once the serpent beguiled Eve, but now I announce to thee the good tidings of joy: O Most Pure, thou shalt remain inviolate and yet shall bear the Lord.[106]

"Be not afraid of me, the chief commander of the armies of the King. For thou hast found the grace that thy mother Eve once lost: and thou shalt conceive and bring forth Him Who is one in essence with the Father.[107]

"Do not fear the servant, for I come to bring thee the Creator. Thou art going to give birth to a Son; so why should my fiery appearance terrify thee?

"Thou art to bring the Lord into the world; why fear a fellow subject? Why dost thou feel fear of me as I tremble before thee? Because of what is going to happen? It was confided to me and I feel assured about it."[108]

Virgin: "I have learned from the Prophet (Isaias), who foretold in times of old the coming of Emmanuel, that a certain holy virgin should bear a child [Is. 7:14]. But I long to know how the nature of mortal men shall undergo union with the Godhead?"[109]

Archangel: "The bush that burnt with fire and yet remained unconsumed [Ex. 3:2] disclosed the secret mystery that shall come to pass in thee, O pure Maiden, full of grace. For after childbirth thou shalt remain ever-virgin."[110]

Virgin: "O Gabriel, herald of the truth, shining with the radiance of Almighty God, tell me truly: how shall I, my purity remaining untouched, bear in the flesh the Word Who has no body?"[111]

Archangel: "In choosing chastity, thou hast found favor with the Lord. Therefore, thou, a virgin shall bring forth a son. "Do not say, 'How can He dwell in me and not consume me?' The fire that thou fearest will be as rain for thee, as David foretold [Ps. 71:6].[112]

"O immaculate one, thou dost ask how the thing I told thee will come to pass? How did the sea appear as dry land to the people [Ex. 14:16] and then again like the sea? Just so will it be with thy womb.[113]

Virgin: "I now have recovered my courage and possess real freedom. I shall raise questions with thee concerning what thou hast said.

"As for the sea that thou hast mentioned to me, the prophet cleft it with his rod [Ex. 14:19-21]. This miracle did not happen without some intermediary: At first it was Moses, then prayers and the rod were intermediaries; now there are none."[114]

"I KNOW NOT A MAN"

Though brought up in a society where women were expected to be inconspicuous, there is nothing automatic about Mary's submission. The Virgin did not doubt the words of Gabriel, but wished to understand the matter better, for she did not welcome an announcement which seemed to involve a forfeiture of her vow. She was perplexed as to the fulfillment of Gabriel's words. Metropolitan Philaret of Moscow
(1849-1867) writes that the all-holy Virgin first inquired concerning the event of her becoming a mother, not because of any lack of faith, not out of curiosity, but from a feeling of reverent awe and out of concern for the preservation of her virginity, which was dedicated to God.[115] Hence, Mary said to Gabriel, "'How can this be, since I do not know a man?'" [Lk. 1:34]. And *how can I bear a son? Who has ever seen a birth without seed?*[116]

Saint Gregory of Nyssa also discusses Mary's response. "The verse, 'How shall this be since I know not a man,' meant that she had the intention, though betrothed, of remaining a virgin." He then says, "The angel announced offspring; but she cleaves to her virginity, preferring her bodily integrity to what the angel manifests. She neither

100

lacks faith nor departs from her promise...because she was bound to preserve her flesh, which was consecrated to God as a sacred gift, untouched. Therefore she says, 'though thou art an angel, though thou come from heaven, though what is shown is beyond human nature, it is nevertheless impossible for me to know man.'"[117]

Theophylactos (+c.1092), Archbishop of Achrida in Bulgaria, asserts that Mary demonstrated wisdom and prudence in desiring to know the manner of the event. The angel understood the reason for her question and did not lay a penance upon her as he had done to Zacharias the priest [Lk. 1:20].[118]

> *Virgin:* "Childbirth comes from mutual love: such is the law that God has given to men....I know not at all the pleasure of marriage: how then dost thou say that I shall bear a child? I fear lest thou speakest in guile."[119]

Saint Photios wishes to comment on the prudence and wisdom of the young Virgin, and remarks, "What did the most holy Virgin reply? Was she immediately softened by these words, and having opened her ears wide with pleasure; did she allow her thoughts to give assent without scrutiny? Not at all. But what says she? 'Now I know clearly that thou hast described to me conception, pregnancy and birth of a son, but thou hast increased my perplexity all the more. For how shall this be to me, seeing I know not a man? For every birth comes from intercourse with a man, while abstention from relations with a man does not so much as permit one even to hear of conception. How then shall I have offspring whose begetter is unknown? How shall this be?'"[120]

> *Archangel:* "O holy Virgin, thou speakest to me of the customary manner whereby mortal men are born. But I tell thee of the birth of the true God. Beyond words and understanding, in ways that He alone knows, He shall take flesh of thee.[121]

> "In His good pleasure shall the Word of God descend upon Thee, as dew upon the fleece" [Judg. 6:38; Ps. 71:6].[122]

> *Virgin:* "I cannot understand the meaning of thy words; for there have often been miracles, wonders worked by the might of God, symbols and figures

contained in the law, but never has a virgin borne a child without knowing a man."[123]

Saint Photios has the Archangel answer: "And who knows how to interpret the Lord's counsel? Who has the strength to scrutinize an inscrutable mystery? One thing I know, one thing I have been taught, one thing I have been sent to tell. This I say: the Holy Spirit shall come upon thee, and the power of the Highest shall overshadow thee. It is that which shall teach thee how thou shalt be pregnant. It shall interpret how thou shalt conceive. It is a participant in the Lord's wish, since they are enthroned together, while I am a slave. I am a messenger of the Lord's commands, not the interpreter of this particular command. I am the servant of His will, not the expounder of His intent. The Spirit shall set everything in order, for it searches all things, yes, the deep things of God [1 Cor. 2:10]. I cry out, 'Rejoice, thou who art full of grace,' and I praise the miracle in song, and worship the birth, but I am at a loss to tell the manner of the conception."[124]

Virgin: "There is no more a prince from Judah's line [Gen. 49:10], but the time is at hand in which Christ, the hope of the nations, shall appear."[125]

Archangel: "He Who promised to thy forefather David that of the fruit of his body He would set upon the throne of his kingdom [Ps. 131:11], He it is that has chosen thee, the only beauty of Jacob [Ps. 46:4], as His spiritual dwelling-place.[126]

"Thou art amazed, O all-blameless Virgin; and amazing indeed is the wonder that comes to pass in thee: for thou alone shalt receive in thy womb the King of all Who is to take flesh. It is thou who art prefigured by the utterances and dark sayings of the prophets and by the symbols of the law."[127]

Saint Photios, in a homily on this Feast, has the Archangel cite Old Testament examples to the Virgin: "If thou wishest to accept credence of my tiding by means of examples, inferring great things from small ones, and confirming the things to come by things past,--thou shalt conceive in thy womb and bring forth a Son in the same manner as Aaron's rod that budded without cultivation, activating like a rooted plant [Num. 17:8]. As the dew from heaven moistened solely the fleece and did not refresh the

102

earth [Judg. 6:37], thus thou too shalt conceive in thy womb and bring forth the Lord. Thy ancestor David, inspired by God of thy pregnancy, announces in advance that He shall come down like rain upon a fleece, and like rain-drops that fall upon the earth [Ps. 71:6]. As the bush received the fire, and feeding the flames was not consumed [Ex. 3:2], thus shalt thou conceive a Son, lending Him thy flesh, providing nourishment to the immaterial fire, and drawing incorruptibility in return. These things prefigured thy pregnancy and represented from afar thy delivery. Those strange things have been wrought that they might confirm thy child's ineffable birth. This happened beforehand that they might delineate the incomprehensibility of the mystery: for the flaming bush, and the bedewed fleece, and the rod bearing leaves would not have contributed anything useful to life, nor would they have incited man to praise the Wonder-worker, nay, the miracle would have fallen to no purpose, unless they had been set down as prefigurations of thy giving birth, and been, as it were, the advance proclamations of the Lord's coming."[128]

THOU SHALT CALL HIS NAME JESUS

"'And, behold, thou shalt conceive in thy womb, and bring forth a Son, and shalt call His name Jesus'" [Lk. 1:31].

Saint Photios interjects here that "Because through Him they will enjoy salvation, they shall call Him Jesus Who has delivered them from their sins. His title comes from His bounty, His fair name from His deeds. They shall call Him Jesus, through Whom the inexhaustible wealth of salvation flows to them; through Whom the sting of death [1 Cor. 15:56] is broken, while the grace of immortality flourishes, and the might of sin collapses, while the nature of the fallen one rises triumphant. He shall be great, and shall be called the Son of the Highest."[129]

"'He shall be great, and shall be called the Son of the Highest; and the Lord God shall give unto Him the throne of His father David: And He shall reign over the house of Jacob forever; and of His kingdom there shall be no end'" [Lk. 1:32-33].

Again, Saint Photios has the Archangel say, "He shall be great, as He had been, although He assumes the smallness of the flesh, although He puts on the humbleness of the body. Nor does the assumption of humanity debase the greatness of

103

divinity, but the humbleness of humanity is rather exalted with it. He shall be great even after the incarnation, or, if thou wilt, even after His labors, even after His sweat has poured down in great drops [Lk. 22:44], even as He takes upon Himself all that the nature of the flesh is wont to suffer. Wherefore, even if thou seest Him hungry, even if sweating, even if laboring, even if insulted and lashed, even if finally crucified, dead and buried, do not consider it with reference to the divine Word as being in any way paltry and unworthy of God."[130]

"THE POWER OF THE MOST HIGH
SHALL OVERSHADOW THEE"

Archangel: "The most Holy Spirit of God shall come upon thee, O pure Lady, thou dwelling-place of the divinity, **'and the power of the Highest shall overshadow thee'** [Lk. 1:34]: and thou shalt bring forth a child Who shall preserve thy virginity unshaken. He is the Son without lineage [Heb. 7:3]; and having appeared, in His good pleasure, He shall save His people [Mt. 1:21]"[131] from their sins.

"When God so wishes, the order of nature is overcome and what is beyond man comes to pass. Believe that my sayings are true, O all-holy Lady, utterly without spot."[132]

This icon of the *Akathist* depicts the overshadowing of the Holy Spirit. The Virgin is depicted enthroned and her companions are seen holding a veil, signifying the hidden mystery of her conception. Divine power is shown as rays coming down from above. Thus, in the *Akathist Hymn*, we chant, *Divine power of the Most High then overshadowed her who knew not wedlock, that she might conceive.*[133]

INCARNATE BY A UNION WITHOUT CONJUNCTION[134]

Saint Paulinus, in a poem, describes the event of the divine conception thus: "In this consecrated virgin, God built

Himself a pleasing temple with a hidden roof-aperture. Silently He glided down like the rain that falls as noiseless dew from a high cloud upon a fleece [Judg. 6:36-40]. None was ever privy to this secret visitation by which God took the form of man from His Virgin-Mother. How remarkable was the artifice of the Lord which sought the salvation of men! Without intercourse, a woman's womb conceived new life. The bride did not submit to a mere husband. She was a mother and bore a child without the woman's role in intercourse. The compact made her a spouse, but she was no wife in body. She became the Mother of a Boy, though she was untainted by a husband."[135]

Saint Ephraim the Syrian writes: "Therefore, He came down, in a manner He knows. He stirred and came in a way that pleased Him. He entered and dwelt in her without her perceiving. She received Him, suffering nothing."[136] In *Homily 41*, St. Ephraim writes: "As lightning illuminates what is hidden, so also Christ purifies what is hidden in the nature of things. He purified the Virgin also and then was born, so as to show that where Christ is, there is manifest purity in all its power. He purified the Virgin, having prepared her by the Holy Spirit, and then the womb, having become pure, conceived Him. He purified the Virgin while she was inviolate; wherefore, having been born, He left her virgin. I do not say that Mary became immortal, but that being illuminated by grace, she was not disturbed by sinful desires." In his homily, *Mary and Eve*, he writes: "The Light abode in her, cleansed her mind, made her thoughts pure, made chaste her concerns, and sanctified her virginity."

Bishop Ignatius Brianchaninov (1807-1867) in his *Exposition* adds: "One who was pure according to human understanding, He made pure by grace."[137]

Saint Gregory Palamas agrees that when the angel appeared to announce that she was to be the Mother of God, she spoke to Gabriel of her faith in the coming of the Spirit "to further purify her nature, and give her the strength to receive the child of salvation."[138]

Saint Gregory then writes that "The King of all...overshadowed her, or rather, the enhypostatic Power of the Most High dwelt in her. He did not manifest His presence through darkness and fire, as in the case of Moses the God-seer, nor through tempest and cloud [Ex. 19:18; Deut. 4:11-12], as with

Prophet Elias [3 Kings 19:12-13]. This time, without mediation or a veil, the power of the Most High overshadowed the sublimely chaste and virgin womb. This was not only simply an overshadowing but an outright union, separated by nothing--not the lower air, the upper, or anything involving the senses. Since what overshadows produces its own form and figure over whatever it casts a shadow, there came to pass in the womb not only a union, but the formation of the incarnate Word of God from both the power of the Most High and the all-holy virginal womb. Thus, in an indescribable manner the Word of God took up His dwelling in her."[139]

The many references to the role of the Holy Spirit in this instance may be summarized in the pithy phrase of Saint Ambrose: "The Offspring of the Virgin is therefore the work of the Spirit."[140] The saint then discusses the verse, "'she was found with child of the Holy Spirit' [Mt. 1:18]....The Greek from which the Latins translated, said *ek Pnevmatos Agiou*, that is, *ex Spiritu Sancto*....thus, if the Virgin conceived as of His operation and power, who will deny the Spirit as Creator?...If, then, the Spirit is Creator, He certainly is not a creature."[141] For what is from someone is either of his substance or of his power.

Saint Ambrose, in his work, *The Mysteries*, writes: "If, then, the Holy Spirit coming upon the Virgin effected conception, and effected the work of generation, surely there must be no doubt that the Spirit, coming upon the Font, or upon those who obtain baptism, effects the truth of regeneration."[142]

Saint Joseph the Hymnographer (c.816-886) chants, *A new wonder, worthy of God: the Lord clearly passes through the closed door of the Virgin, naked at His entry. And God doth manifest Himself as corporeal as He passes out; and yet the gate remaineth shut. Let us magnify her as the Mother of God.*[143]

"'Therefore also that Holy One that shall be born of thee shall be called the Son of God'" [Lk. 1:35].

Saint Cyril of Jerusalem insists on the pure birth of Christ commenting that "The Holy Spirit, coming upon her, sanctified her to receive Him 'through Whom all things are made.'"[144] The saint continues: "His generation was pure and undefiled; for where the Holy Spirit is, there all defilement has been taken away."[145]

Saint Cyril of Alexandria (+444), in a letter, confirms that the Lord Jesus Christ "was made flesh and was made man, and from His very conception He united to Himself a temple taken from her."[146]

Saint Ephraim joyfully sings out: *A wonder is Thy Mother. The Lord entered her and became a servant. The Word entered her and became silent within her; thunder entered her, and His voice was still: the Shepherd of all entered her: He became a Lamb in her, and came forth bleating.*[147] And he also wrote: *Eve and Adam, through sin, introduced death into the created world. The Lord of creation gave us, by His Only-begotten through Mary, new life again. By means of the serpent, the evil one poured out his poison in the ear of Eve. The Good One brought low His mercy and entered through Mary's ear: through the gate by which death entered, Life also entered, putting death to death.*

Saint Cyril of Jerusalem, the catechist, writes: "Of whom in the beginning was Eve begotten? What mother conceived her, the motherless? But  the Scripture saith that she was born out of Adam's side. Is Eve then born out of a man's side without a mother, and is a child not to be born without a father, of a virgin's womb? This debt of gratitude was due to men from womankind: for Eve was begotten of Adam, and not conceived of a mother, but as it were brought of man alone. Mary, therefore, paid the debt of gratitude, when not by man, but of herself alone in an immaculate way she conceived of the Holy Spirit by the power of God."[148]

This day Mary has become for us the heaven that bears God, for in her the exalted Godhead has descended and dwelt. In her It has grown small, to make us great--but Its Nature does not diminish. In her It has woven for us a garment that shall be for our salvation.

107

All creatures were sore amazed at thy divine and great glory, O Maiden, O pure Virgin innocent of wedlock; for thou didst hold in thy womb the God of all things.[149]

BRIDE OF GOD

A constant theme in the Old Testament is that of Israel depicted as the 'Bride of God' when God says, "...I was a husband to them" [Jer. 31:32 or Is. 54:5 (KJV)]. In mystical language, this metaphor may also be found expressed in these verses: "It shall come to pass that as a bridegroom will rejoice over a bride, so will the Lord rejoice over thee" [Is. 62:5]; "And it shall come to pass in that day, saith the Lord, that she shall call Me, 'My husband'....And I will betroth thee to Myself forever; yea, I will betroth thee to Myself in righteousness, and in judgment, and in mercy, and in tender compassions; and I will betroth thee to Myself in faithfulness: and thou shalt know the Lord" [Hos. 2:16, 19-20].

At times marriage was so often taken as the symbol of God's choice, that once "the Woman" appeared prominently in the story of salvation, she was bound to be invested with the "bridal" role, that is 'Bride of God' *(Theonymphe)*. The semitic habit of interchanging personal and corporate roles and attributes made the transference inevitable. Thus, in the New Testament, the "Bride" is the Church, and the Bridegroom is Christ [Mt. 9:15; Jn. 3:29; 2 Cor. 11:2; Rev. 19:7, 21:2,9].

The words of St. Paulinus of Nola confirm this: "What a great mystery was this, by which the Church becomes at once the Lord's Bride and Sister...."[150] In sacred Scripture we learn that "He that hath the bride is the bridegroom" [Jn. 3:29]. Saint Paul will write in his second letter to the Corinthian Church that he had espoused them "to One Husband", so that he might present them "as a chaste virgin to Christ" [2 Cor. 11:2].

Although Mary is nowhere in the New Testament addressed as the 'Bride of God', a study of the writings and hymns of the Orthodox Church would reveal her spousal role. Several Fathers will take up this theme even as early as St. Athanasios of Alexandria (c.295-373) and St. Cyril of Alexandria (+444); St. Ephraim the Syrian (c.306-373) leaves no room for doubt in what is a constant theme for him.

Let's listen to St. Ephraim: *No one quite knows, O Lord, what to call Thy Mother: Should one call her Virgin?*

But her child stood there. Or should one call her a married woman? But no man knew her. If then none comprehended Thy Mother, who can comprehend Thee?

For she alone is Thy Mother, and Thy sister along with all; she became Thy Mother, she became Thy sister. She is Thy Bride too, along with all chaste virgins. Thou, Who art Thy Mother's beauty, Thyself adorned her with everything!

For she was, by her nature, Thy Bride before Thou had come. She conceived Thee in a manner quite beyond nature, O Holy One, and was a virgin when she had brought Thee forth in a most holy fashion.[151]

Then St. Ephraim has the Virgin respond to Christ thus: *I am Thy sister, of the house of David who was the father of us both. Again, I am Thy Mother because of Thy conception, and I am Thy bride of Thy sanctification; also I am Thy handmaid and Thy daughter, from the blood and water wherewith Thou hast purchased me and baptized me.*[152]

Saint Germanos of Constantinople (c.635-733) uses the title *Theonymphe*. Saint John of Damascus addresses Mary as "spouse of the Father" when he writes concerning her Dormition and translation: "It was fitting that the spouse whom the Father had taken to Himself should live in the divine mansion." [153]

The works of St. Neophytos (1134-1220), the Recluse of Cyprus, are heavily laden with many titles for Mary. They are laudatory epithets and deal practically with every Old Testament symbol or type, such as holy Ark, rod of Aaron, promised land, city of God, and others with a connotation of a saving role.[154] To him, Mary is "Mistress *(Despina)* of the world."[155] But especially she is named "spouse". Probably more than any other writer, St. Neophytos applies this title to Mary. She is the "spouse of God," "the Virgin spouse of God," "the spouse and Mother of God," "spouse and daughter of the Immortal Father," "irreproachable spouse of the King," "immaculate spouse," "immaculate spouse of Christ," "spouse of the Father," "pure spouse of the Immortal Father," "blessed, untouched, immaculate spouse, divinely acceptable to the Immortal Father," "holy spouse," and "Virgin spouse Mother."[156] Through the "spouse" metaphor, the saint sees the parallel between Mary and the Church: "We apply, therefore, the words of the Psalm [44] to the Church, spouse and daughter of the King of Glory; but they agree fully also with the most pure Virgin, spouse and daughter of the Immortal Father."[157]

Also St. John Mavropous, Metropolitan of Euchaites (c.+1079), calls her the "spouse of God" and that "through her, He pours out blessing upon the whole race" and "through her the creature is restored and newly fashioned."[158] He also wrote: "Thou hast manifested unto us, O Mother of God and Virgin all pure, the divine mystery unknown to all the incorporeal beings, but known to God alone."[159] To Metropolitan John, even the impossible was possible: "through God, to her, she had thrown down the great wall of enmity and the ancient curse."[160]

Saint John of Kronstadt (1829-1908) also takes up this theme, writing: "The Virgin Mary is the most merciful sovereign of all the sons and daughters of men, as the daughter of God the Father, Who is love; the Mother of God the Word, of our love; the chosen bride of the Holy Spirit, Who is co-essential with the Father and the Word. How can we do otherwise than have recourse to such a sovereign and expect to receive all spiritual blessings from her?"[161]

ELISABETH IS WITH CHILD

The Archangel Gabriel then utters, "**'And, behold, thy cousin Elisabeth, she hath also conceived a son in her old age; and this is the sixth month with her, who was called barren. For with God nothing shall be impossible'**" [Lk. 1:36-37].

Although God ordained marriage as a holy relationship between one man and one woman, as in the example of Adam and Eve, barrenness of the first wife often prompted men to take second wives.

Why then didn't Zacharias take another wife that he might have an heir? Because according to Lev. 21:13-14, the high priest could have only one wife, and she had to have been a virgin from his own tribe.

Saint Photios writes contrasting Elisabeth and Mary: "He Who releases the bonds of barrenness can also make unto Himself a birth without a man's cooperation. He Who has renewed a withered root (Elisabeth) into a fruit-bearing stem, shall also change unto Himself the unmoistened ground (Mary) into fertile land."[162]

Saint Leo the Great, in a sermon, comments, "She (Mary) learns from converse with the angel that what is to be wrought in her is of the Holy Spirit. Nor does she believe it a loss of honor that she is soon to be the Mother of God *(Dei genetrix)*. For why should she be in despair over the novelty of such conception, to whom the power of the Most High has promised to effect it? Her implicit faith is confirmed also by the attestation of a precursory miracle, that of Elisabeth receiving unexpected fertility; in order that there might be no doubt that He Who had given conception to the barren, would give it even to a virgin."[163]

"BEHOLD THE HANDMAID OF THE LORD"

Of the many titles of Mary found in Christian literature, this is the one that she herself chose: "handmaid of the Lord" *(doulee Kyriou)*.

Virgin: "Thou dost appear to me to speak the truth, for thou hast come as an angel messenger, bringing joy to all. Since, then, I am purified in soul and body by the Spirit, be it unto me according to thy word: may God dwell in me."[164] Then the Virgin stretched forth her hands and, raising her eyes to heaven, uttered, "'**Behold the handmaid of the Lord; be it unto me according to thy word**'" [Lk. 1:38].

"Receiving thy glad tidings, O Gabriel, I am filled with divine joy. For thou dost speak to me of joy, a joy without end."[165]

"Thou dost bring me good tidings of divine joy, that the immaterial Light, in His abundant compassion, will be united to a material body."[166]

"He shall borrow flesh from me, that through this mingling He may lead man up unto his ancient glory, for He alone has the power to do so."[167]

Archangel: "Divine joy is given to thee, O Mother of God. All creation crieth unto thee, 'Rejoice, O Bride of God.' For thou alone, O pure Virgin, wast fore-ordained to be the Mother of the Son of God."[168]

"I see thee as a lamp with many lights and as a bridal chamber made by God. As an ark of gold, O spotless Maiden, receive now the Giver of the law, Who through thee has been pleased to deliver the corrupt nature of mankind."[169]

Virgin: "The descent of the Holy Spirit has purified my soul and sanctified my body: it has made of me a temple that contains God, a tabernacle divinely adorned, a living sanctuary."[170] "May the condemnation of Eve be now brought to nought through me; and through me may her debt be repaid this day. Through me may the ancient due be rendered up in full."[171]

Archangel: "God promised to thy forefather Abraham that in his seed the nations would be blessed [Gen. 22:18], O pure Lady; and through thee today the promise receives its fulfillment.[172]

Rejoice, thou restoration of fallen Adam: Rejoice, thou redemption of the tears of Eve.[173]

Here, the Virgin has corrected the shortcoming by which Moses had angered God at the unburnt bush [Ex. 4:14], which is a type of her, because she did not doubt in the least, nor did she raise any objection to God at His selection of her. But by her humble words, "Behold the handmaid of the Lord," she effaced the untoward stuttering of Moses' words; for he tried to excuse himself before God by claiming that he was "weak in speech and slow-tongued" [Ex. 4:10] and, said, "I pray Thee, O Lord, appoint another able person whom Thou shalt send [Ex. 4:13]."[174]

He Who of old commanded Moses to set up the Ark of the Testimony, came to dwell in thee, O Virgin, as in a spiritual ark.[175] *For, Whilst Gabriel was saying, "Rejoice, to thee, O Virgin," at his voice the Master of all became incarnate in thee, the holy ark, as spake the righteous David. Thou wast seen to be more spacious than the heavens while holding thy Creator.*[176]

THE VIRGIN'S OBEDIENCE

In a homily, St. Photios remarks, "What was the reply of the honored virgin, the heavenly chamber, the holy mountain [Ps. 98:10], the sealed fountain [Song 4:12], kept for Him only Who had sealed it? 'Since,' says she, 'thou hast clearly explained that the Holy Spirit shall come upon me, I no longer demure, I no longer object. Be it unto me according to thy word. If I am judged worthy for the Lord, I will gladly serve His will. If the Builder desires the thing built to become a temple to the Builder, let Him construct a house unto Himself as He has pleased. If the Creator rests on His creature, let Him mold in me His flesh as He knows how and wishes. Behold the handmaid of the Lord: be it unto me according to thy word. Let thy words be unto me fulfilled in the act. Let thy words be unto me in accordance with the deeds.'"[177]

Saint Justin Martyr (+c.165) comments, "Eve, being a virgin and incorrupt, conceived the word spoken of the serpent, and brought forth disobedience and death. But Mary the Virgin answered, 'Be it done to me according to thy word.' Mary received faith and grace when the Archangel Gabriel brought her good news that the Spirit of the Lord would come upon her, and the power of the Most High would overshadow her, so that the Holy One born of her is the Son of God. And, indeed, she gave birth to Him, concerning Whom we have shown so many passages of Scripture were written, and by Whom God destroys both the serpent and those angels and men who have become like the serpent, but frees from death those who repent of their sins and believe in Christ."[178]

Saint Irenaeus, Bishop of Lyons, writes: "The Virgin Mary is found obedient, saying, 'Behold thy handmaid, O Lord,....' But Eve was disobedient; though still a virgin she did not obey. For as she, though wedded to Adam, was still a virgin...being disobedient, she became a cause of death to herself and to all mankind. So Mary, having a foreordained husband, but nonetheless a virgin, was obedient and became to herself and to the whole human race a cause of salvation."[179]

Continuing, St. Irenaeus says, "To undo the seduction by which the virgin Eve, betrothed to a man, was wickedly misled, Mary, a virgin betrothed, was given good tidings of truth by an angel. For as Eve was seduced by an angel's talk to turn from God betraying His word, so Mary was given good news by the angel's talk that she should bear God, being obedient to His word. The former had disobeyed God, and the latter was persuaded to obey God, so that the Virgin Mary should become the advocate of the virgin Eve. And as the human race was bound to death by a virgin, by a virgin

113

it was delivered: virginal disobedience is balanced by virginal obedience."[180]

THE ARCHANGEL GABRIEL DEPARTS
"And the angel departed from her" [Lk. 1:38].

Saint Paulinus, in one of his poems, writes: "With these words, he (Gabriel) left her gaze and the earth and made for the upper air which he knows so well with easy motion. Thus, the commands of God were fulfilled."[181]

Saint Photios comments that "The holy and uncorrupted Virgin, for her part, having shown in such words her obedience to the Lord's ambassador, put an end to the conversation....Blessed are thou among women, because thou hast requited the discomfiture of woman's transgression, having turned the reproach of deceit into a laudation of the sex. Because in thee, a virgin, He Who first molded Adam out of virgin earth, today remolds man from thy virginal blood. Having woven the fleshy garment of the Word, thou hast covered up the nakedness of the first-formed."[182]

Saint Gregory of Nyssa, using the image of the "virgin earth", comments: "Wisdom (that is, Christ the Word), according to what is said, built *herself* a house [Prov. 9:1], forming into a man the earth taken from the Virgin, through whom He has mingled with humanity."

Why the feminine metaphor of God? "In the divine Archetype there is no place for sex."[183] Yet, we are told that "God made man, according to the image of God He made him, male and female He made them" [Gen. 1:27]; the creation of human nature is twofold. The image conferred upon our bodies and souls was "godlikeness". In the Old Testament, God often uses "feminine" metaphors, similes and other images to help Israel better understand His love, justice and will. For example: The Spirit of God "hovered over the face of the waters" [Gen. 1:2] and, as an eagle, God watches, yearns, receives and carries His brood on His back [Deut. 32:11]. We read that God "makes" clothes [Gen. 3:21]; "prepares" and nourishes His people with bread [Ex. 16:4, Neh. 9:21] or prepares fish and bread [Jn. 21:9]. God is depicted as the perfect midwife [Ps. 21:10], yet He is like a woman in travail [Is. 42:14]. God also uses the imagery of a nursing mother [Is. 49:15] or a mother who comforts her child [Is. 66:13]. God does not stop with pregnancy, labor or nursing, but personally and lovingly oversees the training and healing of His children [Hos. 11:3-4]. Jesus Himself says that He wanted to gather the children of Jerusalem together, as a hen gathers her chicks under her wings [Mt. 23:37]. However, as a symbol of God's judgment, God is compared to a "she-bear deprived of her cubs" [Hos. 13:8]. Although God cannot be known in His essence, these anthropomorphisms help us understand Him.

THE FIRST BENEFICIARY OF REDEMPTION

Saint Paulinus writes: "The maiden immediately believed, and her ready faith added to the merit of her former life. The seed lay hidden with its causes unrevealed, and fashioned a body which was God's. The holy Burden grew, and her devoted womb cherished the heavenly Lord."[184]

Saint Ambrose writes: "Who was there on whom the Lord had bestowed greater honor?"[185] She was the first beneficiary of the redemption: "Nor is it to be wondered at, that when the Lord was about to redeem the world, He began His work from Mary, so that she, through whom salvation was being prepared for all, should be the first to draw salvation from her Son."[186]

ACCEPTING ALL THINGS OF MAN,
AND MAKING THINE
ALL THINGS THAT PERTAIN TO OUR NATURE[187]

Saint Ambrose writes: "For the flesh of the Lord, generated when the Spirit came to the Virgin, did not await the customary intercourse of male and female union....Although the cause of generation was different, nevertheless the flesh of Christ is of one nature with all men. For childbirth did not change the nature of the Virgin, but established a new method of generating. So flesh was born of flesh. Thus the Virgin had of her own what she gave; for the mother did not give something of another, but she contributed her own from her womb in an unusual manner, but in a usual function. Therefore, the Virgin had the flesh, which by customary right of nature she transferred to the fetus. Therefore, the nature of Mary, who gave birth, and that of the Begotten are the same according to the flesh, and not unlike his human brethren, because Scripture says, 'Wherefore in all things it behooved Him to be made like unto His brethren....'" [Heb. 2:17].[188]

Saint Andrew of Crete praises Mary's holiness thus: "Today the pure nobility of men receives the grace of the first creation by God and thus returns to itself: and the human nature, which clings to the newly born Mother of the Beautiful One, receives back the glorious beauty, which had been dimmed by the degradation of evil, and the best and most marvelous new formation. And this new formation is truly a reformation, and the reformation is a deification, and this restoration is to the first state."[189]

Having sanctified the beginning of human growth and every stage thereafter, and having been made under the law to loose them that were slaves to the law, St. Paulinus adds that "He was made of a woman [Gal. 4:4], a woman by sex and a virgin in childbirth, so that the Creator of both sexes might make both holy; for He became man, and of a woman He was born."[190]

Like a bread baked secretly in thee, mortal nature is purified by having held converse, through thee, with the unendurable Fire of divinity, O all pure Virgin, who wast preserved unhurt therefrom.[191]

Saint Andrew of Crete writes that she conceived the Creator, through the Holy Spirit, according to the good pleasure of the Father; and without alteration or confusion He became what we are.[192] He also chants, *Today there comes glad tidings of joy. Things below are joined to things above. Adam is renewed and Eve set free from her ancient sorrow. The tabernacle of human nature which the Lord took upon Himself, making divine the substance He assumed, is consecrated as a temple of God. O mystery! The manner of His emptying is unknown, the fashion of His conceiving is ineffable. An angel ministers at the wonder; a virgin womb receives the Son. The Holy Spirit is sent down; the Father*

*on high gives His consent; and so the covenant is brought to
pass by common counsel. In Him and through Him we are
saved. Together with Gabriel, let us cry aloud unto the
Virgin, "Rejoice, thou who art full of grace: the Lord is
with thee." From thee has Christ our God and our Salvation
taken human nature, raising it up unto Himself.*[193]

THE VIRGIN'S GESTURES AS DEPICTED IN THE ICONS

The iconographic
depiction of this de-
cisive moment in history
usually emphasizes one
of three moments in the
event. First: the ap-
pearance of Gabriel and
his greeting, to the
perturbation of the holy
Virgin. Hence she turns
about and drops the
purple yarn that she is spinning. The second type depicts
the perplexity, yet prudence, of the Virgin; this is especially
brought out in the hymns for the day. Owing to the fall of
our ancestress Eve, the Virgin Mary is circumspect and does
not at once accept the extraordinary tidings from the world
beyond. Not only does she have in constant remembrance
her vow of virginity, but she recalled the law of nature.
When she says, "How shall this be, seeing I know not a man?
[Lk. 1:34], this might be demonstrated by the gesture of her
hand which she holds before her breast, palm outward, as a
sign of perplexity.[194]

Finally, most icons depict the culmination of the visit--
her consent. Then we may see her bowing her head and
raising her right hand, a gesture of acceptance or obedience.
By her gesture she answers the Sender, not the messenger.
All these interpretations of body language may be combined
together, showing a synthesis of her psychological state.[195]

*Let creation rejoice exceedingly: for the Creator now
makes Himself to be created, and He Who was before all
things now makes Himself known as God newly-revealed.*[196]

THE PATRIARCH JACOB
AND HIS FATHER-IN-LAW LABAN

As a supplementary article to this chapter of the
Annunciation, we wish to bring forward St. Paulinus, who

will interpret, in one of his poems, a biblical account concerning Jacob [Gen. 30: 25-43], which foreshadows the Annunciation.

The Patriarch Jacob, as a shepherd of sheep and goats, agreed to take all the spotted and speckled goats and the grey rams, leaving the white ones to Laban's sons. Jacob then plucked three rods from three trees, peeled them so that stripes appeared, and set them in the water. After summoning the flock, they drank at the watering troughs before the three rods, where they conceived. Later, the progeny of Jacob's flock could be established by their markings; whereas, Laban's flock had no marks on them. [Gen. 30:25-43].

Saint Paulinus explains that "The markings denote life, for Christ will regard those unmarked as marked for death....The Church, so fertile in Her virgin's womb and the Mother of salvation, with Her gaze on the three rods (three Persons of the Trinity) absorbs the moist seed of the Word, and is marked with the brightness of God's immortal countenance--for God supplies plenty to the needy and deprivation to the proud." Continuing, he writes: "In the three rods, if we examine further...is the symbolism of the kingdom. The patriarch chose for himself three rods from three trees. The first was perfumed from the storax tree (incense burning shrub), the second smooth from the plane tree, the third unbending from the almond tree. The storax contains the Virgin, the plane contains the Spirit, and the almond Christ. The plane tree extends its spreading branches to provide shade; thus the Holy Spirit fashioned Christ by casting His shadow over the Virgin. I (continues St. Paulinus) believe that the rod from the storax, the tree of David, is the Virgin who in childbirth brought forth a sweet-smelling Blossom. The rod of the almond tree is Christ, for there is food within that tree, which has an outer casing consisting of bitter bark over its green skin. Here you must recognize the divine Christ clothed in our human body. In that flesh He can be broken; the food lies in the Word, the bitterness in the Cross. His hard covering consists of the tidings of the Cross and the food of that Cross, and it encloses within the divine remedy in the flesh of Christ. Yet in His Cross He is also sweet, because God our life brought forth life from the Tree."[197]

Chapter VII.
The MOTHER OF GOD
Visits
Righteous ELISABETH

+ + +

Saint Ambrose (339-397) writes that "Mary was modest towards her neighbors. And when she knew that she was chosen of God, she became more humble. She then prepared to go forthwith into the hill country to visit her kinswoman, her first-cousin, Elisabeth, the wife of Zacharias the priest, not in order to gain belief by anything external, for she had believed the word of God."[1]

Saint Paulinus of Nola (353-431) says that "her child, though not yet born, impelled holy Mary, in her pregnant state, to journey forth and visit Elisabeth who was now at an age to command respect."[2]

Before going to righteous Elisabeth, the *Protoevangelion* reports that Mary and her companions first passed by Jerusalem to submit the true purple and other threads which they had completed. They brought them to the high priest and, moved by the grace of God, he blessed the Virgin, saying, "Mary, the Lord God hath magnified thy name and thou shalt be blessed in all the generations of the earth."[3]

THE MOTHER OF GOD VISITS EIN KAREM

The Evangelist Luke, who makes greater mention of the significant role of women in the history of redemption, relates this story of Mary's visit to Ein Karem, located about five miles west of Jerusalem, but some 80 miles from Nazareth. To walk this distance would have taken the Virgin and her companions approximately 30 hours.

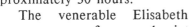

The venerable Elisabeth was a woman of unusual piety, faith and spiritual gifts. According to both the writings of Hippolytos (+235) and the Church *Synaxarion* (25 July), we learn exactly how Mary and

119

Elisabeth were blood relatives. As we already know, Mary's mother was Anna who was the youngest of three daughters of Matthan the priest and Miriam, both of the tribe of Levi. The other two daughters of Matthan and Miriam were one with the same name as her mother, Miriam, and Zoia (Sovee). Ecclesiastical chronicles record that Matthan served as priest during the reign of Queen Cleopatra (c.69 B.C.-30 B.C.), but that he reposed well before the reign of Herod Antipas (4 B.C.-40 A.D.). The eldest daughter, Miriam, was married in Bethlehem, and bore Salome. We shall meet this Salome, a midwife, later in chapter ix of this book. The second daughter, Zoia, was married in Bethlehem, and bore Elisabeth. The third daughter, Anna, was married to Joachim in Nazareth, and after fifty years of marriage, bore Mary Theotokos.[4]

It is possible that Mary, now an orphan, found sympathetic female companionship in her much older cousin, Elisabeth, and desired greatly to visit with her. Throughout Mary's girlhood, growing up in the temple, Elisabeth and her husband, the priest Zacharias, were familiar and loving kin.

Thus, Mary could also claim kinship with the priesthood from her mother's side. This seems to imply that Mary's father's family, of the tribe of Judah, must have held some rank formerly, for only with such did custom sanction any alliance on the part of priests, the tribe of Levi.[5] This, however, is not without precedent, for Aaron (Moses's brother), the high priest, took to wife Elisheba (or Elisabeth), the daughter of Aminadab and sister to Nashon, a ruler in Judah, who was also an ancestor of David [Ex. 6:23; Ruth 4:20; 1 Chron. 2:10]. Although not the usual custom, there are other instances too when the tribes intermingled.

THE BABE LEAPED IN ELISABETH'S WOMB

Then Mary, filled with joy, **"went into the hill country with haste, into a city of Juda; and entered into the house of Zacharias, and saluted Elisabeth. And it came to pass, that, when Elisabeth heard the salutation of Mary, the babe leaped in her womb"** [Lk. 1:39-41].

Saint George (d. after 880), Bishop of Nicomedia and eminent hymnographer, speaks of the prenatal infant John, saying, *The divine Forerunner having recognized thee as the Mother of God, leapt beforehand in his mother's womb and proclaimed beforehand thy great things, O pure Lady."*[6]

Saint Theophanes the Poet (+1381) also makes mention of the unborn John's reaction, chanting, *While yet within thy mother's womb thou wast filled with the Most Holy Spirit and, leaping with gladness, thou hast joyfully announced the fruit of virginity and hast worshipped Him, O venerable prophet.*[7]

Scripture cites cases of great ones who were sanctified, appointed or ordained before they were born and known before they were shaped; as in the case of the forefather Jacob [Gen. 25:23] or the Prophet Jeremias [Jer. 1:5].

Saint Ambrose (339-397) comments in his work entitled *Of the Christian Faith* that the Forerunner John, of whom his holy mother testified that, while he yet lay in her womb, perceived by the Spirit the presence of his Lord, and leaped for joy. John, who prophesied at that moment, was he in existence or not? He surely was in existence who worshipped his Maker. Indeed, Elisabeth was the first to hear the voice of Mary, but John was the first to feel His Lord's gracious presence. Elisabeth heard in the natural manner; he leaped for joy because of the Mystery. She sees Mary's coming; he the coming of the Lord.[8]

BLESSED ART THOU AMONG WOMEN
AND BLESSED IS THE FRUIT OF THY WOMB

The Protoevangelium records that Elisabeth put down the scarlet that she was working and ran to the door and, opening it, **"Elisabeth was filled with the Holy Spirit: And she spake out with a loud voice, and said, 'Blessed art thou among women, and blessed is the fruit of thy womb'"** [Lk. 1:41-42].[9]

Bede (c.673-735) comments that Mary was blessed by Elisabeth with the same words that Gabriel used, thereby, showing that Mary is to be venerated by both angels and men.[10]

Saint Paulinus of Nola (4th c.) writes that "Elisabeth, from a distance, saw Mary gleaming with fiery light. Elisabeth bestirred herself from afar and advanced to meet her with rapid steps. Stretching out adoring hands, she said, 'Rejoice, Mother of the Lord. Rejoice, devoted maiden.

Though thou hast not shared a marriage-bed and know no intercourse with a husband, thou wilt bring forth God. So important was it for thee to be chaste, that thou might win the title and reward of a virgin bride. Now why has the glory of this service fallen to me, when I am undeserving and unworthy of so great a gift? Why has the glory of heaven descended into our hearth and cheap abode, introducing into our dark recesses so powerful a Light? Yet may He show Himself gentle and mild to them that worship Him, and after His birth may He afford the favor which He showed before.' Thus, with these words, Elisabeth clasped Mary in her arms and joined in her embrace, and in reverence to God implanted kisses on that devoted body."[11]

The words of the venerable Elisabeth also bring to mind the Old Testament verses, "Blessed among women be Jael..." [Judg. 5:24] and of Ozias to Judith, "O daughter, blessed art thou of the Most High God above all the women upon the earth" [Judith 13:18] and, especially, "...if thou wilt indeed hear the voice of the Lord thy God..." [Deut. 28:1] which Mary had indeed done, "all these blessings shall come upon thee, and find thee..." [Deut. 28:2], and He (the Lord) "will love thee, and bless thee, and multiply thee: and He will bless the offspring of thy body...." [Deut. 7:13].

ELISABETH, THE PROPHETESS, HATH TAUGHT US TO CRY OUT TO THEE, O MOTHER OF THE LORD![12]

"'And whence is this to me, that the Mother of my Lord should come to me?'" [Lk. 1:43].

Elisabeth's witness must have been an incomparable encouragement to Mary. Elisabeth believed the divine conception and was the first to address Mary as the "Mother of the Lord." Saint Ambrose comments that Elisabeth does not speak as one not knowing; for when she says, "whence is this to me," she knew that it was the favor and work of the

Holy Spirit that the 'Mother of the Lord' should greet the 'mother of the prophet'. In her humility, Elisabeth understood that it was not the consequence of merit or good deeds that this visit was taking place, but a gift of the divine favor.[13]

Old Testament episodes and texts prefigure this moment too. When Elisabeth asks, "whence is this to me, that the Mother of my Lord should come to me?" is reminiscent of David, the Prophet-King, who asks, "How shall the ark of the Lord come in to me?" [2 Sam. 6:9].

Elisabeth is the first to address Mary with the sublime salutation of "the Mother of my Lord" *(ee Meeteer tou Kyriou mou)*. The word *Kyrios*, Lord, that Elisabeth used, was a term which, among Hellenistic Jews, meant only God.

Saint Alexander of Alexandria (+328) is also one of the first to use this most important title of Theotokos. "In this we know the resurrection of the dead; of this the first fruits was our Lord Jesus Christ, Who truly and not in appearance bore flesh, taken from Mary Theotokos."[14]

Saint Athanasios of Alexandria (296-373), a treasure house of apostolic knowledge, writes this about the Mother of God: "The mark and characteristic of Holy Scripture...is that it contains a twofold declaration concerning the Saviour, that He both always was God and that He is the Son, being the Word and brightness and wisdom of the Father, and that afterwards, for our sake, by taking flesh from the Virgin Mary, the Mother of God, He became man."[15] And then after discussing other matters, he writes: "In truth, there have been many saints and men cleansed of all sin. For both Jeremias was sanctified from the womb [Jer. 1:5], and John, as yet unborn, leaped for joy at the voice of Mary, the Mother of God."[16]

This is the most important truth about Mary, that she is the Mother of God. The doctrine is supported by Sacred Scripture, Sacred Tradition, and the teaching authority of the

Church. Apart from St. Elisabeth's exclamation, her title as Mother of God is inferred in Scripture, though not stated explicitly, yet in equivalent terms. Several examples are, as follows: "God sent forth His Son, made of a woman" [Gal. 4:4]; "He shall...be called the Son of the Highest...therefore also that holy thing which shall be born of thee shall be called the Son of God" [Lk. 1:32, 35]; "the Mother of Jesus was there" [Jn. 2:1]; "Is not this the carpenter, the son of Mary...." [Mk. 6:3]; "Then one said unto Him, "Behold, Thy Mother..." [Mt. 12:47]; and, "there stood by the Cross of Jesus His Mother" [Jn. 19:25].

For St. Gregory the Theologian (c.329-c.391), acceptance of Mary as Theotokos was a test of Orthodoxy: "If anyone does not accept the holy Mary as Theotokos, he is without the Godhead."[17] In the West, St. Ambrose (339-397) was the first to use the title *Mater Dei*.[18] Saint Vincent of Lerins (+c.450), in his *Commonitories*, would also write: "Therefore, may God forbid that anyone should attempt to defraud holy Mary of her superiority in divine grace and of her special glory. For by unique favor of our Lord and God she is to be confessed to be the most true and most blessed Mother of God."[19]

The first decisive teaching was at the Council of Ephesus in 431 A.D. The title "Theotokos" (God-birthgiver), was formally sanctioned at this Council. The letter of St. Cyril of Alexandria (+444), illustrious among Fathers, who, acting as representative of Pope Celestine I of Rome, was approved by the Council. The relevant passage from his letter to Nestorius concerning the divine motherhood is, as follows:

"For in the first place, no common man was born of the holy Virgin,...He is said to have endured a generation in the flesh in order to appropriate the producing of His own body. Thus, the holy Fathers did not hesitate to speak of the holy Virgin as the Mother of God."[20] Twenty years later the Council of Chalcedon spoke of our Lord Jesus Christ "indeed born of the Father before the ages according to divinity, but, in the last days, the same born of the Virgin Mary, Mother of God according to humanity."[21]

Moreover, in a letter to priests, deacons and monks, St. Cyril wrote: "I am amazed if some should question at all whether the holy Virgin should be called the Mother of God. For if our Lord Jesus is God, how is the holy Virgin who bore Him not the Mother of God? The inspired disciples transmitted this faith to us, even if they have not made mention of the term. So we have been taught to think by the holy Fathers."[22]

Just over a century later, the second Council of Constantinople (553) condemned an erroneous interpretation of Chalcedon, and ended thus: "Or, if anyone calls her the 'Mother of the Man' or the 'Mother of the Christ', as if the Christ were not God, and does not confess that she is exactly and truly the Mother of God, because God the Word, born of the Father before the ages, was made flesh of her in the last days, and that thus the holy Synod of Chalcedon confessed her to be, let such a one be anathema."[23] The third Council of Constantinople (in the Troullos in 680), condemning the Monothelites, repeated some of the earlier formulas and affirmed that Jesus Christ was born "of the Holy Spirit and the Virgin Mary, rightly and truly the Mother of God according to His humanity...."[24]

BLESSED IS SHE THAT BELIEVED!

Then holy Elisabeth uttered: **"'For, lo, as soon as the voice of thy salutation sounded in mine ears, the babe leaped in my womb for joy. And blessed is she that believed: for there shall be a performance of those things which were told her from the Lord'"** [Lk. 1:44-45].

Mary's excellence is singled out here. The praise of Mary's faith is given a certain force when contrasted with the angel's rebuke to Elisabeth's husband Zacharias, who presently cannot speak as a penance [Lk. 1:20].

Saint Paulinus of Nola, in *Poem 6*, describes what happened when Gabriel came to Zacharias the priest, when he went into the temple of the Lord to burn incense [Lk. 1:8-23]. "The priest stood rooted there, his fearful mind in turmoil. His hesitating heart pondered the promise; he doubted whether he had deserved a kindness so great that the Most High had taken the trouble to send a messenger from the heights of heaven to announce such clear instruc-

125

tions from his Lord to the servant. He feared that he was beguiled; he thought it was a dream. He assessed his own character less generously than was just, proclaiming that he

did not deserve such treatment. So faith itself made him unfaithful, and in his unwillingness to believe himself worthy, he deserved punishment for his skepticism. At once, the tongue in his doubting mouth was tied....He retired in sadness, pondered his grief within his mind, and begged pardon for his fault from the depth of his heart."[25]

"Faith shines forth especially in the Virgin when contrasting her response to that of the Priest Zacharias" [Lk. 1:18], remarks St. Ambrose, "for because she had believed that it would be done, she asked how it would be done. Hence, she deserved to hear 'blessed art thou for believing' (from Elisabeth). And she was truly blessed who excelled the priest, for if the priest had expressed denial, the Virgin remedied his fault."[26]

Saint Ambrose also comments that "Elisabeth, who conceived a son and had hid herself [Lk. 1:24], now begins to exult that within her she was bearing a prophet; she, who before felt shame, now breaks out in blessing. We also see that Mary had not doubted at all, but had believed; therefore, the fruit of faith followed. Every soul that believes, conceives and brings forth the Word of God, and confesses His works."[27]

Both Mary's mother, Anna, and her cousin Elisabeth desired to conceive. Righteous women of the Old Testament, such as Sarah, Rebecca, Rachel, Samson's mother and Hannah, also sought a child. Saint Ephraim [c.306-373] contrasts Mary with these righteous women, writing: *He Who could give moisture to breasts barren and dead--caused them to fail in youth, made them to flow in age--forced and changed*

126

nature, in its season and out of its season. The Lord of natures changed the Virgin's nature.[28]   Hannah with bitter tears asked a child [1 Sam. 1:7]; *Sarah and Rebecca with vows and words, Elisabeth also with her prayer, after having vexed themselves for a long time, yet so obtained comfort. Blessed be Mary, who without vows and without prayer, in her virginity conceived and brought forth the Lord of all the sons of her companions, who have been or shall be chaste and righteous, priests and kings.[29]*

THE MAGNIFICAT

"And Mary said, 'My soul doth magnify the Lord, and my spirit hath rejoiced in God my Saviour'" [Lk. 1:46-47].

Saint Basil (c.330-379) comments that "the first fruit of the Spirit is peace and joy. Therefore, since the holy Virgin had received within herself every grace of the Holy Spirit, rightly does she add that her spirit rejoiced in her Saviour. She speaks of soul and spirit as one thing. The voice of exultation is a familiar one in the Scriptures, conveying to us a certain cheerful and joyous state of mind in them that are worthy. The Virgin, therefore, rejoices in the Lord with an ineffable uplifting of heart, and with a noble and resounding utterance of her love."[30]

In another place, St. Basil discloses that "If at any time light has entered thine heart, to love God and despise bodily things, by this obscure and brief image it will have glimpsed at the perfect state of the just, who serenely and without end rejoice in the Lord; thus, thou may, too, without difficulty, attain to the joy in the Lord."[31]

Bede comments that "The spirit of the Virgin rejoices in the everlasting Godhead of the same Jesus.[32] Saint Ambrose remarks about Mary that "In her dedicated soul and spirit to the Father and to the Son, she adored with fervent love the One God from Whom all things are made. If, according to the flesh, there is one Mother of Christ, yet, according to faith, Christ is the fruit of all men; for every soul that is pure and free from sin, conceives the Word of God, and keeps itself chaste with modesty undefiled."[33]

"'For He hath regarded the low estate of His hand-maiden'" [Lk. 1:48].

Blessed Jerome (347-420) observes that the Virgin says that she is not blessed by her own works and virtue, but by the mercy of God dwelling in her.[34]

Saint Isidore of Pelusium (c.450) adds that since Mary says that "He hath regarded the humility of His handmaid," it was as though she said, "God so ordered; I did not seek; I was content with lowly things.   Now am I called unto ineffable wisdom, uplifted from earth to the stars."[35]

Saint Athanasios comments, "If, according to the prophet, 'Blessed is he that has a seed in Sion, and household friends in Jerusalem' [Is. 31:9], how great should be the praise of the divinely inspired and all-holy Virgin Mary who became, according to the flesh, the Mother of the Word?'"

Saint Aphraates (4th c.) says that Mary's spirit of prayer is lauded and that she would not have found grace otherwise than by her fasting and prayer."[36]

"'For, behold, from henceforth all generations shall call me blessed.   For He that is mighty hath done to me great things'" [Lk. 1:48-49].

Saint Symeon Metaphrastes (c.1000) tells us not to be troubled when she calls herself blessed. She is not troubled by vainglory; where was there place for pride in her who called herself the 'handmaid of the Lord'? But because she was touched by the Holy Spirit, she prophecies those things that are to come.[37]

Bede adds that it was fitting, that as death entered the world through the pride of our first parent, so through the lowliness of Mary was the way to true life thrown open.[38]

Saint Ephraim lauds the Virgin-Mother saying, *"Blessed art thou too, Mary, that thy name is great and exalted because of thy child! Thou cannot tell then how and how long and where He dwelt in thee, the great One in a small room. Blessed be thy mouth that praised and enquired not, and thy tongue that glorified and questioned not!" For if His Mother was uncertain concerning Him, even while she*

carried Him in the womb, who then shall suffice to com-
prehend Him?[39]

Saint Ambrose, as a warning against a certain kind of excess, writes: "Without doubt the Holy Spirit too must be adored when we adore Him Who is born of the Spirit according to the flesh. But let none apply this to Mary: for Mary was the temple of God, not the God of the temple. And therefore He alone is to be adored, who worked in the temple."[40]

"'And holy is His name'" [Lk. 1:49].

Saint Basil explains what is meant by "holy is His name" is not because the name contains in its syllables any special virtue, but because whatever way we contemplate God, we see Him pure and holy.[41] The venerable Bede adds that the very word "holy", in the Greek tongue *agion*, means to be "apart from earth", thereby signifying the supreme eminence of His power and His transcendence over all creatures, far removed from all that He has made.[42]

"'And His mercy is on them that fear Him from generation to generation'" [Lk. 1:50].

Bede remarks that in this statement she is turning from God's special gifts to herself to the general decrees of God. It is as though she were to say, "He that is mighty has not only done great things to me, but in every nation He is pleasing to them that fear God."[43]

"'He hath shewed strength with His arm'" [Lk. 1:51].
The "arm" signifies the Word that is to be born of her.

"'He hath scattered the proud in the Imagination of their hearts'" [Lk. 1:51]. Saint Cyril of Alexandria comments here that "The proud are not only those wicked demons who, together with their prince, fell on account of pride. The proud Greek sages rejected the preaching of Christ and the Cross as folly. The unbelieving Jews were scattered after conceiving unworthy imaginations about the Messiah, the Word of God."[44]

"'He hath put down the mighty from their seats, and exalted them of low degree'" [Lk. 1:52].

Who are the mighty? They could be the scribes and pharisees who sought the chief seats. Saint Cyril of Alexandria believes that the Virgin is referring to the demons who openly claimed mastery over the world. At the coming of the Lord, they had been scattered and those whom the demons had taken captive have now been ushered into Christ's Kingdom.

Great was the haughtiness of the demons, the Greek sages, the scribes and pharisees. But Christ has put them down and exalted tax collectors, harlots and unlettered fisherman who humbled themselves under His mighty hand. He hath given them "power to tread upon serpents and scorpions, and all the power of the enemy" [Lk. 10:19]. Also, the Virgin's prophecy was fulfilled in that the Jews, who gloried in their kingdom, were deprived of it for their unbelief and envy; whereas, the Gentiles, enveloped in the darkness of polytheism, believed the Apostles and were exalted for their faith.[45]

Saint Ephraim chants of the broken power of the underworld: *The evil one and his host fled--he that used to exult in the world. In the high places they sacrificed heifers to him; in the gardens they slew bulls for him. He swallowed up all creation; he filled his belly with prey. Blessed is He Who came and made him disgorge!*[46]

"'**He hath filled the hungry with good things; and the rich He hath sent empty away**'" [Lk. 1:53]. Again, St. Cyril comments that those who hungered were the Gentiles who were pining away in spiritual famine. The Jews were made wealthy by having received the law and the teaching of the prophets. Saint Paul said this about the Jews: "to them pertaineth the adoption, and the glory, and the covenants, and the giving of the law, and the service of God, and the promises" [Rom. 9:4].

Those who were enriched waxed wanton with high feeding. They were swollen with pride at the dignity bestowed upon them. Thus vaunting the fact that they were "sons of Abraham" they disdained to draw humbly to the incarnate Word; hence they were sent away empty, carrying nothing--neither faith, knowledge, nor the hope of blessings. Those Jews who rejected Him became outcasts from the earthly Jerusalem and refused citizenship in the glorious life to come. They denied the Prince of Life and even crucified the Lord of Glory and, abandoning the Fountain of living water, they set at nought the Bread that came down from heaven. On account of this, a famine more severe than any other befell them and a thirst unquenchable and more bitter than any other. Do not think that this is a famine from food and water, but a famine of hearing the word of the Lord [Amos 8:11] and communicating Him. However, the heathen, whose souls were wasting away with deprivation and misery, upon receiving the Lord, were filled with spiritual blessings.[47] The privileges of the children of Israel were then passed over to the new Israel, as He also says, "I will love her that was not loved, and will say to them that were not My people, 'Thou art My people;' and they shall say, 'Thou art the Lord my God'" [Hos. 2:23]; and where it was said, "'Ye are not My people,' even they shall be called the sons of the living God" [Hos. 1:10].

"'He hath helped His servant Israel, in remembrance of His mercy; as He spake to our fathers, to Abraham, and to his seed for ever'" [Lk. 1:54-55].

Saint Cyril remarks that to the many who were Israelites, according to the flesh, and believed, God accomplished what He had spoken to Abraham, that "in thy seed shall all the nations of the earth be blessed" [Gen. 22:18]. The fulfilled promise was Christ, Who was of the seed of Abraham, in Whom the nations are blessed. When the Virgin said, "He hath helped His servant Israel," she did not mean those who were Israelites priding themselves on the bare name, but those true Israelites of the Spirit who would look unto God and believe in Him. The nations are those children that, through the Son, obtained the adoption of sons and the promises made to the prophets and patriarchs of old.[48]

Saint Ambrose, commenting on the meeting of the cousins, Mary and Elisabeth, writes: "Sweet is the harmony of prophecy with prophecy, of woman with woman, of babe with babe. The women speak words of grace, the babes move in a hidden manner. And as their mothers approach one another, so do they engage in mysterious converse of love; and in a twofold miracle, though in diverse degrees of honor, the mothers prophesy in the spirit of their little ones. Who, I ask, was it that performed this miracle? Was it not the Son of God, Who made the unborn to be?"[49]

Some have remarked that the Virgin's majestic words are modeled on the *Psalms*, and especially the *Song of Hannah* [1 Sam. 2:1-20]. Within these verses, the Theotokos praises God, but the general theme is of God's gracious dealing with the humble and poor, while He shows His strong power against the rich and mighty and, finally, the immediate fulfillment of God's mercy promised to Israel.

MARY ABIDES WITH HER COUSIN ELISABETH

Saint Ambrose comments, "As sin began from women so also do our blessings begin with them: hence it does not seem by chance that Elisabeth prophesied before John, and Mary before the birth of the Lord. But it follows that the more Mary excelled in the dignity of her person, the richer would be her prophesying."[50] Saint Basil comments that "The Virgin, with mind upraised, contemplating the immensity of the mystery, advancing as it were more profoundly forward, magnifies God."[51]

Bede further adds that we should not wonder that the Lord, now about to redeem the world, has begun His work from His Mother's womb; so that she, through whom salvation was prepared for all men, might be the first to draw forth the fruits of salvation from her Son. Every soul that conceives the Word of God in its mind, from then on climbs by steps of love to the heights of virtue, to reach the "city of Judah", that is, to the citadel of confession and praise; and as it were to abide there three months, to the perfecting of faith, hope and love.[52]

"Mary abode with her about three months" [Lk. 1:56].

Perceiving herself daily to grow big, and being afraid, Mary went home, and hid herself from the children of Israel.[53] The Gospel is silent as to whether the Virgin remained up to the birth and circumcision of the infant John. Interpreters are divided on the point. Saint Symeon Metaphrastes comments that, on account of her virginal modesty, she naturally would have shunned the attention of the many guests and visitors to welcome the newborn's birth. He then writes that it was the custom of that time for virgins to leave when the time drew near for childbearing.[54]

If we examine the ancient tradition of iconography for the Feast of the Nativity of the Forerunner, Elisabeth is seen lying on a bed as young maidens offer her food and refreshment, while others bathe or fan the newborn. Thus there was nothing shameful about the presence of young virgins at the bed of a woman in childbirth. Nevertheless, the Mother of God is never depicted in this scene.

Saint Elisabeth delivered her firstborn, John, on the 24th of June, three months after the Virgin Mary's conception. Thus, the three-month stay of Mary with her cousin is further adduced to demonstrate the parallel with the Ark which "lodged in the house of Abeddara the Githite three months, and the Lord blessed all the house of Abeddara, and all his possessions" [2 Sam. 6:11].

Chapter VIII.

JOSEPH Reproaches the MOTHER OF GOD

+ + +

JOSEPH RETURNS FROM BUILDING HOUSES

When Mary completed the second trimester of her pregnancy (the end of September), Joseph returned from building houses in Judea. He came to his home Galilee with the intention to marry the Virgin who was betrothed to him.[1] Apart from Mary's cousin Elisabeth, no one knew about the appearance of the angel or her condition.[2]

The *Protoevangelium* relates the following incident: By the sixth month Mary's shape showed that she was with child. Joseph, in the utmost distress, trembled and, smiting his face, threw himself down and cried out, "O Lord God, receive my spirit; for it is better for me to die than to live any longer. With what face can I look up to the Lord my God? What shall I say concerning this young woman? For I received her a virgin out of the temple of the Lord my God, and have not preserved her in purity! Who hath thus deceived me? Who hath committed this evil in my house? Who hath seduced her from me and defiled her?[3]

Then Joseph arose from the ground, and calling Mary, he said, "O thou who hath been so favored by God, why hast thou done this? Why hast thou debased thy soul, O thou who wast educated and reared in the Holy of Holies, and received food from the hands of angels?"[4]

Icons depicting Joseph returning home, only to find Mary with child, causes him to confront her. He is seen

134

pausing at the entrance portico of his house. An icon in the narthex of the Kariye Djami (Monastery of Chora), depicts him with a staff in his hand. The inscription above the icon would liken Joseph to Adam after the fall, when the Lord addresses Eve, saying, "Why hast thou done this?" [Gen. 3:13].[5]

Joseph then thought, "Is not the history of Adam exactly accomplished in me? For in the very instant of his glory, the serpent came and found Eve alone, and seduced her. Thus, the same thing hath occurred to me."[6]

In a hymn from the Nativity of Christ, we chant, *Joseph spoke thus to the Virgin: What is this doing, O Mary, that I see in thee? I fail to understand and am amazed, and my mind is struck with dismay. Go from my sight, therefore, with all speed. What is this doing, O Mary, that I see in thee? Instead of honor, thou hast brought me shame; instead of gladness, sorrow; instead of praise, reproof. No further shall I bear the reproach of men. I received thee from the priests of the temple, as one blameless before the Lord. And what is this that I now see?*[7]

Then with a flood of tears, Mary replied, "I am innocent and have known no man." But Joseph said, "How then art thou with child?" And she only answered, "As the Lord my God liveth, I know not by what means."[8]

Indeed, with her humble acceptance, "...I am the handmaid of the Lord...," would necessarily follow embarrassment, suspicion and misunderstanding concerning her conception.

The *Gospel of Pseudo-Matthew* adds this touching scene: Joseph then was exceedingly afraid and went away from her. The virgins who were staying with Mary then said to him, "Joseph, what art thou saying? We know that no man hath touched her. We can testify that she is a virgin and untouched. We have watched over her and she had always continued with us in prayer. Daily do the angels of God speak with her and daily does she receive food from the hand of the Lord. We know not how it can be possible that sin should be found in her. We suspect that nobody but the Holy Spirit hath caused her to conceive."[9]

Joseph then said, "Dost thou wish to mislead me into thinking that an angel of the Lord hath done this? Perhaps someone pretended to be an angel of the Lord and beguiled her?" Thus speaking, Joseph wept, and said, "With what face shall I look at the temple of the Lord, or with what face shall I see the priests of God?"[10]

Saint Proclos (+446), Patriarch of Constantinople, in a panegyrical sermon to the Theotokos attempts to describe Joseph the Betrothed's tumultuous internal state. Employing rhetorical devices, St. Proclos writes:

"As the Virgin's womb began to grow, so was Joseph's heart wounded. He saw the swelling of the womb and forgot entirely the mystery of chastity. When he saw her to be pregnant, he flew into a rage like a tempestuous and stormy sea. He saw that she was with child, and was convinced that she had been corrupted." Saint Proclos also puts these words into Joseph's mouth, "I will not believe in the manner of conception until I see the birth." He then follows with a dialogue between Joseph and Mary.[11]

Saint Germanos (c.635-733), Patriarch of Constantinople, also takes up the theme of this drama in his *Sermon on the Annunciation of the Most Holy Theotokos*. This type of sermon would be widely used in the pulpit. Saint Germanos also starts out with Joseph's sense of repulsion and wounded honor. He puts these words into the betrothed's mouth: "Leave my home straightway and betake thyself to thy new lover! I do not intend to feed thee anymore! Thou wilt not eat the bread from my table, since, instead of joy, thou hast given me sorrow, disgrace, and dishonor in my old age!"[12] He then reminds her of the judgment and condemnation of the Jewish synagogue,[13] and that they will be tested by the "water of conviction" [Num. 5:11-30].[14]

Saint Germanos continues this poignant narration from his pulpit, saying that she pleads with her betrothed, saying, "Be penitent, O Joseph! Do not drive me in secret from thy home! I am now in a strange place, and am not accustomed to it. I know neither right from left, and I do not know with whom I might find refuge."[15] And, "As the Lord lives, I have not known a man! The stain which comes from a forced bed, and the blemish which comes from carnal desire, I know not!"[16]

But Joseph continues, "If I keep silent concerning thy sin, the very stones will cry out, and the Holy of Holies will sound aloud; for I was to keep thee, but I did not preserve thee."[17]

And, "Tell me who was the traitor who, like a spy and unknown to me, has entered my bedroom!"[18]

"Bring to me him who has committed this sin and I will take his head from his shoulders!"[19]

The all-pure Virgin, in reply, protests her innocence. She reminds Joseph of the judgment to come.[20]

Then, in a calm voice, she recounted to Joseph how she went to the fountain to drink water when she heard, 'Rejoice, full of grace!' She then tells him how she returned and resumed her work with the purple, only to have the angel appear to her. Joseph asks how is it possible to conceive without seed, for such an occurrence has never taken place?[21] She then reminded him of the words of Isaias concerning the words of the sealed book which when given to a learned man, he shall say, "I cannot read it, for it is sealed" [Is. 29:11].[22] She then informs him how Isaias' prophecy of a virgin [Is. 7:14] is fulfilled in her.[23] Saint Germanos then describes the carpenter's heart as beginning to soften."[24]

JOSEPH SEEKS A SOLUTION

Joseph then departed pondering what he would do with his betrothed.[25] He was overcome with great fear, doubt and perplexity, because he did not know what was best for him to do. Being a just man, he was not willing to expose her; nor, being a pious man, to injure her fair fame by a suspicion of fornication. And he said, "If I conceal her crime, I shall be found guilty by the law of the Lord."[26]

He thought about the words in the book of *Deuteronomy*: "If there be a young virgin espoused to a man, and a man should have found her in the city and have lain with her; ye shall bring them both out to the gate of their city, and they shall be stoned with stones, and they shall die; the damsel because she cried not in the city; and the man, because he humbled his neighbor's spouse" [Deut. 22:23-24].

On the other hand, he thought, "If I expose her to the children of Israel, I fear, lest she being with child by an angel, I shall be found to betray the life of an innocent person. Should I hide myself and dwell in secret? What therefore shall I do? I will privately dissolve the contract and dismiss her."[27]

"Then Joseph her husband, being a just man, and not willing to make her a public example, was minded to put her away privily" [Mt. 1:19].

Saint John Chrysostom (354-407) commends the righteous elder on his initial conduct, and writes: "So far from punishing, he (Joseph) was not minded even to make an example of her. Dost thou see a man under self-restraint, and freed from the most tyrannical of passions? For ye know how great a thing jealousy is: and therefore he said, to whom these things are clearly known, 'For full of jealousy is the rage of a husband' [Prov. 6:34]; 'he will not spare in the day of vengeance;' and 'jealousy is cruel as the grave'" [Cant. 8:6].

"Nevertheless, Joseph was so free from passion as to be unwilling to grieve the Virgin even in the least matters. Thus, whereas to keep her in his house seemed like a transgression of the law, but to expose and bring her to trial would constrain him to deliver her to die; he does none of these things, but conducts himself now by a higher rule than the law. For grace having come, there must henceforth be many tokens of that exalted citizenship. Christ, when about to rise from that womb, even before He came forth, shone over all the world. Wherefore, even before her bringing forth, prophets danced for joy, and women foretold what was to come, and John when he had not yet come forth from the belly, leaped in the very womb."[28]

He considered putting her away which could only be done by regular divorce. If it must be so, her letter of divorcement would be handed to her privately, but in the presence of two witnesses. Not willing to have brought the blush to any face, least of all putting Mary to open shame and exposing her to a court of justice, he considers divorcing her secretly. We do not know if this entailed returning the dowry. In any event he could declare either that he had a change of feeling or because he had found just cause [Deut. 24:1], but hesitated to make it known. Though he had a keen sense of personal honor, yet he was not so bound by the law as to be unmoved by kindly feeling. He only wished to procure the divorce on some other grounds less criminal than adultery. Thus, he would leave it open to doubt on what ground he had so acted.

He considered that no one would believe that she had an angelic visitation, therefore, she would be subject to cruel punishment. According to Jewish moral code, the punishment for adultery is death. The death penalty was also imposed upon an affianced woman [Deut. 22:23-24]. The woman caught in adultery is stoned and the first stones are thrown by her own relatives.[29] This death penalty was deemed commensurate to what was considered by the Hebrews as an outrageous crime, because it struck the law of inheritance and inflicted a spurious offspring on the husband.[30]

Knowledge of the practice of divorce among the ancient Hebrews is quite sketchy. It was possible for a man to divorce his wife if he could find "something indecent about her" [Deut. 24:1]. Jewish lawyers interpreted this phrase in different ways. The two chief interpreters of the law in Jesus' time were the Jewish scholars Hill'el (c.60 B.C.-20 A.D.) and Rabbi Shammai. The followers of the conservative school of Shammai, in Jesus's time, believed it referred to adultery or sexual misconduct. The followers of the more liberal Hill'el believed that the phrase allowed divorce for almost any grievance, including the spoiling of a dinner. Divorce might ensue "if," as one tract states, "she goes out with her hair unbound, or spins wool in the street, or speaks with any man." But it was still required that the man give her a written "bill of divorcement."[31]

AN ANGEL APPEARS TO JOSEPH IN A DREAM

"But while he thought on these things, behold, the angel of the Lord appeared unto him in a dream, saying, 'Joseph, thou son of David, fear not to take unto thee Mary thy wife: for that which is begotten in her is of the Holy Spirit. And she shall bring forth a son, and thou shalt call His name Jesus: for He shall save His people from their sins'" [Mt. 1:20-21].

Saint John Chrysostom comments that "the matter then being in this state, and all at their wits' end, the angel comes to solve all their difficulties. Mary had kept silent not thinking to obtain credit with her betrothed husband, in declaring to him a thing unheard of, but rather that she should provoke him the more, as though she were cloaking a sin that had been committed. Since if she herself, who was to receive so great a favor, spoke with such candor, much more would Joseph have doubted--especially hearing it from the woman who was under suspicion. Wherefore, the Virgin says nothing to him, but the angel, the time demanding it, presents himself to him."[32]

Continuing with the homily of St. John Chrysostom, he reminds us that "The angel, speaking to Joseph, calls Mary his wife. He would not have spoken to Joseph had she been corrupted. Further, Scripture is wont to call betrothed husbands sons-in-law even before marriage. But what does the verse mean, 'to take unto thee?' To retain her in his house, for he had intended to put her away. In other words, the angel is saying, 'Consider her committed to thee by God, not by her guardians. God commits her not for marriage, but to dwell with thee, and by my voice doth He commit her.' In the same manner would Christ Himself commit her to His disciple (while on the Cross), so even now to Joseph.

"Joseph had the good tidings declared to him after his suspicions. He had mentioned the fact to no one. But then the angel appears and says the very things which he thought in his mind. This afforded him an unquestionable sign and convincing proof that the angel came from God, because it belongs to Him alone to know the secrets of the heart.

"In other words," comments St. John Chrysostom, "what the angel is saying to Joseph is this: 'Do not imagine that because He is of the Holy Spirit that thou, O Joseph, art an alien to the ministry of this dispensation. Although thou hast no part in the birth, nevertheless, what pertains to a father, though the Virgin abides untouched, this do I give thee, to set a name on that which is born: for "thou shalt call Him [Mt. 1:21]." For though the offspring is not thine, yet thou shalt exhibit a father's care towards Him. Wherefore, I do, straightway, even from the giving of the name, connect thee with Him that is born.'"[33]

Then the angel says, **"now all this was done, that it might be fulfilled which was spoken of the Lord by the prophet, saying, 'Behold a virgin shall be with child, and shall bring forth a son, and they shall call His name Emmanuel, which being interpreted is, God with us'"** [Mt. 1:22-23].

Again, we call upon St. John to comment. "After having established Joseph's faith, the angel rings in the prophet also in good time, to give his suffrage in support of all these. But before introducing the Prophet Isaias, the angel signals that which is beyond all expectation, **'for He shall save His people from their sins'** [Mt. 1:21].[34]

"Upon hearing the prophecy of Isaias, Joseph heard nothing novel, but a verse that was familiar to him. Indeed it had been a long time the subject of his meditations....Thus, the angel, to make his utterance easier to be received, brings forward Isaias.

"How was it then, one may say, that His name was not called Emmanuel, but Jesus Christ? Because the angel did not say, 'thou shalt call,' but 'they shall call,' that is, the multitude, and the issue of events. For here, the angel puts the event as a name. This is customary in Scripture, that is, to substitute the events that take place for names."[35]

JOSEPH TOOK UNTO HIM HIS WIFE

"Then Joseph being raised from sleep did as the angel of the Lord had bidden him, and took unto him his wife" [Mt. 1:24].

141

Saint John Chrysostom comments, "Seest an obedient and submissive mind? Seest thou a soul truly wakened and in all things incorruptible? For neither when he suspected something painful or amiss could he endure to keep the Virgin with him; nor yet, after he was freed from this suspicion, could he bear to cast her out, but he rather keeps her with him, and ministers to the whole Dispensation."[36]

Why did she not conceive before her espousal? St. John Chrysostom explains: "It was thus so that what had been done might be concealed awhile and that the Virgin might escape every evil suspicion. For when he (Joseph the Betrothed), who had most the right of all to feel jealousy, so far from making her a show or degrading her, is found even receiving and cherishing her after her conception, it was quite clear that unless he had been fully persuaded that what was done was by the operation of the Holy Spirit, he would not have kept her with him, and ministered to her in all other things."[37]

Thus Joseph arose and gave thanks unto God, who had given him this grace. He then spoke to Mary and her virgin companions and told them the vision. Joseph then comforted Mary and said to her, "I have sinned, in that I suspected thee at all." And, in accordance with the command of the angel, he kept the Virgin. He did not know her and kept her in chastity, and continued to take care of her.[38]

Saint Germanos, continuing in his dramatic dialogue between Joseph and Mary, writes that Joseph's abhorrence is transformed into veneration as he bows before the Virgin. He is now illumined by the Holy Spirit and, in a contrite voice, he exclaims, "Yesterday I had false suspicions and brought censure upon thy beauty and goodness. But today, having received a word from above, I apologize, and venerate thy magnanimity and bless thy name!"[39]

Nowhere in the Gospels, canonical or apocryphal, is it recorded that the most holy Virgin was given in wedlock to Joseph. It does say that she was betrothed to him [Lk. 1:7; 2:5]. Yet the angel says to Joseph, "fear not to take unto thee Mary thy wife" [Mt. 1:20]; and later, Joseph does "take unto him his wife" [Mt. 1:24]. Although it is not explicitly mentioned, the highest duty towards the Virgin-Mother and the unborn Jesus demanded of Joseph an immediate marriage; that is, payment of the dower (that is, if he had not already

142

taken care of this matter), which would afford not only outward, but moral protection for both.[40]

If we just quickly glimpse into the future at the events to unfold, Jewish custom would not have allowed Mary to travel in company with Joseph to Bethlehem in December. The expression of Luke 2:5 "to register with himself Mary who was betrothed to him as wife", must be read in connection with Matthew's expression that Joseph "took to him his wife."[41]

It is also of interest that according to Jewish law no illegitimate child could enter into the assembly of the Lord [Deut. 23:2], much less be brought into the temple and presented to God. Therefore, if there had been the slightest suspicion of the illegitimacy of Jesus, His Mother would not have been able to present Him in the temple on the 2nd of February.[42] Needless to say, if the Christ was illegitimate, the pharisees and scribes would not have missed the chance to heckle Him about His "born out of wedlock" status and jeer His Mother as having played the harlot in Israel. But, of course, we know that this is not true and that His enemies never spoke thus; moreover, His Mother was always held in the highest regard and was respected by all.

JOSEPH CONSIDERS
HOW THE PROPHETS PROPHESIED MARY

From the kontakia of St. Romanos the Melodist, let us listen how *When Joseph saw the maiden whom God had blessed as highly favored, he was struck with fear and amazement, and he thought to himself, "Just what manner of woman is this? For today she does not seem to me as she did yesterday. Both terrible and sweet does she appear to me now. I gaze upon burning heat in snow; paradise in a furnace. I gaze upon a smoking hill* [Ps. 144:5], *upon a divine flower with young freshness, upon an awesome throne, and yet a pitiable footstool of the All-Merciful One. I do not understand the woman whom I took. How, then, shall I say to her, 'Rejoice, O bride unwedded'?"*[43]

So Joseph, who had never known the Virgin, stood in the presence of her glory, astonished. And he looked upon the appearance of her form, and said:

Joseph: "O shining one, I see a flame and glowing brightness around thee [Ez. 1:4]; and so, Mary, I am struck with amazement. Protect me and do not consume

143

me! Thy chaste womb has suddenly become a furnace full of fire. Dost thou wish that I, too, like Moses long ago, take off my sandals and draw near to thee and listen to thee; and learning from thee, I shall say, 'Rejoice, O Bride unwedded!'?"[44]

Theotokos: "Dost thou seek to draw near me and to be taught what I am? Draw near and learn what I am. A certain winged being appeared before me and, when I heard the name of the Lord, then I assumed a little courage. His salutation, when it struck my ears, was sufficient; it made me luminous, it made me pregnant; yet I do not know about the conception of the child. Now see, I am great with child; and, as thou knowest, my virginity is intact, for thou hast not known me. Who would be a witness of this, if not thyself who protects me? Then make a defense of me that thou may find peace of mind."[45]

Joseph: "I am certainly a witness to this. For me it is clear that the light of thy virginity shines."[46]

Saint Epiphanios writes concerning the giving of the holy Virgin to Joseph was "not for marriage, but that she might be guarded. Joseph would be a witness of things to come, so that at the coming of the incarnate economy Jesus would not appear illegitimate. Thus Joseph showed himself to be a witness to the truth."[47]

Saint Romanos then shows Joseph turning over many things in his mind about this wonderful incarnation, including the words of the prophets and forefathers.

Joseph: "No king considers that his pride is at stake whenever, in his desire to overcome the enemy, he enters into the role of a soldier. For this reason, God, seeking to wound the one who had wounded Adam, assumes flesh from a virgin; and thus a snare for the all-evil one comes about when He takes our form.[48]

"Moses writes that the ark long ago contained manna and an urn of gold [Ex. 16:33-34]. Let us see what this means: For nothing that lies in the Scripture is idle or unclear. The urn of gold: the body of Christ. The manna: the divine Word with which it was united. What then is the ark? The Virgin gives birth and, after birth, remains a virgin.[49]

"The rod of Aaron and Jesse [Is. 11:1]: Mary, who blossomed without being cultivated.[50]

"Also the fire in the bush [Ex. 3:2], which was aflame without burning the bramble, even so now is the Lord in the Virgin. God showed Moses the burning bush, so that He might learn of Christ.[51]

"Adam was thrust out; that is why God devised the renewal for Adam and had Him come from thy womb. A woman formerly cast him down, and now a woman raises him up--a virgin from a virgin (Mary is a descendent of Eve).[52]

"Mary bears my Saviour as He wills it, so that every man may proclaim, 'A virgin gives birth and, after birth, still remains a virgin.'"[53]

THE WATER OF CONVICTION

The following story is taken from apocryphal sources. We make mention of it since it has already been the subject of some sermons and depicted iconographically. What is not apocryphal, however, is that Jewish law required that adultery be clearly established, and that the accused woman would be required to prove her innocence by an ordeal referred to as drinking the 'water of conviction' [Num. 5:11-30]. Saint Germanos describes this very incident vividly in his dialogue between Joseph and Mary, which we examined earlier. Saint Germanos has Joseph say to Mary, "The crime of adultery will fall upon us, and the 'water of conviction' will censure us both!"[54]

This water was "the water of conviction that causes the curse". It was pure water mingled with dust from the floor of the tabernacle of witness. When a woman was suspected of illicit carnal relations, she was brought to drink of this water, a sort of "trial," that was ordered by the Lord. If the woman were guilty, her belly would swell and the thigh would rot. It was the 'water of conviction' that would bring the curse into her. However, if she were innocent the water would have no effect. The trial would be carried out before the Sanhedrin and two witnesses of the alleged adulterous act. If the woman were found guilty, the husband was compelled to divorce her and the accused adulteress lost all her rights accruing from the marriage settlement.[55]

We read in the *Protoevangelium* and *Pseudo-Matthew* that Annas the scribe had come to visit Joseph and said,

"Why hast thou not appeared in our assembly?" Joseph answered, "Because I was weary from my journey and work, and rested the first day." Then Annas turned and beheld that Mary was with child. Annas then hastened to report to the priest that Mary was pregnant, saying to him, "Joseph has defiled the virgin whom he received out of the temple of the Lord. He has taken Mary by stealth and has not revealed it to the sons of Israel." Then Abiathar the priest had Joseph seized by the officers of the temple. Mary was also brought along to appear before the high priest and a tribunal. The priest then said to Mary, "Why hast thou done this? Why hast thou brought thy soul low and forgotten the Lord thy God?" Mary then wept bitterly and said, "As the Lord my God liveth, I am pure before Him, and know not a man."[56]

The high priest and the priests began to reproach Joseph, and said:

"Why hast thou beguiled so great and glorious a virgin, who was fed like a dove in the temple by the angels of God. She never wished either to see or to have a man, and she had the most excellent knowledge of God. If thou hadst not done violence to her, she would still have remained in her virginity."

But Joseph vowed, and swore that he had never touched her at all, saying, "As the Lord liveth, I am pure concerning her."[57]

The priest then said, "Bear not false witness. Give up the Virgin whom thou didst receive out of the temple of the Lord." And Joseph then burst into tears.

To this, the priest answered, "I will give you to drink the water of the Lord's testing [see Num. 5:11-31], and it will make manifest your sins in your eyes."

According to the apocryphal account, both Joseph and Mary were given to drink the 'water of ordeal'. Mary then said, "As the Lord Adonai liveth, the Lord of hosts in Whose presence I stand, I have never known a man; but I am known to Him to Whom from my infancy I have devoted my mind. And I made this vow to my God from my infancy, that with Him Who created me I would abide in integrity, where I trust to live to Him alone: and as long as I live I shall abide without defilement." Having said this, she approached the

altar of the Lord with confidence. Both of them partook and both were sent out separately into the hill country. Both of them then returned after the appointed time unharmed. And all the people wondered. The priest then said, "If the Lord God did not make manifest your sin, neither will I judge you." Then Joseph took Mary and went to his house, rejoicing and glorifying the God of Israel.[58]

The above-described incident had already been made use of by iconographers from ancient times. Its appearance might be seen on the throne of Bishop Maximian, found in Ravenna in the Church of St. Apollinarius. Little by little, depiction of the event became widespread. By the tenth century it was found not only in manuscript miniatures, but on the walls of the great churches of Constantinople, such as the Monastery of Chora (Kariye Djami), and at Kalenic.[59] Also, the Church of Tokali Kilisi I of Goreme in Cappadocia, which was established between 818-845, depicts this event.

The icon here depicted is from the outer narthex of the Kariye Djami. In one sequence we see Joseph asleep on his pallet, his outer robe *(himation)* drawn about him and his head resting on his right hand. Hovering in flight, the angel extends his right hand toward Joseph in a gesture of speaking, assuring him to take Mary [Mt. 1:20-21]. The angel holds a scepter in his left hand. The following sequence portrays the Virgin after she partook of the "water of conviction"  and was sent out into the hill country. She is seen in the company of two of her female companions, outside the city walls of Nazareth, at the foot of a hill.[60]

"AND JOSEPH KNEW HER NOT"

"And [Joseph] knew her not till she had brought forth her firstborn son" [Mt. 1:25].

Saint Ephraim is emphatic about her perpetual virginity and abstention from marital relations, poetically describing her thus: *As for Joseph's bride, not even his breath exhaled from her garments, since she conceived Cinnamon* [Cant. 4:14]. *The Theotokos then says, "A wall of fire was Thy conception unto me, O holy Son."*[61]

In discussing the verse "knew her not till", St. John Chrysostom writes that "The Evangelist uses the word 'till,' *(eos)* not that thou shouldest suspect that afterwards Joseph knew Mary, but to inform thee, that before the birth, the Virgin was wholly untouched by man. But why the word 'till'? It is usual in Scripture often to do this. It uses this expression without reference to limited times. Also, in the account of Noah and the ark likewise, it says, 'The raven returned not till the earth dried up' [Gen. 8:7]. Yet, the raven did not return even after that time. Scripture also says about God, 'From age until age Thou art,' [Ps. 89:2] not as fixing limits in this case. Also in the case, 'in His days shall righteousness dawn forth an abundance of peace, till the moon be taken away' [Ps. 71:7], it does not set a limit to this fair part of creation."[62]

Blessed Jerome (347-420), in his treatise *On the Perpetual Virginity of Blessed Mary*, also adds: "And what does it mean when Scripture says, 'For He must reign, till He hath put all enemies under His feet'? [1 Cor. 15:25]. Is the Lord then to reign only for the time till His enemies shall be under His feet? And David, when he says, 'Behold, as the eyes of servants look unto the hands of their masters, as the eyes of the handmaid look unto the hands of her mistress, so do our eyes look unto the Lord our God, until He takes pity on us' [Ps. 122:2], does not mean that David will have his eyes toward the Lord until he obtains mercy and, then having obtained it, he will direct them toward the earth."[63] Blessed Jerome also comments that when the Saviour speaks to His Apostles, saying, "Lo, I am with you always, even until the end of the world" [Mt. 28:20], it certainly does not mean that after the end of the world, He will step away from His disciples![64]

St. John Chrysostom continues: "In such a manner having become a mother, and having been counted worthy of a new sort of travail and a childbearing so strange, could that righteous man ever have endured to know her and kept her in the place of a wife?"[65]

Saint Basil believed in Mary's perpetual virginity and claimed that "until" could be used indefinitely. "Lovers of Christ cannot hear that the Theotokos ever ceased to be a virgin."[66]

"HER FIRSTBORN SON"

What is the meaning of "her firstborn"? Saint Cyril of Alexandria comments: "The verse 'her firstborn' does not mean the first among several brethren, but One Who was both her first and only Son. For sometimes also the Scripture calls that the first which is the only one: as 'I am the First, and I am hereafter: beside Me there is no God'" [Is. 44:6].[67]

The firstborn son is the name applied to Jesus. He was the first and the only child born to Mary. In the Old Testament, God commanded "sanctify to Me every firstborn" [Ex. 13:2; Num. 3:13], with no view whatsoever as to whether there would be other children after the first or not.

Saint Cyril of Alexandria continues to say, "For though He is the Only-begotten as regards His divinity, yet as having become our Brother, He has also the name of the

Firstborn; that being made the first-fruits as it were of the adoption of men, He might make us also the sons of God. Consider, therefore, that He is called the Firstborn in respect to the divine economy or dispensation of God referring to His incarnation; for with respect to His divinity He is the Only-begotten. Again, He is the Only-begotten in respect of His being the Word of the Father, having no brethren by nature...; but He becomes the Firstborn by descending to the level of created things. When the divine Scriptures address Him as Firstborn, they immediately also add of whom He is the firstborn. They assign the cause of Him bearing this title, such as 'Firstborn among many brethren' [Rom. 8:29] to the fact that He was made like unto us in all things except sin. His title 'Firstborn among the dead' [Col. 1:18] is to mean that He first raised up His own flesh unto incorruption. Moreover, He has ever been the Only-Begotten by nature, as being the Only-Begotten of the Father, God of God, having shone forth as God of God and Light of Light."[68]

Saint Irenaeus (+c.193), Bishop of Lyons, favored this title "firstborn of the Virgin". This is because it would appear to imply an extension of her motherhood to us spiritually, by our regeneration in the faith (through the Church) as linked with that of the Son of God born of the Virgin.[69]

"BEFORE THEY CAME TOGETHER"

From Mt. 1:18, "**Now the birth of Jesus was on this wise: when as His Mother Mary was espoused to Joseph, before they came together, she was found with child of the Holy Spirit**", the verse "before they came together" (*prin ee syneltheen*) simply asserts that the conception was not preceded by a cohabitation. Not wishing to give to much importance to the niceties of usage in Hellenistic Greek, it is a well-know distinction in Attic Greek that *prin* with the infinitive is employed where the action is *not* to have taken place, while it is used with the indicative of a *past fact*; thus St. Matthew would have written *prin syneelthon*.[70]

Saint Ambrose comments in a letter to the Illyrican bishops, which was approved by his own bishops, the following: "The Lord Jesus would not have chosen to be born of a virgin if He judged that she would become promiscuous, that ordinary sexual intercourse would permeate the origin of the Lord's body, the palace of the eternal King."[71]

Saint Ambrose, commenting on the just character of Joseph, says that Joseph considered the purpose of the marriage was the preservation of Mary's good name, "for the Lord preferred that some should doubt His own origin, rather than the chastity of His Mother"[72]--that is, should take Him for Joseph's son. Saint Ambrose also upheld the view of St. Ignatios of Antioch (+c.110) that satan was then kept in ignorance of the virginal conception.[73]

Saint Germanos, Patriarch of Constantinople, also gives his opinion that she was betrothed "in order to mock that ancient and original serpent,· so that being betrothed that serpent would not attack the immaculate daughter, but would pass her by...."[74]

Chapter IX.
The Nativity,
According to the Flesh,
of Our Lord, God and Saviour
JESUS CHRIST,

**the Memory of which the Holy Church
Celebrates on the
25th of December**

+ + +

In the kontakion of the Nativity Feast, composed by St. Romanos the Melodist (c.490-c.556), through the blessing and aid of the Virgin herself,[1] the Church chants, *Today the Virgin giveth birth to Him Who is transcendent in essence; and the earth offereth a cave to Him Who is unapproachable. Angels with shepherds give glory; with a star, the magi do journey; for our sakes a young child is born, Who is pre-eternal God.*[2]

What mysteries beyond mind and speech! God, in His compassion, is born on earth, putting on the form of a servant that He may snatch from servitude to the enemy them that with fervent love cry out: "Blessed art Thou, O Saviour Who lovest mankind."[3]

THE PREACHING OF THE PROPHETS
HAS REACHED ITS FULFILLMENT

Saint Andrew of Crete (c.660-740) comments, "Of thee, O Mary, all interpreters of the Spirit sang." Nowhere in the

152

divinely inspired Scripture can one look without seeing some allusion to her. "Rejoice, Mediatress of the law and of grace, seal of the Old and New Testaments, clear fulfillment of the whole of prophecy, of the truth of Scriptures inspired by God, the living and most pure book of God and the Word in which, without voice or writing, the Writer Himself, God and Word, is everyday read."[4]

Saint Gregory Palamas (+1359) thought that "all divinely inspired Scripture was written because of the Virgin who brought forth God incarnate."[5]

EARLY PROPHECIES

Saint John of Damascus (c.676-c.750) interprets the burning bush [Ex. 3:1-8] as an image of the virgin birth when he chants, *Plainly foreshadowed by the burning bush that was not consumed* [Ex. 3:2], *a hallowed womb has borne the Word. God is mingled with the form of mortal men, and so looses the unhappy womb of Eve from the bitter curse of old* [Gen. 3:16].[6] And, *That which was revealed to Moses in the bush, we see accomplished here in strange manner. The Virgin bore Fire within her, yet was not consumed, when she gave birth to the Benefactor Who brings us light.*[7]

Saint Andrew of Crete also chants elsewhere that *As Thou art one of the Trinity, Thou wast seen to become flesh, not changing Thine essence, O Lord. Neither didst Thou burn the incorrupt womb of her that bore Thee, since Thou art wholly God and fire.*[8]

The burning bush was traditionally interpreted as a type of the Virgin. Saint Gregory of Nyssa (c.335-394) is insistent on the *virginitas in partu*. From the image of the burning bush seen by Moses in Sinai, "we also learn the mystery of

153

the Virgin: the light of divinity, which through birth shone from her into human life, did not wither the flower of her virginity, just as the burning bush was not consumed."[9]

Saint Ildephonsus (607-667), Archbishop of Toledo, wrote that "The Holy Spirit heated, inflamed, and melted Mary with love, as fire does iron; so that the flame of the Holy Spirit was seen and nothing was felt by the fire of the love of God."[10]

Saint Joseph the Hymnographer (c.816-886), borrowing from the book of *Numbers* chants, *Now is Christ born of Jacob,* so Balaam said [Num. 24:19]. *And He shall rule over nations, and His Kingdom shall be exalted in grace and shall remain perpetually.*[11]

That Thou mightest fill all things with Thy glory, Thou hast come and bowed the heavens [Ps. 17:9] *till they touched the earth. For as rain upon the fleece* [Judg. 6:36-38], *hast Thou descended into a virgin womb, from which Thou now camest forth to be born in two natures, O God-Man.*[12]

The poet and brother of St. John of Damascus, St. Cosmas, Bishop of Maiouma, writes: *As dew upon the fleece hast Thou descended into the womb of the Virgin, O Christ, and as drops of rain that fall upon the earth. Ethiopia and Tarshish and the isles of Arabia, the kings of Saba, of the Medes and all the earth, fell down before Thee, O Saviour."*[13]

Saint Romanos in the matinal service writes: *Bethlehem has opened Eden: come, let us behold. We have found joy in this hidden place: come, and let us take possession of the paradise that is within the cave. There the unwatered Root has appeared and flowers forth forgiveness: there is found the undug Well, when David of old yearned to drink* [2 Kings 23:15]. *There the Virgin has borne a babe, and quenched the thirst of Adam and David to cease straightway. Therefore, let us hasten to this place where now a young child is born, the pre-eternal God.*[14]

THE PROPHECY OF ISAIAS

Isaias, as he watched by night, beheld the light that knows no evening, the light of Thy Theophany, O Christ, that came to pass from tender love for us; and he cries aloud: "Behold, a Virgin shall conceive in the womb" [Is. 7:14], *and shall bear the incarnate Word, and all those on earth shall rejoice exceedingly.*[15]

Saint Cosmas the Poet also chants of this virgin: *Lo, the Virgin, as it was said in days of old* [Is. 7:14], *has conceived in her womb and brought forth God made man; and she has remained a virgin. Reconciled to God through her, let us sinners sing her praises, for she is verily the Theotokos.*[16]

Saint Basil the Great (c.330-379) defended the application of Isaias 7:14 to Mary.

He argued that if it did not apply to a "virgin", there really would be no sign. He was aware that in the translation, some proposed to read the Greek word *neanis* instead of *parthenos* for the Hebrew *almah* or *galmah*, but he appealed to Deut. 22:23-28 to justify his interpretation--which was that of all the Fathers.[17] This same Hebrew word *almah* or, in Greek, *parthenos*, translated as "virgin", may also be seen in Gen. 24:23, when referring to Rebecca.

Saint Cyril of Jerusalem (318-c.386) also adds that though the Jews gainsay this by claiming the text says "the damsel" and not "the virgin", he finds truth and writes: "To learn more clearly that even a virgin is called a damsel in the Holy Scripture, hear the Book of *Kings*, saying of Abisag the Somanitess: 'And the damsel (in Greek *ee neanis*, in Hebrew *nah-garah*) was extremely beautiful' [3 Kings 1:4]; that she was chosen as a virgin and brought to David is admitted...." And, "If Scripture says, 'the betrothed damsel

155

cried, and there was none to help her' [Deut. 22:27], does it not speak of a virgin?"[18]

The word *almah* is used nine times in the Old Testament and never for a married woman. The massive patristic witness remains impressive that the verse in Isaias refers to a virgin and not a young woman. Saint Justin Martyr (+165) reminded his Jewish opponent in his *Dialogue with Trypho* that the *Septuagint* used virgin *(parthenos)*. What value as a sign would an ordinary birth have provided?[19] Since the plan of salvation, which God assured [Gen 3:16], comprised a woman in an important role, they who believe the prophet is speaking of a virgin also see an echo of the Virgin in "the seed of her" [Gen. 3:15]. This inference cannot be lightly dismissed.

MARY AS PROPHETESS

Another prophecy of Isaias is: "And I went in to the prophetess and she conceived, and bore a son. And the Lord said to me, Call His name, 'Spoil quickly, plunder speedily.' For before the child shall know his father or his mother, He shall take the power of Damascus and the spoils of Samaria before the king of the Assyrians" [8:3-4].

The Persian sage, monk and bishop, Aphraates (4th c.) speaks of Mary as a "prophetess."[20] Saint Basil, too, considers Mary a "prophetess", because of the Magnificat [Lk. 1:46-55] that she had uttered.[21]

Saint Cyril of Alexandria says that "contemporaneously with the birth of Christ, the power of the devil was spoiled. The name 'Spoil quickly, hastily plunder' or *'Maher-shalal-hash-baz'*, refers to our Lord. The prophetess is the holy Virgin; and the name given to the child suiteth not man, but God; for, saith He, call His name 'Spoil quickly: hastily plunder'. For at His birth, the heavenly and supernatural infant, while yet in swaddling bands and on His Mother's bosom, because of His human nature, stripped forthwith satan of his goods by His ineffable might as God; for the magi came from the East to worship Him...."[22]

Saint Justin Martyr (135-c.165] writes that Isaias' words, "'He shall take the power of Damascus and the spoils of Samaria' meant that the power of the wicked demon that dwelt in Damascus would be crushed by Christ at His birth. This is shown to have taken place. For the magi, held in servitude (as spoils) for the commission of every wicked deed through the power of that demon, by coming and worshipping Christ, openly revolted against the power that had held them captive; and this dominion Scripture [1 Kings 11:23-25; 15:16-22; 22:31-35; 2 Kings 13:3] has shown us to reside in Damascus. Moreover, that sinful and unjust power is termed well in parable, 'Samaria'. Now, even among you none can deny that Damascus was and is a part of the land of Arabia, although it now belongs to Syro-Phoenicia.[23]

Saint Cosmas expounds upon this in his matinal hymn: *Thou hast shone forth from the tribe of Judah, and Thou hast come to plunder the strength of Damascus and the spoils of Samaria* [Is. 8:4], *turning their error into faith beautiful to God.*[24]

Saint Cosmas also incorporates other prophecies of Isaias into his inspired hymns. *As Thou art the God of peace and Father of mercies, Thou hast sent unto us Thine Angel of great counsel* [Is. 9:6], *granting us peace. So are we guided towards the light of the knowledge of God, and watching by night we glorify Thee, O Lover of mankind.*[25]

ROD OF THE ROOT OF JESSE

Here again, St. Cosmas composes hymns by weaving in Old Testament prophecies, showing the Virgin as the rod and the overshadowed mountain: *Rod of the root of Jesse* [Is. 11:1], *and flower that blossomed from his stem, O Christ, Thou hast sprung from the Virgin. From the mountain over-shadowed by the forest Thou hast come* [Hab. 3:3], *made flesh from her that knew not wedlock, O God, Who art not formed from matter.*[26]

Saint Andrew also speaks of the Virgin as the rod and Christ as the Flower: *Let Jesse rejoice and let David dance, for behold, the Virgin, the rod planted by God, hath blossomed forth the Flower, even the everlasting Christ.*[27]

Saint Ambrose (339-397), Bishop of Milan, concurs with this image, writing: "The root is the household of the Jews, the rod is Mary, the Flower of Mary is Christ. She is rightly called a rod, for she is of royal lineage, of the house

and family of David. Her Flower is Christ, Who destroyed
the stench of worldly pollution and poured out the fragrance
of eternal life. As He Himself said, 'I am a flower of the
plain, a lily of the valleys'" [Song 2:1].[28]

Saint Irenaeus (d. after 193) also speaks of Isaias'
prophecy concerning the rod and Flower from the root of
Jesse. "Thereby the prophet says that it is of her, who is
descended from David and from Abraham, that He is born.
For Jesse was a descendant of Abraham, and father of David;
the descendant who conceived
Christ, the Virgin, is thus become
the 'rod'. Moses too worked his
miracles before Pharaoh with a
rod; and among others too of
mankind, the rod is a sign of
empire. And the 'Flower' refers
to His body, for it was made to
bud forth by the Spirit."[29]

From the Akathist Hymn to
the Theotokos, we chant, *Rejoice,
O mystical rod which blossomed
the unfading Flower.*[30] And,
*Rejoice, O Bride of God; thou art
the mystical rod from whom the
unfading Rose blossomed and
budded forth.*[31]

THE LATER PROPHETS

Let us also listen to the hymns as they recount the
later prophecies: "And the Lord said to me (Prophet
Ezekiel), 'This gate shall be shut, it shall not be opened, and

no one shall pass through it; for the Lord God of Israel shall enter by it, and it shall be shut. For the Prince, He shall sit in it, to eat bread before the Lord; He shall go in by the way of the porch of the gate, and shall go forth by the way of the same'" [Ez. 44:2-3].

Saint Amphilochios of Iconium (+after 394) gives his opinion saying, "In what concerns the virginal nature, the virginal doors are in no way opened; as regards the power of the Lord Who was born, nothing is closed to the Lord, but all things are open to Him."[32]

Of old Habakkum the Prophet was counted worthy to behold ineffably the figure and symbol of Christ's birth, and he foretold in song the renewal of mankind. For as a young babe, even the Word, has now come forth from the mountain that is the Virgin [Dan. 2:45], *unto the renewal of the peoples.*[33]

When the prophet [Hab. 3:1, 3] *foresaw Thy birth from a Virgin, he proclaimed, crying, "I have heard Thy report and was afraid"...for from Theman and the holy mountain overshadowed art Thou come, O Christ.*[34]

Saint John of Damascus speaks of Shedrach, Misach and Abdenago, the three children in the Babylonian furnace [Dan. 3], saying, *The children of the Old Covenant who walked in the fire, yet were not burnt, prefigured the womb of the Maiden that remained sealed, when she gave birth in fashion past nature. It was the same grace of God that brought both these wonders to pass in a miracle.*[35]

Saint Cosmas the Poet also speaks of this image, chanting, *The furnace moist with dew was the image and figure of a wonder past nature. For it burnt not the children whom it had consumed, even as the fire of the Godhead consumed not the Virgin's womb into which it had descended.*[36]

Saint Cosmas then speaks of the Prophet Jonas [1:17–2:10], saying, *The sea monster spat forth Jonas as it had received him, like a babe from the womb: while the Word, having dwelt in the Virgin and taken flesh, came forth from her and kept her incorrupt. For being Himself not subject to decay, He preserved His Mother free from harm.*[37]

The person of Jonas and his ordeal within the belly of the sea monster also is a type of Christ in the belly of the earth for three days. *Jonah was compassed but not held fast in the belly of the whale; for serving as a figure of Thy birth and Thine appearing in the flesh, he came forth from the sea-mammal as from a chamber. For, born now in the flesh, Thou shalt in the flesh undergo burial and death, and Thou shalt rise again on the third day.*[38]

With all these prophecies in mind, St. Romanos exhorts the Hebrew nation, saying, *Come, O hard-hearted Israel, cast from thee the mist that lies upon thy soul; recognize the Creator Who is born in the cave. He is the expectation of the nations* [Gen. 49:10]; *He shall abolish thy feasts.*[39]

The prophecy of Baruch clearly declares that God would come unto His own in the world and dwell with them [Jn.

1:10-11,14], "This is our God, and there shall none other be accounted of in comparison of Him. He hath found out all the way of knowledge, and hath given it unto Jacob His servant, and to Israel His beloved. Afterward did He shew Himself upon earth, and conversed with men" [Bar. 3:35-37].

CREATION IS RENEWED AND
LED TO ITS FORMER BEAUTY

Saint Cyril of Alexandria (+444) writes that "she bore Emmanuel, Who is truly God. 'And the Word was made flesh' [Jn. 1:14] and was born according to the flesh so that we might be found to be brothers of Him Who is above all creation."[40] He also writes in another letter that He Who was ineffably begotten of the Father before all ages and finally born as man from a woman, that He is one person and not two.[41]

Orthodox theology of the incarnation is clear in the Church's hymnology. Saint Joseph the Hymnographer chants, *The Son of the Father...has appeared to us...to give light to those in darkness and to gather the dispersed. Therefore, the far-famed Theotokos do we magnify.*[42] This hymnographer also writes that Mary Theotokos ushered in our renewal, saying, *Like a lily, like a fragrant rose, like a divine scent did the All-Divine Word find thee, O all-pure Bride of God; and He made His abode within thy womb, making fragrant our nature which had been full of foetor through sin.*[43] Thus, *in the fullness of time, He raised up man who of old had grievously fallen, leading him up to his pristine beauty.*[44]

Saint Germanos writes: *The express image of the Father* [Heb. 1:3], *the imprint of His eternity, takes the form of a servant and, without undergoing change, He comes forth from a mother who knew not wedlock. For what He was, He has remained, true God: and what He was not, He has taken upon Himself, becoming man through love for mankind.*[45]

Saint John of Damascus chants of our renewal, though Christ did not depart from His own nature yet He shared in our substance. *A most glorious mystery is accomplished today: nature is renewed, and God becomes Man. What He was, He has remained; and what He was not, He has taken on Himself without suffering commingling or division.*[46]

The Only-Begotten of the Father, even after His nativity in the flesh, has remained one in Godhead with the

Father and the Spirit. From the Canon of the Forefeast, we chant, *In the strength of Thy Godhead Thou hast been joined with mortal men, through a union without confusion, O Saviour, in the likeness of the flesh of Adam; and in thus assuming human nature Thou dost bestow upon it immortality and salvation.*[47]

Saint Romanos rejoices, chanting, *The Creator is come, raising up mankind from the earth, making His royal image new again! Rejoice together, ye hosts on high and chant! The middle-wall of enmity is broken down! He is come Who accomplished this! For God becometh man, the King of Israel!*[48]

For St. Joseph the Hymnographer, the role of Mary is clear when he chants, *Through thy incorrupt birth-giving, O august one, thou hast clothed with the garment of incorruption all those denuded through corruption.*[49] He then says that she is the heavenly ladder by which God the Word communicated with men; she is the wound inflicted on demons, the salvation of men, and the ornament of angels.

THE APPELLATION 'THEOTOKOS' OR 'GOD-BIRTHGIVER'

Christ, Who was born of the Virgin, is true God become Man. There are not two sons: a Son of God and a son of the Virgin. He is one Son: from above, motherless out of the Father; from below, fatherless out of a mother. It is proper to call the Virgin Mother 'Theotokos', on the ground that she truly gave birth in the flesh to God.[50]

Saint John of Damascus says, "We hold that God was born of her, not implying that the divinity of the Word received from her the beginning of its being, but meaning that God the Word Himself, Who was begotten of the Father timelessly before the ages, and was with the Father and the Spirit without beginning and through eternity, took up His abode in these last days for the sake of our salvation in the Virgin's womb, and was without change made flesh and born of her. For the holy Virgin did not bear mere man but true God: and not only God but God incarnate, Who did not bring down a body from heaven, nor simply passed through the Virgin as a channel, but received from her flesh of like essence to our own and subsisting in Himself. For if a body had come down from heaven and had not partaken of our nature, what would have been the use of His becoming man?

162

For the purpose of God the Word becoming man was that the very same nature, which had sinned and fallen and become corrupted, should triumph over the deceiving tyrant and so be freed from corruption. Hence, it is with justice and truth that we call the holy Mary the 'Mother of God'. For this name, 'Theotokos', embraces the whole mystery of the dispensation."[51]

Saint John continues, saying, "We never say that the holy Virgin is the Mother of Christ *(Christotokos)*, because this appellation came about in order to do away with the title Mother of God *(Theotokos)*, and to bring dishonor on the Mother of God, who alone is in truth worthy of honor above all creation. It was the impure and abominable Judaizing Nestorius,  that vessel of dishonor, who invented this name for an insult. For David the king and Aaron the high priest are also called 'christ' or 'anointed one', for it is customary to make kings and priests by anointing. Moreover, every God-inspired man may be called 'christ', though he is not by nature God. Yea, the accursed Nestorius insulted Him Who was born of the Virgin by calling Him (Jesus) God-bearer *(Theophoros)*, Who is in truth God incarnate. God the Word deified the nature that He assumed. He was not first made like us and only later became higher than us, but even from the first moment of incarnation, He existed with the double nature, because He is God the Word Himself...."[52]

Saint Andrew of Crete, in his hymns, also declares that she brought forth God in the flesh: *O Mother of God, past speech is thy conceiving and beyond nature is thy childbearing. Thou hast conceived from the Spirit, not from human seed; and thy childbearing has escaped nature's laws, since it was without corruption and above the nature of all birthgiving. For He Whom thou hast born is God.*[53] And, *Thou alone art revealed as the heavenly bridal chamber and ever-virgin bride. Thou hast carried in thy womb and given birth to Him; and He took flesh from thee yet underwent no change. Therefore, as bride and Mother of God, with true veneration all generations magnify thee.*[54]

Two generations before the Council of Ephesus, St. Gregory the Theologian (329-391), Patriarch of Constantinople, was using the term 'Theotokos'. He is very strong when he succinctly states, "If anyone does not consider holy Mary to be the Theotokos, then he does not accept the divinity of Christ."[55] In another epistle he writes: "If anyone does not believe the holy Mary to be Theotokos, he is without the Godhead. If anyone should say that Christ passed through the Virgin as through a channel, and was not formed in her at once in a divine and human way, divine because it was without the work of man, human becomes it was subject to the law of human gestation, he is equally atheistic."[56]

He continues: "For the whole Adam fell by the fatal taste. Accordingly, in a human manner and beyond the human manner, in the venerable womb of the Virgin, He was shown as God and Man, uniting the two natures in one, one hidden, the other manifest to men."[57]

Saint Ambrose also writes: "You should know that Christ is not two, but One, being both begotten of the Father before the worlds, and in the last times [Gal. 4:4] created of the Virgin. And thus the meaning is: 'I, Who am begotten before the worlds, am He Who was created of mortal woman, created for a set purpose.'"[58] He also correctly writes that Jesus was "without a mother according to divinity, because He was begotten of God the Father, of one essence with the Father, but without a father according to the incarnation, because He was born of the Virgin, having neither beginning nor end, for He Himself is the beginning and the end of all things, the first and the last."[59]

AUGUSTUS TAXES ALL THE ROMAN EMPIRE

"And it came to pass in those days, that there went out a decree from Caesar Augustus, that all the world should be taxed. And this taxing was first made when Cyrenius was governor of Syria. And all went to be taxed, every one into his own city [Lk. 2:1-3].

"And Joseph also went up from Galilee, out of the city of Nazareth, into Judea, unto the city of David, which is called Bethlehem, (because he was of the house and lineage of David), to be taxed with Mary his espoused wife, being great with child" [Lk. 2:4-5].

The expression of Luke 2:5, "to register with himself Mary who was betrothed to him as wife", must be read in connection with Matthew's expression that Joseph "took to him his wife" [Mt. 1:24], since Jewish custom would not have otherwise allowed Mary to travel in company with Joseph to Bethlehem.

There are reliable historical records that indicate that a census was taken every fourteen years, and that one was taken about the time of 7-6 B.C.[60] This census, to be taken throughout the Roman Empire, included Egypt, Syria and Palestine. As regards the Roman province of Syria, Cyrenius, the governor, was the well-known Roman senator Publius Sulpicius Quirinius.[61]

Before the era of Christ, years were generally reckoned from the foundation of the city of Rome or from the election of the emperor (*Anno Urbis Conditae*, A.U.C. or Roman Era). With the establishment of Christianity, recording of time was reckoned from the birth of Christ (*Anno Domini*, A.D.). However, an error in the calculation of Dionysios the Younger who, in 526 A.D. introduced the present method of dating, made the birth of Christ to coincide with the Roman year 754. However, further studies since have ascertained that Christ was actually born in 747 or 748 according to the Roman era, that is six or seven years earlier than Dionysios has supposed! From this, results the curious fact that the Christian calendar which we now use, instead of dating from the actual Nativity of our Saviour, actually commenced some six or seven years later. Hence, the birth of Jesus is reckoned to be 6 or 7 B.C., concurrent with the time of the Roman taxation.[62] Furthermore, according to all historical accounts, Herod the Great, the slayer of the children of Bethlehem, died in 4 B.C. In the upcoming chapters, we shall see Christ and His Mother with the venerable Joseph fleeing Herod and his minions. Thus it is evident that the Christ child could not have been born after 4 B.C.

There is a mystical significance that the world was being enrolled in a secular census and the coming of our Lord, because He then appeared in the flesh Who would enroll His elect for eternity.

Saint Ephraim the Syrian comments, *In the days of the king who enrolled men in the book of the dead, our Redeemer came down and enrolled men in the book of the living. He enrolled, and they also: on high He enrolled us, on earth they enrolled Him. Glory to His name!*[63]

The ninth century hymnographer and nun, St. Cassiane, wrote the famous Nativity hymn: *When Augustus reigned alone upon the earth, the many kingdoms of men came to end: and when Thou wast made man of the pure Virgin, the many gods of idolatry were destroyed. The cities of the world passed under one rule; and the nations came to believe in one sovereign Godhead. The peoples were enrolled by the decree of Caesar; and we, the faithful, were enrolled in the name of the Godhead, when Thou, our God, wast made man.*[64]

Saint Germanos writes that *For this cause Caesar published such a decree, since Thy timeless and eternal Kingdom was presently made manifest. Therefore, as we pay our earthly tribute money, at the same time we offer Thee the wealth of our Orthodox Faith, O God and Saviour of our souls.*[65]

THE GENEALOGIES OF THE GOSPELS

The Gospels of Matthew and Luke give the genealogies of Joseph: Matthew, in the opening passage of the Gospel, and Luke, after the story of the baptism. The two lists differ, and various explanations have been given for the discrepancies. Writing in Aramaic to the Jewish community, Matthew's list descends from Abraham, "father of believers," at the origin of the Old Covenant, to Jesus, Author of the New Covenant. The Jews desired to see a glorious king in the person of the Messiah, therefore, St. Matthew cites David the king into His genealogy. King David fathered Solomon, and then a whole line of royal descendants. The Evangelist also introduces women, something that the

Evangelist Luke does not do. And what sort of women? Women who could neither be saved by descent from Abraham (Rahab of Jericho and Ruth the Moabitess), nor by true integrity of character and righteousness (Tamar the daughter-in-law of Judah and Bathsheba the wife of Uriah). According to Jewish tradition, the holy Evangelist did not lose sight either that all the rights and privileges of a family passed on to the oldest of each generation. In Matthew's listing from Abraham and David, it was precisely the elder line that he had to choose everywhere (with the exception of Solomon). David's family line wends its way through Solomon the king and reaches Zorobabel, in whom both lines, Solomon's and Nathan's join together, either through adoption or in accordance with the law of Levirate marriages [Deut. 25:5-6]. Further, David's family runs along the line of Abiud (the elder) and reaches Joseph, the putative father of Jesus. Despite the fact that Joseph was not Jesus' natural father, but only his legal one, he could still pass on rights of inheritance and all the privileges of his family to his "adopted Son". For a Jew, it was the legal relationship of a son to his father that was important, not the natural one.[66] The sense of the word "begat" which is used in Hebrew genealogies was not exact: it indicated immediate or remote descent, and adoptive relationship, or legal heirship, as well as procreation. The Evangelist Matthew's Gospel was intended for the Jews living in Judea and Galilee. He also follows at once with the story of the virgin birth, the work of the Spirit, sign of a wholly new world.

On the other hand, writing in Greek, the glorious Evangelist Luke's longer list ascends to Adam, reflecting the "universalism" which is the feature of his Gospel. The sacred author was writing for both Jews and Greek pagans. Nevertheless, both genealogies contain the name of David, essential to Christ's place among His people. While St. Matthew traces the genealogy of Christ through the kings, and makes Christ appear as a king, St. Luke puts the regal dignity of Christ in second place. Luke lists the descendants of Nathan [2 Sam. 5:14; 1 Chron. 14:4] and not of Solomon the king.[67]

While Joseph is called the husband (*ton andra*) of Mary [Mt. 2:19], he is not represented as the father of Jesus. The word "begat" (*egeneese*) is not used in his case with relation to Jesus. Joseph is only the legal father.

We note that Matthew records that "Jacob begat Joseph" [Mt. 1:16], but Luke records, "Joseph, which was the son of Heli" [Lk. 3:23]. Different solutions have been proposed to explain Joseph's "double fatherhood." One theory appeals to the "levirate marriage" prescribed in Deuteronomy [25:5-7]. If brothers live together and one of them dies without seed, the surviving brother should marry the widow, lest she marry out of the family. The issue of that union shall be named to the deceased brother, that his name not be blotted out of Israel. If this were so in Joseph's case, he would have only one paternal grandfather. He is given Matthan by the Evangelist Matthew and Matthat by the Evangelist Luke, with a different ancestral line to David in each case. The Evangelists were making allowances for the different spelling of names in transliteration from Hebrew or Greek.

To solve this difficulty, Julianus Africanus (c.160-240), known as the "Father of Christian Chronology", suggests a solution that should be considered. "Matthan, Solomon's descendant, begot Jacob. On Matthan's death, Melchi,[68] Nathan's descendent, begot Heli by Matthan's widow Estha. Thus Heli and Jacob had the same mother Estha. Now when Heli died childless, Jacob took Heli's widow and "raised up" offspring to him, begetting Joseph. Therefore, Joseph was by nature Jacob's son, by law Heli's. Thus, Joseph was the son of both."[69]

Scholars and pagan critics have wrestled with the problems of the two genealogies for centuries. Many explanations have been more ingenious than convincing, involving complicated and uncertain inferences. One relatively simple solution was that the genealogy listed by Luke was the physical descent of Jesus through Mary. This view, however, is generally unaccepted. Moreover, it was not customary that female lineage was given, though there are exceptions to be found in the Old Testament [see Num. 26:33; 1 Chr. 2:16-17; Judg. 8:1].

Saint John of Damascus not only asserts that Mary too was of the house and lineage of David, but recites the same solution as that propounded by Julius Africanus.[70] "She who was predestined before the ages in the plan of God's foreknowledge, foreshadowed and foretold by the Holy Spirit in diverse images and words of the prophets, was in the fullness of time, born of the race of David, as had been promised to him."[71]

Also, St. John Chrysostom (354-407) affirms that "the Virgin was of the race of David....[but] it was not the law among the Jews that the genealogy of women should be traced...for if he (St. Matthew) had done this with respect to the Virgin, he would have seemed to be introducing novelties."[72]

Saint John of Damascus also points this out, commenting, "it was neither the custom of the Hebrews, nor of the Scriptures, to note the genealogy of women. It was also the law that betrothals were not to take place between individuals of different tribes."[73] The latter is most especially true in the case of Mary, who was the only surviving child of her father's house which could not be transferred to another tribe.

Saint Justin Martyr states that Mary traces her family descent from David and Jacob and Isaac and Abraham. And he adds, "it is clear that the fathers of girls are also considered the fathers of the children born to their daughters."[74]

Saint Irenaeus also affirmed that the Virgin Mary was of the seed of David and of Abraham. "Besides," he says, "if indeed He had been the son of Joseph, He could not, according to Jeremias the prophet, be either king or heir. For Joseph is shown to be descended from Jehoiakim and Jechonias (also known as Conias or Jehoiachin), as Matthew sets forth in his pedigree [Mt. 1:11-12]. This is because Jechonias, and all his posterity, were disinherited from the kingdom. Jeremias thus declares, 'As I live, saith the Lord, though Jechonias son of Jehoiakim king of Judah were indeed the seal upon my right hand, thence would I pluck thee; and I will deliver thee into the hands of them that seek thy life, before whom thou art afraid...I will cast thee forth, and thy mother that bore thee, into a land where thou wast not born; and there ye shall die. But they shall by no means return to he land which they long for in their souls. Jechonias is dishonored as a good-for-nothing vessel; for he is thrown out and cast forth into a land which he knew not'" [Jer. 22:21-28, LXX].

The prophet then continues speaking, 'Land, land, hear he word of the Lord. Write ye this man an outcast: for there shall be none of his seed at all grow up to sit on the throne of David, or as a prince yet in Juda' [Jer. 22:29, LXX]. And again, God speaks of Jehoiakim, Jechonias' father (whom Matthew [1:11] has omitted, listing the grandfather Josias and then Jechonias the grandson), saying, 'Therefore, thus saith the Lord of Jehoiakim king of Judah: He shall have none to sit upon the throne of David; and his dead body shall be cast out...I will punish him and his seed and his servants for their iniquity'" [Jer. 36:30-31, KJV].[75]

What were the sins of Jekoiakim told by Jeremias the prophet? He had "built his house by unrighteousness and his chambers by wrong;...and used his neighbor's service without wages..." [Jer. 22:13, KJV].

Saint Irenaeus then writes that "Those, therefore, who say that Jesus was begotten of Joseph, and that they have hope in Him, do cause themselves to be disinherited from the kingdom, falling under the curse and rebuke directed against Jechonias and his seed. Thus, learn that not from Joseph's seed is He to be born, but that according to the promise of God, from David's belly, the King eternal is raised up...."[76]

THE JOURNEY TO BETHLEHEM

Christ comes to be born of a maiden who knew not wedlock. Saint Ephraim chants of the humble Maiden and city of His birth. *Blessed art thou, Bethlehem, that the towns envy thee--and the fortified cities! As they envy thee, so the women and the virginal daughters of princes envy Mary. Blessed be the Maiden in whom He deigned to abide, and the city wherein He deigned to sojourn. A poor maiden and a small city is where He chose to humble Himself.*[77]

The apocryphal account of the *Protoevangelium* recounts this episode of Joseph preparing to depart Nazareth for Bethlehem: Joseph thought to himself, "I shall enroll my sons, but what shall I do with this maiden? How shall I enroll her? As my wife? I am ashamed. As my daughter then? But all the sons of Israel know that she is not my daughter. When the time of the Lord's appointment shall come, let Him do as seems good to Him." Joseph then saddled the ass, and put Mary upon it. And his son led it, while Joseph and his other sons, followed after her.[78]

Travel was slow, for both men and animals trod. The length of the day's march depended upon the urgency of the trip. Average travel time for people would be about fifteen miles a day. Donkey caravans tried to make twenty miles a day.

In the icon at the Monastery in Chora, Joseph is depicted with a slight stoop and the mincing gait characteristic of elderly men. His gaze is towards Mary, who turns her head towards him. One of Joseph's sons is seen with a billowing mantle and a bundle of provisions for the journey slung from the end of a staff across his shoulder.[79]

Within three miles of Bethlehem, they rested at a well. One apocryphal account relates that Joseph turned around and saw that Mary was sorrowful. He thought within himself, "Perhaps she is in pain on account of what is in her." But he turned about again and this time he saw her joyful, and remarked, "Mary, how is it that at times I see thee sad of countenance and sometimes I see thee joyful and bright?" Mary replied, "I see two people before me: one is sad and mourning, the other one is glad and rejoicing." That is, one rejoicing in the birth of the Messiah, the other refusing to accept Him.[80]

In a hymn from the Ninth Hour on the eve of the Nativity, we may also hear the Virgin speaking with Joseph, who is still overwhelmed with awe at the mystery. *O Virgin, when Joseph went up to Bethlehem wounded by sorrow, thou didst cry to him: "Why art thou downcast and troubled, seeing me great with child? Why art thou wholly ignorant of the fearful mystery that comes to pass in me? Henceforth, cast every fear aside and understand this strange marvel: for in my womb God now descends upon earth for mercy's sake, and He has taken flesh. Thou shalt see Him according to His good pleasure, when He is born; and filled with joy thou shalt worship Him as Thy Creator, Whom the angels praise without ceasing in song and glorify with the Father and the Holy Spirit."*[81]

171

Saint Justin Martyr writes that God made identical promises to Isaac and Jacob that in their seed all the tribes of the earth shall be blessed [Gen. 26:4; 28:14]. In St. Justin's *Dialogue with Trypho* he tells Trypho that "[God] does not address this blessing to Esau, nor to Reuben, nor to any other, but only to them from whom Christ was to come through the Virgin Mary, in accordance with the divine plan of our redemption. If thou would think over the blessing of Judah, thou would see what I mean. For the seed is divided after Jacob, and comes down through Judah and Phares and Jesse and David.  Now, this was a sign, that some of the Jews would certainly be children of Abraham, and at the same time would share in the lot of Christ; but that others, also children of Abraham, would be like the sand on the beach, which, though vast and extensive, is barren and fruitless, not bearing any fruit at all, but only drinking up the water of the sea. Of this is a great part of the people guilty, drinking in bitter and godless doctrines, while spurning the word of God."[82]

OUR GOD SHALL BE BORN
IN A FASHION PAST WORDS

Bringing with them the few necessaries of a poor Eastern household, the holy travelers neared their journey's end on that short winter's day. Jesus the Messiah was to be born in surroundings of outward poverty. But so far from detracting, they seem most congruous to the divine character. Earthly splendor would here seem like tawdry tinsel, and the utmost simplicity like that clothing of the lilies, which far surpassed all the glory of Solomon's court. Now the way had been long and weary--at least three days' journey. The season of the year also increased the difficulties of the journey. Finally, they reached the rich fields that surrounded the ancient "House of Bread" that is, Bethlehem.

Today a maiden great with child comes to Bethlehem to give birth to the Lord: and choirs of angels go before her. Seeing these things, Joseph, her betrothed, cried out: "What

172

is this strange mystery in thee, O Virgin? And how shalt thou bring forth child, O calf upon whom the yoke has never come?" [Num. 19:2].[83]

THE ENROLLMENT FOR TAXATION

In the iconographic scene of the enrollment in Bethlehem, at the famous Church of Kariye Djami in Constantinople, we see Cyrenius, the governor of Syria, with a fully armed military guard. A scribe is also shown, holding an unfurled scroll, on which he records the names. Mary's tall frame, standing erect in a graceful pose, stands out strikingly before them while being interrogated with her head bowed towards the officers, drawing her *maphorion* modestly about her shoulder. Also, we see Joseph, with his four sons behind him, leaning forward to assist her.[84]

THE CAVE

The little town of Bethlehem was crowded with those who had come from all the outlying district to register their names. Even if the strangers from far-off Galilee had been personally acquainted with any one in Bethlehem who could have offered them hospitality, they would have found every house fully occupied. The inn too was filled.[85] The *Protoevangelium* then relates that when coming to the middle of the road, Mary said to Joseph, "Take me down from off the ass, for that which is in me presses to come forth." But Joseph replied, "Whither shall I take thee, there is no room in the inn and this place is desert?" Then Mary asked Joseph again to take her down. And he took her down. He found a shepherd's cave and led her into it. Then, leaving his sons beside her, he went out to seek a midwife in the district of Bethlehem. This took place at sunset.[86]

In the icons we see the Virgin-Mother reclining on a type of bedroll of a kind such as the Jews were wont to carry when journeying away from home.

THERE IS NO PLACE FOR THY HANDMAIDEN
SAVE THE CAVE THAT BELONGS TO ANOTHER[87]

We learn from the one of the main hymns of this feast the identities of them that ministered at the nativity from times past up to the hour of the virgin birth. *Let us hymn David, the forefather of God, and divine Joseph, the betrothed of the Theotokos, with James, the glorious brother of God, for, with the angels, the magi and the shepherds, they ministered in godly manner at the divine nativity in the city of Bethlehem.*[88]

Listen to the marvelous things that we learn from the Dismissal hymn of the Forefeast: *Mary once, with aged Joseph, went to be taxed in Bethlehem, for they were of the lineage of David; and she bore in her womb the Fruit that had not been sown. The time of the birth was at hand and there was no room in the inn; but the cave proved a fair palace for the Queen. Christ is born, that He may raise again the image that before was fallen.*[89]

Saint Joseph the Hymnographer marvels at how the great God will enter a small cave as a small child. *How shall a small cave receive Thee, for Whom the world cannot find room, O Thou Whom none can comprehend! O Thou, Who with the Father art without beginning, how shalt Thou appear as a small child?*[90] And, *The great King comes in haste to enter a small cave, that He may make me great who had grown small. And, so that by His poverty without measure, He, the transcendent God, may enrich me who had grown poor* [2 Cor. 8:9].[91]

174

Saint Justin Martyr, born in Sichem (Nablus) spoke of the "cave" near Bethlehem. He provides us with one of the earliest testimonies on the subject. "When Joseph could find no lodging place in the village, he went to a cave nearby, and there Mary gave birth to the child and laid Him in a manger."[92]

In icons, the dark background in the cave can be explained by a homily attributed to St. Gregory of Nyssa, where he compares the birth of Christ in a cave and the spiritual light shining forth in the shadow of death that encompasses mankind. Thus, the black mouth of the cave symbolically means the world, stricken with sin through man's fault, in which the "Sun of righteousness" shone forth.[93] The place where Mary brought forth virginally and painlessly was an empty and uninhabited place. It could be compared to the wilderness, as depicted in the Nativity icon. The world did not accept Him, but the wilderness offered refuge. This, too, is a fulfillment of the Old Testament prefiguration when the Hebrew nation departed Egypt for the wilderness of Sinai. It was there, in Bethlehem, the "House of Bread", that the symbol of the Eucharist was given-- manna. Now He Who rained manna upon His people Israel would Himself become the bread of the Eucharist. The wilderness will also offer the manger where He chose to lie, thereby symbolizing the Lamb upon the altar. The cave, the manger, the swaddling clothes are indications of the emptying or *kenosis* of the Godhead, His utter abasement and humility. Also we see foreshadowed here His future death, burial, sepulchre and burial clothes.[94]

In some icons, we see the Virgin-Mother half-sitting or we may see her looking away from her child, as though pondering His miraculous appearance.[95] Her gesture and attitude also bespeak her perplexity at the virgin birth, yet she kept these things in her heart. Later depictions, of western origin, show her kneeling over her Son; thus also indicating a painless delivery and the unneeded service of a midwife to effect delivery.[96]

JOSEPH SEEKS A HEBREW MIDWIFE

The *Protoevangelium* speaks of Joseph lacking perfect knowledge with regard to the virginal birth-giving of Mary. However, his actions confirm the reality of the God-Man's appearing in the flesh and not as some phantom.

After leaving his sons, the holy old man, Joseph, went into the district of Bethlehem to seek a midwife. Then suddenly a woman was coming down from the hill-country when she said to Joseph, "O man, whither art thou going? He replied, "I seek a Hebrew midwife." And she gestured that she was, and then said, "Art thou an Israelite?" Joseph replied, "Yes." The midwife, named Zelomi, then continued, "Who is it that is to bring forth in the cave?" Joseph answered, "A woman betrothed to me." She remarked, "She is not thy wife?" And Joseph said, "It is Mary who had been reared in the temple of the Lord. By lot, I had obtained her as my wife, yet, she is not my wife, but has conceived of the Holy Spirit." The midwife then said, "Is this true?" And Joseph answered, "Come and see." Zelomi then went away with him and they stood in the place of the cave and, behold, a luminous cloud overshadowed the cave. Zelomi remarked, "My soul has been magnified this day, because my eyes have seen strange things, because salvation has been brought forth to Israel.[97]

WHERE GOD WILLS,
THE ORDER OF NATURE IS OVERRULED

"And so it was, that, while they were there, the days were accomplished that she should be delivered [Lk. 2:6].

Concerning His birth, the Prophet Isaias spoke thus, "Before she that travailed brought forth, before the travail-pain came on, she escaped it and brought forth a male" [Is. 66:7]. Saint John of Damascus adds to this saying that "After the normal nine-month gestational period, Christ was born at the beginning of the tenth, in accordance with the law of gestation. It was a birth that surpassed the established order of birthgiving, as it was without pain; for, where pleasure had not preceded, pain did not follow. And just as at His conception He had kept her who conceived Him virgin, so also at His birth did He maintain her virginity intact, because He alone passed through her and kept her shut.

"While the conception was by 'hearing', the birth was by the usual orifice through which children are born, even though there are some who concoct an idle tale of His being born from the side of the Mother of God. For it was not impossible for Him to pass through the gate without breaking its seals. Hence, the Ever-Virgin remained virgin even after giving birth and never had converse with a husband as long as she lived."[98]

Saint Ambrose in his *Synodal Letter 44* writes: "Why is it hard to believe that Mary gave birth in a way contrary to the law of natural birth and remained a virgin, when contrary to the law of nature the sea looked at Him and fled, and the waters of the Jordan returned to their source [Ps. 113:3]. Is it past belief that a virgin gave birth when we read that a rock issued water [Ex. 17:6], and the waves of the sea were made solid as a wall [Ex. 14:22]? Is it past belief that a Man came from a virgin when a rock bubbled forth a flowing stream [Ex. 20:11], iron floated on water [4 Kings 6:6], a Man walked upon the waters [Mt. 14:26]? If the waters bore a Man, could not a virgin give birth to a man? What Man? Him of Whom we read, '...the Lord shall be known to the Egyptians, and the Egyptians shall know the Lord in that day; and they shall offer sacrifices, and shall vow vows to the Lord, and pay them.' [Is. 19:20].

"In the Old Testament a Hebrew virgin (Miriam) led an army through the sea [Ex. 15:21]; in the New Testament a king's daughter (the Virgin Mary) was chosen to be the heavenly entrance to salvation."[99]

Then, the deep was trodden dry-shod by Israel, now, Christ is born seedlessly of the Virgin. The sea, after the passage of Israel, remained untrodden: the blameless one, after the birth of Emmanuel, remained undefiled.[100]

Saint Ambrose also writes in another letter that "A virgin carried Him Whom this world cannot contain or support. And when He was born of Mary's womb, He yet preserved the enclosure of her modesty, and the inviolate seal of her virginity."[101]

Where God so wills the order of nature is overcome. Is anything too hard for Him Who called heaven, earth and the sea into being by His word alone? Nature and the elements are creations of the Creator. Their laws and properties are immediately subject to their Lord Fashioner. Adam and Eve were given dominion over the fish of the sea, the flying creatures of heaven, and over the reptiles and cattle and all the earth [Gen. 1:26]; all were subject to them before the fall. Saint Gregory Palamas comments that when the Logos of God took on human nature, He bestowed on it the fullness of grace and delivered it from the bonds of corruption and death. The consequence of the hypostatic union in Christ of the two natures was the deification of the human nature He assumed.[102] The regeneration of man in Christ was the restoration of Adam and Eve.

The saints, having put on Christ, have often resumed the authority and dominion that our first parents had. Thus, the Prophet Habakkum instantly traversed vast expanses of land, with no effort, and brought food to Daniel in the lion's den. The holy Apostles, too, were transported on clouds to be at the Theotokos' repose in Jerusalem, and their bodily weight proved not to hamper their flight, in defiance to gravity. Our Saviour and the saints performed those things outside the created laws of physics and medicine. By a

178

word, straightway, long and terminal illnesses vanished, limbs that were palsied became sound, those without orbs received the power of vision, and many were raised from the dead. Some of the saints could go long periods without food, water or changes of clothing as St. Paisios the Great of Egypt or St. Mary Golinduc the Persian. Others, by their mere grace-filled presence, tamed wild and ferocious animals. Thus, why should it be difficult to imagine that the Christ infant could not pass through that virginal orifice through which children are delivered without incurring damage or the slightest discomfort to His Mother, despite his newborn height and weight? Later, in life, He would pass through the midst of the mob unscathed as though bodiless and, after His Resurrection, His body would pass through solid and shut doors to meet and greet His anxious disciples [Jn. 20:19].

Concerning the mystery of the incarnation, St. Gregory of Nyssa wrote the following: "When God became known to us in the flesh, He neither received the passions of human nature, nor did the Virgin Mary suffer pain, nor was the Holy Spirit diminished in any way, nor was the power of the Most High set aside in any manner, and all this was because all was accomplished by the Holy Spirit. Thus the power of the Most High was not abased, and the child was born with no damage whatsoever to the mother's virginity."[103]

Saint Hesychios (c.451), a learned priest-monk of Jerusalem, expressed the same truth, writing that "The Theotokos was a woman, yet she did not suffer the pangs of child-birth because the field of marriage had not expe-rienced the plow; the vir-ginal vineyard was not tilled."[104]

OUR LORD HAS SHONE FORTH AS THE DAWN

Who has ever beheld a child whom no father begat, reared on his mother's milk? Or where has a virgin mother ever been seen? Truly, O pure Mother of God, in a manner past understanding thou hast fulfilled both these marvels.[105]

Saint Ephraim the Syrian speaks of how the motherhood of Mary was contrary to nature; that is, "nature" as we know it after the expulsion from Eden. *With Thou, O Lord, Mary underwent all that married women undergo: conception--but without intercourse; her breasts filled with milk--but against nature's pattern. Thou didst make her, the thirsty earth* [Is. 53:2], *all of a sudden into a fountain of milk!*[106]

Saint Ephraim then remarks how God, even as a tender babe, was still enthroned above, governing all things. *If she could carry Thee, it was because Thou, the great Mountain, had lightened Thy weight; if she feeds Thee, it is because Thou had taken on hunger* [Mt. 4:2]; *if she gives Thee her breast, it is because Thou, of Thine own will, had thirsted* [Jn. 4:7]; *if she caresses Thee, it is because Thou, Who art the fiery coal* [Is. 6:7] *of mercy, preserved her bosom unharmed."*[107] And, *Who ever saw a child who beholdeth every place? His look is like one that orders all creatures that are above and that are below! His visage is like that Commander that commandeth all."*[108]

Saint John of Damascus also speaks of her motherhood as unique. *How dost thou give milk, O pure Virgin? This the tongue of mortal man cannot make plain. For thou showest forth a thing unknown to nature, and which utterly surpasses the usual laws of birth.*[109]

Saint Ephraim then has the Virgin-Mother speak to Jesus as she too ponders her excellent motherhood. *How shall I open the fountain of milk to Thee, O Fountain? Or how shall I give nourishment to Thee that nourisheth all from Thy Table? How shall I bring to swaddling clothes One wrapped round with rays of glory?*[110]

Saint Joseph the Hymnographer also treats this subject dramatically in his hymns, putting these words on Mary's lips: *O my sweetest child, how shall I feed Thee Who givest food to all? How shall I hold Thee Who holdest all things in Thy power? How shall I wrap Thee in swaddling clothes, who dost wrap the whole earth in clouds?*[111] We, too, marvel when we hear the Theotokos say, *How shall I look upon Thee without fear, on Whom the Cherubim with many eyes dare not lift their gaze?*[112] *"I hold in my arms as a child Thee Who dost uphold all, and I am filled with amazement,"* said she who had not known wedlock.[113]

We, too, in the following hymn may catch a glimpse of Mary's profound wonder. *Rejoicing at once and weeping, she raised her voice and said: "Shall I give my breast to Thee,*

Who givest nourishment to all the world, or shall I sing Thee praise as my Son and my God? What manner of name shall I find to call Thee, O Lord, Whom none can name?"[114]

Saint Ephraim then writes of Mary speaking thus: *How shall I call Thee a stranger to us, Who art from us? Should I call Thee Son? Should I call Thee Brother? Husband should I call Thee? O Child, I shall call Thee Lord!*[115]

"And she brought forth her firstborn son, and wrapped Him in swaddling clothes, and laid Him in a manger; because there was no room for them in the inn" [Lk. 2:7].

Beyond the pronouncement of this bare fact that the Virgin-Mother "brought forth her firstborn Son...," Holy Scripture, with indescribable appropriateness and delicacy, draws a veil over that most sacred mystery. The pious reader is left with the impression of the Master's utmost humility.

GOD MADE MAN

He Who is equal in honor with the Father and the Spirit, out of compassion, has clothed Himself in our substance...[116]*and He Who before the morning star was begotten without mother of the Father, is today without father made flesh upon earth of thee.*[117]

He was true God and true Man, or, more specifically, the Person and nature of God the Son united with the nature of man from His Mother, a daughter of Adam and Eve. As St. Paul confirms His manhood, saying, "when the fullness of the time was come, God sent forth His Son, made of a woman, made under the law" [Gal. 4:4].

Saint Athanasios (296-373) comments, "Therefore what came forth from Mary, according to the divine Scriptures, was human and the Lord's body was real; real I say, since it was the same as ours. For Mary is our sister, in that we are all sprung from Adam."[118]

The two natures would be united without confusion or loss of identity as God or man. The humanity of Jesus was the same as our own and, according to His Divinity, He was of One Essence with the Father and the Holy Spirit.

Saint Cyril of Alexandria writes that "an ordinary man was not born of the holy Virgin and then the Word descended into Him. United with flesh in her womb, the Word is said to have endured birth according to the flesh, so as to claim as His own the birth of His own flesh....For our sake and for our salvation, He united a human nature to Himself hypostatically and was born from a woman; in this manner, He is said to have been born according to the flesh....We do not hesitate to call the holy Virgin the Mother of God. The holy Fathers do not say that the nature of the Word or His divinity took the beginning of being from the holy Virgin, but that His holy body, animated by a rational soul, was born of her....Thus, the Word's being made flesh is nothing else than that He partook of flesh and blood in like manner with us, and made our body His own, and proceeded man of a woman, without having cast away His divinity....This is what the expression of the exact Faith everywhere preaches; this is the mind we shall find in the holy Fathers."[119]

Saint Cyril goes on to say that "...the flesh was neither turned into the nature of Divinity, nor, indeed, that the ineffable nature of the Word of God was altered into the nature of the flesh, for He is immutable and absolutely unchangeable, always being the same, according to the Scriptures. But when He was visible, and still remained an infant in swaddling clothes, and in the bosom of the Virgin who bore Him, He filled the whole of creation as God, and was Co-Ruler with the One Who begot Him. For the divine is both without quantity and without magnitude, and does not admit of limitation." And in the same letter, he points out that Christ "was born in order that He might bless the very beginning of our existence and, in order that, the curse against the whole race might be stopped. This was sending our bodies from the earth to death, and by abolishing it, He abolished the saying, 'in pain thou shalt bring forth children'" [Gen. 3:17].[120]

Patriarch Germanos of Constantinople (c.635-733) chants, *No more shall women bear children in sorrow: for joy has put forth its flower, and the Life of men has come to dwell in the world.*[121]

Saint Joseph the Hymnographer writes: *Eve hath been delivered from pain, O all-immaculate one; for thou gavest birth without pain unto Christ our God Who hath manifestly healed the sufferings and pain of all.*[122]

Before the coming of Christ, women would bear children in sorrow with the knowledge that their offspring would be subject to sin, death and Hades. Although the physical discomfort of pregnancy and labor still exist to the present day, the hymnographers speak of deliverance from the grief of death and sin to the offspring of those mothers who would be regenerated in Christ through baptism.

Saint Ephraim then speaks of what Mary gained by carrying in her womb the Christ child. *"The Son of the Most High came and dwelt in me, and I became His Mother; and as by a second birth I brought Him forth, so did He bring me forth by the second birth,"* because He put His Mother's garments on, she clothed her body with His glory.*[123]

In the classic passage of St. John of Damascus, he writes: "Hence it is with justice and truth that we call the holy Mary the Mother of God. For this name embraces the whole mystery of the dispensation....Moreover, we proclaim the holy Virgin to be in strict truth the Mother of God. For inasmuch as He Who was born of her was true God, she who bore the true God incarnate is the true Mother of God."[124]

Saint Cyril of Jerusalem also comments that "He did not pass through the Virgin as through a channel, but was truly made flesh from her, and truly nourished with her milk."[125]

In his sermon on the Feast of the Nativity, St. Leo the Great (+461) writes: "The bodily nativity therefore of the Son of God took nothing from and added nothing to His majesty because His unchangeable substance could neither be diminished nor increased. For that 'the Word became flesh' does not signify that the nature of God was changed into flesh, but that the Word took the flesh into the unity of His Person: and therein undoubtedly the whole man was received, with which within the Virgin's womb was made fruitful by the Holy Spirit, whose virginity was destined never to be lost. Thus, the Son of God...Who was born without time of the Father's essence was Himself in time born of the Virgin's womb. We could not otherwise be released from the chains of eternal death but by Him becoming humble in our nature. Thus, our Lord Jesus Christ, being at birth true Man, though He never ceased to be true God, made in Himself the beginning of a new creation, and in the 'form' of His birth started the spiritual life of mankind afresh."[126]

THE NEW ADAM

The false theory that our ancestors' transgression was the author of an "original sin", by which the human race became guilty of their disobedience, is not what the Orthodox Church teaches. The Church teaches that the human race inherited death, becoming enslaved to the devil through the passions. Concurrently, nature, which was subject to our first parents' rule, was now also subject to the same curse: "the bondage of corruption" [Rom. 8:21]. We are not guilty of our first parents' sin, nor are we being punished for it. We sin on account of our mortality. On account of our inheriting death, the "infection", all men "have sinned, and come short of the glory of God" [Rom. 3:23].

Saint Leo the Great wrote that sin could have no origin where the transmission of paternal seed had not reached."[127] And, "Christ was generated in a new nativity, because inviolate virginity, that did not know concupiscence, furnished the material of His body."[128]

Saint Gregory Palamas, concurring with the Church Fathers, taught that mortality was transmitted by natural generation [Ps. 50:5] and led our first parents' progeny to commit sin. In Rom. 5:12, we read: "Wherefore as by one man sin entered into the world, and death through sin; and so death passed upon all men, since all have sinned." The consequence of our first parents' sin is death, a death which became the heritage of all their children. However, the guilt of the actual sin of Adam and Eve is not transmitted by natural generation.

Saint Gregory Palamas, having learned from Greek patristics, thought the concept of "original sin" was above all a hereditary mortality, leading humans to commit sins, but not implying any guilt for the actual sin of Adam and Eve. This mortality was transmitted by natural generation [Ps. 50:5]. That was the essential reason why Christ alone had no human father: "He alone was not conceived in iniquity nor engendered in sin....For the urge of the flesh...brings the original condemnation; it is corruption and, as such, must engender corruption."[129] Elsewhere speaking of Christ, he writes: "If He had come from sperm, He could not have become a new man; belonging to the old race and heir to the error of Adam, He could not have received within Himself the plenitude of the divinity."[130]

The manifold graces which God lavished upon the Virgin Mary, before and after her child-bearing, do not alter the fact that death, which came from Adam, could not be vanquished except in the deified body put on by the hypostasis of the Son of God; therefore, Christ our Saviour alone will be blessed by an immaculate conception in the womb of our Virgin Mary.[131] How else could Jesus have died, save by a violent death? He had no need to suffer a natural death; such death is a result of the fall. Saint Gregory Palamas amplified this by bringing forward the example of St. John the Baptist, the greatest among the children of women. "He had no need to suffer a natural death...he who performed the commandments and who obeyed God in his mother's womb, was not subject thereto; the saints must always give their life for virtue and religion according to our Lord's command, and for that reason a violent death for the sake of the Good suits them best; that is also why the Lord Himself tasted death in this fashion. It was necessary that the death of John should be the forerunner of the death of Christ...."[132]

FRUIT OF THE WOMB

Saint Irenaeus writes that "God promised David that He would raise up from the fruit of his belly (feminine in Hebrew, *behten*, and in Greek, *keelea*), or more correctly 'womb', an eternal King [Ps. 131:11]. He is the same Who was born of the Virgin who was of the lineage of David. On this account also, He promised David that the King would be 'of the fruit of his *belly*,' which was the appropriate term to use with respect to a virgin conceiving. He did not say 'of the fruit of his loins,' nor 'of the fruit of his reins' which is an expression to a generating man and/or a woman conceiving by a man. In this promise, however, Scripture has excluded all virile influence....This promise had fixed and established 'the fruit of the *belly*,' that it might declare the generation of Him Who should be born of the Virgin.

"Elisabeth also testifies to this when, filled with the Holy Spirit, she said to Mary, 'Blessed art thou among women, and blessed is the fruit of thy belly' [Lk. 1:42]. Those who are willing to hear, the Holy Spirit points out that the promise which God had made of raising up a King from the fruit of David's belly, was fulfilled in the birth from the Virgin, that is, from Mary."[133] Although the psalmist does not openly say that the fruit itself is proper to a virgin birth, but only that the choice of his words points to it; the phrase itself being proper to birth of a woman.[134]

The icon shown here from St. Clement, Ochrid, Yugoslavia, is entitled "The Vision of Solomon of the Virgin," and is based on the scriptural verse from *The Song* 3:7-8. In icons depicting the prophets prophesying of the Mother of God, Solomon is shown holding a scroll, saying, 'I foretold thee as a royal couch, O young Virgin, proclaiming thy miracle.'"[135]

King Solomon was aware of what the Lord had sworn to his father David that "of the fruit of thy belly will I set a king upon thy throne" [Ps. 131:11]. And, "When thou (David) shall sleep with thy fathers,...I will raise up thy seed after thee, which shall be of thy belly (*ek tees keeleas su*), and I will establish His kingdom..." [1 Chron. 17:11]. In another place, the Prophet Nathan spoke to David, saying, "I will establish Him in My house and in His Kingdom forever; and His throne shall be set up forever" [1 Chr. 17:14]. We know from many hymns that the Virgin, of the seed of David, is spoken of as the "throne of the Lord". *Rejoice, O throne of the great King, known to Solomon;*[136] *Behold, the divine couch of Solomon,*[137] and *Rejoice, fiery throne of the Lord God.*[138] *Glorious are thy mysteries, O pure Lady, thou wast made the throne of the Most High.*[139] "Then Solomon sat on the throne of the Lord as king instead of David his father" [1 Chron. 29:23 KJV]. This is the only time in Scripture that the term, "throne of the Lord (in Hebrew, *Y'hoh-vah*)" is used, and Solomon understood that the "throne of the Lord" is the Virgin-Mother, of the everlasting King Whose Kingdom would be set up forever. What was spoken of was not Solomon's kingdom, for his kingdom certainly did not last forever and, in fact, for his serious breach of loyalty, God rebuked him, saying that in his son's day the kingdom would be torn apart [3 Kings 11:9-13].

Blessed Jerome asks, "Do you wish to know what sort of a throne our true Solomon, the Prince of Peace, has, and what His attendants are like?" They who are about Solomon have their sword on their thigh and cut short their pleasures, those who have mortified their bodies, the pure virgins. Then the Bridegroom will say to His Bride, "Thou art all fair, my love, and there is no spot in thee." Who is this Bride? She is the Virgin, She is the Church. Thus the Apostle writes that He might present the Church to Himself, glorious, not having spot or wrinkle, or any such thing [Eph. 5:27].[140]

Saint Ambrose, commenting on this verse, writes that for "holy virgins, there is a special guardianship for them who, with unspotted chastity, keep the couch of the Lord holy. No wonder if the angels fight for you who war with the mode of life of angels. Virginal chastity merits their guardianship whose life it attains to. Hence, she is a virgin who is the bride of God."[141]

THY MOTHER IS A CAUSE FOR WONDER

Saint Ephraim the Syrian declares, *Thy Mother is a cause for wonder: the Lord entered into her and became a servant; He Who is the Word entered and became silent within her; thunder entered her and made no sound; there entered the Shepherd of all and, in her, He became the Lamb, bleating as He comes forth.*[142] And, *The Mighty One entered, and put on insecurity from her womb; the Provisioner of all entered and experienced hunger; He Who gives drink to all entered and experienced thirst. Naked and stripped there came forth from her He Who clothes all! Praise to Thee to Whom all things are easy for Thou art Almighty.*[143] In a homily, further marveling at the Lord's condescension, this same saint writes: "He Who measures the heavens with the span of His hand [Is. 40:12] lies in a manger a span's breadth; He whose cupped hands contain the sea [Is. 40:12] is born in a cave; His glory fills the heavens [Is. 6:3] and the manger is filled with splendor."[144]

Saint Ephraim the Syrian continues saying, *The titles of Mary are many and it is right that I should use them: she is the palace* [Prov. 9:1] *where dwells the mighty King of kings. Not as He entered her did He leave her, for from her He put on a body and came forth. Again, she is the new heaven* [Is. 65:17], *in which there dwells the King of kings. He shone out in her and came forth into creation; formed and clothed in her features.*[145]

Saint John of Damascus, who received healing of his severed hand by the Theotokos herself,[146] describes her: *Thou hast been adorned, O thou who art beautiful among women, who hast given birth unto Christ Who is more comely in beauty than all the sons of men."*[147] And St. Joseph the Hymnographer characterizes her, as *having given birth unto the All-Holy God, thou wast shown to be more holy than the Cherubim.*[148]

Saint Leo the Great suggests that Mary is the link between us and Christ in His mystical body, saying, "The generation of Christ is the origin of the Christian people, and the birthday of the Head is also the birthday of the body."[149]

Tradition has it that our Lord and Saviour was born on the first day of the week; for it was on this day that God said, "Let there be light" [Gen. 1:3].

THE MIDWIVES ENTER

Returning to the story in the *Protoevangelium*, the cloud then disappeared and a great light shone in the cave, so that the eyes could not bear it. Little by little, the light gradually decreased. They then beheld the infant at the breast of the Virgin. The old woman then asked the Virgin Mary, "Art thou the mother of this child?" When the Virgin gave her assent, Zelomi said, "Thou art not at all like the daughters of Eve." The Virgin then said, "As my Son has no equal among children, so His Mother has no equal among women."

Saint Ephraim, in his *Hymns on the Nativity*, puts these words on Mary's lips: *Of a sudden the handmaid became the King's daughter in Thee, Thou Son of the King. Lo, the meanest in the house of David, by reason of Thee, Thou Son of David, lo, a daughter of earth hath attained unto heaven by the Heavenly One!*[150] Also, in the same homily, he has Mary speak of herself, saying, *The day that Gabriel came in unto my low estate, he, in an instant, made me free instead of a handmaid: for I was the handmaid of Thy Divine Nature, yet am I also the Mother of Thy human nature, O Lord and Son!*[151]

The midwife then went forth out of the cave and met Salome, another midwife, to whom Zelomi exclaimed, "Salome, I have a strange sight to relate to thee: a virgin hath brought forth, a thing which nature does not admit!"[152]

The aged Salome was a kinswoman of Mary. Salome was Mary's mother's sister's daughter; hence she was Mary's first cousin. When she beheld the most holy Virgin in the shepherd's cave, she did not believe that a virgin brought forth, to which she remarked, "As the Lord my God liveth, unless I receive proof of this matter, I will not believe that a virgin hath brought forth." When Salome stretched forth her hand to the most holy Virgin's body to examine it, after the manner of a midwife, Salome then believed. However, her hand was withered and she groaned bitterly, for she was punished for her impudence and unbelief.

In like manner was Uzzah fatally smitten when he violated the sacred character of the Ark, for he reached out his hand and took hold of it [2 Sam. 6:6-7]. Greatly lamenting, Salome made a supplication unto the Lord, until an angel stood by her and instructed her to reach forth her hand to the child and to carry Him. Straightway, her hand was restored and Salome was filled with joy. And, behold, she heard a voice, saying, "Salome, Salome, tell not the strange things thou hast seen, until the child comes into Jerusalem."[153]

Blessed Jerome writes that on the precise moment of birth, "No midwife assisted at His birth; no women's officiousness intervened. With her (Mary's) own hands she wrapped Him in the swaddling clothes--herself both mother and midwife."[154]

Bearing Emmanuel on thine arm as a babe, O pure and divinely joyous one, thou didst cry out, "O my sweetest child, how can I nourish Thee at my breast Who dost sustain all things? How can I wrap in swaddling clothes Thee Who wrappest the sea in midst?"[155]

Saint Ephraim then speaks of the grace given to the Virgin-Mother: *The bosom of Mary amazes me, that it sufficed for Thee, Lord, and embraced Thee. All creation was too small to conceal Thy Majesty. Heaven and earth too narrow to cover Thy Godhead. Too small for Thee was the bosom of the earth; great enough for Thee was the bosom of Mary.*[156] And, *Who else lulled a Son in her bosom as Mary did?...In fear and love it is meet for Thy Mother to stand before Thee!*[157] Then, the hymnographer puts these words on Mary's lips: *As the Son of Man should I sing unto Thee a common lullaby? For Thy conception is new and Thy birth marvelous. Without the Spirit who shall sing to Thee?*[158]

PERPETUAL VIRGINITY

The virginal conception is affirmed by sacred Scripture --*virginitas ante partum.* At the moment of childbirth she did not lose the physical signs of virginity, *virginitas in partu*, and *virginitas post partum*, meaning she remained a virgin after birth perpetually is supported by the Fathers from the beginning of Christianity.

In a few brief passages on the Virgin Mary, St. Clement of Alexandria (before +215), expressed ideas not then as yet prominent among the Fathers. He speaks of the virginity *in partu* thus, "For certain people say that Mary, examined by the midwife after she had given birth, was found to be virgin."[159]

The title Ever-Virgin *(a-ee-parthenos)* was first used by St. Peter of Alexandria (311), and which St. Athanasios continued to use and was one of the first to argue the perpetual virginity of Mary.[160]

190

Saint John of Damascus also speaks of her perpetual virginity, saying, *The Lord deigned to enter into her, preserving her virginity inviolate after childbirth.*[161]

Saint Ambrose wrote: "Mary had kept the seals of her virginity."[162]   Saint Leo the Great (440-461) wrote: "Mary brought Him forth, with her virginity untouched, as with her virginity untouched she had conceived Him."[163]   He also writes: "The Prophet Ezekiel [44:2] says that he saw the building of a city upon a very high mountain. The city had many gates; of these one is described as shut. What is this gate but Mary? It is shut because she is a virgin. Mary, then, is the gate through which Christ came into the world, born virginally, without loosing the bars of virginity. The enclosure of her purity remained unbreached...and the seals of her integrity kept inviolate, as He went forth from the Virgin....A good gate is Mary, that was closed and was not opened; by her Christ passed, but He opened it not."[164]

Saint Hesychios of Jerusalem insists on the *virginitas in partu*, writing: "Christ did not open but left closed the door of the Virgin; He did not violate nature's seal, did not harm the one giving birth; for her, in reality, He left the sign of virginity."[165]

THE MANGER A THRONE

O Creator, Thou makest new those born on earth by Thyself becoming clay. A manger and swaddling clothes and a cave are the marks of Thy lowliness. The betrothed of Thy Mother, Joseph, is thought by men to be Thy father according to the flesh.[166]

Saint Gregory of Nyssa writes that "The child is wrapped in swaddling clothes and laid in a manger; and the Mother is an incorrupt Virgin after childbirth, and embraces her Son."[167]   The saint then accentuates the note of joy in his writing about the Theotokos. As Eve introduced death through sin and gave birth in sorrow and pain, "it was fitting that the Mother of Life should begin her pregnancy with joy and complete her giving birth in joy."[168]

BATHING OF THE HOLY CHILD

Apart from assisting a mother--though quite unnecessary in the present case--the midwife's duties included washing the baby, rubbing it with salt, water and oil, and then wrapping it in swaddling bands [Ez. 16:4]. The procedure of applying salt was not only used as a disinfectant but, the

191

Jews, at that time, believed that salt rubbed over the skin would harden it.[169] Also they believed that the soft bones would grow straight and firm if they were bound tightly.

The infant would be wrapped in these bands for seven days, then the process was continued, until the child was forty days old. The bandages were 4- to 5- inches wide and 5- to 6- yards long.[170] This was typical postnatal care during the time of Christ.

Byzantine iconographers have often presented the scene of the bathing of the Christ child by two women. Apocryphal accounts identify them as the midwives Zelomi and Salome, the latter being Mary's cousin from Bethlehem. They are shown in the act of bathing Christ with rolled up sleeves. This scene is not taken from the canonical Gospels but from the *Apocrypha*, namely from the *Protoevangelium* and the *Apocrypha of Matthew*. A sixth century Byzantine hymn mentions that the midwife took up the child with joy.[171] These references led iconographers to portray this scene of the bathing. It may be found in both Byzantine monuments as well as in western art.[172]

All complete icons of the Nativity include the bathing scene, as was in the case of the great fresco monuments of the Holy Mountain. This included Theophanes' work at the Great Lavra (1535); and Zorzis' work in the main church (*katholikon*) of the Monastery of Dionysiou (1547); the Protaton, the main church of the Monastery of Stavronikita, and the main churches of the Monasteries of St. Paul, Dochiariou and Chilandari. Unfortunately, due to a misunderstanding of the scene, the monks have erased this graphic incident from many of the frescoes and replaced it with trees or rocks. In fact, these erasures took place at the end of the eighteenth and beginning of the nineteenth centuries.[173]

As we indicated, the incident was received into early Christian art from the *Apocrypha*, as were many other icons were also based on apocryphal writings: St. Joachim praying on the mountain and St. Anna in the garden, the "Entrance of the Virgin into the Temple", the Virgin receiving bread

192

from the Archangel Gabriel, Joseph receiving the Virgin from the temple and several other events. From a dogmatic point of view, there is nothing out of order in the bathing scene. The fact that the Mother of God gave birth painlessly and required no assistance of a midwife, and that our Lord was entirely pure and undefiled, do not constitute reasons for not admitting the scene.[174] As we mentioned earlier, His being bathed and then wrapped in swaddling bands was normal postnatal care in biblical times. The midwives were doing what they habitually performed on numerous newborn infants. Thus, His kinswoman, Salome, proceeded spontaneously to do what she believed had been the accepted standard of care.

The bathing does not signify that Christ was unclean and was enjoined to submit to an act of purification; but He did so out of condescension towards the human race, submitting Himself to human conditions. Thus, we will see that He will submit in a little while to the circumcision of the flesh and, much later, to baptism at the hand of the Forerunner John. Indeed, even the most pure Virgin-Mother had no need to submit to the ritual of purification after childbirth and to be excluded from the temple as being "ceremonially unclean." Nonetheless, she, too, conformed to these practices out of respect for the existing law. In any event, the bathing scene surely emphasizes the incarnation of the Saviour through its very realism. It certainly stresses His true humanity which counters the heresy that He only appeared to be human. In closing, we inform you that no Synod, on any occasion, has opposed or rejected the representation of the bathing. Thus, the erasure from Athonite monuments is the result of misunderstanding.[175]

THE NEW EVE

In this festival of re-creation, Mary is the renewal of all born on earth. She is the new Eve. As the first Eve became the mother of all living people, so the new Eve became the Mother of all renewed mankind, deified through the incarnation of the Son of God. The Virgin Mary is the highest thanksgiving to God, which man, from among all created beings, brings to the Creator.[176]

Saint Andrew, in the Lauds of the Feast, chants, *O Virgin Theotokos who hast born the Saviour, thou hast overthrown the ancient curse of Eve.*[177] Saint Ephraim the Syrian also speaks of the mystery concerning the two virgins,

193

Eve and Mary. *Today Adam has been recalled from error and from the dark deceiving of the adversary, for Christ is made flesh as man from the Virgin; and renewing Adam, He has removed the curse that came from the virgin Eve.*[178] And, *Let women praise her, the pure Mary: that as in Eve their mother, great was their reproach; lo! in Mary their sister, greatly magnified was their honor. Blessed is He Who sprang from women!*[179]

Saint Hesychios of Jerusalem succinctly states that "The Only-begotten Son of God, Creator of the world, was born by her as an infant, He Who refashioned Adam, sanctified Eve, destroyed the dragon and opened paradise, keeping firm the virginal seal."[180]

Saint Gregory the Theologian comments in his work, *In Praise of Virginity*: "When Christ came through a pure, virginal, unwedded, God-fearing and undefiled Mother, without wedlock and without father, and inasmuch as it befitted Him to be born, He purified the female nature, rejected the bitter Eve and overthrew the laws of the flesh."

Saint Gregory Palamas writes that "after dwelling in the Theotokos in an inexpressible manner, He proceeded from her bearing flesh. Then appearing on earth and living among men, He deified our nature and granted us 'things which angels desire to look into'" [1 Pet. 1:12].[181]

Saint John of Damascus sums it up this way: *Today the ancient bond of the condemnation of Adam is loosed. Paradise is opened to us: the serpent is laid low. Of old, he deceived the woman in Paradise, but now he sees a woman become Mother of the Creator. O the depth of the riches of the wisdom and knowledge of God! The agent that brought death upon all flesh, the organ that failed in its purpose has, through the Theotokos, become the first-fruits of salvation for the whole world. For God, the All-Perfect, is born a babe of her and, by His birth, He sets the seal upon her virginity. Through His swaddling clothes He looses the bands of sin, and by becoming a child He heals Eve's pangs in travail.*[182]

JOSEPH'S TRIAL

We see in icons that Joseph is not depicted in the immediate group of the Christ child and His Mother. He is not the father and thus is emphatically separated from them. At times he is depicted as though pondering the wonder of

194

the event which is beyond the natural order of things. In
many icons, the devil, in the guise of an old and bent shep-

herd, is seen standing
before Joseph trying to
tempt him. This scene
bespeaks Joseph's doubts
and troubled state of
soul, which is expressed
by his dejected attitude.
The devil is telling him
that a virgin birth is
not possible, being op-
posed to the laws of
nature and beyond
words or reason.

However, in a
hymn from the Third
Hour on the eve of the
Nativity, let us learn
how Joseph answered
these thoughts: *Tell us,
Joseph, how is it that thou bringest to Bethlehem, great with
child, the Maiden whom thou hast received from the sanctuary? "I have searched the prophets," he said, "and have
been warned by an angel: and I am persuaded that Mary
shall give birth to God, in ways surpassing all interpretation.
And Magi from the east shall come to worship Him with
precious gifts."*[183]

BY A STRANGE SELF-EMPTYING HE PASSED
THROUGH THY WOMB, VASTER THAN THE HEAVENS

*What shall we
offer Thee, O
Christ, Who for our
sakes hast appeared
on earth as man?
Every creature made
by Thee offers Thee
thanks. The angels
offer Thee a hymn;
the heavens a star;
the Magi, gifts; the
shepherds, their*

wonder; the earth, its cave; the wilderness, the manger: and we offer Thee a Virgin Mother, O pre-eternal God, have mercy upon us.[184]

On this occasion of the divine birth-giving, St. John of Kronstadt (1829-1908) comments upon the unsurpassing affection of the Mother to her Son. "The Mother of God is one flesh and blood, and one spirit with the Saviour, as His Mother. So infinitely great was her virtue by the grace of God that she became the Mother of God. She gave Him her most pure and most sacred flesh, nourishing Him with her milk, carrying Him in her arms, clothing Him, caring in every way for Him in His infancy, kissing Him over and over again and caressing Him. O Lord, who can describe the greatness of the God-bearing Virgin?....She is one with God...."[185]

THE SHEPHERDS

"And there were in the same country shepherds abiding in the field, keeping watch over their flock by night. And, lo, the angel of the Lord came upon them, and the glory of the Lord shone round about them; and they were sore afraid. And the angel said unto them, 'Fear not: for, behold, I bring you good tidings of great joy, which shall be to all people. For unto you is born this day in the city of David a Saviour, which is Christ the Lord. And this shall be a sign unto you; ye shall find the babe wrapped in swaddling clothes, lying in a manger.' And suddenly, there was with the angel a multitude of the heavenly host praising God, and saying, 'Glory to God in the highest, and on earth peace, good will toward men'" [Lk. 2:8-14].

The shepherds watched the flocks destined for sacrificial services, in the very place consecrated by tradition as where the Messiah would first be revealed.

196

Not only the earthborn were amazed, but even the heavenly hosts were filled with wonder at the divine condescension. *Before Thy nativity, O Lord, beholding with trembling Thy mystery, the noetic hosts were struck with wonder: for Thou Who hast adorned the heavens with stars wast well-pleased to be born as a babe, and Thou Who holdest all the ends of the earth in the hollow of Thy hand art laid in a manger of dumb beasts.*[186]

Saint Cosmas the Poet writes that *The shepherds abiding in the fields received a vision of light that filled them with terror. For the glory of the Lord shone around them and an angel cried aloud: "Sing praises, for Christ is born."*[187] Then at the announcement of the one angel, he was joined by myriads of others. *At the word of the angel, the hosts of heaven suddenly cried aloud: "Glory to God in the highest, and on earth peace, good will among men; Christ hast shone forth."* [188]

Another hymn makes mention that the angels exhort the shepherds to put aside worldly occupations: *As shepherds were piping songs a host of angels stopped them and called out, saying: "Cease now, ye who abide in the field at the head of your flocks; cry out and sing that Christ the Lord is born, Whose pleasure it is, as God, to save mankind."*[189]

"And it came to pass, as the angels were gone away from them into heaven, the shepherds said one to another, 'Let us now go even unto Bethlehem, and see this thing which is come to pass, which the Lord hath made known unto us'" [Lk. 2:15].

Thus we see in the Nativity icons, angels performing a twofold service: they glorify God and bring good tidings to men. In this festal icon, we also often see angels looking upwards in a posture of singing glory to God or leaning downward towards men, to whom they announce good tidings.

"And they came with haste, and found Mary and Joseph, and the babe lying in a manger" [Lk. 2:16].

Saint John of Damascus attempts to describe the thoughts of the shepherds. *The choir of shepherds abiding in the fields was overwhelmed by the strange sight they were counted worthy to behold: For they looked upon the All-Blessed Offspring of an all-pure bride; and they saw also the ranks of bodiless angels, who sang in praise of Christ the King, incarnate without seed.*[190]

Saint Ephraim puts the following words into the shepherds' mouths: *The shepherds came near and worshipped Him with their staves. They saluted Him with peace, prophesying the while, "Peace, O Prince of the shepherds!" The rod of Moses* [Ex. 4:2] *praised Thy rod, O Shepherd of all.*[191]

Saint Cosmas adds that the shepherds, *coming to Bethlehem, worshipped with her who had given Him birth.*[192] St. Ephraim poetically chants, *Thee then the shepherds praise, because Thou hast reconciled the wolves and the lambs within the fold.*[193]

The very animals that were present therein, the ox and the ass, having Him in their midst, tirelessly attended Him. Then that was fulfilled which was said by Isaias the prophet, "The ox knows his owner, and the ass his master's crib: but Israel does not know Me, and the people has not regarded Me" [Is. 1:3].

Saint Ephraim then mentions the gifts brought by the shepherds. *The shepherds came laden with the best gifts of their flock: sweet milk, clean flesh, befitting praise! They brought and presented a suckling lamb to the Paschal Lamb, a firstborn to the Firstborn, a sacrifice to the Sacrifice, a lamb of time to the Lamb of truth. Fair sight to see the lamb offered to the Lamb!*[194] And, *The lamb bleated as it was offered to the Firstborn. It praised the Lamb, that had come to set free the flocks and the oxen from sacrifices* [Ps. 49:9]*: yea that Paschal Lamb, Who handed down and brought in the Passover of the Son.*[195]

And when the shepherds had beheld Christ, "**they made known abroad the saying which was told them concerning this child. And all they that heard it wondered at those things which were told them by the shepherds [Lk. 2:18].**

"**And the shepherds returned, glorifying and praising God for all the things that they had heard and seen, as it was told unto them**" [Lk. 2:20].

MARY PONDERS THESE THINGS IN HER HEART

"**But Mary kept all these things, and pondered them in her heart**" [Lk. 2:19].

Some hymns attempt to present the hidden thoughts of Mary on this occasion. Hence, the hymnographer asks, *Why art thou filled with wonder, O Mary? Why art thou amazed at that which is come to pass in thee?* "Because I have *given birth in time to the timeless Son, yet understand not how I have conceived Him. I have not known man: how then shall I bear a child? Who has ever seen a birth without seed? But as it is written, 'Where God so wills, the order of nature is overcome.'"*[196]

Saint Romanos depicts Mary pondering the seedless conception, as she speaks to her Son. *Tell me, my child, how the seed was planted in me and how it grew in me? I behold Thee, merciful One, and I am amazed that I, who am unwed, nurse Thee; and though I see Thee in swaddling clothes, still I behold my virginity untouched, for thou hast preserved it, and yet consented to be born a young child, Who is pre-eternal God.*[197]

A Slavonic hymn characterizes her supreme affection for her divine Son. *The undefiled Virgin held Him in her arms and, without ceasing, she kissed Him. Filled with joy, she said aloud to Him: "O Most High God, O King unseen, how is it that I look upon Thee? I cannot understand the mystery of Thy poverty without measure. For the smallest of caves, a strange dwelling for Thee, finds room for Thee within itself. Thou hast been born without destroying my virginity and Thou hast kept my womb as it was before childbirth."* [198]

Saint Joseph the Hymnographer, in the Canon of the Forefeast, also presents the thoughts of Mary, saying, *The all-pure one, fearfully holding Christ in her arms, spake: "What is this great and strange wonder? How do I uphold Thee Who upholdest all the world by Thy word? O my Son Who art without beginning, Thy birth is beyond all speech!"*[199] And, *The blameless Lady was amazed at the height of the mystery, in truth past speech, and said: "The heavenly throne is consumed in flames as it holds Thee: how is it, then, that I carry Thee, my Son?"*[200] Then, the hymnographer has the Virgin-Mother saying, *Thou dost bear the likeness of Thy Father, O my Son. How then hast Thou become poor and taken upon Thyself the likeness of a servant? How shall I lay Thee in a manger of beasts without reason, Who dost deliver all men from irrationalness? I sing the praises of Thy compassion.*[201]

"Thou dost bear the form of Adam, yet Thou art all-perfect, 'being in the form of God' [Phil. 2:6]. *Of Thine own will Thou art held in human hands, Who in Thy might*

199

upholdest all things with Thine hand," spoke the pure and undefiled Virgin. "How shall I wrap Thee in swaddling clothes like a child; how shall I give Thee suck Who givest nourishment to all the world? How shall I not wonder in amazement at Thy poverty beyond understanding! How shall I, who am Thy handmaiden, call Thee my Son? I sing Thy praises and I bless Thee, Who dost grant the world great mercy."[202]

We conclude this chapter with an extract from a poem of St. Romanos who depicts the Virgin-Mother as the mystical vine who put forth the bunch of grapes that were never husbanded and, who with her arms as branches, carried Him and said, *Thou art my fruit, Thou art my life: from Thee have I learned that I remain what I was. Thou art my God: for seeing the seal of my virginity unbroken, I proclaim Thee to be the unchangeable Word, now made incarnate. I have known no seed, and I know that Thou art the destroyer of corruption: for I am pure, yet Thou hast gone forth from me. As Thou hast found my womb, so Thou hast left it. Therefore, all creation shares in my joy and cries to me: "Rejoice, thou who art full of grace."*[203]

Chapter X.
Wise Men Out of the East

+ + +

The wise men or magi referred to a class of priestly scholars, who had great power among the Persians not unlike the Levites among the Jews. This group of intellectuals was occupied with the study of medicine, philosophy, the natural sciences, scientific observation of the stars and planets (astrology) and the interpretation of dreams. We know that the Prophet Daniel, as a youth, was one of the first of the Jewish captives taken to Babylon in 605 B.C. He was renamed Baltasar (or Valtasa) and made chief over this society of scholars that held great honor and respect in the court of the Persian kings. Recognizing Daniel's God as the "God of gods and Lord of kings, Who reveals mysteries," Nebuchadnezzar elevated him to be chief of the enchanters, magicians, Chaldeans and soothsayers [Dan. 2:48; 4:6; 5:11]. The Prophet then asked the king to appoint Sedrach, Misach and Abednago over the affairs of the province of Babylon, which was done [Dan. 2:49].

The wise men of the Gospel were among the last successors of this group, who held a duel priestly (a hereditary priesthood) and governmental office. The writings of their chief magian, Daniel or Baltasar, during the sixth century B.C., concerning the Messianic prophecies, had a profound and motivating effect upon them. Among the prophecies of the holy Daniel which they were most familiar with, was the prophecy concerning the time of the coming of Christ [Dan. 9:25-26]. The Archangel Gabriel had answered Daniel's prayers by revealing the time span that would intervene; "...thou shalt know and understand that from the going forth of the command for the answer and for the building of Jerusalem until Christ the Prince, there shall be seven weeks and sixty-two weeks" [v.25].[1]   They were also familiar with Balaam's prophecy about the star shining forth from Jacob [Num. 24:17].

Saint John Chrysostom (354-407) rebukes an unbelieving Jewish nation when comparing them to the Gentile magi. "The magi sought the Lord Christ, born King of the Jews, among those from whose race they knew that Balaam, a prophet from the Gentiles, had prophesied that He would come. The faith of the magi is the condemnation of the Jews. The magi believed on the authority of their one soothsayer Balaam and the Prophet Daniel; but the Jews, from the testimony of many prophets, refused to believe. Whereas the magi acknowledged that the coming of Christ would terminate their profane knowledge and magical arts, the Jews would not accept the Lawgiver's doing away with their sacrifices and refused to accept the mysteries of the divine dispensation. The magi confessed a Stranger; the Jews rejected their own."[2]

Since the magi believed that there was a mystical influence of the stars upon earthlings, they would constantly study the heavens seeking extraordinary signs which might herald the "Expected One."   As Theophylactos (765-840), Patriarch of Bulgaria, aptly states: "Because the magi were astrologists, the Lord brought them in an ordinary manner, as Peter, being a fisherman, came away from the multitude of the fish."[3]   The famous Dismissal hymn also speaks of them, saying, *for they that worshipped the stars were instructed by a star to worship Thee, the Sun of Righteousness* [Mal. 4:2], *and to know Thee, the Dayspring on high.*[4]

Saint Cosmas the Poet (7-8th c.) writes concerning this: *The magi, beholding the strange course of an unknown and newly shining star that exceeded the brightness of all heavenly light, learned thereby that Christ the King was born on earth in Bethlehem for our salvation.*[5]

Although the Church and Canons forbid us to dabble in astrology and horoscopes, the magi understood that the coming of Christ was the utter destruction of their art.   The great Church doctor, St. Gregory the Great (c. 540-604), Pope of Rome, exhorts us not to believe that one's destiny is determined by the stars, and remarks "far be it from the faithful to believe that there is such a thing as fate. Certain heretics (Priscillan) believe that every person born is

202

subject to the rule of the stars. They assume this to support their error, that a new star came out when the Lord appeared in the flesh. They hold that this same star was His destiny. Let us reflect on the words of the Gospel that speak of this very star: 'until it came and stood over the house where the child was' [Mt. 2:9]. Thus, it is clear that it is not the child that hastens to the star, but the star that hastens to the child. And so, if I may say this, it is not the star that is the child's fate, but rather it is the child Who is the destiny of the star....For it is the Creator Who has made the lives of all men Who alone governs them. Man was not made for the stars, but rather the stars were made for man."[6]

A WORD ON MAGIAN HISTORY

The promise of a divinely-imposed dominion was more than acceptable to the magi. Their own Persian and Medo-Persian history was studded with Jewish nobles, ministers and counselors. For many years their land contained the Jewish dispersion and, moreover, they often came in contact with Jewish Messianic hopes. It is also possible that some of the magi were Jewish descendants from those appointed magi of Daniel's day.[7]

At the time of these magi, they composed the upper house of the Council of the Megistanes whose duties included the absolute choice and election of the king of the realm. With their sudden appearance in Jerusalem, probably traveling in force with all imaginable oriental pomp, and accompanied by adequate cavalry escort to insure their penetration of Roman territory, certainly alarmed Herod and the populace of Jerusalem. Understandably did Herod fear this group of Persian-Parthian king makers, being also aware of the Roman-Parthian rivalry that prevailed during his lifetime. The Romans had been decisively defeated by the Parthians in the last fifty years (Battle of Carrhae), but Roman rule was nominally re-established in Palestine by Herod's father, Antipater. With Parthian collaboration, Jewish sovereignty might be restored. Therefore, Herod also knew that the time was ripe for another Parthian invasion of the buffer provinces, though this was unlikely to happen since, at that time, Parthia had been racked with internal dissension.[8]

Nevertheless, the magi, a group already involved in political maneuvering, apart from being wise and knowledgeable, brought gifts to the newborn King. They were good men who struggled to maintain the purity of their souls. They accepted divine inspiration and were obedient to it. They then understood that the Messianic prophecy of the kingdom would not be fulfilled right then and there, and they obediently departed to their own land to proclaim the newborn Christ; hence, the Persians were the first-fruits of the Gentiles. "And kings shall walk in Thy light, and in Thy brightness" [Is. 60:3].

THE IDENTITIES OF THE MAGI

Thus we see in icons, three magi traveling, either walking or riding spirited horses over mountainous trails in pursuit of the star of Bethlehem. They are often depicted beyond and opposite the cave, for they were not present during those first hours after the virgin birth. One magus is a beardless youth. The second magus is a middle-aged man with a short, dark beard, while the third magus is an old man with a gray beard.[9]

In icons of the Nativity feast, we see both shepherds and magi depicted. On one side of the cave we see simple unsophisticated men, with whom the incorporeals on high enter into communication directly, amid their everyday occupations. Then we see magi, men of learning, who have to undergo a long journey from the knowledge of what is relative to the knowledge of what is absolute. In the shepherds, we witness the first sons of Israel to worship the Christ child. The Church sees the beginning of the Jewish Church. In the wise men, we see the beginning of nations, the Church of the heathen. In the example of the magi, we understand that the Church accepts all human science that leads towards it, provided that the relative light of the extra-Christian revelation bring them that serve it to the worship of the absolute Light. Again, we see that the magi are men of different ages (youth, middle age and old age), which emphasizes that revelation is vouchsafed to men independent of their years and experience.[10]

According to St. Dimitri of Rostov (1651-1709), in his investigation of the identities of these three kings, he asserts that they were kings of small regions in Persia, Arabia and Egypt. They had arrived in Bethlehem very shortly after the birth of Christ. Melchior was old, withered, with long white hair and beard. It was he who offered the Lord the gift of gold. Gaspar or Caspar, was of ruddy complexion, young and beardless. He offered the Lord the gift of frankincense. The third, Balthazar, was dark-skinned and heavily bearded. He gave the gift of myrrh. He further writes that these three wise men represented the three chief races of men that descended from Noah's three sons, that is, Shem, Japheth and Ham: therefore, the Arabian, Gaspar represented Shem; the Persian, Melchior, represented Japheth; the Egyptian, Balthazar represented Ham. Thus, through these three magi, the human race worshipped our incarnate Lord and God.[11]

Saint Cosmas speaks of Babylon in these terms: *The daughter of Babylon once led captive from Sion the children of David, whom she had taken with the sword: but now she sends her own children, the magi bearing gifts, to entreat the Daughter of David in whom God came to dwell.*[12] Then speaking of the magi's gifts, he writes: *Babylon despoiled Sion the Queen and took her wealth captive. But Christ, by a guiding star, drew to Sion the treasures of Babylon, with her kings who gazed upon the stars.*[13]

The Prophet Isaias foretold the coming of the wise men when he spoke: "And the camels of Madiam and Gaepha shall cover thee: all from Saba shall come bearing gold, and shall bring frankincense, and they shall publish the salvation of the Lord" [Is. 60:6]. Saint John Chrysostom interprets Isaias 8:4: "For before the child shall know how to call his father or his mother, He shall take the power of Damascus and the spoils of Samaria before the king of the Assyrians," thusly: "The gold that was offered by the magi, and which the Son of God born a child has received, is interpreted as 'the strength of Damascus'; 'the spoils of Samaria' are the magi themselves, whom He has drawn out of the error of the superstitions of Samaria, that is, the worship of idols; and who formerly because of their false religion were the spoil of the devil, now through the knowledge of Christ have become the spoil of God. The 'king of the Assyrians' means Herod, or at all events the devil, against whom the magi stood forth as adversaries, namely, by adoring the Son of God."[14]

THE WISE MEN ENTER JERUSALEM

"Now when Jesus was born in Bethlehem of Judea, in the days of Herod the king, behold, there came wise men from the east to Jerusalem, saying, 'Where is He that is born King of the Jews?'" [Mt. 2:1-2]

The star appeared in the East at the time of the Annunciation and led the magi about for nine months. The tradition of the Church never held that the star was truly a celestial star but that it was some invisible power transformed into this appearance and made visible to men.

Saint John Chrysostom points out in a homily that "No natural star could have traversed such a course nor could it have shone so brilliantly at midday and, furthermore, it stood still over the child."[15]

In a kontakion of St. Romanos, the melodist writes that the Christ child uttered in spirit to His Mother, *To all appearances, it is a star; but in reality, it is a power. It went with the magi in service to Me; and still it stands outside fulfilling its ministry, and revealing with its beams the place where there has been born a young child, the pre-eternal God.*[16]

In his *Epistle to the Ephesians*, St. Ignatios the God-bearer (+c.110), writes: "A star shown forth in heaven above all the other stars, the light of which was inexpressible, while its novelty struck men with astonishment. And all the rest of the stars, with the sun and moon, formed a chorus to this star, and its light was exceedingly great above them all. And there was agitation felt as to whence this new spectacle came, so unlike to everything else in the heavens. Hence every worldly wisdom became folly; conjuration was seen to be mere trifling; and magic became utterly ridiculous. Every law of wickedness vanished away; the darkness of ignorance was dispersed; and tyrannical authority was destroyed, God being manifested as man, and man displaying power as God. But neither was the former a mere imagination, nor did the second imply a bare humanity; but the one was absolutely true, and the other an economical arrangement. And now that took a beginning which had been prepared by God. Henceforth all things were in a state of tumult, because He meditated the abolition of death."[17]

Patriarch Theophylactos also agrees that what was seen by the magi was "the divine power and an angelic appearance in the form of a star."[18] St. Leo the Great (+461) adds that this light was hidden from the Jews, but shone forth to the heathen.[19]

Also in icons of the Feast of the Nativity of Christ, we see that the star points directly to the cave. It is a long ray which connects the star with a part of the sphere which goes beyond the limits of the icon. Here we have a symbolic representation of the heavenly world. Hence, this star is not merely a cosmic phenomenon, but also a messenger from the world on high, bringing tidings of the birth of the "heavenly One" on earth.

HEROD MAKES INQUIRIES

Entering Jerusalem the wise men asked, "Where is He that is born King of the Jews? We have seen His star in the east." Now when **"Herod the king had heard these things, he was troubled, and all Jerusalem with him"** [Mt. 2:3].

Why was Herod overcome with wrath? This is because His kingdom would soon come to an end. Why was Jerusalem troubled with him? This is because they were living in unrighteousness, and the time of censure had come. Sadly, St. John Chrysostom comments, "See too how the Jewish people are troubled, though they should rejoice that it was a Jewish king that was born. But they were troubled because the wicked can never rejoice at the coming of the just. Hence we have, 'And all Jerusalem with him.'"[20]

The *Protoevangelium* relates the following. Herod then sent messengers to the priests and to the wise men whose names were Melchior, Gaspar and Balthazar, so that he might pose inquiries to them in the public hall. Now when Herod had gathered all the chief priests and scribes of the people together, he demanded of them where it was written concerning Christ the King and where the Christ should be born.[21]

"And when he had gathered all the chief priests and scribes of the people together, he demanded of them where Christ should be born" [Mt. 2:4].

207

Saint John Chrysostom asks, "To what end did Herod, who did not believe in the Scriptures, question them? Or, if he believed, how did he hope to kill Him Whom they said was to be the future King? But Herod was urged on by the devil, who did not believe that Scriptures lied."[22]

The Jews then answered: **"And thou Bethlehem, in the land of Juda, art not the least among the princes of Juda: for out of thee shall come forth a Governor, that shall rule My people Israel"** [Mt. 2:6].

However, what the Prophet Micah had actually said is, as follows: "And thou, Bethlehem, house of Ephratha, art few in number to be reckoned among the thousands of Judah; yet out of thee shall One come forth to Me, to be a Ruler in Israel; and His goings forth were from the beginning, even from eternity" [Mic. 5:2].

Blessed Jerome (347-420) chides the Jews, saying: "Here the Jews are to be reproved for ignorance, since the prophet says, 'And thou Bethlehem Ephratha', but they say, 'Bethlehem of Juda' [Mt. 2:6]. Saint John Chrysostom then remarks that "mutilating the prophecy in this manner, they have become the cause of the slaughter of the infants. For it is written: '...out of thee shall One come forth to Me, to be a Ruler of Israel; and His goings forth were from the beginning, even from eternity' [Mic. 5:2]. If therefore they had quoted the entire prophecy--and properly--Herod, reflecting that this could not be an earthly king, whose days were from the days of eternity, would not have raged so furiously."[23]

Saint Cosmas commends the little town of Bethlehem, chanting, *Be glad, O Bethlehem, for thou art queen among the princes of Judah; for from thee comes forth, before the sight of all, the Shepherd Who tends Israel, He that is seated upon the cherubim, even Christ. He has raised up our horn and reigns over all.*[24]

Saint Gregory the Great writes: "Fitting was it that He was born in Bethlehem; for Bethlehem is interpreted as the 'House of Bread'; for He says of Himself, 'I am the living bread which came down from heaven'" [Jn. 6:51].[25]

Saint John Chrysostom brings to our attention that "since the scribes had not tried to conceal the mystery of the King preordained by God--especially from the sight of an alien king--they became, not preachers of the works of God, but betrayers of His mysteries. Not alone do they divulge His mysteries, but they also cite prophetic testimony[26]--albeit, incorrectly.

Continuing, the "Golden-mouthed" writes: "After Herod had received an answer, he believed it to be credible for two reasons: first, because it was spoken by the priests; and second, because it was confirmed by prophetic testimony. Herod was not inclined towards reverence for the King that was to be born, but rather to the dread evil of the slaughter--and that by treachery. Herod perceived that he could not beguile the magi by flattery, nor frighten them by threats, nor corrupt them by gold, so as to force them to consent to the death of the future King. Accordingly, he planned to deceive them."[27]

Here too, St. John points out a wondrous dispensation: "The Jews and the magi mutually teach each other. The Jews learn from the magi that a star in the East has proclaimed the Christ, and the magi learn from the Jews that of old the prophecies have foretold Him. Thus strengthened by this twofold testimony, the magi desired Him with more ardent faith."[28]

THE WISE MEN BEFORE HEROD
"Then Herod when he had privily called the wise men, inquired of them diligently what time the star appeared" [Mt. 2:7].

209

Herod was struck with amazement, seeing the piety of the magi and, overcome by wrath, he inquired concerning when the Child was born.[29]

And having sent away the chief priests, Herod inquired diligently of the wise men, and said unto them, "What was the sign that did appear concerning the King that is born?" They answered him declaring, "We saw an extraordinarily large star shining among the stars of heaven. It outshined all the other stars, so that they became undiscernible. We knew, thereby, that a great King was born in Israel and, therefore, we came to worship Him."[30] Thus, Herod has a private audience with the magi. Saint John discloses that "he called them secretly, so that the Jews might not see that he suspected them; lest also, perhaps, they, preferring a King of their own race (and rejecting him), might betray his purpose."[31]

Saint Romanos, in a hymn, delves into the diabolical thinking of Herod. *When Herod learned from the magi the power of the child, he uttered cries of suffering mixed with laughter: "O, of all unexpected evils, that a babe should make me afraid! I should tremble before a child whom I have not seen? I rule over sea and land, and an infant terrifies me! What shall I do? Suddenly a star has shone upon the whole earth, and has heralded Him as the mighty King Who will destroy my kingdom, and I mourn that my power will soon be destroyed."*[32]

Saint Leo the Great writes that "Herod here stands for the devil, who then was his inciter; and he is not his unwearied imitator. For he (the devil) is troubled by the calling of the nations. He is tormented daily by the breaking down of his kingdom."[33]

Saint John Chrysostom adds that "Each (Satan and Herod) are troubled by his own greed, and fears a succession to his kingdom. Herod an earthly successor, the devil a heavenly one."[34]

Herod then sent them to Bethlehem and said, "'Go and search diligently for the young child; and when ye have found Him, bring me word again, that I may come and worship Him also.' When they had heard the king, they departed; and, lo, the star, which they saw in the east went before them till it came and stood over where the young child was. When they saw the star, they rejoiced with exceeding great joy" Mt. 2: 8-10].

Herod feigns to revere the child when, in reality, he planned violence. Saint Cosmas characterizes Herod as *the troubled enemy of God, who, in his wild madness, plotted how to he might slay Christ.*[35]

Saint John Chrysostom brings to our attention that when the magi were in that place, "the star had hid from them. Hence, they were compelled to make inquiry in Jerusalem concerning Christ. Thus, at the same time, they made Him known. This took place for two reasons. First, for the confounding of the Jews; for the magi, encouraged only by the rising of a star, have been seeking Christ, and in strange lands, while the Jews, who have been reading from their childhood the prophecies that spoke of Christ, and though He was born in their midst, have not received Him. Secondly, so that the priests, being questioned as to where Christ was born, would make answer to their own con-demnation, 'from Bethlehem'; because they who had instructed Herod concerning Christ, were themselves without knowledge of Him. Thus after the magi made their inquiry, the star appeared. And they, observing the obedience of the star, understood the dignity of the King."[36]

THE WISE MEN ENTER THE HOUSE

The magi, being led by the star, followed it till it came and stood over where the young child was with His Mother [Mt. 2:9]. Now by this time, Joseph had secured a room in Bethlehem for the Theotokos and her Son. Thus, in Ortho-dox iconography of "The Adoration of the Magi", they are depicted in a house, which is in agreement with the words of the Evangelist Matthew that "they (the magi) came into the house" [Mt. 2:11]. The Theotokos is usually seen sitting on a throne with a high polygonal back. The child Jesus is sitting on His Mother's lap.

Several hymns of the Church from the Feast of the Nativity present dialogue between the Theotokos and the visiting magi. Hymns from Slavonic sources recount that *The pure Virgin spoke in wonder...and she said unto them: "Whom do ye seek? For I see that ye have come from a far country. Ye have the appearance, but not the thoughts, of Persians; strange has been your journey and strange your arrival. Ye have come with zeal to worship Him Who,*

211

journeying as a Stranger from on high, has strangely--in ways known to Himself--come to dwell in me."[37] Another hymn portrays the Mother of God turning to her infant Son, saying, *Kings from the east, having learned that Thou wast to be born as King, are come, bringing Thee gifts, O Son, of frankincense and myrrh and gold; and lo, they stand before the doors. Bid them enter and let them behold Thee, held in my arms as a child, Who art older than ancient Adam.*[38]

Saint Ephraim the Syrian (c.306-383) also portrays the Virgin-Mother speaking with her Son, saying, *O Son of the Rich One, Who abhorred the bosom of rich women, who led Thee to the poor? For Joseph was needy and I also am in want, yet Thy merchants have come, and brought gold, to the house of the poor.*[39] The saint then tenderly writes that *The King Whom before the angels of fire and spirit tremble lies in the bosom of a girl, and she cuddles Him as a baby. The heaven is the throne for His glory* [Is. 66:1], *yet He sits on Mary's knees.*[40]

Saint Romanos, rich in imagery, also employs the technique of introducing dialogue into his sermon-like hymns. We will now listen to those hymns taken from his kontakia under the title, *Mary and the Magi.*

The magi then said to her:

Magi: "Who art thou who hast produced and brought forth such an One? Who is thy father? Who is thy mother? For thou hast become the mother and nurse of a fatherless Son. It was His star that we saw when we came to behold a young child, the pre-eternal God.[41]

"Clearly did Balaam reveal to us the meaning of the words which were prophesied, saying that a star would rise up: a star which would dim all prophecies and divinations; a star to destroy the parables of the wise and their teachings and their enigmas; a star much brighter than this star which just appeared, for He is the Maker of the stars about Whom it was written [Num. 24:17].[42]

When Mary heard the words of wonder, she knelt in obeisance to the One from her womb and, crying out, said:

Theotokos: "Great things, my child, great things are all the things which Thou hast done for my humble station; for lo, the magi without are seeking Thee; they

212

that are kings of the east seek thy presence, and the wealthy of the people beg to behold Thee; for truly the people are Thine. They are the ones for whom Thou was known as a young child, the pre-eternal God.[43]

"Since the people are Thine, my child, bid them to come beneath this roof that they may see a poverty full of plenty, and beggary which is honored. I consider Thee a glory and cause for boast, so that I am not ashamed. Thou, Thyself, art the grace and the comeliness of my dwelling. Bid them enter."[44]

Then, uttering in spirit, the Christ child says to His Mother, *Admit the magi, for My word led them, and shone on them that were seeking Me....Now receive them, O revered one, receive them that received Me; for I am in them as I am in thine arms, nor was I away from thee when I accompanied them.*[45]

She, then, opened the door and received the group of magi. Straightway, the magi hastened into the room.[46]

The lights of the east then said to the Virgin:

Magi: "Dost thou wish to know whence we have come here? We came from the land of the Chaldeans where they do not say: 'Lord, God of gods' [Deut. 10:17]; but from Babylon, where they do not know Who is the Maker of the things that they worship. It is from that place that thy Son's spark came and started us on our route, far from the Persian fire. Indeed, we have left behind the fire which is all-consuming and now behold the Fire that refreshes!"[47]

When the Virgin learned of their experiences, she said to them:

Theotokos: "What did Herod the king and the pharisees inquire of you?"

213

Magi: "First Herod and then the chiefs of thy nation inquired in detail about the time of the appearance of this star; but they did not learn. They were not eager to see the One about Whom they asked; for those that search are bound to behold a young child, the pre-eternal God.[48]

"The foolish people suspected us of being senseless, and they asked us, 'Whence and when have you come? How did you follow hidden paths?' But we answered them by referring to what they understood: 'How did you travel through the great desert which you traversed?' The One who led them out of Egypt is the One Who had just guided the men from Chaldea to Him. Formerly, it was with a pillar of fire; now with a star to reveal a newborn babe.[49]

"The star was everywhere guiding our way just as Moses brought his rod for you (Israel), and the light of the knowledge of God shone round about. Long ago manna fed you and the rock gave you to drink; hope of seeing Him satisfied us. So, nourished by His grace, we intended to travel the pathless road and not to turn back into Persia. For we yearn to behold, to worship and to praise a young child, the pre-eternal God.'"[50]

The magi speak of manna, of which St. Gregory of Nyssa (c.335-394) says that the miracle of manna teaches in anticipation the mystery of the Virgin. "You no doubt perceive the true food in the figure of the history: the bread which came from heaven is not some incorporeal thing. For how could something incorporeal be nourishment to a body? Neither plowing nor sowing produced the body of this bread, but the earth which remained unchanged was found full of this divine food, of which the hungry partake."[51]

The journey of the magi brought them no fatigue of mind or body; for none of them felt weariness. Just as Habakkum did not weary when he went to Daniel [Bel and the Dragon, v.33], the same angel, by the aid of the Holy Spirit, guided the kings of Persia to Jerusalem and then Bethlehem.

"And when they were come into the house, they saw the young child with Mary His Mother, and fell down, and worshipped Him" [Mt. 2:11].

Saint Leo the Great remarks that the magi, beheld a child, "small in size, depending on others, powerless to act, differing in no way from any other human infant....for the Son of God had assumed the true nature of man."[52]

Saint John of Damascus (c.676-c.750) writes that *they saw Thee wrapped in swaddling clothes...Who sharest all our suffering. And in joy they gazed upon Thee, Who art at once both mortal and Lord."*[53]

The magi did not see before them either scepter or throne, only utter poverty. Saint John Chrysostom adds that "He was not crowned with a diadem, nor resting on a gilded bed; but scarcely possessing a single tunic, and that served, not for the adorning of His body, but to clothe His nakedness....If, therefore, they had come searching for an earthly king, they would have been rather mortified than filled with exceeding joy, for they would have undertaken the toil of a journey without reward. But now they seek a heavenly King, though they saw in Him nothing regal; yet satisfied by the testimony of a star, their eyes were glad as they looked upon a poor little child; for the Spirit within them showed that He was a Being of awe."[54]

Yet, still, they were moved to adore Him. And as St. John Chrysostom comments, "What moved them to adore Him? For the Virgin bore no distinguishing mark, and the abode was not one of splendor; neither were there any other material circumstances which would either compel them or induce them to do this....What was it then that moved them?....The star and the light that God had placed in their hearts led them step by step to more perfect knowledge."[55]

A hymn from the Slavonic text has the Theotokos invite the magi to enter. *"Come ye and make haste to enter," said the Virgin to the magi, "and behold Him Who is invisible, now visibly manifest and become a child." And they came eagerly and worshipped, bringing gifts in fulfillment of the divine prophecy"* [Ps. 67:30; Is. 60:3,6].[56]

THE MAGI OPEN THEIR TREASURES

"And when they had opened their treasures, they presented unto Him gifts; gold, and frankincense, and myrrh" [Mt. 2:11].

Returning to the narrative of St. Romanos, he writes: *After all the explanations were made, the magi took up their gifts and knelt before the Gift of gifts and the Myrrh of myrrh, saying:*

Magi: "Receive the triple gift like the thrice-holy hymn of the seraphim. Do not reject it as the offerings of Cain, but accept it as the offerings of Abel, for the sake of her who bore Thee."[57]

Then they brought forth out of their treasures. *And eagerly opening their treasures, they offered to Him precious gifts: refined gold, as to the King of the ages, and frankincense, as to the God of all; and myrrh they offered to the Immortal, as to one three days dead.*[58]

What was the significance of these gifts? Hymns from the Canon of the Forefeast disclose their meaning. *The kings, first-fruits of the nations, bring Thee gifts...by myrrh they point to Thy death, by gold to Thy royal power, by frankincense to the dignity of Thy divinity.*[59] Furthermore, *The error of Persia has ceased: for the stargazers, kings of the east, bring gifts of gold, myrrh and frankincense to Christ the King of all at His birth.*[60]

Saint Romanos continues his dialogue, speaking through the Mother of God.

The blameless Virgin then entreated the One Who is Creator and Lord of all, saying:

Theotokos: "Receive the three gifts, my child, and grant three prayers for her who gave Thee birth. I beg Thee in behalf of the heavens above and the fruits of the earth, and them that dwell thereon, be reconciled to all for my sake. I supplicate Thee in behalf of all men. Thou hast made me the pride and boast of all my race [Judith 15:9-11]; for the universe considers me as a powerful protection, rampart and stay. May them that were cast from the joys of Paradise look to me that I may direct them. Save the world, O Saviour; for its sake Thou didst come. Establish Thy Kingdom; for its sake Thou hast let Thy light shine on me and the magi, and all creation."[61]

216

Saint John Chrysostom comments that "at that time, the magi did not perceive to what mystery they tendered in the gifts, or what each single gift might signify, yet there is nothing out of place in their offerings; for the grace that had stirred them to do all these things is the same that orders the universe."[62]   According to St. John Chrysostom, the wise men offered gifts not only free from Judaical grossness, in that they sacrificed not sheep and calves, for it was knowledge, obedience and love that they offered unto Him, in a manner bespeaking the true devotion of the Church.[63]

Saint Gregory, Pope of Rome, writes: "By gold, wisdom is also symbolized, as Solomon testifies, saying, 'A desirable treasure will rest on the mouth of the wise' [Prov. 21:20]; by frankincense, which is burnt before God, the power of prayer is symbolized, according to the psalm, 'Let my prayer be set forth as incense before Thee' [Ps. 140:2]; by myrrh is typified the mortification of the flesh.   To the newborn King, we offer gold, if in His sight we might shine with the light of wisdom.   We offer incense when by the fervor of our prayer we offer up that which is agreeable to Him.   We offer myrrh when by abstinence we mortify the vices of the flesh."[64]

THE MAGI RETURN HOME

"And being warned of God in a dream that they should not return to Herod, they departed into their own country another way" [Mt. 2:12].

Having been warned in a dream--a type of communication most familiar and acceptable to them in that same hour there appeared to them an angel in the form of that star which had before guided them on their journey; and they went away, following the guidance of its light, until they arrived in their own country.

Saint Ephraim composed this hymn concerning their departure.   *The Morning Star cast its bright beams in the darkness, and led them as blind men, and they came and received a great light: they gave offerings and received life, and they worshipped and returned.*[65]

Saint John Chrysostom concludes their journey saying that when "they had returned home, they continued to worship Him, more than before. And they preached Him, and instructed many. Finally, when the Apostle Thomas came to that region they joined themselves to him, and were baptized.

217

They then became his helpers in the work of preaching the Gospel."[66]

Saint John Chrysostom and St. Gregory the Great make an important observation: the magi did not return by the same route. Saint John writes that "It was not possible that having come from Herod to Christ, they would return again to Herod."[67] Concurring with this, St. Gregory writes: "They intimate something here of great import. Our true country is Paradise, to which, having now come to the knowledge of Jesus, we are forbidden to return by the path we left."[68]

JOSEPH THE BETROTHED

What about the beloved and righteous elder Joseph? What were his thoughts?

Joseph, when He beheld the greatness of this wonder, thought that he beheld a mortal wrapped as a babe in swaddling clothes; but from all that came to pass he understood that He was the true God.[69]

Saint Ephraim warmly writes that *Joseph caressed the Son as a babe; he ministered to Him as God. He rejoiced in Him as the Good One, yet he was greatly bewildered and awestruck at Him as the Just One.*[70]

Continuing, St. Ephraim depicts Joseph holding the Christ child, saying, *Who hath given me the Son of the Most High to be a Son to me? I was jealous of Thy Mother, and I thought to put her away, and I knew not that in her womb*

218

was hidden a mighty treasure, that should suddenly enrich my poor estate. David the king sprang from my race, and wore the crown: and I have come to a very low estate, who instead of a king am a carpenter. Yet a crown hath come to me, for in my bosom is the Lord of crowns![71]

Blessed Jerome says, "In His boundless wisdom, God employs the simplest of means. What was the best way to effect the incarnation of the Son of God? To reveal openly the all-holy Virgin's virginal state would have meant to bring attention to the Lord Jesus prematurely, without proper preparation. A threefold purpose was accomplished by Joseph's betrothal to the Virgin: quiet obscurity was assured for Christ until the appointed moment, an impenetrable defense against slander for the all-holy Virgin, and masculine defense was provided for both her and the divine infant. All this was accomplished by the sacred betrothal of St. Joseph to the Virgin-Mother."[72]

What do we assert by the multi-faceted role Joseph would play? Biblical Israel had a patriarchal or father-centered form of family life. From biblical times, as a father and husband, a man would defend his family's right before the judges when necessary [Deut. 22:13-19]. We also know that "the fatherless and the widow," who had no man to defend their rights, were often denied justice [cf. Deut. 10:19]. The stigma of an illegitimate child would have thwarted the divine plan. Furthermore, Mary now had a responsible and respectable man who would provide food, clothing and shelter for her and her infant Son. God ordained the family unit as a vital part of human society. And what a great reward and honor awaited Joseph and all his house! One of his sons would be of the inner Twelve Apostles (Jude); one would become the first Bishop of Jerusalem (James); and his daughter Salome, the myrrh-bearer, would give birth to the two Apostles and "sons of thunder", James and John. Let us not fail to mention Joseph's brother, Cleopas, one of the Seventy Apostles. Then there was Cleopas' son, Symeon, the second martyred Bishop of Jerusalem, as recorded by Hegesippus, Nicephoros Callistos (+c.1335) and Bishop Nikolai Velimirovic (+1956).[73] However the *Synaxarion* in the *Menaion* for the 27th of April records him as Joseph the Betrothed's son.[74] In any event whether

Symeon was Joseph's son or his nephew, it is clear that salvation, honor and glory came to their house.

When the magi were present, St. Romanos the Melodist, puts forth Mary's explanation to the magi concerning the presence of Joseph in the house.

Theotokos: "I shall remind you, O magi, for what reason I have Joseph in my dwelling. It is for the refutation of all who doubt. He himself will tell what he heard about my child. For in his sleep he saw a holy angel who told him whence I conceived [Mt. 1:20]. A divine being, shining like fire, reassured him in the night and settled his thorny doubts. Therefore Joseph is with me to reveal that here is a young child, the pre-eternal God. Clearly he will report the things that he himself saw among the heavenly beings and mortals on earth--how the shepherds sang songs, and the shining ones sang with men of clay; how the star ran ahead of you to light your way and guide you."[75]

Saint Basil the Great (c.330-379) confirms this explanation and description of Joseph as a witness to her purity and whose presence would preserve her from calumny. The saint also remarks that "The virginity of Mary would be hidden from the prince of this world."[76]

The venerable Bede (c.673-735) summarized patristic teaching on their marriage, writing: "Blessed Mary had then a husband who would be the most reliable witness of her integrity and the most faithful custodian of our Lord and Saviour. For the Child Jesus, Joseph would bring to the temple the victims of sacrifice prescribed by the law; in the hour of persecution he would take Him and His Mother into Egypt and bring them back; and finally he would provide many other services called for by the fragility of the nature assumed."[77] Bede elsewhere lists other reasons for the marriage: "The guarantee afforded by Joseph's genealogy, the protection of Mary against stoning as an adulteress, and the concealment of the virginal birth from the evil one."[78]

Saint Ignatios (before 110 A.D.) made the valuable observation that "Now the virginity of Mary was hidden from the prince of this world, as was also her Offspring, and the death of the Lord. Thus, three mysteries of renown, which were wrought in silence, but have been revealed to us."[79]

Chapter XI.
The Circumcision of
Our Lord JESUS CHRIST
in the Flesh,

the Memory of which the Holy Church
Celebrates on the
1st of January

+ + +

"And when eight days were accomplished for the circumcising of the child, His name was called Jesus, which was so named of the angel before He was conceived in the womb" [Lk. 2:21].

As a Jewish mother, the Virgin-Mother fulfilled all the requirements of the law. The first of these was circumcision of her Son, which represented voluntary submission to the conditions of the law, and acceptance of the obligations, but also the privileges, of the covenant between God and Abraham and his seed. The child was then given the name Jesus *(Jeshua* or *Jehoshua)*, meaning 'salvation of Yahweh'.[1]

In the *Synaxarion* of the Feast, we read, "Wherefore then, did He will to be brought to this place by His Mother and Joseph, on the eighth day after His holy birth from the Virgin? Insofar as it was the custom of the Jews to be circumcised, He was circumcised. He accepted the circumcision in the flesh in order to introduce the spiritual circumcision. If Christ our God had not taken on human flesh, then He could not have been circumcised. Therefore, none can say that he did not take on our flesh but only appeared to be born in the flesh."

The Saviour, condescending to mankind, accepted to be wrapped in swaddling clothes. Eight days' old according to His Mother and without beginning according to His Father; He felt no loathing for the circumcision of the flesh.[2]

Saint Cyril of Jerusalem (318-386), in a homily, comments, "It was customary on the eighth day to celebrate the carnal circumcision. On the eighth day (Sunday) Christ rose from the dead, and wrought in us a spiritual circumcision, saying: 'Go ye therefore, and teach all nations, baptizing them...'"[3]

In the Bible, we read that the procedure was done with either a sharp stone [Ex. 4:25] or a sharp knife [Josh. 5:2]. Blood must be shed in the operation, and the inner layer must be torn with the thumbnail. The bleeding would be stopped with wine. In Biblical times, the procedure was done by either the father, the father-in-law (the mother's father) or by a circumciser *(Mohel)*, who recited a special prayer and was unpaid for the service.[4] In Jesus' time, circumcision was performed by a priest. The rite could be performed either in the house or in the synagogue. If the mother desired to be present during the ceremony, it had to be performed outside the temple, since she would not be allowed entry--even into the Court of Gentiles--until the period of her purification had expired [Lev. 12:2-5].[5]

According to the venerable monastic biographer and priest, Bede (c.673-735): "On the same day of His circumcision He received His name....Abram, who first received the sacrament of circumcision, merited in the day of his circumcision, to be blessed in the enlargement of his name (Abraham)" [Gen. 17:5].[6]

In the Matins canon of the Feast, we hear: *Today are depicted the bright and all-shining Nativity of Christ and the mystery of the regeneration to come. For the Saviour is circumcised according to the decree of the law, not as God but as mortal man, as the Fulfiller of the law.*[7] And, *Thou hast not thought it unworthy to put on the form of mortal man but, as a babe, Thou hast lawfully fulfilled the law.*[8] For, *The eighth day, bearing a symbol of future things has been made bright and sanctified by Thy voluntary impoverish-*

ment, O Christ; for on this day hast Thou been circumcised in the flesh according to the law.[9]

The divine Apostle Paul writes: "But when the fullness of the time was come, God sent forth His Son, made of a Woman, made under the law, to redeem them that were under the law, that we might receive the adoption as sons" [Gal. 4:4-5]. In the hymns of the Feast, we learn the following about the purpose of the Law-Giver's condescension and fulfillment of the law: *In fulfilling the law, of Thine own will Thou didst receive circumcision in the flesh, that Thou might make the shadow cease and that Thou might roll away the veil of our passions.*"[10] This is because *The transcendent Word was circumcised unto the ceasing of the law; and He gave us divine first fruits of grace and of life incorruptible.*[11]

Circumcision prefigured Holy Baptism. Now that the Mystery of Baptism had come, the old procedure, circumcision, was superfluous. Saint Athanasios (296-373), Patriarch of Alexandria, comments upon this saying, "Circumcision expressed nothing more than the despoiling of the old man; by this, that part of the body was circumcised which served as the instrument of corporeal generation. This was then done in sign of the future baptism in Christ. And so when that which was prefigured had come, the prefigurement became void; for all that was the old man is taken away by baptism."[12]

Another Patriarch of Alexandria, St. Cyril (+444), writes that after Christ's circumcision: "The rite was done away by the introduction of that which had been signified by it-- baptism; for which reason we are no longer circumcised. Circumcision seems to me to have effected three ends: First, it separated the posterity of Abraham by a sign and seal, and distinguished them from the nations. Second, it prefigured in itself the grace and efficacy of Holy Baptism (for as in ancient times, he that was circumcised was counted among the people of God). Thus, also he that is baptized, having formed in himself Christ the seal, is enrolled into God's adopted family. Third, it is the symbol of the faithful when established in grace, who cut away and mortify the tumultuous rising of carnal pleasures and passions by the sharp surgery of faith, and by ascetic labors; not cutting the body, but purifying the heart, and being circumcised in the spirit, and not in the letter."[13]

The passing away of the shadow of the law may be also heard in these matinal hymns: *By appearing, O Christ Thou hast made the haughty behavior of the Jews with their sabbaths and circumcision to cease; and, by the Spirit, the spring of grace has shone.*[14] And, *Since Christ has become a child and has been shown forth as the fulfillment of the law, the law has become of no effect; and He, by accepting circumcision, has set us loose from the curse of the law.*[15]

Saint Paul writes: "For in Him (Christ) dwelleth all the fullness of the Godhead bodily. And ye are complete in Him,

Who is the Head of all principality and power: In Whom also ye are circumcised with the circumcision made without hands, in putting off the body of the sins of the flesh by the circumcision of Christ: Buried with Him in baptism, wherein also ye are risen with Him through the faith in the operation of God, Who hath raised Him from the dead" [Col. 2:9-12].

At the end of this ritual it is not mentioned in the Scriptures if the holy Joseph took them back to Nazareth or if they tarried in Bethlehem or Jerusalem until the fortieth day after the virginal birth, when the child would be presented in the temple. We do know, however, that on the fortieth day after His nativity (2nd of February), they entered the temple in Jerusalem where they met the Elder Symeon and the Prophetess Anna.

Chapter XII.
The Meeting of Our Lord God and Saviour JESUS CHRIST, in the Temple,

the Memory of which the Holy Church Celebrates on the 2nd of February

+ + +

THE FIRSTBORN

"Sanctify to Me every firstborn, first produced, opening every womb among the children of Israel both of man and beast: it is Mine" [Ex. 13:2]. At first appearance this verse seems to imply that all firstborn are holy and dedicated to God; yet it was only truly fulfilled in the person of Christ. For many firstborn sons of women were neither holy nor dedicated to God. We need only to remember Cain who murdered his younger brother [Gen. 4:8], or Esau who sold his birthright for a platter of lentils, and who was called "Edom" for his unbridled passion [Gen. 25:30-34], or Reuben who defiled his father Jacob's bed [Gen. 49:4].[1] Indeed, Moses wrote this ordinance as a remembrance for the Israelites whom God brought out of the house of bondage when He slew every firstborn in the land of Egypt, but everyone of His firstborn sons He did redeem [see Ex. 13:14-16].

According to the law of Moses, it is written: "The firstborn of your sons ye shall give unto Me. If a woman has conceived seed, and born a man child, in the eighth day, the flesh of his foreskin shall be circumcised. And she shall then continue in the blood of her purifying three and thirty days; she shall touch no hallowed thing, nor come into the sanctuary, until the days of her purifying be fulfilled. And when the days of her purifying are fulfilled, for a son or for a daughter, she shall bring a lamb of the first year for a burnt offering, and a young pigeon, or a turtledove, for a sin offering, unto the door of the tabernacle of the congregation, unto the priest. And if she be not able to bring a lamb, then she shall bring two turtledoves, or two young pigeons: the one for the burnt offering, and the other for a sin offering: and the priest shall make an atonement for her, and she shall be clean. For they are wholly given unto Me from among the children of Israel; instead of the firstborn of the Egyptians have I taken them unto Me and sanctified them for Myself, on the day that I smote every firstborn in the land of Egypt from man to beast, saith the Lord Most High, the Holy One of Israel."[2]

Since God spared the Israelites from the final plague in Egypt, God established a claim on firstborn Israelite male children and cattle, which were henceforth supposed to be dedicated to God's service [Ex. 13:2]. However, in their stead, God placed the tribe of Levi and its cattle [Num. 3:12, 13, 41, 45]. Since there were not enough of them to provide a substitute for all the firstborn, God required the Israelites to "redeem" the remaining firstborn by paying a sum of money [Num. 3:46-51]. In this fashion the firstborn were released from the divine claim upon them and were restored to their families. From that time the firstborn males were redeemed by the payment of a sum of money, a firstborn ass by the substitution of a lamb, etc. [Ex. 13:12,13; 34:19, 20].

Although the all-pure Virgin conceived seedlessly, she did as was commanded in the law of women who conceived by seed. It is evident that the Jews of that time did not perceive who the Virgin Mary and her firstborn Son were in truth.[3]

SAINTS ARE THE FIRSTBORN

Saint Ambrose (339-397), Bishop of Milan, writes in *Letter 76* that, now, the saints are the firstborn. "Accordingly, He then received the Levites instead of the firstborn, just as He does now the saints....They are not holy through their order of birth, but by reason of their duty of holiness. For Levi was the third son of Leah, not the first" [Gen. 29:34]....The firstborn saints are of the firstborn Son of God....Thus, concerning the younger Isaac in his relationship to the older Ishmael, Sarah will say to Abraham, 'Cast out this bondwoman and her son, for the son of this bondwoman shall not inherit with my son Isaac.' This is meant by divine revelation to refer more to the inheriting of virtues than of money. Thus the Lord says to Abraham, 'In all things whatsoever Sarah shall say to thee, hear her voice, for in Isaac shall thy seed be called.' [Gen. 21:12]....Indeed, Abraham put the son of the slave-girl Hagar over nations, handing over, as it were, the full amount of his patrimony. But he gave double the amount to the son of Sarah, on whom were conferred not only temporal but heavenly and everlasting blessings."[4]

Thus, in the Orthodox ceremony for *A Woman on the Fortieth Day*, the mother, having been cleansed and washed, stands at the Church entrance with her infant. On this fortieth day the infant, male or female--whether it be the firstborn or not--is brought to the temple to be churched, that is, to make a beginning of being taken into the Church. A prayer is made on behalf of the mother too that her bodily defilement and the stains of her soul be washed away, and that she be vouchsafed the Communion of the Holy Body and Blood of Christ.

THE RITUAL OF PURIFICATION

"And when the days of their purification according to the law of Moses were accomplished, they brought Him to Jerusalem, to present Him to the Lord" [Lk. 2:22].

The King James Version of the Holy Bible erroneously translated the verse to read "the days of *her* purification". The puristic texts of the Holy Gospel, write thus: "the days for *their* purification" or *(tou katharismou afton)*, that is, of the Jews; because the Theotokos had no need of purification.[5]

The loss of blood (or seed) required ritual purification since it was looked upon as a diminution of the life principle and involved exclusion from Israel's cultic life prior to purification. According to the law, "...the life of flesh is its blood..." [Lev. 17:11; Deut. 12:23], thus the uncleanness came neither from conception nor childbirth. It was in delivery that the mother's vitality (linked with her blood) was diminished. Hence, she was "separated" from Yahweh, the Source of Life, until her integrity was restored by purification.

The flux, being a natural process instituted by God, and having been permitted to occur thus after the transgression, is neither a sin nor an uncleanness; "for these things are not truly sin nor uncleanness," according to St. John Chrysostom. The *Apostolic Injunctions*[6] assert that childbed cannot pollute a woman's nature or separate her from the Holy Spirit; but only impiety and an unlawful act. If actions that occur

227

naturally and without the exercise of human will are unclean, how much more unclean are sins, which we do with the exercise of our will? If God has pronounced these fluxes as "unclean" it was done in order to prevent the husband from having sexual relations with the new mother as a means to protect her in this time of weakness and possible embarrassment. This promotes the modesty of men and the honor of women, according to Isidore; and awe of the law of nature, according to Philo. Both the ancients and medical science today know that children conceived during the time of flux are often weaker in nature. So, for all these reasons, reverence and fear were not only instilled into women, but much more into the impetuous vehemence of the natural instinct of men.[7]

More important these laws reminded the Israelites that sex was not a part of their worship, for men could not worship until they cleansed themselves. All this was done so that they might be set apart from the other ancient cultures and their idolatrous neighbors, for whom fertility rites and temple prostitutes formed an important part of worship.[8]

One sacrifice that only the women gave to the Lord was offered after the birth of her child for her purification [Lev. 12]. She was not always required to be personally present when her offering was being presented. But mothers who were within convenient distance of the temple, and especially the more earnest among them, would naturally attend the temple. In cases such as the Virgin-Mother and her Son, coming from Galilee, it was practicable for the "purification" of the Mother and the redemption of the firstborn be combined.[9]

The book of *Leviticus* prescribes the following for women after giving birth: "And when the days of her purification shall have been fulfilled for a son or a daughter, she shall bring a lamb of a year old without blemish for a whole-burnt offering, and a young pigeon or turtledove for a sin-offering to the door of the tabernacle of witness, to the priest...And if she cannot afford a lamb, then shall she take two turtle doves or two young pigeons, one for a whole burnt-offering, and one for a sin-offering; and the priest shall make atonement for her, and she shall be purified" [Lev. 12:6,8]. Mary accepted the obligation and the purification, though in her case quite unnecessary. Nevertheless, the decision was taken and they brought Jesus also into the temple, which brings to mind the words of the Prophet Malachi, "...and the Lord, Whom ye seek, shall suddenly come into His temple, even the angel of the covenant, whom ye take pleasure in: behold He is coming, saith the Lord Almighty" [Mal. 3:1].

In the case of a poor woman, she would bring a turtle-dove or a young pigeon, one for the whole burnt-offering and one for the sin offering. [Lev. 12:8]. The Virgin-Mother could only afford the pair of turtledoves at the time of her "purification".

THE BURNT AND SIN OFFERINGS

The "sin offering" was that sacrifice which paid off or expiated a worshipper's ritual faults against the Lord. These were unintentional faults, done through ignorance [Lev. 4:13]. A sacrifice for a ceremonial fault would be the offering a woman made after she gave birth, in order to recover her ceremonial cleanliness [Lev. 12].[10]

Why was it written in the law of God that there should be a presentation of "a pair of turtledoves or two young pigeons"? Saint Ambrose informs us that "this is the true sacrifice of Christ: chastity of body and grace of the spirit. Chastity belongs to the turtledove; grace, to the pigeon. It is related that the turtledove, when widowed by the loss of its consort does not seek another, but is utterly weary of the bridal bed and even of the world itself."[11]

Thus we chant in the Canon to the Akathist: *Rejoice, O Ever-Virgin, the Dove that gave birth to the Compassionate One.*[12] Saint Cosmas (7th-8th c.) characterizes Mary as a dove and says, *The pure Dove, the Ewe without blemish, brings the Lamb and Shepherd into the temple.*[13]

When we say "burnt offering", this type of sacrifice was wholly burnt, none of it was eaten by anyone. The worshipper would bring a male animal, without blemish, and placed his hands upon the beast's head; and it was "accepted for him to make atonement for him" [Lev. 1:4]. The animal was then killed at the door. Immediately, the priest collected the animal's blood and sprinkled it about the altar. The priest then quartered the animal, offered its head and entrails on the altar, then washed the legs and entrails in water and offered them. In the case of a bird, it was simply handed over to the priest, who would take it and wring off its head, draining the blood out on the bottom of the altar [Lev. 1:15]. The bird's feathers would be cast aside with the ashes.[14]

REDEMPTION OF THE FIRSTBORN

Saint John of Damascus (c.676-c.750) writes that *He Who is without beginning, the Word of the Father, has made a beginning in time without forsaking His divinity, and as a babe forty days old He is, of His own will, brought by the Virgin, His Mother, as an offering in the temple of the law.*[15]

After the circumcision of the Christ child, there were two other legal ordinances still to be observed. Since all firstborn were God's possession, it was necessary for the family to "redeem" or "buy back" that firstborn infant from God. Therefore, the firstborn son of every household was, according to the law, to be "redeemed" of the priest at the price of five shekels of the sanctuary [Num. 18:16]. The earliest period of presentation was thirty-one days after the child's circumcision, so as to make the legal month quite complete. [Num. 8:16]. The child must be the firstborn of his mother, not his father. The redemption could be made from any priest. As head of the family, the father of the child presented the sacrifices and offerings on behalf of the entire family. The wife need not be present. Evidently, the law took into account the mother's physical condition and the hardship of travel.

The ceremony of the redemption of a firstborn son usually consisted of the formal presentation of the child to the priest, accompanied by two short benedictions--the one for the law of redemption, the other for the gift of a firstborn son, after which the redemption money was paid. It was a very solemn rite.

THE BESTOWER OF THE LAW
FULFILLS THE LAW

In the hymns of this Feast, God the Word made flesh proves beyond all doubt that He appeared among men. *The Ancient of Days for my sake becomes a child; God the most*

230

pure receives purification, that He may confirm the reality of the human flesh, which He took from the Virgin.[16]

This same Ancient of Days, who gave Moses the law on Sinai, places Himself under His own law and fulfills it in His own temple. Appearing in the temple as a babe, *Thou hast placed Thyself under the law, that Thou mightest set all free from the ancient servitude to the law.*[17]

Saint Andrew of Crete (c.660-740) also lists as a reason for the Word's condescension to be offered in His own temple is *to prove that because He received circumcision and was to be carried by Symeon, that His theophany was not in fancy nor in imagination but in very truth has He appeared unto the world.*[18]

THE SEPTUAGINT

Prior to Mary and Joseph bringing Jesus to be offered in the temple, we must interject the story of the priest, elder and translator, Symeon. He is the extremely aged priest to whom the undefiled Maiden will offer her Firstborn.

In the third century B.C., during the reign of the Macedonian Ptolemy II (286-246 B.C.), called Philadelphus, seventy Hebrew scholars gathered to prepare a translation of the Old Testament for Greek-speaking Jews who no longer understood Hebrew. The translation came to be known as the *Septuagint*. One of the teachers and translators was our Symeon.

Alexandria had been the home of a major colony of the Jewish Dispersion, where they occupied the eastern part of this great port. Their strength grew in the city and in both a spiritual and mental context, the Hellenic Jew became a phenomenon of culture. He found himself in a challenging confrontation with the literature and philosophy of the Greeks. The Alexandrian Jew spoke Greek, for such was a condition of citizenship. Indeed, a knowledge of Greek was a prerequisite of trade, business, and social intercourse. The Jew of Alexandria, like any Jew of Tarsus (e.g. the Apostle Paul) was truly the citizen of two world cultures; hence the urge to translate the Hebrew Scriptures into their "other" tongue. Actually, Hebrew was becoming a less familiar medium of communication to the Jews of Alexandria, almost an archaism of the synagogue. This too added to their desire to exalt the wisdom and history of their race and a strong enough motive to inspire the undertaking.[19] But to the all-seeing and knowing God, these were steps taken almost three hundred years in advance, thus ensuring and making available, to Greek-speaking Gentiles, Old Testament Scriptures and prophecies; hence facilitating the evangelic work of the future "Apostles to the Nations."

Further impetus arose to create a translation when Demetrios Phalerios, librarian of the vast and famous library of Alexandria, put before the monarch Ptolemy, who was a bibliophile, a proposal to add to the collection a translation of the "Jewish laws." Thus having learned about the carefully treasured and very ancient historical works written in Hebrew, Ptolemy then sent an embassy to Jerusalem with a letter to Eleazar the high priest, requesting that six elders from each of the twelve tribes should be sent to Alexandria to execute the suggested translation.[20]

The holy elder Eleazar, himself became one of the seventy translators of the Old Testament into Greek. He is better known in the annals of Church history as the teacher of the seven Maccabean sons of the righteous Solomonia. In 167 B.C., Eleazar the priest, together with Solomonia and her sons, suffered martyrdom for the purity of the Israelite faith under King Antiochus Epiphanes (died c. 164 B.C.). The Holy Church celebrates their memory on the 1st of August.[21]

Now let us return to the background history of the *Septuagint*. Eleazar went with sixty-nine elders who were thoroughly skilled in the Scriptures and in both languages. As Symeon and the others called for this work were traveling from Jerusalem, they discussed among themselves certain key verses in the books of the Prophets. Symeon then turned and said to them: "When I commenced to interpret the Prophet Isaias, I saw a verse that read: 'Behold a Virgin shall conceive in the womb, and shall bring forth a Son, and thou shalt call His name Emmanuel' [Is. 7:14]. This verse, my beloved fellows, causes me to marvel exceedingly! How is it possible for a virgin to give birth? Or how is it possible that God should be born? I cannot believe that this will ever happen."[22]

Upon uttering these words of unbelief, suddenly, an unseen hand smote Symeon and he heard a voice say: "Thou wilt behold Christ and will also hold Him in thy hands! Thou wilt not die till this has come to pass."[23]

Young in spirit, yet elderly of body, O Symeon, thou hadst received the promise that thou wouldst not see death until thou wouldst behold a young babe, Who before time is the Creator and God of all."[24]

Coming to himself, they proceeded and, little by little, the other teachers in his party reached a certain river. At that point, Symeon removed the ring from his finger and cast it into the waters, saying: "If the verse of Isaias is true, then I will receive my ring again!" The group then continued to travel on. Upon arriving in a city nearby this river they purchased fish so that they might prepare it for the approaching evening. Then, by God's good will, the same fish that Symeon purchased and began to prepare by slicing it open contained his very own ring within the entrails. Then, he believed the words of the prophecy.[25]

According to St. Irenaeus (c.130-c.236), Ptolemy "wishing to test them individually, and fearing lest they might perchance, by taking counsel together, conceal the truth in the Scriptures by their interpretation, separated them from each other, and commanded them all to make their own translation. He did this with respect to all the books. However, when they came together in the same place before Ptolemy, and they compared their translations among themselves, God was indeed glorified. The Scriptures were acknowledged as truly divine, because all of them read out the same translation, in the very same words and the very same names, from beginning to end, so that even the Gentiles present perceived that the Scriptures had been interpreted by the inspiration of God....Thus the Scriptures had been interpreted with fidelity."[26]

Saint Justin Martyr (+c.165) confirms this narrative, adding the following details: "Lest the work of the translators be interrupted and delayed by outside interference, Ptolemy ordered the construction of individual rooms for each translator, not in the city itself, but about a mile away where the Pharos stood. Another reason for this was to have each scholar make his own translation. Accordingly, attendants were assigned to care for their needs and to prevent one from communicating with another, in order that the accuracy of the work might become more apparent by the uniformity of the translations. When the king learned that the seventy scholars in their respective translations had not only conveyed the same meaning but had done so with the same words, and had not contradicted one another in a single instance, but had described the same things in the same way, he was so astonished that he concluded that the translation had been made by divine power, and he considered the men worthy of praise, since they were so dear to God. Thus, when he sent them back to their own land, he conferred many gifts upon them....This event has also been recorded by Philo,[27] Josephus[28] and many others besides."[29]

The translators' work greatly delighted the Jewish community. They pronounced an appropriate curse on any who might dare to take from the version or add to it. The king too was pleased and it was set in the library. From the first century of the Christian era, evidence of quotes from this version are abundant. As Philo the Jew commented, the version was received in Egypt with the same reverence accorded the original text. This was probably true of the whole Hellenistic world, with the possible exception of Palestine, the seat of orthodox and metropolitan Jewry.[30] Nevertheless, as a landmark in history, the translation was a monument both of literary and historical endeavor. It was a social as well as a religious contribution that cannot be overestimated; for it was a cohesive element to dispersed Jews and gave them the ability to win Gentile converts. And even though it was the Bible of the Diaspora, it also was to be the Bible of the Apostolic Church.[31]

Therefore, decades passed and Symeon waited and waited for the "Consolation of Israel". *It is not the old man who holds Me, but I uphold him: for he begs Me to let him depart.*[32]

Now let us return to the temple in Jerusalem.

+

INTO THE TEMPLE

Saint Cosmas prepares us for the coming event with the following hymn of Vespers. *Adorn Thy bridal chamber, O Sion, and welcome Christ the King; salute Mary, the heavenly gate; for she has been made as the throne of the cherubim [Ps. 79:2], and she carries the King of glory. A cloud of light is the Virgin, who has borne in the flesh the Son begotten before the morning star [Ps. 109:3].*[33]

"As it is written in the law of the Lord, 'Every male that openeth the womb shall be called holy to the Lord;' and to offer a sacrifice according to that which is said in the law of the Lord, 'A pair of turtledoves, or two young pigeons'" [Lk. 2:23-24].

"...the parents brought in the child Jesus, to do for Him after the custom of the law," [Lk. 2:27].

The venerable Bede (c.673-735) comments that Joseph is called the parent of the Saviour, though he was not the father; but that the good name of Mary might be protected, he is regarded by all as His father.[34]

THE PROPHET AND PRIEST ZACHARIAS

When the pure Virgin entered the temple with the child, Zacharias was serving his turn as high priest.

The Ancient of Days, Who in times past gave Moses the law on Sinai, appears this day as a babe. As Maker of the law He fulfills the law and, according to the law, He is brought into the temple.[35]

Saint Theophanes (+1381), Bishop of Nicaea, clearly remarks that the high priest was well aware of the true identity of the child brought into the temple.

Rejoicing, Zacharias, the high priest and preacher of God, paid homage to the Virgin and Mother who beareth the Lord of creation.[36]

He then stood the Virgin Mary in the place reserved for virgins, where women with husbands have no right to stand.[37]

However, the pharisees and priests were amazed at this, and wanted Mary to be placed in that area designated for married women. Nevertheless, Zacharias, enlightened by the Holy Spirit with prophetic power, insisted that Mary was a virgin although she had just borne a Son.

Having ministered to God as a priest according to the law, O Zacharias, thou wast shown to the whole world as a pillar of light, prophesying that Christ would come forth from the Virgin, incarnate of the Holy Spirit, the Orient from the heights of righteousness, Who doth illumine the world.[38]

The famous hymn of St. Romanos (c.490-c.556) also confirms Joseph's confrontation with the priests.

Joseph was amazed at thy seedless conception, O Theotokos, on seeing that which surpasseth nature. But he brought to mind the dew upon the fleece [Ps. 72:6; Judg. 6:37], *the bush that was unconsumed in the fire* [Ex. 3:2-4], *and Aaron's rod which blossomed forth* [Num. 17:8]. *And thy betrothed and guardian bare witness to the priests, crying, "A virgin giveth birth--and after birth still remaineth a virgin."*[39]

Thus Zacharias acknowledged the virgin birth and the divinity of Christ. A hymn of St. Ephraim the Syrian (c.306-383) relates that *Zacharias came and opened his venerable mouth and cried, "Where is the King, for Whose sake I have begotten the Voice (St. John the Forerunner) that is to preach before His face? Rejoice, Son of the King, to Whom also our priesthood shall be given up!"*[40]

On account of their high priest's actions and open declaration, the Jewish elders were discomfited by Zacharias and some even despised and hated him. Turning away from him greatly vexed, the pharisees sought to have him killed and went to advise Herod to do away with him.[41]

Both St. Gregory of Nyssa (c.335-394) and his brother, St. Basil the Great (c.330-379), concur that Zacharias was later slain between the temple and the altar because, after

236

Mary had given birth to Jesus, he brought her to the place reserved for virgins.[42]

SYMEON COMES INTO THE TEMPLE

"And, behold, there was a man in Jerusalem, whose name was Symeon; and the same man was just and devout, waiting for the consolation of Israel: and the Holy Spirit was upon him. And it was revealed unto him by the Holy Spirit, that he should not see death, before he had seen the Lord's Christ. And he came by the Spirit into the temple:" [Lk. 2:25-27].

Saint Andrew of Crete speaks of the symbolic meaning of the pair of doves offered this day. *He Who is borne on high by the cherubim and praised in hymns by the seraphim, is brought today, according to the law, into the holy temple and rests in the arms of the elder as on a throne. From Joseph he receives gifts fitting for God: a pair of doves, symbol of the spotless Church and of the newly-chosen people of the nations;*[43] whereas, the two young pigeons [Lev. 12:8], show Him as the Originator of the two Covenants, both Old and New.

THE MYSTICAL TONGS

The all-pure Virgin cried aloud, "Symeon, receive as a babe in thine embrace the Lord of glory and the salvation of the world."[44] Saint Cosmas adds these words to the Virgin: *O Symeon, knower of mysteries past speech, with rejoicing take in thine arms Christ the Word become a child, concerning Whom thou wast told long ago by the Holy Spirit; and shout aloud to Him: "The whole world has been filled with Thy praise."*[45]

The Virgin is often referred to as "mystical tongs." *Christ the coal of fire, whom holy Isaias foresaw, now rests in the arms of the Theotokos as in a pair of tongs* [Is. 6:6], *and He is given to the elder.*[46] Saint Joseph the Hymnographer also characterizes Mary thusly: *Thou camest to the temple like mystical tongs, bearing the mystical Ember, O all-pure one.*[47]

Saint Cosmas adds these details: *The aged servant of God cried, "Rejoice, O holy Lady; for as a throne dost thou carry God, Lord of the light that knows no evening and King of peace."* And then *The elder bent down and reverently touched the footprints of the Mother of God who knew not wedlock, and he said, "O pure Lady, thou dost carry Fire. I am afraid to take God as a babe in my arms, Lord of the light that knows no evening and King of peace."*[48]

SYMEON TAKES UP THE CHRIST CHILD

Bishop Nikolai Velimirovic (+1956) writes that the elderly Symeon beheld both the child and His Mother bathed in light that shone around their heads like a halo.[49] The Virgin, carrying Jesus in her arms, was rejoicing over Him. Apocryphal sources write that Symeon was filled with the greatest pleasure at the sight of angels praising Him, standing in a circle, like body guards standing by the King.[50]

Saint Romanos also makes mention of this, chanting, *While the angels sang hymns to the lover of man, Mary advanced, holding Him in her arms.*[51] The righteous man was then *constrained by joy and fear, for, with the eyes of the spirit, he beheld the ranks of archangels and of angels standing erect with reverence and glorifying Christ. He then prayed earnestly to himself and cried, "Guard me and do not let the fire of Thy divinity harm me, Thou, the only Friend of man."*[52]

"Then took he Him up in his arms, and blessed God, and said:..." [Lk. 2:28].

The hymnographers of the Church extensively speak through Symeon. Upon receiving the Christ child, St. Cosmas the hymnographer has Symeon speak immediately to the Theotokos: *"Isaias was cleansed by receiving the coal from the seraphim"* [Is. 6:6], *cried the old man to the Mother of God. "Thou dost fill me with light as thou dost entrust to me, with thy hands as with tongs, Him Whom thou holdest,*

Lord of the light that knows no evening and King of peace."[53]

Saint Ephraim points out in his *Homily on Our Lord*, that the infant Christ was actually presenting the priest to His Father and not the priest presenting Him. "Symeon the priest, when he took Him up in his arms to present Him before God, understood as he saw Him that he was not presenting Him, but was being himself presented. For the Son was not presented by the servant to His Father, but the servant was presented by the Son to his Lord. For it is not possible that He, by Whom every offering is presented, should be presented by another. So that He Who receives offerings gave Himself to be offered by another, that those who presented Him, might themselves be presented by Him."[54]

Saint Cosmas then has the priest exclaim: *O Christ that comest from God, Thou art my God.*[55] And, *Thou dost look down upon the earth and make it tremble; how can I, aged and weary, hold Thee in my arms?*[56]

THE ANGELS MARVEL

Saint Romanos declares that the bodiless host was in attendance when the Virgin offered the Christ to be presented. *The bodiless powers, looking at Him from on high, were filled with amazement, saying, "Now we see wondrous and most marvelous things, past understanding and past telling. He Who created Adam is carried as a babe. He Who cannot be compassed is compassed by the arms of the elder. He Who rests uncircumscribed in the bosom of His Father, is voluntarily circumscribed in the flesh but not in divinity, He Who alone loves mankind."*[57]

When they pronounced these words, invisibly they adored the Lord and they called men happy, because the One borne on the wings of the cherubim lived among men and appeared accessible to them on earth, but inaccessible to the angels.[58]

Saint Romanos then describes that while the Lord was being brought in, He was carried along with the burnt offerings of the temple. The melodist then asks, *O Thou, good and philanthropic One, Who hast of old received the offerings of Abel and of other righteous men, to whom, All-Holy One wilt Thou present the sacrifices and burnt offerings? I know that there is no one greater, O Lord Who art not apprehended with mere reason, for Thy Father in no way surpasses Thy substance; Thou art co-essential and co-eternal. But in order that Thou might reveal that Thou art in truth what Thou hast become, that is, protector of Thine own law, Thou hast presented the sacrifice.*[59]

THOU WAST SHOWN TO BE GREATER THAN MOSES

Patriarch Germanos (c.635-733), in a hymn, calls upon the Elder Symeon and the children of the Church to worship Him Who once bestowed the law on Mt. Sinai. *Receive, O Symeon, Him Whom Moses once beheld in darkness, granting the law on Sinai, and Who has now become a babe subject to the law. This is He Who spoke through the law: this is He Whose voice was heard in the prophets, Who for our sakes has taken flesh and has saved man. Let us worship Him.*[60]

"'Lord, now lettest thou Thy servant depart in peace, according to thy word: For mine eyes have seen Thy salvation, which thou hast prepared before the face of all peoples; a light for revelation to the nations, and the glory of Thy people Israel'" [Lk. 2: 29-32].

Thus, in icons, the very ancient holy man, leaning forwards, holds the child in his two hands, which are covered with his garment. This is a sign of veneration. Saint Joseph follows the Mother of God with the offering of poor parents. The turtledoves (*tohr*) symbolize the Church of Israel and that of the nations. Israel has been called a "turtledove" or inferred to as one in Ps. 67:13; 74:19 [KJV], Cant. 4:1; and Is. 60:8. The birds also symbolize the two Testaments, of which Christ is the unique Head. The venerable Symeon appeared with his head uncovered and with the long hair of a Nazarene. The often uplifted head of Anna in the background expresses her prophetic inspiration.[61] The figure of St. Symeon the "God-receiver" is very important. In fact, God appeared to Moses enveloped in darkness, while Symeon carries the incarnate Word in his arms.

Moses was counted worthy to see God through darkness and sounds not clear [Ex. 19:16-19]; *and with his face covered* [Ex. 34:29-33] *he rebuked the unbelieving hearts of the Hebrews.*[62]

In a homily, St. Ephraim writes that the priest testified that he was offered as an offering. "Symeon then, who calls himself His servant [Lk. 2:30], is let to depart in peace to God and is presented as an offering to God. Well did Symeon say that his eyes had seen salvation, for He was freed from the world which is full of snares, that he might go to Eden which is full of pleasures. He who was priest said and testified that he was offered as an offering, that from the midst of the perishing world he should go and be stored up in the treasure house which is kept safe."[63]

Saint Ephraim continues: "It is evident that Symeon inwardly received grace from the child Whom he openly received and carried in his arms; for, through Him Who is glorious, even when He was carried, being small and feeble, he that carried Him was made great. But inasmuch as Symeon endured to carry on his weak arms that majesty which the creature could not endure, it is evident that his weakness was made strong by the strength that he carried. For at that time, Symeon together with all creatures was secretly upheld by the almighty strength of the Son. As far as that majesty stooped to our littleness, so far should our love be raised up from all desires to reach that majesty."[64]

Saint Romanos also point out that the babe that Symeon held in his embrace, in fact, upholds all. *Miserable but a short time ago, I (Symeon) am now made strong, since I have seen Thy salvation, O Lord. Thou art the perfect image of the incomprehensible nature of the Father. Thou, the inaccessible luminary, the unchangeable seal of divinity and the brightness of His glory* [Heb. 1:3] *which, in truth, illuminates the spirits of men, existing before time and the Creator of the universe. For Thou art the light shining from afar, inviolate, infinite and incomprehensible--yet Thou hast become man.*[65]

LET THY SERVANT DEPART!

Realizing the magnitude of the event, one hymn characterizes the priest as filled with dread. *Beholding Thee as a babe, O Word, begotten of the Father before all ages, Symeon the venerable cried aloud: "I am distraught by fear at holding Thee, O Master, in my arms. But now, I pray Thee, lettest Thou Thy servant depart in peace, for Thou art compassionate."*[66]   And, *Mine eyes have seen the mystery hidden from the ages, made manifest in these latter days* [Col. 1:26], *the light that disperses the dark folly of the nations without faith and the glory of the newly-chosen Israel. Therefore, let Thy servant depart from the bonds of the flesh to the life filled with wonder that knows neither age nor end, O Thou Who grantest the world great mercy.*[67]

Symeon, like Zacharias the priest, is called upon to answer for his conduct.   Thus Patriarch Germanos writes: *Symeon, tell us: Whom dost thou bear in thine arms, that thou dost rejoice so greatly in the temple?   To Whom dost thou cry and shout: "Now I am set free, for I have seen my Saviour"?*   And the elder answered, *This is He Who was born of a virgin: this is He, the Word, God of God, Who for our sakes has taken flesh and has saved man.*[68]

The ninth century hymnographer, Andrew Pyros, also chants that Symeon proclaimed *the union of the Godhead with mankind.   And seeing the heavenly God as mortal man, he makes ready to withdraw from earthly things, and raises his cry in joy: "Glory to Thee, O Lord, Who hast revealed to those in darkness the light that knows no evening."*[69]

The Christ child is *Lord of life and Master of death,*[70] and the *Deliverer of souls.*[71]   Saint Joseph the Hymnographer (c.816-886) has Symeon speaking to the child saying, *Let me, Thy servant depart, who has been worn out with the writing of the law and am bowed down with old age.*[72]   Saint Cosmas adds: *Take Thy servant, who is weary of the shadow, and make him a new preacher of the mystery of grace, as he magnifies Thee in praise.*[73]   Thus, *in both fear and joy Symeon held the Master in his arms...singing the praises of the Mother of God."*[74]

Symeon then *pleads to depart from corruption*[75] that he might *depart and declare to Adam that "I have seen the pre-eternal God and the Saviour of the world made a babe without undergoing change."*

Saint Romanos also takes up the theme of Symeon announcing the good news among those souls of the Old Testament.   *Dismiss me, O Holy One, into the presence of Abraham and the patriarchs.   Miserable and wretched are the present circumstances, since they are transitory and always have an end. For this reason Thou hast separated all the righteous from the world here. Thou Who art immortal, send me away from this life, which is mortal: give my body over to mortal death and, as with all Thy friends, grant me, O merciful One, life spiritual and eternal. Since I have seen Thee in the flesh and have been deemed worthy to behold Thee, I perceive Thy glory together with Thy Father and the Holy Spirit; for Thou hast, at the same time, remained on high and come here below.*[76]

Saint Romanos then writes that the *King of heavenly powers received the prayer of the righteous man. And, unseen by others, addressed him: "Now, O My friend, I release thee from the temporal world for an eternal home; to Moses and the other prophets I send thee. Tell them that as they foretold in their prophecies, lo, I have come and have been born of a virgin, I have been seen by men in the world and I have dwelt among them, as they foretold* [Bar. 3:38].[77]

Saint Cosmas concludes with these words of Symeon: *"I depart to declare the good tidings to Adam abiding in hades and to Eve"; and with the prophets he sang rejoicing: "O God of our Fathers, blessed art Thou."*[78]

Saint Ephraim then describes Symeon as having *lulled Him, saying, "...In Thee shall I be raised from the grave into Paradise!"*[79]

When Symeon reposed, Holy Tradition tells us that he was at least three times a centenarian.

THE ELDER BLESSES
THE VIRGIN-MOTHER AND JOSEPH

Saint Romanos then writes that the *immaculate Virgin was amazed hearing these things spoken.* The elder then addressed her: *All the prophets heralded thy Son Whom thou hast produced without seed. Also, a prophet has announced these events and proclaimed the miracle* [Ez. 44:2]*: that thou, Mother of God, art the closed gate, for through thee the Lord has entered and come forth. And the gate of thy chastity was not opened or disturbed; He traveled through it and kept it intact.*[80]

"And Joseph and His Mother marvelled at those things which were spoken of Him. And Simon blessed them..." [Lk. 2:34].

Saint Photios (+c.897), Patriarch of Constantinople, comments that Symeon bestowed upon them a common blessing. Joseph is not deprived of the appearance of fatherhood. But by that which he said to Mary, separately from Joseph, he proclaims that she is the true parent.[81]

After being granted the fulfillment of the prophecies concerning himself, the prophet and priest Symeon will foretell in figures the Passion of her Son.

THE PROPHECIES OF SYMEON, THE GOD-BEARER

Saint Romanos writes the following of Symeon: *Now all-holy, blameless one, I shall prophesy and explain to thee everything about the downfall and the resurrection. Thy Son has in store for Him the life, redemption and resurrection of all. The Lord hath not come so that some might fall and others be resurrected, nor doth the all-merciful One rejoice in the fall of man, nor has He become manifest under the pretext of causing to fall those who are upright; but*

rather, He zealously draws near them that have fallen to raise them up again, redeeming from death His own creature.[82]

"And Symeon...said unto Mary His Mother, 'Behold, this child is set for the fall and rising again of many in Israel; and for a sign which shall be spoken against'" [Lk. 2:34].

Saint Romanos then has Symeon give with exceeding clarity a more detailed account of the Passion. *The manner of the fall and resurrection has been established for the upright in the light of grace. Inspired by Christ, I prophesy to thee that the Cross will be the sign which the lawless will erect for Christ. Some will proclaim Him God crucified; but others will call Him merely man. The opinions of the pious and impious thus are set in opposition.*[83]

Saint Cosmas explains this statement in the following hymn. *Thou hast been set up in Sion as a stumbling stone and rock of offence for the disobedient* [Is. 8:14, Rom. 9:33], *but unto the faithful Thou art salvation which cannot be broken.*[84]

Saint Gregory of Nyssa comments that "He is called the 'salvation that is prepared before the face of all peoples'; but likewise 'the fall and the resurrection of many.' The divine wish is the salvation and the sanctification of each person. Their fall or resurrection is within the will of each person, both of them that believe and disbelieve."[85]

Saint Basil adds that "The Cross in Scripture is called a sign of contradiction. For Moses, it says [Num. 21:19], made a brazen serpent and set it up for a sign. For it is a sign of a wondrous, yet hidden thing; seen by the simple, but understood only by those whose minds are prepared."[86]

Saint John Chrysostom (354-407) speaks, saying, "For whose fall? Without doubt those that believe not, and those that placed the Innocent upon the Cross. For whose resurrection? Those that give thanks; those that turn to Him with a grateful heart."[87]

Saint John continues, "'And for a sign which shall be contradicted.' Of what nature is the sign that is spoken of here? None other than the torment of the Cross: the Sign that the Church proclaims as the salvation of the world. This sign shall be contradicted by the unbelieving and by the impious."[88]

As we know, at that time, the Jews were awaiting, in the person of the Messiah, an awesome king and conqueror, who would subdue all rulers and all thrones to the throne of David, and found a great messianic kingdom, in which the Jews, as the direct descendants of Abraham, would occupy the first place and rule over all. As far as the pagans were concerned, they were not to have any right to this kingdom of the glorious Messiah. When Christ had appeared on the earth, these false messianic hopes of the Jewish people had reached their highest degree of intensity, despite the fact that the traits and course of the true Messiah are depicted completely different in the Old Testament. The death of Christ the Saviour on the Cross would be a stumbling block [1 Cor. 1:23] which caused all those Jews to stumble who were infected by false messianic expectations and narrow nationalistic exclusiveness and aims.[89]

A SWORD SHALL PIERCE THY SOUL

"'Yea, a sword shall pierce through thy own soul also; that the thoughts of many hearts may be revealed'" [Lk. 2:35].

Saint Cosmas chants, *"And a sword shall pierce thy heart, O all-pure Virgin,"* Symeon foretold to the Theotokos, *"when thou shalt see thy Son upon the Cross."*[90]

We reject the faulty tradition that Origen started by associating the oracle of Symeon with doubt or hesitation on her part.[91]

Saint Cyril of Alexandria (+444) comments that the meaning of 'sword' is the pain which she suffered for Christ, in seeing Him Whom she had brought forth crucified. She did not know that He would be mightier than death and rise from the grave.[92]

Saint Romanos here, too, speaks of her maternal anxiety, chanting, *Thine anxiety will be a sword for thee, but after this He will send quick healing for thy heart and unshaken peace to His disciples.*[93]

Saint Paulinus of Nola (353-431), in a letter, writes concerning the blessed Symeon's divine oracle: "Does this relate to her maternal feelings when she later at the time of the Passion stood by the Cross where the child of her own womb was nailed, and was herself pierced by the anguish of a mother's heart? Was the sword which pierced her heart that sword formed by the Cross, which before her eyes had transfixed her Son of the flesh?...Symeon said 'soul' not 'flesh' because devoted love resides within the soul and it is there that the sting of grief pricks like the sword. This is the case when the soul is...tortured by the grief or pain of inward love, as happened with Mary."[94]

Also, Saint Gregory of Nyssa comments that this verse does not mean that she alone would be caught up in His passion. For as some confessed God upon the Cross, so others ceased not from revilings and recriminations. Or this was said in that at the time of the passion the thoughts in the hearts of many persons were revealed, and they were purified in His resurrection.[95]

At this meeting in the temple, the all-pure one did not fully know of the future passion of her Son. Therefore, speaking as a mother, she said to the priest: "What is this that thou dost utter, O Symeon? I have never been sorrowed, for it was with joy that I received Him and with joy that I gave birth unto Him, and it is with joy that I feed Him. Never have I been saddened by Him, for He is the joy and gladness of all the world. I, the Virgin, saddened? In bearing Him, I had none. Therefore, why dost thou say that a sword shall pierce me?"[96]

Yet Symeon continued: "My Lady Virgin, exceedingly glorious, for thou art called the Mother of this child and thou hast become the Queen of the universe and the Mother of God. However, when thou wilt behold that which shall come to pass, then thou shalt bring to mind these words of mine. Then, thou wilt weep and lament for Him; then will a sword enter into thine own heart concerning that of which I have spoken, O all-pure Virgin."[97]

Saint John Chrysostom writes that, in other words, Symeon is saying to her, "And thou, who art His Mother, shall thou also not suffer? Is it perhaps because thou dost avow thyself the Mother of this child, because thou hast brought Him forth to the light, because thou hast sheltered Him in thy womb--for thy womb was the vessel in which was wrought this wondrous work--that thou shalt be free from all trial? It is because thou are called the God-Birthgiver and the Mother of God, and because thou hast conceived without nuptials, and become the Mother of thy Creator, that thou shalt be free from every temptation? Far from it: for even thine own soul a sword shall pierce."[98]

Saint John adds that the aged Symeon, foresaw as a prophet her future suffering, and likened it to a sword in her soul. Indeed, according to the prophecy of the just Symeon, there shall be no one left free of temptation; for the disciples fled and Peter denied Him.[99]

Bishop Nikolai Velimirovic comments that already a sword passed through her soul when the righteous Joseph doubted the source of her conception. But now others would come: when she would flee into Egypt from Herod's sword; when she would witness and learn of the Jewish elders' hatred and plotting against her Son Who daily preached and worked wondrous works among men. But the greatest sword that would pierce her soul would be when she would stand beneath the Cross of her Son and God. This sword was the one foreseen by the holy elder.[100]

Bede comments that "even to the end of this present world, the sword of most dire tribulation will not cease to pierce the soul of the Church, when the sign of faith is contradicted by the wicked."[101]

THE GLORIOUS PROPHETESS ANNA
OFFERS HYMNODY AND CONFESSION

"And there was one Anna, a prophetess, the daughter of Phanuel, of the tribe of Aser: she was of a great age, and had lived with a husband seven years from her virginity; and she was a widow of about fourscore and four years, who departed not from the temple, but served God with fastings and prayers night and day" [Lk. 2:36-37].

Symeon carried the pre-eternal Word of the Father in bodily form, and he revealed the Light of the Gentiles, the Cross and the Resurrection; and Anna was proved to be a prophetess, preaching the Saviour and Deliverer of Israel.[102]

Saint Cosmas brings out the point that it was both Symeon and Anna that were being offered. *Of old, the people offered a pair of doves or two young pigeons [Lev. 12:8]. In their stead, the godly elder and Anna the prophetess, sober in spirit, ministered and gave glory to the child of the Virgin, the Only-begotten Son of the Father, as He was brought into the temple.*[103]

"And she coming in that instant gave thanks likewise unto the Lord, and spake of Him to all them that looked for redemption in Jerusalem" [Lk. 2:38].

Saint Ambrose comments that Anna was so dedicated to the duties of her widowhood, and such was her virtue, that she is deemed worthy to announce to others that the Redeemer of all men had come."[104]

Saint Ephraim comments that *Anna embraced Him, and put her mouth to His lips, and the Spirit dwelt upon her own lips. As when Isaias' mouth was silent, the coal* [Is. 6:6-7] *which approached his lips opened his mouth; so Anna burned with the Spirit of His mouth, yea, she lulled Him, saying, "Son of the Kingdom,...that hearest and art still, that seest and art hidden, that knowest and art unknown, God, Son of Mary, glory be unto Thy name."*[105]

Saint Cosmas tells us that *Anna, sober in spirit, makes terrible things known, as she confesses Christ the Creator of heaven and earth.* The Church then, through St. Cosmas, then asks her to speak: *O daughter of Phanuel, come and stand with us, and give thanks to Christ our Saviour, the Son of God.*[106]

The Words of the Prophetess of God:

"Behold," uttered the prophetess, "O men, what is to be found this day? This small child established firmly heaven and the earth [Heb. 1:2; Is. 40:22]. This small child is the Creator of all the world. Behold this small child! He made the angels. He made the air which we breathe. He made the atmosphere to help warm the earth. He commanded the waters to be so that we might drink. He set the boundaries, and land appeared in the midst of the waters. It is He Who has shut up the sea with doors when it broke forth [Job. 38:8]; this child has brought the winds from out of His treasuries [Ps. 134:8]. He commanded and there came to be

249

tall plants, fruitful trees, ferns and cone-bearing plants. He created the beasts, the great fish of the sea, the winged creatures flying above, quadrupeds and creeping things of the earth. This child covereth the earth with clouds, and prepareth rain for the earth; He giveth snow like wool [Ps. 147:5,7]. Simply put, He is the Creator of the universe.

"He fashioned Adam and breathed upon his face the breath of life and the man became a living soul. In the days of Noah He opened the cataract of heaven [Gen. 7:2]. It was He Who set aright our forefathers. It was this child Who made the covenant with Abraham and confirmed an oath, 'I will bless thee, and I will multiply thy seed as the stars of heaven.' He increased Abraham, multiplied Isaac and expanded and spread Jacob.

"By the rod of Moses He freed our forefathers, saving Moses out of the hands of pharaoh and showed him great wonders when He divided the sea, but the waters overwhelmed our Egyptian foes.

"Behold, O men, this small child Whom Symeon holds in his arms! He delivered our fathers from slavery in Egypt. He dried up the Red Sea and led forth the people that trusted in Him. He was the light at night when we walked. He overshadowed the heat of the day with a cloud [Ex. 13:21]. This child rained manna upon them in the desert [Ex. 16]; He nourished us forty years in the wilderness. He kept us invulnerable from our enemies. He caused water to gush forth from the smitten rock [Ex. 17:6; Num. 20:11]. He sweetened the bitter waters of Merrha [Ex. 15:23]. By the power of this infant, Jesus of Navee slew enemy kings, the walls of Jericho collapsed and Jesus the son of Navee was greatly strengthened [Josh. 6:20]. This infant crushed their strongholds and brought to nought their rule. It was He Who cast out the nations that formerly inhabited this land and established our forefathers therein. He gave our fathers a land flowing with milk and honey as their inheritance [Jos. 6:6].

"This infant preserved the Three Children from the flames of the Babylonian furnace [Dan. 3:21-26]. Yea, this infant, this small one, delivered Daniel out of the mouths of the lions [Dan. 6:27]. It was He Who raised up our people. It was He Who magnified the Hebrew peoples. This child decreed that this temple be dug and raised on high [Esd. 3].

"Esteem not lightly this child, because He is a child, nursed at the breast, resting in the bosom of His Mother, unable as yet through infancy to press the soles of His feet to the earth, and circumcised on the eighth day after the manner of other infants. He Who is a child is co-eternal with the Father. And now, for our salvation, He has come down from on high and taken flesh from this holy Virgin. This child, whom Symeon now holds in his embrace, all of heaven and earth are not able to contain, though He was contained in the womb of this Virgin-Mother. His age is measured within a month, yet there were none who went before Him. This, too, is He of Whom Isaias has told us, saying, 'for a child is born to us, and a Son is given to us' [Is. 9:6]. Note the prophet says the one is born, the other is given. What is born is seen with the eyes; what is given is known by the mind and the thought alone. All this on account of our sins. This infant is hymned by the angels, glorified by the archangels, worshipped by the cherubim, seraphim, thrones, authorities, rulers, and powers. With them, let us worship Him and glorify Him as true God."[107]

Saint Amphilochios (339-400), Archbishop of Iconium, writes: "Such were the words of Anna, such was her wondrous testimony. So was the mission of her widowhood happily fulfilled."[108]

Saint Cosmas says the same similarly of the prophetess: *Holy Anna, sober in spirit and venerable in years, with reverence confessed the Master freely and openly in the temple; and proclaiming the Theotokos, she magnified her before all who were present.*[109] It is not impossible to imagine that the prophetess knew the Virgin Mary when she was growing up in the temple.

According to St. Amphilochios: "Anna is the glory of widowed women; a woman truly in sex and state, but in the order of the prophets. Her life was passed in widowhood, her conversation in heaven. Frail in body and bowed with age, strong and upright of soul. Wrinkles lined her face, but prudence showed itself there. Brought to time's infirmity by years, but vigorous in the knowledge of God, she was given to fasting, and averse to all greediness. She departed not from the temple, not going from house to house. Her delight was in singing the praises of God, not in idle nonsense;

251

prophesying, not in recounting fables; meditating on divine things, not preoccupied with things that are not becoming.

"Anna indeed is to be esteemed above others, for she attained to the gift of prophecy and was a vessel of the Holy Spirit. She pointed out the signs of His Coming to all who awaited the advent of Christ in the flesh.

"Do not, O beloved, pass over lightly the testimony of Anna, in which she described the power of the Lord to all who were present. She acted as a protectress of the Lord, and in His presence spoke in His behalf. O new and unheard of thing! She was but a poor widow, and she makes plain that over which the priests and scribes had long pondered, uplifting the hearts of those who heard her with fervent hope. She made manifest to Israel the salvation of the Lord, which she declared by arguments and by signs; and now she also was to be delivered. Anna discerned the infant Lord. She perceived too the gifts and little offerings which were borne with Him, and for Him. Not on that account was she confused, nor by His helpless and tender age. She confessed that this child was the Lord and the Destroyer of sin."[110]

Saint Gregory of Nyssa adds a very interesting interpretation when he says, "Perhaps someone will say that it was for this reason that Symeon came before her. Symeon stood for the law; for his name means 'obedience'. Anna stands for the dispensation of 'grace', which is the meaning of her name. Between them stood Christ. Accordingly, the Lord dismisses the former, now dying with the law, and cherishes the latter, living on through grace."[111]

Bede, in his *Commentary on Luke*, says, "In a mystical sense Anna stands for the Church, which, in this present world is as it were, widowed by the death of her Spouse. Even the number of the years of her widowhood designates the time in which the Church, continuing on in the body, sojourns afar from her Lord. Seven times twelve make fourscore and four. Seven relates to the full course of this world, which was wrought in seven days. But twelve belongs to the completeness of the apostolic teachings....The period of seven years during which she lived with her husband is in accord with the time of the Lord's incarnation. Here because of the special quality of the Lord's majesty, the simple number of seven years expresses, in sign, perfection, the time in which He taught while clothed in the flesh. It also favors the mysteries of the Church that Anna is interpreted in the Lord's 'grace', that she is the daughter of Phanuel, who is called the 'face of the Lord', and descended from the tribe of Aser, that is, 'blessed with children' [Deut. 33:24].[112]

"And when they had performed all things according to the law of the Lord, they returned into Galilee, to their own city Nazareth" [Lk. 2:39].

In the holy Orthodox Church this festival seems to have been observed since the fourth century, and the iconography associated with the feast developed from the fifth century onwards.[113]

Chapter XIII.
The Massacre of 14,000 Infants,
in Bethlehem and Its Borders,

the Memory of which the Holy Church
Celebrates on the
29th of December

+ + +

"Behold, the angel of the Lord appeared to Joseph in a dream, saying, 'Arise, and take the young child and His Mother, and flee into Egypt, and be thou there until I bring thee word: for Herod will seek the young child to destroy Him' [Mt. 2:13].

"When he arose, he took the young child and His Mother by night, and departed into Egypt" [Mt. 2:14].

She who knew not wedlock said, "O Son without beginning, I am blessed beyond words in Thy strange birth, wherein I have been spared all travail. And as I behold Thee fleeing from Herod with his sword of sorrow, I am torn in soul. But do Thou live and save them that honor Thee."[1]

HEROD, THE FOREIGN KING OF THE JEWS

According to Eusebius, in his *Ecclesiastical History*,[2] Herod was the first foreigner to be king of the Jewish nation, having been entrusted by the Romans with the government of the Jews, thus fulfilling the words of Moses: "A ruler shall not fail from Judah, nor a prince from his loins, until there come the things stored up for Him; and He is the expectation of the nations" [Ex. 49:10].

We, too, acknowledge the fulfillment of these words when we chant, *With the dying away of the princes of Judah's tribe, O all pure one, thy Son and God came down as Ruler and now is truly King over all the earth.*[3]

254

Not long after the magi's visit, Herod left for Rome where he remained for about one year.[4]   Coming back to Judea, Herod knew that he had been mocked by the magi, and his heart swelled with rage. He had the roads searched in his mad desire to have the family seized and put to death; but he could not find a trace of them.[5]

"Then Herod, when he saw that he was mocked of the wise men, was exceeding wroth" [Mt. 2:16].

Saint Ephraim the Syrian (c.306-383) labels Herod a fox and Jesus as the Lion of Judah, when he wrote: *Herod, that base fox, that stalked about like a lion, as a fox crouched down and howled, when he heard the roaring of the Lion Who came to sit in the kingdom according to the Scriptures. The fox heard that the Lion was a whelp and a suckling. The fox then sharpened his teeth and then lay in wait to devour the Lion before He grew up and the breath of His mouth should destroy him.*[6]

Saint Romanos (c.490-c.556) relates how Herod listened to the sayings of the prophets that He might ascertain better Who the child was and where He might be found. *The anxiety, which Herod had always feared, now came to him when he did not wish it; for what he had not expected he learned on hearing the sayings of the prophets. Isaias wrote: "For a child is born to us, and a Son is given to us, Whose government is upon His shoulder: and His name is called the Angel of great counsel." He is a strong God upon His throne and in the manger; and He is everywhere, and infinite. Herod, frightened, deeply feared Him, and investigated carefully to learn where the King of the universe had been born.*[7]

HEROD SUMMONS HIS SOLDIERS

Saint Cosmas (7th-8th c.) writes that *Herod reckoned the time the guiding star had appeared, which brought the magi to Bethlehem, there to worship Christ with gifts. Led back to their own land by that same star, they returned not to Herod, but mocked the wicked perpetrator of infanticide* [Mt. 2:7-12].[8]

Mulling over his thoughts, Herod pondered how he could most quickly destroy the infant whom the magi proclaimed. Then, after calculating the time from the appearance of the star to the Magi (which was nine months before they entered Jerusalem), he added the year of his own absence abroad, and

255

counted twenty-one months. Desiring to be certain of the Christ child's death, he would slay those infants twenty-four months and younger, instead of twenty-one months old. Then he called forth his army and commanded them to slay all male children under two years of age.

"Herod...sent forth, and slew all the children that were in Bethlehem, and in all the coasts thereof, from two years old and under, according to the time which he had diligently inquired of the wise men" [Mt. 2:16].

Herod commanded his men not only to enter Bethlehem, but also into the large province of Juda, on account of the misquoted verse of the chief priests and scribes who said, "Bethlehem of Juda" [Mt. 2:6]. What the Prophet Micah actually prophesied was the small hamlet of "Bethlehem, house of Ephratha, art few in number to be reckoned among the thousands of Juda" [Mic. 5:2]. Thus, the mutilated scripture verse ushered in the mutilating deaths of thousands of children.

Saint Romanos then describes a demented Herod whose *mind was unhinged and his reason darkened--not by drunkenness but by envy.*[9]

Saint Romanos then presents the following scene:

Calling his army, Herod gave them license. He spoke to them in a rough voice, as follows:

Herod: "Go quickly into cities and the country-side, in full armor, bearing yourselves proudly. Assuming a garb of mercilessness, slay all the sons of Bethlehem. This war has no difficulty, no cause for timidity. I send you against babes, tender two-year olds; no one opposes a royal order. All the people tremble."[10]

When the army heard this, at once, they answered Herod, saying:

Army: "We are afraid to bring about what thou hast commanded, for fear that we be ridiculed. For who of foolish men will not laugh that we make war on babes?"[11]

Nevertheless, Herod sternly reminded them that they were men under authority and best not dare to defy the order, making them accomplices to treason and no friend of Caesar; for Rome had only one king, who would not share his glory with another, especially a Hebrew subject Who would not worship their many deities.

His men then complied, reasoning among themselves, that it was a tradition of Bethlehem to produce kings.

Army: "Hitherto, Bethlehem produced David, the great king; therefore, if it seems best to thee, O king, let all Bethlehem and its boundary be searched so that among the infants slaughtered there, we may find this babe Who has been born and destroy Him with the others. The birth was revealed to thee and the place made known to thee; the magi mocked thee and the prophets terrify thee. Command thy followers, then, and we shall wipe from the earth the One Who desires to overthrow thy kingdom. Do not be fearful that thy power will soon be destroyed."[12]

HEROD,
THE ENEMY OF THE CHILDREN OF BETHLEHEM

Saint Romanos characterizes Herod as *lamenting that his power should be so soon destroyed and, therefore, he mowed down the children like wheat.*[13] The melodist now calls Herod a wolf in pursuit of the Whelp, saying, *The wolf, having tracked down the great Whelp, arouses the wicked dogs against Him. They run in and outside of Bethlehem, seeking their prey. He mangles the lambs, but not the Lion, for he cannot with his glance meet Him face to face.*[14]

We know that the wicked slayer of children did not slay the Christ child; though *he reaped a bitter harvest of children, he failed to seize and slay the wheat ear of life. For being the Giver of life, as God, He escaped from the pursuer by His divine power.*[15]

What about the innocent slain? How has the Church accepted their sacrifice? Let us hear the Dismissal hymn for this occasion: *As acceptable victims, as newly-picked flowers and divine first-fruits and newborn lambs were ye offered unto Christ, Who was born as an infant.*[16] And, *The ungodly king seized the multitude of infants and transformed them into martyrs, for he knew not that they, being citizens of the kingdom on high, would expose his madness unto the ages.*[17]

The *Synaxarion* of the day adds that "Herod labored in vain, not knowing that man cannot forestall the counsel of God. Whereby sending those infants into the Kingdom of the Heavens, he prepared for himself eternal torment."

RACHEL WEEPS FOR HER CHILDREN

"Then was fulfilled that which was spoken by Jeremias the prophet, saying, 'In Rama was there a voice heard, lamentation, and weeping, and great mourning, Rachel weeping for her children, and would not be comforted, because they are not'" [Mt. 2:17-18; Jer. 31:15, KJV].

The terrible command was carried out to the letter. The gruesome slaughter began and infants were transfixed to the points of swords. Herod's soldiers cut off some of the children's heads with their swords, dashed others on the stones, trampled some of them underfoot and drowned others with their own hands.

Icons at the Kariye Djami show mothers attempting to shield their sons, with their hair disheveled in despair and grief. To the side is often depicted a pile of dismembered infants.[18]

Saint Romanos gives us a painful description of the scene of soldiers pursuing nursing mothers. *For they pursued the mothers and, when they caught up with them, they snatched the child from their arms. With bared swords, the soldiers met the mothers carrying their children in their arms. So that each one cried, "Kill them, but the bosom of Abraham will receive them like faithful Abel." Thus the lawless one shed the innocent blood of blameless children.* And, also, one must consider Zacharias (father of the Forerunner) who would bring his accusation before God against them that murdered him.[19]

The saint further describes the massacre. *With daggers they are slain mercilessly. Some were transfixed and breathed their last horribly; others were cut in two. Still others had their heads cut off as they suckled and drew milk from the breasts of their mothers. Then, as a result of this, the cherished heads of the babes hung from the breasts, and the nipples were still held within their mouths by their delicate teeth. Then the distress of the women who were nursing the infants redoubled and became intolerable as they were physically torn from their two-year old infants.*[20]

Thus, *Mothers were made childless and, at an untimely age, infants were bitterly harvested, paps grew dry and sources of milk were stopped. Great was the calamity!*[21]

In Scripture, the repose of our righteous foremother Rachel is the first related instance of a mother's death in childbirth. After hard labor in bringing forth Benjamin, she gave up the spirit and was buried near the road to Ephratha, in the district of Bethlehem [Gen. 35:17-19].

Saint Ambrose (339-397) writes in his *Letter 45*: "And Rachel died in childbirth because, even then, as the patriarch's wife, she saw Herod's wrath which spared not the tenderest years. Likewise, in Ephratha she gave birth to that Benjamin of surpassing beauty, the last in the order of mystery, namely, Paul, who was no small grief to his Mother (the Church) before his birth, for he persecuted Her sons (the Christians). She died and was buried there, that we, dying and being buried with Christ, may rise in the Church."[22] In another letter to the same priest, he comments that "Rachel wept for her babes that were washed with her tears and offered to Christ."[23]

A hymn also confirms this of Rachel that she foresaw in the spirit, the massacre of the infants. *Rachel was without consolation, beholding the unjust slaughter and timeless death; and she wept for them while suffering in her womb, but now she rejoiceth, beholding them in the bosom of Abraham.*[24]

Saint Ephraim reminds us that *Rachel had cried to her husband, and said, "Give me children"* [Gen. 30:1]. *But blessed be Mary, in whose womb, though she asked not, Thou didst dwell, O Gift, that poured itself upon them that received it.*[25]

RIGHTEOUS ELISABETH

One of the mothers who understood that her eighteen-month old child was in mortal peril was righteous Elisabeth, the Virgin's first cousin on her mother's side. Elisabeth's son, John, the firstborn and only son of the high priest was certainly a target for Herod's soldiers. In the *Protoevangelium*, we learn that when the soldiers were searching for

John, the elderly and venerable Elisabeth took the lad and went up into the hill-country, and kept looking where she might conceal him; but there was no secret place to be found.

Going up into the mountain, the elderly Elisabeth, groaned with a loud voice--for she could not climb up--and uttered, "O mountain of God, receive mother and child." Straightway, the mountain cleaved and received Elisabeth and her son. A light then shone about them and an angel of the Lord was with them, watching over them.[26] This scene is confirmed in both the icons and hymns of the Church.

Saint Andrew of Crete (c.660-740), borrowing from apocryphal sources, chants, *The lawless Herod seized suckling*

260

infants from their mothers' embraces: and Elisabeth, taking up John, prayed to God before a rock, saying, "Receive a mother with her child." And the mountain received the Forerunner.[27]

THE NURSLING OF THE WILDERNESS

As we said, an angel of God was sent to minister to them. According to Bishop Nikolai Velimirovic (+1956), the place where Elisabeth hid with John was a cave that had opened. Then, by God's power, a spring flowed and a fruit-bearing palm grew.[28]

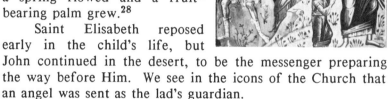

Saint Elisabeth reposed early in the child's life, but John continued in the desert, to be the messenger preparing the way before Him. We see in the icons of the Church that an angel was sent as the lad's guardian.

The Evangelist Luke then simply states that "the child (John) grew, and waxed strong in spirit, and was in the deserts till the day of his showing unto Israel" [Lk. 1:80].

Thus, we chant, *O Baptist, thou hast come forth as a messenger from a barren womb, and from thy very swaddling clothes hast thou gone to dwell in the wilderness. Thou wast made the seal of the prophets: for the prophets saw Him in many forms and foretold dark sayings, but thou wast counted worthy to baptize Him in the Jordan.*[29]

HEROD SLAYS THE HIGH PRIEST

According to the *Protoevangelium*, in the meantime, Herod made a search for the infant John. He decided to send his officers to his father, Zacharias the priest. At that moment, Zacharias was ministering at the altar when they said to him, "Where hast thou hid thy son?" Zacharias replied, "I am a minister of God and a servant at the altar. I sit constantly in the temple of the Lord. I do not know where my son is."

The officers then departed and made their report to Herod. Herod then was incensed and said, "Is not his son likely to be a king in Israel?" And Herod remembered the malice and complaints of the priests and pharisees towards Zacharias in some other temple matters.[30]

Therefore, Herod again dispatched his servants to Zacharias, saying, "Tell us the truth, where is thy son?; for thy life is in Herod's hand." Zacharias then replied to them, "I am a martyr for God, and if he shed my blood, the Lord will receive my soul. Moreover, know this, ye shall shed innocent blood."

Then, carrying out Herod's order, they slew the high priest before the dawn, that the slaying of him might not be prevented by the people. And they slew him in the vestibule of the temple, at the entrance of the altar.[31]

The hymns of St. Zacharias' feast day, the 5th of September, characterize the holy prophet thusly: *As a pure priest thou didst enter into the Holy of Holies and, clad in sacred vesture, didst blamelessly minister unto God, observing the law like Aaron and leading the tribes of Israel like Moses, in the pure signaling of the little bells. Wherefore, thou wast slain.*[32] The hymns also confirm the place of his death as *in the midst of the temple thou wast unjustly slain, O right-glorious one, finishing thy godly course in martyrdom.*[33]

Bishop Nikolai Velimirovic writes that the high priest, in the midst of his priestly service,[34] was slain and that his blood spilled over the marble and, clotting, stained the stone so that it could not be removed. Thus it remained as a testimony to Herod's wickedness. Forty days after the holy Zacharias' repose, blessed Elisabeth, his wife, also entered into rest, leaving behind the lad John in the wilderness where he was fed by an angel and guarded by God's providence.[35]

Concerning the violent murder of the holy prophet and priest, one tradition ascribes his death to the scribes and pharisees, on account of his proclaiming the virgin birth. The other tradition, taken from the *Protoevangelium*, claims that the holy man was slain by the orders of Herod during the massacre of the innocents and, thus, he suffered with them for the newly born Saviour of the world.

The two traditions need not be contrary to one another. His death was wanted by both his own people and the Romans, each for their own malicious reasons. It is unlikely that the Hebrews themselves would destroy their own high priest before the altar in the very act of ministering; it is more probable that they instigated Herod and his minions to do away with him. The scribes and pharisees  bided their time until a convenient moment arose when they might incite Herod's fears and thus have him eliminate Zacharias. Hence, Gentile soldiers found admittance into the holy place. Similarly the Jews would seek to destroy Jesus by the hands of others [Mt. 27:2; Mk. 15:1; Lk. 23:1; Jn. 18: 28, 31].

Christ Himself uttered "that upon you may come all the righteous blood shed upon the earth, from the blood of righteous Abel unto the blood of Zacharias, son of Barachias, whom ye slew between the temple and the altar" [Mt. 23:35; Lk. 11: 50-51]. There are some who thought that Christ was referring to the slaying of Zacharias, the son of Jehoida the priest, who was stoned at the commandment of King Joash, in the court of the house of the Lord [2 Chron. 24: 20-22]. However, in this instance, He was referring to Zacharias the High Priest, son of Barachias.

HEROD'S DESPICABLE END

After warring against God and slaughtering the children that were in the Christ child's age group, Herod turned on the Jewish elders, who had previously revealed to him where the Messiah was to be born. He slew Hyrcanes the High Priest and seventy elders from the Sanhedrin. This Hyrcanes was the grandfather of his best-loved wife Mariamne. A little later, Mariamne herself was put to death. In 6 B.C., her sons, Alexander and Aristobulus, were condemned and executed. In 4 B.C., a few days before Herod's death, Antipater, his eldest son, who had been instrumental in the condemnation of Alexander and Aristobulus, was slain by his orders. These murders were accompanied by many other friends and kindred, who were constantly falling under suspicion of treason.

However, immediately after the crime perpetrated against our Saviour and the other infants, the punishment sent by God drove him on to his death. In the seventeenth book of his *Antiquities of the Jews*, Josephus writes as following concerning Herod's end: "The disease grew more severe, God inflicting punishment for his crimes. He had a terrible desire for food which it was not possible to resist. He was affected also with ulceration of the intestines, and with especially severe pains in the colon, while a watery and transparent tumor settled about his feet. He suffered also from a similar trouble in his abdomen. Nay more, his privy member was putrefied and produced worms. He found also excessive difficulty in breathing, and it was particularly disagreeable because of the offensiveness of the odor and the rapidity of respiration. He had convulsions also in every limb, which gave him uncontrollable strength."[36]

At the time of his death, he recalled that there were many captive Jews in prison. So that they might not rejoice in his evil demise, he ordered them all slaughtered, saying, "that all Judea and every house may weep for me even against their will."[37] Shortly thereafter, this cruel and demented tyrant lost his inhuman soul and was given over to eternal torments.

Relics of the Holy Innocents,
Grotto of the Nativity, Bethlehem.

Chapter XIV.
The Flight Into Egypt

+ + +

AN ANGEL APPEARS TO JOSEPH

Before Herod gave the command to slay the children from two years old and under that were in Bethlehem, and in all the coasts thereof [Mt. 2:16], the goodly and just elder Joseph was then warned by God in a dream. **"The angel of the Lord appeared to Joseph in a dream, saying, 'Arise, and take the young child and His Mother, and flee into Egypt, and be thou there until I bring thee word: for Herod will seek the young child to destroy Him'"** [Mt. 2:13].

Thus gentle and mild-mannered Joseph, when he arose, began to set his household affairs in Nazareth in order. Then, full of faith, Joseph took his son James[1] and, complying with the bidding of the angel, **"he took the young child and His mother, by night, and departed into Egypt"** [Mt. 2:14]. The Virgin rode a donkey, carrying the young child in her arms. Joseph or James strode in front, taking turns in leading the beast.

According to St. Cyril of Alexandria (+444), Joseph fled into Egypt by the command of an angel in the month of March, in order that "the lamb be not killed in the milk of his mother..." [Ex. 23:19].[2]

Tradition places the entry of the Lord into Egypt as the 1st of June.[3]

Saint Ephraim the Syrian (c.306-383) chants, *As a young dove* [Cant. 6:8], *she carried the Eagle, the Ancient of Days* [Dan. 7:9], *singing lovely praises as she carried Him:* "O my Son most rich, in a tiny nest Thou hast chosen to grow. O

265

melodious harp, Thou art silent like a child, please let me sing to Thee with the lyre whose cords stir the cherubim; pray let me speak to Thee."[4]

Saint John Chrysostom (354-407) comments that "as soon as He was born the tyrant rages; then comes flight, and a journey into exile; and without cause His Mother is forced to fly into a land of strangers. Indeed, she, who scarcely ever went outside her home, is bidden to set out on a long and wearisome journey, because of this wondrous newborn child and His miraculous birth."[5]

IN PRAISE OF JOSEPH

At the venerable age of eighty, when most men have entered that stage of life of retirement and reflection, Joseph is called to active service. Saint John Chrysostom comments that "The elderly Joseph is not offended at hearing that he must flee home, family and occupation and fly, secretly, as a fugitive. He was a man of faith. Note that he does not make inquiry when he might return from

THE FLIGHT INTO EGYPT

MAP 1

dwelling in a strange land, although the angel had spoken in an indefinite manner. Neither was he regretful at the command, but submissive and obedient, bearing these trials with cheerfulness."[6]

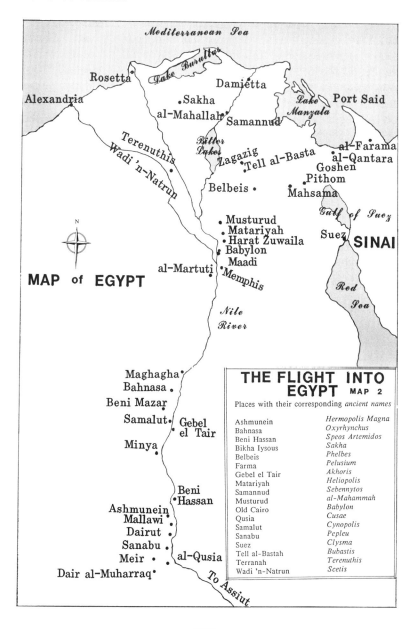

MAP of EGYPT

THE FLIGHT INTO EGYPT MAP 2

Places with their corresponding *ancient names*

Ashmunein	*Hermopolis Magna*
Bahnasa	*Oxyrhynchus*
Beni Hassan	*Speos Artemidos*
Bikha Iysous	*Sakha*
Belbeis	*Phelbes*
Farma	*Pelusium*
Gebel el Tair	*Akhoris*
Matariyah	*Heliopolis*
Samannud	*Sebennytos*
Musturud	*al-Mahammah*
Old Cairo	*Babylon*
Qusia	*Cusae*
Samalut	*Cynopolis*
Sanabu	*Pepleu*
Suez	*Clysma*
Tell al-Bastah	*Bubastis*
Terranah	*Terenuthis*
Wadi 'n-Natrun	*Scetis*

267

ENTERING EGYPT

After consulting numerous sources, the present chapter will reconstruct the route taken by the holy refugees from Palestine to Dair al-Muharraq in Upper Egypt. Many traditions will be drawn upon. Interested pilgrims may visit most of these sites to this day. Details concerning the sites today were also extracted from contemporary scholars, Coptologists, guide books and maps.

It is most probable that the divine travelers avoided the well-traveled routes when escaping and fleeing into Egypt. During that time, there were many Jewish descendants to be found in Alexandria, in the Delta and the Nile Valley. Leaving Nazareth, they first went to the ancient Philistine city and seaport of Askelon. Askelon was where Samson slew thirty Philistines [Judg. 14:19]. At the time of their visit, Askelon was a strong and beautiful center of Hellenistic culture.

From Askelon, in a southerly direction, for about forty kilometers, there is the site of the ancient Canaanite stronghold of Gaza [Gen. 10:19]. At the time of Christ this city too was a center of Hellenistic culture. By taking the route that runs parallel to the shore of the Mediterranean Sea, the divine travelers would have crossed, in two hours, the Wadi Gaza. A day's journey from Gaza, brought them to the ancient township of Jenysos. Today, this village is part of the Gaza Strip and is known as Khan Yunis.[7] The next town on their route would have been Raphia (Rafah). Continuing along the caravan route, about forty-four kilometers or two days travel, they would cross a stream, the Wadi al-Arish, which formed a type of natural boundary between Palestine and Egypt. A little further on, they would have arrived at the city of Rhinocoroura (Rhinocolura), the present-day al-Arish or El-Arish. The first town which they would have reached after El-Arish was Ostrakini. Ostrakini has since disappeared, though there is a village called Straki, which is situated in the vicinity of al-Arish.[8]

Situated between al-Arish and Port Said, almost at the southwestern end of the caravan route, from Judea to Egypt, there is the celebrated city of Pelusium (al-Farama), seaport and key to Egypt. Pelusium had many marshes, water holes and swamps lying around it. Saint Epiphanios (c.315-403) also makes mention that the holy family visited this historical city. Thus the holy family entered the land of Pharaoh when Gaius Turranius (7-4 B.C.) was the Roman Prefect of Egypt.[9] It has also been calculated that for someone to reach the nearest point in Egypt traveling from Nazareth would be about fourteen days.

The travelers then crossed the narrow isthmus at al-Qantara (the bridge), today a small village along the Suez Canal. It was over this isthmus, which separates Lake Manzala from Lake Ballah, that the ancient caravan route from Judea to Egypt passed. Of further interest, it was this same route that had been used centuries before by both the Patriarchs Abraham and Jacob and his sons. Hence, in the steps of the patriarchs, the holy travelers entered the province of Goshen.[10]

In icons depicting their flight, Mary is seen riding. We also see James, Joseph's youngest son, leading the donkey on which Mary is seated. Joseph strode behind the animal. Often we see the infant Jesus astride on Joseph's shoulders. There are other icons in which we see the child Jesus and Joseph following behind the animal. Mary then is depicted turning about in the saddle and extending her arms to her Son, who responds in like manner. It is not certain if other sons of Joseph accompanied them into Egypt.[11]

Thus were the words of the Prophet Isaias fulfilled: "In that day shall Israel be third with the Egyptians and the Assyrians,...and blessed be My people that is in Egypt, and that is among the Assyrians, and Israel Mine inheritance" [Is.

19:24-25]. In his Nativity morning sermon, St. John Chrysostom comments, "What dost thou say, O Judah, who was first and has become third? The Egyptians and Assyrians are placed before thee, and Israel, the firstborn, is last? Rightly shall the Assyrians be first, since they, through the magi, first adored Him. The Egyptians, after the Assyrians, received Him flying from the treachery of Herod. Israel is numbered in third place, for only after the ascent from the Jordan was He acknowledged by His Apostles."[12]

Saint John also comments that "since Babylon and Egypt, more than the rest of the world, burnt with the fire of iniquity, the Lord, manifesting even from the beginning that He desired to restore both these regions to Himself and bring them to worthier things, by correcting and amending them. At the same time, He intimates to the whole earth that His gifts and bounties were now to be looked for: to Persia, He sends the magi, and to Egypt He goes Himself with His Mother."[13]

Most of the adventures of the holy travelers, as described in the apocryphal gospels, are believed by many to be fabrications. We have gleaned from these sources a few incidents that have a more sober content and which clearly are maintained in the ancient traditions of the Egyptian Orthodox who are the guardians of many of these holy sites, which can be seen to this day.

We have avoided using those narratives which make the child Jesus appear as a precocious infant behaving well beyond His tender years. Saint John Chrysostom is adamant on this point when he writes: "Now if He had performed miracles as a child, the Israelites would not have needed another to declare Him. For He Who came among men, and by His miracles was so made known, not to those only in Judea, but also to those in Syria and beyond, and Who did this in three years only, or rather Who did not need even these three years to manifest Himself, for immediately and from the first His fame went abroad everywhere. He, I say, Who in a short time so shone forth by the multitude of His miracles, that His name was well known to all, was much less likely, if while a child he had from an early age wrought miracles, to escape notice so long. For what was done would have seemed stranger as done by a boy, and there would have been time for twice or thrice as many, and much more.

270

But in fact He did nothing while He was a child, save only that one thing to which Luke has testified, that as the age of twelve years old He sat hearing the doctors, and was thought admirable for His questioning.

"Besides, it was in accordance with likelihood and reason that He did not begin His signs at once from an early age; for they would have deemed the thing a delusion. For if when He was of full age many suspected this, much more, if while quite young He had wrought miracles, would they have hurried Him sooner and before the proper time to the Cross, in the venom of their malice; and the very facts of the dispensation would have been discredited."[14]

What is accepted by holy ecclesiastical tradition, and is expressed in both Orthodox hymnology and iconography, is the destruction of the idols of Egypt: In fact, it was prophesied by the Prophet Isaias that the Lord Himself would enter Egypt: "Behold, the Lord sits on a swift cloud, and shall come to Egypt: and the idols of Egypt shall be moved at His presence, and their heart shall faint within them" [Is. 19:1]. Very often, in the background of "The Flight Into Egypt" icons, there are depicted the cities of Egypt and demons leaping off the walls.

Saint Athanasios the Great, of Alexandria (296-373), asks, "Who (but Christ) among the righteous ones or of the kings came into Egypt and the statues fell before them?"[15]

IN THE NILE DELTA

The holy travelers then entered the Nile Delta. The first town they visited was Bubastis (Tell Basta), two kilometers south of Zagazig. As soon as the Christ child entered the town, the idols and statues collapsed before Him. This event greatly exasperated the heathen priests and the inhabitants refused them hospitality and even ill-treated them. However, a good person of Tell Basta suggested to them a village nearby the town.[16]

THE AREA INFESTED WITH THIEVES

Apocryphal sources relate an incident that took place in the desert country. According to the *Egyptian Synaxarion*, the following meeting with two brigands took place in Basatah (Bubastis or Tell al-Bastah). We are told it was an area that was infested with robbers. Therefore, the Virgin and Joseph purposed to pass by that territory under the cover of night. As they were journeying, they beheld two

271

robbers that appeared to be asleep in the road, but there was a great number of their confederates also asleep in a place close by.[17] The names of these two thieves were Dismas and Gestas. Dismas, roused from his sleep, arose and went across the road to the Mother of God to see what she held at her breast. Seeing the Christ child, he marvelled at His beauty and remarked, "If God were to take human flesh, He would not be more beautiful than this child!" Then Dismas turned to Gestas and said, "I beseech thee to let these persons go by quietly. Let not our comrades be roused and perceive the coming of these people." However, Gestas would not consent. Again, Dismas turned to him and said, "I will give thee forty drachmas and, as a pledge, take my belt. Dismas gave it to his companion before he finished speaking that he might not open his mouth or make a noise.[18]

The Lady Theotokos, full of gratitude for the kindness rendered unto them by this robber, turned and said to Dismas, "My child will reward thee richly for having spared Him this day. The Lord God will receive thee to His right hand and grant thee pardon of thy sins."

Indeed, more than thirty years later, at the Crucifixion of her Son and God, it was those very two thieves that were also crucified on either side of Jesus. Dismas would be to Christ's right hand and Gestas to the left. Dismas, while on his cross, repented of his whole life, and said, "This Man hath done nothing amiss" [Lk. 23:41]; he even rebuked Gestas who had reviled the Lord. And, as we well know, Dismas was that same day with Christ in Paradise [Lk. 23:43].[19]

AL-MAHAMMAH

Leaving this area, they went and camped under the shade of a tree for several days. It was there that Christ caused a spring to flow, into which the Virgin bathed the child and washed His clothes. This place today is called Al-Mahammah or the "Bath". A tremendous number of visitors, both Egyptians and foreigners still frequent this place. Some reports state that the divine travelers passed through this way on their return back home.[20]

THE TREE OF THE VIRGIN

We know that from Al-Mahammah they left for Belbeis (Bilbais), alongside the modern Ismailia Canal where, on the way, they also rested in the shade of a tree that since has been known as "The Tree of the Virgin Mary."[21]

After they visited Bubastis, a day's journey further south, they reached the towns of Bilbais, alongside the modern Ismailia Canal. Commemorating their visit to Bilbais, in the center of town, the Uthman ibn al-Haris al-Ansari Mosque is on the very site; there is also the Coptic Church of St. George, situated in the northeastern part of town.[22]

Traveling northwards along the Nile Delta, they departed for Meniet Genah,[23] then they reached the town of Sebennytos (Samannud or Samanoud), which is situated along the Damietta branch of the Nile. The local tradition in Samannud related that the present Egyptian Church of Apa Nub was built on the ruins of an ancient church dedicated to the holy Virgin, which, in turn, was built on the site where the family stayed.[24]

Having crossed the Damietta branch of the Nile towards the west, they then went on to Burulus and to Al-Mahallah, where they crossed the Nile to the western bank. They then stayed some days at the village of Sakha, situated about two kilometers south of Kafr ash-Shaikh. It is claimed that Jesus put His foot on a stone, and the mark of the sole of His foot remained upon the stone. The place became known as Bikha Isous, that is to say, the "footprint of Jesus" or "Jesus' heel."[25]

THE DESERT OF SCETIS

After Bikha Isous, the family traveled westward and crossed the Rosetta branch of the Nile. Continuing their journey, they beheld from afar the Desert of Scetis (the Wadi an-Natrun). An Orthodox tradition states that Jesus blessed this desert place.[26]

Indeed, it is evident that their presence blessed this place, for, in the future, it became the sight of many monasteries and hermitages, filled with ascetics and spiritual fighters that served God night and day. The renown of these thousands of choirs of angels in human form and the multitudes of martyrs, of the early centuries of Christianity, is well documented.[27]

The area that they passed was to have more than fifty monasteries, of which only four are inhabited today by about 320 monks.

Although there is no tradition to support it, they would most probably have seen the Desert of Scetis from the town of Terranah, the ancient bishopric of Terenouti, fifteen kilometers north of al-Khatatba. It is about forty kilometers from the fourth century Monastery of St. Macarios (Dair Abu Maqar).

IN THE NILE VALLEY

Continuing their journey southward, the travelers reached the city of On, the biblical Beth-Shemesh (Heliopolis). At that time, the city of On or Heliopolis was deserted, not having yet recovered from the destruction it incurred at the time of the Persian invasion in 525 B.C. It was only natural that the family would have avoided lodging in a deserted pagan city. Consequently, they sought some dwelling place nearby where Jewish families had been living on account of its proximity to the Jewish center at Leontopolis.[28] Thus they put in at the site of the present village of Matariyah or Mataria, now a suburb of Cairo.

MATARIA

They arrived in Ein Shams, now called Al-Matariyah, northeast of Cairo (near Heliopolis), where, after troublesome effort, they found rest under a tree. The place is still shown to this day and is also named after the holy Virgin.

Near the village, they saw a sycamore fig tree (*ficus sycomorus*). While Joseph went into the village, the holy Virgin found shelter with the Lord under this tree. She had become greatly fatigued by the excessive heat of the desert sun. This type of tree, which is known to attain a height of sixty feet, then bowed its crown down to the ground and gave shade to the holy travelers.

274

Its lower branches opened in such a way that mother and child could go under it and rest.[29]

Then, by divine power, a miraculous spring of water gushed up under the tree. The Virgin then washed the clothes of the Christ child from that water and then threw the water around that place. Again, by God's grace, a tree exuding balsam grew; balsam appeared only in this place.[30]

Joseph then found a hut nearby and the family settled therein, all the while being greatly refreshed by the wonderful spring.

This was the only spring of water to be found in Egypt, for all other water in Egypt finds its source in the Nile River, which branches out into innumerable channels.[31]

THE IDOLS FALL

Another apocryphal account preserves the following tradition: At length, they drew near to a great city of the Egyptians, in which there was an idol, to which the worshippers of other idols and deities of Egypt brought their offerings and vows. There was a priest that ministered to this idol who, as often as satan spoke out of the idol, this priest would relate the things he heard to the inhabitants of the land.

This priest had a son who was about three years old. The young lad was possessed and tormented by a great many demons. Through the boy, they would utter many strange things. When the demons seized him, he would walk about with torn clothes or naked and cast stones at whomever he encountered.

It was nearby to this idol that there was the inn of the city, into which Joseph had taken them. It was then that all the magistrates and priests of the idols assembled before that idol and made inquiry, saying, "What means all this dread and consternation which has befallen all in our land?" The idol then answered them, saying, "The unknown God is come hither, Who is truly God; nor is there any one besides Him, who is worthy of divine worship; for He is truly the Son of God. Wherefore, on account of His coming, there is the present commotion. We ourselves are affrighted by the greatness of His power."

When the demonized son of the aforementioned priest had his usual disorder befall him, he came into the inn where

Joseph brought them. When the Virgin had finished washing the clothes of the Lord Jesus, she hung them out to dry on a post. Now the possessed lad took down one of the articles of clothing and laid it upon his head. Straightway, the demons fled from out of the lad's mouth in the shape of crows and serpents. From that time, the lad was healed and he began to sing praises and give thanks to the Lord Who had healed him. When the priest beheld his son completely restored and in his right mind he inquired after the cure he received. The lad answered, "When the demons seized me I went to the inn. I found there a very handsome woman with a boy. She had just finished washing his swaddling clothes and hung them out to dry. I took one of these and, upon putting it on my head, the demons fled from me." At this, the priest rejoiced and said to the lad, "My son, perhaps this boy is the Son of the living God Who made the heaven and the earth."

Then, straightway, this idol, the chief of them all, fell down. Whereupon, all the dwellers of the land, besides others, ran together. For as soon as the Christ child came among them, not only this idol was broken to pieces, but all the idols that were in that land fell down and turned into hills of sand, for they were destroyed by a greater power.[32]

In accordance with the Prophet's words, O Virgin, in truth, we call thee a light cloud; for, sitting on thee, the Lord hath come to overthrow the Egyptian hand-wrought images of deception, and to enlighten them that serve them.[33]

Saint Ambrose (339-397) comments on the light cloud, saying, "This signified the Lord Jesus, who was to come in a light cloud, that is in the Virgin Mary, who was a cloud on account of the inheritance of Eve, but light because of her virginal integrity. She was light because she did not seek to please man, but God. She was light because she did not conceive in iniquity, but begot a child under the over-shadowing Spirit; nor did she bring forth in fault, but with grace."[34]

Bishop Nikolai Velimirovic (+1956) gives a dual meaning to the term "light cloud" on which the Lord will come into Egypt. He writes: "It means the Lord's body, in which He will clothe His divinity, for a man's body is like a thick cloud in which the soul is shrouded. This is, then, a prophetic vision of the incarnate Lord....However, other interpreters think that the "light cloud" also refers to the most pure Mother of God, who, by long fasting and prayer and other ascetic labors, made her body as light as a cloud. This cloud--the body of the Mother of God--was especially light from her conquest of the passions that weigh down the bodies of men."[35]

Saint Romanos chants, *At the very time Jesus arrived in Egypt, straightway, all of the statues fashioned by man were shaken down. For the One Who caused trembling in Herod also brought on the quaking of the idols. He was hidden in the arms of His Mother, but He acted as God. He proceeded into Egypt and an angel from on high ministered to His flight.*[36]

Indeed, we commemorate this event when we chant in the *Akathist Hymn to the Theotokos: Lighting in Egypt the illumination of truth, thou didst dispel the darkness of falsehood. And unable to bear Thy strength, O Saviour, her idols fell; and they that were set free therefrom cried to the Theotokos, "Rejoice, uplifting of men! Rejoice, downfall of demons! Rejoice, thou who didst trample upon the delusion of error! Rejoice, thou who hast censured the deceit of idols! Rejoice, sea which drowned the noetic pharaoh!"*

THE PROPHECY OF JEREMIAS

In his old age, the Prophet Jeremias lived in Egypt [Jer. 43:8-9 KJV], after being forced by some Jews to go with them to Egypt.

Bishop Nikolai Velimirovic (+1956) writes that the prophet sojourned there for fours years and prophesied to the Egyptian pagan priests that their idols would fall and all their graven images would be destroyed when a virgin mother with a child, born in a manger, would enter Egypt.[37]

After being stoned by his own countrymen, the Prophet Jeremias was almost deified by the Egyptians who interred him with honor befitting a king. After his repose, he was

277

revered as a wonder-worker.[38]   Indeed, the Egyptian priests remembered this prophecy and, in accordance with it, depicted a similar scene in their temples.   They venerated this image which portrayed a virgin resting in bed, and a child, wrapped in swaddling bands, placed in a manger beside her.   In later years, when Pharaoh Ptolemy inquired of the priests the meaning of the image, they replied that it was a mystery.   A mystery that was foretold by a Hebrew prophet to their forefathers and that they were awaiting its fulfillment.

BABYLON

Then the holy travelers headed southward, to Babylon of Old Cairo. They stayed there for some time, in a cave. The cave is now part of St. Sergios (Abu Sarga) Church.[39]

LEAVING UPPER EGYPT

According to oral tradition, the holy travelers, leaving for Upper Egypt, which is to the south, went by Memphis. In a sailing boat, they set out from the spot where the present Church of the Holy Virgin with its three cupolas at Maadi lies, some twelve kilometers south of Cairo.[40]

According to oral tradition, there was at that time a synagogue in that place, to which the family attended. Joseph then had become acquainted with the sailors of the Nile boats.   The holy family was then invited to be taken south to Upper Egypt.   They stopped in Munyat as-Sudan, on the western bank of the Nile, about twenty-five kilometers south of Cairo, that is south of Badreshein.   Later a church was founded by the Christians dedicated to the Virgin, and was called al-Martuti, which is loosely taken from the Greek words *Meeter Theou* or Mother of God.[41]

Thus, sailing southward on the Nile, they passed Maghagha.   Twelve kilometers southwest of Maghagha is the village of Ishnin an-Nasarah.   Local tradition there relates that the waters of the well, about eighty meters north of the Church of St. George, were also blessed by the child Jesus, when the family passed through this village, on their way to

Baysus (Dair al-Ganus), about seven kilometers west of Ishnin. The sacred well of Dair al-Ganus is located at the western end of the south aisle of the Church of the Virgin.[42]

Ten kilometers in a southerly direction, on the edge of the desert, there is the ancient city of Oxyrhynchus, the present town of al-Bahnasa.[43] According to local oral traditions, they came to a place east of Bahnasa, near Beni Mazar. The place was later called "the house of Jesus". They stayed there four days.[44] It is recounted that they were given refuge on a high place with water springs and that was good for grazing. Today, in al-Bahnasa, there is only one church.[45]

Near ancient Cynopolis, the present village of al-Kais, the travelers took a boat to travel southward. Thirty-five kilometers from that site, they then crossed the eastern bank, where they stopped at Gebel El Tair or Gabal at-Tair "the mount of birds", which is almost opposite Samalut and Bayahu. There is some local tradition there that when the family passed by this mountain, a large rock was about to fall on the boat, and the holy Virgin was very frightened. Jesus, however, stretched forth His hand and prevented it from falling, but the imprint of His left hand remained on the rock.[46] Since then, the mountain has become known as the Palm Mountain. The famous Church of the Blessed Virgin Gabal at-Tair may only be reached by boat. Saint Helen, the mother of St. Constantine the Great, is reputed to have built the church which also came to be known as "Our Lady of the Palm." Some ten thousand pilgrims come annually to this church which may be reached after ascending 166 steps cut in the face of the cliff.[47]

From Gabal at-Tair, the family sailed southward, passing on their way, the first port of Khoufou, the present day Minya (El Minya), then the rock temple of the goddess Pekhet, called by the Greeks Speos Artemidos. The site of that temple is now the present-day Bani Hassan ash-Shuruq (Beni Hassan). Finally, they passed the temple of Ramses II, on the ruins of which the Roman Emperor Hadrian built the town of Antinoupolis in 130 A.D. This particular site is occupied now by the village of ash-Shaikh Abada.[48]

Opposite the ruins of Antinoupolis there is the town of ar-Rodah, which is built on the site where the family disembarked, in order to proceed to the famous city of Khmunu, the Hermopolis Magna of the Greeks. At present, this is the village of al-Ashmunain (Ashmunein).[49] Records show that the Romans collected a large number of various taxes that became a burden to the Egyptians. Although the holy family traveled extensively, they too must have paid a toll when they traveled to Upper Egypt, that is south on the Nile.[50]

IN HERMOPOLIS OF EGYPT

When the divine refugees drew near the city of Hermopolis (Ashmunein), wearied from their long journey, they went up to a tree to rest a little. But the tree was very tall and did not render much shade. This particular tree was called "Persea" by the natives and they worshipped it as a god. They believed that some divinity was hidden within it but, in fact, an evil spirit dwelt within the tree. As the family approached, the tree trembled and, the evil spirit, greatly terrified at the presence of the Christ Child, fled. The tree then bent its crown down and worshipped its Maker like a rational creature. Thus the tree gave them much shade and they found rest. From that day, the tree received miraculous healing power from Christ the Lord, to heal every human sickness.[51]

Sozomen (4th-5th c.) in his *Ecclesiastical History* also mentions that in Hermopolis of the Thebaid "there survived a huge palm tree, of which the branches, the leaves, and the least portion of the bark, are said to heal diseases, when touched by the sick. The Egyptians relate that when Joseph fled with Christ and the Virgin, from the wrath of Herod, they went to Hermopolis. When entering the gate, this largest tree, as if not enduring the advent of Christ, inclined to the ground and worshipped Him. I relate what I have heard from many sources concerning this tree....The inhabitants of Egypt and of Palestine testify to the truth of these events, which took place among themselves."[52]

THE TEMPLE OF 365 IDOLS

*I have gone down into the land of Egypt, but, O
Mother, I have laid low with an earthquake the idols of
Egypt made by the hands of man. And sending into Hades
the enemies that seek My life in vain, with the power that I
alone possess, I shall lift up and save them that honor
thee.*[53]

When the divine refugees were
in the regions of Hermopolis, they
entered into a certain city of
Egypt which is called Sotinen
(Sotrina). They knew no one from
whom they could ask hospitality.
Wherefore, they went into the
temple which is called the "Capitol
of Egypt". In this temple there
was to be found 365 idols that
were set up so that divine honors
and sacred rites could be performed
in front of one for every day of
the year.

It is noteworthy that blessed
Jerome (347-420) remarks in *Isaias*
that "No nation was so given to
idolatry and worshipped such a
countless number of monsters as
the Egyptians."

It came to pass that when the
blessed Virgin entered the temple
with her Son, that all the idols fell
on their faces shattered and broken
to pieces. Thus, they plainly
showed that they were nothing.

According to the *Gospel of
Pseudo-Matthew*, when Aphrodosios,
the governor of the city, heard the news, he went to the
temple with all his army. The priests of the temple assumed
that Aphrodosios and his men would see vengeance taken
upon those on whose account their gods had fallen. However, when the governor entered the temple and beheld the
gods lying prostrate in pieces, he went up to the blessed
Mary, who was carrying the Lord in her bosom, and adored

Him. He then turned to his army and friends and addressed them: "Unless this were the God of our gods, our gods would not have fallen on their faces before Him. By their silence they confess Him as their Lord. Unless we, too, confess Him, we may run the risk of His anger and come to destruction. Thus it happened to our pharaoh who, not believing in powers so mighty, was drowned with all his army." Wherefore, all the people of that city believed in the Lord God.[54]

The ruins of the Basilica of Hermopolis Magna are situated just outside the village of Ashmunein. About ten kilometers southward, the family stayed a few days in Manlau, the present town of Mallawi. There are numerous churches, now Coptic, in this town and two are dedicated to the holy Virgin.[55] One local tradition says that they stayed at a nobleman's house and he was very hospitable to them. However, he suffered many evils for their sakes, but was blessed by the child Jesus.

FURTHER SOUTH IN UPPER EGYPT

Two days further traveling in a southerly direction, the family came to the town of Phyls or Philes in the Thebaid. Local tradition has it that this town was very charitable and the family remained with them several days. Today, there may be seen the Dyrout Monastery, some twenty kilometers south of Ashmunein.[56]

From Philes, the present Dairut ash-Sharif, they traveled via Pepleu, the present Beblaw, to the town of Sanabo or Sanabu.

According to the *Infancy Gospel*, the holy family always received sufficient provision for their journey from the people who received them.[57]

THE DEMONIAC WOMAN

Near Sanabu there was a demoniac woman beset by satan. She could not bear to wear clothing nor live in a house. As often as they bound her with chains or thongs, she rent them asunder and fled naked into the waste places. At times she would be seen standing at crossroads or in cemeteries where she would throw stones at people. All her activities brought heavy calamities upon her acquaintances.

It happened that the blessed Virgin saw this woman and greatly pitied her affliction. Upon this, satan, in the form of a young man, immediately fled the possessed woman, crying out, "Woe to me, because of thee, O Mary, and thy Son!" Therefore, the woman was delivered from her torment and restored to her senses. Then she blushed on account of her nakedness and, shunning the sight of men, went to her home and friends. She then gave an account of the entire matter to her father and relations, who were the chief notables of the city. They, in turn, received the Virgin and Joseph with the greatest honor and finest hospitality.[58]

THE DUMB BRIDE

The following morning, after having received sufficient supply of provision for the road ahead, they departed. That evening they arrived in another town where a marriage was about to be solemnized. However, by the arts of satan and the practices of some ill-intentioned enchanters, the bride had become dumb and could not utter a word. When the Lady Mary entered the town carrying the Lord Christ, the dumb bride espied them and approached the Christ child to take Him in her arms. Thus doing, she closely hugged Him and kissed Him and then the string of her tongue was loosed, her ears opened, and she began to sing praises unto the God that had restored her. That evening, all the inhabitants exulted with great joy believing that God and His angels had come down among them. In this town, they remained three days, where they were entertained with the greatest respect and offered splendid hospitality.[59]

After being furnished provisions for the road, they departed to another city. There are also traditions existing that Christ cured both a young girl and an infant boy of leprosy when they were washed in His leftover bath water.[60]

THE CITY OF CUSAE

After staying a few days, they left for the city of Cusae (Qus-qam) or old Qoussieh, but now known as the village of al-Qusia.[61] According to Aelianus, Venus Urania and her cow were worshipped in that place. As the an-  cient city of Gosu, it had served as the capital of the Lower Sycamore Nome. At the time when the holy travelers arrived, the Temple of Idols was surmounted by an idol arrayed with seven veils. When Jesus had reached the gate of Cusae, the seven veils were rent asunder and the idol fell and was dashed to pieces. Then the demons that had inhabited the idol cried out to the priests of the temple, "If thou dost not pursue that Woman and the Child Who is with her, and the old man and the boy with them, and drive them away from this town, they will put an end to your service and we will depart from this town!" When the one hundred priests of the idols heard this threat, they pursued the holy ones with rods and axes in order to strike them.[62] Thus ill-treated and driven away, in their weariness and fatigue, they escaped to the village of Mirah or Meir, some six kilometers to the west.

Not far away, about eight kilometers south of Meir, the family discovered a well by the Qousqam Mountain. They sojourned six months in this place in a certain house.

According to a local tradition, the child Jesus, no longer an infant, predicted that holy monastics would one day abide there. Even to this day, a monastery is located there, the Monastery of the Holy Virgin, known as Dair al-Muharraq, located at the foot of the western mountain. Tradition has it that this was the first church built in Upper Egypt. Although the monastery dates from the fourth century, the church dates back to the first century. Most believe that it was erected immediately after St. Mark's arrival in Egypt, in about 60 A.D. It was the existence of the historic Church of the Holy Virgin that inspired Abba Pachomios the Great (294-405), to choose this spot to build a monastery.[63] The present church at this location may be assigned to the twelfth or thirteenth century.[64]

THE TURNING POINT

Taking a route that led a little further south, some ten kilometers southwest of the ancient city of Lycopolis (Asyut or Assiut), at Establ Antar, the holy elder Joseph brought them to a mountain range rising west of Asyut. There are large rock tombs there from the 9th to the 12th Dynasty. There is a Church dedicated to the Virgin at Dair al-Adra, situated east of the cave in which the family hid and rested.[65] This seems plausible considering that, as refugees, they had grown accustomed to taking and following the unbeaten track and seeking shelter in caves.[66] Oral tradition continues that from Lycopolis, the holy family returned to the site of the present Dair al-Muharraq Monastery.[67]

Nearly all historical and ecclesiastical sources assert that Al-Muharraq Monastery was the last spot in Upper Egypt reached by them on their journey. It was there, in a cave, that it is claimed that Joseph had been told in a dream to return to Israel.

THE END OF THE JOURNEY

"But when Herod was dead, behold, an angel of the Lord appeareth in a dream to Joseph in Egypt, saying, 'Arise, and take the young child and His Mother, and go into the land of Israel: for they are dead that sought the young child's life'" [Mt. 2:19-20].

Thus after living about three years in Egypt, till the death of Herod (4 B.C.), that prophecy was fulfilled spoken by the Lord, **"Out of Egypt have I called My Son"** [Mt. 2:15]. Saint John Chrysostom says that "this makes the Virgin also in no common degree glorious and distinguished; that the very thing which was the whole people's special endowment in the way of praise, she also might henceforth have for her own. I mean, that whereas they (Israel) were proud of their coming up from Egypt, and used to boast of it...this pre-eminence belongs to the Virgin likewise."[68]

Christ did not return to Nazareth till after the death of Herod, which history records as April in 4 B.C. According to Egyptian tradition, the holy family found refuge in Egypt for about three years. Thus we arrive at the date of Christ's birth as 7 B.C., which also coincides with the date of the census which is recorded to have taken place in about the years 7 or 6 B.C., when Cyrenius was governor [Lk. 2:2].[69]

THE RETURN HOME

Then having left Cusae, they came again to the town of Hermopolis Magna (al-Ashmunain), where they were received with joy and jubilation. A local oral tradition in the village of Dair al-Barsha, on the east bank of the Nile opposite Mallawi, states that the holy family visited their village and remained for some time in a cave nearby. The Magharat al-Adra, the Cave of the Holy Virgin, is situated in the mountains west of Dair al-Barsha. The cave is still visited by pilgrims annually.[70]

There is good reason to believe that the divine travelers returned to Palestine by the same way they had come. On the return trip, the holy travelers again lodged in the cave that is now beneath the Church of St. Sergios in Old Cairo, the ancient Babylon of Egypt.[71]

It is believed that they remained for some time at Babylon. Since the days of the Exile (597-538 B.C.), Jews continued to live there. An ancient synagogue was known to have been there and, according to Jewish tradition, the Prophet Jeremias had preached there. No doubt the divine refugees would have been attracted to put in at this place for a awhile, so as to be among their own people and familiar language and culture. Another local oral tradition states that Joseph even had some family at Babylon with whom they were persuaded to spend some time.[72] The tradition of their visit to Babylon is well attested by *Synaxaria* and reports of ancient pilgrims.

From Babylon, the family continued their way northwards, stopping again at On, near the site of the present village of al-Matariyah. It was here that they bathed Jesus. In the Church of the Holy Virgin at Musturud, about three kilometers west of Matariyah, on the western bank of the Ismailia Canal, there is to this day a well which was blessed by the holy travelers. This well is situated in the northeast corner of the church, east of the cave where the family found shelter.[73] Thousands of pilgrims annually visit the cave.

Again, on their return trip, they visited al-Mahammah or the "place of bathing". In ancient times, a temple with many idols stood there. When the holy travelers approached, the temple collapsed and broke into pieces. A source of water there commemorates the place where the family bathed. The practice of frequent ceremonial purifications, partial or entire, was enjoined on all Jews by the law.

This would explain, to some extent, the emphasis laid on springs and wells as stopping places for the family.[74]

From al-Mahammah, the next stopover was Leontopolis, known today as the ruins of Tell al-Yehudiyah, or Vicus Judaeorum in old Roman maps. Local tradition states that the family visited their countrymen who had settled around the Temple of Onias. The high priest Onias IV went to Egypt in 154 B.C. and, with the permission of Ptolemy IV, he built at Leontopolis a temple which, though comparatively small, was modeled on that of Jerusalem which had been desecrated by Antiochus Epiphanes (170 B.C.). Today the ruins of the temple of Onias are buried in rubbish.[75]

From Tell al-Yehudiyah, the family returned to Judea along the same route they used to enter Egypt. They passed through Bilbais, the Wadi Tumilat, the isthmus at al-Qantara, and then traveled on the caravan-route from Egypt to Palestine, along the Mediterranean coast.[76] Another local tradition holds that the family also rested for several days near Gaza, in a garden between the Gabal Muntar and Gaza.

In Egypt today, the flight of the Christ child, the Virgin Mary, Joseph and James is both a significant and living tradition;[77] for, with but a few exceptions, they were accepted by the citizens of that land and treated well.

Therefore, from the haven of Egypt, Joseph **"arose, and took the young child and His Mother, and came into the land of Israel. But when he heard that Archelaus did reign in Judea in the room of his father Herod, he was afraid to go thither: notwithstanding, being warned of God in a dream, he turned aside into the parts of Galilee [Mt. 2:22].**

"And he came and dwelt in a city called Nazareth: that it might be fulfilled which was spoken by the prophets, 'He shall be called a Nazarene'" [Mt. 2:23].

This Archaelaus ruled Judea from 4 B.C. to 6 A.D. Herod Antipas ruled Galilee and the land beyond Jordan from 4 B.C. to 39 A.D.

Icons at the Kariye Djami depict a donkey laden with a bundle of provisions. James, Joseph's youthful son, carrying a staff, leads the beast. Mary is seen walking close behind her child and Joseph. Jesus is astride Joseph's shoulders, yet He turns to look back at His Mother. The town of Nazareth, behind a battlemented wall, is shown is the background.[78]

Joseph then returned to Nazareth and abode there, resuming his former occupation as a carpenter. **"And the child grew, and waxed strong in spirit, filled with wisdom; and the grace of God was upon Him"** [Lk. 2:40].

Chapter XV.
Daily Life

+ + +

GALILEE

Galilee at the time of Jesus was not only of the richest fertility, cultivated to the utmost, thickly covered with populous towns and villages, but the center of every known industry, and the busy road of the world's commerce. The area is approximately sixty miles long from north to south and thirty miles wide from east to west. The entire region is watered by springs, heavy mountain dew, and an annual precipitation of about twenty-five inches. At Herod's death in 4 B.C., Galilee fell to  Herod Antipas who made his capital on the western shore of the Sea of Galilee, calling it Tiberias after the Roman emperor.[1] At least twenty-two species of fish have been classified from the streams and the Sea of Galilee, which is approximately 685 ft. below sea level.[2] This beautiful blue lake reaches a depth of 150 ft. and is approximately twelve and a half miles long and eight miles at its widest point.[3] It was in this area by the Sea of unrivalled beauty, quaint villages and lovely retreats that the fisherman plied his vocation.

Galilee was notably favored with a fine climate, a rich forest growth, great fertility of soil, and a wealth of vegetation. The town of Nazareth is nestled on the side of a mountain, in the territory of Zebulon. It is about halfway between the south end of the Sea of Galilee and Mt. Carmel. It was the scene of tranquil and homely beauty. Just outside the town, to the northwest, bubbled the only spring or well. Beyond it stretched lines of houses, each with its flat roof standing out distinctly against the clear blue sky. One could see watered, terraced gardens and gnarled wide-spreading fig trees, graceful feathery palms, scented oranges, silvery olive-trees, thick hedges, rich pasture land, and then the bounding hills to the south.[4]

Lower Galilee was easy labor for the agriculturist, for the area produced the best wheat. Galileans planted fall wheat as the winter rains were beginning, harvesting it between May and June.[5] It was a beautiful country and one might say that the Law-Giver had this province specially in mind when He promised the Hebrews that they were to enter "a good and extensive land, where there are torrents of waters, and fountains of deep places issuing through the plains and through the mountains: a land of wheat and barley, wherein are vines, figs and pomegranates: a land of olive oil and honey" [Deut. 8:7-8].

Proverbially, fruit grew to perfection and altogether the cost of living was about one-fifth of that in Judea to the south. Pomegranates thrived near Mt. Carmel and the grapes of Napthali were famous.[6] Galilee also had a busy teeming population. Josephus writes that in his day the population of Galilee was about three million. We cannot ignore his account about the 240 towns and villages of Galilee, each with about 15,000 inhabitants.[7] This would help explain the crowds that would follow Jesus.

It is noteworthy that eleven of our Saviour's disciples were Galileans. Old Testament notables include Barak, Gideon, and the Prophets Jonas and Elias. Other famous personages include Deborah, the authoress of a triumph song; the judges Ibzan, Elon and Tola who judged Israel forty years. The men of that area had a reputation of courage.[8] In the future great struggle with Rome, from 66-70 A.D., they were the strongest defenders of liberty of whom the Jewish nation could boast. The hardest fighting of the war would be done on Galilean soil, when during that long and bloody battle, 150,000 of her inhabitants fell.[9]

One of the great caravan routes, *Via Maris* or "the Way of the Sea", led from Acco on the sea to Damascus, and then through Nazareth; hence there was a stream of commerce. Men of all nations, would then appear in the streets of Nazareth. Apart from this, Nazareth was also one of the great centers of Jewish temple life. Nazareth was one of the priest-centers.[10] Although Nazareth was close to important trade routes, the population remained exclusively Jewish. For this reason it would be one of the towns chosen as the residence of a group of priests who were forced to leave Jerusalem when the temple was destroyed in 70 A.D.[11]

Yet, Galilee was still "the Court of the Gentiles" to Judaism.[12] On account of its position as a frontier town on the border of Zebulon, its inhabitants fostered a certain aloofness from the rest of Israel.   For this reason, strict Jews scorned the people of Nazareth.[13]   There was a general contempt in Rabbinic circles for all that was Galilean.   Yet the traits of the inhabitants of Galilee were admired by all. They had a reputation of being healthy, industrious, able to develop their resources and were known to be skilful merchants, shipping their commodities to all parts of the world.[14]

Although the Judean or Jerusalem dialect was far from pure, the people of Galilee were especially blamed for neglecting the study of their language, charged with errors in grammar, and especially with absurd mispronunciation.[15] An example of this was when the chief of the disciples, Peter, a native of Bethsaida of Galilee, was accused by one of the maids of the high priest as being a Galilean because his "speech agreeth thereto' [Mk. 14:70].   The opprobrium also was attached to Nazareth because it seems from history that its people were given to sedition and rebellion.[16]

JOSEPH THE CARPENTER

The custom then among the Jews was that when the bride was chosen, they had a life-right of residence in their husband's house.   Such was the case of the maiden Mary when she was brought to Joseph's home.[17]

The Virgin Mary was then the wife of the village carpenter in Nazareth.   Joseph worked with his hands to build houses and to make furniture and other articles for the home. Saint Justin Martyr (+c.165), who was a native of that area (Sichem or Nablus), said the carpenter of Nazareth also made "ploughs and yokes; by which He taught the symbols of righteousness and an active life." Although a worker in wood, none were demeaned by that occupation. Jesus' labor as a carpenter accentuates the wonder of His incarnation. His example, too, makes all productive labor honorable.

The trade of the carpenter is mentioned in scriptures [cf. Gen. 6:14; Ex. 37] and that he was usually a talented wood carver [1 Kings 6:18,19]. The Galilean hills were considered to have been heavily forested in early times with an abundance of trees: Some cypress and cedar grew north, sycamore (a type of fig tree) in the foothills region, and olive everywhere. There might have been oak and ash in the area too. But none of these trees yielded long timber.[18] Woodworkers recognized the virtues of different woods and used them according to their properties. Olive wood, for example, was ideal for carving, so the cherubim of Solomon's Temple were carved from that wood; but the holm oak, on the other hand, made the best plow for a farmer.

Carpentry was a rough, tough job that demanded a good deal of physical strength and endurance as well as great skill. There were two aspects to the carpenter's work: firstly, building and, secondly, the making of smaller objects that included furniture. Roofs were constructed by laying timber beams from wall to wall and filling in the gaps with matting that was plastered down with mud. The carpenter had to cut down trees and square up logs so that they could be used as beams. This was done with a hand adz or by sawing the length with a primitive saw. Either way, it was hard physical work.

As we said, the carpenter had to fell the tree and cut it up into usable units. If boards were to be made, the trunk sections had to be ripsawed into boards, which required skill to keep the boards of equal width. Beams could be shaped with an adz from tree sections approximately the size of the beam desired. Only certain sections would require the carpenter to use other skills if a house were made of stone or mud brick. Some houses had a second story. If the house used wooden columns he would shape these but would plant them on a wide stone base. Stairs could be made out of wood or stone. Some homes had gates that the carpenter would make.

Working on the ground outside his dwelling, the carpenter also undertook smaller jobs, such as making doors, door frames, window lattices, locks, low tables and chests for inside the home.[19]   Agricultural instruments were also part of the carpenter's work, and that included yokes, ploughs, ox goads, shovels, pitchforks and threshing sledges.   Farmers and merchants also needed wagons, but this took extra skill because of the wheels.   Also wooden frames for the pack saddles used on donkeys and camels, the making and repairing of chariots, and oars for ships came within the province of the woodworker.

His tools consisted of a measuring line, used as much as we would use a tape measure or ruler today.   He had a plumb line to measure and check the vertical line of a structure.   He used a stylus for a marking device and a compass to mark a circle or portions of a circle.   The adz was used to shape wood, for the blade of this too was curved and attached to the handle at a right angle.   He had an awl used to poke holes in wood or leather.   A copper saw would be fitted into a wooden handle.   Axe heads were made of bronze and were lashed to a shaft.   The ancient carpenter used nails and also a hammer that was usually made of heavy stone.   The maul mentioned in Prov. 25:8 was thought to have been a heavy wooden mallet.   Joseph probably also had a copper chisel, which looked something like a wide screwdriver.   The Bible [2 Kings 12:9], together with archaeological discoveries indicate that a type of drill was used to bore into wood.[20]   The fact that the tools were relatively crude meant that obtaining a good finish required great expertise on the part of the carpenter.[21]

Some thirty Old Testament texts teach the necessity and the dignity of manual work.   In biblical times, a man who would not provide for his family was guilty of a serious offense.   A man who failed to do this was shunned and mocked by society.   Acceptance of this ideal would also be exemplified by the tentmaker, St. Paul, the great Apostle to the nations.   In the future, the Apostle would identify the man who would not provide for his family as one who had "denied the faith, and is worse than an infidel" [1 Tim. 5:8].

According to Jewish tradition, a father had several responsibilities towards his son, besides teaching him the law, which began from three years of age: to circumcise his son

293

[Gen. 17:12]; redeem him from God if he was the firstborn [Num. 18:15-16]; teach the lad a trade; and, if need be, find him a wife [Gen. 24:4].[22] Joseph had the Christ child circumcised and "redeemed" Him as the firstborn. Jesus was not only the carpenter's "son" [Mt. 13:55], but we may infer with great probability that He adopted the trade of His putative father [Mk. 6:3].

Although Joseph was a descendant of the royal house of Israel, his status in the community was limited by his calling. He could have owned a small plot of ground to keep a few beasts, perhaps for a little tillage.

Among the Jews, contempt for manual labor did not exist. Disdain for it was one of the characteristics of heathenism. On the contrary, work was considered a religious duty. Frequently and most earnestly insisted upon was the learning of some trade, provided it did not minister to luxury, nor tend to lead away from the observance of the law. Indeed, Jewish sentiment asserted the nobility of manual labor, and advised that intellectual prowess and physical activity go hand and hand. An early Jewish tractate insists: "Whosoever does not teach his son work, teacheth him to rob."[23] Thus, Jewish tradition sought to produce a man who could both think and act.[24]

There was not such a separation between rich and poor like there is with us. While wealth might confer social distinction, the absence of it in no way implied social inferiority. How could it be otherwise? Their lives were so simple and their wants few.[25]

JEWISH CHILD LIFE

Jesus passed his early years in Nazareth. The evangelic narrative has left us the briefest notice of His childhood: that **"the child grew, and waxed strong in spirit, filled with wisdom: and the grace of God was upon Him"** [Lk. 2:40].

Great loving care was bestowed upon Jewish child life. Education began in the home where character and moral upbringing were imparted by influence and example. The reverence and affection between Jewish parents and children, is known to every reader of the Old Testament.

The relationship of father has its highest sanction and embodiment in that of God towards Israel; the tenderness and care of a mother in that of the watchfulness and pity of the Lord over His people. It was a special relationship between parents and children.   From the child's first days of existence, he was surrounded by a religious atmosphere.

The first education was necessarily the mother's, whether she recited the tribe's history or taught the child prayers.   Before the child went to school, indelibly pressed upon his mind were the private and united prayers at home, the domestic rites, the weekly Sabbath or the festive seasons. Together with the wife, the father was to "train up a child in the way he should go..." [Prov. 22:6].   The father, too, was bound to teach his children the knowledge of the law [Deut. 6:7-9].

When the child first learned to speak, no doubt his religious instruction began with such verses of Holy Scripture that were part of their corporate worship.   The words of the *shema* (creed) were basic: "Hear O Israel: The Lord our God is one Lord.   And thou shalt love the Lord thy God with all thy mind, and with all thy soul, and all thy strength" [Deut. 6:4].   Josephus relates in his *Contra Apion*[26] that both the Scriptures and the traditions were taught in every city to Jewish boys "from our first consciousness."   Thus all little boys were immersed in such a curriculum, being taught both in the home and in the synagogue.[27]

Despite the wording, far more than outward duties were required in the reverencing of parents in the Fifth Commandment.   Indeed, no punishment was more prompt as a result of its breach [Deut. 21:18-21].[28]   Jesus was to condemn many Jews of His day for not honoring their parents [Mt. 15:4-9].

After their journey and experiences in Egypt, Mary always stayed close to home.   As with the custom of mothers in those years, she nursed her child until the age of two or three.   Mothers were also responsible for watching the children and keeping them clean.   All children spend their formative years close to their mother.   Eventually, sons went with their fathers to employment.

Saint Cyril of Alexandria (+444) recorded a story with a few human touches when he wrote how Mary "would take hold of Jesus' hand and lead Him along the paths, saying, 'My darling, walk a little way.' And He clung to her with His little hands, stopping now and then, and hanging on to her skirts...until she would lift Him up in her arms and carry Him."[29]

In ancient Israel, education was an informal process. There were no classrooms and structured curriculum. We know from the Old Testament that Samuel set up an assembly of prophets in Ramah [1 Sam. 19:18-21], and some kind of theological schools developed from this [2 Kings 2:5-7]. The origin of the practice of calling a priest "father" began here, for he exercised the role of the father in teaching the children [2 Kings 2:3,12].[30] By New Testament times, the Jews had adopted a more formal approach to education. At about the time of Christ, Rabbi Joshua ben Gamala instituted schools apart from the homes in every town and village in Palestine and, because of the intercourse with Greece, especially in Galilee, it is likely that the Greek language was also studied. Each Sabbath, though, Jews faithfully gathered at the synagogue to hear the rabbi read the Scriptures and explain the law. The synagogue would then sponsor classes to which boys could come during the week. As we indicated earlier, these classes were to supplement religious education outside the home.[31]

Several key passages of Scripture were to be mastered. Of primary importance was the creedal statement of the Jews [Deut. 6:4-5]. Next in importance were Deut. 11:13-21 and Num. 15:37-41. The student was also required to learn the *Hallel* ("Praise") that is, Psalms 112-117 [LXX], as well as the Creation story [Gen. 1-5] and the sacrificial laws [Lev. 1-8]. As boys grew older they examined the *Book of Leviticus*. At the synagogue, where the *Torah*[32] scrolls were kept, they would receive lessons.

The classroom itself contained a small raised platform where the teacher sat cross-legged. Before him on a low rack were scrolls containing Old Testament passages. The only "textbooks" were the law, the Prophets and writings. Later, from ten to fifteen years old, they were allowed to discuss questions of the law with the pharisaic teachers. Although school was year-round, during the hot summer months school was no more than four hours per day. Hours were before 10 a.m. and after 3:00 p.m.[33] Writing was done in wax on a wooden tablet. If writing was done on broken pottery, it was done with pens made of hard cane and sharpened to a point. Ink was made from soot, resin, olive oil, and water.³⁴ At times the student would write on the ground.

It is likely that Mary's Son would have attended such a school in Nazareth when he was about six years old. As was the custom, the boys sat in a semicircle on the floor, facing the teacher. Much of the teaching was done by repetition, and the memorizing led to the common practice of reading aloud.³⁵

All Jewish boys were grounded in the teaching of the *Pentateuch* from their earliest schooling. The book of *Leviticus* was, in fact, their first textbook. It was the parents' responsibility to instruct their children in minutiae of ceremonial law as the various festivals came around, and the synagogue service would serve the same purpose.³⁶

FAMILY OBSERVANCES

The Lord commanded all of the adult Hebrew males to congregate regularly at a central place of worship, as attested to in Ex. 23:17 and Deut. 16:16-17. The three great pilgrim feasts were the Passover, the Feast of Weeks (Pentecost) and the Feast of Tabernacles (or Booths). Mary, however, would accompany Joseph to Jerusalem with the Christ child. Therefore, festival times especially focused upon the temple, when pilgrims from all other parts of Palestine and the empire would attend. Temple worship was highly organized, with twenty-four divisions of priests, as set up by the Prophet-King David. The priests would work on a rotation system to insure continuity and efficiency.³⁷

Only the Sabbath and festivals, whether domestic or public, would be occasions to bring forth the best foods. Music was also much a part of their feasts [Is. 5:12].³⁸ Religious festivals, of which feasting was very much a part, may be grouped as follows: (1) the Sabbath, the feast of new moons, the sabbatical year, and the Year of Jubilee; (2) the Passover, Pentecost, and the Feast of Tabernacles; (3)

the Feasts of Purim and of the Dedication. All labor ceased on these principal feast days. The seven day Passover celebration called for no work on the first and seventh day [Lev. 23]. Moreover there were feasts for marriages [Jn. 2:1-22], at sheep-shearing [1 Sam. 25:2,36], and burials [Jer. 16:5].[39]

Hebrew men also wore phylacteries *(tephillin)*: one worn on the forehead between the eyebrows, and one worn on the left arm. The frontlet (one worn on the forehead), contained four pieces of parchment that were wrapped in animal skin, and upon which were written the scriptural verses of Ex. 13:1-3, 11-16 and Deut. 6:4-9; 11:13-21. The one worn on the arm had two rolls of parchment. Phylacteries were to be worn for morning and evening prayers, though some only wore them in the morning prayers, together with a head covering.[40] Every male over the age of thirteen was required to wear it at daily morning prayer. At the time of our Saviour, the Pharisees were chided by Christ Who, though not condemning this practice, had said, "All their works they do for to be seen of men: they make broad their phylacteries, and enlarge the borders of their garments" [Mt. 23:5]. Christ was condemning their ostentation that prostituted an ancient custom in the interests of outward display. Indeed, many of the Pharisees attached the greatest importance to these material reminders or sensible signs of their obligations under the law.

DWELLINGS

The home was central to people's lives. It was both a social center and a work place, as well as somewhere to eat and sleep.

The houses of Israel tended to be squarish, with a flat roof and external staircase. Houses were most often built with white limestone rocks, but the stone of Galilee was normally black basalt. These types of houses became the pattern because of climate, availability of building material, and the need to conserve space. Homes were made out of bricks fired in a kiln or squared stone. The walls were thick, of mud brick or of rough stone and rubble, and contained niches for the storage of food and utensils.

Many houses were built with a single thickness of large, undressed stones. Smaller stones were packed into the gaps and the rough wall was faced with a layer of mud plaster.

There was usually a foundation below ground level, and sometimes wooden stakes were driven into the ground along the length of the wall to give it extra stability. A plumb line enabled builders to keep the wall vertical.[41]

Without glass, a single window was small and high and sometimes had a wooden lattice to keep out intruders. In the winter the lattice might be covered with a skin or some form of curtain. The main source of light was through the single open door, which was shut with a wooden bar at night. Wooden doors were fixed to heavy posts which turned on stone sockets by the doorsill and were held in the frame by the lintel. All Jewish homes had a box fixed to the doorpost, the *mezuzah*, which contained small portions of scripture within [Deut. 6:9;11:20]. It was a reminder of God's presence and the people's redemption from the Egyptians. Jews would kiss the *mezuzah* by touching their lips with their fingers and raising the fingers to it when entering or leaving the home. Inside the houses there might be only curtains to close the entrances to the rooms. Light was provided at night by an oil lamp standing on a projection from the wall, in an alcove, or some form of utensil.[42]

The basic house for the poorest members of the community in the country was a single room, about ten feet square. The floors were usually bare mud, trodden hard, or plastered. They were often covered with straw mats. The area nearest the door was levelled and stamped-down earth, but at the back of the room was a raised platform of stone that was used for family activities such as eating, sitting, and sleeping. The state of the floor and the lack of light would certainly make it difficult to find a lost coin [Lk. 15:8]. A fire for heating and for cooking was sometimes set on the lower floor, with the smoke left to find its own way out.[43]

The roofs were constructed by laying brushwood across rough sycamore beams and binding them together by using mud. At that time, the hill country was heavily wooded. However, long timbers were hard to obtain, so most rooms were quite narrow.[44] A heavy roller was kept on the roof to compact the material after rain. November to March was the rainy season and roofs were not watertight. The flat roofs did have their advantages though: one could go up and find quiet and a vantage point to view the neighborhood; for the drying of crops and storage, or even to sleep on a hot summer's night. By law, a parapet had to be built around it so that people could not fall off. In the city, such houses were literally joined house to house. It is interesting that the Romans introduced the tiled sand gabled roofs and tiled floors. Not until Roman times was the earthenware oven invented in which the firebox was separated from the cooking area and so made the possibility of thicker loaves of bread.[45]

For the Hebrew family, fasting was also an essential part of life. Fasts were prescribed among the Jews for the Day of Atonement by the Mosaic Law [Lev. 16:30], to commemorate the breaking of the tablets of the law, and for other such events in their history. Further, garments of sackcloth, ashes sprinkled on one's head, unwashed hands, and an unanointed head were signs that a person was observing a fast.

After the conquests of the Prophet Jesus of Navee, for centuries the standard type of building for the "middle class" was the "four-roomed house", usually on one floor. The plan was simple, though there were many variations of this theme. From the street you entered a courtyard. On one side were one or two rooms for storage; on the other for animals. The roof was flat, and strong enough for people to work and rest. An outside staircase or ladder gave access to the roof. Pillars rather than walls, often separated the side rooms from the courtyard, so these rooms would have been light and airy, little more than shelters from rain. Some houses were set in a larger walled courtyard where a donkey, sheep and goats may have been kept. The yard probably resembled a modern farmyard, cluttered with animals, a work area, stores of fodder and piles of debris. Some of the four-roomed houses were further subdivided to provide extra rooms. Others were more enclosed, with only a single line of pillars down the center supporting the roof. Each room had a door of its own, set in the corner of the room so that only one door post was needed. Rooms were roughly equal in size. Walls dividing them were about 2 ft.-3 in. thick while the northern exterior wall was 4 ft.-9 in. thick and built of dressed stone.[46] Again, the roof was a place where all kinds of domestic activities could take place: weaving, washing, drying out dates, figs and flax; and even evening prayer.[47]

Heating the home and cooking were done by fire, using natural combustible materials such as dried animal manure, sticks, dried grass, thorn bushes, and charcoal. The fire could be made in the open or in a depression in the earth floor or contained in some kind of earthenware cooking box. Better homes were provided with a chimney. Fire would be kindled by flint or by friction. Heating was important in the hill country; winters were cold and damp and there were snowfalls. Furnishings were simple: a bed, table and chairs.[48] Although the word "bed" could mean a variety of things from a straw mat to a wooden-framed bed.

HOME LIFE, FOOD AND MEALS

Jewish home life in the country was the simplest. We must remember that life then was difficult and uncomfortable. It was also socially and economically insecure; war and famine were constant threats. Despite these harsh realizations, everyday home life persevered amid the Romans and zealots.

The morning and midday meal must have been of the plainest, and even the larger evening meal of the simplest, in the home at Nazareth. The morning meal was usually eaten sometime between 9 o'clock and noon. It was a light meal and consisted of bread, fruits, olives and cheese. As the heat of the day approached, it was time for siesta and out of the sun. In the village, the heavier evening meal was eaten about two hours before sundown, when the air was cooler. Vegetables, butter, and wine were consumed at the evening meal.[49] Although meat was not part of the normal diet, it was used by the more affluent. Sheep and goat meat were to be found at banquets and feasts, though some beef was consumed. Vegetable products were an important part of diet, and they were boiled. Garden beans, flavored with oil and garlic were boiled and enjoyed. Also for vegetables they had lentils, cucumbers, onions and garlic. Olives were grown for eating and for use as cooking oil. Olive oil was mixed with flour and used for frying. Herbs were used to add flavor to meals. Seasonings were salt, seeds, whole or ground, including anise, coriander, cumin, dill, thyme, mint and others. Bread was eaten by itself or with something to increase its flavor, such as salt, vinegar, broth, or honey. Fruits were a favorite part of the diet that could include grapes, raisins, pomegranates, apples and figs. Almonds, pistachio nuts and other nuts were also included in vegetable stews or eaten raw.[50]

Hebrews drank the milk of camels, sheep and goats. The camel's milk was especially rich and strong, but not very sweet.[51] Some milk was fermented to produce yogurt. Some of it was churned to produce butter. Milk would be placed in a skin bag, and the bag was alternately shaken and squeezed until the butter was formed. Milk was also used to make cheese. Salt was used to both flavor and preserve food.[52]

Although we read about sacred vessels [Ex. 25:29] to include plates, flagons and bowls, table utensils were not used among the Hebrews, other than a 3-pronged fork for removing meat from a cauldron and a spoon for soup dishes. Cups resembled small bowls without handles. The sop was a piece of bread used to dip in the soup or broth which sat in the center of the table. As we know Jesus was to dip a sop and give it to Judas [Jn. 13:26].[53]

Although earlier Jews sat on mats on the floor to eat, later they adopted the custom of using a table with couches on which they reclined. The washing of one's hands was considered essential and was observed as a religious duty. Then a short prayer or blessing was offered before eating. Traditionally recited was: "Blessed art Thou, *Adonai* our God, King of the world, Who causes to come forth bread from the earth." *Adonai* being a divine name, translated as "the Lord" and signifying sovereignty or God is the ruling Lord. Whenever Hebrew readers would find the tetra-grammaton forming the word *Yahweh*, they substituted *Adonai*, as the name of God was regarded as too sacred to be pronounced.[54]

Nazareth was not a city of the wealthy or influential, thus simplicity prevailed in dress and manner. But close and loving were the bonds which drew together the members of a family, and deep the influence which they exercised on each other.[55] Also common in that day was the evening circle where all the men gathered in an open-air meeting place, where they sat or lay in a large circle with the older or more respected men in the center. On the outer edges, older boys would stand and listen.[56] Nevertheless, usually once the evening meal was over and darkness came, people went to bed early, so as to be up with the sun the following morning.[57]

THE LIFE OF A HOUSEWIFE
Domestic Activities

Each family member had a well-defined role within the community and home. Most of the household chores fell to the women. This included baking and cooking. The average Israelite mother was up each morning, before the sun was up, starting a fire in the hearth or oven. She would use thorns, stubble, or straw. Often, children usually had the job of finding the fuel.

While the men were at work, women would take a hand-mill from its place on the platform and place it on a square of clean cloth. The mill was made of two disc-shaped stones about 12 to 18-inches lengthwise. The lower stone had an upright wooden stake that passed through an ample opening in the upper stone, usually made of basalt, a lightweight rock. An upright handle fixed to the upper stone made it possible to rotate the stone about the wooden stake or pivot. Either barley grains or wheat grains were put into the pivot hole as the top stone was being turned. The grain would then be crushed between the two stones and came out onto the cloth as flour.[58] A woman could do the milling by herself, but a larger mill was easier with a companion. Grain would either be stored in large pottery jars or in a stone-lined silo sunk in the floor or in the ground outside the house.[59]

Hebrew women used special tools in preparing food for the family, the preparation of which was done in the courtyard. Bread was the all-important staple food of the Near East. Preparing grain for food was a strenuous and backbreaking task. After grinding the wheat and barley into flour, in a wooden bowl, they then kneaded the flour, yeast, olive oil, and water or milk into a dough that was stretched thin for baking. The dough would be made into circular cakes, pricked, and baked around a jar or in a bowl. A woman could also then bake flat cakes by sticking them to the sides of the oven or placing them over a fire on heated stones [Lev. 2:4; 11:35; 26:26]. Generally, fresh bread was baked every day.[60] If the bread was to be leavened, a piece of dough from the previous day (the leaven) was put into the new dough with salt and the whole lump left by the fire

303

until the yeast in the old dough had permeated the whole; it was then baked. Also, sometimes a metal tray was put on the fire so that grains could be placed over the fire. As the grains "popped" they formed popped corn or "parched corn".[61]

The oven was generally in the courtyard. The Hebrews had three types of ovens: (1) a sand oven, in which a fire was built on clean sand and then removed when the sand was hot. Dough would then be spread on the hot sand in thin layers to bake; (2) the earth oven was a hole in the earth in which stones were heated. Dough would be spread in thin layers on the stones after the fire had been removed; or (3) portable ovens that were made of clay. When hot inside, thins layers of dough were spread on the stones lining the bottom of the oven after the ashes had been removed. They were hollow at the top with a 24-inch diameter at the base, being constructed by alternating layers of clay and pieces of broken pottery.[62] Cooking pots were generally made from pottery, but bronze ones were known to be used in the tabernacle and the temple.[63]

Apart from preparing foods, the floor of the house had to be swept carefully and the place made tidy. The fire had to be fanned into a flame so that cooking could proceed.[64]

Every family needed water. Water was fetched from the local well or spring at the beginning or end of the day. Some families had their own private cistern to store rain water, but most often the water came from a spring or well in the middle of the village. Young women would fill their water jugs and carry them home on their heads every day.

When filled to the top with water, each jug weighed as much as fifty pounds.[65] Nazareth had only one spring and, doubtless, the Theotokos would fetch water here for the needs of her little family. Apocryphal sources state that the boy Jesus would accompany His Mother to this fountain to carry water with her. Today it is still flowing and the water is excellent. On the site today is situated the Greek Orthodox

Church of the Annunciation. Excavations have proven that the fountain's main source is under a cave within that Greek Orthodox Church.

Although the Jewish diet was generally good for health, their biggest health problem concerned water, which was easily polluted through animal usage, washing, sewerage, and plain dirt. This included water that had been collected in a cistern. For this reason wine was a staple drink.[66]

Shopping

Two jobs outside the house, usually performed by women, were collecting water and shopping. Shopping was usually a daily task, simply because food would not keep for more than a day in the hot climate, without recourse to drying or salting. Some families would collect bread that had been baked in the community oven.[67]

The marketplace was normally an open place inside the city gate that served a market square, and streets leading from the square would have served as dwellings for traders. It was an area where the villagers brought in their produce, craftsman their wares, and traders from other parts of the country displayed their wares. There were stalls of fresh food. Goods were displayed at ground level, while the seller sat among the goods. Special markets would be set up when a caravan passed through Nazareth. Prices were seldom fixed, so that every purchase needed some form of bargaining. Goods in kind were accepted as exchange, as well as weighed amounts of metal or coinage. Dry goods were always measured full and pressed down.[68]

The marketplace was generally a busy and happy place, as there were many people about it. Public speaking and teaching could be done therein. Children played games such as "wedding" and "funeral" [Mt. 11:16-17]. The unemployed ventured there in the hope that someone might hire them. Somewhere in this area could also be found the public oven.[69]

The narrow streets running off from the market area were unpaved and could be full of rubbish--mud bricks, broken pottery, and litter--often higher than the floor level of the houses themselves. The streets were dark and cut at odd corners, and dirt and dust were everywhere. The odors in the streets were unpleasant, that of disease, unclean bodies, smoke, drainage, cooking, refuse, animal droppings, all would have been familiar in the streets of the towns.

Clothing and Washing

The average housewife spent hours each day preparing meals and making clothes from wool. This could also include rugs and coverings for the home. Clothes were not easy to come by for most people and were very costly. Out of necessity, the wife was expected to make her family's clothes. And as we already know, Mary was quite adept from her girlhood at embroidery. The embroidery then, however, was not our idea of embroidery. The embroiderer wove cloth with a variety of colors and then sewed a pattern onto it. Thus the decorated part of the cloth was on one side of the fabric. In contrast, the "artistic or cunning work" was done by weaving gold thread or figures right onto the fabric [Ex. 26:1, 31; 28:6]. But this sophisticated type of embroidery was only on garments worn by the priests.

Spinning wool was mainly the occupation of women. Since the spinning wheel was unknown in the Virgin's time, women used distaff spinning to make cloth. She would attach wool or flax to the distaff (a rod or stick), and then use a spindle to twist the fibers into threads. After she spun the raw materials into thread, they could then be used to weave cloth. Lengthwise threads are called the warp and cross threads the woof. The spinner would then attach the woof to a shuttle, an instrument that held the thread so that it could be passed over and under the threads of the warp. The warp was attached to a wooden beam at the top or the bottom of the loom, and as she wove she stood.[70] Most clothes would be woven in two or three pieces before being sewn together by hand. With her work-basket at her side, the Virgin-Mother would mend or spin. But during the day, she would take an intermission from her tasks and recite the prescribed psalms and blessings. On the Sabbath all work was set aside.

The Theotokos also made clothing for her Son and husband. The clothing of men consisted of a lightweight sleeveless inner garment that reached below the knees. A V-shaped opening was cut for the head and two slits in the two corners for the arms. This garment was usually colored and made from two pieces of material seamed. A loin cloth was worn under the sack-like garment. Indeed, experts have commented that Jesus' tunic (*chiton*) was of the most recent fashion because it was without the center seam [Jn. 19:23]. Looms able to accommodate the full length tunic were invented only in His lifetime.[71] A man's girdle was actually a belt or band of cloth or a cord. It could also be leather and was fastened. The outer garment was a square or oblong cloth. It was called a robe or mantle. Jewish men would wear fringes with blue ribbons on the border, or hemline, of the garment [Num. 15:38]. The fringes were to remind them of the constant presence of the Lord's commandments and to do them.

During the winter, people wore skins or fur dresses. Among the poor, cattle skins were worn. In the country during winter where warmth was important, cloaks were made by wrapping thick woolen material around the body, seaming it at the shoulders, and providing slits for the arms to go through. Most men at that time wore a skull cap with a piece of material folded into a ban around the turn-up edge, so that it gave the appearance of a turban.[72] When one entered a house it was the usual practice to take off one's sandals, because otherwise dirt from the unpaved streets and pathways would defile the house. If the floors were carpeted, the carpets would be ruined. Removal of shoes was therefore a mark of consideration and respect. Those coming in would then proceed to wash their feet.[73]

The clothing of women was very similar to that of the men. The Virgin also wore an inner garment. Women's tunics were usually ankle-length and blue, with embroidered edges to the V-neck, which in some cases identified the village or region of the wearer. It could be made out of wool, linen or cotton. However, the woman's outer garment differed from that of the man. It was longer, with enough border and fringe to cover the feet. It was secured at the waist by a girdle. The front of a woman's outer garment was long enough for her to tuck it up over the girdle to serve as an apron. Hebrew women did not wear a veil at all times.

Covering the head was an act of modesty that usually indicated that a woman was married. Women of the New Testament times covered their heads for worship, but not necessarily their faces.[74] Women did wear a square of material, folded to make a sun shield for the eyes and allowed to fall in folds over the neck and the shoulders to give full protection from the sun, especially since tanned skin for women was never considered beautiful or in vogue in that part of the world. This square of material was held in place by a plaited cord. A light veil was sometimes worn over the head if a woman did not wish to show her face in public. All respectable women went out with their heads covered.

Indeed, short hair suggested that the woman was a prostitute. Only prostitutes displayed their faces and showed off their hair in order to attract men. Thus Hebrew women wore their hair long and braided. The *Talmud* mentions that women used combs and hairpins.[75]

Archaeologists have found headbands at various sites; for women, as well as men sometimes, wore their hair long. Later on, the Apostle Paul would urge women to keep their hair long, as her glory and for a covering [1 Cor. 11:15], and not give cause for the heathen to entertain unseemly thoughts towards a Christian woman. Furthermore, the Apostle commands laymen to wear short hair, so as not to appear effeminate.

Also, more than likely, the Virgin also carried a handkerchief and wore simple sandals of either leather or wood.

The cleaning of clothes could be done by allowing the swift current of a stream to pass through the coarse-woven cloth, washing the dirt out and away, or else by placing the wet clothes on flat stones and pounding out the dirt. Soap was made either from olive oil or from a vegetable alkali.[76]

As far as bathing was concerned, small houses seldom had bathing facilities. More common was a shallow earthenware bowl with a ridge in the middle for the feet.[77] There were no lavatories in homes and, as a rule, human excrement was to be disposed of in the soil in a convenient patch of waste ground. Cess-pits were regularly emptied by carts during the night.[78]

Transportation

For transportation, the basic pack animal was the donkey. It could carry people as well as goods. The saddle was made of three layers--felt, straw, and haircloth. Sacks were either roped together and hung over the saddle, being tied together underneath for security, or else they were hung from a cradle that had been put across the saddle. Boxes

308

and baskets could also be hung from the cradle, and children were sometimes carried in the boxes.[79]

POLITICAL SITUATION

The Roman occupation of Palestine brought with it many benefits, but had incurred the implacable hatred of the Jewish people. The occupying forces were, in their eyes, a threat to their national heritage and aspirations. During the time while Jesus was in Nazareth, Antipas, the son of Herod the Great, was made tetrach of Galilee. He would not be banished by Caligula till 39 A.D.[80]

One feature of the political situation was the considerable measure of self-government allowed to the Jews. Much of the government of Palestine was in the hands of the ruling religious party and was conducted in accordance with Old Testament principles. There was a central council (Sanhedrin) in Jerusalem and local councils in various other centers. The central council consisted of elders, chief priests and scribes.[81]

Although throughout the empire there was a fair degree of political stability, the Romans found that the Jews were among the most turbulent of their subjects, mainly because of what they described as Hebrew religious "peculiarities" and nationalistic aspirations. In the time of our Saviour, Jewish society was roughly divided into the following groups:

(1) The Pharisees were apart from the everyday people. They were educated, middle class Jews who regulated all of life by many rules which teachers of the law, or Scribes, derived from Scripture and tradition. They believed in the resurrection and immortality of the soul, which were denied by the Sadducees.

(2) The Sadducees were rich land owners and priests who managed the temple and emphasized the laws found in Scripture rather than tradition. The Pharisees had the dominant religious influence, although the Sadducees were more politically powerful.

(3) The Herodians or members of Herod's party [Mk. 3:6; 12:13] supported rule by descendants of Herod the Great.

(4) The Zealots or patriots [Lk. 6:15; Acts 1:13] wanted to use force to gain freedom from the Romans.

(5) The Essenes lived in the desert west of the Dead Sea. This group stressed the coming of the Messiah.

THE CULTURAL SITUATION

There is strong evidence that people commonly spoke Aramaic in the New Testament period. It was in Aramaic too that Jesus would speak to Jairus' daughter to arise *(Talitha qumi)* [Mk. 5:41]; or when He said, "Be opened" *(Ephphatha)* [Mk. 7:34]; and His cry from the Cross, "My God, My God, why hast Thou forsaken Me? *(Eloi, Eloi, lama sabachthani?)* [Mt. 27:46; Mk. 15:34]; Nevertheless, Hebrew was still spoken by some Jews, especially in Jerusalem, and was normal in religious circles.

In the northern district of Palestine, there were many Hellenistic cities, to which Greek ideas and practices flourished. This is not only true of the cities known as the Decapolis, but also true of other cities on the borders of Palestine. They could not help but have an impact on certain sections of Jewish culture. However, the Pharisees were particularly resistant to the inroads of Greek culture. Although we know that Jesus used and spoke Aramaic, there is a possibility that He did not exclusively use this language, but possibly Greek when he was in Galilee. There is no certain answer whether He did or not, but many people in Galilee were speaking Greek. In all probability the area was bilingual. It need not be considered incredible that at times He expressed His teaching in forms which would have affinity with Greek modes of thought, as appears at times in the Gospel of the Evangelist John.[82]

COMMENTARY

The Virgin-Mother believed from the very beginning in the Messiaship of her Son and that Scriptures were fulfilled through Him, yet, she behaves just as she was before all these great gifts and graces came upon her. Amid obscurity and a mundane existence, she leaves all to God and claims no works, honor or reputation for herself. She continued to do the most menial of tasks. Each day the same tasks would be endlessly repeated. She is not swollen with pride nor vaunts herself; she brings no attention to herself as someone special or as the "Mother of the Messiah", but remains in the shadows. Her whole existence can only be viewed in relation to her Son.

Saint Sophronios (+c.638), Patriarch of Jerusalem, wrote that "divine love so inflamed her that nothing earthly could enter her affections; she was always burning with this heavenly flame and, so to say, inebriated with it."[83]

In closing, we bring to mind the words of St. John of Kronstadt (1829-1908), who wrote: "Truly she is most holy, firm, steadfast, immovable, unchangeable through all eternity in her most exalted God-given holiness; for the all-perfect God, her Son, has made her also all-perfect, on account of her great humility, of her love of purity and of the source of purity--God, of her entire abandonment of the world and entire attachment to the heavenly kingdom, and above all because she gave herself to Him to be His Mother, bore Him in her womb, and afterwards in her immaculate arms, nourished Him with her immaculate milk--He Who feeds all creatures!--cared for Him, caressed Him, suffered and sorrowed for Him, shed tears for Him, lived her whole life for Him alone, and was wholly absorbed in His Spirit, one heart and one soul with Him, one holiness with Him! How exalted, how wondrous, is the unity in love and holiness of the immaculate Virgin Mary with her divine Son, the Lord Jesus Christ!"[84]

Chapter XVI.
CHRIST at Twelve Years Old
in the Temple

+ + +

Only once in the canonical Gospels is the great silence broken which lies over the history of Christ's early life. The passages concerning the "finding of Jesus in the temple" give us our only direct information on the life of Jesus between His infancy and His entry into public life. This childhood story foreshadows future greatness.

In strict law, personal observance of the ordinances, and hence attendance on the feasts at Jerusalem, devolved on a youth only when he was of age, that is, at thirteen years old. But in this case, the legal age was anticipated by one year. It was in accordance with this custom, that, on the first Passover after Jesus had passed His twelfth year, His parents took Him with them in the company of the Nazarenes to Jerusalem.[1]

We note that, although women were not bound to make such a personal appearance, Mary always gladly availed herself. The *Mishnah*[2] explains that "the observance of all the positive ordinances that depend on the time of year is incumbent on men but not on women." In other words, women were exempt from any requirement which necessitated their leaving the home for any period of time. Consequently, they were exempt from studying the *Torah*[3] at school, as well as traveling to Jerusalem at the Feasts of Passover, Pentecost and Tabernacles. However, women did attend local synagogue services. According to Jewish thought and practice, the primary role of women was that of homemaker, thus they were not encouraged to leave their homes. Also, Jewish culture feared the possibility of unchastity if their women were to mingle with other men.

By New Testament times, a boy of thirteen became a "son of the law or commandment" (*bar mitzvah*). Only after the age of thirteen did a child take upon himself the full obligation of the law, and more promising lads were directed into rabbinic schools under abler teaching.[4] At thirteen a young man could qualify to become one of the ten men who could constitute a synagogue.[5]

Saint Ambrose (339-397) comments that "the public teaching of the Lord had its beginning from His twelfth year, for herein should be foreshadowed the number of those announcing the faith that was to be preached."[6]

"Now the parents of Jesus went to Jerusalem every year at the Feast of Passover. And when He was twelve years old, they went up to Jerusalem after the custom of the feast" [Lk. 2:41-42].

Concerning the conduct of the Virgin-Mother, St. Ambrose comments that "The Virgin went every year with Joseph to Jerusalem at that solemn day of the Passover. Indeed, Mary did not even go to the temple without the guardianship of her modesty, Joseph."[7] And "Joseph is ever in her company in eager devotion and a zealous guardian of her chastity. The Mother of God is not puffed up either, as though secure of her own virtues, but the more she realized her position, the more fully did she pay her vows, the more abundantly did she perform her service, the more fully did she discharge her office, the more religiously did she perform her duty and fill up the mystic time."[8]

Saint Ambrose then lauds the Virgin saying, "Mary was such that her example alone is a lesson for all....How many kinds of virtues shine forth in one virgin? She possessed the secret of modesty, the banner of faith, and the service of devotion, which showed through whether within the house, as a companion for the ministry, or the mother at the temple."[9]

Bede (c.673-735) also comments that "our Lord went each year with His parents to Jerusalem for the Passover, and that this indicates His humility as man. For it is in the nature of men to come together to offer sacrifice to God, and to join in prayer to Him."[10]

Joseph's fatherhood is restricted to a legal context, as during the presentation of the Lord in the temple and now for the Passover; these were duties outlined in the law.

Joseph is significantly not called father until Jesus is born, and the birth proclaimed by a heavenly sign.

THE PILGRIMAGE ROAD

The pilgrimage road from Nazareth to Jerusalem was not easily trod. The direct and shorter route passing through ancient Samaria was generally avoided, since there was great hostility between the Jews and Samaritans. Thus, most pilgrims took the longer route through Perea, on the eastern side of the Jordan River. The itinerary included flourishing Beth Shean (also known as Scythopolis), a city of Decapolis. Although it was a Roman city with pagan customs, many

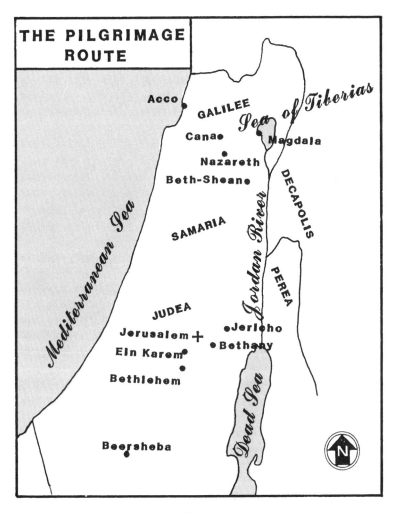

pilgrims would remain there over night. The following day, pilgrims would cross the Jordan River and head south descending a steadily sloping valley. Reaching the area of the Dead Sea, five miles north they would reach the oasis of Jericho. The final day of their trek would be spent climbing from Jericho to Jerusalem, from 820 feet below sea level to 2,700 feet above. This means traversing through thirteen miles of road through the Judean Desert. When pilgrims from Galilee would reach Bethany, two miles east of Jerusalem, they would ascend the Mount of Olives where they could view the temple. They would then descend to Gethsemane and the valley of the brook of Kidron. After this followed the ascent to the mount of the temple where they could enter by one of the eastern gates and purify themselves in the pool of Bethsaida. Some record that for them that lived far from Jerusalem, such as the Galilean Jews, the requirements for pilgrimages to Jerusalem were modified so that only a Passover pilgrimage was required.[11]

JESUS WITH THE DOCTORS OF THE LAW

"And when they had fulfilled the days, as they returned, the child Jesus tarried behind in Jerusalem; and Joseph and His Mother knew not of it" [Lk. 2:43].

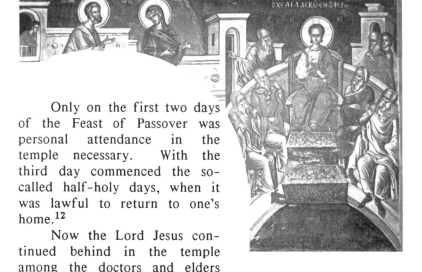

Only on the first two days of the Feast of Passover was personal attendance in the temple necessary. With the third day commenced the so-called half-holy days, when it was lawful to return to one's home.[12]

Now the Lord Jesus continued behind in the temple among the doctors and elders and learned men of Israel, to whom He proposed several questions of learning, and also gave them answers. According to apocryphal sources, Jesus is presented as a child possessed of great wisdom. Therein, it is written that He said to the Jews, "Whose son is the Messiah?" And they answered, "The son of David." He then said, "Why then does he in the spirit call him Lord, when he says, 'The Lord said unto my Lord, "Sit Thou at My right hand, until I make Thine enemies the footstool of Thy feet"'?" [Ps. 109:1].

A principal rabbi asked Him, "Hast Thou read the books?" And Jesus answered that He had read them and the things which were contained in other books. He then explained to them the books of the law, and the precepts, and the statutes, and the mysteries which are contained in the books of the prophets; things which the mind of no creature could reach.

Turning to the other doctors, that rabbi remarked, "I hitherto have neither attained to nor heard of such knowledge: Who, pray, do you think that boy will be?"[13]

Bede comments that in order to show He was a man He humbly listened to men, as to teachers; to show that He was God, He answered them, wondrously and admirably, with wisdom from on high. The divine tongue showed forth the divine wisdom, but the tender years exhibited human frailty. Hence, the Jews, between the sublimity of what they hear and the lowliness of what they see, that is, a mere lad, are troubled with doubting wonder.[14]

Saint Epiphanios (c.315-403) writes that "it was after twelve years, not after His thirtieth year, that Christ is found to be astonishing in utterances of power. Accordingly, it may not be said that after the Spirit descended upon Him in baptism He became the Christ, that is, was anointed with divinity, but that from very childhood He acknowledged both temple and Father."[15]

Now the Virgin and Joseph, supposing that Jesus **"to have been in the company, went a day's journey; and they sought Him among their kinsfolk and acquaintance. And when they found Him not, they turned back again to Jerusalem, seeking Him** [Lk. 2:44-45].

The priest-monk Bede remarks, "Someone may ask how could the Son of God, cherished with such care by the Virgin and Joseph, be forgotten and left behind? To which we answer, that it was the custom of the children of Israel that

316

when they were either going or coming from Jerusalem, at the time of the festival, that men and women journeyed separately. Infants and children could go with one or the other parent. Hence, both the Virgin and Joseph thought Jesus was with the other."[16]

We also read here that Mary and Joseph were traveling among kinsfolk. Families at that time were large and included every member of the family--aunts, uncles, cousins, step-brothers, and servants. We would call them extended families.

THE THEOTOKOS AND JOSEPH
RETURN TO JERUSALEM

"And it came to pass, that after three days they found Him in the temple, sitting in the midst of the doctors, both hearing them, and asking them questions. And all that heard Him were astonished at His understanding and answers" [Lk. 2:46-47].

Saint Ephraim the Syrian (c.306-383) describes it thus in his hymn: *In the twelfth year, they saw the child when He sat among the old men. Let the holy temple praise Him. The priests were silent when the Lamb of the feast bleated in His feast. Blessed be His propitiation!*[17]

Although He had attained an age of discretion, being twelve years old in the flesh, He did not abruptly unveil His wisdom. This too is a parable for the young, even though they might be learned, they should rather desire to hear their elders than wish to teach them and, thereby, leave themselves open to boasting. Indeed, the young Jesus questioned, not that He needed to learn from them, but that by questioning He might instruct; for He questioned and answered wisely, as He is the Source of knowledge.

Saint John Chrysostom (354-407) comments that "the Lord performed no miracles in His childhood. Luke, however, discloses this single event, through which He is seen to be astonishing."[18]

Saint Ambrose remarks that "after three days He is found in the temple as a sign that after the three days of His triumphal passion, He would rise up; He Who was believed dead would reveal Himself to our faith in the heavenly Seat, surrounded with divine honor."[19]

"And when they saw Him, they were amazed: and His Mother said unto Him, 'Son, why hast thou thus dealt with us? Behold, Thy father and I have sought thee sorrowing'" [Lk. 2:48].

"Thy father" does not mean physical paternity when applied to Joseph. Saint Cyril of Alexandria (+444) writes that "The Virgin certainly knew that Jesus was not the child of Joseph, but she so speaks to avoid the suspicions of the Jews."[20]

Saint Ephraim confirms this in a hymn, chanting, *My mouth knows not how I shall call Thee, O Thou child of the Living One: for to venture to call Thee as the child of Joseph, I tremble, since Thou art not his seed: yet I am fearful of denying the name of him to whom they have betrothed me.*[21]

The apocryphal narrative then narrates that the teachers and doctors asked Mary whether He were her Son. And when she said that He was, they said, "Blessed art thou, O Mary, who hast brought forth such a Son!"[22]

"And He said unto them, 'How is it that ye sought Me? Did ye not know that I must be about My Father's business?' And they understood not the saying which he spake unto them" [Lk. 2:49-50].

Bede explains the Lord Jesus' remark in this way: "He is not chiding them for seeking Him as a son, but rather He compels them to raise the eyes of their mind to what is due to Him of Whom He is the eternal Son."[23]

"And they understood not the saying which Jesus spake unto them" [Lk. 2:50]. Bede answers "because namely, He spoke to them of His divinity."[24]

Saint Cyril of Alexandria comments that "here He lays bare His own divinity, making mention of Him Who is truly His Father. When His Mother asks, 'Why hast Thou so done unto us?' then at once He shows Himself to transcend the measure of human beings, and teaches her that she had been the handmaid of the dispensation in giving birth to the flesh,

318

but that He by nature and in truth was God, and the Son of the Father that is in heaven."[25]

Bede comments that he believes that Joseph knew that Jesus was greater than he, and so with trepidation ruled Him. Let each one remember that oftentimes he that is the subject is the greater: which if he understands he will not swell with pride who is higher in dignity, being aware that his subject is more worthy.[26]

"Then Jesus went down with them, and came to Nazareth, and was subject unto them" [Lk. 2:51].

Saint Basil the Great (c.330-379) confirms this in his *Monastic Institutions* that the Christ child was "obedient to His parents from His earliest years. He humbly and reverently undertook any physical labor."[27]

Saint Ambrose aptly comments here that "This is the submission of filial piety, not of weakness or dependence. He obeyed the Handmaid, He obeyed His reputed father; need you wonder if He obeyed God?"[28]

"But His Mother kept all these sayings in her heart" [Lk. 2:51].

This was the practice of the Virgin throughout all her life. Nothing that was said or done by Him fell idly on her mind. She dwelt in meditation on His words and actions, cherishing them in her heart. She waits to have revealed to her with greater clarity what she beholds in the present. Bede comments that she wished to disclose to no one the secrets of Christ which she knew, but she waited reverently for the time and the manner to disclose them."[29]

JESUS INCREASED IN WISDOM AND STATURE

"And Jesus increased in wisdom and stature, and in favor with God and man" [Lk. 2:51-52].

Saint Cyril of Alexandria correctly writes that "As the Word He did not grow, for He is perfect as is the Father".[30] Not as the Word did He become more wise, but that He unveiled His wisdom gradually. Therefore, the divine nature revealed its own wisdom with the growth of the bodily stature.

Saint Cyril of Alexandria reminds us that "The Word incarnate knew the age of childhood and adolescence. Yet, at all ages of His earthly life, He reined as the same hypostatical Wisdom of the Father which was made manifest before the doctors of the law." The Patriarch of Alexandria

319

then points out to us "that Christ took all our disabilities upon Himself, for our sakes, that He might bring us to a better state; and that in man He might make a beginning of every good."[31]

Further on he comments: "A certain natural law forbids that a man be not endowed with more wisdom than the age of the body sustains, but that wisdom grows in us at equal pace with the body's growth. The Word had become man in flesh...He was perfect. He was the Wisdom and Knowledge of the Father. Since, however, as man He had to endure the manner of growth of His nature--lest he seem strange and diverse from it--so, with His body's growth, He revealed Himself to them that saw and heard Him as growing in wisdom from day to day."[32]

Patriarch Theophylactos of Bulgaria (765-840), also concurs with this writing: "Not that as He grew He became more wise, but that He unveiled His wisdom gradually. He did this in speaking with the scribes, asking them questions with regard to the law, to the astonishment of all who heard Him....The progress of His wisdom consists in the manner of its being shown. Thus, the Evangelist immediately adds 'age' to 'Jesus advanced in wisdom and age'; for the increase of age is, he says, itself growth of wisdom."[33]

Saint Amphilochios (339-400), Archbishop of Iconium, writes that He advanced therefore in age, His body advancing towards manhood; in wisdom, by means of those who, by Him, were instructed in divine things...."[34]

Hence, from this time, Christ would remain in subjection to His parents in Nazareth for eighteen years, thus sanctifying obedience. Perhaps during those years, Mary and Joseph were catching from His lips the secrets of the Kingdom which He set up in their hearts.

320

Chapter XVII.
The Repose of
the Righteous Elder JOSEPH,

**Whose Memory the Holy Church
Celebrates on the
First Sunday after the
Nativity of Christ**

+ + +

The just Joseph, of the royal lineage of King David, though his hands were covered with callouses, yet his spirit was refined and elevated with the knowledge of the sacred Scriptures to which he lived in accordance.

Though he took no part in the incarnation of Jesus Christ, nevertheless, he was chosen to be the betrothed of the Virgin and to be called the father of the Lord. He fulfilled all the duties of a father towards a son. He called His name Jesus [Mt. 1:25], had Him circumcised and paid the redemption for the firstborn, fled with the divine infant and His Mother into Egypt, and then chose their place of residence to be Nazareth.

In Nazareth, Joseph resumed his trade of carpentry, earning his living by the work of his hands, for he never sought to live by another's labor. Church tradition tells us that the Lord Himself worked along side His foster father as a carpenter.

JESUS' STEP-BROTHERS

As we mentioned, Joseph's first marriage to Salome produced sons and daughters. At the time of the elder Joseph's repose, most of Jesus' step-brothers and step-sisters had already married and were living in their own houses. This included his daughter, also named Salome, who had married Zebedee and had two sons, James and John, the "sons of thunder" and future Apostles. However, Jesus' step-brothers, Jude and James, were still living at home.

Jude had been born in Nazareth[1] and, according to tradition, his mother was Salome, the wife of Joseph and the daughter of Haggai. This Haggai was the son of Barachias and the brother of Zacharias, the father of the holy Prophet

John. Thus, this Salome was first-cousins with the famed St. John the Baptist.

The holy Theophylactos (765-840), Patriarch of Bulgaria, writes that, in their early years, Jude and others of his family did not believe in the God-Man Jesus. Whence came this disbelief in Him? It came from their own foolish will and from envy; for it is more characteristic of kinsfolk to envy their own relatives than for outsiders to do so. Thus it was clear that Jude sinned against the Lord in his lack of faith.[2]

However, Jude also showed a lack of brotherly love towards Jesus, in the following instance. Before nearing the end of his earthly sojourn, Joseph began to divide his land among his children born of his first wife Salome. He also wished to give a portion to the Lord Jesus Who was born supernaturally of the all-pure Mary. Three of Joseph's sons did not want Jesus to have a share, since He was born of another mother. Only James accepted Jesus as co-owner of his own portion.[3] Later in life, James, the "brother of the Lord", became the first Bishop of Jerusalem, and is commemorated by the Church on the 23rd of October.

However, soon in the public ministry of Jesus, Jude repented of his former doubts and became one of the inner twelve disciples of his Brother. Nevertheless, Jude, thereafter, always deemed himself unworthy to be addressed as the "brother of the Lord" and would introduce himself as "the brother of James".

THE ELDER JOSEPH'S REPOSE

The apocryphal account, *The History of Joseph*, a 4th century document, describes Joseph's last years: At length, the elder arrived at a very advanced age. He did not, however, labor under any bodily weakness, nor had his sight failed, nor were any of his teeth missing. His mind was still clear and never wandered and, like a youth, he displayed youthful vigor in his business. His limbs remained unimpaired and free of pain. But his old age was greatly prolonged.[4]

When Joseph knew that he would soon repose, he arose and went to Jerusalem, into the temple of the Lord, and poured out his prayer before the sanctuary. He besought the Lord to send the great Michael, the prince of the holy angels, to remain with him when his soul would depart. He begged forgiveness for his sins and besought the Lord's compassion.[5]

He then returned to Nazareth and was suddenly seized by disease, making him keep to his bed. The sickness weighed heavily upon him. According to the most ancient tradition, dating from the time of the Apostles, Christ Himself heard the righteous man's confession, an account of his entire life. Then, going beside his bed, Jesus said, "Hail, my father Joseph, thou righteous man." And Joseph answered him, "Hail, my well-beloved Son. Indeed the agony and fear of death has encompassed me. But as soon as I heard Thy voice, my soul was at rest. O Jesus of Nazareth! Jesus, my Saviour! Jesus, the deliverer of my soul! Jesus, my protector! Jesus, O sweetest name in my mouth, and in the mouth of all that love it! O Eye that seest and Ear that hearest, hear me! I am Thy servant; this day I most humbly reverence Thee and before Thy face I pour out my tears. Thou art altogether my God!"[6]

Jesus then closed his foster father's eyes. He then buried him in the royal sepulchre in the Valley of Jehosaphat near Jerusalem, after having embraced him and wept over him.

The soul of Joseph then departed peacefully to his ancestors, where he gave witness to the joyful news of the long-awaited Messiah.[7] According to St. Epiphanios of Cyprus (c.315-403), the Elder Joseph lived to a profound old age, having entered into rest at the age of one hundred and ten years old. He reposed just before Christ entered His public ministry to preach the Gospel.

Saint Joseph's virtue is summed up in the words of the Evangelist Matthew that he was "a just man" (*deekaos*). This was the eulogy of Holy Writ itself.

Chapter XVIII.
The Marriage at Cana

+ + +

The mystery of marriage as performed in the Orthodox Church may be found in the *Small Evchologion*. Within the text we may find references to this very Gospel reading of the Lord's attendance at the marriage in Cana [Jn. 2:1-11].[1] The service contains the following entreaty on behalf of the new Orthodox couple: "That this marriage may be blessed as was that of Cana of Galilee; let us pray to the Lord." And in another prayer of the same service: "O God most pure...Who through Thy unspeakable grace and plentiful goodness was present in Cana of Galilee, and blessed the marriage there, that Thou might show a lawful union, and that the generation therefrom, is according to Thy will...."

Saint Romanos the Melodist (c.490-c.556) speaks of Christ God's presence at the marriage in these terms: *"God, honoring virginity, inhabited a virgin's womb. He was born of her without seed; He did not break the seals of her purity. He Himself has espoused the Church, virgin and bride....He has made the bridal chamber (the Virgin's womb) a heaven. Even though He was born of a virginal and holy womb, He does not feel disgust at the union of wedlock; He Who has in wisdom created all things.*[2]

The event at Cana is set by the venerable monastic and historian Bede (c.673-735) in the context of the Church as the spouse of Christ. "It was not by chance, therefore, but by the grace of a certain mystery that Christ came to the marriage celebrated on earth. He came down from heaven to earth that He might join the Church to Himself with spiritual love. The bridal chamber was the womb of the incorrupt Mother of God, where He was joined with human nature and from where He went forth as Bridegroom to associate the Church with Himself."[3]

Saint Cyril of Alexandria (+444) makes the following observations: "Many noteworthy things were achieved by this one first sign. Honorable marriage is sanctified and the curse against women is lifted; no longer will they give birth to children in pain, since Christ has blessed the very beginning of our coming to life."[4] In a letter, he writes that

324

in order to bless the beginning of our existence, "according to the economy, He Himself both blessed the marriage and attended it when invited in Cana of Galilee along with his holy Apostles."[5] In another place, the saint remarks that "Thus Christ came, not so much as to partake of the wedding feast, but to perform His miracle; and furthermore, that He might sanctify the beginning of human generation in that which pertains to the flesh."[6]

Saint Romanos also speaks of the condescension of Christ into everyday human life. *He Who alone is borne upon the wings of the Cherubim, He Who exists in the bosom of the Father, inseparable from Him, reclined in a mortal home. He Who knew no sin, dined with sinners, in order that He might, by His presence, show that marriage is to be honored.*[7]

Saint John Chrysostom (354-407) writes: "For He Who disdained not to take the form of a servant, did not disdain to come to the nuptials of simple people."[8]

Saint Basil the Great (c.330-379) also comments on marriage, saying that "Virginity should be honored and marriage not despised."[9] Saint Romanos commends marriage: *For virgins are radiant because of marriage, since they were born in marriage. Indeed the Mother of God, the holy Virgin, even though she remained a pure virgin after childbirth, still it was marriage which brought her forth.*[10]

TUESDAY IN CANA

"And the third day there was a marriage in Cana of Galilee; and the Mother of Jesus was there. And both Jesus was called and His disciples, to the marriage" [Jn. 2:1-2].

The third day is what we call "the day after tomorrow." An example of this kind of reckoning may be seen in Lk. 13:32; "I do cures today and tomorrow, and the third day I shall be perfected." This exact specification of time probably infers that the author, the Apostle John, was present at the wedding feast. We note that Joseph is not mentioned, because the righteous man had already reposed.

The most probable identification of the village of Cana is Kefr Kenna, five miles northeast of Nazareth, on the road to the Lake of Galilee. It may be seen as built on the slope of a hill, with its houses rising terrace upon terrace. This was also the home of the future Apostle Nathaniel (Bartholomew) [Jn. 21:2].

In his poetic hymns reflecting on this episode in the Gospels, St. Romanos will unfold a religious drama for us. The scene opens in the room of the wedding feast in Cana.

"THEY HAVE NO WINE"

When Christ was present at the marriage feast, the crowd of guests were faring sumptuously when the supply of wine failed them, and their joy was turned into distress. The bridegroom was upset and the cupbearers muttered unceasingly. There was this one sad display of penury, and there was no small clamor in the room. Recognizing it, the all-holy Mary came at once and said to her Son:[11]

Theotokos: **"They have no wine [Jn. 2:3]**, but I beg thee, my Son, show that thou canst do all things, Thou Who hast in wisdom created all things."[12]

Bishop Theophan the Recluse (+1894) reminds us to "learn compassion from her who could not indifferently bear the shame of another family on the occasion when wine was insufficient at the wedding."

The Cana incident is frequently chosen to illustrate the Theotokos' intercession. Here the Mother takes the initiative. She alone mentions wine and is the intermediary between her Son and the bridegroom and, then, bypasses the chief steward, and the waiters too.

Some have commented that her words show intimacy with the family of the bridegroom, and that she knew of the failure of wine and wished to relieve the embarrassment.

Saint Romanos then poses this query to the Mother of God: *We beg of thee, O holy Virgin, from what sort of miracles did thou know how thy Son would be able to offer wine?; for the Evangelist John, inspired of God, wrote that never before had He worked wonders and made trial of His miracles.*[13]

In spirit, St. Romanos tells us the Theotokos' answer.

Theotokos: "Listen, my friends, instruct yourselves and know the mystery; I have seen my Son working miracles even before this miracle. John was not yet His disciple at the time when He performed those miracles ....I shall now touch upon matters of which I have knowledge. For I know that I did not know a husband, and yet I bore a Son--beyond natural law and reason. And I know that I remained a virgin as I had been....After my conception, I myself heard Elisabeth call me 'Mother of the Lord' [Lk. 1:43] before the actual birth; after the birth, Symeon praised me in song [Lk. 2:25-35]; Anna greeted me with joy [Lk. 2:36-38]; the magi from Persia hastened (to the newborn), for a heavenly star proclaimed the birth in advance; shepherds and angels heralded joy, and creation rejoiced with them. What would I be able to ask for greater than these miracles?"[14]

St. Cyril of Alexandria says that she asks, desiring Him to use His wonted goodness and kindness.[15] And as St. Romanos writes in regard for her desire for a miracle, *to the Merciful One, a tender Mother is fitting.*[16]

"WHAT IS IT TO ME AND THEE?"

"Jesus saith unto her, 'Woman, what is it to Me and thee?'" [Jn. 2:4].

Although the word "woman" might appear disrespectful in modern English, it was not an unusual form of address in the ancient East. The term "woman" or *gynai*, in the East, was one of respect, not equivalent to our casual use of "woman." In the Greek tragedians, the term *gynai* is constantly used in addressing queens and persons of distinction. Augustus addresses Cleopatra (1st c. B.C.), Queen of Egypt, as *gynai*. In this same Gospel, when dying on the Cross, Christ again addressed His Mother as "woman" and entrusted her to His beloved disciple [Jn. 19:26].

The King James Version of the Bible erroneously translates Jn. 2:4: "Woman, what have I to do with thee?" The correct translation is: "What is it to Me and thee" (*tee emee ke see, gynai*). These words are not a gentle rebuff, and in no way show that mothers are to be despised, but, as we will see, only emphasize the importance of the miracle and one which He indeed performed at her request.

The word "woman" was the name given to our first mother Eve; for Adam said, "This now is bone of my bones, and flesh of my flesh; she shall be called woman" [Gen. 2:23]. Now the Mother of Christ is the new Woman of whom the New Adam was born seedlessly. When the Lord God said to the serpent, "I will put enmity between thee and the woman and between thy seed and her seed; He shall bruise thy head, and thou shalt bruise His heel" [Gen. 3:15], He spoke of Himself as that Seed. And, as Eve (in Greek *Zoe*) was the "mother of all living" [Gen. 3:20], Mary is the new Woman, the new Eve, and Mother of the new humanity restored and deified through the incarnation of the eternal Son, Who is the new Man, Who would crush the head of the spiritual serpent, though He was subject to violence. According to the prediction, the condemned serpent and his seed have great malice towards the Woman; but the insults, enmity and blasphemy directed against her would be brought down on his head and his seed, thus destroying their power.

Thus, we hymn to the Theotokos: *Rejoice, O dwelling of the Light; thou hast dispelled the gloom of night, and didst wholly annihilate the darksome ranks of the demon's hosts.*[17]

Eve as the mother of the race of Adam became subject to the devil, death and corruption. However, Mary, Eve's anti-type, is the Mother of Christians and offspring freed from these destructive influences and powers, having become "partakers of the divine nature" [2 Pet. 1:4]. Speaking about this, St. Justin Martyr (+165) writes "that He is born of the

Virgin, in order that the disobedience caused by the serpent might be destroyed in the same manner in which it had originated."[18]

Saint John of Kronstadt (1829-1908) also makes mention that the demons tremble before our Lady, writing: "The demons tremble even at the sight of the life-giving Cross, because the Son of God was nailed to the wood of the Cross and sanctified it by His sufferings upon it. How much more do the demons tremble before our Lady, the Mother of God, and even at her most holy name? Our Lady is like the brightest star. She is all radiant with the Light--in God, she is like a glowing ember in a large fire, all-luminous and full of fire. As God is Light and Holiness, she, too, is eternal light and eternal holiness."[19]

"MINE HOUR IS NOT YET COME"

What is the meaning of "Mine hour is not yet come" [Jn. 2:4]? Saint Neophytos (1134-1220), the Recluse of Cyprus, takes the "hour" to mean that of His miracles. Some feel that the "hour" mentioned by Jesus may refer to Golgotha [Jn. 12:27], when He again addresses her as "Woman". In Johannine usage throughout the Gospel, "hour" refers to death or glorification. The Greek Fathers thought mostly of the "hour" as the beginning of miracles.

According to St. Romanos, *certain men made use of this saying as a pretext for impiety. They said that Christ submitted to necessity; they said that He was a slave to periods of time; but they do not understand the meaning of His phrase. However, the mouths of the impious that practice evil have been stopped, because straightway He performed the miracle.*[20]

The explanation given by St. John Chrysostom for Christ's answer, "My hour is not yet come" was not because He was subject to the need of the times, or because He was governed by the hour, but He desires to make plain that He does all things at a fitting time.

Returning to the dialogue in St. Romanos' hymns, Christ addresses His Mother, and reveals to her the following.

Christ: "I knew before thou told me, O revered Virgin, that the wine was just beginning to give out for them. I know all the concerns of thy heart that thou hast set in motion in this matter. For within thyself thou hast reasoned as follows, 'Necessity now summons my Son to a miracle and He puts it off under the pretext of "the time".' Holy Mother, learn now the meaning of the delay, for when thou wilt know it, I shall grant thee this favor.[21]

"Lift up thy heart at these words, and know, O chaste one, what I am saying. At the time when I brought forward heaven and earth and all things from a state of nonexistence, I would have been quite able at that time to arrange in order at once all that I had produced; but I introduced a certain well-regulated order. Creation was accomplished in six days--not that I did not have the power, but in order that the chorus of angels, seeing what I did, each deed in turn, would glorify Me, singing a hymn: 'Glory to Thee, O Powerful One, Who hast in wisdom created all things.'"[22]

And this is true, for we read in the *Book of Job*: "When the stars were made, all My angels praised Me with a loud voice" [Job 38:7].

Christ: "Listen carefully, O holy one. I did allow being conceived and born as a man, taking milk at thy breasts, O Virgin, and everything in Me progressed in order. For as far as I am concerned nothing is without order. And so now I am willing to accomplish the miracle in a well-regulated order.[23]

"But now, contrary to order, before the teaching, thou hast asked for miracles. It is for this reason that I delayed a short time in answer to thee. But since it is necessary that parents be honored by their children, I shall pay observance to thee, O Mother, for I am able to do all things."[24]

Saint John Chrysostom further explains this verse saying that "Christ was not yet known to those present, nor did all immediately realize that the wine was failing. He wished them to be fully apprised that there was a need, and then they would appreciate more the benefit received."[25]

THE SERVANTS ARE BROUGHT FORWARD

Christ: "Quickly then, tell the members of the household that they are to serve under My directions, and they will thereafter be the witness of a miracle for themselves and for others. For I do not wish Peter to serve Me, nor yet John, nor Andrew, nor any one of My disciples; so that no suspicion of lack of accomplishments come to men because of them. But now I want these servants to assist Me, so that they themselves may be witnesses that I can do all things."[26]

His Mother wisely brought forward the waiters, that He might be requested by many, for she was His Mother and this might render the miracle suspect. Saint John Chrysostom also comments upon this point saying that "the request ought to have come from them that were in need, not  from His Mother. And why so? Because what is done at the request of one's friends, great though it be, often causes offense to the spectators; but when they make the request who have the need, the miracle is free from suspicion, the praise unmixed, the benefit great."[27]

Here, St. Cyril of Alexandria remarks, "The Woman, having, as was fitting, great authority over the Lord, her Son, persuades Him to work a miracle. She also prepares the way for it, bidding the waiters of the feast to be at hand, and to have prepared that which the Lord will presently command."[28]

The Virgin-Mother was to be the "instrument" of His first public miracle and, again by her intercession, a countless procession of miracles would ensue through the ages.

"His Mother said unto the servants, 'Whatsoever He saith unto you, do it'" [Jn. 2:5]

Bede remarks that "Although He seems to refuse her by His response to her, she knew that He was kind and merciful." Moreover, her response is not that of one who was either rebuffed or thrust aside. Saint John Chrysostom then writes that "She knew that He did not refuse from want of power, but because He was retiring, and neither did He wish to appear to hasten to perform this wonder."[29]

We see here that the all-holy one, the *Panagia*, perceived the anxiety of those at the wedding feast. She saw their worried faces and was sympathetic to their plight and decided to help them. But she did not focus the attention on herself, but rather, she said to her Son, "they have no wine." She awaited help from Him alone. Turning to the servants, she did not say "whatever I say, do it," but "whatsoever He says to you, do it;" because salvation, glory, honor and power is unto the Lord our God [Rev. 19:1].

THE TRUE BRIDEGROOM

The Theotokos was not insensitive to the needs of others. Indeed, Christ Himself, much like His Mother, will later say to His disciples, "I have compassion on the multitude, because they continue with me now three days, and have nothing to eat: and I will not send them away fasting, lest they faint in the way" [Mt. 15:32]. The All-Merciful One is also tender-hearted and sympathetic towards the needs of others. Moreover, "can the  children of the bride-chamber fast, while the Bridegroom is with them? As long as they have the Bridegroom with them, they cannot fast" [Mk. 3:19]. According to Jewish custom, there was no fasting of any kind at a wedding feast. Therefore, how could it be that our Lord, the Bridegroom, would allow the lack of wine?

Saint Ephraim the Syrian (c.306-383) here chants, *Bridegrooms with their brides rejoiced. Blessed be the babe, whose Mother was bride of the Holy One! Blessed be the marriage feast where Thou was present, in which when wine was suddenly wanting, in Thee it abounded again!"*[30]

Saint Cyril of Alexandria analyzed the interplay of petition and response between Mother and Son, and the respect that Jesus showed His Mother: "Besides, Christ shows that the greatest honor is due to parents when, through reverence for His Mother, He undertakes to do that which He did not wish to do."[31]

At the Kariye Djami or Church of the Saviour in Chora, outside the old city walls of Constantinople, two scenes may be seen above the figure of Christ at the entrance to the second narthex: the marriage at Cana and the multiplication of the loaves with the distribution of the bread to the hungry crowd. The marriage feast is a symbol of the Messianic Banquet foreshadowed and anticipated in the Eucharist and the Bread of Life symbolized in the feeding miracles and received in the Eucharist. Thus when one enters the monastery-church in "Chora", meaning "land" of the living, those two icons over the entrance mean to indicate the truth that one is entering into the heavenly Kingdom of Christ in receiving the Eucharist.[32]

THE SIX WATERPOTS

"And there were set there six waterpots of stone, after the manner of the purifying of the Jews, containing two or three firkins apiece" [Jn. 2:6].

Everything connected with this marriage in Cana was strictly Jewish. We hear that there are six waterpots for purification--for the washing not only of hands before and after eating, but also of the vessels used.

One firkin held 10.3 U.S. gallons.[33] Purification was one of the main points of rabbinic sanctity. By far the largest and most elaborate of the six books into which the *Mishnah*[34] is divided is exclusively devoted to this subject *Seder Tohoroth*.[35] Thus, it is symbolic that the six water-pots represent these six books. Furthermore, we understand through Christ's actions that He would not offer the rabbinical laws for outward purification by water, but would offer His own wine, His Blood, for our sanctification.

"Jesus saith unto them, 'Fill the waterpots with water, And they filled them up to the brim'" [Jn. 2:7].

Saint John Chrysostom explains the reason for the Lord's directives. "That none might suspect that the lees from wine might have remained, and then water poured into them to make a very diluted wine, He indicates waterpots, showing wine had not been in these vessels. He then has them fill the pots with water, making them witnesses that what will be forthcoming is not an illusion."[36]

REJOICE, WINE-BOWL POURING FORTH JOY![37]

"And He said to them, 'Draw some out now, and take it to the master of the feast.' And they took it" [Jn. 2:8].

Rejoice, true vine that did bear the truly ripe Cluster of grapes, dripping with the wine that does gladden all the souls of them that glorify thee most faithfully, O Virgin.[38]

333

Saint Romanos reminds us that, *through the power of miracles, the Egyptians, and Hebrews in bondage, witnessed the nature of the water miraculously changed to blood. And now at the marriage feast, again He transforms nature, He Who has in wisdom created all things.*[39]

"When the ruler of the feast had tasted the water that was made wine, and knew not whence it was (but the servants that drew the water knew), the governor of the feast called the bridegroom, and saith unto him, 'Every man at the beginning doth set forth good wine; and when men have drunk well, then that which is worse: but thou hast kept the good wine until now'" [Jn. 2:9-10].

Saint John Chrysostom then explains the position and role of a "governor of the feast": He is the "chief steward who gives his opinion of the wine; for he was sober having the special obligation to conduct everything at the nuptials celebration in an appropriate manner. The Christ calls him to witness what has taken place as one who could best discern."[40]

In spirit, St. Romanos hears Christ saying:

Christ: "Draw the wine which was not harvested and, after that, offer drinks to the guests; replenish the dry cups. Let all the crowd and the bridegroom himself enjoy it; for I have, in marvelous fashion, given pleasure to all."[41]

In the following hymn, St. Romanos will describe the reaction of the guests and of us who are partakers of the banquet in Church. *When Christ, as a sign of His power, clearly changed the water into wine, all the crowd rejoiced, for they considered the taste marvelous. Now we all partake at the banquet in the Church, for Christ's Blood is changed into wine and we drink It with holy joy, praising the Great Bridegroom; for He is the true Bridegroom, the Son of Mary, the Word before all time Who took the form of a servant, He Who has in wisdom created all things.*[42]

Rejoice, thou who hast borne the Grape of Life, Who hath poured forth the wine of salvation![43]

APOSTLE SIMON ZELOTES

The bridegroom at the marriage in Cana was the future disciple and Apostle of Christ, Simon the Zealot. When the Saviour made water into wine at his wedding, at the behest of His all-pure Mother, Simon's heart was smitten with the

334

love for Christ so much so that he forsook his own bride. He then left the wedding festivities and his very home and followed after Jesus.[44]

At the wedding in Cana, I made water into wine at the behest of My all-pure Mother. There also, O Simon, I made thy heart zealous to follow Me in faith; I Who alone know what is in the heart.[45]

Although at most weddings the bride is the center of attraction, St. Ephraim points to the beauty of the Bridegroom.

Let the wedding feast thank Him Who multiplied its wine jars, for six wonderful miracles took place there: six jars of splendid wine changed from water! The King Himself, Whom they had invited, poured out the wine for them! How happy was he who was a guest there, who could turn away from the bride's beauty and gaze at Thee, our Lord, and see how fair Thou art![46]

Saint Ephraim also writes of the Apostle Simon, saying, *Let Cana thank Thee for bringing joy to her wedding feast. The bridegroom's crown honors Thee, since Thou hast honored him.*[47]

"This beginning of miracles did Jesus in Cana of Galilee, and manifested forth His glory; and His disciples believed on Him" [Jn. 2:11].

This verse is explained by St. John Chrysostom: "Now if He had wrought miracles at an earlier age, the Israelites would not have needed another to go before Him to announce Him, namely, St. John the Baptist. If He wrought wonders as a child, He would have seemed fantastic. Fittingly, therefore, He did not begin as a child to perform wonders, for then men might have regarded the incarnation as but a semblance of humanity. And, His enemies, overwhelmed by envy, would have hastened Him to the Cross before the appointed time"![48]

Chapter XIX.
CHRIST Shows Who is His
Mother, Brother and Sister

+ + +

The Saviour grew up in the pious Hebrew family of his reputed father, Joseph. They were a model Jewish family that fulfilled the whole law and certain traditions of the elders. Suddenly, the order of this family was infringed upon. Jesus, the youngest son, left the family and began to lead a singular life. He went throughout all Galilee, preached in synagogues and, what is more, associated with people of dubious repute [Mt. 9:11; 11:19; Lk. 19:7].[1]

THE PEOPLE OF NAZARETH WONDER AT
AT JESUS' GRACIOUS WORDS

The synagogue had become the center of a new social and religious life. The reading of the Torah and prayer took the place of sacrifice. According to the *Mishnah*[2] the service of the synagogue consisted of five parts: (a) the *Shema* or creed was read [Deut. 6:4-9; 11:13-21; Num. 15:37-41]; (b) synagogue prayers were recited; (c) the reading of the Law; (d) the reading from the prophets; and (e) the benediction.[3]

The mystery of the hidden years of Jesus' childhood is deepened by the obvious hardness of the people who knew Him. Evidently, the inhabitants of Nazareth did not expect Him to show forth such wisdom and to do mighty works, as evidenced by their astonishment when His ministry began.

The month was September when, for the Jews, it was the beginning of the civil year [Ex. 12:2]. It was a month for the gathering of fruits and the bring-ing of sacrifices of  thanksgiving to God. It was at this time, on the Sabbath, that the Lord Jesus went into the synagogue in Nazareth, to read.

The choice of reader and preacher was left to the ruler of the synagogue, and he could invite anyone capable of doing it. He exercised a great deal of influence and was regarded with respect. **"And there was delivered unto Him the book of the Prophet Isaias"** [Lk. 4:17]. The impact of His words before the synagogue in Nazareth was immense when He said, "'The Spirit of the Lord is upon Me, because He hath anointed Me to preach the Gospel to the poor; He hath sent Me to heal the broken-hearted, to preach deliverance to the captives, and recovering of sight to the blind, to set at liberty them that are bruised, to preach the acceptable year of the Lord'" [Is. 61: 1:2; Lk. 4:18-19].

And then, "'This day is this Scripture fulfilled in your ears'" [Lk. 4:21].

Many wondered at His gracious words, but said, "'Is not this Joseph's son?'" [Lk 4:22]. And Jesus went on to tell them that **"No prophet is accepted in his own country'"** [Lk. 4:24]. Then after Jesus cited the examples of the Prophets Elias [3 Kgs. 17:8-16] and Eliseus [4 Kgs. 5:1-14], who were accepted by strangers, all those in the synagogue were filled with wrath [Lk. 4:28].

Although astonished at His wisdom with which He taught, especially in view of His humble family connections, yet they were offended because of Him and they disbelieved in Him. **"And they rose up, and thrust Him out of the city, and led Him unto the brow of the hill whereon their city was built, that they might cast Him down headlong. But He, passing through the midst of them, went His way"** [Lk. 4:29-30].

His conduct appeared incomprehensible and possibly scandalous to some of the inhabitants of the provincial town of Nazareth. Many in His family were disturbed and decided to take steps to return Jesus to an ordinary mode of life. Understandably, the family of Jesus was alarmed, for He was not only threatened with general censure, but they believed His life to be in danger.[4]

JESUS HEALS ALL MANNER OF DISEASE

"Jesus went about all Galilee, teaching in their synagogues, and preaching the gospel of the kingdom, and healing all manner of sickness and all manner of disease among the people [Mt. 4:23].

"And His fame went throughout all Syria: and they brought unto Him all sick people that were taken with divers diseases and torments, and those which were possessed with devils, and those which were lunatic, and those that had the palsy; and He healed them" [Mt. 4:24].

AT CAPERNAUM

Early in His public ministry, at Capernaum, Christ healed many, absolved sins, and rebuked unclean spirits, yet the Pharisees sought how to destroy Him [Mk. 3:6].

"And they (Jesus and His Twelve Disciples) went into a house. And the multitude cometh together again, so that they could not so much as eat bread. And when His friends heard of it, they went out to lay hold on Him: for they said, 'He is beside Himself'" [Mk. 3:19-21].

The words "lay hold" of Jesus could hardly be attributed to His Mother. The all-holy Virgin, having witnessed so many prophecies fulfilled in her Son and the many miracles He performed, could hardly be disturbed by His conduct. Nor did she believe that He was of a weak mind and needed to be bound, though we read that several of His kindred desired to do this. We read that His relatives *(ee par aftoo)* and friends thought that He was "beside Himself" [Mk. 3:21]. Scribes from Jerusalem remarked that **"He hath Beelzebub, and by the princes of the devils casteth He out devils'"** [Mk. 3:22]. But it is impossible to believe that the Virgin-Mother conceived of any abnormality or possession in her Son.[5]

"There came then His brethren and His Mother, and, standing outside, sent unto Him, calling Him. And the multitude sat about Him, and they said unto Him, 'Behold, Thy Mother and Thy brethren outside seek for Thee'" [Mk. 3:31-32].

338

While Jesus was preaching the way of life and the kingdom of God, and actively engaged in the healing of infirmities of both body and soul, His brethren arrive, though His disciples were always in attendance with Him. His relatives are absent and, now that they turn up, they cannot wait, but prefer to interrupt Him and wish to call Him away from His great and solemn work. Indeed, persons so near to Him "stood without", while strangers hung on His every word.

Blessed John Maximovitch (1896-1966) comments that "even though full of grace, she did not yet fully understand in what the service and the greatness of her Son would consist. The Hebrew conceptions of the Messiah were still close to her, and natural feelings caused her to be concerned for Him. This included preserving Him from labors and dangers which appeared excessive."[6]

Continuing, he writes that she supported His mission and preaching. However, in this case she did not voluntarily desire to interrupt His preaching, but was pressed by the brethren to accompany them in their seeking Him outside.[7]

When they brought Jesus' Mother with them, it was only that their meeting with Jesus might have greater authority. They knew that they could not prevent Him, for, according to Jewish law, a man over thirty years of age could be independent and had the right to interpret Scripture in the synagogue.

The conflict in Jesus' family was not brought about by the all-holy Virgin, but by the conduct of His brethren who decided to interfere in His preaching, "for neither did His brethren believe in Him" [Jn. 7:5].[8]

These actions evoked His asserting the superiority of spiritual to bodily kinship.

"And He answered them, saying, 'Who is My mother or My brethren?' And He looked round about on them which sat about Him, and said, 'Behold My mother and My brethren! For whosoever shall do the will of God, the same is My brother, and My sister, and mother'" [Mk. 3:33-35].

Out of all humanity, who else might be named as the one who most did the will of God? Is it not His Mother?

Keeping in mind the deep reverence among Jews for parents, He, of all in Israel, would never be disrespectful to His Mother. There was a higher meaning to His words. Once again, as when He was a twelve year old lad, He is again saying to His beloved Mother that He was about His Father's business [Lk. 2:49].

Saint Cyril of Alexandria (+444) says, "Do not let anyone imagine that Christ spurned the honor due to His Mother, or contemptuously disregarded the love owed to His brethren; for He it was Who spake the law by Moses, and clearly said, 'Honor thy father and thy mother, that it may be well with thee.' And how, I pray, could He have rejected the love due to brethren Who even commanded us to love not merely our brethren, but those who stand in relation to us of foes? For He says, 'Love thine enemies' [Mt. 5:44; Lk. 6:27, 35]. What, therefore, does Christ wish to teach? His object then is to highly exalt His love towards those who are willing to bow the neck to His commandments....The greatest honors, and the most complete affection is that which we all owe to our mothers and brethren. If, therefore, He says that they who hear His word and do it are His mother and brethren, is it not plain to every one, that He bestows on those who follow Him a love thorough and worthy of their acceptance? Thus He would make them readily embrace the desire of yielding themselves to His words, and of submitting their minds to His yoke, by means of complete obedience.

"In order, then, that Christ may win us all unto obedience, He promises us surpassing honors, and deigns us the highest love, saying, 'My mother and My brethren are those who hear the word of God and do it.' Therefore, when bowing our neck to the Saviour's commands, we become His followers, so also are we in relation to Him as a mother and as brethren. And how will He regard us at the judgment

340

seat? Is it not with gentleness and love? What doubt can there be of this? What is comparable to this honor and goodness? What is there worthy of being matched with a gift thus splendid and desirable?"[9]

Saint Ambrose (339-397) based his doctrine of spiritual fecundity on the words of Jesus. "Through the Gospel there are many fathers and many mothers who bring forth Christ. Who then will show me the parents of Christ? He Himself did so when he said, 'Who is My mother? And who are My brethren?' And He stretched forth His hand toward His disciples, and said, 'Behold My mother and my brethren! For whosoever shall do the will of My Father Who is in the heavens, the same is My brother, and sister, and mother' [Mt. 12:48-50]. Do the will of the Father that thou mightest be a mother of Christ. Many have conceived Christ, but did not give birth to Him."[10]

Hence, from this event, we draw this conclusion: The Saviour desired to show that spiritual kinship is higher than blood relationship. Saint Basil (c.330-379) rightly comments "that intimacy with the Lord is not to be explained in terms of kinship according to the flesh, but it is achieved by alacrity in doing the will of God."[11] Christ will also utter, "Ye are My friends, if ye do whatsoever I command you" [Jn. 15:14]. Family relationships cannot be placed on a higher level than service to God. Christ foreknew that His disciples would encounter not only enemies from without, but they would encounter enmity and malice from their blood relatives.

Before sending the disciples out to preach, He said to them, "Think not that I am come to send peace on earth: I came not to send peace, but a sword....A man's foes shall be those of his own household" [Mt. 10:34, 36].

Elsewhere, we hear the Master saying, "He that loveth father or mother more than me is not worthy of me: and he that loveth son or daughter more than Me is not worthy of Me" [Mt. 10:37]. Later in the Gospel of St. Mark, the Lord tells His disciples that assuredly "there is no one who has left house or brothers or sisters or father or mother or wife or children or lands, for My sake and the Gospel's who shall not receive a hundredfold now in this time--houses and brothers and sisters and mothers and children and lands, with persecutions--and in the age to come, eternal life" [Mk. 10:29-30]. How strange it would have seemed to His

341

audience, after having taught them not to esteem mother, or father, or brothers, as highly as the word of God, that He should abruptly break off from them and leave the word of God as soon as His relatives are announced to Him.

Saint Hilary of Poitiers (+358), on this incident, proposes that "since He came into His own and His own did not receive Him, in His Mother and brothers the synagogue and the Israelites are foreshadowed, refraining from entry and approach to Him."[12]

Some have gone so far as to say that the Virgin-Mother did this out of maternal vanity or ostentation to summon Jesus to her outside the house. On the contrary! The opposite could well have been her motive. On account of her past history of reservedness, modesty, diffidence and meekness, she would not have wished to make a show of herself in front of so great a crowd; for she did everything out of love and humility.

THE KINSMEN OF CHRIST

Blessed John Maximovitch writes that it is incorrect to think that the brothers and sisters of Christ were the uterine children of His Mother, the Ever-Virgin Mary. The name brother and sister signified a certain kinship between people. Saint Epiphanios of Cyprus (c.315-403) asserts that nowhere can it be seen in the Gospel that the siblings of Jesus were considered the children of Mary. On the contrary, it was known that they were the children of Joseph.[13]

Extended family appellations, such as cousin or nephew, have no distinguishing word in the Hebrew and Aramaic. For example, since they have no word for "cousin", the Hebrew word *'ah* (brother) is used in the Old Testament for kinsman. The *Septuagint* has translated this word as *adelphos*. Thus, Laban will call his nephew Jacob *adelphos* or brother [Gen. 29:15]. The righteous Elisabeth, who is first cousins with the Virgin, is called her "kinswoman" (*syngenis*). In modern Greek the word *anepsios* has taken on the meaning of "nephew", and never to be interchanged with "brother" (*adelphos*) or "cousin" (*exadelphos*). Yet, in the Old Testament, the Greek word *anepsios* is translated as "cousin" [Num. 36:12; Tobit 7:2]. In the New Testament Greek, the word describing Marcus' relationship with Barnabas is that of *anepsios*, which has also been translated as cousin [Col.

4:10]¹⁴ or, as in the King James Version, "Marcus, sister's son to Barnabas", which really makes Marcus the nephew of Barnabas. The Aramaic of the *Peshitta* translates it as the "cousin to Barnabas."¹⁵ But the influence of the Septuagint, if used strictly, would dictate use of the other word, *adelphos*. Papyri from contemporary Egypt show similar use of the broad meaning of the word *adelphos*. We also see the broad use of the word *adelphos* occur in the Gospels, Epistles and Revelation with the same general sense. Thus, when we read of the "brethren of the Lord", we must understand it as His foster brothers or His extended family of cousins or nephews, and not as uterine brothers.

JESUS REPROVES HIS KINSMEN

After a while we learn that **"Jesus walked in Galilee: for He would not walk in Jewry, because the Jews sought to kill Him. Now the Jews' Feast of Tabernacles was at hand. His brethren said unto Him, 'Depart, hence, and go into Judea, that Thy disciples also may see the works that Thou doest. For there is no man that doeth any thing in secret, and he himself seeketh to be known openly. If Thou doest these things, shew Thyself to the world.' For neither did His brethren believe in Him"** [Jn. 7:1-5].

What is the attitude of Christ's brethren? These verses do not seem to indicate that His brothers did not believe that He wrought miracles, but that they had not submitted to His claim to be the Messiah. They required to see Him publicly acknowledged before they could believe. Thus they urge Him to present Himself in Jerusalem, though the Jews sought to slay Him. However, we just read that He would not walk in Jerusalem of Judea. Saint Basil comments here that "We should retreat in good time before them that seek to ensnare us" and "that no one should place himself in the way of temptation before God permits, but we should pray not to fall into temptation."¹⁶

St. John Chrysostom (354-407) comments that "They exhort Him to work miracles. But their words came from their unbelief, their insolence, and unseasonable freedom of speech. Owing to their relationship with Him, they address Him boldly. Their words seem to be that of friends but, in truth, they are words of great maliciousness and bitterness. They reproach Him with cowardice and vainglory. When they say, 'no man doeth anything in secret,' is the expression of charging Him with cowardice and then to add the words, 'he seeketh to be known' was accusing Him of vainglory. Their unbelief came from an evil mind and from envy; for superiority among kindred is wont somehow to be envied by them that are not likewise exalted."[17]

Hence, the Lord reproves His kinsmen for their ambition and boldness, saying, "**My time is not yet come: but your time is always ready. The world cannot hate you; but Me it hateth, because I testify of it, that the works thereof are evil. Go ye up unto this feast: I am not yet going up to this feast; for My time has not yet fully come**" [Jn. 7:6-8].

In closing, the kinsmen of the Lord ultimately came to believe in our Saviour, and became His disciples.

Chapter XX.
CHRIST Shows Who is Blessed

+ + +

"And it came to pass, as He spake these things, a certain woman of the company lifted up her voice, and said unto Him, 'Blessed is the womb that bore Thee, and the breasts which Thou hast sucked'" [Lk. 11:27].

In the midst of the provocation and the blaspheming of the scribes and pharisees, a certain woman, possessed of marvelous faith, proclaimed the Lord's incarnation. By this declaration, she put to shame both the calumny of them that stood about her and the unbelief of future heretics.

Just prior to this the Jews had blasphemed the works of the Holy Spirit, saying that Jesus cast out devils through Beelzebub, the chief of devils [Lk. 11:15]. Thus, they denied that Jesus was the true Son of God and co-essential with the Father.

In later generations there would be those heretics that would deny that the blessed Ever-Virgin Mary gave the Only-Begotten One the substance of His flesh,...and that He was true Son of man and consubstantial with His Mother. He had united Himself hypostatically to the flesh in His Mother, the all-holy one, for He is no stranger to her who bore Him and whose breasts gave Him suck.

"But He said, 'Yea, rather, blessed are they that hear the word of God, and keep it'" [Lk. 11:28].

The KJV translates the Greek word *menounge* as "yea, rather"; the New KJV translates it more correctly as "more than that". This Greek word *menounge* is a particle that is used especially in answers to emphasize or correct, even contrary to usage. Used at the beginning of a clause it means, rather, "on the contrary" or "indeed".[1]   In the KJV, see Romans 9:20, where the word *menounge* is translated as "nay but"; the *Peshitta* as "however".[2]   Again, see Romans 10:18, when the word *menounge* is translated as "yes verily"; the Aramaic of the *Peshitta* translates it as "but I say".[3]

The response given by Jesus to the honest woman's blessing on His Mother, taught her not to merely think that to be the mother of an illustrious son constituted happiness and blessing. Jesus treats the joy of natural motherhood as entirely subordinate to that of disciplehood. Indeed, the Virgin was blessed to become the instrument of the incarnation of the Word, but was more blessed in that she remained an undying keeper of His beloved word. Mary Theotokos welcomed the words of her Son during His preaching. Thus Jesus called blessed, not her alone who was vouchsafed worthy to give birth bodily to the Word of God, but likewise to all them that, from the hearing of faith, spiritually conceive the same Word; and then they labor through good works to bring it forth and nourish it, as it were, either in their own hearts or their neighbor's.

Saint John Chrysostom (354-407) comments "that He did not say this as repudiating His Mother, but to show that His birth would have been no gain to her unless she was also good and faithful in all things. Certainly, if it would have been no gain to her to have Christ born of her if she did not possess virtue, much less will it avail us that we have a virtuous father or brother or son, and we ourselves are far from virtue. For there is only one nobleness, to do the will of God."[4]

Saint Ambrose (339-397) also explains this verse [Lk. 8:21] saying, "Therefore, the Mother...is not denied; however, the accomplishment of heavenly commandments is preferred to physical relationship. This may also be understood in another way: through the figure of parents, He shows the community of the Jews, from whom He came in the flesh, but it is His Church, which believes, that is to be preferred."[5]

The venerable Bede (c.673-735) remarks that in Jesus' response to the woman in the crowd, "He sought to reprimand those 'wise ones' among the Jews who neither hear nor keep the Word of God but, rather, deny it and blaspheme it."[6]

346

THE THEOTOKOS AND WOMEN DISCIPLES OF JESUS

Although the Theotokos keeps in the background, her Son is ever on her mind. As He goes about Galilee and Judea, preaching and healing, His fame spreads throughout the country. She follows His progress with all the anxieties of a worried mother. She is aware that He oft has "no where to lay His head" [Mt. 8:20; Lk. 9:58], that sometimes He went without food, and that there were those in the crowd who envied Him and wished to catch Him in His words.

In first century Jewish society, women did travel more freely in the countryside than in the cities. The norm for a woman was to be localized around the household or the courtyard. Activity in public was to be done only when necessary and then it had to be done carefully. Women who did take an active part in public life were in danger of a charge of promiscuity; hence most participated little in public life. Respectable women did not travel alone nor with their hair unbound or unveiled. At times the Theotokos risked the hazards of traveling to catch a glimpse of her Son addressing the crowds. She is also among the women who would comfort Him and the disciples by ministering to them [Mk. 15:41; Lk. 8:1-3]. Understandably, the women disciples who followed Jesus traveled in a group, thereby making it possible for them to appear respectable.

Our Saviour did not allow the fear of immorality to prohibit Him from having female disciples in His immediate group. Consequently, He demanded the highest chastity from the men when He said, "But I say to you that whoever looks at a woman to lust for her has already committed adultery with her in his heart" [Mt. 5:28].

Chapter XXI.
The Passion of
Our Lord JESUS CHRIST

+ + +

The Theotokos, now about forty-eight years old, had always been well-read and steeped in the Old Testament Scriptures and prophecies. She knew what was foretold about her Son [Is. 50:6; 53], and the time now arrived that He would be betrayed [Mt. 26:47; Mk. 14:43; Lk. 22:47; Jn. 18:2], delivered up to the chief priests and elders, and accused and brought bound before Pilate [Mt. 27; Mk. 15; Lk. 23; Jn. 18:28-40].

Christ is then rejected by the multitude and Barabbas set free [Mt. 27:16-26; Mk. 15:7-15; Lk. 23:18-25; Jn. 18:40]. Christ then condescends, in His love for man, to His saving and dread Passion, and stoops down and raises us up. For us, He willingly endured the spittings, the scourgings, the buffetings, the scorn, the mocking, and purple robe [Mt. 27:28-31; Mk. 15:15-20; Jn. 19:1-5]; the reed, the sponge, the vinegar, the nails, the spear, and above all, the Cross and Death.[1]

A hymn from Holy and Great Thursday relates how every member of His holy body endured dishonor for us: *Thy head, the thorns; Thy face, the spittings; Thy cheeks, the smiting; Thy mouth, the taste of vinegar mixed with gall; Thine ears, the impious blasphemies; Thy back, the lash; Thy hand, the reed; Thy whole body, extension on the Cross; Thy joints, the nails; and Thy side, the spear, O Thou Who didst suffer for us, and set us free from suffering...O, Almighty Saviour, have mercy on us.*[2]

THE SWORD OF SYMEON

Bede (c.673-735) interprets the "sword" that Symeon spoke of as the Virgin's pain and grief, but not as hesitation or doubt [Lk. 2:35]. "Without bitter pain, she could not see Him crucified and dying. She was grief-stricken by the death of one taken from her flesh. Yet she in no way doubted that, as God, He would rise from the dead."[3]

One of the many *Theotokia*, also brings out the Theotokos' motherly grief: *"A sword hath gone through my heart, O Son," said the Virgin in her grief, as she beheld Christ her Son and Master hanging on the Tree, "and my heart is sorely rent, O Master, from my grief, as Symeon once told me of old. But do Thou now arise, O Word. And I pray Thee, O Immortal One, do Thou glorify Thy Mother and handmaid with Thee."*[4]

The suggestion of hesitance in the soul of Mary is opposed to Christian belief and piety, and theological reasoning, and to the words of Scripture regarding her fullness of grace and extraordinary personal experiences. The Elder Symeon is speaking to her of trial and temptation, yet there is no question of her consenting. Our Saviour Himself was also subject to temptation but did not succumb [Mt. 4:1-11; Mk. 1:13].

Saint John of Damascus (c.676-c.750) comments that she "who was deemed worthy of gifts that are supernatural, suffered pains in the hour of the Passion that she had escaped at birth. For when she beheld Him, Whom she knew to be God by the manner of His generation, slain as a malefactor, she endured the rending of the bowels from motherly sympathy. And her thoughts pierced her as a sword."[5]

Saint Theodore the Studite (c.759-826), in his lenten hymn, writes that *The pain which, in ways surpassing nature, Thy Mother did not undergo at Thy birth, she suffered at Thy holy Passion. For she was filled with agony when she saw Thee nailed of Thine own will by the Jews upon the Cross, O Thou Who hast set the earth upon the foundation of the waters.*[6]

Also, when the Theotokos saw Him pierced on the Cross, she was *smitten with the nails of most bitter grief, and her soul itself was pierced as with a sword.*[7] And, in another hymn we hear her exclaiming, *Woe! The prophecy of*

349

the Elder Symeon findeth fulfillment; for the sword whereof he spake hath now pierced my heart, rending me with sorrow, O Emmanuel.[8]

This same theme is also heard during the Resurrection Canon, when we chant: *On beholding Thee nailed to the tree, O Christ, the Virgin who had borne thee painlessly, did suffer a mother's anguish.*[9] And, *when the most pure Virgin saw thee impaled, O Logos, a mother's dirge she sang thee.*[10]

In speaking of the greatest sufferings of the Theotokos during her earthly sojourn, St. Dimitri (1651-1709), Metropolitan of Rostov and Yaroslav, records that a certain holy father was standing in prayer and, being in ecstasy, heard the voice of our Lord speaking to the Theotokos, saying to her, "Tell me, My Mother, which were the greatest of thy sufferings when thou didst live in the world which thou didst suffer for My sake?" The Virgin-Mother replied, "My Son and God, five times I endured my greatest suffering for Thee: First, when I heard from the Prophet Symeon that thou wast to be slain; second, when I looked for Thee in Jerusalem and did not see Thee for three days; third, when I heard that thou wast seized and bound by the Jews; fourth, when I saw thee on the Cross crucified between the robbers; and fifth, when I saw Thee placed in the tomb."[11]

THE DAUGHTERS OF JERUSALEM

"And there followed Him a great company of people, and of women, which also bewailed and lamented Him [Lk. 23:27].

"But Jesus turning unto them said, 'Daughters of Jerusalem, weep not for Me...'"[Lk. 23:28].

This brings to mind the prophecy of Zacharias, "...they shall look upon Me, because they have mocked Me, and they shall make lamentation for Him, as for a beloved friend, and they shall grieve intensely, as for a firstborn son. In that day the lamentation in Jerusalem shall be very great, as the mourning for the pomegranate grove cut down in the plain. And the land shall lament in separate families, the family of the house of David by itself, and their wives by themselves; the family of

350

the house of Nathan by itself, and their wives by themselves..." [Zach. 12:10-12].

When the spotless Ewe-lamb saw her Lamb driven of His own will as Man to the slaughter, she wept and said, "O Christ, Thou dost now hasten to make me who bare Thee, childless. O Deliverer of all, what is this thing that Thou hast done? Yet I pause and glorify Thine extreme goodness, O Thou Who lovest mankind."[12]

WHAT HAVE THEY RETURNED TO THEE
FOR THE BOUNDLESS BLESSINGS THEY ENJOYED,
O SOVEREIGN LORD?

The hymns during Holy and Great Thursday and Friday of Holy Week utilize a poignant and lyrical poetry wherein Christ is portrayed conversing to the people. Let us listen to the religious drama unfold in the hymns chanted by the Church.

When Thou wast led to the Cross, O Lord, Thou didst say:

Christ: "For what act do ye wish, O Jews, to crucify Me?

Is it because I raised your dead as from sleep [Mt. 9:18-19, 23-26; Mk. 5:22-24, 35-43; Lk. 7:11-16; 8:41-42, 49-56; Jn. 11:1-46], healed the woman with an issue of blood [Mt. 9:20-22; Mk. 5:25-34; Lk. 8:43-48], and showed mercy upon the Canaanite woman [Mt. 15:22-28]?

For what act, O ye Jews, desire ye My death? But ye shall behold Him Whom ye have pierced, O law-transgressors and know that He is Christ."[13]

"O My people, what have I done unto you? Wherewith have I harmed you? Thy blind have I given sight [Mt. 9:27-31; 20:30-34; Mk. 8:22-26; 10:46-52; Lk. 18:35-43; Jn. 9]; thy lepers have I cleansed [Mt. 8:2-4; Mk. 1:40-45; Lk. 5:12-16; 17:12-19], and the man on the couch have I raised [Mt. 9:2-8; Mk. 2:3-12; Lk. 5:18-26]. O my people, what have I done unto you, and wherewith have ye rewarded Me? Instead of manna [Ex. 16:4-31], gall; and in place of water [Ex. 17:5], vinegar; and instead of loving Me, thou didst nail Me to the Cross. I can endure no more. I will call the nations, and they will glorify Me with the Father, and the Spirit. And I will grant them everlasting life."[14]

When the lawless nailed Thee upon the Cross, O Lord of glory, Thou didst cry unto them:

"Wherein have I caused you sorrow? Wherein have I angered you? And who before Me delivered you from sorrow? And now wherewith do ye reward Me? Instead of goodness, evil; instead of the Pillar of fire [Ex. 13:21, 32; 14:19-20], ye nailed Me on the Cross; for the clouds, ye kept a watch at the tomb."[15]

During the service of the taking down from the Cross or the unnailing *(apokatheelosis)*, which is usually sung after the Royal Hours on Holy and Great Friday, again, we hear in the hymns, a similar theme of extreme ingratitude on the part of the recipients of His kindness. *How did the lawless synagogue condemn to death the King of all creation? Were they not ashamed when He recalled the benefits with which He had shielded them, saying to them, "My people, what have I done unto you? Have I not filled Judea with miracles? Have I not raised the dead by My word? Have I not healed all manner of sickness and disease? How then have ye*
recompensed Me? How have
ye forgotten Me? Instead
of healing, ye inflict unto
Me wounds; instead of life,
death. Ye hang upon the
tree as a malefactor, your
Benefactor; as lawless, the
Law-Giver; as a convict, the
King of all." O long-
suffering Lord, glory to
Thee![16]

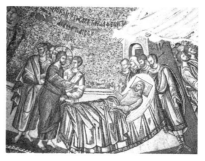

CHRIST HASTENS TO HIS VOLUNTARY DEATH

The highly dramatic and figurative strophes of the Syrian, St. Romanos the Melodist (c.490-c.556), one of the greatest of the Byzantine poets, composed the following moving strophes for Great Friday. The composition is one of his best known poems. In his poem-sermon, the melodist desired to put into poetic form the Virgin-Mother's laments. Through this hymnographic technique, we learn from the dialogue the purpose of His death and Resurrection. Thus, St. Romanos proves his theological points in what later became known as *kontakia*.

The Virgin Mother, seeing her own Lamb led to the slaughter, followed wailing with the other women, and she cried:

Theotokos: "Whither goest Thou, O my child? Why dost Thou travel along so fast? Surely there is not another wedding in Cana? Whither dost Thou speed in order to turn for them water into wine [Jn. 2:1-10]? Shall I come with Thee, O child, or tarry for thee? Give me a word, O Thou, Who art the Word. Pass me not by in silence, O Thou Who didst keep me, holy; for Thou art my Son and my God.[17]

"I did not think, Son, to see Thee among these people, nor did I believe until now that these lawless ones would rage and lay hands on Thee unjustly. For still their children cry out to Thee, 'Hosanna' [Mt. 21:9; Mk. 11:8-9]; still the road is lined with palms and bear witness to all of the general praise of the unrighteous for Thee. Then why hast the worse counsel prevailed? Woe is me, would that I knew! How is my light extinguished! How is He nailed to the Cross? O my Son and my God![18]

"Thou dost advance, my child, to an unjust death, and no one suffers with Thee. Peter does not accompany Thee--he who said to Thee, 'I shall never deny

Thee, even if I die' [Mt. 26:35; Mk. 14:31]. Thomas has left Thee--he who said, 'Let us all die with Him' [Jn. 11:16].

"And again the others, well-known and intimate friends, destined to judge the tribes of Israel, where are they now? Not one of them is here (save John). But the One above all, Thou, alone, O Son, art to die so that they may be saved, my Son and my God."[19]

THE WOMEN AT THE CROSS

"And many women were there beholding afar off, which followed Jesus from Galilee, ministering unto Him: Among which was Mary Magdalene, and Mary the mother of James and Joses, and the mother of Zebedee's children" [Mt. 27:55-56].

Blessed Jerome (347-420) affirms that the Mary mentioned in this verse as "'the mother of James (the less) and of Joses', is the Lord's Mother. James is called the 'less' to distinguish him from James the 'greater', who was the son of Zebedee."[20]

Saint Gregory of Nyssa (c.335-394) also remarks that "the mother of James and Joses" was really the Theotokos, and that this device was used by the evangelists to conceal the virgin motherhood from the Jews. Saint Gregory felt that, at this time, had they known the mystery concerning her, they would have slain her too.[21]

Saint John Chrysostom (354-407) praises the women who followed Jesus in His public ministry and who showed their quality especially by fidelity in His Passion. "These things the women see done, they who were most inclined to feel for Him, who were most of all bewailing Him. And mark how great their assiduity. They had followed Him ministering to Him, and were present even unto the time of danger. Wherefore they saw all: how He cried out; how He gave up the spirit; how the rocks were rent; and all the rest."[22] But who were they? His Mother, for she is called "mother" of James (actually step-mother), and the rest.[23]

Continuing, St. John writes that "the Evangelist Luke [Lk. 22:48] says that many lamented over the things that were done, and smote their breasts, which above all shows the cruelty of the Jews, for that they gloried in things for which others were lamenting, and were neither moved by pity, nor checked by fear."[24]

Saint John then remarks, "But the women stood by the Cross, and the weaker sex then appeared the manlier; so entirely henceforth were all things transformed."[25]

Standing by the Cross with many others who suffered and shed tears with the Mother of the Lord, St. Mary Magdalene uttered, *What a strange wonder is this, that He Who sustains the whole creation is pleased to suffer. Glory to Thy power!*[26] And, *How is He, Who put death to death slain and dying, He Who by nature is life?"*[27]

Similarly, the Theotokos, on seeing His unjust slaughter, cried out in grief:

"O most sweet child, how is it that Thou diest lawlessly? How is it that Thou Who hast suspended all the earth upon the floods of waters art now Thyself suspended from the Tree?"[28]

"Now there stood by the Cross of Jesus His Mother, and His mother's sister, Mary the wife of Cleopas, and Mary Magdalene" [Jn. 19:25].

There are two opinions as to the identity of Mary, the wife of Cleopas. The fact that Cleopas and Joseph were natural blood brothers was stated by Hegessipus (2nd c.).[29] Hence, Mary, the wife of Cleopas, was Mary Theotokos' sister-in-law.[30] Others, however, believe that Mary, the wife of Cleopas, was a half-sister of the Theotokos. How so? They purport that the Theotokos' father, Joachim, on account of the levirate law, when his brother died childless, he took his sister-in-law and raised up seed and named the child Mary.[31] We believe the latter untrue. Righteous Joachim did not have other children after he had deposited his daughter in the temple with Zacharias the priest. Moreover, a father with two daughters does not give them identical first names!

Saint Ambrose (339-397) writes this about Mary Theotokos on Calvary: "Mary was to show in her wisdom she was not ignorant of the heavenly mystery."[32] She was to manifest fortitude of soul and, in his view, "The Mother stood before the Cross and, as the men fled, she stood fearless. Consider whether the Mother of Jesus could alter her chaste behavior when she did not alter her spirit. With loving eyes she gazed at the wounds of her Son, through Whom she knew would be the world's salvation. The Mother stood--no unworthy sight--and did not fear the slayer. Perhaps she thought through her own death she would give herself for the common weal. But Jesus had no need of a helper in redeeming all, for He saved all without a helper. Therefore He says, 'I am become as a man without help, free among the dead' [Ps. 87:4]. Indeed He received the devotion of His parent, but He did not seek another's aid."[33] The uniqueness and sufficiency of Christ's redemptive act must be maintained. Although Christ accepted the love *(affectum)* of a mother, He sought no help of man.[34]

Continuing, St. Ambrose comments, "We have here a teaching on devotion; the reading teaches us what maternal love should imitate, what filial reverence should follow, that the former should come forward in a moment of danger to their sons, while for sons beholding the anxiety of their mothers, this should be a greater grief than the sadness of their own death."[35]

If Mary had fainted, the eyewitness and Evangelist John would have told us so, but he forthrightly declared that she stood by the Cross. All her hope and strength of soul is summed up in these few words. Thus when others called Him a malefactor and ridiculed Him, she stood at His Cross, blessing Him and weeping silently for Him. She stood not only in a physical sense, but her soul, as well. As a real mother, she does not doubt her Son. She now seeks to serve Him by being quiet and by taking a hold of herself. Saint Ambrose, in a funeral oration, writes: "Even the blessed Mary stood by the Cross of her Son, and the Virgin watched the passion of the Only-Begotten. I read of her standing; I do not read of her weeping."[36]

Thus, in icons of this event, she is depicted holding herself upright, her contracted facial expression is one of grief contained, dominated by intrepid faith and belief in the mystery of salvation which would be accomplished in her Son. Saint John, the beloved disciple, appears profoundly grief-stricken and his expression bespeaks intense sorrow.

Her conduct was majestic and moving; she was peerless in her nobility. She had seen her place within God's plan for man's salvation; she had read of herself in the prophets; she had spoken with angels, God's heralds. Now she knew that all that came upon her was from God, and she never grumbled in her pain. She was able to endure the affliction by the grace given her by Christ, her Son and Lord. *For Mary saw Him on the Cross and said, "Even though Thou sufferest crucifixion, yet Thou art My Son and God."*[37]

THE THEOTOKOS AT THE CROSS

Thy Mother stood near and, with a mother's lamentation, uttered:

Theotokos: "How is it possible that I should not mourn, and that my whole being should not be overwhelmed, when I see Thee naked and hanging as a criminal on the Tree?[38]

"I see Thee lifted on high, and because of Thy suffering there is neither form nor beauty in Thee; yet when first I saw Thee incarnate in the flesh, Only-Begotten Son, Thou wast fairer than all the sons of men; O salvation of all, manifest Thy glory!

"I am rent with grief, and my heart with woe is torn and broken, as I see Thee slain unjustly, O Word of God. Woe is me, my Son!...Lo, I see Thee now condemned to hang on the Cross, Thee Whom I had hoped to see a mighty King.[39]

Returning to the religious drama of St. Romanos, Christ answers the words of Mary, which she called out from her deep grief and cried out from great suffering.

357

Christ: "Banish thy grief, O Mother, banish it, for it is not fitting for thee to grieve, since thou wert called blessed....O all-wise Virgin, thou art in the middle of My bridal chamber, (meaning she will be of central importance in the Church)....Consider them in the bridal chamber as thy slaves, for everyone shall run with fear and trembling to hear thee call, O august one, when thou dost say, 'Where is my Son and my God?'[40]

"My Mother, it is for thee and through thee that I save them. If I had not desired to save them I would not have dwelt in thee, I would not have caused My Light to arise from thee, and thou would not have been called My Mother.[41]

"So that I may renew man's corrupted and subverted nature, I gladly, in My flesh, take death on Me. Wherefore, Mother, be not stricken with lament."[42]

Saint John Chrysostom writes that "by dying He rescued from death them that were dying, so by taking upon Himself the curse, He delivered them from it."[43]

Theotokos: "Why dost Thou say to me, my child, 'Do not go along with the other women?' For indeed, just as they bore in their wombs, so I, in mine bore Thee and gave Thee milk at my breasts; how is it then that Thou dost wish, my Son, that I do not lament for Thee as Thou dost hasten to submit unjustly to a death which will raise up the dead, O my Son and my God?'[44]

"Woe is me, my most beloved child! What has the ungrateful assembly of the Jews done to Thee, wishing to leave me childless...O most beloved One?[45] With what hath the iniquitous and thankless assembly of the Jews, which hath delighted in Thy many and great gifts, rewarded Thee, O my Son? I hymn Thy divine condescension!

"O my beloved Son, where is Thy surpassing beauty gone? I magnify Thy mercy, for by Thine own free choice Thou sufferest for all mankind.[46]

"Yet, why dost Thou say to me, O babe of my womb, 'If I do not suffer, Adam is not healed'?"[47]

Christ: "In thy heart, O Mother, thou dost know the truth of what I am saying. This poor Adam...was sickened, not only in body but also in soul. Willingly he suffered, not hearkening to Me, and endangered himself. Thou knowest what I say; therefore, weep not, O Mother. Yea, rather, cry aloud, 'Mercy for Adam and pity Eve, my Son and my God.'[48]

"By insubordination and gluttony did Adam become ill and was cast into lowest Hades, where he weeps in the sorrow of his spirit. Eve, who instructed him to sin, also sighs with him, having become ill together.... Dost thou understand now? Art thou fully aware of what I say? Again, O Mother, cry, 'If Thou dost forgive Adam, also forgive Eve, my Son and my God.'"[49]

As she heard these words, the blameless Ewe lamb spoke to the Lamb of God about her concern of seeing Him again while she was still in this world.

Theotokos: "My Lord, yet again would I speak; be not wroth with me. I shall tell Thee what I have in mind so that I may learn in detail from Thee what I wish. If Thou dost suffer and die, wilt Thou come to me again? If Thou goest to provide for Adam and Eve, shall I behold Thee again? For this I fear, that perhaps after the tomb Thou wilt rise up to heaven, and then I will seek to see Thee and shall mourn and cry out, 'Where is my Son and my God?'[50]

"Thus, when shall I behold Thee, O my Saviour and God, the Eternal Light, my Joy and my heart's delight?[51] O most-merciful Benefactor, do not leave me, Thy Mother and handmaid alone."[52]

Our Saviour, Who knows all things before they take place, answered His Mother:

Christ: "Be of good courage, Mother, since thou shalt be the first to see Me from the tomb. I shall come to show thee what I endured to redeem Adam. I shall also show the prints of the nails in My hands to My friends. Then, later, O Mother, thou shalt see Eve alive as formerly; and thou shalt say with joy, 'He has saved my ancestors, He Who is my Son and my God.'[53]

"Bear up for a short time, O Mother, and thou shalt see how, like a physician, I strip and go where they lie and cure their wounds, cutting their callousness and malignity with the lance. I take the vinegar and use it as an astringent on the wound. When I have opened up the cut with the surgical lancet of the nail, I shall use My cloak as dressing. I shall use My Cross as a remedy, O Mother, so that thou mayest sing with understanding: 'He has redeemed suffering by suffering, my Son and God.'[54]

"Lay aside thy grief, O Mother, and advance with joy. I now hasten to that for which I came: to do the will of Him Who sent Me [Jn. 6:38]. From the first this was ordained for Me by My Father. Never was it displeasing to My spirit to become man and suffer for the fallen. Hasten, O Mother, to tell the people that, by suffering, He strikes down the enemy of Adam and, having conquered, He comes, my Son and my God."[55]

Theotokos: "I shall conquer, my child, I shall conquer my pain. Truly, I shall not mourn when I am in my chamber and Thou art on the Cross--I in my house and Thou in the tomb. Grant that I come with Thee for it helps me to look upon Thee [Jn. 3:14; Num. 21:8].

"I know the boldness of those that trusted Moses; for Moses made a serpent of brass, and put it on a pole, so that those who were bitten, when they beheld the serpent of brass, would live [Num. 21:9]. Then the blind were taking vengeance on Moses, so now they have come to slay Thee. Moses said to Israel that the time would come that they would see Life upon the tree [Deut. 28:66]. Who is the Life? It is my Son and my God.'"[56]

She is a real mother who sees her child on the threshold of death and does not abandon herself completely to grief and despair. She is watchful and strives to keep her courage lest she add to her child's suffering the sight of her own distress. Here St. Photios interjects that "Even at the Lord's Passion, no word of blasphemy or indignation passed the Virgin's lips, which distressed mothers are wont to do at such great suffering of their children."[57]

Christ: "If thou comest, then do not weep, O Mother. Do not again be distressed if thou seest the elements of the universe dashed together, for such a reckless and daring act utterly confounds all creation. The vault of heaven is blinded and will not open its eye till I command [Mt. 27:45; Mk. 15:33; Lk. 23:44]....The temple will rend its veil before such deeds of daring [Mt. 27:51; Mk. 15:38; Lk. 23:45]. The mountains will shake, tombs will be emptied [Mt. 27:51-52]. When thou beholdest these things, if, as a woman, thou art frightened, cry out to me, 'Spare me, my Son and my God.'"[58]

O ye hills and valleys, all ye mountains and dales, and thou multitude of mankind, weep and lament, crying "Woe!" with me, the Mother of our God.[59]

Saint Romanos finishes his poem with the following words: *Thou art, as human, able to suffer, but as God, Thou knowest no suffering. Dying, Thou art saving. Thou dost grant to the holy Virgin fearless confidence to cry to Thee, "My Son and my God."*[60]

Saint Cyril of Alexandria (+444) also affirms that "God, Who is beyond suffering, suffered in His own flesh as a human being. In becoming man, though God, in no way did He cease being God;...becoming a part of creation, He also remained above creation;...being Legislator, He came to be 'under the law' [Gal. 4:4];...being Master according to His divinity, He 'took upon Him the form of a servant' [Phil. 2:7], yet He still has the inseparable dignity of a Master; ...being the Only-Begotten, He became 'the firstborn among many brethren' [Rom. 8:30]. So the all-wise Paul says that Christ Jesus, Who, being 'in the form of God' [Phil. 2:6] and equal to God the Father, 'became obedient unto death, even the death of the Cross'" [Phil. 2:8].[61]

THE SAVIOUR COMMENDS HIS MOTHER TO JOHN

"When Jesus therefore saw His Mother, and the disciple standing by, whom He loved, He saith unto His mother,

'Woman, behold thy son!' Then saith He to the disciple, 'Behold thy Mother!' And from that hour that disciple took her unto his own home" [Jn. 19:25-27].

The Apostle John then regarded her as his own mother, serving her with much respect. John's natural mother, Salome (who married Zebedee), was Joseph the betrothed's daughter from his first marriage. Therefore, Salome had Mary as her stepmother and Jesus as her Stepbrother.[62] We meet St. Salome earlier in the Gospels when she requests of Jesus that her two sons, James and John, may sit in His kingdom, the one at His right hand and the other at His left hand [Mt. 21:21; Mk. 10:37].

At the end of His earthly life, Christ voices His filial love and does His filial duty. Thus, St. John Chrysostom writes that when Christ was "on the Cross, He committed His Mother to the disciple, teaching us even to our last breath to show  every care for our parents....Here He showeth much loving affection and committeth her to the disciple whom He loved. Again John conceals himself, in modesty...for it was no little thing for him to be honored with such a dignity, and to receive the reward of steadfastness. But do thou consider, I pray, how even on the Cross He did everything without being troubled, speaking with the disciple concerning His Mother, fulfilling prophecies, holding forth good hopes to the thief. Yet before He was crucified, He appeareth sweating, agonized, fearing. What then can this mean? Nothing difficult, nothing doubtful. There indeed the weakness of nature had been shown, here was being shown the excess of power."[63]

The Universal Motherhood of the Theotokos

Saint Ephraim (c.306-383) identifies Mary as a symbol of the Church,[64] in his commentary on the *Diatessaron*: "He freed His Church from circumcision and replaced Jesus of Navee with John who was a virgin, to whom He entrusted Mary, His Church, as Moses entrusted his flock to Jesus of Navee" [Num. 27:22, 23; Deut. 31:14, 15, 23].[65]

"Hence," writes St. George of Nicomedia (d. after 880), "Mary is constituted as a guide for the disciple. She is Mother not only to John, but to all other disciples who will honor her as their Mother. If none but Christ should be called 'Father' on this earth; likewise, none should be honored as 'Mother' save Mary."[66]

That the Mother of God is our Mother too is a teaching accepted by the Orthodox for centuries. It was St. Epiphanios (c.315-403) who applied to her the title "Mother of the living," an extension of the Eve typology [Gen. 3:21].[67] Saint Nilos the Abbot (c. +430) speaks thus: "She indeed is shown as the true Mother of all who live in harmony with the precepts of the Gospel, not allowing their souls to fail in unbelief."[68] In the West, St. Ambrose thought of Mary as having a parental role, *munus parentis*, towards virgins. Blessed Jerome was more explicit when he wrote: "She is a perpetual virgin and Mother of countless virgins."[69]

A notable exponent of her universal motherhood is St. Theophanes (+1381), Poet and Bishop of Nicaea, who wrote: "In the same way as she became the Mother of the incarnate God, she is Mother of all them that are deified according to grace."[70]

Saint Gregory Palamas (+1359) also writes of her as the "Mother of us all" for she "alone, placing herself between God and the whole human race, made of God a Son of Man and transformed men into sons of God."[71] And as "she stands on the borders of created and uncreated nature, being the first to realize in her own life the fact of human deification, she represents the way and the prototype of the God-oriented man."[72]

Saint Ambrose poses an interesting insight as to why Mary was commended to John and he to her. "There is a mystery in the fact that Mary is committed to John, the youngest of the Apostles; and it does not take a strange ear to understand...for His action is related to the Mystery of the Church: formerly united with her ancient people in type, but not effectively, and after giving birth to the Word, and having sown Him in the bodies and souls of men by faith in the Cross and by burial in the Body of the Lord, she has, by God's command, chosen the society of the youngest people (i.e., the Gentiles)."[73] Thus, he has presented Mary as the Old Testament type of the Church whose first children were to be the Jews, but welcomes the "younger", that is, the Gentiles, as typified by St. John. For St. Ambrose, Mary is the Mother of all Christians who are the siblings of the Christ. He was the "firstborn among many brethren" [Rom. 8:29], and she is the spiritual Mother of all them that belong to her Son.

Saint Ambrose also exhorts us to follow the Apostles James and John, saying, "Thou wilt be a 'son of thunder' [Mk. 3:17], if thou art a son of the Church; since from the gibbet of the Cross, Christ speaks to thee also: 'Behold thy Mother'; and also He says unto the Church, when you see Christ victorious on the Cross...the son of the Church is he who sees in it a triumph and who recognizes the voice of the triumphant Christ."[74]

Saint John of Kronstadt (1829-1908) also speaks of the universal motherhood of the Virgin Theotokos, writing: "The world is a house. The Builder and the Master of this house is the Creator, and the Father of the Christian people living in it is God. The Mother in this house is the most holy Mother of the Lord. Always walk in the presence of thy Father, in love and obedience to Him; likewise in the presence of our common Mother, the most holy Mother of the Lord, in holy love, reverence and obedience to her. In thy bodily and spiritual needs, in thy sorrows, misfortunes and sicknesses, turn to her with faith, hope and love. Be holy, as the Lord God thy Creator and Father is holy; as our Lady, the Mother of God, and thy Mother, too, in accordance with the Saviour's words, 'Woman, behold thy Son;...behold thy Mother.'

"In order that we should not doubt our right to call the most exalted Mother of the Most High God, the most holy, most pure, most blessed, glorious Lady, our Mother, her eternal, divine Son, the Lord Jesus Christ, had solved our doubt by directly allowing us, or those of us who are zealous after holiness, to call her our Mother. It was in the person of St. John the Theologian that the words 'Behold thy Mother' was also said to us Christians. Yes, she is indeed our most tender, most provident, and all holy Mother, guiding us, her children, to holiness."[75]

No Other Uterine Children

It is evident that the so-called brothers and sisters of the Lord were not the children of His Mother from the fact that the Lord entrusted His Mother, before His death, to His beloved disciple John. Why should He do this if she had other children besides Him? They themselves would have taken care of her. The sons of Joseph, the reputed father of Jesus, did not consider themselves obliged to take care of one they regarded as their stepmother, or at least did not have for Her such love as blood children have for parents, and such as the adopted John had for her.[76]

Saint Athanasios of Alexandria (296-373) was probably first among the Fathers to use Jn. 19:25-27, as an argument for perpetual virginity: "By saying, 'Woman, behold thy son,' He teaches us that Mary had no other sons but the Saviour. If, in fact, she had another son, the Saviour would not have neglected him and entrusted His Mother to others....But because she was a virgin after having been His Mother, He gave her to the disciple as Mother."[77]

Saint Hilary of Poitiers (c.315-367), the most prominent Latin theologian of his time, followed the Greek Fathers in thinking that the "brothers of the Lord" were sons of Joseph by an earlier marriage: "If they had been Mary's sons and not those taken from Joseph's former marriage, she would never have been given over in the moment of the Passion to the Apostle John as his mother. The Lord had bequeathed filial love to a disciple as a consolation to the one desolate."[78]

Saint Epiphanios also is in agreement here when he writes: "If there were other children born to Mary, then for what cause did the Lord give Mary to John?...If she had a husband, if she had a house, and if she had other children, then she would not have departed from her own to dwell in a strange place."[79]

Saint Paulinus (353-431) writes in a letter that Jesus, "Himself was young, and He chose a younger disciple so that He could appositely trust His Virgin-Mother to a virgin Apostle. In this one sentence He taught us two things. First, He bequeathed to us an example of dutiful love when He showed care for His Mother, so that when He left her in the flesh He should not renounce His anxiety for her; though in fact He was not leaving her in the flesh, because after seeing Him die she was later to see Him restored to life. Secondly, by means of that utterance He carried out the secret design of the divine plan, for He demonstrated the mystery of His dutiful love which brings salvation, so that it might impinge on the faith of all men: He delegated to another His Mother so that John might look upon her as his Mother and console her in turn; and on the other hand He gave her a new son in place of His own physical appearance. I might even say that He 'begot' a son for her, to show that she had no son past or present except Him Who had been born of her virgin womb, for had He not been her only Son the Saviour would not have shown such concern that she was being left unsupported."[80]

In conclusion, St. Ambrose writes, that upon commending Mother and Apostle to each other, He "desired to leave them the heritage of His love and His grace."[81]

Now let us hear the Virgin-Mother's response to her Son's careful solicitude: *O my Son, behold Thy well-beloved disciple and Thy Mother; let us, as aforetime, hear Thy sweet voice again.*[82]

LIFE FALLS ASLEEP

In the tradition of iconography, Christ is represented naked, by having only a white cloth covering His loins. The flexion of the body is towards the right with bowed head. His closed eyes indicate His death. His face, turned towards His Mother, preserves a grave expression of majesty in suffering, an expression which gives the impression of sleep. The Cross is placed upon the rocky summit of Golgotha, "the place of the skull". Beneath the Cross there is a dark space with the skull of Adam.

Saint John Chrysostom comments that "some say that Adam died there (Golgotha) and lieth at the place of the skull. Thus in the place where death reigned, Jesus set up the trophy. For He went forth bearing the Cross as a trophy over the tyranny of death."[83] Saint Epiphanios adds that "Adam was restored to life by the drops of Christ's blood that fell on his skull."[84]

By Thy death, O Saviour, Thou hast led back to life Adam, who of old, by malice was made to die; Thou wast seen as the new Adam in the flesh.[85]

HIS SIDE IS PIERCED

"But when they (the soldiers) came to Jesus, and saw that He was dead already, they did not break His legs: but one of the soldiers with a spear pierced His side, and forthwith came there out blood and water" [Jn. 19:33-34].

366

Today there is hung upon the Tree He that suspended the earth upon the waters. A crown of thorns is placed upon Him, Who is the King of the angels. With false purple is He wrapped about, He that wrappeth the heavens with clouds. Buffetings did He receive, Who freed Adam in the Jordan. With nails was He affixed, He that is the Bridegroom of the Church. With a lance was He pierced, He that is the Son of the Virgin. We worship Thy Passion, O Christ. Show also unto us Thy glorious Resurrection.[86]

Saint Gregory Palamas, who saw death as being directly related to sin, thought how else could Jesus have died, save by a violent death? He had no need to suffer a natural death which is the result of the fall.[87]

Saint John Chrysostom comments, "Yet they, to gratify the Jews, pierced His side with a spear, and now insulted the dead body. O abominable and accursed purpose!...Be not confounded, for the things which these men did from a wicked will, served on the side of truth. There was a prophecy, 'They shall look on Him Whom they pierced' [Zach. 12:10]. With this too an ineffable mystery was accomplished; for 'there came forth water and blood.' Not without a purpose, or by chance, did those founts come forth, but because by means of these two together the Church consisteth. And the initiated know it, being by water indeed regenerated, and nourished by the blood and the flesh. Hence the mysteries take their beginning; that when thou approach to that awful Cup, thou mayest so approach as drinking from the very side."[88]

Saint John of Damascus writes: "He caused the fountain of remission to well forth for us out of His holy and immaculate side: water for our regeneration, and the

367

washing away of sin and corruption; and blood to drink as the earnest of life eternal."[89]

Saint Ambrose comments that "Indeed He died in that which He took from the Virgin, not in that which He had from the Father, for Christ died in that in which He was crucified....He took on flesh and bones that on that Cross the temptations of our flesh might die. For He took on what He was not, that He might conceal what He was; He concealed what He was, that He might be tempted in it, and that which He was not might be redeemed, that He might call us to that which He was, through that which He was not. O, the divine mystery of that Cross!"[90]

Saint John of Kronstadt also makes mention that after the Crucifixion, it was our Lord's intention that His Mother, after Himself, be everything to us. He writes that "It was for our sakes that the Lord was incarnate, suffered, was crucified, died and rose from the dead. It was for our sakes also that He adorned His Mother, the most pure Virgin Mary, with all virtues, and endued her with all divine powers, so that she, the most merciful and the most perfect, should be, after Himself, everything to us. And, therefore, let not God's grace, with which our Lady is filled, be fruitless for us. Let us all come with boldness and trust to the Virgin's wonderful, ever-helpful and most pure protection."[91]

The King and God goes forth wearing the purple dyed from thy blood, O all-undefiled. He has renewed all mankind in His compassion.[92]

THE NOBLE JOSEPH, TAKING THINE IMMACULATE BODY DOWN FROM THE TREE, AND HAVING WRAPPED IT IN PURE LINEN AND SPICES, LAID IT FOR BURIAL IN A NEW TOMB[93]

"And when evening had come, there came a rich man of Arimathea, named Joseph, who also himself was Jesus' disciple. He went to Pilate, and begged the body of Jesus. Then Pilate commanded the body to be delivered" [Mt. 28:57-58].

The Evangelist Luke adds that Joseph was "a good man and just: the same had not consented to the counsel and deed of them. He was of Arimathea, a city of the Jews; who also himself waited for the kingdom of God" [Lk. 23:50-51].

After Christ's death, the approach of sunset made it difficult for the disciples--unprepared as they were, even if they had recovered their courage--to arrange duly for the reverent interment of the Master before the Sabbath began. Enter Joseph, hitherto faint-hearted, who rose to the occasion. The spectacle of the crucified Saviour had quickened his faith and love. His boldness is the more notable, because, to all human appearances, he was showing sympathy with a "ruined cause" at the risk of persecution or death. His example, presumably, moved the blessed Nicodemos to similar courage.

Saint John Chrysostom lauds him by saying, "This was Joseph, who was concealing his discipleship of late; now, however, he had become very bold after the death of Christ. For neither was he an obscure person, nor of the unnoticed; but one of the Council, and highly distinguished; from which circumstance especially one may see his courage. Joseph exposed himself to death, taking upon him enmity with all, by his affection to Jesus, both having dared to beg the body, and not having desisted until he obtained it.[94]

Saint Ephraim the Syrian comments that the choice of St. Joseph of Arimathea for the burial of Christ was "so that full honor should be given to the name of Joseph, which presided at His burial as at His birth in the cave."[95]

We chant in Matins for Great Saturday: *Once a Joseph bare Thee into exile, Saviour; another doth inter Thee.*[96]

Saint Romanos also reminds us of the Christ-type figure to be found in righteous Joseph the All-Comely when he was waylaid by his brothers and cast into a pit [Gen 37:18, 20, 24]. *When, after the Crucifixion, the God of Joseph, Who once saved Joseph from the well, was laid in the tomb by a Joseph.*[97]

O Thou Who puttest on light like a robe, when Joseph, with Nicodemos, brought Thee down from the Tree and beheld Thee dead, naked, and unburied, he mourned outwardly and grievously, saying:

Joseph: "Woe is me, sweet Jesus, Whom but a while ago, when the sun beheld suspended upon the Cross, it was shrouded in darkness, the earth quaked with fear, and the veil of the temple was rent asunder. Albeit, I see that Thou willingly endurest death for my sake. How then shall I array Thee, my God? How shall I wrap Thee with linen? Or what dirges shall I chant for Thy funeral?

"Wherefore, O compassionate Lord, I magnify Thy passion, and praise Thy burial with Thy Resurrection, crying, 'Lord glory to Thee.'"[98]

NICODEMOS, THE PHARISEE AND DISCIPLE OF JESUS

"And there came also Nicodemus, who at the first came to Jesus by night, and he brought a mixture of myrrh and aloes, about a hundred pound weight" [Jn. 19:39].

Nicodemos was a Pharisee and a ruler of the Jews which meant that he was a member of the court of seventy elders, known as the Sanhedrin, which was the highest religious body among the Jews. As a secret disciple, he attempted to defend Jesus before the Sanhedrin, insisting, "Doth our law judge any man, before it hear him, and know what he doeth?" [Jn. 7:51]. The taunting reply that he received was: "Art thou also of Galilee? Search and look: for out of Galilee ariseth no prophet" [Lk. 7:52]. Conveniently, they

370

seemed to have overlooked the eighth century Prophet Jonas who was born at Geth-chopher [2 Kings. 14:25], in the territory of Zebulon, about five miles north of Nazareth in northern Galilee![99]

The Evangelist John reports that Nicodemos brought a "mixture of myrrh and aloes" [Jn. 19:39], which brings to mind the statement of the prophet, "Myrrh and stacte and cassia exhale from Thy garments" [Ps. 44:7].

Myrrh is a symbol of burial. Aloes is a very refined form of myrrh. When the aromatic herb is squeezed, whatever part of it is liquid is separated as aloes, but the denser part which is left is called myrrh. Cassia is a very delicate and fragrant bark which is tightly stretched around a woody stalk. Saint Basil comments in his *Homily 17, On Psalm 44 (LXX)* that "you have myrrh because of burial; aloes, because of the passage down to the lower world (since every drop is borne downward); and cassia, because of the dispensation of the flesh upon the wood of the Cross.[100]

THE BURIAL OF JESUS

"And when Joseph had taken the body, he wrapped it in clean linen cloth, and laid it in his own new tomb, which he had hewn out in the rock: and he rolled a great stone to the door of the sepulchre and departed" [Mt. 27:59-60].

According to Jewish tradition, burial never took place on a Sabbath or a holy day [Jn. 19:31]. The body was normally washed and wrapped loosely in linen cloth. In the exceptional case of our Saviour, the body was covered in spices and in paste, and these were tied to the body by layers of white roller bandage. The paste hardened and impregnated the bandages until a hard preservative mold or cocoon was formed about the body. A cap was placed on the head, and often the jaw was held in position by a bandage under the chin. The body was then carried to the burial place on a wooden stretcher. All this was performed for Jesus by these two wealthy men, Joseph and Nicodemos.[101]

In iconography, Christ is shown wrapped, after the unnailing, in one large sheet. Subsequently, He is depicted in winding roller bandage.

JOSEPH AND THE BLESSED DISCIPLE NICODEMOS TEND THE LIFE-GIVING BODY[102]

Dirges at the tomb did blest Joseph sing with Nicodemos, chanting unto Christ, Who hath now been put to death; and in song with them are joined the seraphim. And, *wrapping Thee, O Christ, in myrrh oils in a manner unwonted, Nicodemos and the most noble Joseph cried, "Be thou terrified and quake with fear, O earth!"*[103]

Overcome with holy fear, Joseph cried:

Joseph: "The centurion knew Thee as God even when they slew Thee. How then, O my God, dare I touch Thee with my hands? I do shudder.

"Ah, those eyes so sweet, and Thy lips, O Word, how shall I close them? How shall I entomb Thee as doth befit the dead?"[104]

The Evangelist John also adds that **"they took the body of Jesus, wound it in linen clothes with the spices, as the manner of the Jews is to bury"** [Jn. 19:40]. And he also remarks that the sepulchre was near at hand. **"Now in the place where He was crucified there was a garden; and in the garden a new sepulchre, wherein was never man yet lain"** [Jn. 19:41].

Saint John Chrysostom remarks that "not by taking the body only, nor by burying it in a costly manner, but by laying it in his own new tomb, he showed his love, and his courage. And this was not so ordered without purpose, but so there should not be any bare suspicion, that one had risen instead of another."[105]

A LAMENTATION OF THE THEOTOKOS

Now all these things, the Crucifixion, the death, the piercing, the unnailing and the burial, the most pure Virgin witnessed with profound grief.

Prosaical lamentations entitled *The Lamentations of the Theotokos When the Honorable Body was Wrapped*, written in the ninth century, by St. Symeon the Translator *(Meta-*

phrastes), are mixed with agony and theology. The essential fragments of this work are presented herein:

"O sweetest Jesus! I remember that the wise men who arrived in Bethlehem at the time of thy birth and brought Thee not only gold as a King, and frankincense as God, but also myrrh as prefiguring Thy death! I remember what Symeon said that a sword would pierce my soul!...

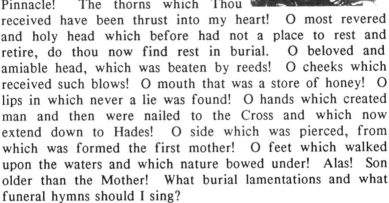

"Which member of Thy body escaped the Passion? O Divine Pinnacle! The thorns which Thou received have been thrust into my heart! O most revered and holy head which before had not a place to rest and retire, do thou now find rest in burial. O beloved and amiable head, which was beaten by reeds! O cheeks which received such blows! O mouth that was a store of honey! O lips in which never a lie was found! O hands which created man and then were nailed to the Cross and which now extend down to Hades! O side which was pierced, from which was formed the first mother! O feet which walked upon the waters and which nature bowed under! Alas! Son older than the Mother! What burial lamentations and what funeral hymns should I sing?

"How was it that only Nicodemos pulled the nails from Thy hands and feet and took down Thy body from the Cross. And he laid it in my arms....Before I made Thee infant's garments, now I am busy with Thy funeral garments! O paradox!...Then I was freed from the pains of birth, but now at Thy funeral I accept all grief! Many times I remained sleepless, holding Thee as an infant to my breast, but now Thou dost sleep among the dead!....But now, as Thou hast

said, rebuild in three days the Temple [Mk. 8:31; Jn. 2:19] which Thou hast demolished!"[106]

Hasten and arise, that I also may behold Thy Resurrection from the dead on the third day.[107]

After interring Christ's body, St. Joseph of Arimathea was fettered by the Jews and cast into prison. The risen Lord appeared to him and brought him to belief in His Resurrection from the dead. The Jews then released Joseph and drove him out of Judea.

Traveling all about preaching the Gospel, the holy man also preached in England where he entered into rest.[108]

THE DESCENT INTO HADES

Christ's victory over Hades, the deliverance of our first parents and of the righteous of the Old Testament is the main theme of the icon, "The Descent into Hades." Thus we see, in all these icons, broken doors, chains, keys and nails that symbolize the despoiling of Hades. At times, there is also depicted a bound and dark figure, personifying death.

The following hymns from Holy and Great Friday and Saturday Vespers, help explain the meaning of this icon.

When Thou, the Redeemer of all, had been laid for all in the new tomb, Hades, the respecter of none, saw Thee and crouched in fear. The bars broke, the gates were shattered, the graves were opened, the dead arose. Then Adam, thankfully rejoicing, cried out to Thee, "Glory to Thy condescension, O Merciful Master."[109]

Today hell groans and cries aloud, "My dominion has been swallowed up; the Shepherd has been crucified and He has raised Adam. I am deprived of them that once I ruled; in my strength I devoured them, but now I have cast them forth. He Who was crucified has emptied the tombs; the power of death has no more strength." **And,** *Today hell groans and cries aloud, "It had been better for me, had I not accepted Mary's Son, for He has come to me and destroyed my power; He has shattered the gates of brass, and as God He has raised up the souls that once I held."*[110]

And, When Thou, O Christ, didst submit in the flesh to be committed to the tomb, though Thou wert by nature of the Godhead and still remained infinite and limitless, then didst Thou shut up and empty out all the store-houses and palaces of Hades and of Death, then also didst Thou honor this Sabbath with Thine own splendor and divine blessing and glory.[111]

375

Chapter XXII.
The THEOTOKOS and the Myrrh-bearers:
MARY MAGDALENE, MARY, JOANNA,
SALOME, SUSANNA, MARY and MARTHA,

Whose Memory the Holy Church
Celebrates on the
Sunday of the Myrrh-bearing Women,
the Third Sunday of Pascha

+ + +

Each of the four Evangelists contributes valuable details concerning the events of the Resurrection of our Lord Jesus Christ. Not all these distinctive items of information are contained in all four Gospels. However, nothing could be clearer than that all four testify to the event that the same Jesus Who was crucified on Great Friday rose again in His crucified body early Pascha morning.

By Jewish reckoning it was the third day from His death. It is interesting to note that the third day was also spoken of by the Prophet Hosea in connection with the resurrection from the dead: "After two days He will heal us: in the third day we shall arise, and live before Him" [Hos. 6:3].

Each of the four writers contributed individual details from his own perspective and emphasis, yet inspired by the Holy Spirit. A careful examination of all four records in comparison with one another demonstrates that they are not in any way contradictory, despite the charges of some critics. It will be helpful to our study to consolidate the evidence given in all four accounts in order to arrive at a fuller picture of what took place that Sunday morning. If we knew all the circumstances, we would see that they are all harmonious.

SYNOPSIS

Let us propose the following synopsis of the events which took place involving the myrrh-bearers, to facilitate understanding the various Gospel readings concerning the first paschal morning. Before the first day of the week, the women disciples determined to meet at the sepulchre. Coming from various points in the city, they proceeded in two or more groups. This explains why in icons of this scene the number of myrrh-bearers varies from one to six or more.

It happened that there was an earthquake when an angel of the Lord descended and rolled back the stone [Mt. 28:2]. Saint Gregory Palamas (+1359], in his *Homily On the Sunday of the Myrrh-bearing Women*, believes that Mary Theotokos, together with Mary Magdalene, were first to arrive and witnessed the descent of the angel who rolled back the stone at the time of the earthquake. At that time it was still dark, but beginning to dawn [Mt. 28:1; Jn. 20:1]. The Myrrh-bearer, Mary Magdalene, seeing the stone taken away from the sepulchre [Jn. 20:1] and the soldiers [Mt. 28:4], ran immediately to notify Simon Peter and John [Jn. 20:2], leaving the Virgin at the sepulchre. It is at this time when the Virgin was alone at the sepulchre that her Son appeared to her first. Later in this section we will put forward the writings of the hymnographers, Saints Romanos, Theophanes, George of Nicomedia, Gregory of Nyssa, Hesychios of Jerusalem, Gregory Palamas and Cyril of Alexandria supporting this point.

As the sun was rising [Mk. 16:2] Mary Theotokos was joined by Salome [Mk. 16:1] and Joanna [Lk. 24:10] who brought the sweet spices and ointments that they all had earlier bought [Mk. 16:1] and prepared before the Sabbath [Lk. 23:56]. Certain other women were with them [Lk. 24:1] whom we know through holy Tradition were the Myrrhbearers Mary (the wife of Cleopas), Susanna, Martha and Mary. In all likelihood Lazarus' sisters Mary and Martha, both from Bethany, had been staying in Jerusalem.

These other women, not realizing then that the angel had already rolled away the stone, said among themselves, "Who shall roll away for us the stone at the door of the sepulchre?" [Mk. 16:3]; for it was very great [Mk. 16:4]. When the women looked, they saw that the stone was rolled away [Mk. 16:4].

Then the women beheld an angel sitting upon the stone that had been rolled back [Mt. 28:2]. And his countenance

377

was like lightning, and his raiment white as snow [Mt. 28:3]. Meanwhile, the guards, for fear of the angel, became as dead men [Mt. 28:4].

The angel then addresses the women saying, "Fear not: for I know that you seek Jesus Who was crucified [Mt. 28:5]. He is not here; for He is risen, as He said [Mt. 28:6]. The angel then invites the women saying, "Come, see the place where the Lord lay" [Mt. 28:6].

The women entered into the sepulchre [Mk. 16:5; Lk. 24:4], but did not find the body of the Lord Jesus [Lk. 24:3]. The Evangelist Mark describes that they found an angel inside who was sitting on the right side, clothed in a long white raiment; the women were afraid [Mk. 16:5]. This angel then says to them, "Be not afraid. Ye seek Jesus of Nazareth Who was crucified. He is risen. He is not here. Behold the place where they laid Him!" [Mk. 16:6].

It came to pass, as the women were very perplexed [Lk. 24:4] that the angel from the outside also entered in. Now, two angels stood by the women in shining garments [Lk. 24:4]. The women now, still afraid, bowed down their faces to the earth [Lk. 24:5]. The angels then addressed them saying, "Why do you seek the living among the dead?" [Lk. 24:5] He is not here, but He is risen. Remember how He spoke unto you while He was in Galilee [Lk. 24:6]. He said, 'The Son of Man must be delivered into the hands of sinful men, and be crucified, and the third day rise again'" [Lk. 24:7]. And the women disciples remembered His words [Lk. 24:8].

The angel that had met the women outside, then says, "Go quickly, and tell his disciples that He is risen from the dead" [Mt. 28:7]. The angel whom they had found inside sitting on the right side also says, "Go your way, tell His disciples", but he adds, "and Peter" [Mk. 16:7]. Then both angels told the women that the Lord would go before them into Galilee and that they would see Him there [Mt. 28:7; Mk. 16:7], just as He said [Mk. 16:7]. The angel who had met them outside then closes the dialogue, saying, "Lo, I have told you" [Mt. 28:7].

The Theotokos and her myrrh-bearing companions quickly departed from the sepulchre with fear and great joy, and hastened to bring the men disciples word [Mt. 28:8]. The Evangelist Mark characterizes the women as fleeing from the tomb, for they trembled and were amazed. They did not say anything to any man, for they were afraid [Mk. 16:8]; that is, they did not pause to talk to anyone save the eleven, and to the rest of the disciples [Lk. 24:9]. Saint Gregory Palamas is of the opinion that only the Theotokos truly understood the import of the angels' words.[1]

While the women departed to disclose what they had seen and heard, Mary Magdalene, who earlier had hastened from the sight of the rolled away stone [Jn. 20:2], told Simon Peter and John, "They have taken away the Lord out of the sepulchre, and we do not know where they laid Him" [Jn. 20:2]. She said this because she had not heard the words of the angels, nor had she seen the Lord yet. Saint Gregory Palamas also brings forward this observation about Mary Magdalene.[2]

Then arose Simon [Lk. 24:12] and he went out [Jn. 20:3] together with the other disciple John, and they went to the sepulchre [Jn. 20:4]. Now the two men ran, but the youthful John outran Peter [Jn. 20:4]. Though John first reached the sepulchre and stooped down to look in, he did not enter [Jn. 20:5]. Simon Peter finally caught up and he entered the sepulchre. He noted the grave clothes and how they were positioned. The napkin that was about the Lord's head was not with the linen clothes, but wrapped in its place by itself [Jn. 20:7]. Then John entered and saw and believed [Jn. 20:8]; for as yet they knew not the Scripture that He must rise again from the dead [Jn. 20:9]. Without ever mentioning the disciple John at all, the Evangelist Luke records that Peter departed and wondered in himself at that which came to pass [Lk. 24:12]. However, John records in his Gospel that the disciples, that is, Peter and himself, went away again to their own home [Jn. 20:10].

After this, St. Mary Magdalene came to the tomb and stood outside weeping. As she wept, she stooped down and looked into the sepulchre [Jn. 20:11]. She saw two angels sitting in white garments: the one at the head and the other at the feet where the body of Jesus had lain [Jn. 20:12]. The angels addressed Mary saying, "Why weepest thou?" She answered, "Because they have taken away my Lord, and I do not know where they have laid Him" [Jn. 20:13]. After saying this, she turned herself back and saw One standing there. He said to her the same thing, "Woman, why weepest thou?" But He adds, "Whom seekest thou?" Now Mary supposed that He was the gardener, and said, "Sir, if Thou hast borne Him hence, tell me where Thou hast laid Him, and I will take Him away" [Jn. 20:15].

Jesus then calling her by name, "Mary," caused her to turn, and she said, "Master" [Jn. 20:16]. Then He said to her, "Touch Me not; for I am not yet ascended to My Father. But go to My brethren and say to them, 'I ascend unto My Father, and your Father, and to My God, and your God'" [Jn. 20:17]. Mary then hastened to report to the other disciples those things she had seen and heard from the Lord [Jn. 20:18].

Now the other myrrh-bearers had already departed the tomb site to announce the glad tidings to the brethren. It is not improbable that Mary Magdalene might have overtaken the other women and joined them before Jesus appeared to His Mother and to the other myrrh-bearers. He met them with the greeting, "Rejoice" *(Chairete)* [Mt. 28:9]. They, too, attempted like Mary Magdalene to take hold of Him [Jn. 20:17]. Yet, St. Gregory Palamas believes that it was His pure Mother who actually held Him by the feet,[3] but all worshipped Him [Mt. 28:9].

Jesus then encouraged His women disciples, saying, "Be not afraid. Go and announce to My brethren to go into Galilee, and there they shall see Me" [Mt. 28:10]. The Theotokos, Mary Magdalene, Joanna and the other women that were with them did in fact relate all these things to the apostles [Lk. 24:10]. But their words seemed to them as idle tales, and they believed them not [Lk. 24:11]. The Evangelist Mark also adds that Mary Magdalene, to whom Jesus appeared "first" went and told the others, as they mourned and wept [Mk. 16:9-10]. But when they heard that He was alive and that she herself had seen Him, they did not believe her either [Mk. 16:11].

However, we learn that afterwards, the Lord appeared to the eleven as they sat at meat and He upbraided them for their unbelief and hardness of heart, because they believed not them that had seen Him after He arose [Mk. 16:14].

We will now discuss, point by point, the events of that great and holy Friday, Saturday and Sunday.

+

THE HOLY SEPULCHRE

From the Feast of the Sunday of the Myrrh-bearing Women, we learn, *"Joseph asked for the body of Jesus and laid it in his new sepulchre; for it was meet that He should come forth from the grave, as from a bridal chamber. O Thou Who didst crush the might of*

death, and didst open the gates of paradise unto man, glory be to Thee![4]

"And that day was the preparation, and the Sabbath drew on. And the women also, which came with Him from Galilee, followed after, and beheld the sepulchre, and how His body was laid" [Lk. 23:54-55].

"And Mary Magdalene and Mary the mother of Joses beheld where He was laid" [Mk. 15:47].

"And there was Mary Magdalene, and the other Mary, sitting over against the sepulchre" [Mt. 27:61].

A hymn in the Matins service to St. Mary Magdalene remarks, *Gazing at the tomb with expectation, she cried out, "Thou hast been pleased to suffer: Glory to Thy power."*[5]

Saint Gregory Palamas (+1359) identifies the myrrh-bearers as "all those women who followed with the Mother of the Lord, stayed with her during those hours of the salvific passion, and with pathos anointed Christ with myrrh."[6] Saint John Chrysostom (354-407) comments, "See thou the courage of the women? Dost thou behold their affection?"[7]

Saint Gregory of Nyssa (c.335-394) thought that the Theotokos was "the other Mary" who, according to Mt. 28:1, came to the tomb on Pascha morning with Mary Magdalene.[8] Saint Gregory Palamas also writes: "With the expression, 'and the other Mary', the Evangelist means, without a doubt, the Mother of Christ. She was also called the mother of James and Joses, who were the children of Joseph, her betrothed."[9] In the same spirit, Nicephoros Callistos (+c.1335) writes that the "other Mary" was the Theotokos, who burned with longing and melancholy as did Mary Magdalene, and so she accompanied her to the tomb.[10]

Well does the blessed Jerome (347-420) comment to Helvidius, saying, "What a poor and impious view we take of Mary, if we hold that when other women were concerned about the burial of Jesus, she, His mother, was absent; or if we invent some kind of a second Mary; and all the more because the Gospel of St. John testifies that she was there present, when the Lord upon the Cross commended her, as His Mother and now widow, to the care of John."[11]

In the *Lamentations*, we see that the Theotokos was indeed at the sepulchre: *Thy pure Mother, weeping bitter tears over Thee, cried to Thee, "O my Jesus, O my Saviour, O my Son, how can I lay Thee in the grave?"* And, *"Gone the Light the world knew! Gone the Light that was mine! O my Jesus, my Beloved and Desired One!"* So the Virgin spake lamenting in her grief.[12]

"And they returned, and prepared spices and ointments; and rested the Sabbath day according to the commandment" [Lk. 23:56].

The names of seven of the myrrh-bearers that have come down to us are: St. Mary Magdalene (commemorated by the Holy Church on the 22nd of July and the 4th of May); St. Salome, the mother of the sons of Zebedee (3rd of August); St. Mary the wife of Cleopas (23rd of May); St. Joanna, the wife of Chuza (27th of July); SS Mary and Martha, the sisters of St. Lazarus (4th of June);  and St. Susanna (third Sunday after Pascha). Again, the identity of "Mary the mother of James" [Mk.16:1; Lk. 24:10] and "Joses" [Mt. 27:56] is none other than the Theotokos. Theophylactos (765-840) also identifies Mary as the "stepmother" of St. Joseph the Betrothed's sons.[13]

THE MYRRH-BEARING WOMEN DRAW NIGH
AT DEEP DAWN TO THE TOMB OF
THE GIVER OF LIFE[14]

"Now upon the first day of the week, very early in the morning, they came unto the sepulchre, bringing the spices which they had prepared, and certain others with them" [Lk. 24:1].

Saint John Chrysostom lauds the women disciples, writing: "Dost thou see their noble spirit? For they had brought ointments, and were waiting at the tomb, so that if the madness of the Jews should relax, they might go and embrace the body. Dost thou see their noble spirit even unto death? Let us imitate the women; let us not forsake Jesus in temptations. For Him, though dead, they spent so much and exposed their lives."[15]

The Sabbath then was past and the women decided to go back to the tomb of Joseph of Arimathea, where they had seen Christ's body laid away on Friday at sundown. They would bring with them sweet spices that they might anoint Him [Mk. 16:1], beyond those which Nicodemos and Joseph had already used on Friday. They prepared them [Lk. 24:1] and bought [Mk. 16:1] additional spices with their own means.

It is not unlikely that there were two or more parties of women disciples starting from different places; this would account for the slight differences in identifying which women were grouped together. Mary Theotokos and Mary Magdalene started their journey from Jerusalem, even though it was very early morning, though still dark. By the time the others arrived, dawn was glimmering in the east that Sunday morning [Mt. 28:1; Mk. 16:2]. Saint Gregory Palamas remarks that "it seems that the Evangelists disagree somewhat concerning both the time of the visits and the number of women that are involved. This is attributable to the fact that the myrrh-bearers were many; that they did not come to the sepulchre one time only, but two and three times--and not always in the same groups; that all the visits were at dawn but not at exactly the same hour.

The venerable Mary Magdalene came not only as part of the group, but alone too. Each of the Evangelists, therefore, relates one trip of some of the women and leaves off recounting the others trips."[16]

Saint Gregory then discloses, "I conclude, consequently, that the Theotokos was the first who came to the grave of her Son and God, together with Mary Magdalene."[17]

What were the thoughts and hopes of the Mother of Jesus at that time? We may hear from her in the *Lamentations*, when she cried aloud, *O Word and God eternal, O my Joy and Delight, how shall I endure Thy three-day entombment? My maternal bowels are rent with grief for Thee.* And, *"When shall I behold Thee, O my Saviour and God, the Eternal Light, my joy and my heart's delight,"* thus the Virgin cried out in her great distress.[18] The troparion also contains this hope-filled utterance: *Rise, O Life-Bestower ....Hasten, Word, to rise now, and release from sorrow the spotless Maiden that bare Thee.*[19] And, *She that gave Thee birth, poured libations of tears for Thee, Christ God, when Thou, in the flesh, wast laid in a tomb of stone; and she cried, "Arise, O Christ, as Thou didst say."*[20]

"And they said among themselves, 'Who shall roll away the stone for us from the door of the sepulchre?' [Mk. 16:3].

See how faith propels them, though the stone would require enormous strength to roll it upward through its track, they did not bring tools, ropes or levers with them, only their love and genuine care.

Continuing in the religious drama of St. Romanos, he "eavesdrops" on the women hastening to the tomb when he writes: *To the Sun Who before the sun had sunk in the tomb, the young women bearing incense hastened towards the dawn, as though seeking day. And they said to one another, "O friends, come let us anoint with spices the body, life-bringing and buried, the flesh which resurrects fallen Adam which lies in the tomb. Let us go, let us hasten like the magi, and let us kneel down and bring with us the spices as gifts--not to Him in swaddling clothes but to Him wrapped in a shroud. Let us weep and cry out, 'O Master, arise, Thou Who dost offer resurrection to the fallen.'"*[21]

The Evangelist Matthew then records: **"And, behold, there was a great earthquake: for the angel of the Lord descended from heaven and came and rolled back the stone from the door, and sat upon it. His countenance was like lightning, and his raiment white as snow. And for fear of him the keepers did shake, and became as dead men [Mt. 28:2-4].**

The earthquake could not have been one in the ordinary sense, nor was it that extensive to have roused the sleeping inhabitants of the city. However, it was sufficient to break the seal placed over the circular stone at the time of interment and roll the stone away from its settled position in the downward slanting groove along which it rolled. The angel, thus, removed the stone from the entrance of the sepulchre, not to enable the risen Christ to exit, as had to be done in the case of Lazarus [Jn. 11:41], but to clearly exhibit that the sepulchre was empty.

WHERE ARE THE WATCHMEN
AND THE SECURE SENTRY?[22]

So blinding was the angel's glorious appearance that the guards specially assigned to the tomb were completely terrified and swooned away, losing all consciousness.

A hymn from the *Octoechos* identifies the principle angel at the burial site as the Archangel Gabriel: *Descending from the heights above, Gabriel came unto the stone wherein the Rock of Life lay, and arrayed in white, he cried out to the weeping women, "Cease your tears and your wail of lament, O ye that ever possess loving compassion."*[23]

Saint Gregory Palamas also names the angel as Gabriel, saying, "It was after all, the same angel of the Annunciation, Gabriel. He watched the Theotokos proceed rapidly towards the grave and thus he immediately descended. He who in the beginning had told her, 'fear not, Mary, thou hast found grace with God,' now addresses her with the same exhortation. It was to her, who had seedlessly borne Him, that he came to announce His Resurrection from the dead; to roll the stone away, to reveal the empty tomb and the grave clothes. In this manner would the good news be verified by her."[24]

Life lay in the grave, and a seal was placed over the stone. The soldiers guarded Christ as a sleeping King; but having smitten His enemies with blindness, the Lord hath risen.[25]

Saint Romanos chants, *Outside the tomb were soldiers; within was war between Christ and Death.*[26]

There was a sublime irony in contrast between man's elaborate precautions by setting a watch at the tomb and the ease with which the divine hand can sweep them aside. We recall the prophetic declaration: "He that dwelleth in the heavens shall laugh them to scorn, and the Lord shall deride them" [Ps. 2:4].

Saint Romanos the Melodist chants, *Without the aid of human hands, the Stone cut from the mountain* [Dan. 2:34] has risen--just as once from the womb of the Virgin, so now from the tomb has the Lord risen.[27]

The saint then realistically reports the reaction of the guards in the following poem: *As we were watching over the tomb and taking care lest something happen, suddenly we perceived fiery hands taking away the stone from the tomb, and a voice cried out, "The Lord is risen." By him (the angel) the stone was rolled away, and all our force was weakened and nothing was left for us by way of aid, no word, no thought, for we were all dead men--we who guarded the dead. And all our wisdom was consumed suddenly at what we beheld was accomplished. For the one that rolled the stone away looked sternly at us who did not cry, "The Lord is risen."*[28]

Saint Romanos continues to interview the guards: *You may marvel at this: he (the angel), the fiery one, was approachable by the women, but to us wretched men he was not approachable. He conversed with them; he threatened death to us. Them he strengthened; and humbled us with fear. And overtaking us, he buried us. To the women he was joyous; with us he became as one dreaded. He mortified us, but he enlivened them to cry, "Fear not, the Lord is risen."*[29]

Saint Gregory Palamas is of the opinion that "other women came after the earthquake...and found the grave open and the stone rolled back. Albeit, the Virgin-Mother was there when the earthquake took place, when the stone was rolled back, when the sepulchre opened with the guards present, though they were completely overcome with fear. That is why the guards immediately thought of fleeing when they recovered and showed signs of life. However, the Mother of God rejoiced without fear at what she beheld." The saint then comments, "I believe that the life-bearing grave opened first to the Theotokos. It was for her and by her grace that all things were revealed unto us--everything that is in heaven above and on the earth below. For her sake, the angel shone so brightly, so that, even though it was dark, she beheld by means of the angelic light not only the empty sepulchre, but also the burial garments which were neatly arranged, thereby witnessing the Resurrection of her Son."[30]

THE ANGEL SPEAKS TO THE WOMEN DISCIPLES

After the earthquake and the arrival of the other women, "[T]he angel answered and said unto the women, 'Fear not ye: for I know that ye seek Jesus Who was crucified. He is not here: for He is risen, as He said. Come, see the place where the Lord lay. And go quickly, and tell His disciples that He is risen from the dead; and, behold, he goeth  before you into Galilee; there shall ye see Him: lo, I have told you'" [Mt. 28:5-7].

Saint Romanos, speaking through the guardians of the tomb, writes: *When the women stood still, and wisely looked in the vault, the incorporeal one spoke to them, saying, "The One Whom you seek is risen. But if you do not believe and consider me a phantom, follow me and behold the place where the Lord was lying." And they went within. At that time we (the guards) fled, and said thus, "If the servant (the angel) has come and has jolted the earth, what, then, happens now that the Lord is risen?"*[31]

The Evangelist Matthew then records that "some of the watch came into the city, and reported to the chief priests all the things that had happened. And when they were assembled with the elders, and had taken counsel, they gave a large sum of money to the soldiers, saying, "Say ye, 'His disciples came by night, and stole Him away while we slept'" [Mt. 28:11-13]. One wonders how the guards could see anyone while they slept! However, "they took the money, and did as they were taught" [Mt. 28:15].

Longinus the centurion, who was on duty as the officer in charge, both at the Crucifixion and in the watch outside the tomb, refused to accept the bribe, together with two fellow soldiers. When the Jews conspired to kill Longinus, by slandering him to Pilate, he resigned from the military and removed his army belt. Subsequently, he received baptism, and secretly left for Cappadocia. He was still pursued by Pilate's soldiers, and was beheaded by them. He is commemorated by the Holy Church on the 16th of October.

Let us now return to the sepulchre. Saint John Chrysostom speaks of the fact that the angel came after the Resurrection. "Why did he come and take away the stone? Because the women had seen Him when He was in the sepulchre for burial. Therefore, that they might believe that Christ was risen, they see the sepulchre void of the body. For this cause, he removed the stone; for this cause, also an earthquake took place, that they might be thoroughly roused and awake. For they came by night to pour oil on Him and it was likely that they had become drowsy.

"Why does the angel say, 'Fear not ye'? First he delivers them from dread, and then tells them of the Resurrection. And the 'ye' is of one showing them great honor, and indicating, that extreme punishment awaits them that had dared to crucify Christ...except they repent. For to be afraid is not for you, the angel means, but for them that crucified Him.

"Having delivered them from fear by his words, and by his appearance (for his form was brilliant, as bearing such good tidings), he went on to say, '...I know that ye seek Jesus Who was crucified.' The angel is not ashamed to call Him 'crucified;' for this is the source of blessings.

"'He is not here: for He is risen.' Whence is this evident? The angel asserts that Jesus Himself had said it [Mk. 8:31]. Hence, if ye refuse to believe me (the angel), remember His words, and neither will ye disbelieve me.

"Then also another proof: 'Come, see the place where the Lord lay.' For this reason the angel lifted up the stone, in order that from this too they might receive proof. 'And go quickly, and tell His disciples that He is risen from the dead; and, behold, He goeth before you into Galilee.' The angel prepares them to bear good tidings to others. Well did

Christ utter, 'in Galilee,' thereby freeing them from troubles and dangers (existent then in Judea), so that fear might not hinder their faith."[32]

Saint Romanos, who exceeds most in poetical genius, then dramatically describes the scene between the incorporeal and the women. He portrays the God-loving women advancing, like in a procession, saying, *"The words of thy divine mouth, like drops of moisture will now refresh us, so that we may not die from terror."* Then the angel who was sitting on the stone spoke, *"Be ye not afraid; but the men who guard the*

tomb tremble, cower in fear, and are deadened from fear of me, in order that they may learn that He is Lord of the angels, He Whom they now guard but Whom they do not control. For the Lord is risen, and they do not know how He has roused Himself."[33]

The drama continues for St. Romanos when the angel says, *Henceforth be immortal, women; do not be subject to death. Ye seek to behold the Creator of angels, then why do ye fear the sight of one angel? I am the servant of the One Who inhabited the tomb; I have the rank and nature of a slave. As I have been commanded, I am here to announce to you, "The Lord is risen."*[34]

The women then, *taking a commendable courage from the voice of the angel, respond wisely, "Truly the Lord is risen [Lk. 24:34], as thou dost say. Thou hast proved to us by thy words and attitude that the Merciful One has risen; for if He had not risen and departed from the tomb, thou would not be seated. For when would a soldier of the king be seated and conversing if the king were present? Indeed such things are not done on high where there is the invisible throne and the ineffable One seated thereon."*[35]

WHO HATH TAKEN AWAY A NAKED AND ANOINTED BODY, THE ONLY CONSOLATION OF HIS MOTHER?[36]

The Evangelist Luke also concurs that the women found the stone rolled away from the sepulchre.

"And they entered in, and found not the body of the Lord Jesus" [Lk 24:3].

Sidestepping the unconscious soldiers, all the women enter the tomb. Once inside, they behold another angel, appearing as a young man with blazing white garments [Mk. 16:5]. Soon after, this angel was joined by the Archangel Gabriel who had been sitting outside the tomb. The angels then spoke to the women disciples the following words of encouragement.

"And it came to pass, as they were much perplexed thereabout, behold, two men stood by them in shining garments: And as they were afraid, and bowed their faces to the earth, they said unto them, 'Why seek ye the living among the dead? He is not here, but is risen: remember how He spake unto you when He was yet in Galilee, saying, "The Son of man must be delivered into the hands of sinful men, and be crucified, and the third day rise again."' And they remembered His words" [Lk. 24:4-8].

Saint Cyril of Alexandria (+444) comments that "for their love's sake unto Christ, and their earnest zeal there-unto, they were counted worthy of seeing holy angels, who even told them the joyful tidings, and became the heralds of the Resurrection....And more firmly to settle the faith of the women in these things, the angels recall to their minds what Christ had said."[37]

WHY MOURN YE THE INCORRUPTIBLE AMID CORRUPTION?[38]

Saint Gregory Palamas writes that the Evangelists record that the women both prepared [Lk. 23:56] and bought [Mk. 16:1] spices and fragrant oils. They did not yet clearly know that He is truly the 'Perfume' of life for them that approach Him with faith; just as He is the 'odor' of death for them that remain unbelievers. The myrrh-bearers did not yet clearly know that the fragrance of His clothes and His own body is greater than all perfumes and that His name is like myrrh that is poured out to cover the world with divine fragrance. For them that desired to remain close by the body, they contrived an antidote of perfumes that they might anoint it for the supposed stench of decomposition."[39]

The hymnographer, St. Theophanes the "Branded" (1381), writes elsewhere: *Thy flesh beheld not corruption in the sepulchre, O Master; but as it was composed without seed, it received not corruption in conformity with nature, for in a transcendent manner it was not subservient thereto.*[40]

On the Sunday of the Holy Myrrh-Bearers, the Church chants: *Unto the myrrh-bearing women did the angel cry out as he stood by the grave: "Myrrh-oils are meet for the dead, but Christ hath proved to be a stranger to corruption. But cry out, 'The Lord is risen, granting great mercy to the world.'"*[41] Indeed, another hymn of the same Feast mentions that though myrrh-oils were not needed, yet, *their compassionate purpose was pleasing unto God.*[42]

Saint Gregory Palamas continues to write that "they prepared the myrrh and spices and rested on the Sabbath according to the commandment. They had not yet experienced the true Sabbath, nor did they yet understand that exceedingly blessed Sabbath that transports us from the confines of Hades to the perfection of the bright and divine heights of heaven."[43]

GO, PROCLAIM THE RESURRECTION UNTO THE APOSTLES!

"And they departed quickly from the sepulchre with fear and great joy; and did run to bring His disciples word" [Mt. 28:8].

Having heard the words of holy joy from the angels sitting upon the stone at the grave of the Word, those blessed women showed exceeding haste as they ran. Thus they left behind their previous rank of myrrh-bearers and were seen to be proclaimers unto the initiates of Him Who became incarnate for our sakes of the most joyous and good tidings of His rising from the chambers of dark Hades.[44]

The women disciples then turned away from the tomb and go *to meet the Apostles; and they said, "Why are you disheartened? Why do you hide your faces? Lift up your hearts, Christ is risen....Therefore, do not be downcast, but take courage."*[45]

We hear in the Resurrection troparion that *the women disciples of the Lord spoke to the Apostles exultantly, "Death is despoiled and Christ God is risen, granting great mercy to the world!"*

Saint John Chrysostom continues then to explain why they departed from the sepulchre with fear and joy. "They had seen an amazing thing, and beyond expectation, an empty tomb, where they had before seen Him laid. Wherefore, also he (the angel) had led them to the sight, that they might become witnesses of two things: His tomb and His Resurrection.

"For the women considered that no man could have taken Him, unless He raised up Himself. For this cause also they rejoice and wonder, and receive the reward of so much continuance with Him, that they should first see and gladly declare, not what had been said only, but also what they beheld."[46]

However, the Evangelist Mark makes mention that the women **"went out and fled from the sepulchre; for they trembled and were amazed: neither said they any thing to any man; for they were afraid"** [Mk. 16:8]. What this means is that they did not pause to inform anyone else as they hurried back.

Saint Gregory Palamas interjects at this point, saying, "I am of the opinion that Mary Magdalene and the other women who had come up to that point were still frightened. They did not yet understand the meaning of the angel's powerful words, nor did they contain to the end the power of the light so as to see and understand with great exactitude. But I think that the Mother of God made this great

392

joy her own, since she comprehended the words of the angel. Her whole person radiated from the light, for she was all-pure and full of divine grace. She firmly appropriated all these signs as the truth. She believed the Archangel Gabriel, since, previously, he showed himself worthy of trust. The Virgin was an eyewitness to these events; therefore, why should she not comprehend what had occurred with divine wisdom? She beheld the earthquake and the great angel descending from the heights like lightning. She beheld the guards fall as dead men, the rolling away of the huge stone and the empty tomb. She also was an eyewitness to the great miracle concerning her Son's burial garments in that they were kept in place by myrrh and aloes, though they contained no body. Together with all these signs, she beheld the joyous countenance of the angel and heard his joyful message."[47] On the other hand, "some of the women left the tomb frightened and ecstatic without saying anything." At this juncture, St. Gregory then says, "Other women followed the Mother of the Lord and because they happened to be with her they saw and heard the Lord too. Now Mary Magdalene had earlier parted their company, hastening to Peter...but then she re-united with the women."[48]

THE WOMEN DISCIPLES CAST OFF
THE ANCESTRAL CONDEMNATION[49]

"**And as they went to tell His disciples, behold, Jesus met them, saying, 'All Rejoice'** (*Chairete*). **And they came and held Him by the feet, and worshipped Him. Then said Jesus unto them, 'Be not afraid: go tell My brethren that they go into Galilee, and there shall they see Me'"** [Mt. 28:9-11].

Saint John Chrysostom comments that the women "first see Jesus; and the sex that was most condemned, this first enjoys the sight of the blessings, this most shows its courage. And when the disciples had fled, they were present."[50]

Saint John Chrysostom then says that they departed with emotions high from the sepulchre: "with exceeding joy and gladness they ran unto Him, and received by the touch also, an infallible proof, and full assurance of the Resurrection. And they worshipped Him.

"And what then does He say to them? 'Be not afraid.' Again, He casts out their fear, making way for faith, 'Go tell My brethren that they go into Galilee, and there shall they see Me.' Note how He Himself sends good tidings to His disciples by these women, bringing to honor, as I have often said, that sex, which was most dishonored, and to good hopes; and healing that which was diseased."[51]

Saint Cyril of Alexandria writes that when they departed the sepulchre, after "having been taught the mystery by the voice of angels, the women ran to tell these things to the disciples. Indeed it was fitting that this grace--though so splendid--should be granted unto women. For she who of old was the 'minister of death' is now freed from her guilt by ministering unto the voice of the holy angels, and by being the first both to learn and tell the adorable mystery of the Resurrection. The female sex, therefore, gained both acquittal from their reproach and the reversal of their curse. For He Who of old had said unto them, 'In pains thou shalt bear children' [Gen. 3:16], gave them deliverance from their misfortune, by having met them in the garden, as another Evangelist mentions [Mt. 28:9], and said, 'Rejoice.' To the holy Apostles, however, the account of the Resurrection seemed to be absolutely but an idle tale and a falsehood; for even they did not know the inspired Scripture, and so they were incredulous. Thus, they mocked the news and rejected it."[52]

Eve had hearkened to the word of the serpent and went astray; the women disciples hearkened to the word of the angel and did well. Eve instructed Adam and he hearkened. The women disciples proclaimed the news to the men disciples, but they considered their words as false. Adam and Eve hid in the garden from our Saviour, but in another garden, He greets the women with "Rejoice!", but to His disciples He upbraids them for their unbelief.

The Evangelist Luke records that, after leaving the sepulchre, they "told all these things unto the eleven, and to all the rest" [Lk. 24:9].

"It was Mary Magdalene, and Joanna, and Mary the mother of James, and other women that were with them, which told these things unto the apostles. And their words seemed to them as idle tales, and they believed them not" [Lk. 24:10-11].

Saint Gregory of Nyssa adds to his Eve-Mary theme that since Mary "is the root of joy" it is fitting that she should spread the joyous news of the Resurrection.

Thus we chant, *Most glorified art thou, O Virgin Theotokos.*

We praise thee, for through the Cross of Thy Son, Hades was cast down and death was slain. Having been put to death, we were raised up and were deemed worthy of life. We received Paradise, the ancient bliss.

Wherefore, in thanksgiving, we glorify Christ our God, since He is mighty and alone abundant in mercy.[53]

CHRIST FIRST APPEARS TO HIS MOTHER

The Evangelist Mark, citing St. Mary Magdalene as first to behold the risen Lord, does not mention the Theotokos, when he writes: **"Early the first day of the week, He appeared first to Mary Magdalene...and she went and told them that had been with Him, as they mourned and wept"** [Mk. 16:9-10]. It is evident that the testimony of Christ's Mother as the first to behold Him might be construed as suspicious or, at best, the hysterical longings of a bereaved mother.[54] Therefore the Evangelist Mark left it for the

Evangelists Matthew and John to narrate how the Theotokos and St. Mary Magdalene met the risen Lord, albeit not at the same moment. Thus, the Evangelist Mark writes that He had first appeared to St. Mary Magdalene [Mk. 16:9].[55]

It is not unusual to find Orthodox hymnographers of different centuries concurring that Christ first met His Mother. Thus, the Resurrection hymn notes that *Mary stood by the grave seeking Thine immaculate body. Thou didst despoil Hades and was not tried thereby. Thou didst meet the Virgin, and didst grant us life.*[56]

In St. Romanos' poem, *Mary at the Cross*, he writes about Christ consoling His Mother from the Cross: *Be reassured, O Mother, thou wilt be the first to see Me leave the tomb.*[57]

One of the hymnographers composing hymns for the Feast of the Myrrh-bearers, St. Theophanes the Poet chants, *As thou beholdest thy Son and God arisen, thou rejoicest with the Apostles, O pure one, graced of God, and wast the first to hear the greeting, "Rejoice", as thou art the cause of the joy of all, O all-blameless Mother of God.*[58]

Saint Hesychios of Jerusalem (+ c.451) speaks of Mary since she "who introduced virginity, contained God in her womb, gave birth in the flesh to the Creator, first welcomed Jesus coming back from the dead, and began to proclaim the Resurrection, thus revealing joy to the disciples."[59]

Saint George of Nicomedia (c. 880) devotes a homily to the Virgin at the sepulchre of the dead Christ, in which he adheres to a tradition already established in the East, that Christ appeared first after the Resurrection to Mary, His Mother. "Thus accordingly...upon her the clear light and joy of the Resurrection shone."[60]

Sharing this idea also, St. Gregory Palamas writes: "Before all others, the good news of the Resurrection of Christ was received by the Theotokos from the Lord Himself. This, verily, is meet and right. She was the first to see Him after the Resurrection and she had the joy of hearing His voice first. Moreover, she not only beheld Him and heard Him, but with her hands she was the first to touch His immaculate feet. The Evangelists do not mention these points clearly. They do not want to present the Mother's witness, for it might promote suspicion among non-believers."[61]

Saint Gregory Palamas also makes the following comparison: "The Resurrection of the Lord was the regeneration of human nature...and re-creation of the first Adam, whom sin led to death. The Resurrection is the return to immortal life. Whereas, no one saw the first man Adam when he was created and given life...woman was the first person to see him after he had received the breath of life by divine in-breathing....Likewise, no one saw the second Adam, that is, the Lord, rise from the dead....Following the Resurrection, however, it was a woman (the new Eve) who saw Him first."[62]

Archbishop Nikon of Vologda and Totma (+1917), in a sermon, comments: "Sacred tradition says that immediately upon His arising from the tomb, the resurrected Lord hastened to comfort His beloved and most-blameless Mother. He had appeared to her before appearing to anyone else. Before greeting anyone else, He greeted His Mother with His all-joyful, 'Rejoice.' Only because of her ineffable humility did the most holy Virgin not desire that this event, the appearance of her Son to her upon His Resurrection, an event which concerned her personally, be added to the account of the holy Evangelist."[63]

THE DISCIPLES AT THE TOMB

The Evangelist John, writing from his own perspective, gives a greatly abridged version of St. Mary Magdalene at the tomb, specifically, not mentioning her companion myrrh-bearers. Writing exclusively about her, he records that, leaving at dark and coming to the tomb, she finds the stone taken away. Among the myrrh-bearers, it is she alone who runs to inform both him (the author John) and Peter that the body is missing; and, therefore, he writes solely about her.

Saint Romanos warmly writes about this Mary saying, *It was dark, but love lighted the way for her.*[64]

She then makes her announcement **"to Simon Peter, and to the other disciple (John), whom Jesus loved, and said unto them, 'They have taken away the Lord out of the sepulchre, and we know not where they have laid Him'"** [Jn. 20:2].

After this declaration, "we know not where", it is evident that she went not alone, nevertheless, she was absent when the angels told her other companions that the Lord was alive and had risen. Having seen the stone rolled away, in her amazement she could not understand what had become of the body; where could that body now be? It was for this reason that she wanted the pre-eminent disciple Peter to go back there and see what he could find out.

Saint Gregory Palamas writes about St. Mary Magdalene, saying, "In responding to the announcement of the angel, Mary acted as though she did not hear at all. The angel had not, in fact, spoken directly to her. After running to Peter and to the other disciple, as St. John says, she testifies only to the empty tomb and says nothing about the grave clothes. The Mother of God went to the sepulchre where she met the other women....Just as the Theotokos alone understood the power of the angelic words--even if she heard the good news of the Resurrection together with St. Mary Magdalene--when she met her Son and God with the other women, she saw and recognized the risen One before all the other women. Falling down, she touched His feet and became His Apostle to His Apostles."[65]

Saint Romanos relates the following about Mary Magdalene: *And so she saw the great stone rolled away from the entrance of the tomb, and she returned and said, "Disciples, learn what I saw, and do not keep secret what you understand. The stone no longer covers the tomb. Would they have taken away my Lord?...Would He not have risen, He Who offers resurrection to the fallen?"*[66]

The younger and faster disciple John outran Peter, which St. Romanos describes thus: *When Cephas and the son of Zebedee heard this, immediately they ran as though in a race with one another.*[67] John was first, but gave place, due to seniority, to Peter who went inside the chamber and found it indeed empty. He then noticed the linen clothes *(othonia)*, because they were lying in a remarkable position. Instead of being spread out in a long, jumbled strip, it was still all wrapped together in one spot *(entetyligmenon ees ena topon)*. Moreover, the handkerchief *(soudarion)* that had been wound around the head of Jesus was not unwound and tossed on the shroud, but was still wrapped together and lying right about it. Jesus' body passed through the cocoon of spice-impregnated bandages; they had retained the form they had when covering the entombed body, that is, wrapped together.

Saint John Chrysostom comments, "they drew near, and seeing the linen clothes lying, which was a sign of the Resurrection. For neither, if any persons had removed the body, would they before doing so have stripped it; nor if any had stolen it, would they have taken the trouble to remove the napkin and roll it...and lay it in a place by itself; but how? They would have taken the body as it was. On this account, the Evangelist John tells us by anticipation that it was buried with much myrrh, which glues linen to the body not less firmly than lead; in order that when thou hearest that the napkins lay apart, thou mayest not endure those who say that He was stolen. For a thief would not have been so foolish as to spend so much trouble on a superfluous matter. For why should he undo the clothes? And how could he have escaped detection if he had done so? For it would have required much time in so doing, and he would have been caught delaying and loitering. But why do the clothes lie apart, while the napkin was wrapped together by itself? That thou mayest learn that it was not the action of men in confusion or haste, the placing some in one place, some in another, and the wrapping them together. Now to separate, and to place one thing by itself, and another, after rolling it up, by itself, was the act of some one doing things carefully, and not in a chance way, as if disturbed."[68]

"Then went in also that other disciple (John), which came first to the sepulchre, and he saw, and believed" [Jn. 20:8].

But behold the disciples hastening to the tomb, how they surmised His Resurrection from the funeral shrouds and the napkin that had lain upon His face; and they remembered the Scriptures concerning Him.[69]

In other words, no one had removed the grave clothes from the corpse in the usual way; it was as if the body had simply passed right out of the head cloth and shroud and left them empty. John then believed that no one had removed the body from that tomb. The body had simply left the tomb and left the grave clothes on its own power, passing through all those layers of cloth without unwrapping them at all. Jesus had not been removed by other hands; He had raised Himself from the dead.

Saint Romanos then joyfully exclaims, *Even if Thou didst descend into the tomb, O Immortal One, still Thou hast overthrown the power of Hades and Thou hast risen victor, O Christ God; to the women bearing incense Thou hast said, "Rejoice" [Mt. 28:9], and on Thy Apostles Thou hast bestowed*

399

peace [Jn. 20:19], *Thou who dost offer resurrection to the fallen.*[70]

MARY MAGDALENE RETURNS TO THE TOMB

Apparently, Mary Magdalene came along at a slower pace, after the runners, Peter and John. In fact, she had gotten back to the tomb only when Peter and John had already departed. She arrived alone, but did not immediately enter until she had paused to weep for a little while outside.

Saint John Chrysostom remarks, "Full of feeling somehow is the female sex, and more than men inclined to pity. Mary weeps bitterly at the tomb, while Peter was in no way so affected. Mary did not know yet accurately the account of the Resurrection; whereas the two disciples having seen the linen clothes and believed, departed to their own homes in astonishment. However, the Evangelist John himself comments that both Peter and he had not known **"the Scripture, that He must rise again from the dead"** [Jn. 20:9].

Our rhythmical poet, St. Romanos, believes that what has happened is in accordance with the divine plan: that women, who were first to fall, would be the first to see the resurrected One. He also writes that Christ's greeting of "Rejoice", would be a sign to them (womankind) that mourn.

The saint conceives of Mary Magdalene's words and tears [Jn. 20:11] to mean that she indeed understood--though not perfectly--that He resurrected, and says this about her as she remained at the tomb:

She truly believed that the body had been raised up. And so she cried out, not with words but with tears, "Woe is me, my Jesus, where have they taken Thee? How didst Thou endure, Immortal One, to be lifted up by dishonored hands. The six-winged ones...cry, 'Holy, Holy, Holy' [Is. 6:3]; and their shoulders can scarcely carry Thee, yet did the hands of deceivers lift Thee up?"[71]

Saint John Chrysostom continues: "Mary stood at the place, for, even the sight of the tomb tended greatly to comfort her. And she received no small reward for her zeal. For what the disciples saw not, this woman saw: Angels sitting, the one at the feet, the other at the head, in white; even the appearance was full of much radiance and joy."[72]

O Lord, Mary Magdalene was present at Thy tomb and thinking Thee to be a gardener, she wept, crying aloud, saying, "Where hast thou concealed Him that is eternal life?

400

Where hast thou placed Him that sitteth on a cherubic throne? For they that guarded Him became as dead for fear. Either give me back my Lord, or cry out with me, 'O Thou that wast among the dead and hast raised up the dead, glory be to Thee!'"[73]

St. Romanos then continues her soliloquy: *"Arise, stand up, and be revealed to them that seek Thee, Thou Who dost offer resurrection to the fallen."* Then, *He Who sees all, conquered by her weeping and touched by her suffering, was at once moved to pity.*[74] The Saviour then appears and speaks to her.

Knowing that *Mary would recognize His voice, like a shepherd, calling His crying lamb, He says, "Mary." And she at once recognized Him.*[75] Mary heard her name in those well-remembered accents that had first unbound her from seven-fold demoniac power and called her into a new life. This was another unbinding, into a new life.

From this sequel, Mary Magdalene's actions and responses bespeak of one who left the tomb before the other women. She did not yet have the benefit of the angels' explanation and exhortation, nor had she as yet seen the neatly arranged burial clothes.

Saint Gregory Palamas affirms this making the following observation of St. Mary Magdalene when he remarks that "she had not yet seen Him nor had been informed of the Resurrection." The saint continues, saying, "If she has seen and touched Him with her hands and heard Him speak, how could she say the words, 'if thou hast borne Him hence, tell me where thou hast laid Him, and I will take Him away'?....And when the angels appeared and addressed  her, 'why weepest thou?', she answers as if she thought He were dead by asking where He is lain. It was not until Christ called her by name and showed her that He was the same did she understand."[76]

A FEW WORDS ABOUT ST. MARY MAGDALENE, EQUAL-TO-THE-APOSTLES

A virgin until her repose, Mary Magdalene, of the town of Magdala, situated on the west side of the Sea of Galilee, was raised and thoroughly educated in the law and prophets by her parents, especially her father. Although she was orphaned at ten, she lived an exemplary life before God. She was virtuous, prayed continually, and was like a bee collecting the honey of virtues. From her adolescence, she could be found either at home or in the synagogue. She never spoke to men. She did, however, have female companions of like mind, who would visit and minister to the infirm and sick. Her manner of life was ascetical. She never laughed in a disorderly manner, but would just smile modestly when the occasion demanded it.

"Was she the virgin that Isaias spoke of?" wondered satan. Believing her to be, she was assailed by seven evil spirits that they might cause her to fall into grievous sin and destroy her virginity. Therefore, her early life was one of fierce struggle and spiritual warfare. Seven demons assailed her: those of pride, fornication, judging others, lying, stealing, murder and unbelief. But she valiantly withstood them and never opened the door to any of them that they might take her captive, until Christ came and cast them away [Mk. 16:9; Lk. 8:2].[77]

Therefore, the casting out of seven demons does not mean that Christ had rescued a social derelict. There is no evidence that she was promiscuous, much less a harlot for hire; that she was a woman of means is evident from her ability to support Jesus from her means [Mt. 27:56]. Her obvious leadership and prominence among the women is seen in the fact that her name is mentioned more often than most, and usually first; this hardly reflects a scarlet past.

"TOUCH ME NOT"

But let us return to the story in the Gospel of John by listening to a hymn of St. Romanos. Then, Mary *carried away by the warmth of her affection and by her fervent love, the maiden hastened and wished to touch Him, the One Who fills all creation without being confined by boundaries. The Creator did not find fault with her eagerness; but lifted her to the divine when He said, "Touch Me not; or dost thou consider Me merely human?* [Jn. 20:17]. *I am God, do not*

402

touch Me. O holy woman, lift up thine eyes and consider the heavenly spheres. Seek Me there, for I ascend to My Father, Whom I have not left. For I share His throne, and with Him I am without time and beginning, I Who offer resurrection to the fallen."[78]

Saint Leo the Great (+461) comments that when Christ said to Mary Magdalene, "'Touch Me not; for I am not yet ascended to My Father' [Jn. 20:17], that is, 'I would not have thee come to Me as to a human body, nor yet recognize Me by fleshly perceptions: I put thee off for higher things, I prepare greater things for thee: when I have ascended to My Father, then thou shalt handle Me more perfectly and truly, for thou shalt grasp what thou canst not touch and believe what thou canst not see.'"[79]

The Saviour then commissions her: *Hasten Mary, and gather together My disciples. I use thee as a trumpet with a powerful voice; sound forth peace to the fearful ears of My concealed friends. Arouse them all as from sleep...saying, "The Bridegroom has arisen from the tomb, and nothing has been left in the tomb."*[80]

Saint Mary Magdalene then went and spoke exultantly to the disciples and to the women of their group. *When the grave had been opened, and Hades was lamenting, Mary cried unto the hidden Apostles: "Come forth, ye workers of the vineyard. Preach the word of the Resurrection. The Lord is risen, granting great mercy to the world."*[81]

CHRIST IS RISEN!

Thou, O Saviour, didst come forth unbegotten from the Virgin's womb, leaving her virginity unsullied; just so now Thou hast abolished death by death. Thou hast left in the tomb the fine linen of Joseph, but Thou hast raised from the tomb the ancestor of Joseph. Adam came following Thee; Eve came after Thee. Eve serves Mary, but all the earth is prostrate before Thee as it sings the song of victory, "The Lord is risen."[82]

Saint Ephraim the Syrian (c.306-383) chants, *Eve lifted up her eyes from Sheol and rejoiced in that day, because the Son of her daughter as the Medicine of life came down to raise up the mother of His Mother. Blessed Babe, that bruised the head of the serpent that smote her!*[83]

Saint Gregory the Theologian (329-391) writes that "The Resurrection of Christ is the Feast of feasts and the Celebration of celebrations; it excels all other festivals, as the sun excels the stars; and this is true not only of human and earthly feasts, but also of those belonging to Christ and celebrated for Christ."[84]

The descent into Hades and the Resurrection of Christ transcends us and is not accessible to our perception. The Paschal canon by St. John of Damascus succinctly explains that *Thou didst descend into the deepest parts of the earth, and didst shatter the everlasting bars that held fast them that were fettered, O Christ. And on the third day, like Jonas from the sea monster, Thou didst arise from the grave.*[85] Although the Evangelists say nothing of this event, the Apostle Peter speaks of it when he says, "He (Jesus) went and preached unto the spirits in prison" [1 Pet. 3:19].

Within the same Paschal Canon, St. John the Damascene chants, *Having kept the seals intact, O Christ, Thou didst rise from the tomb, O Thou Who didst not break the seal of the Virgin by Thy birth.*[86]

Before Thy conception, O Lord, an angel brought the greeting, "Rejoice," to her that is full of grace; and, at Thy Resurrection, an angel rolled away the stone of Thy glorious tomb. The one, instead of sorrow, announced the tokens of gladness. The other, instead of death, proclaimed the life-giving Master unto us. Wherefore, we cry aloud unto Thee, Benefactor of all: "Lord, glory be to Thee."[87]

Just like His birth from the Virgin-Mother, so is His Resurrection from a virgin tomb. This is an ineffable mystery, inaccessible to all inquiry. In like manner would Christ come to His disciples through shut doors, which He did not open [Jn. 20:19].

404

Chapter XXIII.
The Ascension of
Our LORD JESUS CHRIST,

the Memory of which the Holy Church
Celebrates on the
40th Day or 6th Thursday
After Pascha

+ + +

**AND HE MOUNTED UPON CHERUBIM AND FLEW,
HE FLEW UPON THE WINGS OF THE WINDS[1]**

Christ had been seen first by the women and then by His Apostles for forty days after His Resurrection. During this time, He taught His disciples the Mysteries of the Church. Then on the fortieth day, the The-otokos and the holy Apostles were on the Mt. of Olives where, for the last time, Christ com-manded them not to depart Jerusalem, but to await the promise of the Father [Acts 1:3-4].[2]

O Lord and life-giving Christ, as the Apostles beheld Thee being lifted up in the clouds, they were filled with sorrow and wept with lamenta-tion, saying in their grief, "O Master, leave not as orphans Thy servants whom Thou didst love in Thy mercy, since Thou art compassionate. But as Thou didst promise, send us Thine All-Holy Spirit, to illumine our souls."[3]

Christ then blessed them and **"He was taken up; and a cloud received Him out of their sight. And while they looked steadfastly toward heaven as He went up, behold, two men stood by them in white apparel who also said, 'Ye men of Galilee, why stand ye gazing up into heaven? This same Jesus, Who was taken up from you into heaven, shall so come** in like manner as ye have seen Him go into heaven" [Acts 1:9-11].

The Lord was taken up into the heavens that He might send the Comforter unto the world. The heavens made ready His throne and the clouds His mount. The angels wondered as they beheld a Man more exalted than themselves. The Father received Him Whom He had with Him eternally in His bosom. The Holy Spirit commanded all His angels: "Lift up your gates, O ye princes. All ye nations, clap your hands; for Christ has ascended whither He came." [4]

Beholding Thee being taken up from the Mount of Olives, O Christ, the powers cried one to another, "Who is this?" And it was said unto them, "He is the Mighty One and Potentate. He is the Mighty One in war. He is in truth the King of glory. And wherefore are His garments red? Because He cometh from Bosor, which is the flesh." But Thou, being God, didst sit at the right hand of majesty and sent us the Holy Spirit, that He may guide and save our souls. [5]

Saint John Chrysostom (354-407) asks, "Why did a cloud receive Him? [Acts 1:9]. This too was a sure sign that He went up to heaven. Not fire, as in the case of Elias, nor a fiery chariot, but 'a cloud received Him;' which was a symbol of heaven, as the Prophet David says, 'Who appointeth the clouds for His ascent' [Ps. 103:4]. Divine power appeared on the cloud." [6]

AND HIS FEET SHALL STAND IN THAT DAY ON THE MOUNT OF OLIVES, WHICH IS BEFORE JERUSALEM ON THE EAST [7]

The icon depicts Christ enthroned as He ascends in glory. He is blessing with His right hand, and in His left hand He is holding a scroll. His garments are gold, thus depicting His majesty and victory; red garments, as we read

406

in the above hymn, refer to His humanity. The concentric circles of the mandorla with gold rays symbolize the high heavens. We may also see two angels bearing aloft the mandorla. In the foreground, we see the Mother of God, in the center, sur-rounded by the Apostles and two angels in white. In sacred Scriptures there is no direct mention of her presence, neverthe-less holy Tradition affirms her attend-ance.

Saint John of Damascus (c.676-c.750) also testifies of her attendance with the disciples and angels when the Church chants in the Canon of the Feast: *Rejoice, O Theotokos, Mother of Christ God. Him Whom thou didst conceive, didst thou magnify today together with the angels as thou didst behold Him ascending from the earth.*[8]

As is evident from the icon, the Theotokos occupies a singularly special and central position, standing directly below her Son; in some icons she is on higher ground than the pre-eminent Apostles.

In the icon, we also note the presence of the holy Apostle Paul who, in fact, was not historically present. The Apostle himself remarks that he was "as one born out of due time" [1 Cor. 15:8]. What is depicted and meant in the icon is the full complement of the Church. The Mother of God who had become the temple of the incarnate Word is the personification of the Church, the body of Christ whose Head is the ascending Lord; for the Father of glory "hath put all things under His feet, and gave Him to be the Head over all

407

things to the Church, which is the body, the fullness of Him that filleth all in all" [Eph. 1:17, 22-23].

Therefore, as the embodiment of the Church, Mary Theotokos is placed immediately below Christ. Her uplifted hands are positioned in the ancient gesture of prayer, revealing the intercessory role and faith of both her and the Church, which she expresses. Her hieratic and stationery pose seems to manifest the immutability of the truth, of which both she and the Church are the keeper. The Apostles, on the other hand, are represented with a diversity of movements in their limbs which seem to express the multitude of means in expressing that truth.[9] However, the focus of their eyes and gestures is directed towards the Source of the life of the Church, whose Head abides in heaven.

Saint Leo the Great (+461) comments that "Christ's Ascension is our uplifting, and the hope of the body is raised, whither the glory of the Head has gone on before."[10]

L. Church of the Ascension, Jerusalem.
R. Imprint of Christ's Foot on the Mount of Olives.

The Church of the Ascension at the
Russian Convent on the Mount of Olives

408

Chapter XXIV.
The Descent of the HOLY SPIRIT
on the Pentecost,

the Memory of which the Holy Church
Celebrates on the
50th Day or 8th Sunday
After Pascha

+ + +

After Christ's Ascension into heaven [Acts 1:9-11], the holy Evangelist Luke writes: "Then they returned unto Jerusalem from the Mount called Olivet, which is near Jerusalem, being a Sabbath's day journey. And when they had entered, they went up into the upper room, where abode both Peter, and James, and John, and Andrew, Philip, and Thomas, Bartholomew, and Matthew, James the son of Alphaeus, and Simon the Zealot, and Jude, the brother of James. These all persevered with one accord in prayer and supplication, with the women, and Mary the Mother of Jesus, and with His brethren" [Acts 1:12-14].

With the others, Mary awaits the coming of the Spirit at Pentecost. Her special position is emphasized by the title "Mother of Jesus" and even the little word "and" *(kai)* separating her from others in the group [v.14].

After the Ascension of Jesus Christ, the Theotokos was the one consolation for His disciples, their joy in sorrow and their firm teacher in the faith. All the words and wondrous events which she had laid up in her heart, from the beginning, she then disclosed to them. She related to them the Archangel Gabriel's joyful tidings regarding the seedless conception and the incorruptible birth of Christ from her virgin womb. She strengthened her Son's disciples when she spoke to them about His earlier years prior to His baptism by the Forerunner John.[1]

THE DESCENT OF THE HOLY SPIRIT
"And when the day of Pentecost was fully come, they were all with one accord in one place" [Acts 2:1].

Awaiting the much desired Comforter in that upper room, they continued constant in prayer and entreaty for the reception of the gifts of the Holy Spirit, promised by the Lord, from the Father. Saint John Chrysostom (354-407) remarks: "Observe, how when one is continuing in prayer, when one is in charity, then it is that the Spirit draws near."[2]

Then, on the fiftieth day after the Resurrection of our Lord, "**suddenly there came a sound from heaven as of a rushing mighty wind, and it filled all the house where they were sitting. And there appeared unto them cloven tongues like as of fire, and it sat upon each of them**" [Acts 2:2-3].

In icons we see small tongues of fire placed within the haloes, immediately over their heads. Thus the Spirit alighted upon them in the form of tongues, about which St. Gregory the Theologian (329-391) comments that "as a sign of sanctification both of the principal controlling member of the body and of the mind itself" and "showing that the Holy Spirit rests in the saints." He then says, "the Holy Spirit appears in the shape of separate tongues, owing to the diversity of gifts."[3]

Thus the Holy Spirit descended upon every member of the Church separately, and though there are "diversities of gifts, but the same Spirit" [1 Cor. 12:4] and "the manifestation of the Spirit is given to each one for the profit of all" [1 Cor. 12:7]. "For to one is given by the Spirit the word of wisdom; to another the word of knowledge by the same Spirit; to another faith by the same Spirit; to another the gifts of healing by the same Spirit; to another the working

410

of miracles; to another prophecy; to another discerning of spirits; to another divers kinds of tongues; to another the interpretation of tongues" [1 Cor. 12:8-10]. For "God hath placed some in the Church: first apostles, secondly prophets, thirdly teachers, after that miracles, then gifts of healing, helps, governments, diversities of tongues" [1 Cor. 12:28].

Saint John Chrysostom makes this comment about the "tongues like as of fire" (*glossae osee pyros*): "Observe how it is always, 'like as'; and rightly: that you may have no gross sensible notions of the Spirit. Also, 'as (*osper*) of...wind;' but it was not a wind. 'Like as of fire.' For when the Spirit was to be made known to John (the Baptist), then it came upon the head of Christ as in the form of a dove [Jn. 1:32]: but now, when a whole multitude was to be converted, it is 'like as of fire.' And it sat (*ekathise*) upon each of them. This means that it remained and rested upon them; for sitting signifies settledness and continuance.

"Was it only upon the Twelve that it came? No, but upon the hundred and twenty. **'They were all filled with the Holy Spirit, speaking with other tongues, as the Spirit gave them utterance'** [Acts 2:4]. It would not have said 'all' unless the rest also were partakers."[4] Thus, the nativity of the Church took place at Pentecost, the fiftieth day after the Resurrection.

If we carefully examine the icon, we see the Apostles of the Twelve and of the Seventy. We also observe St. Paul who is sitting with St. Peter at the head of the circle; among the Apostles of the Seventy, we see the two Evangelists, Luke and Mark. Hence, the Holy Spirit descended not only on the chosen Twelve, but also upon all them that were in the house, thus fulfilling the prophecy of Joel 2:28-29: "And it shall come to pass afterward, that I will pour out of my Spirit upon all flesh; and your sons and your daughters shall prophesy, and your old men shall dream

411

dreams, and your young men shall see visions. And on My servants and on My handmaids in those day will I pour out My Spirit."

We also see in the icon of the Pentecost the figure of a king, who symbolically represents the world (in Greek, *Cosmos*). He is garbed in red and set against a black background. He is old with a white beard and crowned. He holds in his hands a white cloth, containing twelve scrolls.

The old man personifies the ancient earth, clothed in red because of the pollution of blood sacrifices to idols. He is crowned because sin ruled in the world, blackened with the darkness of unbelief. The white cloth with the twelve scrolls foreshadows the conversion of the world, by the Twelve Apostles, to the pure Faith.

REJOICE, THOU WHO ART INCONTESTABLY MORE EXALTED THAN THE CHERUBIM AND SURPASSEST THE SERAPHIM!

The gifts of the Holy Spirit were also poured out upon the most blessed Virgin, and in greater abundance than upon the Apostles--just as a larger vessel can contain more water. The Theotokos was a vessel most rich in the gifts of the Holy Spirit, for she had been a worthy temple of Him before this, in which He constantly dwelt. The Theotokos was possessed of all the virtues in her blessed soul. She is higher than the Apostles, Prophets and all the Saints.[5]

Hence, the Church chants with St. George of Nicomedia (d. after 880): *O pure Virgin, thou art truly highly exalted above all!*[6] Saint John of Damascus (c.676-c.750) writes: *Rejoice, O Bride of God, thou who art more sacred than the noetic hosts and higher than all created nature!*[7]

The following hymn explains why the Theotokos is highly exalted. *O pure Ever-Virgin, thou art incomparably higher than all creation both visible and invisible; for thou*

412

hast brought forth the Creator, Who was pleased to be incarnate in thy womb. Boldly, then, intercede with Him that He save our souls.[8]

According to St. Gregory Palamas (+1359), Mary's destiny, through the divine maternity, has a vastness which inclines all creatures in its influence and calls for the highest gifts in her person. "Mary is the cause of what had gone before, the pioneer of what has come after her; she distributes eternal goods. She is the thought of the Prophets, the head of the Apostles, the support of Martyrs, the certainty of doctors. She is the glory of the earth, the joy of heaven, the  ornament of creation. She is the principle, the source, and the root of ineffable good things. She is the summit and the fulfillment of all that is holy."[9]

The idea of mediation on the part of the Theotokos is not open to doubt or question for St. Gregory Palamas, who is quite explicit when he says, "No divine gifts can reach either angels or men, save through her mediation. As one cannot enjoy the lamp...save through the medium of this lamp, so every movement towards God, every impulse towards good coming from Him is not realizable save through the mediation of the Virgin. She does not cease to spread benefits on all creatures, not only on us men, but on the celestial incorporeal ranks, as well."[10]

It behooveth us to praise the life-giving Maiden, who alone gave passage through her womb unto the Word, Who healed the diseased nature of mortals, and sat at the right hand of the Father, and now sends the grace of the Spirit.[11]

Saint Gregory Palamas also says that Mary received gifts of knowledge precociously. The mutual love between her and Jesus was perfect.[12]

AFTER THE DESCENT OF THE HOLY SPIRIT

At that time, the Apostles cast lots that they might determine where each should go and preach the Gospel. The Virgin-Mother also requested a lot for herself, so that she might share in the preaching. Thus, she said, "I, too, want to take part in the preaching of the Gospel and wish to cast my lot with you to receive the land which God will show." Then with fear and reverence, they cast for the Theotokos, and her lot fell on the Iberian land (now Georgia in southern Russia). The most pure Mother of God then joyfully accepted her lot.[13]

After the day of Pentecost, the Theotokos was planning to set out for Iberia at once, but the Archangel Gabriel appeared to her, restraining her, saying, "Virgin Birth-giver of God, Jesus Christ Who was born of thee, thus commands: Thou shalt not depart from the land of Judea, that is, Jerusalem. The place assigned as thy lot is not Iberia but Macedonia's peninsula, Mount Athos. After some time thou wilt have the work of preaching in the land to which God will guide thee. This place shall be greatly blessed and illuminated in the light of thy face."[14] The Archangel then revealed to her the following about the Iberian land: "The land which fell to thee will be enlightened in the latter days, by another woman, and thy dominion will be established there."

These words were fulfilled three centuries later when the blessed Virgin Mary sent Saint Nina, "Equal-to-the-Apostles" (commemorated January 14th), whom she blessed and helped in proclaiming the Gospel to the Iberians.[15]

O all-pure Virgin Mother of God, the holy virgin **Nina** *was the vessel of thy blessedness and has enlightened* **the** *land that was thy lot.*[16]

SAINT MARY MAGDALENE,
COUNTED IN THE RANKS OF THE APOSTLES[17]

After the Ascension, Mary Magdalene's life again became quiet and peaceful. She lived with the Theotokos in the home of the Evangelist John in Sion. Mary Magdalene was about seven years younger than the Theotokos and esteemed and attended the Theotokos as a sister dearly beloved.

On the day of Pentecost, St. Mary Magdalene, too, received the Holy Spirit. The strong desire then entered her heart to expose them that unjustly condemned and slew the Teacher Christ. She resolved to go to Rome and present her case before Emperor Tiberius against Pilate, Annas and Caiaphas.

Greatly moved in her heart to accomplish this, she went before the holy Virgin with tears in her eyes, and said:

"My Lady and Mother of the King of All, Christ our God: Grant to thy unworthy handmaid thy blessing to depart. I desire to make a long journey for two reasons: The first is to lodge a complaint with Tiberius Caesar of the unlawful tribunal where they unjustly condemned thy righteous Son; the other reason is that I might preach to whomever I meet concerning the Faith of the risen Jesus. I will tell them that the Resurrection was not a fable, but an indisputable event that is both true and sublime, which I myself witnessed."

The Theotokos then looked upon Mary with loving eyes. Mary Magdalene then continued, "O, how shall I be separated from the affection and friendship of such a beloved soul? How much will I be deprived of thy company and our many spiritual bonds? How can I not behold thy blessed eyes which were vouchsafed to gaze upon thy risen Son and which have rendered me tender consolation?"

After this, the Theotokos gave Mary her blessing to depart. Then as a genuine mother, the Virgin-Mother helped Mary prepare and pack for the trip, for she understood that it was  God's will that Mary depart. Mary had no fear of traveling such a long distance with all its attendant dangers and perils. She was secure in her belief that the unsleeping God would navigate her little sailing vessel across the waves to Rome.[18]

A hymn taken from the service of St. Mary Magdalene lauds her in these words: *Nothing on earth hast thou preferred to the love of Christ our God. Smitten by His excellencies alone and by the flashes of light sent down on thee directly, O honored saint, thou hast trodden in His footsteps, crying aloud, "I magnify Thee of many mercies."*[19]

The apostle of Christ, Mary of Magdala, arrived safely in Rome. She went before Tiberius Caesar and presented him with a red egg, greeting him with the words: "Christ is Risen!" At the same time, she denounced Pilate to Caesar for his unjust condemnation of the Lord Jesus. And Caesar listened to her.

In conjunction with St. Mary Magdalene's complaint, Eusebius (263-339), the historian of Christian antiquity, records that Tiberius also heard that Pilate's soldiers had slaughtered some Samaritans unjustly. Therefore, he deemed it necessary to summon Pilate to Rome to answer for his actions. However, Pilate, upon reaching Rome, found Tiberius dead, and Caius upon the throne. Pilate, unable to defend himself, fell under imperial displeasure. He was banished to Vienne in Gaul, where some accounts state that he committed suicide.[20]

Of further interest is the life of Pilate's wife, Procula Claudia, who, when Christ was delivered bound before Pilate, sent to her husband, saying, "Have nothing to do with that just Man, for I have suffered many things in a dream because of Him" [Mt. 27:19]. After the Passion, she came to believe in Christ and lived a holy life. After suffering greatly for the Lord's sake, she reposed peacefully. She is commemorated by the Holy Church on the 27th of October.

Chapter XXV.
The Early Years of the Church
In Jerusalem

+ + +

The Saviour had left His immaculate Mother among the living, so that by her presence, guidance, teaching and fervent prayers, the children of the Church might be established and increase. The Theotokos strengthened all, comforted all with the joy of her presence. Also she emboldened many who were called to lay down their lives in martyrdom for the Lord and the Faith.[1]

The holy Apostles did not at once scatter throughout the world to preach the Gospel, but tarried a long while in Jerusalem, protected by the power of God. This is evident from the *Acts of the Apostles*, as recorded by the Evangelist Luke.

The Apostles wrought many miracles, thereby increasing the number of the faithful. When the high priest and the Sadducees rose up against them, they laid their hands on them and cast them into the common prison [Acts 5:18]. The Mother of God especially prayed with a tender heart for their deliverance. And an angel of the Lord opened the prison doors and brought them forth, commanding them to go and speak in the temple [Acts 5:19-20].

At that time, the Mother of God dwelt in the house of St. John the Theologian, which was on the highest elevation in Jerusalem, Mt. Sion.[2] The Apostle John had taken her to his home, and regarded her as his own Mother, serving her with much respect, from the time when the Lord commended her to his care [Jn. 19:27]. The Theotokos influenced many and strengthened the desire for virginity in not a few. On account of her companionship, the Evangelist John spoke more than others of divine mysteries. The Theotokos remained constant in the ascetic labor of fasting and prayer, yet always harbored a fervent desire to behold her Son.[3]

During the early ninth century, Epiphanios the Monk reported that "She healed many sick people and freed those overcome by impure spirits; she gave alms and sympathy to the poor and to the widows."[4]

We read in the *Acts of the Apostles* that the Jerusalem community was close-knit after the day of Pentecost. Many had anticipated the return of Christ within their lifetimes. We note that the Christians in Jerusalem shared all their material goods [Acts 2:44-45]. Many sold their property and gave the proceeds to the Church, and distribution was made to all according to their need [Acts 4:34-35]. Although the Christians still went to the temple to pray [Acts 2:46], they began partaking of the Lord's Mystical Supper in their own homes [Acts 2:42, 46]. God worked miracles of healing through these early Christians. Sick people would gather at the temple, so that the Apostles might touch them on their way to prayer [Acts 5:12-16]. The Church grew very rapidly so that the Apostles had to appoint seven men to distribute goods to the needy widows [Acts 6:1-3].

THE PROTO-MARTYR AND ARCHDEACON STEPHEN

Stephen's name, meaning "crown" in Greek, could indicate that he was a Hellenist or Greek-speaking Jew. The significance of the Hellenists is seen first in their numbers and the need for seven men to be in charge of the distribution of relief. Historical records indicate the presence of thousands of Christians in Jerusalem whose native tongue was Greek. [Acts 6:1,3,7].

The Hellenists had a crucial part in the early transition of the Gentiles into the Church. Though Jews and Gentiles were separated by the major barriers of race, geography and language, the Hellenistic Jews, many of them who lived outside of Palestine, had overcome part of the barriers and had learned to live with Gentiles. When converted to Christianity, they readily adapted the message to a Greek context and, of course, had access to the *Septuagint*.

Now Stephen, full of faith and the Holy Spirit, did great wonders and miracles among the people [Acts 6:5,8]. According to Acts 6:13, he was accused by his critics of speaking against the temple and the law. These charges were brought forth by Hellenistic Jews, who considered their ancestral faith the one thing worth living for; therefore, they were bitterly opposed to anything that might undermine their traditional faith.

But Stephen had discovered the inadequacy of a mere formalism and ceremonialism in the temple worship. Christ's own words, to the Samaritan woman, had indicated to him and the early Church that true worship of God is not confined to the temple [Jn. 4:20-24; Mk. 13:2]. Jesus had defended laxity in matters of tradition and had supported a freer attitude toward Sabbath observance [Mk. 2:15f.; 7:1-27; Lk. 15:1f.]. Jesus had granted consideration to Gentiles [Mt. 8:5-13; Mk. 7:24-30]. On rare occasions He had superseded the law [Mt. 5:33-37; Mk. 10:2-12]. Many of our Saviour's followers were the common people "who heard Him gladly" [Mk. 12:37]; and it is clear that the observance of legal minutiae was not an absorbing concern with many of these people. Therefore, Stephen, with his broad background among those of the Dispersion, maintained these important aspects of Jesus' messages and conduct and opened the way for future advance into Gentile evangelism.

Stephen did not hesitate to preach his views in the Hellenistic synagogues. Naturally, others arose and disputed with him, but they could not gainsay or resist the wisdom and power of his words. Worsted in debate, they secretly induced some men to falsely accuse Stephen and they stirred up the people, the elders and the scribes. How did they stir up the people against the spiritual insights of the arch-deacon? They misrepresented Stephen's views and aroused Jewish suspicions and fears. Seizing him, he was brought before the assembled council and, before pre-arranged false witnesses, charged with blasphemy [v. 12-14]. The accusations were twofold: a charge that he spoke against Moses, which would make Stephen a blasphemer against God; and they charged him with radical and revolutionary statements concerning the temple and the law. Indeed the accusations against Stephen will be remarkably similar to those levelled against Christ [Mt. 26:64; Mk. 14:58; 13:2; 15:29]. Therefore, the archdeacon was accused of implied approval of the destruction of the temple and the change of the law. To them, Christianity threatened to overthrow their religion and Jewish nationalism.

The holy Stephen was then permitted to answer their accusations in the council. While Stephen judged Old Testament history from the prophetic viewpoint, the council represented the legalistic view. For Stephen, the new religion was only the divinely ordered development of the old. The real blasphemers were the disobedient Jews who rejected the revelation and slew Christ. When the archdeacon declared that he beheld the opened heavens and Jesus at the right hand of God [7:56], this caused the council to break loose and forget the formality of pronouncing sentence.

Why was Christ pleased to appear in this attitude to Stephen? Saint John Chrysostom (354-407) comments that the idea of Jesus sitting at the right hand of God was offensive to the Jews.[5] By standing it shows that He is in a position to succor His martyr; for thus it is said, "...Arise unto my help [Ps. 34:2]; "...now will I arise, saith the Lord; I will establish them in salvation, I will be manifest therein" [Ps. 11:5]; and "Arise, O Lord, save me, O my God, for Thou hast smitten all who without cause are mine enemies..." [Ps. 3:8].

But that He "is seated with Him as God with God, and Lord with Lord, and as Son with His Father in truth, being this by nature even though He is known to be with flesh" is affirmed by St. Cyril of Alexandria (+444), who also says, "When Christ had completed the dispensation with us, trampled on satan, thrown down all his power and 'destroyed the power of death' [Heb. 2:14] itself, He restored for us a new and living way by having ascended 'into the holy places' and having 'appeared in the presence of God for us' [Heb. 9:24], as it is written. He is seated with Him even in the flesh, not as a man considered separately and a different Son besides the Word, nor as a man having Him in-dwelling, but as the Son being truly the one and only Son even when He became man."[6]

This irregular outbreak of priests purposed to stone Stephen as a blasphemer, though technically he was uncondemned [Deut. 17:7; Lev. 24:14-16], because he was not really guilty of blasphemy by their law; he did not pronounce the ineffable name. Thus, at most, he should have received forty stripes lacking one. Furthermore, the Romans had not granted the Sanhedrin the power of capital punishment. Much later, the execution of James, the brother of the Lord, would be declared illegal. Agrippa quickly held responsible the high priest Annas II and removed him from office.[7] However, it is not difficult to believe that when Jewish authority perpetrated some illegality, which to the Romans was not particularly significant, it could be conveniently overlooked.[8]

When the proto-martyr was led to the place of execution, the Mother of God followed at a distance. When they reached the Valley of Jehosaphat, by the brook of Kedron, she stood at a distance on a nearby hill with St. John the Theologian.[9]

Meanwhile, the witnesses laid down their clothes at a young man's feet, named Saul, who, not only consented to Stephen's death [Acts 8:58], but failed to show any pity for one of his own blood who was being put to death.[10] Saul, who claimed to be a Hebraic Jew, trained in the most worthy traditions of his fathers, whose Pharisaic qualifications could hardly be surpassed was, perhaps, in his misguided zeal that lacked true knowledge, basing his actions against Stephen on Deut. 13:6-10. "And if thy brother...or thy friend who is equal to thine own soul, entreat thee secretly saying, 'Let us go and serve other gods...' thou shalt not consent to him, neither shalt thou hearken to him: and thine eye shall not spare him, thou shalt feel no regret for him, neither shalt thou protect him: thou shalt surely report concerning him, and thy hands shall be among the first to slay him, and the hands of all the people at the last. And they shall stone him with stones, and he shall die, because he sought to draw thee away from the Lord thy God...."

Witnessing his martyric end, the most holy Theotokos fervently prayed to the Lord that He strengthen His martyr and receive his soul into His hands.

While the innocent Stephen was sustaining the rain of blows from the stones, he knelt down and, with a loud voice, he cried, "Lord, lay not this sin to their charge." After he uttered this, in imitation of His Master Christ, he fell asleep [Acts 7:58-60].[11]

Commenting upon the martyr's final words, St. Basil (c.330-379) remarks that "It behooves us to make suitable requests in prayer, even if we are at the very point of death."[12]

And great lamentation was made over the young Stephen, whose face shone like that of an angel's. Moreover, his death was a kind of double loss, for he was held by all as one most gracious and amiable. The Holy Church commemorates the day of his martyrdom on the 27th of December.

For our sake the Master entered the cave of life through condescension; and Stephen, chief among the martyrs, departed from human burdens, overcome by the love of the Master.[13]

The effects of Stephen's death were enormous. The proto-martyr's relics were left by the Jews for the dogs to eat. However, God's providence disposed otherwise when, at night and two days later, as the martyr's body lie in an open place, the Jewish sage and teacher of Saul, Gamaliel [Acts 5:34], who was a secret follower of Christ, came and took up Stephen's relics and went to Caphargamala. Gamaliel buried the precious relics on his own land in a cave.[14]

It is also recorded that on the very same day, St. Nicanor,[15] one of the Seventy Apostles, who was also one of the seven deacons serving with St. Stephen [Acts 6:5], suffered and was slain in Jerusalem with two hundred others, at the hands of wicked Jews.[16] Thus, a persecution followed, scattering the Church [Acts 8:1]. In this instance, too, the prophecy of our Saviour was fulfilled: "They shall put you out of the synagogues: yea, the time cometh that whosoever killeth you will think that he doeth God service. And these things will they do unto you, because they have not known the Father, nor Me" [Jn. 16:2-3].

SAUL PERSECUTES THE CHURCH

"As for Saul, he made havoc of the Church, entering into every house and, dragging off men and women, committing them to prison. Therefore, those who were scattered abroad went everywhere preaching the word" [Acts 8:3-4].

Saul now assumes the role of persecutor after officiating at the martyrdom of his kinsman, St. Stephen [Acts 8:1,3]. In Jewish eyes, Stephen's message was teaching laxity of the law and apostasy of the foulest kind. Saul sensed the whole basis of Judaism threatened. Saul's drastic actions related to his fear that transgression and apostasy within the Jewish nation would delay the messianic age. Saul's zeal for the law was consonant with pharisaic endeavors, in large part, to keep Israel unified in its worship of God, especially during this time of what they considered the messianic travail. Therefore, Saul received the right to extradite the Christians, seeking primarily the Hellenistic Jewish believers.

It appears that the young rabbi Saul was modeling his own life and justifying his actions biblically. In Num. 25:1-5, Moses orders the destruction of immoral Israelites at Beelphegor, just prior to their entrance into Canaan. In the same chapter we read of the much-lauded Phinees, who received God's praise for his zeal to put apostasy out of Israel, even slaying the chief offenders himself [Num. 25:6-15]. The activities of Mattathias some two centuries earlier in rooting out apostasy among their own people may have also been a model to Saul [1 Mac. 2:23-28, 42-48]. Perhaps after all his reading, together with the following passage, "For it is a token of His great goodness, when wicked doers are not suffered any longer time, but forthwith punished" [2 Mac. 6:13], he thought himself as justified to carry out activities against the new Church. Thus motivated to do God's will as he then understood it, Saul later would acknowledge that he "did it ignorantly in unbelief" [1 Tim. 1:13].

Here, too, the Mother of God prayed on behalf of Saul to her Son and God. With warm tears, she entreated Christ that Saul, the Benjamite, might change from a ravening wolf [Gen. 49:27],[17] into a meek lamb, from an enemy into an Apostle, from a persecutor into a disciple and universal teacher. Then, miraculously, on the road to Damascus, he was stricken down to the earth and then called to apostleship [Acts 9].[18]   Saint Athanasios of Alexandria (296-373) commented that St. Paul later would receive his ideas about virginity from Mary Theotokos' example.[19]

THE APOSTLES

During this period, while the Apostles were traveling, from time to time, they would return to Jerusalem, as in the case with both Apostles Peter and James,[20] the brother of John the Theologian.

The Apostles loved to see the Mother of God as often as possible to learn from her. They honored her as the pro-locutress of their assembly, and would gaze upon her most glorious countenance as that of Christ Himself. Listening to the gracious words of the blessed Virgin filled them with ineffable joy. The sweetness of her words made them forget the bitterness of their troubles and misfortunes.[21]

Many wished to visit with the Mother of God and to learn from her. They would travel from far and distant lands in order to behold her and to partake of her words of wisdom. Thus as the preaching of Christ went out into all the earth, more and more people, after learning about the Theotokos, were drawn to her in Jerusalem.[22]

There are also two epistles of St. Ignatios the God-bearer (+c.110), written from Antioch, to St. John the Theologian, of whom he was a disciple. According to Holy Tradition, St. Ignatios came to be identified with the child whom Christ [Mt. 18:2] set before His disciples as a pattern of humility. Hence, St. Ignatios received the appellation *Theophoros* or "God-bearer". The following epistles have been attributed to him.

+

"Ignatios, and the brethren who are with him, to John the holy presbyter:

"There are many women among us who desire to behold the Mother of Jesus. They often endeavor to find an opportunity to come to thee, O Apostle John, that they might visit with her and lean on the bosom that nourished the Lord, and to learn from her certain mysteries. Among us, she is glorified as the Mother of God and Virgin, full of grace and virtue.

"I have heard it said that she is joyful in troubles and persecutions, free from murmuring in the midst of penury and want, and never gets angry with them that offend her, but does more good unto them. She is grateful to those that injure her and rejoices when exposed to troubles. She sympathizes with the wretched and the afflicted as sharing in their affliction, and is not slow to come to their assistance as much as she is able.

"Moreover, she shines forth gloriously as contending in the fight of faith against the pernicious conflicts of vice. She is the Lady and teacher of our new piety and the guide for all the faithful in every good work. Indeed, all who behold her experience delight. She is indeed devoted to the humble, and she humbles herself more devotedly than the devoted, and is wonderfully magnified by all, while at the same time she suffers detraction from the scribes and pharisees. And how humble she is when the Jewish lawyers and pharisees laugh at her!

"Now there are some people, worthy of all credibility, who declare that in Mary, the Mother of Jesus, there is an angelic purity of nature allied with human nature. Such reports as these have greatly excited our emotions, and urge us eagerly to desire a sight of this--if it be lawful to so speak--heavenly prodigy and most sacred marvel. But do thou in haste comply with this our desire; and fare thou well. Amen."[23]

+

In a second epistle to the Apostle John, St. Ignatios writes:

"To John, the holy presbyter, from his friend, Ignatios:

"If thou wilt give me leave, I desire to go up to Jerusalem, and see the faithful saints who are there, especially Mary the Mother, whom they report to be honorable, affable, an object of admiration and of affection to all. For who would not rejoice to behold and to address her who bore the true God from her own womb?--provided he is a friend of our faith and religion.

"In like manner, I desire to see the venerable James, who is surnamed 'Just', whom they relate to be very much like Christ Jesus in appearance, in life, and in method of conduct, as if he were a twin-brother of the same womb. They say that if I see him, I see also Jesus Himself, as to all the features and aspect of His body. Moreover, I desire to see the other saints, both male and female. Alas! why do I delay? Why am I kept back? Kind teacher, bid me hasten to fulfil my wish, and fare thou well. Amen."[24]

+

Indeed, all who beheld the Mother of God considered themselves fortunate. Truly blessed were the eyes that beheld her and the ears that were granted to hear her most precious words which renew us to the spiritual life; verily, what joy and grace they received![25] Elsewhere, St. Ignatios commented that "he who is devout to the Virgin Mother will certainly never be lost."[26]

THE APOSTLE AND EVANGELIST LUKE, FIRST OF THE ICONOGRAPHERS

Saint Luke, holy writer of the Gospel of Jesus Christ, was an eloquent orator, a most learned physician and teacher of every form of knowledge and science.

Acceding to the pious desire of many early Christians, Luke clearly manifested his divine love when, through the Holy Spirit, he received wisdom and depicted the form of the most holy Virgin, carrying the pre-eternal Infant, our Lord Jesus Christ, in her arms.

Luke, the divinely eloquent recorder of the Gospel, at the behest of God, set down thine all-immaculate image, O Theotokos, depicting the pre-eternal infant in thine arms.[27]

426

He painted her holy image on a panel in varied colors, a face which he himself had seen. He then painted two other icons of the all-holy Theotokos and brought them to the Mother of God for her approval. Upon beholding and approving the sacred images, she said: "May the grace of Him Who was born of me, through me, be imparted to them (the icons)".[28] The Theotokos then repeated the hymn that she had once said in the house of her cousin Elisabeth: "My soul doth magnify the Lord, and my spirit hath rejoiced in God my Saviour..." [Lk. 46-55].[29]

However, the Theotokos, during her earthly life, avoided the glory which belonged to her as the Mother of the Lord. She preferred to live in quiet and to prepare herself for the departure into eternal life.

After that, the holy Luke painted on wooden boards the images of the holy Apostles Peter and Paul. The Evangelist Luke, thus, was himself the initiator of the good and blessed sacred art of iconography, to the glory of God, the Theotokos and all the saints, and for the adornment of the holy Orthodox Churches and for the instruction of the faithful.

Of the highly-venerated miraculous images of the Orthodox Church those five directly ascribed to the painter-Apostle are: the Blessed Virgin of Megaspilaon on Morea (Peloponnese, Greece); the Kykkou Icon of Cyprus; the Mother of God of Mount Soumela, in the former empire of Trebizond on the Black Sea; the Saydanaya Icon of the Theotokos in Syria; and Panagia (All-holy one) of the Salutations of the Akathist, Monastery of Dionysiou on the Holy Mountain.

For centuries, the Mother of God has mercifully visited us in her wonder-working icons that are resplendent with grace, and have illumined and helped them that approach to venerate them with love. Through this well-spring, countless people have been freed from ailments of spiritual and bodily suffering. Through her holy images, many have been granted aid amid necessities, consolation amid sorrows, and deliverance amid misfortunes. As a mighty helper and fervent mediatress for the faithful, she has chosen the holy icons through which she has bestowed great mercy in her maternal protection. Indeed angels reverence her precious image and demons flee from the image of the all-pure one.

HEROD PERSECUTES THE CHRISTIANS

"Now about that time, Herod, the king, stretched forth his hands to vex certain of the Church. And he killed James, the brother of John, with the sword. And because he saw it pleased the Jews, he proceeded further to take Peter also" [Acts 12:1-3].

About ten years had now passed since the Ascension of our Saviour when the pre-eminent Apostle Peter was shut up in prison, and prayer was made without ceasing to God on account of him. Then an angel of the Lord was sent who led him forth out to the street [Acts 12:10]. The year was then about 37 A.D. (Christ having been born in about 6 B.C.).

Shortly thereafter, it became necessary for the Apostles to leave Jerusalem. However, before dispersing, they compiled the *Symbol of Faith* and the *85 Apostolic Canons*, so that the preaching and planting of the holy Faith of Christ might be achieved harmoniously. Whereupon, James, the brother of the Lord, who was chosen as first Bishop of Jerusalem by the Lord Himself, was the only one who remained in the Holy City.[30]

THE VIRGIN TRAVELS ABROAD

In Ephesus

To escape persecution, St. John the Theologian thought it prudent to flee with the Mother of God. Therefore, they departed Jerusalem and went to Ephesus, for this lot fell to the Apostle. Ephesus is located at the western end of Asia Minor (Anatolia), which today is within the Turkish Republic. It is 680 km. south of Constantinople (Istanbul), 10 km east from the Aegean Sea, and near by Smyrna (Izmir). In Ephesus, the Panagia and Apostle John spent some time. Here, she spent her time in prayer and meditation.[31]

Much later, the city of Ephesus, fully conscious of paying honor to the Virgin Mary, erected the first church and basilica constructed in honor of Mary Theotokos. It was built adorned with columns in a classical style in the middle of a large open space. The classical church was 260 m. in length and was built on the columns and adapted into a fine basilica with baptistry. The church was formally dedicated after the saintly King Constantine decreed permission for the public performance of Christianity in 313 A.D. Today only the ruins of the church remain.[32]

Later in 431 A.D., about 200 bishops and 111 general consults convened the Third Ecumenical Synod. In the minutes of that meeting, it is recorded: "In Ephesus, where lived John the Theologian and the Virgin Theotokos, holy Mary." But this is not to be construed that she reposed and was buried in that Asian city. It is a well founded and ancient tradition that she did not repose in Ephesus, but that her Dormition took place in Jerusalem (where she was born) and that she was buried in Gethsemane.

The Virgin and the Apostle John did not confine their period abroad to only Ephesus, but traveled to other cities where the Mother of God illuminated many with the light of Christian teaching. The Apostle John would return to Ephesus later (after 53 A.D.) with St. Prochoros, after the honored and glorious repose of the Theotokos.[33]

In Antioch

Holy Tradition also says that the Theotokos visited with St. Ignatios in Antioch. He had sent a letter to her writing:

+

"I desire with my whole heart to obtain information concerning the things which I have heard from thee, who was always intimate and allied with Him, and Who wast acquainted with all His secrets. I have also written to thee at another time, and have asked thee

429

concerning the same things. Fare thou well; and let the neophytes who are with me be comforted of thee, and by thee, and in thee. Amen."[34]

+

The reply of the blessed Virgin to this letter stated her pending arrival.

"The lowly handmaid of Christ Jesus to Ignatios, her beloved fellow-disciple:

"The things which thou hast heard and learned from John concerning Jesus are true. Believe them, cling to them, and hold fast the profession of that Christianity which thou hast embraced, and conform thy habits and life to thy profession. Now I will come in company with John to visit thee and them that are with thee.

"Stand fast in the faith,[35] and show thyself a man; nor let the fierceness of persecution move thee, but let thy spirit be strong and rejoice in God thy Saviour.[36] Amen."[37]

+

It is manifest and noteworthy that, in the last paragraph written by the Theotokos, she has uttered a prophecy concerning the future "fierce" manner of martyrdom that awaited St. Ignatios in the stadium.

As Bishop of Antioch, Saint Ignatios governed the Church of God as a good shepherd. It so happened that many years after the Theotokos' repose, he refused to offer sacrifice to the idols when Emperor Trajan urged him. The saint was then put in irons and sent to Rome, escorted by ten bestial soldiers, to be thrown to the wild beasts. It was a long and difficult journey, but the saint rejoiced to be suffering for Christ and prayed that the wild beasts might be the tomb of his body.

In the stadium, before the Roman crowd, the bishop announced that he was not being punished for any wrongdoing, but was condemned for the sake of his God Whom he desired with an insatiable desire. He also said, "I am His wheat; may I be ground by the teeth of beasts, that I may be His pure bread." Indeed he was thrown to the lions in the circus and they tore him to pieces and devoured him, leaving only a few of the larger bones. The holy man's precious relics were taken back to Antioch, by the Christians, as a great treasure. Later, St. John Chrysostom (354-407) would comment that, consumed by love for Christ, "St. Ignatios put off his body as easily as a man takes off his clothes."

Saint Ignatios always proclaimed that he had Christ in his heart. He, therefore, was given the appellation of "God-bearer" (*Theophoros*). He suffered on December 20, 106 A.D.[38]

THE RETURN TO JERUSALEM

After visiting Ephesus and Antioch, the Theotokos again returned to Jerusalem, and dwelt in the house of St. John the Evangelist. The all-powerful right hand of God preserved His Mother from the envious snares of the synagogue of the Jews, for the Lord overshadowed the living ark of God, so that she was not touched by the hands of the unbelieving.

431

Chapter XXVI.
The THEOTOKOS on
Mount Athos

+ + +

SAINT LAZARUS

Returning from Ephesus and Antioch, the Mother of God then remained in Jerusalem for a considerable period. During this time, St. Lazarus, whom the Lord had raised from the dead on the fourth day of his repose [Jn. 11:14-44], was living on the island of Cyprus. The Apostle Barnabas had consecrated him as bishop.

Now St. Lazarus had a great longing to behold the Theotokos whom he had not seen in a long while. However, he dared not enter Jerusalem for fear of the Jews, who still sought him. The Theotokos learned of this and wrote St. Lazarus, the true friend of her Son, a letter wherein she comforted him. She asked him to send a ship to her that she might visit him in Cyprus, for she would never demand of him to come to Jerusalem for her sake. When the holy Lazarus read her letter, he was filled with tremendous joy and, at the same time, he wondered at her great humility.

Without a moment's delay, he sent a ship for her together with a letter of reply. Whereupon, the Theotokos, together with Christ's beloved disciple, John, and others, who reverently accompanied them, set sail.[1] It is said that she had sewn St. Lazarus an *omophorion* (a bishop's stole, pall) with *epimanikia* (cuffs) and that she wished to present them to him personally.[2] The year was 52 A.D.

A STORM AT SEA

The Virgin and her company set sail from the Holy Land on a bright and glorious day. As the ship parted from the shore, the Virgin prayed to her almighty Son that He pilot their vessel, according to His will. It happened that, after a time at sea, a violent sea storm raged and the sailing vessel was forced off course. By divine intervention, as the storm abated, they found themselves outside the port of Clemes (Clementos) on Athos. Athos was the farthest east of the three promontories of Chalkidiki, a Greek peninsula that stretches into the Aegean Sea between the Thermaic and

432

Strimonic gulf. It is some seventy km. in length, varying in width from eight to twelve km., covering in all an area of about 400 sq. km.[3]

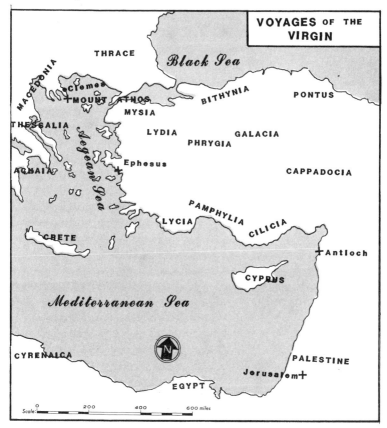

VOYAGES OF THE VIRGIN

At that time, Athos was inhabited by pagan tribes. However, in ancient times, the citizens of that region were mostly young virgins dedicated to the goddess Diana and destined to become priestesses to serve in the idolatrous temples of Greece. To this purpose, young girls were sent there from all parts of Greece. It was forbidden, under penalty of death, for men to enter; especially "Kerasia", which is today the area of the Holy Monastery of Great Lavra. The name "Kerasia" being a corrupted form of the Greek word *korasia*, meaning "virgin maiden".[4]

Agapios the Cretan writes that when the ship carrying the Virgin Mary approached Athos, Jupiter's statue, at the

433

top of the Mountain, fell and shattered to pieces in a thunderous noise.[5] The presence of this statue is mentioned in ancient history. Plutarch and Anaximander and others also mention that at the top of Athos there was a great gold-ivory statue of Jupiter which, instead of eyes, bore two large gems, reflecting the starlight. Emitting flashes by night, they served as lighthouses to the seaman sailing around Athos.[6]

THE VIRGIN GOES ASHORE

It is said that they came ashore close to the present Monastery of Iveron which is situated above a picturesque inlet on the northeastern side of the peninsula. There, the holy Virgin rested for awhile and, overwhelmed by the beauty of the place, she asked her Son to give her the Mountain, despite the fact that the inhabitants were pagans. A voice was then heard saying, "Let this place be thine inheritance and garden, a paradise and a haven of salvation for those seeking to be saved." The Virgin then brought to mind the words of the Archangel Gabriel, who told her some twenty years earlier, after the Pentecost, that her lot would be a Macedonian peninsula, Mount Athos. Thus it was consecrated as the inheritance and garden of the Mother of God,[7] and immediately acquired the name *Aghion Oros* or Holy Mountain, because our Lady the Theotokos chose this Mountain and placed it under her own protection.

Upon asking and receiving Athos as a heavenly gift, in that moment, the ground shook and the pagan statues in all the temples fell prostrate and broke into pieces. Then, even the trees of the peninsula bent forward, as though offering veneration to the Theotokos who had reached the port of Clemes.

THE INHABITANTS OF ATHOS

On the peninsula there was a great temple and shrine of Apollo. Diabolic works such as fortune telling, divining and witchcraft took place here. All the pagans greatly honored this place as one chosen by the gods. In fact, people from all over the world gathered there to worship. Therein, they would receive answers to their questions from the diviners. Therefore, when the Mother of God entered port, and all their idols had collapsed, shouting, confusion and uproar were heard from all the idols in Athos. Cries could be heard, saying, "Men of Apollo, get ye all to Clemes harbor and welcome Mary, the Mother of the Great God Jesus!" Thus, all the demons inhabiting the idols, forced against their will, could not resist the power of God and they proclaimed the truth.

Whereupon, all the inhabitants of Athos hastened from all parts to that port. Once there, they welcomed the Theotokos. Meeting her with honor, they took the Theotokos, St. John and all their fellow passengers to the common hall, called the *Synagogeion* (meeting house or assembly room).

They then asked her, "What God didst thou bear and what is His name?" Opening her divine lips, she explained, in detail, to the people everything about Christ. The natives diligently posed questions concerning the mystery of providence in the divine incarnation. They even wondered at how she, a Hebrew woman, explained everything to them in the

435

Greek language. As a result of all the excellent and super-natural occurrences attendant with her arrival, they believed. Upon being catechized by her teaching, they accepted the Christian faith.

They then fell down to the ground and worshipped the God Who was born of her and showed great respect to the Virgin who bore Him in the flesh. The Mother of God also worked many miracles on the Holy Mountain. After their baptism, she appointed a leader and teacher for the newly-illumined from among them that were in her traveling party.

TRULY GREAT IS THY FORETHOUGHT FOR US, O EVER-VIRGIN![8]

Rejoice, O all-holy Lady, who hast hallowed Athos by thy coming! Rejoice, thou who cast down the idols in that place! Rejoice, thou who didst plant the true Faith on the Mountain! Rejoice, thou who didst drive unbelief from thence![9]

Rejoicing in Spirit, the Theotokos said, "Let this place be my lot given to me by my Son and God." After these words, the Theotokos blessed the people.

When God divided the nations according to the number of His angels, then He foresaw that thou, O Virgin, would be His all-pure Mother, and He set the great Mount Athos apart for thee as an inalienable inheritance.[10]

Most pleased with the place, she prayed for it and said, "My Son and my God, bless this place, this lot of mine. Pour Thy mercy upon it and keep it free from harm till the end of this world, together with them that dwell therein for Thy holy name and mine. And, through their little fatigue and through the struggle of repentance, may their sins be forgiven. Fill their lives with every good and necessity in this age, and with eternal life in the future age. Glorify this place above every other place and show Thy miraculous power in every way. Fill it with men from every nation under the sky, who are called by Thy name and extend their habitations in it from end to end. Exempt them from eternal punishment, save them from every temptation, from visible and invisible enemies and from every heresy, and pacify them in right worship (Orthodoxy)."[11]

Rejoice, thou who hast chosen Mount Athos as thy portion! Rejoice, thou whose will it hath been to be the helper of that place! Rejoice, bestower of earthly blessings upon the faithful who abide there! Rejoice, surety of their eternal salvation![12]

REJOICE, THOU WHO BY THE GRACE OF GOD HAST PLANTED A SPIRITUAL GARDEN IN THE MIDDLE OF THINE INHERITANCE![13]

In the life of St. Peter the Athonite (681 A.D.), commemorated the 12th of June, he beheld a vision of the Theotokos speaking with St. Nicholas the Wonder-worker and Bishop of Myra, saying, "There is a Mountain in Europe, both beautiful and great, extending into the sea, facing Libya. Of all the places on the earth, I have chosen this Mountain, and it is to be the monk's proper residence. I myself have come to know it and have received it from my Son and God as an inheritance, for them

that desire to forsake the cares and tumults of the world,

that they might betake themselves there and serve God in peace without hindrance. Henceforth this place shall be 'holy' and my garden. Exceedingly do I love that place. I will especially aid them that come to dwell there and that labor with all their souls for God."[14]

Thou, O all-pure Virgin, hast promised ever to fight with all who on Mount Athos contend against the adversary who wageth war on men. Wherefore, O Mistress, mindful of thy promise, forsake us not, we beseech thee.[15]

Continuing, the Theotokos uttered, "The time will come when, from every direction, it will be filled with a multitude of monks. On account of this my soul rejoices and is exceedingly glad because they will praise and glorify the name of my Son and God. If those monks shall labor for God with all their hearts and faithfully keep His commandments, I will vouchsafe them great gifts on the great day of my Son. And, while even here on earth, they will receive great aid from me. I shall lighten their afflictions and labors. I will be for the monks an invincible ally, invisibly guiding and guarding them, a healer, a source nourishing them, and make it possible for them, with but scant means, to have sufficiency for life."[16]

How great is thy forethought for Mount Athos, O Mistress! For thou didst say that thou wilt be an instructor and teacher in the virtues to all who live virtuously thereon, and a nurturer and physician for their bodies and souls.[17]

Then she said, "I will, therefore, ask my Son and God, warmly entreating Him, to forgive the sins of them that will spend their lives here in a God-pleasing manner."[18]

Rejoice, O fervent mediatress for those who live within thy portion! Rejoice, thou who hast promised that place the mercy of thy Son until the end of time! Rejoice, thou who hast foretold that His grace would never be removed

438

therefrom! Rejoice, O joy and salvation of our souls![19]

Thou art the Mistress of the world, O Ever-Virgin, and even more art thou the Mistress and intercessor of Mount Athos, saving it from all trials and misfortunes.[20]

DEPARTING FOR CYPRUS

After praying for the new flock on the Holy Mountain, the Theotokos and those with her entered the ship with joy, and set sail for Cyprus. Upon arriving in Cyprus, she found the holy Lazarus in great sorrow, for he feared that her delay had been caused by a storm. He was unaware that divine providence had brought her to Mount Athos. However, her arrival speedily changed his sadness into joy. The Theotokos then presented him with the *omophorion* and *epimanikia* that she made for him. She then related to him all that had happened in Jerusalem and on the Holy Mountain. They then offered up thanksgiving for everything.[21]

After staying in Cyprus for a short while and consoling the Christians there, she blessed them and journeyed back to Jerusalem.[22]

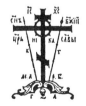

Chapter XXVII.
The THEOTOKOS in Jerusalem

+ + +

Amid the hatred and enmity of the Jews in Jerusalem, the Mother of God dwelt like a sheep among wolves and a lily among thorns. She often repeated the words of her forefather, the Prophet and King David: "The Lord is my light and my Saviour; whom then shall I fear? The Lord is the defender of my life; of whom then shall I be afraid? Though a host should array itself against me, my heart shall not be afraid; though war should rise up against me, in this have I hope" [Ps. 26:1, 3]. And, "'though I should walk in the midst of the shadow of death, I will fear no evil' [Ps. 22:4], for Thou, my Son and God, art with me."

At this time, tradition tells us that St. Mary Magdalene returned to Jerusalem after traveling to Rome, France, Egypt, Pamphylia, Syria and many other countries preaching the Gospel. Straightway, she went and dwelt again with the Theotokos and told her about all her travels and the people of the West. Saint Mary would remain with the Theotokos until her blessed Dormition and glorious bodily translation.[1]

After the Dormition of the Theotokos, St. Mary Magdalene also went to Ephesus and struggled alongside the Evangelist John in preaching the saving doctrine of Christ. It is not within the scope of this work to describe her hardships, afflictions, scourging and imprisonments that she endured for the Gospel. Then St. Mary Magdalene, "Equal-to-the-Apostles", ended her days in Ephesus and was interred by the beloved disciple John.[2] Later on, Emperor Leo the Wise would transfer her incorrupt relics to Constantinople.[3]

ST. DIONYSIOS THE AREOPAGITE

When the Apostle Paul entered Athens in about 50-51 A.D., the Greeks brought him to the Areopagus that they might hear his new doctrine. One of the men in the audience, a member of the highest court in Greece, was Dionysios. He was a nobleman from a pagan family who, when he heard the words of the divine Paul, believed [Acts 17:19-34]. Together with his wife, Damaris, his whole household was baptized.

The divine Paul then consecrated Dionysios as Bishop of Athens. Then taking leave of his wife, sons and status, for the love of Christ, Dionysios traveled widely with the Apostle Paul and came to know the other Apostles. Three years after his conversion, Dionysios had a strong desire to behold the Theotokos. Therefore, with the Apostle Paul's blessing, he visited Jerusalem.

Upon beholding the Theotokos he was filled with immeasurable spiritual joy, after which he wrote a letter to the holy Paul describing his visit:

+

"I have seen with my own eyes the most holy Mother of our Lord Jesus Christ, who surpasses in sanctity all the angels of heaven. By the grace of God, the good favor of the Apostles, and the unutterable goodness and mercy of the gracious Virgin, I was granted this meeting. Again, I confess before the Almighty God, before the grace of the Saviour, before the great glory of the Virgin, His Mother, that when I was introduced to the beautiful and most pure Virgin, together with John--the first among the Evangelists and Prophets, who, while living in the flesh, shines like the sun in heaven--a great divine radiance shone about me from without and lit up my soul. At the same time, I sensed such a wonderful fragrance that my spirit and body could hardly bear this manifestation of glory and foretaste of eternal bliss. From divine grace and glory, my heart and spirit were prostrated.

"I bear witness before God, Who dwelt in that most honorable virginal womb, that I would have taken her for the true God and would have honored her with the adoration due to God alone, if my newly-enlightened soul had not retained thy divine instructions and laws. No honor and glory of men can compare with that beatitude that I experienced, unworthy though I be. That moment in time for me was one of extreme happiness. I thank my most high and most gracious God, the divine Virgin, the great Apostle John, and thee, O Paul, the adornment of the Church and invincible leader, for having mercifully granted me such a great blessing!"[4]

+

From St. Dionysios' letter, we, too, clearly see what divine grace must have been present in the face of the all-revered Mother of our God. During her lifetime, all those souls that beheld her were enlightened and their hearts were filled with spiritual joy.

Saint Gregory Palamas (+1359) adds: "Must not the one who was to give birth to the fairest among the sons of men have been comparable to Him in everything and been clothed by her Son with marvelous beauty? This Son, was in fact, to resemble her in every aspect so that whoever would see Jesus would at once recognize, because of this perfect resemblance, the Virgin, His Mother."[5]

The sweet-voiced and immortal mouth of the Church, St. John Chrysostom, cries out, "Wherefore, in life there is none other such as the Theotokos Mary. You may wander about the earth, look round about the sea, examine the air thoroughly, the heaven in thy mind, search all the invisible hosts, remember, and see if there be any other such miracle throughout the creation."[6]

One of the greatest of the Greek Fathers, the priest-monk and hymnographer, St. John of Damascus (c.676-c.750), clearly uninhibited in expressing his devotion towards Mary, writes: "What is sweeter than the Mother of God? She holds my mind captive; she has seized my tongue; on her, I meditate day and night. Since she is the Mother of the Word, she has words abundant."[7] Saint John had consecrated his mind, soul, and body to her...with psalms, hymns, spiritual canticles and hymns, although he was convinced of the utter inadequacy of human language to describe her.[8]

THE VIRGIN AT THE HOLY PLACES

Newly baptized men and women journeyed from all parts of the world to visit the Theotokos, and, as a true Mother, she received all, without distinction or partiality. She bestowed upon all the bounties of her grace, by granting healing to the sick, health to the weak, and comfort to the sorrowing. She confirmed all in the faith, strengthened their

442

hope, instilled divine joy and love, and brought sinners to amendment.

Thus, the pure Mother of God lived among the first Christians for many years. She was filled with great spiritual joy at the spread of the Gospel of her Son throughout all the world. Indeed, within her own lifetime, she beheld the fulfillment of those words that she had uttered as a very young woman: "Behold, from henceforth all generations shall call me blessed" [Lk. 1:48]. Indeed, for wherever Christians glorified Christ as God, they also blessed His most pure Mother.

In Jerusalem, as we mentioned, she remained in the home of the Apostle John. She was wont to frequent those places that her beloved Son had sanctified, by His footsteps and the shedding of His  blameless blood. At times, she would visit Bethlehem where she gave birth to Christ. However, she especially favored those places where our Saviour suffered His voluntary Passion. It was in these places, that the force of nature, that is, maternal love, caused her to weep. And then she would say, "Here, my beloved Son was scourged. Here, He was crowned with a crown of thorns. Here is where He walked carrying His Cross; here, He was crucified."[9]

At the Holy Sepulchre, the Theotokos would then be filled with ineffable happiness and, with tears of joy, cried, "And here, He was buried and on the third day He rose with glory!"[10]

THE JEWS COMPLAIN ABOUT
THE MOTHER OF JESUS

The Jews often attempted to seize the Mother of God in order to torture and kill her; but they could do nothing. Then, at that time, some Jews reported to their chief priests and scribes that Mary, the Mother of Jesus, had the habit of daily visiting the places of the Crucifixion and the Tomb of her Son. They further informed them that she had the custom of kneeling, weeping and burning incense at these sites. Moreover, she often was followed by other men and women. From this practice of the Mother of God, the pious custom of making pilgrimages to holy sites to offer up prayers had already begun.[11]

In regard to her tormenters, St. Ephraim the Syrian (c.306-383), puts these words on the Virgin-Mother's lips: *All the chaste daughters of the Hebrews and the virgin daughters of the chief men are astonished at me! For Thee does the daughter of the poor meet with envy; for Thee, the daughter of the weak encounters jealousy.*[12]

Filled with malice and conspiring to murder, it was then decided that guards were to be placed before these sites so that no Christian might approach for veneration; and if the Mother of Jesus was to approach, she was to be slain. Nevertheless, when the Theotokos came with a company of others to the Holy Sepulchre, God did not allow His Virgin-Mother or her company of followers to be seen by the guards. Therefore, after a considerable time of observing nothing, the guards departed the sepulchre and, with an oath, assured the chief priests and scribes that they saw no one at Jesus' tomb.[13]

THE VIRGIN IS SLANDERED

The enemies of Christ also aimed to defame the fair reputation of the most pure Virgin. Seeing that Christianity was spreading everywhere, they began to spread vile slanders about the Christian Faith. A common slander of the time was that Jesus was the illegitimate son of a Roman soldier called Panthera, and that Jesus had come from a base and immoral environment.[14]

Here, again, St. Ephraim has the Theotokos say, *For Thy sake I, too, am hated, Thou Lover of all. Lo! I am persecuted who have conceived and brought forth One House of refuge for men.*[15]

However, the ugly lie was too evident and this fiction did not attract serious attention. The whole family of Joseph and Mary herself were well known by the inhabitants of Nazareth and the surrounding countryside in their time. In small towns, the family matters of everyone are well known. Indeed, a very strict watch was kept over the purity of married life.

Would people really have behaved with respect towards Jesus and called Him to preach in the synagogue, if He had been born of illegitimate cohabitation? To Mary, the law of

Moses would have been applied, which commanded that such women be stoned to death. Would the scribes and pharisees have missed such an opportunity to reproach Christ many times for the wanton conduct of His Mother? Would not His enemies have reproached Him if His birth were tainted; for in accordance with their law, "one born of a harlot shall not enter into the assembly of the Lord" [Deut. 23:2]. But just the contrary was the case. Mary enjoyed enormous respect. At Cana she was an honored guest at the wedding. And even when her Son was condemned, no one allowed himself to ridicule or censure His Mother.[16]

THE VIRGIN AT THE MT. OF OLIVES

Often the Theotokos ascended the Mount of Olives, where our Lord had ascended into the heavens before His Mother and His disciples [Acts 1:9]. The site where He had ascended was marked by His footprint that had been

impressed into the rock. Kneeling down, the Theotokos would kiss the imprint. Ofttimes she would pray to her Son and God that He might take her from among the living to Himself. How she yearned to depart and be with her Son Christ and would recite the words of the psalmist: "When shall I come and appear before the face of God? My tears have been my bread by day and by night" [Ps. 41:2-3]. She would then continue saying, "When shall I see my beloved Son? When shall I come to Him Who sits at the right hand of God the Father? When shall I stand before the throne of His glory? When shall I be satisfied with the vision of Him? O sweetest Son and my God!" And then she would utter, "'Thou shalt rise up and have pity on Sion, for it is time to have compassion' [Ps. 101:13] on me, Thy Mother, who, till now, am sorrowing at not beholding Thy face in the sorrowful valley of this world. Take my soul out of my body, as out of prison. 'As the hart panteth after the fountains of

445

water, so panteth my soul after Thee, O God' [Ps. 41:1], that it may be delighted when Thy glory shall appear to me."[17]

THE VIRGIN AT THE GARDEN OF GETHSEMANE

At the foot of the Mt. of Olives there was the Garden of Gethsemane where a small plot belonged to the house of Zebedee. The Theotokos would visit the very place where our Lord kneeled down and fell on His face [Mt. 26:39], praying to God the Father. She would prostrate herself on this spot and, watering the earth with her tears, she offered up fervent prayers. However, towards the end of her earthly sojourn, she received consolation from the Lord's angel when he revealed her imminent departure to heaven.[18]

Chapter XXVIII.
The Dormition of Our Most Holy Lady
the THEOTOKOS and EVER-VIRGIN MARY,

the Memory of which the Holy Church
Celebrates on the
15th of August

+ + +

Saint John of Damascus (c.676-c.750) writes: *If her Fruit, Whom none may comprehend, on Whose account she was called a heaven, submitted of His own will to burial as a mortal, how should she, who gave Him birth without knowing a man, refuse it?*[1]

In accordance with divine providence, the Theotokos, having come from mortal loins, had a death conformable to nature for the consolation of all people, so that they too might not fear to proceed to heaven by the same gates of death through which the Queen of Heaven passed, sharing the lot of all the earthborn. Saint John of Damascus writes: "It was necessary that that which was composed of earth should return to earth and only then pass to heaven, having embraced on earth a most pure life through the subjection of the flesh. It was necessary that the body should be purified through death, as gold through fire, from every darkness and coarse burden of filth, and should rise from the grave incorrupt, pure and illumined by the light of immortality."[2]

O pure Virgin, sprung from mortal loins, thine end was conformable to nature: but because thou hast borne the true Life, thou hast departed to dwell with the divine Life Himself.[3]

Saint John of Damascus' brother, St. Cosmas, speaks of the Virgin's death as *a crossing into a better and eternal life*, that is, it has translated her from *this mortal life to that which knows no end and is indeed divine*, where she may *look with joy upon* her Son and Lord.[4]

THE THEOTOKOS PRAYS FOR RELEASE
FROM THE BONDS OF THE FLESH

The Theotokos had now reached an advanced age. If she was born in about 20 B.C., when construction of Herod's

Temple commenced, and St. Dionysios the Areopagite came to visit her and received her blessing after 52 A.D., she had to be about seventy years old.

As we know, she dwelt many years among the first Christians, for our Lord Jesus Christ intended to have her live among His disciples. It was their desire to behold her most holy countenance constantly and to receive strength, grace, and spiritual reinforcement throughout their afflictions, misfortunes and adversities of life. Thus, through her personal presence, holy sayings and sweet words, the Apostles indeed received strength, energy, and consolation, and accorded her reverence and glorified and blessed her.[5] With the rapid advance of the young Church, the Theotokos would rejoice at her Son's boundless mercy, and over all the faithful and them that fear Him.[6]

Nevertheless, her fervent and unceasing desire was to leave the body and be with her beloved Son and God and to behold His sweet face. She shed copious tears and prayed that the Lord might remove her from this vale of tears to the blessed abodes on high.[7]

The Mother of God did not fear death, nor did she seek to avoid it. She knew that death had already been overcome by her Son and God. One Church account records that she asked the Lord for one thing: "that I may not see the dismal sight of the demons," for they are vile and foul. It is natural for chastity and modesty to seek to avoid all contact and even proximity with those who bear filth, impudence or shamelessness.[8]

One account records the following: She would call to mind her Son's words to her before His Passion when she asked Him many things and about her own future departure. She said to Him, "O most dear Son, I pray Thy holiness, that when my soul goes out of my body, that Thou wilt let me know on the third day before; and do Thou, O beloved Son, with Thy angels, receive it, and cause all the Apostles to be present at my departure.

Christ answered His beloved Mother's prayer, saying, "O palace and temple of the living God, O blessed Mother, O Queen of all saints, and blessed above all women, before thou didst carry Me in thy womb, I always guarded thee, and caused thee to be fed daily with My angelic food, as thou knowest. How can I desert thee, after thou hast carried Me, and nourished Me, and brought Me down in flight into Egypt, and endured many hardships for Me? Know, then, that My angels have always guarded thee, and will guard thee even until thy departure. After I undergo suffering for men, as it is written, and rise again on the third day, and after forty days ascend into heaven, thou shalt see My Archangel Gabriel coming to thee with a palm which I shall send to thee from heaven. Know then that I shall soon come to thee, together with My disciples, angels, archangels, and the saints and virgins. Know for certain that thy soul will be separated from the body, and I shall carry it into the heavens, where it shall never have tribulation or anguish." Then the Theotokos rejoiced and exulted, and kissed the knees of her Son, and blessed the Creator of heaven and earth, who gave her such a gift through Jesus Christ her Son.[9]

THE ARCHANGEL CRIED, "REJOICE, THOU WHO ART MAGNIFIED BY THE MESSAGE OF THY DEPARTURE UNTO THY SON!"

At that time she still lived in the house of St. John the Theologian on Mount Sion. She often went from there to the Mount of Olives, to the very place of the ascension into the heavens of her Son and Lord. There, in solitude, she would offer up her fervent prayers. As she was thus praying on the Mount of Olives that the Lord quickly take her to heaven, there appeared before her the Archangel Gabriel. It was the very Archangel who had served the Virgin from her earliest childhood; for he fed her in the Holy of Holies, announced to her the good news of the birth of her Divine Son, and constantly guarded her throughout her life on earth. With a radiant face, the celestial ambassador disclosed to the Theotokos the following: "Thus saith thy Son: 'The days are approaching when I will take My Mother unto Me.' Thus, my Mistress and my Lady, Queen of heaven, and the Creator's most immaculate Mother, thine only-begotten Son and God sent me to tell thee that He calls thee unto Him, to His Kingdom, to His ineffable glory, that thou might sit at the right hand of His throne. He awaiteth thee. Therefore, do not be troubled over these words, but receive it with delight, for thou shalt be translated to life eternal."[10]

Thus the Virgin heard those much longed for words which she received with gladness. The Archangel then said, "Thy Son and our God, with the Angels, Archangels, Cherubim and Seraphim, and all the heavenly spirits and the souls of the righteous will receive thee, His Mother, into the heavenly Kingdom that thou mayest live and reign with Him forever."[11]

Tradition has it that this occurred on a Friday. Thus after three days, on a Sunday, she would depart and be with Christ. The Archangel then told the Virgin the hour of her death. Again, as in her youth, he said that she should receive his words with joy, since she was being called to immortal life and to the eternal King of glory.

As a sign of all this, the Archangel gave into her hand a date palm branch from paradise, which shone with the light of heavenly grace. It signified that bodily death would not have power over her, just as spiritual death had not had dominion over her. She would merely fall asleep for a short time and, then, as if waking from sleep, would rise and shake off death like sleep from the eyes. She would then see in the light of the Lord's face the immortal life and glory to which she would go with shouts of joy and spiritual happiness. The Archangel informed her that the branch was to be carried before the bier of her most honorable and pure body. Upon hearing these words, the Theotokos was filled with ineffable joy and spiritual rapture; for what could be more joyous and acceptable to her than life in Heaven with her Son and the happiness of contemplating His face? Then, falling to her knees she fervently thanked her Creator.[12]

That the Virgin should receive in advance a pledge or assurance from Paradise will not be an unheard of occurrence in the history of the Orthodox Church. Others, too, have received gifts from Paradise, such as St. Methodios, Patriarch of Constantinople, St. Irene Chrysovolantou and St. Euphrosynos the Cook.

Saint Germanos (c.635-733), Patriarch of Constantinople, comments that this palm branch given to her was a symbol of victory, which was given to convince her that in leaving this life she would overcome corruption, just as Christ conquered Hades. Such palms had the God-loving children of the Hebrews held when Christ was approaching His Passion, and was soon to become victorious over death.[13]

Then she uttered the following prayer to God: "I would not have been worthy to receive Thee, O Lord, into my womb, unless Thou Thyself had mercy on me, Thy slave. I kept the treasure entrusted to me and, therefore, I have the boldness to ask Thee, O King of glory, to protect me from the power of Gehenna. If heaven and the angels tremble before Thee, how much more man, made of the dust, who has nothing good of his own except what he has been given by Thy goodness. Thou, O Lord, art God, blessed forever."[14]

The Theotokos also desired to behold the holy Apostles who were then scattered throughout the world preaching the Gospel.[15]

When our Lady knelt and offered her petition and thanksgiving to her Creator, her prayer was accompanied by a wonderful manifestation: the olive trees growing on the Mount of Olives bowed with the Theotokos as though they were animate. When the Theotokos knelt, the trees bent down; when she arose, the trees straightened themselves out again. Thus, even trees revered and honored the Lady and Mistress of the universe.[16]

THE THEOTOKOS RETURNS TO HER HOME

After completing her prayer, the Theotokos returned to her home. Then by the invisible power of God, the Theotokos shone forth with the glory of God. Her lovely face, which always shone with the grace of God--more so than the face of Moses who spoke to God on Sinai--became even more radiant with indescribable glory.[17]

The Theotokos then prepared for her repose. She told the matter to the beloved disciple John, who had taken her into his home as his own mother. She also showed him the flowering branch from Paradise and told him to carry it before her bier.[18]

The plant of chastity, the fragrant myrrh...O John the Apostle, who hast lain on the bosom of the

Master and made the word to fall on the world like rain, thou hast guarded the Virgin as the apple of thine eye."[19]

Both SS. Sophronios (566-638) and Symeon Metaphrastes (c.1000) say, without any hesitation, that the Theologian never left the Virgin, but as a true son he served her and gave her shelter in his home till her repose. Occasionally, he visited for a very short time the surrounding areas, but he did this with her consent and blessing, and then would return to her in Jerusalem. In his absence, the Theotokos was served by her stepson, St. James, the brother of the Lord, who never left his diocese of Jerusalem.[20]

The Virgin then disclosed her pending repose to the rest of the household and virgins, Mary Magdalene, Sepphora, Abigail and Jael that dwelt with her, and they bewailed their orphanhood. But she consoled them saying that she would in-tercede for them and all the world. She then ordered that her bed and room should be decorated, and that incense and as many lamps as possible to be lit in it. She then changed her clothes. Simply put, all necessary preparations for her burial were made.[21]

THE FAITHFUL GATHER

Saint John the Theologian at once sent for the Lord's brother, James, the first Bishop of Jerusalem. John also sent for all their relatives and neighbors, informing them of the imminent repose of the Mother of God. Saint James, too, also informed all the Christians, both them that were in Jerusalem and in the surrounding towns and villages. Thus, a great multitude of the faithful gathered around the Theotokos.[22]

Then, in the hearing of all, the Theotokos told all them that had gathered of the message brought to her by the Archangel Gabriel concerning her translation into heaven. In confirmation, she then showed them the date palm branch from Paradise which, like a ray of the sun, shone with the light of heavenly glory. Upon uttering these words, the faithful could not restrain their tears. The whole house was then filled with weeping and lamentation. All implored the merciful Lady, as the common Mother of all, not to leave them orphans. The Theotokos, however, asked them not to weep for her, but to rejoice at her repose. She said that she would be able to pray to her Son with greater boldness after her death, for she would be standing nearer to the throne of God and gazing face to face upon her Son and God and would converse with Him. She promised that she would not leave them orphans after her departure, but that she would visit the whole world and attend to its needs and help those in trouble. These comforting words dried their tears and brought solace to their sorrow.[23]

The Theotokos then made a will concerning her two garments. She desired that they be given to two poor widows who had faithfully served her and received their maintenance from her. With regard to her pure body, the Mother of God made her will known that it should be buried on the Mount of Olives, not far from Jerusalem, in the Garden of Gethsemane. There also were interred her parents, the righteous Joachim and Anna, and her spouse, St. Joseph. The tombs lay in the Valley of Jehosaphat between Jerusalem and the Mount of Olives.[24]

THE CHOIR OF APOSTLES IS MOST WONDROUSLY BROUGHT TOGETHER FROM THE ENDS OF THE WORLD

While the Theotokos was making these arrangements, all of a sudden a noise was heard, similar to a clap of thunder. A cloud then encircled the home of St. John the Theologian. By the command of God, angels had seized the Apostles that were scattered to the ends of the world and brought them on clouds to Jerusalem. All, save the Apostle Thomas, were then placed on Sion before the door of the house where the Theotokos dwelt.[25] Some are of the opinion that St. John the Theologian had also been caught up in a cloud like the others; no doubt it was from some place close by.[26]

Why should we wonder at this miraculous occurrence of their transferral? We have read of this when the Prophet

Habakkum carried food to Daniel, who was in the lion's den in Babylon, and quickly returned to Judea [Bel and the Dragon, vers. 33-37] or in the case of the Apostle Philip who, after baptizing the eunuch from Ethiopia, the Spirit caught him and brought him to Azotus [Acts 8:39].

Saint Cosmas (7th-8th c.), in describing the conveyance of the Apostles, writes: *Carried to Sion as it were upon a swift cloud, the company of the Apostles assembled from the ends of the earth to minister to thee, O Virgin.*[27]

Saint John of Damascus also makes mention of the purpose of the attendance of both the Apostles and angels when he wrote that they might *minister in fitting manner at thy burial, O Lady.*[28] In another hymn, we learn that *It was right that the eyewitnesses and ministers of the Word should see the Dormition of His Mother according to the flesh, even the final mystery concerning her: hence, they might be witnesses not only to the Ascension of the Saviour but also to the translation of her who gave Him birth. Assembled from all parts by divine power, they came to Sion, and sped on her way to heaven the Virgin who is higher than the cherubim.*[29]

Therefore, on seeing one another, the holy Apostles rejoiced, but at the same time they wondered, saying, "Why has the Lord gathered us together in this place?" Saint John the Theologian then went out to them and greeted them with joyful tears. He then informed them of the speedy departure of the most holy Mother of God. Then the holy Apostles understood that the Lord had gathered them from the various parts of the world to be present at the blessed end of His immaculate Mother, and for the honorable burial of her body, as is meet. Nevertheless, her departure from among them brought intense sorrow to their hearts.[30]

Entering the house, they beheld the Theotokos wearing a joyful countenance, sitting upon her bed. Then, *Reaching thine immaculate body, the source of Life, they (the Apostles) saluted it with mighty honor.*[31]

The holy Apostles then greeted the Mother of Life with these words: "Blessed art thou of the Lord Who made heaven and the earth!" The immaculate Lady replied, "Peace to you, brethren, chosen by the Lord Himself." Then she asked, "How did you arrive here?" Then the holy Apostles revealed how, by the power of the Spirit of God, each of them was caught up from the place where he had been preaching the Gospel. Then when the Theotokos heard that Peter came from Rome, Mark from Alexandria, Matthew had been on a boat, and the others where they were carried from, she glorified God Who had hearkened to her prayer and fulfilled the desire of her heart to behold the holy Apostles at the hour of her death.[32]

REJOICE, HONORABLE CROWN OF THE DISCIPLES!

Then during this conversation, the chosen vessel arrived--the holy Apostle Paul. Falling at the feet of the Theotokos, he opened his mouth, praising and blessing her, "Rejoice, Mother of my life and my preaching! Gazing on thee now, I think that I see thy Son." Already the divine Paul's close disciples had arrived, that is, St. Dionysios the Areopagite, St. Hierotheos, Apostle Timothy and other godly-wise hierarchs. Also present were the rest of the Seventy Apostles. All had been gathered by the Holy Spirit that they might be granted the blessing of Mary Theotokos. Moreover, their presence also increased the solemnity of her burial. Then the immaculate Lady called each of the holy Apostles by name to herself, and she praised their faith and labors in the preaching of Jesus Christ. To each one, she wished eternal beatitude and she prayed for the peace of the whole world.[33]

After, with great joy, she said to them, "Stay awhile, my children, that I may bid thee farewell, for today I will go to my Son, my Beloved. The Archangel Gabriel who announced the conception of my Son to me, again came and gave me this palm branch, saying, 'Rejoice, O God-Birthgiver, and know that after three days thou shalt be translated from earth to the heavens.' And, thus, I thank my Son and God for gathering you all here that I may behold you." Upon hearing this, they all wept.[34]

Then she addressed them, saying, "The Lord has brought you here for the consolation of my soul which, as our mortal nature demands, is soon to be separated from the body. Already the time appointed by my Creator draws nigh." In sorrow, they then replied, "During thy life on earth, O Lady, we were consoled by gazing upon thee as upon our Lord and Master Himself. But now, deprived of thy presence, how shall we bear the heavy sorrow that envelops our souls? But now, by the will of Him Who was born of thee, Christ God, thou art going away to the heavenly abodes, and it is impossible for us not to rejoice at the decision of God regarding thee, though at the same time we cannot refrain from weeping that we are to be left orphans, for we shall no longer see thee, our Mother and comforter." At these words the holy Apostles wept.[35]

She then said, "Watch and pray with me, that when the Lord comes to receive my soul, He may find you watching. Then all promised and prayed the whole night, with psalms and chants.[36]

Then the beloved disciple John said, "My Lady Mother of God and my Mother, thy beloved Son had left thee as a consolation; and now thou shalt leave us? In all the world what will we humble Apostles have as our consolation? Who will teach us and who will guide us? What else shall we have on earth to encourage us if thou should leave us?"[37]

This, too, caused the Theotokos to weep, and she said, "Do not sorrow, my children, for you make me sad when I see you cry so. Although I will be going to my Son, O friends of my Son, I will not be apart from you, nor from them that call upon me. Nay, I shall be an intercessor and mediatress for all the Christians before my beloved Son.[38] Therefore, do not weep, friends and disciples of my Son and God. Do not darken my joy by your sorrow and mourning. Much rather, rejoice with me, for I am going away to my Son and God. My body, which I have myself prepared for burial, commit to the earth in Gethsemane. Afterwards, return again to the preaching of the Gospel appointed to you. If the Lord wills, ye shall see me after my departure."[39]

Then the Apostle Paul spoke up and again said, "O Lady and Mother of God, I did not behold thy beloved Son, the Christ, while He was in the flesh on earth, but when I behold thee it is as if I behold thy Son. Now thou too shall leave me? Who will counsel me in my many temptations? Who will grieve with me in my reproaches? Whom will I, the lowly one, have to exhort and encourage me in my afflictions and torments?" Panagia then said to him, "O Paul, friend of my Son and me, my Son and my grace shall comfort thee and the other disciples."[40]

When the translation of thy most pure tabernacle was being prepared, the Apostles surrounded thy deathbed and looked upon thee with dread. And as they gazed at thy

456

body, they were filled with awe. In tears, Peter cried aloud to thee: "O undefiled Virgin, I see thee who art the life of all mankind lying here outstretched, and I am struck with wonder: for He Who is the delight of the future life made His dwelling in thee. Pray, then, fervently to thy Son and God to save thy city from harm."[41]

St. Peter

St. Paul

Peter wept and then said, "Lady Theotokos, earlier, I tarried here and did not venture to depart for fear that I might not see thee before thy repose. I always thought that thou would be here to exhort and console me. But now thou shalt leave? The loss of thy Son was not enough, and now thou dost wish to depart?"[42]

The Theotokos then said to him, "My beloved Peter, do not cry anymore. As thou had me with thee while on earth, thou wilt have me spiritually as a help and solace from this day. But thou, O Peter, art the eldest, therefore, thou must, for the time that remains, encourage the younger brethren, strengthen the weak, and be not distressed at my death."[43] Then the other Apostles said to the Theotokos, "Indeed, O Lady, thou wilt be translated to the heavens, then, at least, comfort us and leave us a word of counsel from thy holy mouth, that thy slaves may have a remembrance."[44]

Saint Gregory Palamas (+1359) comments here that the "precepts and encouragements which she gave to God's heralds (the Apostles) were sent throughout the whole world. Thus she herself was both a support and comfort while she was both heard and seen among men. She labored with the

457

rest in every way for the preaching of the Gospel. In such wise, she led a most strenuous manner of life proclaimed in mind and speech."[45]

In the famous *Akathist Hymn* to the Theotokos, we chant: *Rejoice, thou who dost fill the nets of the fisherman. Rejoice, thou who dost draw us from the depths of ignorance. Rejoice, thou who dost enlighten many with knowledge.*[46]

The Theotokos has been called the Church's greatest theologian, for as St. Cyril of Jerusalem (318-c.386) remarks, "the Virgin Mother of God is His witness."[47]

THE THEOTOKOS SPEAKS A PARABLE

Our Lady, the Theotokos, then spoke to them, saying, "My beloved children, hearken to my brief words and small instruction, for this I wish and seek. My children, do you see this world? It is a festival. God is as a king, and you, His servants, are the merchants of my beloved Son. Now listen to this parable: There was a great and powerful king who had two servants. The king then heard that there was a great fair where there would be very many goods and products that would bring great gain. Therefore, the king summoned these two servants and said, "Make great haste to go into this country where the festival is being held and, for one month, do business. If any of you delay, he will lose his life!" Straightway, the two servants took money and went to the fair. However, one of them was senseless and foolish; he purchased items that were useless to the king, such as houses, shops and fields. All these things the king had no need of, nor would they bring him any gain. Moreover, the undiscerning servant delayed in returning because it took time to sow the fields, and to refurbish and complete the shops and the houses, because they were in disarray. Thus it took him about three to four months to return to the king. Now the other servant was prudent and purchased precious stones, and returned punctually to the king. The king honored and glorified this servant, for he found him trustworthy. As for the other servant, an order was issued that he be executed as one who was an enemy of the king.[48]

"The same situation is also before you, O Apostles of my Son. My beloved Son has sent you as merchants into the world of deceived mankind, to win those souls who will hearken to His name. Whichever of you, O my friends and children, is a friend of thy Teacher and my Son, He will honor in His Kingdom. Those that will not obey the commands of the Teacher, he knows what he will suffer. On account of this, my beloved children, go and preach. Enlighten and guide those of the world that are led astray, and gain them and direct them to the Kingdom of my Son.[49]

"Always have love and peace among you, and rejoice and be glad for great will be your reward in the Kingdom of the heavens. And, though, my friends, I go to the Kingdom of my Son and God, I am ever with you, and I will strengthen and comfort you in your afflictions." This and other things the all-holy one uttered to the Apostles.[50]

THE THEOTOKOS DELIVERS HER SOUL,
FULL OF LIGHT

It was the Lord's day, and the fifteenth day of the month of August, when that blessed hour that all were awaiting drew near. It was the third hour of the day (9:00 a.m.). In the room a number of lamps were burning. The holy Apostles were offering praise to God. Upon a beautifully adorned bed, the Theotokos was lying and preparing herself for her blessed end when her beloved Son and Lord would come to her.[51] She then greeted each Apostle with a blessing.[52]

She then stretched her hands to heaven and prayed, saying, "I adore, praise and glorify Thy much to be praised name, O Lord, because Thou hast looked upon the lowliness of Thine handmaiden, and because Thou that art mighty hast done great things for me; and, behold, all generations shall call me blessed [Lk. 1:48]. After this prayer, she said to the Apostles, "Cast incense and pray, because Christ is coming with a host of angels; and, behold, Christ is at hand, sitting on a throne of cherubim." When they had prayed, there was thunder from heaven and there came a fearful voice, as if of chariots; and, behold, a multitude of a host of angels and powers, and a voice, as if of the Son of Man was heard.[53]

Then there shone in the room an ineffable light of divine glory which dimmed the lamps. Those that were granted this vision were awestruck. Many beheld the roof of the apartment open and the glory of the Lord descending from heaven. It was Christ the King of Glory with hosts of angels and archangels, and all the heavenly powers. Also with them were the holy fathers and prophets who prophesied of old concerning the pure Virgin, and all the righteous souls, approached His immaculate Mother.[54]

Saint John of Damascus also mentions that some of the most famous and righteous prophets of the Old Testament were in attendance.[55] The text of *Pseudo-John*, in describing the events, records that the Theotokos' mother, Anna, and her cousin Elisabeth appeared with Abraham, Isaac, Jacob and David and all the choirs of saints, singing praising and venerating the body of the Mother of the Lord.[56]

REJOICE,
FULFILLMENT OF PROPHETIC FORETELLING!

The theme of Mary as Theotokos and mediatress is a theme of great emphasis for St. Andrew of Crete. Nowhere in divinely inspired Scripture can one look without seeing some allusion to her. "Rejoice, Mediatress of the law and of grace, seal of the Old and New Testaments, clear fulfillment of the whole of prophecy, the truth of Scriptures inspired by God, and the living and most pure book of God and the Word."[57]

Saint Gregory Palamas also points out that the prophets and angels glorified God Who came from her, and that all creation renders her everlasting praise. "The Prophet Ezekiel was taken up by the spirit, and he heard, 'Blessed be the glory of the Lord from His place' [Ez. 3:12]. The Patriarch Jacob, beheld the ladder as a type, and exclaimed, 'How fearful is this place! This is none other than the house of God, and this is the gate of heaven' [Gen. 28:17]. The Prophet-King David, too, says, 'I shall commemorate thy name in every generation and generation. Therefore shall peoples give praise unto thee for ever, and unto the ages of ages'" [Ps. 44:16-17].[58]

Let us listen to select verses of the *Akathist Hymn of the Dormition: Rejoice, thou who wast prefigured by the patriarchs. Rejoice, thou foretelling of the prophets. Rejoice, thou perfect scroll of the law and prophets.*

Rejoice, O noetic ark, raised on the mountains above the flood of mortality. Rejoice, O twig of the dove in the hands of Noah. Rejoice, O heavenly ladder, foreseen by Jacob. Rejoice, O bush unburnt, foreseen by the law-giver (Moses). Rejoice, O rod of Aaron, sprouting forth incorruption. Rejoice, O animate ark of holiness of the Lord. Rejoice, O tabernacle overshadowed by the cherubim. Rejoice, O holy of holies, spoken of by the seraphim. Rejoice, O star of Jacob, prophesied by Balaam. Rejoice, O fleece bedewed of Jesus, symbolized by Gideon. Rejoice, O sun, dwelling of Christ, revealed by the psalmist. Rejoice, O God-inspired flute of David, the ancestor of God. Rejoice, O rising glory of his prophecy, psaltery and harp most beautiful. Rejoice, O throne of the great King, known to Solomon. Rejoice, O gate impassible, foreseen by Ezekiel. Rejoice, O holy mountain, discerned by the man of desire (Daniel). Rejoice, thou who didst bring to fulfillment all the prophetic words forespoken of thee. Rejoice, thou who didst bring to perfection the economy of the Highest for the salvation of the world.[59]

Rejoice, O sound of the prophet's words; Rejoice, thou blest adornment of the Apostles' choir.[60]

BE IT UNTO ME ACCORDING TO THY WORD

At the sight of the approach of her Son, the Theotokos cried with great joy unto her son, "My soul doth magnify the Lord and my spirit hath rejoiced in God my Saviour" [Luke 1:46-47].[61]

And, behold, a stream of light came upon the Virgin because of the presence of her Son, and all the powers of the heavens fell down and adored Him. He then said, "Mary." And she answered, "Here am I, Lord."[62]

Raising herself from her bed as if she were trying to go to meet her Son, she worshipped the Lord. Looking at her with love, He said, "Arise, come my beloved, My fair one, My dove [Song 2:10]. Arise from the dead with authority, because Thou art My Mother. Arise and come to My Kingdom, for Thou art the Queen of all. Arise to receive My divine glory, O My sweet Mother. Arise and come unto Me, My fair dove, for thou art escorted by My angelic hosts. Take up thy soul on thy virginal, incorrupt and divine body that thou mayest soar to the heights of heaven, and go through My spiritual hierarchies, and come unto Me, that thou mightest sit at My right hand, in order to enjoy the throne of thy Kingdom which is prepared for thee since the foundation of the world. Gird thyself with the glorious and gold-embroidered royal garment of thy virtues. Adorn thyself with the luminous glory of thy divine blessedness. Arise, come My beloved, My fair one, My dove; yea, come" [Song 2:13].[63]

Bowing, the Mother of God replied, "Blessed is Thy name, O Lord of Glory and my God, Who was pleased to choose Thy humble handmaid for the service of Thy mystery. Remember me, O King of glory, in Thy eternal Kingdom. Thou knowest that I have loved Thee with all my heart and have kept the treasure entrusted to me. And now receive my soul in peace and defend me from all the snares of the dark power of satan."[64]

The Lord then consoled His Mother with words full of love and persuaded her not to fear the power of satan which was already conquered by her. He called her with love to pass fearlessly from earth to heaven.[65]

Saint Gregory Palamas comments on the love between Son and Mother, thus: "Wherefore, she loves and is loved in return more than any other...for He was her only Son. Moreover, she alone among women gave birth knowing no spouse, so that the love of Him, that was of her flesh, was twofold. Who will the Only-Begotten love more than His Mother, He Who came forth from Her in an indescribable manner, without a father, in this last age, even as He came forth from the Father without a mother before the ages? He that came down and fulfilled the law, how could He not multiply the honor due His Mother above and beyond the law?"[66]

And the Lord remained by her and said, "Behold, presently thy soul will be translated to the heavens, to the treasures of My Father in exceeding brightness, where there is peace and joy of the holy angels, and many other things. Then the Mother of the Lord answered and said to Him, "Lay Thy right hand upon me, O Lord, and bless me." Then the Lord stretched forth His undefiled right hand and blessed His Mother.[67]

She then took hold of His hand and kissed it, saying, "I adore this right hand, which created the heaven and the earth; and I call upon Thy much to be praised name Christ, O God, the King of the ages, the Only-Begotten of the Father, to receive Thine handmaid, O Thou Who didst deign to be brought forth by me, in a low estate, to save the race of men through Thine ineffable dispensation; do Thou bestow Thine aid upon every one calling upon, or praying to, or naming the name of Thine handmaid."[68]

While uttering this, the Apostles, went up to her feet and venerated her, saying, "O Mother of the Lord, leave a blessing to the world, since thou art going away from it. For thou hast blessed it, and raised it up when it was ruined, by bringing forth the Light of the world." The Theotokos then prayed and spoke thus, "O God, Who through Thy great goodness hast sent from the heavens Thine only-begotten Son to dwell in my humble body, Who hast deigned to be born of me, humble as I am, have mercy upon the world, and every soul that calls upon Thy name." And again she prayed, and said, "O Lord, King of the heavens, Son of the living God, accept every man who calls upon Thy name, that Thy birth may be glorified." Then she continued shortly after, saying, "O Lord Jesus Christ, Who art all-powerful in heaven and on earth, in this appeal I implore Thy holy name: in every time and place where there is made mention of my name, make that place holy, and glorify them that glorify Thee through my name, accepting from such persons all their offerings, and all their supplications, and all their prayers."[69]

Having thus prayed, the Lord said to His Mother, "Let thy heart rejoice and be glad; for every grace and every gift has been given to thee from My Father in heaven, and from

Me, and from the Holy Spirit. Every soul that calls upon thy name shall not be ashamed, but shall find mercy, and comfort, and support, and confidence, both in the world that now is, and in that which is to come, in the presence of My Father in the heavens."[70]

Saint Cosmas then speaks of the Virgin interceding for us. *As she departed, the Virgin without spot, lifted up her hands--those hands that had held God incarnate in their embrace--and, with the boldness of a Mother to her Son, she said, "Keep unto all ages those whom Thou hast made mine and who cry aloud unto Thee, 'We, who have been delivered, praise the one and only Creator and exalt Him above all forever.'"*[71]

She then rose up and blessed each of the Apostles with her own hand, and all gave glory to God.[72] Then addressing her Son and His disciples, she uttered, *O ye Apostles, assembled here from the ends of the earth, bury my body in Gethsemane: and Thou, O my Son and God, receive my spirit.*[73]

Then she said, "Ready is my heart, O God, ready is my heart" [Ps. 107:2]. Then she repeated the words once said by her, "Be it unto me according to Thy word" [Lk. 1:38], and then lay down on the bed.[74]

Feeling unspeakable joy at the sight of the radiant face of her Son and Lord, the Theotokos, filled with spiritual rapture out of love for Him, surrendered her pure soul into the hands of the Lord. And the Lord stretched forth His undefiled hands and received her holy and blameless soul. She felt no pain whatsoever, but it was as if she had fallen into a sweet sleep. He Whom she conceived without destroying her virginity and bore without pain, now received her soul from her pure body.[75]

Saint John of Damascus also speaks of how the Law-Giver fulfilled His law concerning mothers. *He Who, taking*

464

flesh, strangely made His dwelling in thy pure womb, Himself received thine all-holy spirit and, as a Son paying His due, He gave it rest with Himself.[76]

At once there began wonderful and joyous angelic singing repeating the former words of Gabriel: "Rejoice, thou who art full of grace, the Lord is with thee: Blessed are thou among women" [Lk. 1:28].[77]

At this point, St. Cosmas describes the scene in this manner. *The angelic powers were amazed as they looked in Sion upon their own Master, bearing in His hands the soul of a woman: for as befitted a Son, He said to her who without spot had borne Him, "Come, honored among women, and be glorified together with thy Son and God."*[78]

With such triumphant hymns did the heavenly hosts accompany the holy soul of the Theotokos as she went in the arms of the Lord to the dwelling above. The holy Apostles, who were found worthy to behold this vision, followed the Mother of God with tender eyes, as once they had followed the Lord when He ascended from the Mount of Olives [Acts 1:9]. For a long time now they looked steadfastly toward heaven as if they were in a swoon. When they came to themselves, the disciples worshipped the Lord Who had raised His Mother's soul to heaven with glory, and they surrounded her bed with weeping.[79]

At a divine command the chief Apostles hastened from the ends of the earth to bury thee, and when they beheld thee taken up from earth to heaven they shouted with joy the words of Gabriel, and cried unto thee, "Rejoice, thou bearer of the divinity: Rejoice, thou who alone by thy childbirth hast brought together earthly things and things on high."[80]

THE APOSTLES AT THE BIER

The face of the Theotokos shone like the sun and a splendid and sweet perfume emitted from her most pure body; it was a scent that is impossible to find here on earth. With piety and fear, the holy Apostles kissed the most pure body and were sanctified by contact with it.[81]

Describing the thoughts and feelings of the Apostles, St. Cosmas writes that *The glorious Apostles knew thee, O Virgin without spot, to be a mortal woman and, at the same time, beyond and above nature, the Mother of God: therefore they touched thee with fearful hands, as they gazed upon thee shining with glory, the tabernacle that had held God."*[82]

In their hearts they felt the activity of divine grace and were filled with spiritual joy. Then all the faithful then reverently venerated her most pure body and kissed it with awe. Then from the precious relics of the Theotokos there went out sanctifying power which filled with joy the hearts of all who touched her. The sick received healing, the blind regained their sight, the ears of the deaf were opened, the lame were made to walk and devils were driven out. In a word, every disease vanished completely, merely by touching the bed of the Theotokos. Then many others came, seeking to be cured of their diseases, who also obtained healing. And there was unspeakable joy that day among the multitude of them that had been cured, as well as of them that looked on. All then glorified Christ our God and His holy Mother, and kept festival with psalms and spiritual songs.[83]

At thy departing, O Virgin Theotokos, to Him Who was ineffably born of thee, James the first bishop and brother of the Lord was there, and so was Peter, the honored leader and chief of the disciples, and the whole sacred fellowship of the Apostles. In discourses that showed forth heavenly things they sang the praises of the divine and amazing mystery of the dispensation of Christ our God; and they rejoiced, O far-famed Virgin, as they buried thy body, the origin of the Life and holder of God.[84]

Describing the actions of the holy Apostles, St. Cosmas writes that while *Standing round thy body that had held God, the choir of the Apostles looked upon it with awe and saluted it, saying with clear voice: "As thou departest to the heavenly mansions unto thy Son, do thou ever save thine inheritance.*[85]

And, *The inspired tongues of the Apostles rang out louder than trumpets, as they sang in the Spirit the burial hymn to the Theotokos, "Rejoice, incorruptible source of God's life-giving incarnation, that brings salvation unto all."*[86]

THE SOLEMN PROCESSION

In the midst of these events which had accompanied the Dormition of the Theotokos, they began the solemn procession to inter her most honorable body. The Apostles bore her bier aloft on their shoulders; towards the head were St. John the Theologian and St. Peter on the other side, then St. James and St. Paul opposite him.[87] The other Apostles and hierarchs proceeded chanting, while St. John the Theologian also carried the branch from paradise which shone brightly. The rest of the faithful, with lights and censers, walked close by, surrounding the bed.[88]

All sang the funeral prayers. Then at the command of the Saviour, the pre-eminent Apostle Peter began chanting one of the Psalms of David: "When Israel went out of Egypt, and the house of Jacob from among a barbarous people. Alleluia. Judea became His sanctuary, Israel His dominion. Alleluia..." [and the rest of Ps. 113], together with the other Apostles who sang with most sweet voices.[89]

The solemn procession conveyed the sacred body of the Theotokos from Sion through Jerusalem to Gethsemane. Hovering over the bier and accompanying the procession there appeared a circular cloud reminiscent of a crown which shone with a bright radiance. In the hearing of all, there resounded ceaseless angelic singing from out of the cloud that filled the air. Saint Theophanes the Poet (+1381) incites us to honor her with these words: *Come, let us crown the Church with song, as the ark of God goes to her rest.*[90]

467

ARISE, O LORD, INTO THY REST
THOU AND THE ARK OF THY HOLINESS[91]

Saint Hesychios (c.451), adverting to this verse, comments, "The ark of Thy sanctification is the Virgin Theotokos surely. If Thou art the Pearl, then she must be the ark."[92] Many have spoken of Mary as the ark, such as: St. Romanos (c.490-c.556);[93] St. Andrew of Crete (c.660-740);[94] and St. John of Damascus.[95] Saint John of Damascus also writes reminding us that in Old Testament times the ark of the Lord was transferred by way of Mount Sion [Ps. 9:11] to the most sacred village of Gethsemane.[96]

THE MOB IS ROUSED

Many of the Jews who did not believe in Christ, on hearing the unusual chanting and witnessing the triumphant procession, left their homes and joined the multitude. They too, went along, and followed the procession out of the city, astonished at the glory and honor that was given to the most honorable body of the Theotokos. When the chief priests and scribes learned of this, they burned with the heaviest hatred and began to reason frivolously. Indeed, they would become inflamed at anything that reminded them of Christ. They stirred up many of the people and sent temple servants and soldiers to overtake the procession and disperse it. They also ordered them to slay the disciples of Christ and to burn the body of Mary, for they claimed that the nation of the Jews was ruined by this woman.[97]

Then satan entered and incited the mob. They then quickly began to arm themselves as if for battle. Furiously, they hastened to overtake the procession. Gradually, they began to catch up with them when, suddenly, the circular cloud that was floating in the air descended and surrounded, like a wall of protection, the holy Apostles and the rest of the Christians. Indeed, the pursuers only heard chanting, but could see no one behind the wall of the cloud. Then the holy angels, invisibly hovering over the sacred relics and the Christians, struck the malicious persecutors with blindness.[98]

Struck with blindness, the persecutors began striking their heads against the walls, and then struck each other. Others, not knowing where to go, looked for someone who might lead them.

THE JEWISH PRIEST ATHONIOS

At that time, a Jewish priest called Athonios (some texts give his name as Jephonias) was out on the road. When the cloud had lifted by the command of God, he beheld the holy Apostles and a multitude of Christians who, with lights, were chanting about the bier of the Mother of Jesus. No tongue of clay could adequately describe the joyful procession. But Athonios was filled with envy and had a storm of disbelieving thoughts assail

him. Then with great malice in his heart, he blurted out, "Look, what honor surrounds the body of her who bore the imposter Who destroyed the law of our fathers![99]

Being a strong man by nature, he rushed with mad fury through the crowd of Christians and, running up towards the bier, he attempted to cast the Virgin's body to the ground. When the audacious hands of the priest barely touched the couch, an invisible angel at once struck them off at the elbows with the immaterial sword of divine vengeance. Thus, Athonios' hands clung fast to the bed, while he collapsed to the earth wailing, "Woe is me!"[100] The Jews that beheld this sight of their priest, then cried out, "Verily, He that was brought forth by thee is the true God, O Mother of God, Ever-Virgin Mary."[101]

LET NO PROFANE HAND TOUCH
THE LIVING ARK OF GOD![102]

The Lord guarded with the glory of the Godhead the honor due to the living ark in which the Word took flesh; and in His just vengeance He intervened to cut off the sacrilegious hands of the presumptuous unbeliever.[103]

This incident was prefigured in times of old when King David was having the ark brought to Jerusalem. Uzzah presumptuously reached out to steady the ark and was fatally smitten. His death was attributed to the violation of the sacred character of the ark, in that he presumed to handle the sacred object [2 Sam. 6:7; 1 Chron. 13:10].

Saint Andrew of Crete, in his *Great Canon*, makes mention of this Old Testament incident. *When the ark was being carried in a cart and the ox stumbled, Uzzah did no more than touch*  it, *but the wrath of God smote him. O my soul, flee from his presumption, and respect with reverence the things of God.*[104]

Now David was greatly distressed at this incident, and immediately cancelled plans to enshrine the ark in Jerusalem. Instead, he deposited the sacred object in the home of Obed-edom (Abeddara the Gethite), where it remained for three months [2 Sam. 6:11]. In like manner, we shall see the Theotokos' earthly tabernacle remain in the tomb for three days until she was bodily assumed into the Jerusalem on high by her Son.

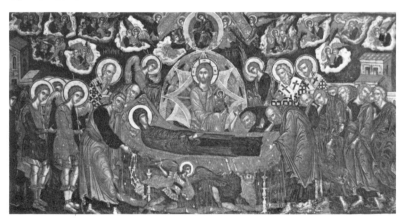

Acknowledging his sin, Athonios repented and turned to the holy Apostles and said, "Have mercy on me, servants of Christ!" The pre-eminent Apostle Peter then ordered the procession to stop. He then said to Athonios, "Now thou hast received thy just fruits. Know that 'the Lord is the

God of vengeance; the God of vengeance hath spoken openly' [Ps. 93:1], and, thus, we cannot heal thee of thy wounds. Only our Lord Himself can do this, Whom you had unjustly rose up against, seized and killed. Even He will not bestow healing upon thee till thou wilt believe in Him with all thy heart and confess with thy mouth that Jesus is the true Messiah, the Son of God."[105]

Then Athonios cried aloud, "I believe that He is the Saviour of the world foretold by the prophets--He is the Christ. From the very first we saw that He was the Son of God but, being darkened by malicious envy, we did not acknowledge the greatness of God openly, but delivered Him to death, though He was guiltless. But by the power of His divinity He arose on the third day, putting us all to shame. We attempted to conceal His resurrection by bribing the soldiers, but we could do nothing, as the glory of the Resurrection was manifest and spread abroad."[106]

When Athonios uttered this confession and repented of his sin, the holy Apostles and all the faithful rejoiced with the joy of the angels over a penitent sinner. The holy Apostle Peter then ordered Athonios to put the wounds of his severed arms to the limbs hanging on the bier. He then told him to call upon the most holy Mother of God with faith. Athonios did as he was instructed and, at once, the severed arms were joined at the mark where they had been severed; only a red line remained about his elbows.[107]

Athonios then fell down before the bier, and worshipped Christ God Who was born of the Virgin Mary. He then blessed with many praises His immaculate Mother. Then Athonios began to recite prophesies from Holy Scripture that testified both to the Virgin Mary and to Christ. Therefore, all were doubly amazed at beholding Athonios' miraculous healing and hearing from him the wise words with which he glorified the Lord Jesus and praised the Mother of God. Athonios then joined the procession, following behind the bed with the other Christians to Gethsemane. He was later baptized.

Some, who were part of the rushing mob that were struck with blindness, also acknowledged their sin and penitently approached the honorable bier and touched it with faith. When the Apostle touched their faces with the heavenly palm branch,[108] they regained their bodily sight together with the eyes of their soul. Thus, the merciful Mother of all, our most holy Lady, as by her birth she had given joy to the whole world, so at her falling asleep she did not wish to sadden anyone. As the good Mother of the good King, she mercifully consoled even them that were her enemies with gracious gifts.[109]

The initiates and eyewitnesses of the Word then continued to hear the angels singing lofty hymns. They, too, desirous to give honor pleasing to God, cried aloud, *Rejoice, thou who didst swiftly avenge the evil boldness of the Jew. Rejoice, thou who did grant healing to the same. Rejoice, thou who didst turn the unbelief of Athonios into belief. Rejoice, thou who didst receive his faithful confession.*[110]

Saint Gregory Palamas writes that her "death was also life-bearing, translating her into a celestial and immortal life." And that her falling asleep was "a joyful event and festivity for the entire world. It not only renewed the memory of her wondrous deeds, but also added the novel delivery from faraway nations of the sacred Apostles to her most holy burial." We learn also that the Apostles and hierarchs composed their God-revealing hymns and encomia. "The presence of the angelic choirs was standing by, aiding and presiding. Together with the Apostles, the incorporeals went on before, followed after, assisting, opposing, defending and being defended. Both celestial and terrestrial beings labored and chanted together to their uttermost with them who also venerated her life-originating and God-receiving body; for she is the healing and saving remedy of our race and the majesty of all creation. But they (the angelic hosts) strove against and opposed with a concealed hand those Jews who fought against God by rising up against and attacking that body. Nonetheless, the Son of the Ever-Virgin and Lord of Sabaoth was present Himself. Into His hands she commended her God-bearing spirit, through which and with which its yoke-fellow, her body, was translated into the celestial regions, as was meet."[111]

ANGELIC HOSTS STOOD AT SION
GUARDING THEIR MASTER,
DIRECTING A FEMALE SOUL

Saint Cosmas the Poet also confirms that at the burial of the far-famed Theotokos, *The spiritual hosts that dwell in*

472

heaven attended thy divine body in Zion;[112] as they *stood by with their own Master.*[113]

We learn that the celestial hierarchies came to escort the Theotokos' soul as it was transported into the heavenly realms and eternal life. *The dominions and the thrones, the rulers, the principalities and the powers* [Rom. 8:38; Col. 1:16], *the cherubim and the fearful seraphim glorify thy Dormition.*[114] Also, with them were the *prophets, and the whole creation: and thy Son Who received into His immaculate hands thy spotless soul.*[115]

Among the prophets in attendance, we find the Theotokos' ancestor David. *Cry out, O David: what is this present feast? And he said, "Christ has translated into the heavenly mansions her who bore Him without seed, of whom I sang in the book of Psalms, calling her daughter, child of God, and Virgin* [Ps. 44]. *Therefore, mothers and daughters and brides of Christ, rejoice and cry, 'Rejoice, thou who art translated into the heavenly Kingdom.'"*[116]

Saint John of Damascus comments that "it was fitting that the bride whom the Father had espoused should dwell in the heavenly bridal chambers."[117]

Saint Gregory Palamas writes: "Today we celebrate her holy Dormition or translation to another life. While being 'a little lower than the angels' (referring to her mortality), by her proximity to the God of all...she has ascended higher than the angels and the archangels and all the hosts that are found beyond them."[118]

In accordance with the hymnography of the Church, the gates of heaven were lifted, and the angels sang. *Open wide the gates and receive above the world the Mother of the everlasting Light.*[119]

GLORIOUS ARE THY MYSTERIES, O PURE LADY. TODAY THOU ART TRANSLATED FROM EARTH TO HEAVEN

Meeting the Queen, the cherubim stood behind with rejoicing and the seraphim glorified her with joy.

Saint Cosmas chants, *The gates of heaven were opened wide and the angels sang, as Christ received the virgin treasure of His own Mother. Cherubim withdrew before thee in thine exultation, while seraphim glorified thee in thy joy.*[120]

Saint John of Damascus continues writing that *The spiritual powers receive her with the honors due to God.*[121] Then, the heavenly mansions of God fittingly received the Queen. *Joyously adorned as a Bride without spot, thou standest beside our King and God.*[122]

Saint Theophanes also mentions the conduct of the incorporeals. *The hosts of angels, present with the fellowship of the Apostles, gaze in great fear at her who bore the Cause of life, now that she is translated from life to life.*[123]

**REJOICE, O BEAUTY AT THE RIGHT HAND
OF THE LORD, WHO DOST EMBELLISH
ALL THE HEAVENLY DWELLERS
WHO BLESS THEE!**

Before the angelic hierarchies, she is closer to God and deemed worthy of greater audience, according to St. Gregory Palamas. The Prophet Isaias wrote: "And seraphs stood round about Him..." [Is. 6:2]; yet David speaks concerning her, "at Thy right hand stood the Queen" [Ps.44:8]. Saint Gregory comments, "Do you see the difference in station? From this you may comprehend the difference in the dignity of their positions. The seraphim are round about God, but the Queen of all is solely beside Him....God Himself proclaims her by the mighty deeds enacted with respect to Him. And, as it said in the *Song of Songs*: 'Thou art fair my companion' [6:3], for where Christ sat in the heavens, that is, at the 'right hand of the majesty on high,' [Heb. 1:3] there, too, she takes her stand, having ascended from earth to heaven. She is truly His throne, and wherever the King sits, there His throne is set also....The Prophet also wrote that 'I saw the Lord sitting on a high and exalted throne...' [Is. 6:1], thus declaring that the position of the Mother of God far transcends that of the heavenly hosts."[124] *For her excellence is past understanding.*[125] *For through her the salvation of all mankind has come. We have not the strength to look upon her, and are unable to render honors worthy of her.*[126]

Continuing his explanation, St. Gregory Palamas writes that "throughout the course of ages, she shall never cease from rendering benefactions to all creation, not only terrestrial creatures but celestial also." He brings forward the Prophet Isaias to show that only through her both the heavenly hosts and we partake of and touch God. To better perceive this, St. Gregory reminds us that Isaias beheld the seraphim take the coal from the altar without mediation, but with tongs, by means of which the coal touched the prophetic lips and purified them [Is. 6:6-7]. Moses, too, beheld "the tongs" of that great vision of Isaias when he beheld the bush aflame, yet unconsumed. "Indeed, who does not know that the 'tongs' and the 'bush' are the Virgin-Mother? She conceived the Divine Fire without being consumed....and through her, He touched mankind; thus, by that ineffable touch and union, He cleansed us. Therefore, she is the frontier between created and uncreated nature. No man shall come to God unless he is truly illumined through her, the lamp radiant with divinity. Thus says the Prophet, 'God is in the midst of her, she shall not be shaken.'" [Ps. 45:5].[127]

Saint John of Damascus supports this vision, too, saying, "She stands at His right as a real Queen, with much boldness, clad in golden garments, attired in embroidery, according to the prophetic saying [Ps. 44:8]. Yea, she stood upon the royal throne glittering as the glorious Queen of heaven and earth, and shining inside and outside with the lightings of the gifts of the Holy Spirit, as the ever-illuminating Bride and Mother of the heavenly King of glory, Jesus Christ, our God and Saviour. Ever since then she stands at the right side of the Son, embroidered in the virtues and gifts of purity, of holiness, everything beautiful, chosen, innocent, as the holiest of all saints, the noblest of the cherubim, and incomparably more glorious than the seraphim and of all the heavenly hosts, being thus, next to God, venerated, glorified, and praised above all beings in heaven and earth."[128]

Saint John of Kronstadt (1829-1908) also speaks in similar terms of the exalted position of the Theotokos, writing: "Our Lady, the Mother of God, is the most beautifully adorned temple of the Holy Trinity. She is, after God, the treasury of all blessing, of purity, holiness, of all true wisdom, the source of spiritual power and constancy."[129]

Rejoice, O all-desirable and sweet vision of the saints. Rejoice, O gateway to the paradisiacal dwellings of the righteous. Rejoice, O beginning of man's salvation. Rejoice, O fulfillment of all good desires. Rejoice, O Theotokos and Queen, who reignest after God the King. Rejoice, O Lady and Sovereign, who rulest after the Lord our Master.[130]

THE GARDEN OF GETHSEMANE, THE SACRED ABODE OF THE THEOTOKOS

The tomb in the Garden of Gethsemane was east of Jerusalem, across the Kidron Valley. Finally, the holy Apostles with all the multitude of the Christians reached the Garden. When they laid down the bier with the most precious body, again the Christians began to weep.

All bewailed their orphanhood at the loss of such a treasure. In giving the last kiss, the Christians fell down before the body of the Theotokos. Kissing it, they shed copious tears, so that only towards evening could the most honorable body be placed in the new tomb.[131] Her sacred relics were laid with the greatest honor, while chanting and weeping took place. When the Apostles stepped before her bier to bid her farewell, each according to the inspiration of the Holy Spirit, they uttered psalms of triumph and thanksgiving and chanted prayers.[132]

REJOICE, EMBELLISHMENT OF HIERARCHS AND GOODNESS OF PRIESTS!

However, of all the hymns of praise *(encomia)*, St. John of Damascus comments that the most exquisite was that composed by the Athenian, St. Hierotheos (commemorated the 4th of October). He was the close friend of the Apostle Paul and St. Dionysios the Areopagite.

Saint John of Damascus records that St. Hierotheos was *Wholly beside himself and transported; his whole self consecrated to God, the chosen vessel of the Lord surpassed himself in hymns to thee, O far-famed Theotokos and Virgin. And in the sight of all he proved himself to be in the very truth inspired by God.*[133]

According to tradition, his divine singing and heartfelt joy proved him to be greatly inspired. The Apostles themselves admired his words and retained them in their memory.[134] An extract of St. Hierotheos' encomium, we present here:

"When was such a wonder of wonders ever seen by men? How does the Queen of all lie breathless? How has the Mother of Jesus reposed? Thou, O Virgin, wast the preaching of the prophets; thou art heralded by us. All the people venerate thee; the angels glorify thee. Rejoice, thou who art full of grace, the Lord is with thee, and through thee, with us. With Gabriel we hymn thee; with the angels we glorify thee; and with the prophets we praise thee, for they announced thee.

"Habakkum beheld thee as an overshadowed mountain, for thou art covered with the gifts of the Holy Spirit. Daniel beheld thee as a mountain from whom, seedlessly, the solid and strong King, the Christ, issued forth. Jacob saw thee as a ladder upon Whom Christ came down to eat and drink with us. And although we, His slaves, contemplate ascending into the heavens, yet thou hast ascended before all. Rejoice, O Virgin, for Gideon beheld thee as a fleece. David saw thee as the virgin daughter of the King. Isaias called thee Mother of God and Ezekiel a gate. All the prophets prophesied thee![135]

"What shall we call thee, O Virgin? Paradise. It is meet, for thou hast blossomed forth the flower of incorruption, Christ, Who is the sweet-smelling fragrance for the souls of men. Virgin? Verily, a virgin thou art, for without the seed of man thou gavest birth to our Lord Jesus Christ. Thou wast a virgin before birth, and virgin at birth, and still a virgin after. Shall we call thee Mother? This is meet too; for as a Mother thou gavest birth to Christ the King of all. Shall we name thee Heaven? This thou art also, for upon thee rose the Sun of righteousness. Wherefore, rejoice, O

Virgin, and hasten to thy Son's rest and dwell in the tents of His beloved. Hasten there and make ready a place and remember us and all thy people also, too, O Lady Mother of God, for both we and thyself are of the race of Adam. On account of this, intercede on our behalf; for this supplicate thy Son Whom thou hast held in thine embrace, and help us in our preaching and then afterwards that we may find rest in our hopes. Go forward, O Virgin, from earth to heaven, from corruption to incorruption, from the sorrow of this world to the joy of the Kingdom of the heavens, from this perishable earth to the everlasting Heaven. Hasten, O Virgin, to the heavenly light, to the hymns of the angels, to the glory of the saints from all the ages. Hasten, O Virgin, to the place of thy Son, to His Kingdom, to His power, where the angels chant, the prophets glorify and the

Archangels hymn the Mother of the King, who is the lit lampstand, wider than the heavens, the firmament above, the protection of Christians, and the mediatress of our race."

Thus, with these words of praise he bid farewell and embraced the body of the all-holy one, the Panagia.[136]

Saint Germanos, in a simple narrative, writes that "...the body was placed in the tomb, and also a linen cloth upon her body, leaving her hands uncovered."[137]

Saint John of Damascus marvels, saying, "O! the lightnings that did shine that night. O! the angelic attendance that adorned the repose of the life-giving Mother. O! the apostolic orations that blessed the burial of the divine body."[138]

Then even after an enormous stone had been rolled into place before the mouth of the tomb, the faithful did not wish to depart, held by their intense love for the Mother of God. Thus, the holy Apostles also stayed by her tomb and did not leave Gethsemane for three days, chanting psalms continually.

During all this time, there could be heard in the air the wonderful chanting of the heavenly hosts that were praising God and blessing His immaculate Mother.[139]

DESCENT INTO HADES

The soul of the Theotokos was then received into the hands of her Son. Panagia then asked her Son if she could visit Hades to see where He Himself had gone to deliver the forefathers [1 Pet. 3:19]. Then radiant angels escorted the soul of the Theotokos to this region.[140] Saint John of Damascus makes mention of this in a matinal hymn of the Feast, chanting, *A strange wonder it was to see the living heaven of the Ruler of all descend into the hollows of the earth.*[141]

Rejoice, O thou who didst trample upon the all-destructive Hades. Rejoice, thou who didst open the gates of Paradise to the Christian race who ever blesseth thee.[142]

From his *Spiritual Psalter*, Saint Ephraim entreats: "O my Lady, do not leave me in the terrible hour of death, but hasten to my aid and deliver me from the bitter torments of the demons. For if thou choosest, thou hast the power to accomplish this, for thou art truly the Mother of God, who reignest over all."

ICONS OF THE DORMITION

Icons of Dormition depict Christ in glory, surrounded by a *mandorla*, looking at the body of His Mother stretched on a litter, which is a richly draped bier. The Virgin is clad in her red and blue garments. We see Christ holding, in His arms, a small figure of a child clothed in white and crowned with a halo; it is the all-luminous soul of Mary, represented as a newborn infant, that He has just taken to Himself.

By the end of the eleventh century, the Dormition scene had begun to appear in representations of the Orthodox Church cycle of Feasts, which adorn the walls and vaults of Byzantine churches. Some of the earliest wall paintings of this Feast may be seen above the entrance of the Monastery of Daphne and the Perivlepto of Mystra, which dates from the fourteenth century. As in the Monastery of Chora (Kariye Djami), the icon usually took its place on the west wall of the nave above the entrance door. As in so much of Christian art, the iconography of the Dormition is based upon literary sources, of which the most important is the Greek apocryphal text of the fourth or fifth century, entitled, *The*

Discourse of St. John the Theologian Concerning the Dormition (Keemeesis) of the Holy Mother of God.[143]
IN THY FALLING ASLEEP,
DEATH WAS WITHOUT CORRUPTION[144]

It must be remembered that it is not the Assumption that the Holy Orthodox Church observes on the 15th of August, but the Dormition *(Keemeesis)* or "falling asleep" of the holy Virgin. This most sacred Feast marks the falling asleep of the Mother of God which was followed by the translation of her sacred body three days later into heaven. This Feast, therefore, marks her soul being commended into her Son's hands and the short sojourn of her body in the tomb. Death is not the annihilation of our existence, but a passage from earth to heaven.[145]

It was St. Juvenal, Patriarch of Jerusalem, in the fifth century, who related to St. Pulcheria, the earliest traditions concerning the translation of the relics of the Theotokos.[146] At the end of the sixth century, Emperor Maurice (582-602) dated her august Dormition as the fifteenth of August and ordered that the Feast be celebrated throughout the universe.

Unlike the Resurrection of Christ, the mysterious character of her death, burial, resurrection and ascension were not the subject of apostolic teachings, or at least there are no extant epistles; yet it has been revealed to the inner consciousness of the Church. Inaccessible to the view of those outside the Church, the glory of the Theotokos' Dormition can be contemplated only in the inner light of Tradition. The glorification of the Virgin-Mother is a result of the voluntary condescension of the Son who is incarnate of her and made "Son of Man", capable of dying. The Mother of God is now established beyond the general Resurrection and the Last Judgment, having passed from death to life, from time to eternity, from terrestrial condition to celestial beatitude. Hence, the feast of August 15th is a second mysterious Pascha, since the Church celebrates, before the end of time, the secret first-fruits of its eschatological consummation.[147]

O marvelous wonder! The source of life is laid in the tomb, and the tomb itself becomes a ladder to heaven. Thy glory is full of majesty, shining with grace in divine brightness.[148]

Chapter XXIX.
The THEOTOKOS is Bodily Translated
On the Third Day

+ + +

THE HOLY APOSTLE THOMAS

While Thomas was enlightening the lands of India by preaching the Gospel, the honored Dormition of the Mother of God took place. All the Apostles had been caught up from various lands on the clouds of heaven, and were transported to Gethsemane, to the bier of the all-blessed Virgin. By God's special arrangement, Thomas was not brought hither. This was permitted by the will of God, that the faithful might be assured that the Mother of God was bodily assumed into Heaven. For just as they were more greatly assured of the Resurrection of Christ, through

the disbelief of Thomas, so did they learn of the bodily assumption into heaven of the all-pure Virgin Mary, the Theotokos, through the delay of Thomas.[1]

On the third day after the burial, Thomas was suddenly caught up in a cloud in India and transported to a place in the air above the tomb of the Virgin. From that vantage point, he beheld the translation of her body into the heavens, and cried out to her, "Whither goest thou, O all-holy one?" And, removing her cincture, she gave it to

481

Thomas, saying, "Receive this, my friend." And then she was gone.[2]

Thereafter, he descended to find the other disciples keeping watch over the sepulchre of the Theotokos. He sat down beside them, with the cincture in his hand, greatly saddened that he had not been there when she reposed, as had been the other Apostles. Hence, he said, "We are all disciples of the Master; we all preach the same thing; we are all servants of one Lord, Jesus Christ. How, then, is it that ye were counted worthy to behold the repose of His Mother, and I was not? Am I not an Apostle? Can it be that God is not pleased with my preaching? I beseech you, my fellow disciples: open the tomb, that I also may look upon her remains, and embrace them, and bid her farewell!"[3]

Taking pity on him, the Apostles then did as Thomas requested and opened the tomb that he might at least behold and venerate the sacred relics. The holy Apostles then rolled away the stone and opened the tomb. All were aghast when they discovered that her remains had vanished, not realizing that just moments before she had been bodily transported to paradise. All that remained were the burial clothes, which emitted a wonderful fragrance. Thus they stood in amazement and then each of them kissed the burial clothes which were lying in the tomb. They then prayed to the Lord that He would reveal to them where the body of the Theotokos had been transported.[4]

THE CINCTURE OF THE VIRGIN

In Biblical times, the cincture or girdle was made of leather or cloth. It is significant that the Virgin left her cloth cincture to the Apostle Thomas and, subsequently, to the Church. The girdle, placed around the middle and the loins, wherein is the seat of desire, signifies the mortification of carnal desires. We know that the immaculate Virgin-Mother subdued the passions. We chant during the service of the Deposition of the Cincture of the Theotokos (commemorated on the 31st of August) that *thy cincture as the garment of thy virginity and bridehood, is truly shown to be a most honorable wedding chamber, O Theotokos.*[5] Saint Joseph the Hymnographer understood that the precious relic of the Virgin's cincture or girdle was left to us as a surety of her mediation and assistance to Orthodox strugglers for purity and chastity. Hence, he chants, *The heart is renewed which touches the sacred cincture of the Virgin with fervent faith, for it is girded about with invincible power against impure passions and remains unscathed by incorporeal foes.*[6] Thus, it is meaningful when, in the taking of the Great Angelic Habit, the candidate receives the girdle and is told to "gird his loins with the power of truth, for mortification of body and renewal of spirit, and for courage and caution, in fulfillment of Christ's commandment."[7]

THE QUEEN GOES TO DWELL WITH HER SON AND TO RULE WITH HIM FOR EVER[8]

It is noteworthy that the zealous pastor, St. Gregory of Tours (538-594), in his *Book of Miracles*, testifies to his belief in the Dormition of the Virgin--the first of its kind in the West: "Finally when blessed Mary having completed the course of this life, and was to be called from the world, all the Apostles gathered to her house from their different regions. And when they had heard that she was to be taken from the world, together they kept watch with her; and lo, the Lord Jesus came with His angels. Taking her soul, He gave it to the Archangel Michael and withdrew. At dawn the Apostles raised her body with a pallet and they placed it in a vault and they guarded it awaiting the coming of the Lord. And lo, a second time the Lord stood by them and he ordered the holy body to be taken and borne to Paradise; there having rejoined the soul exultant with His elect, it enjoys the good things of eternity which shall know no end."[9]

Again, using the imagery of the *Apocrypha*, St. Gregory of Tours speaks of Mary's body being "taken up and borne on a cloud into Paradise where, now, reunited with her soul and rejoicing with the elect, it enjoys the good things of eternity which shall never come to an end."[10]

Saint Joseph the Hymnographer (c.816-886), confirming her bodily assumption, writes that *Thy tomb declared that thou wast buried, and it now openly shows that thou hast been bodily borne to the heavens.*[11]

Saint Cosmas (7th-8th c.), also speaking of her bodily translation, writes: *The Lord and God of all gave thee as thy portion the things that are above nature. For just as He kept thee virgin in thy childbirth, so did He preserve thy body incorrupt in the tomb; and He glorified thee by a divine translation, showing thee honor as a son to his mother.*[12]

The great doctor of the Dormition, St. John of Damascus (c.676-c.750), writes: "But even though, according to nature, thy most holy and happy soul is separated from thy most blessed and stainless body, and the body as usual is delivered to the tomb, it will not remain in the power of death and is not subject to decay. For just as her virginity remained inviolate while giving birth, when she departed from life her body was preserved from destruction and only taken to a better and divine tabernacle which is not subject to any death."[13]

Continuing, he writes: "It was fitting that she, who in childbirth had kept her virginity undamaged, should also, after death, keep her body free from all corruption."[14] He then speaks of the benefit of her translation. *For Christ translates her, as His own Mother, into a dwelling far better and more divine, the Holy of Holies.*[15]

Saint Gregory Palamas (+1359) writes that "the 'Ark of holiness' was resurrected, as was Christ Who had risen from the dead on the third day. Her burial clothes afforded the Apostles a demonstration of her resurrection from the dead.

As in the case of their Master, her burial clothes, too, alone remained in the tomb for their scrutiny."[16]

Saint Modestos of Jerusalem (+634), confirming her eternal bodily incorruptibility, writes: "As the most glorious Mother of Christ, our Saviour and God Who is the Giver of Life and immortality, she has been endowed with life by Him. She has received an eternal incorruptibility of the body, together with Him Who has raised her up from the tomb, and has taken her up to Himself in a way known only to Him."[17]

Saint Neophytos the Recluse (1134-1220) also speaks of her bodily translation, writing: "That pure and holy body, placed by the Apostles in the sacred place of Gethsemane, was borne to the God of the Apostles and delighted in those things which 'eye hath not seen, nor ear heard, neither have entered into the heart of man'" [1 Cor. 2:9].[18]

Under the presidency of the great Patriarch Dositheos, a statement was made at the Council of Jerusalem, in 1672, that "though the immaculate body of Mary was locked in a tomb, yet, like Christ, she was assumed and translated into the heavens on the third day."[19]

AFTER THE DORMITION: SHE ENTREATS HIM WITHOUT CEASING TO GRANT THE INHABITED EARTH PEACE AND GREAT MERCY

In describing her rank and authority in the heavenly realms, let us listen to the following hymn. *By thy deathless Dormition thou has sanctified the whole world. Thou hast been translated to the places above the world, there to perceive the beauty of the Almighty and, as His Mother, to rejoice in it exceedingly. Thou art attended by ranks of angels, O pure Virgin, and by the souls of the just.*[20]

Saint John of Damascus describes the conduct of the heavenly host at her translation. *At thy translation, O Mother of God, the angelic hosts, in fear and joy, with their holy wings covered thy body, that had been spacious enough to harbor the divinity.*[21]

Seized with dread, they (the powers of heaven) accompanied thine inviolate body that had held God, and they went on high before thee, crying, unseen, to the hierarchies above, "Lo, the Queen of all, the Maiden of God, is nigh."[22]

Saint John Mavropous (+c.1079), Metropolitan of Euchaites in Pontus, also comments that now "Mary is above the angels and is accompanied by thousands of them."[23]

485

Saint Ambrose (339-397), Bishop of Milan, lauding her bodily translation, says, "What a procession shall that be, what joy of applauding angels when she is found worthy of dwelling in heaven who lived on earth a heavenly life! Then, too, Miriam (Moses' and Aaron's sister), taking up her timbrel, shall stir up choirs of virgins singing to the Lord, because they have passed through the sea of this world, without suffering from the waves of this world [Ex. 15:20]. Then each shall rejoice, saying, 'I shall go in unto the altar of God, unto God Who giveth gladness to my youth' [Ps. 42:4]; and, 'Sacrifice unto God a sacrifice of praise, and pay unto the Most High thy vows'" [Ps. 49:14].[24]

Her role in heaven, as it was on earth, is intercessory. The kontakion of the Feast speaks of her as an unfailing hope and mediation. *Neither the tomb nor death had power over the Theotokos, who is ever watchful in her prayers and in whose intercessions lies unfailing hope. For as the Mother of Life she has been translated unto life by Him Who dwelt in her ever-virgin womb.*[25]

Saint John of Damascus comments upon the victory she has obtained for us. "Through her, our reconciliation with God has been consecrated, and peace and grace have been bestowed;...she has won for us all good things."[26]   And, "Thus thou art also the fountain of true light, the inexhaustible treasury of life itself, the most fruitful source of blessing, who has won for us and brought us all good things --though for a while thou wast covered corporeally with death; nonetheless, thou dost pour out pure and inexhaustible streams of immense light, immortal life and true happiness, rivers of grace, fountains of healing, and everlasting blessing."[27]

Thus, *From all generations we call thee blessed, O Virgin Theotokos....Blessed also are we in having thee as our succor: for day and night thou dost intercede for us, and the scepters of kings are strengthened by thy supplications.*[28]

Saint Andrew of Crete (c.660-740) associates great things with Mary, writing: "Blessed in Heaven, and glorified on earth, every tongue piously and with grateful sentiment preaches thee, glorifying thee as the Mother of Life. Every creature is filled with thy glory. All things have been made holy by the odor of thy fragrance; through thee the occasion of sin has been abolished; the woes of the first parent have been transformed into joy. Through thee all the angels sing with us, 'Glory in heaven; peace on earth.'"[29] And, "Mary is the first of the divinely re-created, to enter the Kingdom of the heavens standing at the right hand. She enters because she is the Church, the deified body of Christ. If she were not welcomed before the throne of God, body and soul, then neither could those identified with her as children to their 'virginal' Mother stand before Him in the age to come. What has been done for the saved in the age to come has been accomplished in the Theotokos. She has passed into the 'Church triumphant.' Thus, now she is beyond death, beyond the resurrection and beyond the Last Judgment."

THE CUSTOM OF THE "PANAGIA"

The Virgin also appeared to the holy Apostles after her repose, as did her Son. After the Ascension of our Lord, whenever the Apostles shared a meal together, it was their custom to leave a place at their table for the Master Christ.

After her bodily disappearance from the tomb, it was towards evening and they sat down in order to refresh themselves with a little food.

As was their custom, they would cut a cube of bread and place it at the head of the table as Christ's portion. And when they finished the meal and offering thanks, they would elevate this portion, proclaiming, "Great is the name of the Holy Trinity! O Lord Jesus Christ, help us!" And each would partake of a small piece thereof as a blessing.[30] This custom continued not only when they were together but even when they were far from one another.[31]

At this meal, however, they spoke and thought of nothing but of the Virgin's empty tomb. Now when they had finished eating and had come to the conclusion of their prayers, they again followed their custom of lifting up the portion of bread put aside to honor the Lord and glorify the Trinity. Suddenly, they heard angelic singing. Raising their eyes, they beheld standing, in the air, the Theotokos, who was surrounded by a multitude of angels. She was suffused with an ineffable light, and said to the Apostles, "Rejoice, for I am with you all the days of your lives!"[32] Indeed, she is not only with her Son's Apostles, but she is also with all the faithful and devout Orthodox Christians of all the ages.

Upon seeing her, they were filled with joy and cried aloud, "All-holy Mother of God, save us!" This is what they exclaimed instead of the usual, "Lord Jesus Christ, help us." Thus they were all convinced that the Mother of God, like her Son, had risen on the third day and had been translated bodily into the heavens. Ever since, a piece of bread has also been set aside in her name, hence the appellation, *Panagia*, or All-holy (one).[33] For a precious keepsake, the Apostles then returned to the tomb and took the shroud for the consolation of the sorrowful and as authentic evidence of her rising from the tomb.[34]

Thus, they were convinced that the Mother of Life, although she had died, yet rose, like her Son, to eternal life; and that her body, having been raised, was lifted up to Heaven by Jesus, her Son and the Saviour of our souls.

Thus, in the pure Virgin, vanquished were the laws of nature. Her virginity was preserved in birthgiving, and life was united with death. And remaining a virgin after giving birth, and alive after death, she prays unceasingly, as our Mother, for her inheritance.

Then, Peter, in fervent faith and abundant tears, exclaimed: *Rejoice, Mother of the Creator, ascending to the world on high. Rejoice, thou who wast taken above the heavens, being more spacious than heaven. Rejoice, thou who brought gladness unto the heavenly hosts with thy passage above. Rejoice, thou who art received into the most splendid Jerusalem on high. Rejoice, thou who art entering most joyfully the temples not made with hands. Rejoice, Queen of the cherubim and seraphim. Rejoice, refuge and deliverance of the faithful. Rejoice, help and defense of thy*

heritage. Rejoice, O intercessor unto God for all the Chris-
tian world. Rejoice, O all-good bestower of all that is
good.[35]

As we know, through divine providence, the Apostle
Thomas was not present during the funeral procession.
Having thoughts within himself, he also rejoiced in her
Dormition and translation, and cried out, *Rejoice, thou who*
wast taken from the earth in the hands of thy Son. Rejoice,
thou who ascended on high to enjoy His glory. Rejoice, thou
who wast escorted above by all the leaders of the angels.
Rejoice, thou who wast extolled with majestic hymns at the
gates of heaven by the superior hosts. Rejoice, O earthly
heaven raised up unto the tabernacle on high. Rejoice, O
throne of the Lord, who ascended from earth into the
heavenly kingdom. Rejoice, O our intercessor and strong
defense. Rejoice, intercessor of sinners unto salvation.
Rejoice, Queen of them that call themselves by thy Son's
name and, who, after God, art the hope of the heavenly
kingdom. Rejoice, Mother of Life who, after the Lord, art
unto us hope of eternal life.[36]

Then the same cloud by which the Apostles had been
brought carried them back each to his own place. Thus,
they were *witnesses not only to the Ascension of the Saviour*
but also to the translation of her who gave Him birth.[37]
Each Apostle then continued preaching and telling the great
things of God, and praising our Lord Jesus Christ.

REJOICE, THOU WHOSE INCORRUPTIBLE BODY
IS GLORIFIED TOGETHER WITH THE SOUL!

From that time, the tradition of the Holy Orthodox
Church affirms the bodily assumption of the Theotokos into
heaven on the third day after her burial. We observe two
things from this occurrence: that it was not fitting that the
Mother of Life should remain in the tomb and partake of
corruption and we see that the Law-Giver proved a doer of
the law that children should honor their parents. Hence, He
bestowed upon his Mother the same honor as Himself. As He
was raised on the third day in glory, thus He raised His
Mother with glory on the third day and took her to Himself.[38]

Saint John of Damascus rejoices, saying, "The earth
could not bear her divine body and dissolve it, as with other
mortals. Nay, though necessary that it be delivered to death,

three days thereafter, her relics were delivered incorruptible into angelic hands. She becomes incorruptible, rises, and is translated to heaven. There, she stands before Her Son and God in a living body."[39]

This glorious St. John also writes: "The Theotokos, today commences a second existence, which is the resurrection by Him Who gave her the commencement of the previous existence." And again the same writes: "For thy soul was not forsaken in Hades, neither did thy flesh see corruption; nor was thine immaculate and pure body taken by the earth, but by heaven. The Queen, the Lady, the Mistress, the God-Mother, the true Mother of God, is translated."[40]

Our holy God-bearing father, Germanos (c.635-733), Patriarch of Constantinople, in his encomium asserts: "How could the dissolution of the flesh turn thee to earth and dust, which through thy Son's incarnation has delivered man from the corruption of death? Impossible....Thou didst become one of us, and thereupon wast unable to avoid the common human death, even as thy Son, and God of all, Who died on behalf of the human race, also tasted of the same death. He shall glorify thy tomb also in death....For the death-corrupting and dissolving earth could not contain thee, the God-containing vessel. Since the God Who emptied Himself in thee, was even from the beginning everlasting Life, it behoved Him to have the Mother of Life also the companion of Life. And as thou didst fall asleep on thy Dormition, even so hast thou risen and been translated unto life." He then continues saying that "she has filled Paradise with her glory and has her rest in the heavenly life. She is also the co-dweller of God in His contentment."[41]

The defender of Orthodoxy, St. Mark of Ephesus chants in one of his odes: "For thou wast dead and art risen again, as the Lord's Mother, to the assurance of the last resurrection whereunto we hope." And again, "the Mother of Life welcomes death, and having been put in the grave, she arises forever gloriously on the third day, reigning with her Son, entreating the forgiveness of our faults."[42]

Nicephoros Theotokes (18th century) also wrote that her body was awarded a great exception, "for it joined the soul before the common resurrection. It was translated from earth and ascended to the heavens incorruptible. Such a glory and exception was awarded only to the divine body of the God-Man Jesus. Such a glory, superior to all glories, was received by the Theotokos, so that she became incorruptible before the common resurrection. She became incorruptible before the time of incorruptibility. She was examined and glorified before the judgment. She received her recompense before the day of recompense. Finally, she was honored with prerogatives such as her Son's."[43] Saint Nicodemos of the Holy Mountain (+1809) also agrees to this, saying, "...not only was she translated, but...her all-illuminating soul was again united to her body."[44]

Saint Gregory Palamas believes also that Mary was bodily assumed, "for there was no need for her to remain on the earth, except for a short while, as did her Son and God for forty days. Therefore, she ascended immediately on the third day from the grave to the heavenly space."[45]

The manifold graces which God lavished upon the Virgin Mary, before and after her childbearing, do not alter the fact that death, which came from Adam, could not be vanquished except in the deified body put on by the hypostasis of the Son of God.[46] Saint Gregory recognizes the bodily glorification of the daughter of the righteous ones, Joachim and Anna, as a consequence of the divine maternity: "If a soul in which grace dwells rises to the sky when it has separated itself from things here below...how could the body which received in itself the eternal and unique Son of God, the inexhaustible Source of grace, and which even gave birth thereto, fail to be lifted up from earth to heaven?"[47]

Saint Gregory Palamas comments that "she alone, in her body, became immortal after death and dwells together with her Son and God. And for this reason she pours forth from thence abundant grace upon them that honor her, for she is a receptacle of great graces and lavishly bestows sublime gifts, including our ability to look towards her. In her goodness, she never ceases to provide a fruitful and plentiful gain....She is for virtue and for them that live virtuously....To her has been vouchsafed the excellent inheritance of every good, and this allotment far exceeds in holiness the portion of them that are divinely-graced."[48]

It is meet that the Mother of God now has her dwelling in heaven, for this is a suitable place for her. She now stands at the right hand of the King of all, "arrayed in a vesture of in-woven gold, adorned in varied colors" [Ps. 44:8].

Saint Gregory Palamas comments that the verse "vesture wrought with gold" is to be understand that she is adorned with every virtue. She alone, in her body, glorified God and now enjoys the celestial domain with her Son, the King of all. From the super-celestial realm, she flashes forth radiant and divine illuminations and graces upon the earth; thus is she rightly venerated and hymned by all the faithful.[49]

Thus we are correct to beseech her intercession for light and grace when we chant in the Dismissal Hymn for the Transfiguration of Christ on August 6th: *Shine forth Thou on us who are sinners all Thy light ever unending, through the prayers of the Theotokos, O Light-Bestower, glory to Thee!*[50] Saint Gregory continues lauding the Mother of God saying, that God was "willing to set up an image of all goodness and beauty to make clearly manifest His own therein to both angels and men. He fashioned a being supremely good and beautiful, and united within her all good, seen and unseen, which when He made the world He distributed to each thing and thereby adorned all."[51]

REJOICE, FOR THY MATERNAL ENTREATY MOVETH GOD TO RELENT!

Saint Gregory Palamas aptly glorifies the Virgin Theotokos when he writes that "she cooperated and suffered with that divine emptying *(kenosis)* and condescension in His incarnation, when He took the form of a servant [Phil. 2:7]. She also rightly is glorified and exalted together with Him....After her ascent into heaven, she rivaled her former great works that were through Him and that had surpassed mind and speech, by mighty and many-faceted labors through her prayers and her zealous and earnest attention for the world."[52]

And, "in truth, many were vouchsafed divine favor, glory and power, however, Prophet David writes: 'But to me, exceedingly honorable are Thy friends, O Lord; their principalities are made exceedingly strong. I will count them, and they shall be multiplied more than the sand; I awoke and am still with Thee' [Ps. 138:16-17]. And according to Solomon: 'Many daughters have obtained wealth, many have wrought valiantly; but thou hast exceeded, thou hast surpassed all' [Prov. 31:29]. For while she stood between God and the whole human race, God became the Son of Man and made men sons of God. She made earth heavenly. She deified the human race. She alone of all women was shown forth to be a mother by nature and the Mother of God transcending every law of nature, and by her ineffable childbirth--the Queen of all creation....Hence she has exalted them under her through herself. She partook of a more excellent power because, while on earth, she hearkened and obeyed heavenly things rather than things earthly. By the divine Spirit, she received ordination from out of the heavens and became the most sublime of the sublime and the blessed Queen of a blessed race."[53]

Blessed Archbishop John Maximovitch (1896-1966) comments in his Orthodox treatise on her veneration that "The end of the earthly life of the Theotokos was the beginning of her greatness. Being adorned with divine glory, she stands and will stand, both in the Day of the Last Judgment and in the future age, at the right hand of the throne of her Son. She reigns with Him and has boldness toward Him as His Mother, according to the flesh. She is one in spirit with Him--as one who performed the will of God and instructed others [Mt. 5:19]. Merciful and full of love, she manifests her love towards her Son and God in love for the human race, which she intercedes for before the Merciful One. Going about the earth, she helps men, as one having experienced all the difficulties of earthly life. She sees every tear, hears every groan and entreaty directed to her. Especially near to her are them that labor in the battle with the passions and are zealous for a God-pleasing life."[54]

Saint Cyril of Alexandria writes: "Through thee, the Trinity is glorified; through thee, the Cross is venerated in the whole world...through thee, angels and archangels rejoice, through thee, demons are chased...through thee, the fallen creature is raised to heaven...through thee, churches are found in the whole world, through thee, peoples are led to conversion."[55]

Through the Theotokos alone did the Lord come to us and appear and live on earth among men, being invisible to all before this time. The Virgin Mother is incomparably superior to all. "Likewise" says St. Gregory Palamas, "in the endless age to come, without her mediation, every emanation of illuminating divine light, every revelation of the mysteries of the Godhead, every form of spiritual gift, will exceed the capacity of every created being. However, she alone has received the all-pervading fullness of Him that fills all things. Through her, all may now attain it, for she dispenses it according to the power of each, in proportion and to the degree of the purity of each. Thus, she is the treasury and presides over the riches of the Godhead.[56]

Saint Gregory then finishes his *Homily on the Dormition*, thus: "It is through her that as many as partake of God do partake, and as many as know God understand her to be the enclosure of the Uncontainable One, and as many as hymn God hymn her together with Him. She is the cause of what preceded her, the protectress of what came after her and the patroness of things eternal. She is the subject of the prophets, the chief *(archee)* of the apostles, the steadfast base of the martyrs, and the foundation *(kreepis)* of teachers. She is the glory of the earthborn, the sweetness of the heavenly beings, and the adornment of all creation. She is the beginning and the fountain and the root of all those ineffable good things. She is the head *(koreefee)* and consummation of all that is holy."[57]

REJOICE, O JOYFUL ONE, WHO IN THY DORMITION HATH NOT FORSAKEN US!

Together then with St. Theophanes the Poet (+1381), let us chant, *Forget not, O Lady, thy ties of kinship with those who commemorate in faith the Feast of thine all-holy Dormition.*[58]

Appendix A:
MARY THEOTOKOS and the CHURCH

+ + +

From what we have previously read, we see that the Virgin Mary is more than an example of piety. She is more than a saint. She is "All-holy", "Ever-Virgin" and "Mother of God". She is the Church's greatest theologian. She is the one human--body and soul resurrected, united and complete--and now deified person who is "more honorable than the cherubim and beyond compare more glorious than the seraphim."

"In her," writes St. John of Damascus (c.676-c.750), "the whole mystery of the divine economy" is personified.[1]

As we have seen, the Scriptures say more about the Theotokos than most people perceive, albeit, in a hidden manner, revealed only to the faithful through Holy Tradition and the writings of the holy Fathers. If there was a general silence about her in the early Church, it was intentional, to avoid comparisons with the pagan religions which provide anti-typical divine mother and child similarities, such as the Egyptian Isis and Serapis or the Oriental Cybele and Attis. Only later, during the fourth and fifth centuries, did circumstances demand an elucidation of the Virgin Mary's role in the plan of salvation.

Since Mary Theotokos is one flesh with her divine Son, she is, therefore, necessarily the Mother of those baptized into His body, the Church. Not without purpose does St. Epiphanios of Cyprus (c.315-403) write that she is "the holy Jerusalem, Virgin of Christ, His Bride"; for what is granted in the flesh to the Virgin is granted spiritually to the Church. Let us see how, in the writings of the holy Fathers, the Theotokos is, among other things, portrayed as the Church; for as St. Andrew of Crete (c.660-740) chants, she is "the living city of the King and God, in which Christ hast dwelt, and worked our salvation."[2]

Saint Cyril of Alexandria (+444), in his famous litany of praise spoken after the Council at Ephesus, where he was a dominant figure, ends with these words: "Let us give glory to Mary, Ever-Virgin, that is to the holy Church, and her Son and Immaculate Spouse; to Him be glory for ever and ever."[3]

Saint Clement of Alexandria (d. before 215) points to the Mary-Church parallel, saying, "O mysterious wonder! There is only one Father of all, only one Word of all, and the Holy Spirit is also one and He is everywhere. There is but one Virgin Mother. I like to call her the Church...she is both virgin and mother--immaculate as a virgin and loving as a mother. She calls her children and feeds them with holy milk: the Word, a child."[4]

Therefore, in giving birth to the body of Christ, Mary gave birth to the Church, the unity of all them that are incorporated into Christ. She is the progenitress of the Christian race, that is, the historical Church which is forever united to divinity.

Saint Ildefonsus (+667), Archbishop of Toledo, affirms that "the form of our Mother the Church is according to the form of the Lord's Mother."[5] The mysteries of the Virgin's life are daily renewed in the Church, for, as one wedded yet, at the same time immaculate. As a virgin she conceives us by the Spirit, yet brings us forth without pain, so the venerable Bede (c.673-735) was to write.[6] The influence of Saint Ambrose (339-397) is also evident here. "Mary is truly espoused but a virgin, because she is a type of the Church which is immaculate but wedded." And, "What was prophesied of Mary was as a type of the Church."[7] In another place, he writes: "How beautiful are those things which have been prophesied of Mary under the figure of the Church."[8] In other words, she is the Church because she is the Mother of Christ, even as she is Mother to all Orthodox, His "brethren."

Since Mary Theotokos is the Church, the perpetual virginity of Mary also signifies the "perpetual virginity" of the Church, that is, Her inviolate fidelity to Christ. Deny the one, and one must deny the other: the Church and the Theotokos stand together; ecclesiology and Mariology safeguard each other. Thus, too, the Orthodox Church insists upon the "all-holiness" of the Virgin Mary, for the same reason that She speaks of the Church as "holy". She is *Panagia* or "All-holy", because she is the Church.

The types of the Virgin are everywhere associated with the types of the Church. It may seem strange that she, the Virgin, is sometimes cast in the role of Mother, Sister, Daughter, Bride and Child of Christ, but those are the relationships found in old Israel between God and His people. This explains why the Church (the Virgin), the new Israel, is depicted as the "Bride of Christ" while, at the same time, His body.

Saint Paulinus (353-431), Bishop of Nola (near Naples) writes:

"What a great mystery was this, by which the Church became wedded to Christ and became at once the Lord's Bride and His Sister! The Bride with the status of Spouse is a Sister....So She continues as Mother through the seed of the eternal Word, alike conceiving and bringing forth nations. She is Sister and Spouse because Her intercourse is not physical but mental, and her Husband is not man but God. The children of this Mother comprise equally old and infants; this offspring has no age or sex. For this is the blessed progeny of God which springs from no human seed but from a heavenly race.

"This is why the teacher Paul says that 'there is neither male nor female, for ye are all one in Christ Jesus' [Gal. 3:28] and 'there is one body, and one Spirit, even as ye are called on one hope of your calling; one Lord, one faith, one baptism' [Eph. 4-5]. For all of us who acknowledge Christ as Head of our body [Col. 1:18] are one body, and are all Christ's limbs [1 Cor. 12:27]. Because we have now all put on Christ and stripped off Adam, we are at once advancing towards the shape of angels. Hence for all born in baptism there is the one task; both sexes must incorporate the perfect man, and Christ as all in all [Eph. 4:13] must be our common Head, our King Who hands over His limbs to the Father in the Kingdom. Once all are endowed with immortal bodies, the frail condition of human lives forgoes marriage between men and women" [Mt. 22:30].[9]

+

The Woman in Revelation, Chapter Twelve

A most difficult passage in a difficult book, the *Revelation:* "And there appeared a great wonder in heaven; a woman clothed with the sun, and the moon under her feet, and upon her head a crown of twelve stars. And she being with child cried, travailing in birth, and pained to be delivered" [Rev. 12:1-2]. The word "woman" was given a collective meaning by most ancient writers as describing the people of God by a female figure. There are many though who identify the "woman" as being the Virgin Mary, who shows herself forth as an image of the Holy Church. As she remained virgin bringing forth a Son, so the Church at all times would bring forth members (sons and daughters) without losing Her virginity (pure Orthodoxy). The pains the Church suffers refers to Her spiritual motherhood, for neither the Church of the Old Testament or the New Testament "cried out in pangs of birth...and brought forth a male child"--Christ. Israel, as a community, did not give birth by natural generation to the Messiah--but it did issue the Virgin-Mother. A woman was at the heart of the mystery and, at the essential moment, the transition of Israel to a new and final destiny would be conveyed by the figure of a woman. This woman was the Virgin Mary who, without pain, gave birth to Christ.

The outstanding commentator and noted father, Hippolytos (c.170-c.236), clearly states, that the Evangelist meant "the Church, endued with the Father's Word, Whose brightness is above the sun. And by 'the moon under her feet' he referred to her being adorned, like the moon, with heavenly glory. And the words, 'upon her head a crown of twelve stars,' refer to the twelve apostles by whom the Church was founded. And that 'she, being with child, cried, travailing in birth, and pained to be delivered,' means that the Church will not cease to bear from her heart the Word that is persecuted by the unbelieving world. 'And she brought forth,' he says, 'a man child' [Rev. 12:5], a man child of God, who is declared to be God and man, becomes the instructor of all the nations."[10]

Saint Methodios, Bishop of Tyre (+311) also sees the "woman" in a collective sense, the Church. He writes about the significance of the moon, saying, "and her standing on the moon...refers by way of allegory to the faith of them that have been purified from corruption by baptism...for all moist substances depend on the moon...She labors and brings forth natural men as spiritual and under this aspect is she indeed their mother. For just as the woman receives the unformed seed of her husband and after a period of time brings forth a perfect human being, so too the Church, one might say, is constantly conceiving those who take refuge in the Word, and shaping them according to the likeness and form of Christ, after a certain time makes them citizens of that blessed age. Hence it is necessary that she stand upon the laver, as the mother of those who are washed. The function that she exercises over the laver is called the moon because those who are thus reborn and renewed shine with a new glow, that is, with a new light....Hence, they are designated by the expression 'the newly enlightened.' She continues to reveal to them the spiritual full moon in her periodic presentation of His Passion, until the full glow and light of the great day shall appear."

He then continues speaking of the "man child," saying, "Remember that the mystery of the incarnation of the Word was fulfilled long before the *Apocalypse*, whereas John's prophetic message has to do with the present and the future. Christ was not the 'child who was caught up unto God, and to His throne' [Rev. 12:5] for fear lest he be injured by the serpent; rather, He descended from the throne of His Father and was begotten precisely that He might stay and check the dragon's assault on the flesh."

Then St. Methodios brings forward the Prophet Isaias, saying, "Before she that travailed brought forth, before the travail-pain came on, she escaped it and brought forth a male. Who has heard such a thing? And who has seen after this manner?" [Is. 66:7-8].[11] Yet, it is obvious that such a prophecy could only be applied to the Virgin who experienced no pain in birthgiving.

Saint Methodios then represents "the Church...to bring forth a man child, because the enlightened spiritually receive the features and image of Christ. The likeness of the Word is stamped on them and is begotten within them by perfect knowledge and faith, and thus Christ is spiritually begotten in each one. Thus the Church is with child and labors until Christ is formed and born within us, so that each of the saints by sharing in Christ is born again as Christ....Those who are baptized in Christ become, as it were, other 'christs' by a communication of the Spirit, and here it is that the Church effects this transformation into a clear image of the Word."

Therefore, St. Methodios believes that the Woman who has brought forth continues to bring forth a male child, the Word, in the hearts of the faithful; and this same Woman went forth into the desert undefiled and unharmed by the wrath of the beast. This Woman is our Mother, the Church. He then explains that the seven heads of the dragon, the devil, signify the seven vices.[12]

Saint Andrew of Caesarea explains that the Church is pained for each one who is reborn by water and the Spirit until Christ shall be formed in them. The same also writes that the devil always arms himself against the Church and increasingly strives to make those reborn by her his food. Concerning the man-child, St. Andrew concurs with St. Methodios, that "in the person of those who are baptized, the Church ceaselessly gives birth to Christ; just as, according to the Apostle, we come 'unto the measure of the stature of the fullness of Christ'" [Eph. 4:13].[13]

Saint Ambrose writes that most authors seem to interpret the moon as representing the Church when referring to certain passages [Ps. 135:8-9; Ps. 103:21]. The Church, like the moon would have her seasons, namely of persecution and peace. Though the moon seems to lose light, she does not. She can be cast in a shadow, but she cannot lose her light. The Church, for example, is weakened by the desertion of some in time of persecution, but is replenished by the witness of Her martyrs. In fact, the moon undergoes a diminution of its light, not, however, of its mass...so that it may borrow from the sun.[14]

Who was clad with Christ, the Sun of righteousness? Who had the moon as a footstool? Who was crowned on the head with the twelve stars? Who else but the most holy Mother, the Virgin Mary. This is the virgin woman whom the beloved disciple saw clad with the Sun, and crowned by twelve stars, namely, the Apostles, and under her feet the moon, the sacred Church of God, imploring her intercessions for the salvation of her children.[15]

If we examine the work of the hymn-writers of the two *Akathist Hymns* for the Dormition of the Mother of God, they see in the Evangelist's divine revelation the holy Theotokos at the right of her Son as a great sign in heaven.

The twenty-four stanzas of the Akathist written in commemoration of her Dormition, as celebrated on the Holy Mountain, explain St. John's vision as a type of her glory: *The heavenly sign was a type of thy glory, O Mother, which I beheld in the Revelation; for thou didst then appear unto me as a woman clad with the intellectual Sun, Who illumines and enlightens all, crying unto thee: Rejoice, thou who art clad with the Lord. Rejoice, thou that art embroidered before Him. Rejoice, thou that bearest the twelve-star crown on thy head. Rejoice, thou that hast the moon as a disk by thy feet. Rejoice, thou Mother of Christians.*[16]

Arethas Caesaria writes: "That woman some accepted as the Mother of the Lord...others, too, say she is the Church, clothed in the Sun of righteousness, and of the moon, the synagogue...under her feet."[17]

Thus, in icons depicting the *Apocalypse of St. John, the Painter's Manual* or *Hermeneia* illustrates chapter 12 of the *Revelation* with the Virgin upon clouds, wearing a purple robe and with angel's wings; around her crown are twelve stars and the rays of the sun surround her from her head to her feet. Under her feet is the moon, and before her is a red dragon with seven heads and ten horns and wearing seven crowns; out of its mouth pours water, like a river, and the land opens up and swallows the river. Behind it is a mass of stars, and above the Virgin are two angels holding the child Christ in a veil; many clouds surround them.[18]

Rejoice, thou who art clothed in the Sun, who dost irradiate grace and glory upon all the universe.[19]

Appendix B:
The Gospel Reading
for the
Feasts of the Theotokos

+ + +

At that time, Jesus "entered into a certain village: and a certain woman named Martha received Him into her house.

"And she had a sister called Mary, who also was sitting alongside, at Jesus' feet, and heard His word.

"But Martha was distracted about much serving, and, came to Him, and said, 'Lord, dost Thou not care that my sister hath left me to serve alone? Bid her therefore that she help me.'

"And Jesus answered and said unto her, 'Martha, Martha, thou art careful and troubled about many things: but one thing is needful; and Mary hath chosen that good part, which shall not be taken away from her.'" [Lk. 10:38-42].[1]

INTRODUCTION

This Gospel reading is used for many of the Feasts of the Mother of God, such as her Nativity, her Entrance into the Temple, and her Dormition. What is the significance of using this Gospel reading involving SS Martha and Mary, in which Mary Theotokos is not mentioned, nor is it known if she were one of the guests?

As indicated in the previous chapter, entitled *Mary Theotokos and the Church*, the Theotokos is a symbol of the Church, the body of Christ. There is a relationship between the two sisters, Martha and Mary, and the antithesis between the married and the unmarried woman [see 1 Cor. 7:34-35], which characterizes women in the Church. The married woman, caring for the things of the world, is like unto Martha; whereas, the unmarried woman cares about the things of the Lord, much like Mary of Bethany. The Virgin Mother of God may be cast in the role of her "who cares for the things of the Lord, that she may be holy both in body and in spirit" [1 Cor. 7:34]. And though she had a husband, it was as though she had none [1 Cor. 7:29]. Nevertheless, this Gospel need not be addressed only to the roles of women in the Church, but men too. Our Saviour was simply comparing, metaphorically, a life of works and a life of contemplation.

MARY IS COMMENDED

Both Martha and Mary belong in the gallery of famous women of the Bible. The two sisters lived in Bethany, a quiet village on the southeast of the Mount of Olives, beside the Jericho Road. It was a short and pleasant walk from here over the Mount of Olives to the temple at Jerusalem.

The Evangelist Luke's statement that Martha received Jesus into her house (v. 10:38) implies that Martha was mistress of the house. The home of Lazarus, Martha and Mary was comfortable and they were people of means. Both house and garden were inviting, for Martha excelled as a homemaker. Martha, an Aramaic name, not found in Hebrew, means "mistress" or "lady". She takes the lead in a way that implies she is the elder sister. Although Mary might be socially subordinate to her sister Martha, she is the spiritual heroine. Mary's posture of sitting at the feet of Jesus signifies a receptive mind and devoted spirit. Mary was sitting before Jesus; she was not sitting in the back of the crowd. We can be sure that Mary was not selfish in her withdrawal from homemaking, but that she knew her sister had the ability to carry on without her.

However, Martha is in no placid mood when she looks upon her sister, at that moment, as being idle. Martha made every effort to entertain Jesus in a manner that she thought was worthy of such an illustrious Guest, that it might also be a blessing to her home.

Blessed Jerome comments that "Martha, in her anxiety to be hospitable, was preparing a meal for the Lord and His disciples. But it was Mary's actions that were preferred. Be then like Mary; prefer the food of the soul to that of the body. Leave it to thy sister to run to and fro and to seek how she may fitly welcome Christ. But do thou, having once and for all cast away the burden of the world, sit at the Lord's feet and say, 'I have found Him Whom my soul loves:

I held Him, and did not let Him go' [Song 3:4]. And He will answer, 'My dove, My perfect one...she is the only one of her mother; she is the choice of her that bare her' [Cant. 6:8]. Now the mother of whom this is said is the heavenly Jerusalem" [Gal. 4:26].[2]

In all likelihood, Martha had prepared too lavish a meal, when a simple one would have sufficed. Our Saviour was more interested in food for the soul than the body. Martha, however, becomes distracted and bustled. Perhaps the visit had been unexpected and the guests too numerous.

Saint Basil the Great comments that "the Lord did not praise Martha for being anxious about much serving...that is, the preparation of the meal. But one thing, that is, the purpose of the meal, should be to satisfy need. You are well aware, also, of what sort of food the Lord Jesus Himself placed before the five thousand" [Mt. 16:9; Mk. 8:19]. There was no need for delicacies and sumptuous appointments.[3] The divine Paul writes: "Whether therefore ye eat, or drink, or whatsoever ye do, do all to the glory of God" [1 Cor. 10:31].

In another place, Christ, when teaching His own disciples, says, "Therefore, I say unto you, take no thought for your life, what ye shall eat, or what ye shall drink; nor yet for your body, what ye shall put on. Is not the life more than meat, and the body more than raiment?" And again, "Seek ye first the kingdom of God, and His righteousness; and all these things shall be added unto you" [Mt. 6:25, 33].

However, Jesus speaks to Martha gently, with a touch of pity, saying that she is over-occupied. Jesus did not condemn Martha's work, nor did he speak derogatorily about housework or hospitality. But He did remark about her excessive attention to material provision, which disturbed her peace of mind, prompted criticism of both Jesus and her sister, and robbed her of the benefit of receiving the Lord's instruction. He passes easily and swiftly from the natural to the spiritual. Mary having chosen the good portion was not to be blamed and cannot be deprived of it. Thus, He would not sanction Martha's demand for Mary to participate in a lower vocation.

For the first century Jew, to sit at someone's feet, was an act symbolizing formal education. Sitting at a rabbi's feet was a position typical of rabbinic students expressing respect

504

to their rabbi. Since teachers sat on a raised place in order to teach [see Lk. 4:20-21], students had to sit on mats on the floor to be in a lower position than their teacher. The Apostle Paul describes his own rabbinic training in similar language, when he told a crowd of Jews that he was reared in Jerusalem "at the feet of Gamaliel, and taught according to the perfect manner of the law of the fathers" [Acts. 22:3]. Thus, indirectly, the evangelist is telling us that Mary was taking a position typical of a rabbinic student, a position unusual for a woman and moreover generally disapproved. Martha stresses in her question to Jesus that she is all alone and commands Him to tell Mary to help her.

Martha allowed her frustration to turn to the Lord and, inappropriately, she commanded her honored Guest to do her bidding. Nevertheless, Martha's indignation was perfectly understandable in the light of her culture. A Jewish woman's primary role was that of homemaker. All women were exempt from synagogue school and rabbinic training, and received no distinction for learning the law. Martha, at that moment, was not thinking about Mary's spiritual growth nor about the one concern that she herself should have had. Martha assumed that her demand to have Mary's help superseded Mary's desire to learn.

Saint Clement of Alexandria remarks that Martha "blamed her sister, because, leaving serving, Mary sat herself at His feet, devoting her time to learning." In another place and time, Jesus said to the rich man who also was busy about many things, "if thou wilt be perfect...come and follow me" [Mt. 19:21]. Here, St. Clement writes: "So also Christ bade him to leave his busy life, and cleave to the One and adhere to the grace of Him Who offered everlasting life."[4]

How does the "Rabbi" Jesus respond to Martha's command? Jesus' love for Martha is shown by the tender way in which he repeats her name and shows her what she is feeling. The Saviour does show concern for Martha's feelings, but He would not allow Martha, or anyone else, to stop Mary from learning as His other disciples would learn. Jesus had completely reversed the priorities of ancient Jewish life. A woman's role as homemaker is not primary.

Later, the divine Paul would write that "Faith comes by hearing, and hearing by the word of God" [Rom. 10:17]. But, "How shall they believe in Him of Whom they have not heard?" [Rom. 10:14]. If Israel apostatized and followed other deities so many times in her history, might it not be attributed in part to the fact that women were left ignorant and uneducated in the law, thus making them easy prey to the religions of the nations? Our Saviour desired to return His people to that original injunction in Deuteronomy 31:12 that men, women, children and the stranger that is in their cities are to learn to fear the Lord and to hearken to the words of God.

In the *Conferences of St. John Cassian*, he records Abba Moses saying "that the soul should ever cleave to God and to heavenly things. What is alien to this, however great it may be, should be given the second place, or even treated as of no consequence, or perhaps as hurtful. We have an excellent illustration of this state of mind and condition in the Gospel example of Martha and Mary: Martha was performing a service that was certainly a sacred one, since she was ministering to the Lord and His disciples, but Mary, being intent only on spiritual instruction, was clinging close to the feet of Jesus....She is shown by the Lord to have chosen the good part, and one which should not be taken away from her....You see that the Lord makes the chief good consist in meditation, that is, in divine contemplation, whence we see that all other virtues should be put in the second place, even though we admit that they are necessary, useful and excellent, because they are all performed for the sake of this one thing.

"He makes the chief good consist not in practical work --however praiseworthy and rich in fruits it may be--but in contemplation of Him, which indeed is simple and 'but one'; declaring that 'few things' are needful for the perfect bliss....When he says that Mary chose the good part, although He says nothing of Martha--and certainly does not appear to blame her--yet, in praising the one sister, He implies that the other is inferior. He also shows that 'Martha's portion' can be taken away (for bodily ministry cannot last forever with a person), but teaches that 'Mary's desire' can never have an end."[5]

From all the above evidence, it can clearly be seen that this Gospel reading concerning Mary of Bethany was intentionally chosen to illustrate Mary the Theotokos who, from her infancy, always chose the good part, delighting in the words of God.

Epilogue:
The THEOTOKOS as Mediatress

+ + +

"Thy name, O Mary, is a precious ointment,
which breathes forth the fragrance of divine grace.
Let this ointment of salvation
enter the innermost recesses of our souls."
Saint Ambrose (339-397).[1]

What then of Mary Theotokos as Mediatress? What is the significance of Orthodox Christians chanting hymns such as the following from the *Paracletike*: *Unto thee do I ever ascribe my salvation; in thee do I hope to be saved, O all-holy Virgin. Do thou, therefore, snatch me out of every harm, corruption, passion, and unexpected evil?*[2] The answer arises from the life and practice of the Church, for historical evidence will be found in the inspired writings, hymns and iconography of Orthodoxy. All the saints held the common truths of the faith about the Theotokos and cherished devotion towards her. In each case greater or less emphasis arises from temperament, character, vocation and circumstance. Yet, there was always a universal consciousness of her personality and power.

A mediator or mediatress, in religion, is one who acts as an intermediary between God and man. Christ is the perfect Mediator as the Son of God and true Man, for He partakes of both natures. Saint John Chrysostom (354-407) comments that "Christ would no longer be a mediator, if He were connected with one (nature) but separated from the other."[3]

507

However, Christ also works and rests in His saints, thus, vouchsafing them the role of mediator or mediatress. Therefore, when we read the words of St. Paul that "there is one God, and one *(eis)* Mediator between God and men, the man Christ Jesus; Who gave Himself a ransom for all" [1 Tim. 2:5-6], we understand the use of the word "one" as emphasizing our Saviour's transcendence as a Mediator. The word "one" was translated from the Greek word *eis* meaning the numeral "one", and not *monos* meaning "only" or "alone". We also must understand the context of this verse by the Apostle's verses preceding it. Saint John Chrysostom remarks that the divine Paul is referring to the salvation of the heathen,[4] when he wrote: "(God, our Saviour), Who will have all men to be saved and come unto the knowledge of the truth" [1 Tim. 2:3-4]. Hence, when the Apostle is speaking of the perfect Mediator, he is referring to the unique value of Christ's redemptive death. Christ, since He is true God and true Man, is the only ransom for the Jew and Gentile alike.

Saint Peter, also referring to Christ's relationship with the uninitiated, says that "Neither is there salvation in any other; for there is no other name under heaven given among men, whereby we must be saved" [Acts 4:12].

Therefore, the practice of addressing the Theotokos as a mediatress or the saints as intercessors, need not be impeded by either text, since their relationship is to those of the Church. Hence, throughout Church history, to Mary Theotokos, the word mediatress or *mesitevsasa* (in Latin translations, mediatrix) will be used.

Thus, we chant to the Virgin-Mother: *We praise thee, the Mediatress for the salvation of our race, O Virgin Theotokos; for thy Son and our God hath deigned to endure the Passion in the flesh taken from thee, and hath redeemed us from corruption, since He is the Friend of man.*[5]

O MISTRESS OF CREATION
MAKE ENTREATY UNTO THE ONE BORN OF THEE!

How do the holy Fathers of the Church perceive the Theotokos as an intercessor? We shall examine, chronologically and briefly, a few of their writings.

The First One Thousand Years A.D.

Saint Irenaeus (d. after 193), in a highly rhetorical passage, writes also that the Virgin Mary had become the

508

patroness or advocate *(advocata)* of the virgin Eve.[6] "For what the virgin Eve had bound fast through unbelief, this did the Virgin Mary set free through faith."[7]

The corpus of Mariology is substantial in the works of **St. Ambrose**. Studying the Greek Fathers, he saw the link between the incarnation and redemption when he wrote: "Alone Mary has worked the salvation of the world and conceived the redemption of all."[8] Through her, "salvation was given to all."[9] Saint Ambrose also attributes to Mary a share in the overthrow of satan's power, saying, "Mary, who gave birth to the Victor, has defeated thee (satan). Without her virginity being lessened, she brought forth Him Who, when crucified, would defeat thee and, when dead, would bring thee into subjection. Thou art conquered today so that the woman should defeat his attacks."[10]

By the fourth century the Eve-Mary doctrine was expressed by the great biblical scholar, **Jerome** (347-420) thus: "Death *through* Eve, life *through* Mary."[11] The use of the preposition *through*, in all languages hereafter, will always have some reference to a mediating role.

In the greatest Marian sermon of antiquity, the pre-eminent doctor of the Church, **St. Cyril of Alexandria** (+444), the dominant figure at the Council of Ephesus, related the mediation of the Virgin to her office as Mother of God and her relationship with the Most Holy Trinity. "Rejoice, Mary Theotokos, venerable treasure of the whole world, light unextinguished, crown of virginity, scepter of Orthodoxy, indestructible temple, which contains the uncontainable...it is through thee that the Holy Trinity is glorified and adored; through thee, the precious Cross is venerated and adored throughout the whole world; through thee that heaven is in gladness, that angels and archangels rejoice, and that demons are put to flight; through thee that the tempter, the devil, is cast down from heaven; through thee that the fallen creature is raised up to heaven; through thee that all creation, once imprisoned in idolatry, has reached knowledge of the truth, that the faithful obtain baptism and the oil of joy, churches have been founded in the whole world, and that peoples are led to conversion."[12] The reason is that, through Mary, the only Son of God shone as a light on those who are in darkness and the shadow of death. And thereafter, "...the

Apostles announced salvation to the nations, and the dead are raised...."[13]

Saint Proclos, Patriarch of Constantinople (+446), spoke of Mary as "the glory of virgins, the joy of mothers, the support of the faithful, the diadem of the Church, the model of the true Faith, the seat of piety, the dwelling-place of the Holy Trinity."[14] Elsewhere he writes that she is "the nuptial chamber wherein the Logos wedded the flesh, the burning bush of nature, which did not burn in the fire of divine travail, the handmaid and Mother, the Virgin and heaven, the only bridge between God and man, the fearful web of providence whereunto was the garment of unity ineffably woven."[15]

In the sixth century, **St. Romanos the Melodist** (c.490-c.556), sets the doctrine of Mary's mediation in a distinctive relationship to Adam and Eve. He dramatizes figuratively the Theotokos speaking to Adam and Eve: *End your lamentations, I shall be your intercessor (presbis) before my Son. And restrain your tears, receive me as your mediatress with Him Who is born of me.*[16]

This theme is also brought out in every Resurrection Matins service in the *Evlogitaria: By giving birth to the Giver of Life, O Virgin, thou didst rescue Adam from sin, and thou didst grant Eve joy instead of sorrow; for the God and Man Who was incarnate of thee guided back to life those that had fallen away therefrom.*[17]

Again, the great Byzantine melodist Romanos then writes: *For I (Theotokos) am not simply Thy Mother, O merciful Saviour,...but I supplicate Thee in behalf of all men. Thou hast made me the pride and boast of all my race* [cf. Judith 15:9-11]; *for Thy universe considers me as a powerful protection, rampart and stay. May those that were cast from the joys of Paradise look to me that I may direct them to a perception of all things. Grant this to me who gave birth to Thee, a newborn babe, the pre-eternal God.*[18]

The *Akathist Hymn*, has been assigned by some to St. Romanos; others to Patriarch Sergios of Constantinople (7th c.)[19] or George from Antioch in Pisidia (610-640), a deacon under Patriarch Sergios, who was distinguished for composing iambic verses. The inspired hymnographer of the *Akathist Hymn* uses language both profound and imaginative. Pure lyricism, philosophical thought, and theological and dogmatical teaching are all part of these verses written in honor of the Theotokos who miraculously preserved the great city of Constantinople from attack by Arians and Persian barbarians. It was adopted for liturgical use wherein it expresses the idea that Mary is one *through whom* certain spiritual benefactions were achieved. *Rejoice, thou through whom creation is renewed....Rejoice, thou through whom and in whom the Creator is adored....Rejoice, heavenly ladder, through whom God has descended....Rejoice, bridge leading those on earth to heaven....Rejoice, supplication before the Righteous Judge....O thou who didst bear the world's Salvation, through thee are we raised from earth unto heaven's heights....Rejoice, O fiery pillar that doth lead all mortal men to the life on high.*

In the eighth century, the great trio of Eastern Fathers, Saints Andrew of Crete, John of Damascus and Germanos of Constantinople taught the doctrine of Mary's mediation in an explicit and plenary manner.

 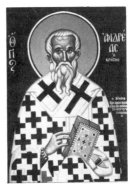

Saint Andrew of Crete (660-740) called her, "Mediatress of the law and grace," saying also, "She is the mediation between the sublimity of God and the abjection of the flesh, and becomes the Mother of her Maker."[20] He also wrote the *prosomion* (a special hymn) to her that begins, as follows: *Rejoice with God, ranking second only to the Trinity.*[21]

Saint John of Damascus (+c.750) called Mary "Mediatress". He introduces the concept with a favorite Old Testament image which he liked to apply to her: Jacob's ladder. Addressing the Theotokos, he wrote: "By fulfilling the office of Mediatress *(Mesitevsasa)*, and being made the ladder of God descending to us, that He should assume our weak nature, and join and unite it to Him...thou hast brought together what had been separated."[22] He also said that "To serve Mary and to be her courtier is the greatest honor one can possibly possess, for to serve the Queen of Heaven is already to reign there, and to live under her commands is more than to govern."[23]

Saint Germanos (635-733), who spoke of himself as our Lady's slave *(doulos)*,[24] is the doctor of the Theotokos' universal mediation. In his oration on the Annunciation, he calls her "truly a good Mediatress for all sinners."[25] In his second homily on the Dormition, he writes: "Man was made spiritual when thou, O Theotokos, became the dwelling of the Holy Spirit. No one is filled with the knowledge of God save through thee, O most holy one. No one is saved except though thee, O

Theotokos; no one is ransomed save through thee, Mother of God *(Theomeetros)*; no one secured a gift of mercy save through thee, who holds God;...thou cannot fail to be heard, since God, as to everything, through everything, and in everything, behaves towards thee as His true and unsullied Mother...in thee all peoples of the earth have obtained blessing, for there is no place where thy name is not held in honor."[26]

Saint Theodore of Studion (c.759-826), who defended the sacred icons of the Theotokos, has a devotion that is evident in his homilies and anti-iconoclastic writings. "For having left the body she is

with us in spirit, and, entering heaven, she puts demons to flight, becoming our mediatress with the Lord. Formerly death, by the ancestress Eve, made entry and held the world in its sway; now having assailed her blessed Daughter, it has been routed, being overcome from the very point whence formerly it had taken its power."[27] Mary enjoys in heaven royal power "which through her authority as Mother she obtained from the Lord of all."[28]

Saint Tarasios (+806), Patriarch of Constantinople, clearly taught Mary's role in the universal salvation, for she was the "abyss of miracles, the fount of good things, the untarnished supply of riches."[29]

She is "the cause of salvation of all mortals," "the reconciler in the second regeneration with God," "the restoration of the whole world," "the expiation of Adam's curse, price of Eve's debt," and "the one who frees us from the curse pronounced against our first parent Eve." Consequently, she is Queen of the whole universe, "the Mediatress of all who are under heaven."[30]

Saint George, Metropolitan of Nicomedia (+c.880), a friend of St. Photios, when writing about the Virgin's intercession, chants, *Lady, I dedicate to thee my understanding and my counsel, my expectation, my body, soul and spirit. Deliver and save me from grievous adversaries and temptations, and from every threat to come;*[31] and *O Virgin, who hast born the Light that no man can approach, with thy light-saving radiance disperse the darkness of my soul: take me by the hand and guide my life into the paths of salvation.*[32]

The liturgical poet, **Joseph the Hymnographer** (816-886), hymns, *O Theotokos, thou art more glorious than the cherubim and seraphim and all the heavenly hosts. With them, O Virgin undefiled, entreat Him Who took flesh from thee, God the Word from the Father without beginning, that we may all be counted worthy of eternal blessings.*[33]

And the same wrote: *O pure Virgin, through thee, our earthly and corruptible nature is made heavenly: By thy fervent intercession, bring our prayers and petitions before thy God and King of all men.*[34]

Saint Photios (+c.897), Patriarch of Constantinople, a scholar of encyclopedic knowledge, speaks of the Theotokos in his homilies writing: "The Lord is with thee, delivering through thee the whole race from its ancient sorrow and curse;"[35] and "...for she, the descendant, was able to repair the ancestral defeat, who brought forth the Saviour of our race by a husbandless birth, and molded His body."[36]   In the saint's homily, entitled *Attack of the Russians*, he prays to the Theotokos with characteristic Byzantine trust in the Mediatress: "Let us set her up as our mediatress *(mesitis)* before her Son our God, and make her the witness and surety of our compact; she who conveys our  requests and rains down the mercy of her Offspring, and scatters the cloud of enemies, and lights up for us the dawn of salvation."[37]

The Holy Protection of the Mother of God

The Feast of the Holy Protection (in Greek, *Aghia Skepi*; in Slavonic, *Pokrov)* or Veil, celebrated on the 1st of October, commemorates the appearance of the Mother of God in the Church of Blachernae in Constantinople in the tenth century.   The Russian Church has always celebrated this festival with particular solemnity.   The account of the appearance is to be found in the life of St. Andrew (+956), the Fool for Christ, whose memory is celebrated by the Church on the 2nd of October and the 28th of May.   At that time, in the Church of Blachernae, the Panagia's robe, veil and part of her girdle (belt) were preserved.   During the office of the vigil, at 4:00 a.m., St. Andrew and his disciple, St. Epiphanios, beheld a majestic Woman advancing towards the ambo, escorted by St. John the Baptist and St. John the Theologian, and several other saints with the choirs of angels. On reaching the center of the church, the Theotokos knelt down and remained long in prayer, and her face was bathed in tears.   When she prayed yet again before the altar table, she removed her veil which shone like lightning.[38]

A Matins sticheron of this Feast exclaims: *As they beheld the Queen of all,...with outstretched arms in the air, she prayed for the peace of the world, the confirmation of Orthodox Christians, and the salvation of our souls.*[39]

Then with great solemnity, she held her veil high up and extended it over all the people present in the church.

However, only the holy Andrew and Epiphanios were vouchsafed to behold her visitation and the veil that shone like the glory of God. The covering was over the people for a considerable time, and as long as she was present it was visible. When she departed it became invisible, but the grace of this visitation remained with the people. The invisible protection of the Mother of God, interceding with her Son for the whole universe, protection that St. Andrew could contemplate in the form of a veil covering the faithful, constitutes the central idea of this festival.[40]

The icon of our Lady's Protection portrays her standing on a small cloud, hovering in the air above the crowd of faithful. Clothed in her traditional *maphorion*, she has both her arms outstretched in a gesture of prayer, which expresses her prayer of intercession on our behalf. Again we see our beloved melodist, St. Romanos, from the sixth century clothed in his deacon's dalmatic holding an open role of the Nativity kontakion. The anachronism is easily explained: the memory of St. Romanos, celebrated on the 1st of October, coincides with the festival of the Protection. One may see St. Andrew and his disciple, the witnesses of the appearance, standing at the right of the ambo.[41]

The Second Thousand Years A.D.

The summit of Byzantine Marian theology, however, was to be found among the Palamites. The mediation of the Theotokos was part of their vision of the cosmic Christ, the center and purpose of creation. The incarnation was brought about in her and by her; the person of Christ is inseparable from that of His Mother.

Saint Gregory of Palamas (+1359) saw her "standing alone between God and the whole human race," making God the Son of man and men the sons of God. He is not thinking of the person of Mary taken by herself but of "her who begat God". Thus, for St. Gregory and for the whole tradition of the Orthodox Church, this Mariology asserts both the full divinity and full humanity of Christ; without Mary, this union could not have been realized in the person of Jesus.

Thus St. Gregory will write that the Mother of God "is the source and root of the race of liberty;"[42] her body, the temple of God, is "the saving balsam for our race;"[43] and "the Virgin Mother alone dwells on the frontier between created and uncreated natures, and those who know God recognize also in her the habitation of the infinite;"[44]

However, the Palamite, **St. Theophanes** (+1381), Bishop of Nicaea, also known as "the branded" with his brother Theodore, is unequalled in all literature as an exponent of the Theotokos' universal mediation. His critics have accused him of some of the most daring synthesis ever proposed on the primacy of Mary and her relationship to the Trinity.

To St. Theophanes, he sees the entire cosmos turning around the Theotokos, when he wrote: "It cannot happen that anyone, of angels or of men, can come otherwise, in any way whatsoever to participation in the divine gifts flowing from what has been divinely assumed, from the Son of God, save through His Mother."[45]

Saint Theophanes used the metaphor of the neck to express her place in the Mystical Body: "Since then the Head of every principality, power and of our Church is the only way which leads to the Father, so that the sacred neck is the only way leading to the Head of all."[46] Mary Theotokos, for this brilliant confessor and hymnographer, was the "dispenser and distributor of all the wondrous uncreated gifts of the divine Spirit."[47] As the fountain, the beginning of life, "she receives wholly the hidden grace of the Spirit and amply distributes it and shares it with others, thus manifesting it."[48]   All things were created for her and are governed through her.   No one attains the fullness and the goal of life in Christ "without her cooperation or without the Spirit's help."

He then speaks of her spiritual motherhood over us, saying:

"The Mother of Him--Who through His unspeakable goodness willed to be called our Brother--is the dispenser and distributor of all the wondrous uncreated gifts of the divine Spirit, which make us Christ's brothers and co-heirs, not only because she is granting the gifts of her natural Son to His brothers in grace, but also because she is bestowing them on these as her own true sons, though not by ties of nature but of grace."[49]

A latter-day father, **St. John of Kronstadt** (1829-1908), writes in his memoirs, the following: "Holy Virgin, our Lady! Thou, whose love towards Christians surpasses the love of every earthborn mother, of every wife, hear our prayers and save us! May we constantly remember thee! May we always pray fervently to thee!   May we ever undoubtingly and unfailingly take refuge beneath thy holy protection!"[50]

Saint John also writes that it was "through the incarnation of the Word that the all-holy Virgin has been given to us as an all-powerful intercessor, who protects us from sins, misfortunes and disasters. Praying for us day and night, our Queen, whose power no enemy visible or invisible can withstand, truly is our mother by grace in accordance with the words uttered by Christ on the Cross to the beloved disciple, 'Behold thy Mother!' and to her, 'Behold thy son!'"[51]

In another place, St. John writes that "she has the all-merciful power of driving away from us, at her sign, the sub-celestial spirits of evil--those ever-vigilant and ardent sowers of enmity and malice among men.

"Yet, to all who have recourse with faith and love to her powerful protection, she soon speedily gives both peace and love....She is the highest of all creatures, the Mediatrix for the whole race of mankind. Strive to train thyself in the spirit of humility, for she herself was more humble than any mortal, and only looks lovingly upon the humble. Recall what she said to her cousin Elisabeth, 'He hath regarded the low estate of His handmaiden'" [Lk. 1:48].[52]

He also writes: "We pray to the all-merciful and most pure Mother of God--and she prays for us. We glorify her--she who is above all glory--and she prepares eternal glory for us. We often say to her, 'Rejoice," and she asks her Son and God, 'My beloved Son, give them everlasting joy in return for greeting me with joy.'"[53]

SUMMARY

The Eastern Fathers, using the Apostle Paul's word *mesitis*, borrowed it without stirring the slightest fear that the dignity of the One Mediator or *Mesitis* would be compromised. Although throughout, the context of the word varied, certain essential aspects are clearly distinguishable: The role of the Theotokos in the work of salvation and her ceaseless and heavenly activity on our behalf.

The following well-known hymns bring out her role:

Seeing that we have no boldness on account of our many sins, do thou beseech Him that was born of thee, O Virgin Theotokos; for the supplication of the Mother availeth much to win the Master's favor.[54]

As the treasury of our salvation, O all-hymned one, do thou lead forth from the pit and abyss of offenses them that hope in thee; for those that were guilty because of sin hast thou saved by giving birth to Salvation, O thou who before childbirth wast virgin, and in childbirth wast virgin, and after childbirth against remainest virgin.[55]

No mediation is greater than that made in our behalf by the Theotokos, the Mother of all the saints, living and dead. Orthodox Christians also honor the saints as vessels of grace and examples for us. We seek their mediation, for the fervent prayer of the righteous availeth much before God [Jas. 5:16]. Hence, in the kontakion for "All Saints", we chant: *To Thee, the Planter of Creation, the world doth offer the God-bearing martyrs as the first-fruits of nature. By their supplications, preserve Thy Church in perfect peace, through the Theotokos, O greatly Merciful One."*[56]

Saint John of Damascus writes that "The Master Christ, made the relics of saints to be fountains of salvation to us, pouring forth manifold blessings and abounding in the oil of sweet fragrance. Let none doubt it.....Therefore...in psalms and hymns and spiritual songs, in contrition and pity for the needy, let us believers venerate the saints, as by this God is most worshipped. Let us raise monuments to them and visible icons, let us ourselves become, through emulation of their lives, living icons and monuments of them. Let us give honor to her who bore God as being strictly and truly the Mother of God...the Prophet John as Forerunner and Baptizer...martyrs...holy Fathers, the God-possessed ascetics...the patriarchs...prophets...in order that we may be sharers with them in their crowns of glory."[57]

PLACEMENT OF THE ICONS OF THE
VIRGIN THEOTOKOS

The special importance given to the universally accepted icons of the Virgin, by placing them to the right of Christ, finds its justification in Scripture. The Virgin Mary is said to have "found favor with God" [Lk. 1:30] and to have been "overshadowed" by the power of the Highest [Lk. 1:35], to have miraculously conceived and given birth to the Son of God, Jesus Christ.[58] And, "at Thy right hand stood the Queen" [Ps. 44:8].

In most Orthodox Church domes, the Mother of God is depicted just beneath and to the east of the main icon of Christ, the *Pantocrator*, "Ruler of All" or "Almighty". In an attitude of prayer, she is on the same plane as the angelic host and St. John the Baptist. If there is another dome in the same church, she is depicted holding Christ as a child. This too is justified in the hymnography of the Church, when we chant the composition of the Archangel Gabriel and St. Cosmas the Poet (7th-8th c.), *It is truly meet to call thee blest, the Theotokos, the ever-blessed and all-immaculate and Mother of our God. More honorable than the Cherubim, and beyond compare more glorious than the Seraphim, thee who without corruption gavest birth to God the Word, the very Theotokos, thee do we magnify.*

The Icon of the Platytera

Second only in importance to the central dome of a church, is the icon in the main eastern apse.

In accordance with ancient tradition, the dominant figure in the semi-dome is that of the Virgin-Mother, known as the *Platytera ton uranon* or "She who is more spacious than the heavens."

The heavens were astonished and stood in awe, and the ends of the earth, O Maiden, were sore amazed, for God appeared bodily to mankind as very man. And lo, thy womb hath proved to be vaster and more spacious than heaven's heights. For this, O Theotokos, the choirs and assemblies of men and angels magnify thy name.[59]

In this icon she is depicted in one of two ways: (1) She is shown half-stature with her arms outstretched in prayer. In front of her is the Christ child, Who is blessing with two hands. (2) The Theotokos is shown enthroned, holding the Christ child in her lap. He is blessing with His right hand and holding a scroll in His left Hand. This icon may also have full-length angels on either side. Often the Theotokos will be flanked by the Archangels Michael and Gabriel, to her right and left respectively.

The placement of the Platytera icon in this section of the church, which unites the roof of the church with the floor, allegorically symbolizes her uniting heaven and earth. She hovers over the earth, as it were between heaven and earth. And as we recite in the *Akathist Hymn*, the Theotokos is *the heavenly ladder, whereby God has descended* and the *bridge leading those on earth to heaven*.[60] Thus, the Theotokos stands between heaven and earth as the intercessor of our race by means of the divine Child in her arms.[61]

Also, the rubrics in the celebration of the Eucharist contribute to her placement in the main eastern apse. During the Divine Liturgy, the celebrant, at various times, will face and bow before the eastern wall or apse, uttering the following prayer: "Blessed art Thou on the throne of Thy glory." Thus, the celebrant is addressing Christ and His "throne", the Virgin.

The Icon of the Deisis

The word *deisis* in Greek means entreaty. Thus this icon of entreaty frequently is seen with Christ enthroned and on either side of Him are the Virgin to His right and St. John the Baptist to His left, both in postures of supplication, as intercessors.

Later icons will depict others in the company of the Virgin and the Baptist interceding for humanity at the judgment seat of Christ. In the present icon, we see the Virgin-Mother as the Bride of God and St. John the Baptist as the "friend of the Bridegroom" [Jn. 3:29], who in the plan of salvation had a central part to play.

In this icon, Christ is, at times, seen in the sacerdotal vestments of an archbishop. He is wearing a *Sticharion* (Dalmatic), *Epitrachilion* (Stole), *Phelonion* (Chasuble) and *Omophorion* (Pall or Bishop's Stole), thus emphasizing His liturgical office of the "Great High Priest."

When the two brothers and disciples of Christ, SS James and John requested of Christ, "Grant unto us that we may sit, one at Thy right hand, and the other at Thy left hand, in Thy glory" [Mk. 10:37], St. John Chrysostom comments that Christ wished to show His two disciples that they were not requesting something spiritual, and that if they had known what it was they asked, they would not have ever dared to ask. He immediately draws them away from notions of crowns and honors. He speaks to them of struggles, of the sweat of toils. This is not the time for rewards, neither shall My glory now be revealed; the present hour is one of slaughter, of wars, and of dangers. They, in fervor of spirit, promise themselves to Him immediately, not knowing really what they said. Nevertheless, He foretold great things of them, "But to sit at My right hand and at my left hand is not Mine to give; but it shall be given to them for whom it is prepared." [Mk. 10:40].[62]

Enthroned as Lord, thy Son hath placed thee (O Virgin) at His right hand, for thou art arrayed in the gold-embroidered raiment of the holy virtues; and He giveth thee the honor that is due thee, O immaculate one.[63]

The Odegitria Icon

The reverence and honor rendered to the Theotokos is not idolatrous. She is not the Lord, but the Handmaid of the Lord. She is not the King, but the Throne of the King. She is not the self-illumined Sun, but the Moon which reflects the Sun. She is not the Fountain, but the Conduit. She is not the bank of the River, but the Bridge which carries people to the other side. She is not the One who saves, but she is the one who leads the people to Him Who saves; thus she is aptly named "the Directress" or *Odegitria*.[64]

This type of image, according to tradition, was originally painted from life by the Evangelist Luke. The blessed Virgin bears the Christ child on her left arm, and supplicates and points with her right hand to Christ, Who said of Himself, "I am the way" [Jn. 14:6]. This kind of depiction never appears without Christ, thus conforming to Orthodox belief, which stipulates that the Theotokos is the "Pointer of the Way" to heaven or as a "Preparer of the Way to Salvation" in conjunction with her Son.

It is this style of icon, on the iconostasion, where the Mother of God stands before us as a symbol and type of the Church and the Christian vocation: to point away from self to Christ. The Virgin and the Church point to Him with holiness, gentleness, love, firmness and inner conviction.[65]

LIST OF ICONS, ILLUSTRATIONS, LAYOUTS AND MAPS

528

529

XXIX. THE THEOTOKOS IS BODILY TRANSLATED

APPENDICES

EPILOGUE: THE THEOTOKOS AS MEDIATRESS

BACK OF BOOK

533

END NOTES

PREFACE

1. *De Virginibus*, II, 2,15.

2. *On the Incomprehensibility of God.*

3. M.D. Toal, D.D., *The Sunday Sermons of the Great Fathers*, 3rd ed., vol. I, (Chicago: Henry Regnery Co., 1964), 168-169.

4. Saint John of Damascus, *Exposition of the Orthodox Faith*, Book III, The Nicene and Post-Nicene Fathers of the Christian Church, Second Series, vol. IX, trans. by Rev. S.F.D. Dalmond, D.D., F.E.I.S. (Grand Rapids, MI: Wm. B. Eerdmans Pub. Co., 1976), ch. xii.

5. Henry Barclay Swete, D.D., F.B.A., *An Introduction to The Old Testament in Greek*, Rev. by R.R. Ottley, M.A. (Peabody, MA: Hendrickson Pub., 1989).

6. Savas J. Savas, *Hymnology of the Eastern Orthodox Church*, (MA: Byzantine Melodies, 1983).

7. Saint Romanos the Melodist, *Introduction*, Kontakia of Romanos, Byzantine Melodist, vol. I, trans. and annot. by Marjorie Carpenter (MO: University of Missouri Press, 1970), xix.

8. After the iconoclastic controversy, these kontakia were revived and became a part of the later canon. In time, the kontakia were shortened and they lost their homiletic character and dialogue. Scholars suggest that the manner of its delivery resembled the recitative of an oratorio. It is not within the scope of this work to discuss Byzantine music in detail. This prolific writer-composer was considered inspired.

Of the genuine and extant kontakia, we clearly see that he used biblical sources for most of the kontakia and in several instances, apocryphal sources, such as the *Protoevangelium*. One must admire the manner in which a point in theology is woven into a dramatic situation and given poetic flavor by the use of antithesis and figure of speech. The poet-preacher presents a very simple theology in his kontakia. His work reflects the preoccupation of the sixth-century Greek Christian with theological disputes. However, he always supported the Orthodox point of view. Within the kontakia that we have incorporated into our work, Romanos' works often subtly or openly refute Arianism, Docetism, Nestorianism and Monophysitism. Ibid., i.

9. Leonid Ouspensky and Vladimir Lossky, *The Meaning of Icons*, trans. by G.E.H. Palmer and E. Kadloubovsky (Crestwood: St. Vladimir's Seminary Press, 1983, repr.), 145.

10. A group of early Christian papyri form the collection of M. Martin Bodmer of Geneva and began to be published in 1954. Among this collection are Greek and Coptic texts of biblical documents, such as the *Gospel of John* in Greek, and also *Apocrypha* such as the *Nativity of Mary*. Merrill C. Tenney and Steven Barabas, eds., *Pictorial Encyclopedia of the Bible*, vol. 1-5 (Grand Rapids: Regency Reference Library & Zondervan Publishing House, 1975), 632.

The oldest manuscript of apocryphal work is the Papyrus Bodmer V, published in 1958, and dated by its editor, on grounds of its paleography to the third century, the first half of it possibly the fourth century. See, E. de Strycker, *La forme la plus ancienne du Protoevangile de Jacques* (Brussels, 1961), 14, n.3.

In addition there are versions in Syriac, Armenian, Ethiopian, Georgian and other languages. The manuscripts have been exhaustively examined by de Strycker, who concludes a remarkable homogeneity and continuity. None-theless, the document has been in existence long enough for error to creep in, though most are superficial.

A critical edition was made by Fr. de Strycker on the basis of three papyri and several manuscripts from the Syrian, Sahidic, Armenian and Georgian versions. It was then believed that the whole work was from 150-200 A.D. However, this does not mean that the book itself was already in existence. De Strycker claims that the Bodmer text is not the original version, but an abridgement that presupposes a longer version. Tenney and Barabas, *Pictorial Encyclopedia of the Bible*, vol. 3, pp. 402-403; de Strycker, pp. 403-404.

11. Saint Cyril of Jerusalem, *Catechesis IV, On The Ten Doctrines: Of The Holy Scriptures, Vol. 1*, The Fathers of the Church, vol. 61, trans. by Leo P. McCauley, S.J. and Anthony A. Stephenson (Washington, D.C.: The Catholic University of America Press, 1969), 137.

12. PL 30, 307ff.

13. Prof. M. B. Riddle, D.D., *Apocrypha of New Testament: Introductory Notice*, The Ante-Nicene Fathers, The Writings of the Fathers Down to A.D. 325, vol. VIII (Grand Rapids, MI: Wm. B. Eerdmans Publishing Co., 1986), 352.

14. PG 97, cols. 881-913.

15. PG 98, cols. 320-340.

16. PG 10, cols. 1172-77.

17. On the use of *Apocrypha* by George of Nicomedia [cf. L. Brehier, *Les miniatures des 'homilies' du moine Jacques* (quaest, 151, PG 101, col. 813).

18. PG 93, cols. 1453 sq.; Saint Photios, *Homily V: The Annunciation*, The Homilies of Photius, Patriarch of Constantinople, trans. by Cyril Mango (Cambridge, MA: Harvard University Press, Dumbarton Oaks Studies Three, 1958), 111-112.

19. Constantine D. Kalokyris, "The Content of Orthodox Iconography: Art of High Theology," *The Essence of Orthodox Iconography*, trans. by Peter A. Chamberas (Brookline: Holy Cross School of Theology, 1971), 20-21.

20. John Baggley, *Doors of Perception* (Crestwood, NY: St. Vladimir's Seminary Press, 1988), 53.

21. Ibid., p. 47.

22. Ibid., p. 23.

23. Ibid., p. 24.

24. Ibid., p. 36.

25. Andre Grabar, *Byzantine Painting*, trans. by Stuart Gilbert (NY: Rizzoli International Publications, Inc., 1979), 137.

26. Constantine D. Kalokyris, *Athos, Themes of Archaeology and Art* [in Greek and English] (Athens: Astir Publishing, Al. & E. Papademetriou, 1963), 324.

27. Grabar, loc. cit.

28. Megalynarion, Tone Plagal Fourth.

I. CONCEPTION BY RIGHTEOUS ANNA

1. *Homily 2, On the Birth of the Theotokos*, PG 96, 708.

2. *Sermon on the Theotokos at Her Presentation (or Entrance) to the Temple*, PG 98, 313.

3. *Homily on She Who Bloomed from a Barren Womb*, PG 107, 1.

4. *Homily 37 on the August Dormition of Our Most Immaculate Lady Theotokos and Ever-Virgin Mary* [in Greek], PG 151, 461.

5. Rev. Alexander Roberts, D.D. and James Donaldson, LL.D., eds., *Apocrypha of the New Testament: The Gospel of the Nativity of Mary*, The Ante-Nicene Fathers, The Writings of the Fathers down to A.D. 325, vol. VIII (Grand Rapids, MI: Wm. B. Eerdmans Pub. Co., 1986), 384.

6. Rev. Alexander Roberts, D.D. and James Donaldson, LL.D., eds., *Apocrypha of the New Testament: The Gospel of Pseudo-Matthew*, The Ante-Nicene Fathers, The Writings of the Fathers down to A.D. 325, vol. VIII (Grand Rapids, MI: Wm. B. Eerdmans Pub. Co., 1986), 368.

7. Rev. Alexander Roberts, D.D. and James Donaldson, LL.D., eds., *Apocrypha of the New Testament: The Protoevangelium of James*, The Ante-Nicene Fathers, The Writings of the Fathers down to A.D. 325, vol. VIII (Grand Rapids, MI: Wm. B. Eerdmans Pub. Co., 1986), 361.

8. Roberts and Donaldson, *The Gospel of Pseudo-Matthew*, p. 368; *The Gospel of the Nativity of Mary*, p. 384.

9. Bishop Nikolai Velimirovic, *The Prologue from Ochrid*, Pt. 3, Trans. by Mother Maria (Birmingham: Lazarica Press, 1986).

10. Blessed Archbishop John Maximovitch, *The Orthodox Veneration of the Mother of God*, trans. by Fr. Seraphim Rose, (Platina, CA: St. Herman of Alaska Brotherhood, 1987), 50.

11. *The Gospel of Pseudo-Matthew*, p. 369; *The Gospel of the Nativity of Mary*, p. 384.

12. Ibid.

13. Matins Kathisma, 9 Dec., Tone Four.

14. Roberts and Donaldson, *The Gospel of the Nativity of Mary*, loc. cit.

15. Saint Romanos the Melodist, *On the Nativity of the Virgin Mary*, Kontakia of Romanos, Byzantine Melodist, vol. II, trans. and annot. by Marjorie Carpenter (MO: University of Missouri Press, 1970), Tone Four, strophe 3, p. 3.

16. Roberts and Donaldson, *The Protoevangelium of James*, loc. cit.

17. Alpha House, *The Gospel of the Birth of Mary*," The Lost Books of the Bible (NY: Meridian Books, 1974), p. 18; Roberts and Donaldson, *The Protoevangelium of James*, loc. cit.

18. *The Gospel of Pseudo-Matthew*, loc. cit.; Blessed Archbishop John Maximovitch, *The Orthodox Veneration of the Mother of God*, p. 50.

19. *The Protoevangelium of James*, loc. cit.

20. *On the Nativity of the Virgin Mary*, Tone Four, strophe 2, p. 2.

21. Roberts and Donaldson, *The Protoevangelium of James*, p. 361.

22. Alpha House, *The Protoevangelion*, The Lost Books of the Bible (NY: Meridian Books, 1974), p. 26; Roberts and Donaldson, *The Protoevangelium of James*, pp. 361-362.

23. Ikos of Matinal Canons, 8 Sept.

24. Saint Ephraim Syrus, *Hymns on the Nativity, Hymn 14*, Nicene and Post-Nicene Fathers of the Christian Church, Second Series, vol. XIII, trans. by Rev. J.B. Morris, M.A. (Grand Rapids, MI: Wm. B. Eerdmans Pub. Co., 1976), p. 251.

25. Alpha House, *The Gospel of the Birth of Mary*, pp. 18-19; Roberts and Donaldson, *The Gospel of the Nativity of Mary*, loc. cit.

26. Roberts and Donaldson, *The Gospel of the Nativity of Mary*, pp. 384-385.

27. Ibid.

28. Alpha House, *The Gospel of the Birth of Mary,* p. 19; Roberts and Donaldson, *The Gospel of the Nativity of Mary,* p. 385.

29. Roberts and Donaldson, *The Protoevangelium of James,* p. 362.

30. Ibid.

31. Aposticha of Vespers, 9 Dec., Tone Plagal First.

32. Roberts and Donaldson, *The Gospel of the Nativity of Mary,* loc. cit.

33. Matins Canon, 9 Dec., Ode Four, Tone Four.

34. Alpha House, *The Gospel of the Birth of Mary,* p. 14; Roberts and Donaldson, *The Gospel of the Nativity of Mary,* loc. cit.

35. Kontakion of Feast, Tone Four.

36. Roberts and Donaldson, *The Gospel of Pseudo-Matthew,* p. 370; *The Protoevangelium of James,* loc. cit.

37. Roberts and Donaldson, *The Gospel of the Nativity of Mary,* loc. cit.

38. Dismissal Hymn of Feast, Tone Four.

39. Roberts and Donaldson, *The Gospel of the Nativity of Mary,* loc. cit.

40. *The Gospel of Pseudo-Matthew,* p. 370; *The Protoevangelium of James,* loc. cit.

41. Matins Canon, 21 Nov., Ode Six, Tone Four.

42. "Against the Collyridians", *Panarion,* taken from Blessed Archbishop John Maximovitch's, *The Orthodox Veneration of the Mother of God,* p. 40.

43. *Against the Antidikomarionites,* taken from Blessed Archbishop John Maximovitch's, op. cit., p. 41.

44. Great Vespers, 8 Sept., Tone Plagal Second by Sergios.

45. *Commentary on Luke,* ch. 2, taken from Blessed Archbishop John Maximovitch's, loc. cit.

46. Maximovitch, *Orthodox Veneration,* p. 45.

47. Matins Canon, 15 Aug., Ode Three, Tone Four.

48. Maximovitch, *Orthodox Veneration,* p. 44.

49. Ibid., p. 45.

II. THE NATIVITY OF THE VIRGIN MARY

1. *Theotokarion of St. Nikodemos* [in Greek] (Volos, GR: Sot. Schoina, 1979), Prosomion after Canon for Sunday, Tone Plagal First, Crete, p. 108.

2. *Vide St. Ambrose* in Luke PL 15 col. 1368, 42,42.

3. Matins Canon, Ode Six, Tone Plagal Four.   Unless otherwise specified hymns in this section are taken from the Feast on the 8th of September.

4. Saint Gregory Palamas, *Homily 37 on the August Dormition of Our Most Immaculate Lady Theotokos and Ever-Virgin Mary* [in Greek], *PG* 151, 461B.

5. *Homily 57,* ed. Oikonomos (1861), cited from John Meyendorff, *A Study of Gregory Palamas,* trans. from French by George Lawrence (London: Faith Press, 1964), 216. See also PG 151.

6. Saint Photios, *Homily IX: The Birth of the Virgin,* The Homilies of Photius, Patriarch of Constantinople, trans. by Cyril Mango (Cambridge, MA: Harvard University Press, Dumbarton Oaks Studies Three, 1958), 165.

7. Ibid., pp. 167-170.

8. Matins Canon, Ode One, Tone Plagal Four.

9. *Patrologia Orientalia,* vol. 3, 530.

10. *Nativity of the Virgin,* The Great Synaxaristes of the Orthodox Church [in Greek], 5th ed., vol. IX (Athens, 1978), 185.

11. Lity, Tone One.

12. Doxastikon of Small Vespers, Tone Two.

13. Matins Canon, Ode Seven, Tone Two.

14. Vespers Sticheron, Ideomelon, Tone Plagal Second.
15. Matins Sessional Hymn, Tone Four.
16. Vespers Doxastikon of the Aposticha, Tone Plagal Fourth.
17. Matins Sessional Hymn, Tone Four.
18. Matins Canon, Ode Four, Tone Plagal Four.
19. Vespers Sticheron, Ideomelon, Tone Plagal Second.
20. Rev. Alexander Roberts, D.D. and James Donaldson, LL.D., eds., *Apocrypha of the New Testament: The Protoevangelium of James*, The Ante-Nicene Fathers, The Writings of the Fathers down to A.D. 325, vol. VIII (Grand Rapids, MI: Wm. B. Eerdmans Pub. Co., 1986), 362.
21. Constantine Callinicos, *Our Lady the Theotokos*, trans. and rev. by Rev. George Dimopoulos (Upper Darby, PA: Christian Orthodox Editions, 1987), 12-13.
22. Saint John of Damascus, *Exposition of the Orthodox Faith, Book IV*, The Nicene and Post-Nicene Fathers of the Christian Church, Second Series, vol. IX, trans. by Rev. S.F.D. Dalmond, D.D., F.E.I.S. (Grand Rapids, MI: Wm. B. Eerdmans Pub. Co., 1976), ch. xiv.
23. Matins Canon, Ode Six, Tone Two; and Ode Three, Tone Two.
24. Vespers Aposticha, Tone Four.
25. Saint Romanos the Melodist, *On the Nativity of the Virgin Mary*, Kontakia of Romanos, Byzantine Melodist, vol. II, trans. and annot. by Marjorie Carpenter (MO: University of Missouri Press, 1970), strophe 6, pp. 3-4.
26. Matins Canon, Ode Four, Tone Plagal Four.
27. Kontakion of the Feast, Tone Four.
28. Matins Canon, Ode Seven, Tone Plagal Four.
29. Lity, Tone Two.
30. Matins Sessional Hymn, Tone Plagal Fourth.
31. Song 2:1.
32. *Sermon on the Birth of the Theotokos*, 6, 11. PG 96, 669-677.
33. Paul A. Underwood, *The Kariye Djami, Vol. 1, Historical Introduction and Description of the Mosaics and Frescoes*, Bollingen Series LXX (NY: Pantheon Books, 1966), 71.
34. Roberts and Donaldson, *The Protoevangelium of James*, loc. cit.
35. Ibid.
36. Ibid.
37. Lity, Tone Two by Anatolios.
38. *On the Nativity of the Virgin Mary*, Kontakia of Romanos, Tone Four, strophe 4, p. 3.
39. *The Protoevangelium of James*, loc. cit.
40. Vespers Aposticha, Tone Four.
41. *The Protoevangelium of James*, loc. cit.
42. Underwood, *The Kariye Djami*, 70.
43. Saint Romanos the Melodist, *On the Nativity of the Virgin Mary*, Tone Four, strophe 4, p. 3.
44. *The Protoevangelium of James*, loc. cit.
45. Ibid.
46. Underwood, *The Kariye Djami*, pp. 223-224.
47. *Homily IX: The Birth of the Virgin*, p. 172.
48. Ibid., pp. 174-175.
49. Ibid.
50. Ibid., p. 172.
51. Matins Canon, Ode Six, Tone Two.

III. ENTRANCE OF THE VIRGIN INTO THE TEMPLE

1. Vespers Sticheron, Prosomion, Tone One. Unless otherwise specified, hymns in this section are taken from the Feast on the 21st of November.
2. Leonid Ouspensky and Vladimir Lossky, *The Meaning of Icons*, trans. by G.E.H. Palmer and E. Kadloubovsky (Crestwood: St. Vladimir's Seminary Press, 1983, repr.), 153.
3. Vespers Sticheron, Prosomion, Tone Four.
4. Rev. Alexander Roberts, D.D. and James Donaldson, LL.D., eds., *Apocrypha of the New Testament: The Protoevangelium of James*, The Ante-Nicene Fathers, The Writings of the Fathers down to A.D. 325, vol. VIII (Grand Rapids, MI: Wm. B. Eerdmans Pub. Co., 1986), 362.
5. Ibid.
6. Matins Canon, Ode Four, Tone Two by Basil the Monk.
7. Matins Sessional Hymn, Tone Four.
8. Saint Gregory Palamas, *Homily 37 on the August Dormition of Our Most Immaculate Lady Theotokos and Ever-Virgin Mary* [in Greek], PG 151, 461C.
9. Roberts and Donaldson, *The Protoevangelium of James*, loc. cit.; Rev. Alexander Roberts, D.D. and James Donaldson, LL.D., eds., *Apocrypha of the New Testament: The Gospel of the Nativity of Mary*, The Ante-Nicene Fathers, The Writings of the Fathers down to A.D. 325, vol. VIII (Grand Rapids, MI: Wm. B. Eerdmans Pub. Co., 1986), 385.
10. Matins Canon, Ode One, Tone Two by Basil the Monk.
11. Vespers Aposticha, Tone Plagal First.
12. Matins Canon, 8 Sept., Ode Six, Tone Plagal Fourth.
13. Small Vespers Sticheron, Prosomion, Tone One.
14. Vespers Sticheron Prosomion, Tone Four.
15. Matins Sessional Hymn, Tone Four.
16. Vespers Sticheron, Prosomion, Tone One.
17. Matins Canon, Ode Eight, Tone Four.
18. Alpha House, *The Protoevangelion*, The Lost Books of the Bible (NY: Meridian Books, 1974), 28.
19. *Sermon at the Feast of the Presentation*, 5, PG 126, 136.
20. Matins Canon, Ode Nine, Tone Two by Basil the Monk.
21. Matins Canon, Ode Nine, Tone Four.
22. Sessional Hymn of Matins Canon, Tone Four.
23. Matins Canon, Ode Nine, Tone Four.
24. Matins Canon, Ode Four, Tone Four.
25. Ibid.
26. *Entrance of the Virgin in the Temple*, The Great Synaxaristes of the Orthodox Church [in Greek], 5th ed., vol. II (Athens, 1978), 577.
27. Matins Canon, Ode Three, Tone Two by Basil the Monk.
28. *Entrance of the Virgin in the Temple*, Great Synaxaristes, loc. cit.
29. Matins Canon, Ode Eight, Tone Four.
30. Ibid.
31. Vespers Sticheron, Prosomion, Tone Four.
32. Matins Canon, Ode Eight, Tone Four.
33. Ibid.
34. Matins Sessional Hymn, Tone Plagal Fourth.
35. *Entrance of the Virgin in the Temple*, Great Synaxaristes, loc. cit.
36. Matins Canon, Ode Five, Tone Four.
37. Vespers Aposticha, Tone Plagal First.
38. Alpha House, *The Gospel of the Birth of Mary*, The Lost Books of the Bible (NY: Meridian Books, 1974), 20.
39. Matins Canon, Ode Three, Tone Two by Basil the Monk.

40. Matins Canon, Ode Nine, Tone Two by Basil the Monk.

41. Bishop Nikolai Velimirovic, *The Prologue from Ochrid*, Pt. 3, Trans. by Mother Maria (Birmingham: Lazarica Press, 1986), 307.

42. *Hom. 53*, ed. Oikonomos (1861), pp. 145-6, cited in John Meyendorff, *A Study of Gregory Palamas*, trans. from French by George Lawrence (London: Faith Press, 1964), 233.

43. Matins Canon, Ode Nine, Tone Four.

44. Matins Canon, 15 Aug., Ode Six, Tone One.

45. To indicate that the "glory of the Lord" filled the temple after the installation of the ark and the holy vessels [3 Kings 8:11], the iconographer at the *Kariye Djami* had placed a large arc of heaven above the scene. Although the ray emitting therefrom is now nearly effaced, its path, can be traced Paul A. Underwood, *The Kariye Djami, Vol. 1, Historical Introduction and Description of the Mosaics and Frescoes*, Bollingen Series LXX (NY: Pantheon Books, 1966), 228-229.

46. Saturday Matins of the Third Week of Lent, Theotokion of Lauds, Tone Two.

47. Canon of the Akathist, Ode Five, Tone Four.

48. Josephus, *The Antiquities of the Jews*, The Works of Josephus, trans. by William Whiston, A.M. (Peabody, MA: Hendrickson Pub., 1988), XV.xi.6.

49. J.A. Thompson, *Handbook of Life in Bible Times* (Downers Grove, IL: Inter-Varsity Press, 1986), 347-349.

50. Ralph Gower, *The New Manners and Customs of Bible Times* (Chicago: Moody Press, 1987), 353.

51. Alfred Edersheim, M.A. Oxon., D.D., Ph.D., *The Life and Times of Jesus the Messiah* (McLean, VA: MacDonald Publishing Co.), 244-245; Gower, pp. 350-352.

52. James Hastings, M.A., D.D., *A Dictionary of the Bible*, vol. 4 (Peabody: Hendrickson Pub., 1988), 425.

53. Gower, pp. 343, 352-353; J.A. Thompson, *Handbook of Life in Bible Times*, 332; and, Merrill C. Tenney and Steven Barabas, eds., *Pictorial Encyclopedia of the Bible*, vol. 1 (Grand Rapids: Regency Reference Library & Zondervan Publishing House, 1975), 656.

54. J.A. Thompson, p. 341.

55. Ibid., p. 332.

56. Gower, p. 353.

57. The Moslem mosque, the Dome of the Rock, presently sits on the site.

58. Thompson, p. 333.

59. Gower, loc. cit.

60. Hastings, vol. 4, p. 715.

61. Edersheim, pp. 244-246.

62. Canon of the Akathist Hymn, Ode Three, Tone Four.

63. Josephus, *The Wars of the Jews*, The Works of Josephus, trans. by William Whiston, A.M. (Peabody, MA: Hendrickson Pub., 1988), V, v.5'.

64. Fragment 8, ed. W.W. Harvey, (1857), cited in Michael O'Carroll, C.S.Sp., comp. and ed., *Theotokos* 3rd ed. (Wilmington, DE: Michael Glazier, Inc., 1988), p. 50.

65. In *Patrologia Syriaca*, 23(22), *apud* Theodoret. "Dial I" in *Die griechischen christlichen Sriftsteller der ersten drei Jahrhunderte*, Leipzig-Berlin (1897), 1,2,147 (tr. adjusted by J.H. Crehan). Cf. *In Daniel 4*, in GCS, 1,1,246; *Sources Chretiennes*, (Lyons), 14, 188.

66. *De S. Maria Deip.*, in PG 93, 1464.

67. In *S. Mariam Deip.*, in *Patrologia Orientalia*, 19, 338.

68. *Hom. VI*, in PG 65, 720C.

540

69. *Hymns* in SC, 110,122-3], the *Akathist Hymn*, PG 92, 1345D.
70. *Homilies*, in PG 97, 869C.
71. *Homilies*, in PG 96, 724.
72. Gower, p. 369; Tenney and Barabas, pp. 306-307.
73. The word in Hebrew is translated as "almond". See, Jay P. Green, Sr., ed. and trans., *The Interlinear Hebrew-Aramaic Old Testament*, Vol. 1, 2nd ed. (Peabody, MA: Hendrickson Pub., 1985), 79. The *Septuagint* has translated the Hebrew word for "almond" into the Greek word *kareeon*, which is any kind of nut. Some versions of the Old Testament have translated this word as almond, walnut or chestnut. However, in this case, it is more properly an almond tree. See, Henry George Liddell and Robert Scott, compilers, *Greek-English Lexicon*, revised and augmented by Sir Henry Stuart Jones and Roderick McKenzie (Oxford at the Clarendon Press, 1968), 881.
74. *Poem 27(235,256,272,288)*, Ancient Christian Writers, vol. 40, pp. 279-280.
75. Hastings, vol. 1, p. 67; Tenney and Barabas, vol. 1, p. 108.
76. *Hom. 53*, ed. Oikonomos (1861), p. 157, cited in Meyendorff, *A Study of Gregory Palamas*, p. 233.
77. *Homily 53*, p. 161, cited in Meyendorff, pp. 233-234.
78. *Hom. 14*, col. 177A.
79. Matins Canon, Ode Five, Tone Four.
80. Matins Canon of Wednesday in the First Week of Great Lent, Ode Eight, Tone Two.
81. Canon of the Akathist, Ode Four, Tone Four.
82. Matins Canon, Ode Three, Tone Two by Basil the Monk.
83. Tenney and Barabas, vol. 1, p. 306.
84. Monday in the First Week of Great Lent, Matins Ode Eight, Tone Two.
85. Ode Three, Tone Four.
86. Tenney and Barabas, loc. cit.
87. Ibid., p. 307.
88. Tenney and Barabas, loc. cit.
89. Tenney and Barabas, vol. 4, p. 190.
90. Saint Ambrose, *Letter 19, To Felix* (dated c.380), The Fathers of the Church, vol. 26, trans. by Sister Mary Melchior Beyenka, O.P. (Washington, D.C.: The Catholic University Press, 1987; repr.), pp. 103-104.
91. Gower, p. 370; Tenney and Barabas, vol. 1, p. 306.
92. Gower, loc. cit.; Tenney and Barabas, vol. 1, p. 652; Ibid., vol. 2, p. 332; Ibid., vol. 5, p. 850; Thompson, loc. cit.
93. Matins Canon, Ode One, Tone Two by Basil the Monk.
94. "The Presentation of the Most Holy Theotokos in the Temple," *Orthodox Life*, no. 5 (Sept-Oct. 1971): 22.
95. Underwood, *The Kariye Djami*, p. 74.
96. Matins Canon, Ode Nine, Tone Four.
97. Matins Canon, 8 Sept., Ode One, Tone Plagal Fourth.
98. Doxastikon of Vespers, Tone Plagal Fourth.
99. Matins Canon, Ode Four, Tone Two by Basil the Monk.
100. Vespers Aposticha, Tone Plagal First.
101. Saint Romanos the Melodist, *On the Nativity of the Virgin Mary*, Tone Four, strophe 5, p. 3.
102. PG 98, 292-309.
103. Matins Canon, Ode Three, Tone Four.
104. *Homily 37*, PG 151, 461.
105. Matins Canon, Ode Six, Tone Two by Basil the Monk.

106. Kontakion, Tone Four.

107. Aposticha of Small Vespers, Tone Two.

108. Matinal Lauds, Tone One.

109. Matins Canon, Ode Three, Tone Four.

110. *Saint Paisios the Great*, (Jordanville, NY: Holy Trinity Monastery, 1983): 32.

111. *The Life and Struggles of Our Holy Mother Among the Saints, Golinduc, in Holy Baptism, Mary (13th of July)* in The Lives of the Saints of the Holy Land and the Sinai Desert, trans. by Holy Apostles Convent (Buena Vista, CO: Holy Apostles Convent Publications, 1988), 296.

112. Lity Doxastikon, Tone Plagal First, by Leo the Master.

113. Aposticha Doxastikon, Tone Plagal Second by Sergios of the Holy City.

114. *De Virginitate B. Mariae*, ed. by V. Blanco Garcia (Madrid, 1937, 2d ed. Saragossa, 1954): I, 61.

115. Matinal Laud, Tone One.

116. Matins Canon, Ode Five, Tone Four.

IV. THE VIRGIN GROWING UP IN THE TEMPLE

1. Rev. Alexander Roberts, D.D. and James Donaldson, LL.D., eds., *Apocrypha of the New Testament: The Gospel of Pseudo-Matthew*, The Ante-Nicene Fathers, The Writings of the Fathers down to A.D. 325, vol. VIII (Grand Rapids, MI: Wm. B. Eerdmans Pub. Co., 1986), 371.

2. Blessed Archbishop John Maximovitch, *The Orthodox Veneration of the Mother of God*, trans. by Fr. Seraphim Rose, (Platina, CA: St. Herman of Alaska Brotherhood, 1987), 50.

3. *Exposition of the Teaching of the Orthodox Church on the Mother of God*, cited in Blessed Archbishop John Maximovitch, *The Orthodox Veneration of the Mother of God*, pp. 50-51.

4. Cited in Blessed John Maximovitch, *The Orthodox Veneration of the Mother of God*, pp. 50-51.

5. Roberts and Donaldson, *The Gospel of Pseudo-Matthew*, loc. cit.

6. *The Gospel of Pseudo-Matthew*, loc. cit.

7. Paul A. Underwood, *The Kariye Djami, Vol. 1, Historical Introduction and Description of the Mosaics and Frescoes*, Bollingen Series LXX (NY: Pantheon Books, 1966), 76.

8. *The Gospel of Pseudo-Matthew*, loc. cit.

9. Blessed Archbishop John Maximovitch, *The Orthodox Veneration of the Mother of God*, p. 50.

10. *The Gospel of Pseudo-Matthew*, loc. cit.

11. *Hom. 53*, ed. Oikonomos (Athens, 1861), p. 169, cited in John Meyendorff, *A Study of Gregory Palamas*, trans. from French by George Lawrence (London: Faith Press, 1964), 235.

12. Leonid Ouspensky and Vladimir Lossky, *The Meaning of Icons*, trans. by G.E.H. Palmer and E. Kadloubovsky (Crestwood: St. Vladimir's Seminary Press, 1983, repr.), 153.

13. Ibid., pp. 153, 155.

14. Saint Ephraim Syrus, *Hymns on the Nativity, Hymn VI*, Nicene and Post-Nicene Fathers of the Christian Church, Second Series, vol. XIII, trans. by Rev. J.B. Morris, M.A. (Grand Rapids, MI: Wm. B. Eerdmans Pub. Co., 1976), 239.

15. Michael O'Carroll, C.S.Sp., comp. and ed., *Theotokos* 3rd ed. (Wilmington, DE: Michael Glazier, Inc., 1988), 385; Merrill C. Tenney and Steven Barabas, eds., *Pictorial Encyclopedia of the Bible*, vol. 5 (Grand Rapids: Regency Reference Library & Zondervan Publishing House, 1975), 3.

16. J.A. Thompson, *Handbook of Life in Bible Times* (Downers Grove, IL: Inter-Varsity Press, 1986), 847-848.

17. Thompson, p. 847.

18. James I. Packer, A.M., D. Phil., Merrill C. Tenney, A.M., Ph.D., William White, Jr., Th.M., Ph.D., eds., *The Bible Almanac* (Nashville: Thomas Nelson Publishers, 1980), 327.

19. Blessed Archbishop John Maximovitch, p. 51.

20. St. Ephraim, *Church Hymns*, 36, 2, in *Corpus Scriptorum Christianorum Orientalium*, (Louvain, 1903), 199, 88.

21. Saint John of Damascus, *Exposition of the Orthodox Faith, Book IV*, The Nicene and Post-Nicene Fathers of the Christian Church, Second Series, vol. IX, trans. by Rev. S.F.D. Dalmond, D.D., F.E.I.S. (Grand Rapids, MI: Wm. B. Eerdmans Pub. Co., 1976), ch. xiv, p. 85.

22. Ed. of Sophocles Oikonomos, (Athens, 1861, copy in Bollandist Library), 6, 214.

23. PG 105, 993D.

V. THE VIRGIN COMES OF AGE

1. Alpha House, *The Gospel of the Birth of Mary*, The Lost Books of the Bible (NY: Meridian Books, 1974), 21.

2. Saint Romanos the Melodist, *On the Nativity of the Virgin Mary*, Kontakia of Romanos, Byzantine Melodist, vol. II, trans. and annot. by Marjorie Carpenter (MO: University of Missouri Press, 1970), Tone Four, strophe 9, p. 4.

3. Constantine Callinicos, *Our Lady the Theotokos*, trans. and rev. by Rev. George Dimopoulos (Upper Darby, PA: Christian Orthodox Editions, 1987), 15-16.

4. Rev. Alexander Roberts, D.D. and James Donaldson, LL.D., eds., *Apocrypha of the New Testament: The Gospel of Pseudo-Matthew*, The Ante-Nicene Fathers, The Writings of the Fathers down to A.D. 325, vol. VIII (Grand Rapids, MI: Wm. B. Eerdmans Pub. Co., 1986), 371.

5. Ibid.

6. Josephus, *The Antiquities of the Jews, Book III*, The Works of Josephus, trans. by William Whiston, A.M. (Peabody, MA: Hendrickson Pub., 1988), section 54.

7. Saint Gregory of Nyssa, *On Virginity*, Nicene and Post-Nicene Fathers of the Christian Church, Second Series, vol. V, trans. by William M.A. Moore and Henry Austin Wilson, M.A. (Grand Rapids, MI: Wm. B. Eerdmans Pub. Co.), ch. 19, pp. 264-365.

8. Rev. Alexander Roberts, D.D. and James Donaldson, LL.D., eds., *Apocrypha of the New Testament: The Gospel of the Nativity of Mary*, The Ante-Nicene Fathers, The Writings of the Fathers down to A.D. 325, vol. VIII (Grand Rapids, MI: Wm. B. Eerdmans Pub. Co., 1986), 386.

9. *Sermo in nat. Dni*, in PG 46, 1140A.

10. PG 46, 1140D.

11. Roberts and Donaldson, *The Gospel of the Nativity of Mary*, loc. cit.

12. Rev. Alexander Roberts, D.D. and James Donaldson, LL.D., eds., *Apocrypha of the New Testament: The Protoevangelium of James*, The Ante-Nicene Fathers, The Writings of the Fathers down to A.D. 325, vol. VIII (Grand Rapids, MI: Wm. B. Eerdmans Pub. Co., 1986), 363.

13. *Homily on the Theotokos*, 6, PG 96, 709.

14. Roberts and Donaldson, *The Protoevangelium of James*, loc. cit.

15. Roberts and Donaldson, *The Gospel of the Nativity of Mary*, loc. cit.

16. *Annunciation*, The Great Synaxaristes of the Orthodox Church [in Greek], 5th ed., vol. III (Athens, 1979), 481.

17. Roberts and Donaldson, *The Gospel of Pseudo-Matthew*, 372.

18. Roberts and Donaldson, *The Gospel of Pseudo-Matthew* and *The Protoevangelium of James*, loc. cit.

19. *Sunday of Pascha in the Pentecostarion*, The Great Synaxaristes of the Orthodox Church [in Greek], 5th ed., vol. XIV (Athens, 1979), 38.

The actual name of the third daughter is unknown to us; possible suggestions include Martha, Lydia, Thamar or Assia.

20. *Against Heresies III*, 2,7, PG 42, 708-709.

21. In *Gen.*, in PG 69, 325C.

22. *The Gospel of Pseudo-Matthew* and *The Protoevangelium of James*, loc. cit.

23. Ibid., p. 80.

24. Roberts and Donaldson, *The Gospel of Pseudo-Matthew*, loc. cit.

25. Roberts and Donaldson, *The Protoevangelium of James; The Gospel of Pseudo-Matthew;* and *The Gospel of the Nativity of Mary*, loc. cit.

26. *On the Nativity of the Virgin Mary*, Tone Four, strophe 9, p. 4.

27. *The Protoevangelium of James* and *The Gospel of Pseudo-Matthew*, loc. cit.

28. *The Protoevangelium of James*, loc. cit.

29. Roberts and Donaldson, *The Gospel of Pseudo-Matthew* and *The Gospel of the Nativity of Mary*, loc. cit.

30. Bishop Nikolai Velimirovic, *The Prologue from Ochrid*, Pt. 3, Trans. by Mother Maria (Birmingham: Lazarica Press, 1986), 299.

31. *Against Heresies III*, 2,7, PG 42, 708.

32. *Ecclesiastical History*, PG 145, 652.

33. *Homily on the Theotokos*, PG 96,709.

34. Saint John of Damascus, *Exposition of the Orthodox Faith, Book IV*, The Nicene and Post-Nicene Fathers of the Christian Church, Second Series, vol. IX, trans. by Rev. S.F.D. Dalmond, D.D., F.E.I.S. (Grand Rapids, MI: Wm. B. Eerdmans Pub. Co., 1976), ch. xiv, p. 85.

35. *The Gospel of Pseudo-Matthew* and *The Gospel of the Nativity of Mary*, loc. cit.

36. Ralph Gower, *The New Manners and Customs of Bible Times* (Chicago: Moody Press, 1987), 65.

37. Alfred Edersheim, M.A. Oxon., D.D., Ph.D., *The Life and Times of Jesus the Messiah* (McLean, VA: MacDonald Publishing Co.), pp. 149-159, 353-354.

38. George M. Lamsa, *Idioms in the Bible Explained and A Key to the Original Gospel* (San Francisco: Harper & Roe, Pub., 1985), 90.

39. Underwood, *The Kariye Djami*, p. 81.

40. Rev. Alexander Roberts, D.D. and James Donaldson, LL.D., eds., *Apocrypha of the New Testament: The History of Joseph the Carpenter*, The Ante-Nicene Fathers, The Writings of the Fathers down to A.D. 325, vol. VIII (Grand Rapids, MI: Wm. B. Eerdmans Pub. Co., 1986), 389.

41. Roberts and Donaldson, *The Protoevangelium of James*, loc. cit.; Underwood, *The Kariye Djami*, pp. 83-84.

42. *The Protoevangelium of James* and *The Gospel of Pseudo-Matthew*, loc. cit.

43. Underwood, *The Kariye Djami*, p. 77.

44. Roberts and Donaldson, *The Gospel of the Nativity of Mary*, pp. 373-373.

45. J.A. Thompson, *Handbook of Life in Bible Times* (Downers Grove, IL: Inter-Varsity Press, 1986), 179.

VI. THE ANNUNCIATION

1. Saint Photios, *Homily VII: The Annunciation*, The Homilies of Photius, Patriarch of Constantinople, trans. by Cyril Mango (Cambridge, MA: Harvard University Press, Dumbarton Oaks Studies Three, 1958), 141.
2. Matinal Lauds, Tone One. Unless otherwise specified, hymns in this section are taken from the Feast on the 25th of March.
3. Dismissal Hymn of Feast, Tone Four.
4. *Demonstratio apostolicae praedicationis*, 32, English tr. by J. P. Smith, in "Ancient Christian Writers," 68; Blessed Archbishop John Maximovitch, *The Orthodox Veneration of the Mother of God*, trans. by Fr. Seraphim Rose, (Platina, CA: St. Herman of Alaska Brotherhood, 1987), 23.
5. Doxastikon of Matins, Tone Two.
6. Canon of the Akathist, Ode One, Tone Four.
7. *The Works of Saint Cyril of Jerusalem*, (Washington, 1969, 1970), Clavis G., vol. xii, 15, p. 235.
8. Ep. 63, 33 PL 16, 1198.
9. *De Obitu Theod.*, 44, PL, 16, 1400.
10. *De coemet. et de cruce*, 2, in PG 49, 396.
11. PG 720.
12. PG 712.
13. *In SS Deip Annunt.* 22 PL 87c, 3241.
14. *Homily VII: The Annunciation*, p. 142.
15. Matins Canon, Ode Nine, Tone Four by St. John of Damascus.
16. Matins Canon, 21 Nov., Ode Four, Tone Two by Basil the Monk.
17. Matins Canon, Ode Nine, Tone Four by St. John of Damascus.
18. Matins Canon, Ode One, Tone Four St. John of Damascus or St. Theophanes.
19. Matins Canon, 21 Nov., Ode Four, Tone Two by Basil the monk.
20. Hypakoe of Matinal Canons, 8 Sept., Tone Two.
21. Matins Canon, 8 Sept., Irmos of Ode Seven, Tone Two.
22. Matins Canon, Ode Nine, Tone Four by St. John of Damascus.
23. Saint Ambrose, *Concerning Virgins*, The Nicene and Post-Nicene Fathers of the Christian Church, Second Series, vol. X, Philip Schaff, D.D., LL.D. and Henry Wace, D.D., eds. (Grand Rapids, MI: Wm. B. Eerdmans Pub. Co., 1979), ch. 2, pp. 374-375.
24. *Corpus Scriptorum Christianorum Orientalium* (Louvain, 1903), 60-61.
25. *Letter to the Virgins*, ed. Th. Lefort, Le Museon, 42(1929), 256-259.
26. *De Virg.*, ed. E. Cazzaniga, *Corp. Script. Lat. Parav.*, (1948), 2, 7-15, 36-40.
27. *Exhort. Virg.* V, 31, PL, 16, 345.
28. *Exp. in Luc.* X, 132, *Corpus Scriptorum Ecclesiasticorum Latinorum* (Vienna, 1866), 32(iv), 505.
29. Saint Ephraim Syrus, *Hymns on the Nativity, Hymn III*, Nicene and Post-Nicene Fathers of the Christian Church, Second Series, vol. XIII, trans. by Rev. J.B. Morris, M.A. (Grand Rapids, MI: Wm. B. Eerdmans Pub. Co., 1976), 232.
30. *De Virginitate*, II, in PG, 324B.
31. *Serm. 21*, in PL 54, 191.
32. *Ep. 124*, 9, in PL 54, 1068; Saint Leo the Great, *Sermons*, The Nicene and Post-Nicene Fathers of the Christian Church, Second Series, vol. XII, Philip Schaff, D.D., LL.D. and Henry Wace, D.D., eds. (Grand Rapids, MI: Wm. B. Eerdmans Pub. Co., 1979), 95.
33. In *Lucan I*, in *Corpus Christianorum, Series Latina*, Turnhout, (1953), 120, 33.

34. PG 96, 684C.

35. Saint Photios, *Homily IX: The Birth of the Virgin*, The Homilies of Photius, Patriarch of Constantinople, trans. by Cyril Mango (Cambridge, MA: Harvard University Press, Dumbarton Oaks Studies Three, 1958), pp. 174-175.

36. *Homily VII: The Annunciation*, pp. 142-143.

37. *Homilies of St. Gregory Palamas*, comp. and ed. by S. Oikonomos (Athens, 1861). This rare edition may be found in Migne, *PG* 151. *Homily 55*, p. 142, cited in John Meyendorff, *A Study of Gregory Palamas*, trans. from French by George Lawrence (London: Faith Press, 1964), 234.

38. *Hom. III in Dorm.*, 1092D.

39. *Hom. 52*, Oikonomos (1851), p. 123, cited in Meyendorff, *A Study of Gregory Palamas*, loc. cit. These verses are not, as some have implied, upholding the doctrine of the Immaculate Conception. When one reads St. Gregory's view of sin and the way it was transmitted, it cannot be reconciled with the doctrine of the Immaculate Conception, as defined by Rome. See, Meyendorff, pp. 234-236.

40. Saint John of Kronstadt, *My Life in Christ*, trans. by E. E. Goulaeff (Jordanville, NY: Printshop of St. Job of Pochaev, 1984), 269.

41. Saint John of Kronstadt, *Spiritual Counsels of Father John of Kronstadt*. Select passages from *My Life in Christ*, edited and introduced by W. Jardine Grisbrooke (London: James Clarke & Co. Ltd., 1967), 59.

42. *The Assumption of Our Most Holy Lady, The Mother of God and Ever-Virgin Mary*, translated from the Menology of St. Dimitri of Rostov (Jordanville, NY: Holy Trinity Monastery, 1976), 18.

43. Constantine Cavarnos, "Iconography of the Holy Virgin" in *Byzantine Sacred Art* 2d ed. Belmont, MA: Institute for Byzantine and Modern Greek Studies, 1985): 107, 110.

44. Ibid., p. 110.

45. Cavarnos, loc. cit.

46. Alpha House, *The Protoevangelion*, The Lost Books of the Bible (NY: Meridian Books, 1974), 29, 30.

47. Vespers Sticheron, Prosomion, 26 March, Tone One.

48. Ibid.

49. Ibid.

50. *Annunciation*, The Great Synaxaristes of the Orthodox Church [in Greek], 5th ed., vol. III (Athens, 1979), 472.

51. Ibid., p. 478.

52. Saint Romanos the Melodist, *On the Annunciation I*, Kontakia of Romanos, Byzantine Melodist, vol. II, trans. and annot. by Marjorie Carpenter (MO: University of Missouri Press, 1970), Tone One, strophe 2, pp. 9-10.

53. Doxastikon of Vespers Sticheron, Tone Plagal Second.

54. p. 19, 1.2; James Hastings, M.A., D.D., *A Dictionary of the Bible*, vol. 1 (Peabody: Hendrickson Pub., 1988), 405.

55. Saint John Chrysostom, *Homilies on the Gospel of St. Matthew, Homily IV*, The Nicene and Post-Nicene Fathers of the Christian Church, First Series, vol. X, Philip Schaff, D.D., LL.D., ed. (Grand Rapids, MI: Wm. B. Eerdmans Pub. Co., 1975), 22.

56. Saint Cyril of Alexandria, *Commentary on the Gospel of Saint Luke, Homily I*, trans. by R. Payne Smith (NY: Studion Publishers, Inc., 1983), 48.

57. Saint Athanasios, *Letter 59, to Epictetus*, Nicene and Post-Nicene Fathers, Second Series, vol. IV, trans. by Philip Schaff, D.D., LLD. and Henry Wace, D.D. (Grand Rapids, MI: Wm. B. Eerdmans Pub. Co., 1975; repr.), 572.

546

58. Alpha House, *The Protoevangelion*, The Lost Books of the Bible (NY: Meridian Books, 1974), 29.

59. Leonid Ouspensky and Vladimir Lossky, *The Meaning of Icons*, trans. by G.E.H. Palmer and E. Kadloubovsky (Crestwood: St. Vladimir's Seminary Press, 1983, repr.), 173.

60. Doxastikon of Small Vespers, Tone One by Byzas.
    September for the Hebrews being the first of the year, therefore, March would be the sixth month.

61. Small Vespers, Aposticha, Tone Plagal Fourth.

62. Small Vespers Sticheron, Tone Four.

63. Vespers Sticheron, Prosomion, Tone Plagal Second.

64. Matinal Lauds, Tone One.

65. Lity, Tone One.

66. Exapostilarion, Tone Two.

67. Leonid Ouspensky and Vladimir Lossky, *The Meaning of Icons*, trans. by G.E.H. Palmer and E. Kadloubovsky (Crestwood: St. Vladimir's Seminary Press, 1983, repr.), 172.

68. *Homily VII: The Annunciation*, pp. 143-144.

69. PG 35, 325B, 633C.

70. *Patrologia Orientalia*, vol. 19, 477. (Hereinafter referred to as PO).

71. *Homily on the Entrance*, ed. Sophoclis, Athens, 1861, p. 123, PG 151, 178.

72. *Homily 57*, ed. by S. Oikonomos (Athens, 1861), p. 214. Cited in Meyendorff, *A Study of Gregory Palamas*, 234.

73. Saint Gregory Palamas, *Homily 37 on the August Dormition of Our Most Immaculate Lady Theotokos and Ever-Virgin Mary* [in Greek], PG 151, 460-474.

74. Matins Resurrection Canon, Ode Nine, Tone Four.

75. Great Canon of St. Andrew of Crete, Theotokion of Ode Eight, Tone Plagal First.

76. John Baggley, *Doors of Perception* (Crestwood, NY: St. Vladimir's Seminary Press, 1988), 128.

77. *Homily on the Lord's Nativity*, 2, PG 65, 712.

78. *On the Theotokos*, 1, PG 65, 681.

79. Rev. Alexander Roberts, D.D. and James Donaldson, LL.D., eds., *Apocrypha of the New Testament: The Gospel of the Nativity of Mary*, The Ante-Nicene Fathers, The Writings of the Fathers down to A.D. 325, vol. VIII (Grand Rapids, MI: Wm. B. Eerdmans Pub. Co., 1986), 386.

80. Saint Photios, *Homily V: The Annunciation*, The Homilies of Photius, Patriarch of Constantinople, trans. by Cyril Mango (Cambridge, MA: Harvard University Press, Dumbarton Oaks Studies Three, 1958), pp. 114-115.

81. *Homily VII: The Annunciation*, p. 146.

82. *Homily V: The Annunciation*, pp. 115-116.

83. Ibid., p. 116.

84. Sermo de Annunt., in PG 765.

85. PG 46, 1148AB.

86. *Hom. V de SS. Deip. 1*, in PG 93, 1461.

87. *Hom. V de SS. Deip. 4*, in PG 93, 1465; *Hom. V in SS. Deip.*, in M. Aubineau ed., 164.

88. Matins Canon, Ode One, Tone Four by St. Theophanes.

89. Ibid.

90. Ibid.

91. *Annunciation*, The Great Synaxaristes of the Orthodox Church, p. 473.

92. Saint Paulinus of Nola, *Poems 6(108)*, Ancient Christian Writers, vol. 40, trans. and annot. by P.G. Walsh (NY: Paulist Press, 1975), 43.

93. Matins Canon, Ode Eight, Tone Four by St. John of Damascus.

94. Matins Canon, Ode Three, Tone Four by St. Theophanes.
95. Small Vespers Aposticha, Tone Plagal Fourth.
96. Vespers Sticheron, Prosomion, Tone Plagal Second.
97. Small Vespers Sticheron, Tone Four.
98. *Annunciation*, The Great Synaxaristes of the Orthodox Church, loc. cit.
99. Small Vespers Sticheron, Tone Four.
100. *Annunciation*, The Great Synaxaristes of the Orthodox Church, p. 474.
101. Matinal Lauds, Tone One.
102. *Homily V: The Annunciation*, pp. 116-117.
103. *In SS Deip Annunt. 22* PL 87c, 3237.
104. Matins Canon, Ode Four, Tone Four by St. Theophanes.
105. Matins Canon, Ode Three, Tone Four by St. Theophanes.
106. Theotokion of Lity, Tone Two, by St. Cosmas.
107. Small Vespers Sticheron, Tone Four.
108. Saint Romanos the Melodist, *On the Annunciation I*, Kontakia of Romanos, vol. II, Tone One, strophe 4, pp. 10-11.
109. Matins Canon, Ode Four, Tone Four by St. Theophanes.
110. Matins Canon, Ode Four, Tone Four St. John of Damascus or St. Theophanes.
111. Matins Canon, Ode Four, Tone Four by St. Theophanes.
112. Saint Romanos the Melodist, *On the Annunciation II*, Kontakia of Romanos, Byzantine Melodist, vol. II, trans. and annot. by Marjorie Carpenter (MO: University of Missouri Press, 1970), Tone Four, strophe 12, p. 23.
113. Saint Romanos the Melodist, *On the Annunciation I*, Kontakia of Romanos, Tone One, strophe 8, p. 12.
114. Ibid., strophe 9, p. 13.
115. *Homily on the Feast of the Annunciation*, by Metropolitan Philaret of Moscow. Translated from *The Works of Philaret, Metropolitan of Moscow and Kolomna, Sermons and Discourse*, Vol. V (Moscow, 1985), pp. 71-75. Cited in *Orthodox Life* 28, No. 2 (March-April 1978): 9.
116. Matins Sessional Hymn, Tone Four.
117. *De natali Christ*, PG 46, 1140D-1141C.
118. PG 123, 75.
119. Matins Canon, Ode Eight, Tone Four by St. John of Damascus.
120. *Homily V: The Annunciation*, pp. 118-119.
121. Matins Canon, Ode Eight, Tone Four by St. John of Damascus.
122. Matins Canon, Ode Four, Tone Four by St. Theophanes.
123. Matins Canon, Ode Five, Tone Four by St. Theophanes.
124. *Homily V: The Annunciation*, p. 119.
125. Matins Canon, Ode Three, Tone Four by St. Theophanes.
126. Matins Canon, Ode Five, Tone Four by St. Theophanes.
127. Ibid.
128. *Homily V: The Annunciation*, pp. 119-120.
129. Ibid., p. 117.
130. Ibid., pp. 117-118.
131. Small Vespers Aposticha, Tone Plagal Fourth.
132. Vespers Sticheron, Prosomion, Plagal Second.
133. Akathist Hymn, First Station of the *Salutations*, subdivision Delta.
134. Resurrection Theotokion, Tone Four.
135. *Poem 25*, Ancient Christian Writers, vol. 40, p. 250.
136. Saint Ephraim the Syrian, *Homily on the Nativity*, The Harp of the Spirit, trans. by Sebastian Brock (England: Fellowship of St. Alban & St. Sergius, 1975), 66.

137. Bishop Ignatius Brianchaninov, *Exposition of the Teaching of the Orthodox Church on the Mother of God*, cited in Blessed Archbishop John Maximovitch, *The Orthodox Veneration of the Mother of God*, p. 52.

138. *Hom. 14*, col. 176D. Cited in Meyendorff, *A Study of Gregory Palamas*, p. 235.

139. *Homily 37 on the August Dormition of Our Most Immaculate Lady Theotokos and Ever-Virgin Mary*, PG 151, 461D.

140. Saint Ambrose, *The Holy Spirit, Book II, Theological and Dogmatic Works*, The Fathers of the Church, vol. 44, trans. by Roy J. Deferrari, Ph.D. (Washington, D.C.: The Catholic University Press, 1987; repr.), ch. 1(38), 110.

141. Ibid., ch. 1(42-44), p. 111.

142. Saint Ambrose, *The Mysteries, Theological and Dogmatic Works*, The Fathers of the Church, vol. 44, trans. by Roy J. Deferrari, Ph.D. (Washington, D.C.: The Catholic University Press, 1987; repr.), ch. 9(59), p. 28.

143. Canon of the Theotokos, Ode Nine, Tone Three.

144. *The Works of St. Cyril of Jerusalem*, 2 vols., (Washington, 1969, 1970), Clavis G., vol. 2, xvii, 6, p. 100.

145. Ibid., xii, 15, p. 235.

146. Saint Cyril of Alexandria, *Letter 39*, The Fathers of the Church, vol. 76, trans. by John I. McEnerney. Washington, D.C.: The Catholic University of America Press, 1987, p. 149.

147. *Hymns on the Nativity, Hymn VII*, Nicene and Post-Nicene Fathers of the Christian Church, p. 242.

148. *Catechesis* 12, 29, PG 33, 761.

149. Canon of the Akathist, Ode Five, Tone Four.

150. *Poem 25*, Ancient Christian Writers, vol. 40, p. 167.

151. *Hymns on the Nativity, Hymn VIII*, The Harp of the Spirit, p. 35.

152. *Hymns on the Nativity, Hymn X*, Nicene and Post-Nicene Fathers of the Christian Church, p. 245.

153. PG 96, 741, Hom *II in Dormit.*, 14.

154. *Marianum* (Rome, 1974), 36. (Hereinafter referred to as MM).

155. MM, 240-248.

156. PO 5, 542; MM 220, 222, 218, 234, 262, 236, 266, 276, 264, 270, 294, 300, 298.

157. MM, 218.

158. PG 120, 1081C, 1085, 1105A, *Sermo in SS. Deip. Dorm.*

159. *Can. 6, 4, apud* E. Follieri, 141.

160. *Can. 8, 7, apud* E. Follieri, 179.

161. *My Life in Christ*, p. 170.

162. *Homily V: The Annunciation*, p. 120.

163. Saint Leo the Great, *Sermons*, The Nicene and Post-Nicene Fathers of the Christian Church, Second Series, vol. XII, Philip Schaff, D.D., LL.D. and Henry Wace, D.D., eds. (Grand Rapids, MI: Wm. B. Eerdmans Pub. Co., 1979), Serm. 21, 1, pp. 128-129.

164. Matins Canon, Ode Eight, Tone Four by St. John of Damascus.

165. Matins Canon, Ode Six, Tone Four by St. Theophanes.

166. Matins Canon, Ode Seven, Tone Four by St. Theophanes.

167. Vespers Sticheron, Prosomion, Tone Plagal Second.

168. Matins Canon, Ode Five, Tone Four by St. Theophanes.

169. Matins Canon, Ode Seven, Tone Four, by St. Theophanes.

170. Ibid.

171. Matins Canon, Ode Five, Tone Four by St. Theophanes.

172. Ibid.

173. Matins Ikos.

174. Archbishop Nathanael of Vienna and Austria, "The Holy Righteous Abraham, Moses and Elias as Preparers of Man's Salvation," *Orthodox Life* 28, no. 6 (November-December, 1978): 14. Translated by Seraphim F. Englehardt from *Orthodox Observer* (Montreal), No. 27, July, 1959.

175. Matins Canon for Sunday of Orthodoxy, Theotokion of Ode Six, Tone Four by St. Theophanes.

176. Resurrection Theotokion, Tone One.

177. *Homily V: The Annunciation*, p. 120.

178. Saint Justin Martyr, *Dialogue with Trypho*, The Fathers of the Church Series, vol. 6, trans. and ed. by Thomas B. Falls, D.D., Ph.D. (Washington, D.C.: Catholic University Press, 1977), ch. 100, p. 305.

179. *Adversus Haereses, III*, 22,4 in *Sources Chretiennes*, (Lyons), SC 34, 378-380; PG 7, 958-960; SC 211, 438-444 (hereinafter referred to as SC).

180. Ibid., V10, 1, in SC 152, 248-250; PG 7, 1175-1176.

181. *Poem 6(138)*, Ancient Christian Writers, vol. 40, p. 43.

182. *Homily V: The Annunciation*, p. 121.

183. *Contra Apollin.*, 9 in PG 45, 1141C; *On the Making of Man* XVI, 14.

184. *Poem 6*, loc. cit.

185. *De Inst. Virg., VI*, PL 16, 317B.

186. *Exp. in Luc. X, 42*, cited in *Corpus Scriptorum Ecclesiasticorum Latinorum* (Vienna, 1866), 32(iv), 470.

187. Sunday of the Paralytic, Matins Second Sessional Hymn, Tone Three.

188. Saint Ambrose, *The Incarnation, Theological and Dogmatic Works*, The Fathers of the Church, vol. 44, trans. by Roy J. Deferrari, Ph.D. (Washington, D.C.: The Catholic University Press, 1987; repr.), ch. 9(103-104), p. 257; *De Incar. 1, 9, 104*, PL 16, 843CD.

189. *Hom. 1 in Nativ.*, 812A, tr. H. Graef.

190. Saint Paulinus of Nola, *Letter 23, Vol. 2*, Ancient Christian Writers, vol. 36, trans. and annot. by P.G. Walsh (NY: Paulist Press, 1967), p. 16.

191. Resurrection Canon, Tone Four, Ode Three.

192. Canon of Great Compline on the Eve of the Saturday of St. Lazarus, Ode One, Tone One.

193. Doxastikon of Vespers Aposticha, Tone Four.

194. Ouspensky and Lossky, *The Meaning of Icons*, p. 172.

195. Ibid.

196. Nativity Canon of Forefeast, Ode Nine, Tone Plagal Second.

197. *Poem 27(235,256,272,288)*, Ancient Christian Writers, vol. 40, pp. 279-280.

VII. THE MOTHER OF GOD VISITS RIGHTEOUS ELISABETH

1. Saint Ambrose, *Concerning Virgins, Book II*, The Nicene and Post-Nicene Fathers of the Christian Church, Second Series, vol. X, Philip Schaff, D.D., LL.D. and Henry Wace, D.D., eds. (Grand Rapids, MI: Wm. B. Eerdmans Pub. Co., 1979), ch. 1, p. 375.

2. Saint Paulinus of Nola, *Poem 6, In Praise of St. John*, Ancient Christian Writers, vol. 40, trans. and annot. by P.G. Walsh (NY: Paulist Press, 1975), pp. 43-44.

3. Alpha House, *The Protoevangelion*, The Lost Books of the Bible (NY: Meridian Books, 1974), 30.

4. Nicephoros Callistos, *Ecclesiastical History, II, 3*, PG 145, 700; Bishop Nikolai Velimirovic, *The Prologue from Ochrid*, Pt. 3, Trans. by Mother Maria (Birmingham: Lazarica Press, 1986), 307. *The Menaion of July* (25), [in Greek], Athens: Apostolikes Diakonias of the Church of Greece, 1974), 132.

5. Alfred Edersheim, M.A. Oxon., D.D., Ph.D., *The Life and Times of Jesus the Messiah* (McLean, VA: MacDonald Publishing Co.), 149.

6. Matins Canon, 24 June, Theotokion of Ode Six, Tone Four.
7. Synaxis, 7 Jan., Matins Canon, Ode One, Tone Two.
8. Saint Ambrose, *Of the Christian Faith, Book IV,* The Nicene and Post-Nicene Fathers of the Christian Church, Second Series, vol. X, Philip Schaff, D.D., LL.D. and Henry Wace, D.D., eds. (Grand Rapids, MI: Wm. B. Eerdmans Pub. Co., 1979), 277.
9. Rev. Alexander Roberts, D.D. and James Donaldson, LL.D., eds., *Apocrypha of the New Testament: The Protoevangelium of James,* The Ante-Nicene Fathers, The Writings of the Fathers down to A.D. 325, vol. VIII (Grand Rapids, MI: Wm. B. Eerdmans Pub. Co., 1986), 364.
10. M.D. Toal, D.D., *The Sunday Sermons of the Great Fathers,* 3rd ed., vol. IV (Chicago: Henry Regnery Co., 1964), 413.
11. *Poem 6,* op. cit., p. 44.
12. Saint Theophanes the Hymnographer calls righteous Elisabeth as a prophetess. [Matins Canon, 5 Sept., Ode Six, Tone Plagal Fourth].
13. Toal, op. cit., p. 414.
14. *Epist. as Alexand. Byzant.,* 1, 12 PG 18, 568C.
15. *Contra Arianos* 3.29, PG 26, 385-388.
16. Ibid., 3.33, PG 26, 393-396.
17. *Ep. 101,* in PG 37, 177C.
18. Michael O'Carroll, C.S.Sp., comp. and ed., *Theotokos* 3rd ed. (Wilmington, DE: Michael Glazier, Inc., 1988), 258.
19. Saint Vincent of Lerins, *Commonitories,* The Fathers of the Church, vol. 7, trans. by Rudolph E. Morris (Washington, D.C.: The Catholic University Press, 1970; repr.), ch.15, p. 296.
20. A. Schonmetzer, S.J., *Enchiridion Symbolorum,* Denziger-Bannwart, ed. 33., p. 251. Hereinafter referred to as ES.
21. Ibid., p. 301.
22. Saint Cyril of Alexandria, *Letter 1,* The Fathers of the Church, vol. 76, trans. by John I. McEnerney (Washington, D.C.: The Catholic University of America Press, 1987), p. 15.
23. ES, op. cit., p. 427.
24. Ibid., p. 555.
25. *Poem 6(84-85),* op. cit., p. 42.
26. *Exp. in Luc. II, 17,* cited in *Corpus Scriptorum Ecclesiasticorum Latinorum* (Vienna, 1866), 32, 51.
27. Toal, op. cit., pp. 413, 415.
28. Saint Ephraim Syrus, *Hymns on the Nativity, Hymn XIV,* Nicene and Post-Nicene Fathers of the Christian Church, Second Series, vol. XIII, trans. by Rev. J.B. Morris, M.A. (Grand Rapids, MI: Wm. B. Eerdmans Pub. Co., 1976), p. 251.
29. *Hymns on the Nativity, Hymn VI,* op. cit., p. 239.
30. *Psalm 32,* cited in Toal, op. cit., pp. 415-416.
31. *Psalm 31(1),* cited in PG 29, col. 323.
32. Toal, op. cit., p. 416.
33. Ibid.
34. Saint Jerome, *Against the Pelagians, Book I,* The Nicene and Post-Nicene Fathers of the Christian Church, Second Series, vol. VI, Philip Schaff, D.D., LL.D. and Henry Wace, D.D., eds. (Grand Rapids, MI: Wm. B. Eerdmans Pub. Co., 1983), p. 457.
35. Toal, loc. cit.
36. *Demonst.,* III, 14, 130-131, *Patrologia Syriaca,* vol. 1.
37. Toal, op. cit., p. 417.
38. Ibid.

39. *Hymns on the Nativity, Hymn XVIII*, op. cit., p. 260.
40. *De Spirit Sancto, III, 80*, PL 16, 795A.
41. Toal, op. cit., p. 417.
42. Ibid., pp. 417-418.
43. Ibid., p. 418.
44. Saint Cyril of Alexandria, *Commentary on the Gospel of Saint Luke*, trans. by R. Payne Smith (NY: Studion Publishers, Inc., 1983), p. 39.
45. Ibid.
46. *Hymns on the Nativity, Hymn XV*, op. cit., p. 254.
47. *Commentary on the Gospel of Saint Luke*, op. cit., p. 40.
48. Ibid., pp. 40-41.
49. *Of the Christian Faith*, loc. cit.
50. *Psalm 32*, op. cit., p. 415.
51. Ibid.
52. Ibid.
53. *The Protoevangelion*, loc. cit.
54. *On Virginity 4*, PG 115, 534.

VIII. JOSEPH REPROACHES THE MOTHER OF GOD

1. Rev. Alexander Roberts, D.D. and James Donaldson, LL.D., eds., *Apocrypha of the New Testament: The Gospel of the Nativity of Mary*, and *The Protoevangelium of James*, The Ante-Nicene Fathers, The Writings of the Fathers down to A.D. 325, vol. VIII (Grand Rapids, MI: Wm. B. Eerdmans Pub. Co., 1986), pp. 387 and 364, respectively.
2. John Meyendorff, *A Study of Gregory Palamas*, trans. from French by George Lawrence (London: Faith Press, 1964), 52.
3. Alpha House, *The Protoevangelion*, The Lost Books of the Bible (NY: Meridian Books, 1974), 30.
4. Ibid., p. 31.
5. Paul A. Underwood, *The Kariye Djami, Vol. 1, Historical Introduction and Description of the Mosaics and Frescoes*, Bollingen Series LXX (NY: Pantheon Books, 1966), p. 84.
6. Alpha House, *The Protoevangelion*, loc. cit.
7. Eve of Christ's Nativity, First Hour, Tone Plagal Fourth.
8. Alpha House, *The Protoevangelion*, loc. cit.
9. Rev. Alexander Roberts, D.D. and James Donaldson, LL.D., eds., *Apocrypha of the New Testament: The Gospel of Pseudo-Matthew*, The Ante-Nicene Fathers, The Writings of the Fathers down to A.D. 325, vol. VIII (Grand Rapids, MI: Wm. B. Eerdmans Pub. Co., 1986), p. 373.
10. Ibid.
11. *Sermon to the Theotokos*, 8-9, PG 65, 736-737.
12. Saint Germanos, Patriarch of Constantinople, *Sermon on the Annunciation of the Most Holy Theotokos* [in Greek], PG 98, 332D.
13. Ibid., PG 98, 332B.
14. Ibid., PG 98, 333A-B.
15. Ibid., PG 98, 332D.
16. Ibid., PG 98, 333A.
17. Ibid., PG 98, 333D.
18. Ibid., PG 98, 332D.
19. Ibid., PG 98, 332C.
20. Ibid., PG 98, 332B.
21. Ibid., PG 98, 336A.
22. Ibid., PG 98, 332C.
23. Ibid., PG 98, 336A-B, D.
24. *On the Annunciation*, PG 96, 332-340; PG 100, 1334-1456.

25. Roberts and Donaldson, *The Gospel of Pseudo-Matthew*, p. 373.
26. Roberts and Donaldson, *The Gospel of the Nativity of Mary*, loc. cit.;
Alpha House, *The Protoevangelion*, loc. cit.
27. Ibid.
28. Saint John Chrysostom, *Homilies on the Gospel of St. Matthew, Homily IV*, The Nicene and Post-Nicene Fathers of the Christian Church, First Series, vol. X, Philip Schaff, D.D., LL.D., ed. (Grand Rapids, MI: Wm. B. Eerdmans Pub. Co., 1975), p. 23.
29. George M. Lamsa, *Idioms in the Bible Explained and A Key to the Original Gospel* (San Francisco: Harper & Roe, Pub., 1985), p. 90.
30. James Hastings, M.A., D.D., *A Dictionary of the Bible*, vol. 1 (Peabody: Hendrickson Pub., 1988), p. 521.
31. Merrill C. Tenney and Steven Barabas, eds., *Pictorial Encyclopedia of the Bible*, vols. 3 and 2 (Grand Rapids: Regency Reference Library & Zondervan Publishing House, 1975), pp. 159 and 150, respectively; Ralph Gower, *The New Manners and Customs of Bible Times* (Chicago: Moody Press, 1987), p. 70. See, also *m. Ketub.* 7:6.
32. *Homily IV*, op. cit., p. 24.
33. Ibid., p. 25.
34. Ibid., pp. 24-25.
35. Ibid., p. 32.
36. *Homily IV*, op. cit., p. 33.
37. Ibid., p. 22.
38. Alpha House, *The Protoevangelion*, p. 24; Roberts and Donaldson, *The Gospel of Pseudo-Matthew*, p. 373.
39. *On the Annunciation*, PG 98, 337D.
40. Alfred Edersheim, M.A. Oxon., D.D., Ph.D., *The Life and Times of Jesus the Messiah* (McLean, VA: MacDonald Publishing Co.), pp. 155-156.
41. Ibid., p. 156.
42. Lamsa, op. cit., pp. 90-91.
43. Saint Romanos the Melodist, *On the Annunciation I*, Kontakia of Romanos, Byzantine Melodist, vol. II, trans. and annot. by Marjorie Carpenter (MO: University of Missouri Press, 1970), Tone One, strophe 13, pp. 14-15.
44. Ibid., strophe 15, pp. 15-16.
45. Ibid., strophes 16-17, p. 16.
46. Ibid., strophes 17-18, p. 17.
47. *Against Heresies III*, 2,7, PG 42, 708-709.
48. Saint Romanos the Melodist, *On the Annunciation II*, Kontakia of Romanos, Byzantine Melodist, vol. II, trans. and annot. by Marjorie Carpenter (MO: University of Missouri Press, 1970), Tone Four, strophe 2, 20-21.
49. Ibid., strophe 3, p. 21.
50. Ibid., strophe 4, p. 21.
51. Ibid., strophe 5, p. 21.
52. Ibid., strophe 8, p. 22.
53. Ibid., strophe 1, p. 20.
54. *On the Annunciation*, PG 96, 332-340; PG 100, 1334-1456.
55. Tenney and Barabas, *Pictorial Encyclopedia of the Bible*, vol. 1, p. 66.
56. Roberts and Donaldson, *The Protoevangelium of James*, p. 364.
57. Roberts and Donaldson, *The Protoevangelium of James* and *The Gospel of the Nativity of Mary, op. cit.*, pp. 364 and 373, respectively.
58. Alpha House, *The Protoevangelion*, p. 32.
59. Diehl, *Manuel d'art*, Ry2, p. 535. Dalton Ry2 Art, p. 268. Adamantius Adamantiou, Vol. 1, 1910.
60. Underwood, *The Kariye Djami*, p. 87.

61. Saint Ephraim Syrus, *Hymns on the Nativity, Hymn XI,* Nicene and Post-Nicene Fathers of the Christian Church, Second Series, vol. XIII, trans. by Rev. J.B. Morris, M.A. (Grand Rapids, MI: Wm. B. Eerdmans Pub. Co., 1976), p. 246.

62. Saint John Chrysostom, *Homilies on the Gospel of St. Matthew, Homily V,* The Nicene and Post-Nicene Fathers of the Christian Church, First Series, vol. X, Philip Schaff, D.D., LL.D., ed. (Grand Rapids, MI: Wm. B. Eerdmans Pub. Co., 1975), p. 33.

63. *On the Ever-Virginity of Blessed Mary,* cited in Blessed Archbishop John Maximovitch, *The Orthodox Veneration of the Mother of God,* trans. by Fr. Seraphim Rose, (Platina, CA: St. Herman of Alaska Brotherhood, 1987), 23.

64. Blessed Archbishop John Maximovitch, *The Orthodox Veneration of the Mother of God,* op. cit., pp. 23-24.

65. *Homily V,* loc. cit.

66. PG, 31, 1468A.

67. Saint Cyril of Alexandria, *Commentary on the Gospel of Saint Luke, Homily 1,* trans. by R. Payne Smith (NY: Studion Publishers, Inc., 1983), 48.

68. Ibid., p. 49.

69. *Adv. Haer., IV, 33, 4,* in Sources Chretiennes, (Lyons), 100, 810-812.

70. Saint Basil, *Prolegomena,* Nicene and Post-Nicene Fathers of the Christian Church, Second Series, vol. VIII, trans. by Philip Schaff, D.D., LLD. and Henry Wace, D.D. (Grand Rapids, MI: Wm. B. Eerdmans Pub. Co., 1975; repr.), p. xli, f.n. 6.

71. *Ep. de Bonoso,* PL, 16, 1173C.

72. *Exp. Luc. II, 1,* cited in *Corpus Scriptorum Ecclesiasticorum Latinorum* (Vienna, 1866), 32(iv), 41.

73. *To Smyrna* 19, PG 5, 660.

74. *Homily on the Theotokos,* PG 98, 316.

IX. NATIVITY OF CHRIST

1. Before the commencement of the services on the eve of the Nativity of Christ, the deacon, St. Romanos, was in the Church of Blachernae in Constantinople, and, as was his custom, he was praying before the famous Kyriotissa icon of the Theotokos. He always prayed for help in his chanting, and especially tonight since it would be his turn that evening. He knew that he could not sing as well as the other chanters, nor could he compose beautiful poetry to glorify God. After praying very long, he slumbered from exhaustion and, in a vision, the holy Virgin appeared to him. She spoke to him, and said, "Open thy mouth wide so that I may place this kontak inside." The deacon quickly obeyed and she placed a scroll on his tongue and told him to eat it. Trusting in his patroness and spiritual Mother, he obeyed and ate the scroll. Immediately, he was roused from sleep, but beheld no one. He only sensed a pleasant sweetness on his tongue and recalled the wonderful vision. That evening, he went and took his place among the chanters. He then went forward to receive his vestment and the blessing of the patriarch. Then, in the midst of the Church, he opened his mouth to chant. Then a most miraculous thing occurred! His voice had became strong and clear, and he began to chant the glorious kontakion of the Feast in the Third Tone. All were amazed at the beauty of the hymn. Thus, from the Virgin's marvelous intercession and blessing, the deacon received the gift of chanting and the ability to compose kontakia.

2. Kontakion of Feast, Tone Three by St. Romanos the Melodist with the aid of the Virgin.

Unless otherwise specified, hymns in this section are taken from the Feast on the 25th of December.

3. Matinal Lauds of Forefeast, Tone Plagal Second.

4. *Hom. IV in Dorm.*, PG 97, 865A.

5. Michael O'Carroll, C.S.Sp., comp. and ed., *Theotokos* 3rd ed. (Wilmington, DE: Michael Glazier, Inc., 1988), 162.

6. Matins Canon of Nativity, Ode One, Tone One.

7. Matins Canon of Theophany, Ode Nine, Tone Two.

8. Matins Canon of Wednesday of Mid-Pentecost, Ode Three, Tone Plagal Fourth.

9. Saint Gregory of Nyssa, *The Life of Moses*, trans. by Abraham J. Malherbe and Everett Ferguson (NY: Paulist Press, 1978), p. 59; PG 46, 1136B.

10. *The Wisdom of the Saints*, compiled by Jill Haak Adels (NY: Oxford University Press, 1987), p. 20.

11. Canon of Forefeast, Ode Five, Tone Two.

12. Canon of Forefeast, Ode One, Tone Plagal Second.

13. Matins Canon of Nativity, Ode Four, Tone One.

14. Matins Ikos of Nativity.

15. Irmos of Canon of Forefeast, Ode Five, Tone Plagal Second.

16. Matins Canon of Nativity, Ode Five, Tone One.

17. O'Carroll, *Theotokos*, p. 71.

18. Saint Cyril of Jerusalem, *Catechesis XII, On the Incarnation, Vol. 1*, The Fathers of the Church, vol. 61, trans. by Leo P. McCauley, S.J. and Anthony A. Stephenson (Washington, D.C.: The Catholic University of America Press, 1969), p. 240.

19. PG 6, 673.

20. O'Carroll, *Theotokos*, p. 37.

21. PG, 30, 464A-465B, 477B.

22. Saint Cyril of Alexandria, *Commentary on the Gospel of Saint Luke, Paschal Homily 17*, trans. by R. Payne Smith (NY: Studion Publishers, Inc., 1983), p. 53, f.n.2.

23. Saint Justin Martyr, *Dialogue with Trypho*, The Fathers of the Church Series, vol. 6, trans. and ed. by Thomas B. Falls, D.D., Ph.D. (Washington, D.C.: Catholic University Press, 1977), ch. 78, p. 273.

24. Matins Canon of Nativity, Ode Four, Tone One.

25. Matins Irmos of Nativity, Ode Five, Tone One.

26. Matins Irmos of Nativity, Ode Four, Tone One.

27. Matins Canon for the Sunday of the Myrrh-bearers, Ode Nine, Tone Two.

28. Saint Ambrose, *The Patriarchs, Exegetical Work*, The Fathers of the Church, vol. 65, trans. by Michael P. McHugh (Washington, D.C.: The Catholic University Press, 1985; repr.), pp. 252-253.

29. Saint Irenaeus, *Proof of the Apostolic Preaching, Part C: Christ in the Old Law*, Ancient Christian Writers, trans. and annot. by Joseph P. Smith, S.J. (NY: Newman Press, n.d.), sect. 59, p. 87.

30. Canon of the Akathist Hymn, Ode Seven, Tone Four.

31. Ibid.

32. PG 39, 49.

33. Matins Irmos of Nativity, Ode Four, Tone One by St. John of Damascus.

34. Hiermos of Matins Canon on Sunday of the Myrrh-bearers, Ode Four, Tone Two.

35. Matins Irmos of Ode Eight, Tone One.

36. Matins Irmos of Nativity, Ode Eight, Tone One.

37. Matins Irmos of Nativity, Ode Six, Tone One.

38. Irmos of Canon of Forefeast, Ode Six, Tone Plagal Second.

39. Matinal Lauds of Forefeast, Tone Plagal Second.

40. Saint Cyril of Alexandria, *Letter 18, To the Priests, Deacons and People of Constantinople,* The Fathers of the Church, vol. 76, trans. by John I. McEnerney (Washington, D.C.: The Catholic University of America Press, 1987), p. 94.

41. *Letter 42, To Bishop Rufus of Thessalonica,* The Fathers of the Church, vol. 76, op. cit., p. 183.

42. Canon of Forefeast, Ode Nine, Tone Two.

43. Matins Canon, 3 Feb., Ode Eight, Tone Four.

44. Sedalen of Forefeast, 20 Dec., Tone Plagal Fourth.

45. Nativity Vespers Sticheron, Tone Two.

46. Aposticha, 26 Dec., Tone Plagal Fourth.

47. Canon of Forefeast, Ode Four, Tone Plagal Second.

48. Matinal Lauds of Forefeast, 20 Dec., Tone Plagal Second.

49. *Canon 4, In depositione pretiosae vestis SS. Deiparae in Vlachernis,* in PG 105, 1005B.

50. D. Cummings, trans., "Concerning the Holy and Third Ecumenical Council" in *The Rudder (Pedalion),* (Chicago: The Orthodox Christian Educational Society, 1957), p. 221.

51. Saint John of Damascus, *Exposition of the Orthodox Faith, Book III,* The Nicene and Post-Nicene Fathers of the Christian Church, Second Series, vol. IX, trans. by Rev. S.F.D. Dalmond, D.D., F.E.I.S. (Grand Rapids, MI: Wm. B. Eerdmans Pub. Co., 1976), ch. xii, p. 56.

52. Ibid., p. 56.

53. Canon to Small Compline in Wednesday of Holy Week, Ode Four, Tone Plagal Second.

54. Canon to Small Compline in Wednesday of Holy Week, Ode Nine, Tone Plagal Second.

55. *Letter 91,* PG 37, 177.

56. *Ep. 101,* in PG 37, 177C.

57. *Poemata dogmatica, 9,* in PG 37, 460A.

58. Saint Ambrose, *Of the Christian Faith, Book III,* The Nicene and Post-Nicene Fathers of the Christian Church, Second Series, vol. X, Philip Schaff, D.D., LL.D. and Henry Wace, D.D., eds. (Grand Rapids, MI: Wm. B. Eerdmans Pub. Co., 1979), ch. ix(60), p. 251; cf. *Ep. 63, 49.*

59. Saint Ambrose, *The Mysteries, Theological and Dogmatic Works,* The Fathers of the Church, vol. 44, trans. by Roy J. Deferrari, Ph.D. (Washington, D.C.: The Catholic University Press, 1987; repr.), ch. 8(46), p. 22.

60. Merrill C. Tenney and Steven Barabas, eds., *Pictorial Encyclopedia of the Bible,* vol. 1 (Grand Rapids: Regency Reference Library & Zondervan Publishing House, 1975), p. 772.

61. Dr. Otto F.A. Meinardus, *The Holy Family in Egypt* (Cairo, Egypt: The American University In Cairo Press, 1986), p. 15.

62. *The Gospel of Jesus,* MIMEP [Pessano] Milano, (Vincenza, Italy: Edizioni Istituto S. Gaetano, 1969), 31.

63. Saint Ephraim Syrus, *Hymns on the Nativity, Hymn XIII* Nicene and Post-Nicene Fathers of the Christian Church, Second Series, vol. XIII, trans. by Rev. J.B. Morris, M.A. (Grand Rapids, MI: Wm. B. Eerdmans Pub. Co., 1976), p. 247.

64. Doxastikon of Nativity Vespers, Tone Two.

65. Matins Doxastikon of Nativity, Tone Plagal Second.

66. "The Genealogy of Christ," *Orthodox Life* 24, no. 6 (Nov-Dec. 1974): 10-14. (Trans. from *The Russian Pilgrim*, 1895, Nos. 51, 51).

67. Ibid.

68. Melchi, who is here given as the third from the end, is in our present texts of Luke the fifth. Matthat and Levi standing between Melchi and Eli. It is highly probable that the text which Africanus followed omitted the two names Matthat and Levi [see Westcott and Hort's, *Greek Testament*, Appendix, p. 57]. It is impossible to suppose that Africanus in such an investigation as this could have overlooked two names by mistake if they had stood in his text of the Gospels. Cited in Eusebius, *Church History, Book I*, The Nicene and Post-Nicene Fathers of the Christian Church, First Series, vol. I, trans. by Rev. Arthur Cushman McGiffert (Grand Rapids, MI: Wm. B. Eerdmans Pub. Co., 1961), ch. 7, pg. 91, f.n.6.

69. Ibid.

70. *Exposition of the Orthodox Faith, Book IV*, loc. cit., ch. xiv, p. 85.

71. Ibid. See also, PG 94, 1156A. Cf. *Hom. 1 in Nativ. B.V.M.*, 7, in PG 96, 672C.

72. Saint John Chrysostom, *Homilies on the Gospel of St. Matthew, Homily I*, The Nicene and Post-Nicene Fathers of the Christian Church, First Series, vol. X, Philip Schaff, D.D., LL.D., ed. (Grand Rapids, MI: Wm. B. Eerdmans Pub. Co., 1975), p. 12.

73. *Exposition of the Orthodox Faith, Book IV*, op. cit. See also, PG 94, 1156.

74. *Dialogue with Trypho*, op. cit., ch. 100, p. 304.

75. Saint Irenaeus, *Against Heresies*, Book III, Ante-Nicene Fathers, The Writings of the Fathers down to A.D. 326, vol. I, Rev. Alexander Roberts, D.D. and James Donaldson, eds. (Grand Rapids, MI: Wm. B. Eerdmans Pub. Co., 1987; repr.), ch. 21(9), p. 453.

76. Ibid., p. 454.

77. *Hymns on the Nativity, Hymn XVIII, op. cit., p.* 260.

78. *Rev. Alexander Roberts, D.D. and James Donaldson, LL.D., eds., Apocrypha of the New Testament: The Protoevangelium of James*, The Ante-Nicene Fathers, The Writings of the Fathers down to A.D. 325, vol. VIII (Grand Rapids, MI: Wm. B. Eerdmans Pub. Co., 1986), 365; Alpha House, *The Protoevangelion*, The Lost Books of the Bible (NY: Meridian Books, 1974), 32.

79. Paul A. Underwood, *The Kariye Djami, Vol. 1, Historical Introduction and Description of the Mosaics and Frescoes*, Bollingen Series LXX (NY: Pantheon Books, 1966), p. 88.

80. Rev. Alexander Roberts, D.D. and James Donaldson, LL.D., eds., *Apocrypha of the New Testament: The Gospel of Pseudo-Matthew*, The Ante-Nicene Fathers, The Writings of the Fathers down to A.D. 325, vol. VIII (Grand Rapids, MI: Wm. B. Eerdmans Pub. Co., 1986), p. 374.

81. Nativity Eve, Ninth Hour, Tone Two.

82. *Dialogue with Trypho*, op. cit., ch. 120, p. 333.

83. Nativity Eve, Sixth Hour, Tone Plagal First.

84. Underwood, *The Kariye Djami, p.* 89.

85. *Alfred Edersheim, M.A. Oxon., D.D., Ph.D., The Life and Times of Jesus the Messiah* (McLean, VA: MacDonald Publishing Co.), pp. 184-185.

86. Roberts and Donaldson, *The Protoevangelium of James, p.* 365.

87. Saint Romanos the Melodist, *On the Nativity (Mary and the Magi)*, Kontakia of Romanos, Byzantine Melodist, vol. I, trans. and annot. by Marjorie Carpenter (MO: University of Missouri Press, 1970), strophe 3, Tone Three, p. 5.

88. Exapostilarion of Sunday After Nativity, Tone Two.

89. Apolytikion of Forefeast, Tone Four.

90. Canon of Forefeast, Ode Six, Tone Two.

91. Canon of Forefeast, Ode Five, Tone Two.

92. *Dialogue with Trypho*, ch. 78; see also PG 6, 657-660.

93. Leonid Ouspensky and Vladimir Lossky, *The Meaning of Icons*, trans. by G.E.H. Palmer and E. Kadloubovsky (Crestwood: St. Vladimir's Seminary Press, 1983, repr.), p. 157.

94. Ibid.

95. Ibid., p. 159.

96. Constantine D. Kalokyris, *Athos, Themes of Archaeology and Art* [in Greek and English] (Athens: Astir Publishing, Al. & E. Papademetriou, 1963), p. 323.

97. Roberts and Donaldson, *The Protoevangelium of James*, loc. cit.

98. *Exposition of the Orthodox Faith, Book IV*, ch. xiv.

99. Saint Ambrose, *Letter 44, To Pope Siricius, et. al.*, (dated c.389), The Fathers of the Church, vol. 26, trans. by Sister Mary Melchior Beyenka, O.P. (Washington, D.C.: The Catholic University Press, 1987; repr.), 227-228.

100. Resurrection Theotokion of Saturday Vespers, Tone Plagal First.

101. *Letter 59, To the Church at Vercelli*, (dated 396), Fathers of the Church, op. cit., pp. 332-333.

102. Georgios L. Mantzaridis, *The Deification of Man: St. Gregory Palamas and the Orthodox Tradition*, trans. by Liadain Sherrard (Crestwood, NY: St. Vladimir's Seminary Press, 1984), 29.

103. *Against Eunomius, Hom. II*, PG 45, 492.

104. *Sermon on the Presentation*, PG 93, 1469.

105. Matins Canon, 8 Sept., Ode One, Tone Plagal Four by St. Andrew of Crete.

106. Saint Ephraim the Syrian, "Hymns on the Nativity", *The Harp of the Spirit*, trans. by Sebastian Brock (England: Fellowship of St. Alban & St. Sergius, 1975), p. 35.

107. Ibid.

108. *Hymns on the Nativity, Hymn IV*, Nicene and Post-Nicene Fathers of the Christian Church, op. cit., p. 236.

109. Matins Canon, 25 Mar., Ode Nine, Tone Four.

110. *Hymns on the Nativity, Hymn IV*, Nicene and Post-Nicene Fathers of the Christian Church, loc. cit.

111. Canon of Forefeast, Ode Nine, Tone Two.

112. Matinal Lauds of Forefeast, Tone Six.

113. Aposticha of Forefeast (Slav), Tone One.

114. Vespers Sticheron of Forefeast, Tone Four.

115. *Hymns on the Nativity, Hymn X*, Nicene and Post-Nicene Fathers of the Christian Church, op. cit., p. 245.

116. Vespers Sticheron of Forefeast, Tone Four.

117. Kontakion 26 Dec., Tone Plagal Second.

118. PG 26, 1061B.

119. *Letter 4 to Bishop Nestorius*, The Fathers of the Church, op. cit., pp. 40-41.

120. *Letter 17 to Bishop Nestorius*, The Fathers of the Church, op. cit., p. 83.

121. Vespers Aposticha, 9 Sept., Tone Four.

122. Matins Canon, 20 Aug., Ode Six, Tone Four.

123. *Hymns on the Nativity, Hymn XI*, Nicene and Post-Nicene Fathers of the Christian Church, op. cit., p. 245.

124. *Exposition of the Orthodox Faith, Book II*, op. cit., ch. xii, pp. 55-56.

558

125. *Catechesis IV, On the Ten Doctrines*, Vol. 1, The Fathers of the Church, op. cit., p. 123.

126. Saint Leo the Great, *Sermon 27(ii)*, The Nicene and Post-Nicene Fathers of the Christian Church, Second Series, vol. XII, Philip Schaff, D.D., LL.D. and Henry Wace, D.D., eds. (Grand Rapids, MI: Wm. B. Eerdmans Pub. Co., 1979), pp. 139-140.

127. *Serm. 22, 3,* in PL 54, 196C.

128. *Tome of Leo, 4,* in PL 54, 768A.

129. *Hom. 16,* PG 151, 192C.

130. PG 151, 192C; *Hom. 58, Homilies of St. Gregory Palamas,* comp. by S. Oikonomos (Athens, 1861), p. 230 (note: This rare edition may be found in Migne, *PG* 151). Also cited in John Meyendorff, *A Study of Gregory Palamas,* trans. from French by George Lawrence (London: Faith Press, 1964), p. 235.

131. Meyendorff, *A Study of Gregory Palamas,* p. 236.

132. *Hom. 40,* PG 151, col. 513C, cited in Meyendorff, *A Study of Gregory Palamas,* p. 236.

133. *Against Heresies*, Book III, Ante-Nicene Fathers, op. cit., ch. 21(5), 453.

134. Saint Irenaeus, *Proof of the Apostolic Preaching: Christ in the Old Law,* Ancient Christian Writers, op. cit., end note 180, p. 175.

135. Dionysius of Fourna, *The Painter's Manual,* trans. by Paul Hetherington (London: Sagittarius Press, 1974), 146.

What does the scriptural verse from The Song 3:7-8, have us contemplate when it says, "Behold Solomon's bed; sixty mighty men of the mighty ones of Israel are round about it. They all hold a sword being expert in war: every man has his sword upon his thigh because of fear by night"? Saint Gregory the Great comments that "the sword is put upon the thigh when the evil suggestion of the flesh is subdued by the sharp edge of holy preaching. Every man's sword is put upon his thigh because of the fears of the night. By night, is expressed the blindness of our infirmity." [Saint Gregory the Great, *The Book of Pastoral Rule*, The Nicene and Post-Nicene Fathers of the Christian Church, Second Series, vol. XII, Philip Schaff, D.D., LL.D., Henry Wace, D.D., Rev. James Barmby, D.D., trans. and eds. (Grand Rapids, MI: Wm. B. Eerdmans Pub. Co., 1979; repr.), ch. XXXII, p. 64.]

136. "Akathist to the Most Holy Theotokos in Honor of Her Dormition" *Orthodox Life* 34, No. 4 (July-August, 1984): 19-29.

137. Matins Canon, 31 August (Deposition of the Virgin's Cincture, Ode Nine, Tone Plagal Fourth, by St. Joseph the Hymnographer.

138. The Great Supplicatory Canon to the Theotokos. A poem of Emperor Theodore Ducas Lascaris, chanted during the first fourteen days of August, that is, the Fast of the Mother of God. Ode Eight, Tone Plagal Fourth.

139. Vespers Sticheron, Tone One.

140. Saint Jerome, *Against Jovianus, Book I*, The Nicene and Post-Nicene Fathers of the Christian Church, Second Series, vol. VI, Philip Schaff, D.D., LL.D. and Henry Wace, D.D., eds. (Grand Rapids, MI: Wm. B. Eerdmans Pub. Co., 1983), 369.

141. Saint Ambrose, *Concerning Virgins*, The Nicene and Post-Nicene Fathers of the Christian Church, Second Series, vol. X, Philip Schaff, D.D., LL.D. and Henry Wace, D.D., eds. (Grand Rapids, MI: Wm. B. Eerdmans Pub. Co., 1979), ch. IX, p. 371.

142. *The Harp of the Spirit*, op. cit., p. 36.

143. Ibid.

144. Ibid., p. 64.

145. Ibid., p. 67.

146. *The Life and Struggles of Our Holy Father Among the Saints, John, the Priest of Damascus (4th of December)* in The Lives of the Saints of the Holy Land and the Sinai Desert, trans. by Holy Apostles Convent (Buena Vista, CO: Holy Apostles Convent Publications, 1988), 439-440.

147. Canon to the Theotokos, Ode Eight, Tone Plagal Fourth.

148. Matins Canon, 27 Jan., (Slav) Ode One, Tone Plagal Second.

149. *Serm. 26, 6,* in PL 54, 213B.

150. Saint Ephraim Syrus, *Hymns on the Nativity, Hymn IV,* Nicene and Post-Nicene Fathers of the Christian Church, op. cit., p. 235.

151. Ibid.

152. Roberts and Donaldson, *The Protoevangelium of James,* op. cit., p. 365.

153. Bishop Nikolai Velimirovic, *The Prologue from Ochrid,* Pt. 4, Trans. by Mother Maria (Birmingham: Lazarica Press, 1986), pp. 385-386; Alpha House, *The Protoevangelion,* op. cit. 34; Roberts and Donaldson, *The Protoevangelium of James,* p. 366.

154. *The Perpetual Virginity of Blessed Mary,* The Nicene and Post-Nicene Fathers of the Christian Church, p. 339; PL 23, 192A.

155. Theotokion, 4 Mar., Ode Nine, Tone Plagal Fourth.

156. *Hymns on the Nativity, Hymn XVI,* op. cit., p. 256.

157. *Hymns on the Nativity, Hymn VI,* op. cit., pp. 239-240.

158. *Hymns on the Nativity, Hymn XI,* op. cit., p. 245.

159. PG, 9, 529,30; *Stromata VII,* 16, in *Die griechischen christlichen Sriftsteller der ersten drei Jahrhunderte* (Leipzig-Berlin, 1897), 17, 66.

160. *Or. II c. Arianos, 7,* in PG 26, 161B; *Corpus Scriptorum Christianorum Orientalium,* (Louvain, 1903), 59.

161. Matins Canon, 8 Sept., Ode Three, Tone Two.

162. *Epist. 63, 33,* PL 16, 1198C.

163. *Letter of Flavian, the Tome, Leo I,* E. Schwartz, ed., *Acta Conciliorum Oecumenicorum* (Strasburg, 1914), 2,2,1,25; PL 54,759.

164. *On the Institution of Virginity,* VIII, 52.

165. *Hom. 1 in Praesent. 3, 6-9,* PG 93, 1453-1477.

166. Canon of Forefeast, Ode Five, Tone Plagal Second.

167. PG 46, 1141B.

168. *In Cant. Canticorum, 13,* in PG 44, 1053C.

169. James I. Packer, A.M., D. Phil., Merrill C. Tenney, A.M., Ph.D., William White, Jr., Th.M., Ph.D., eds., *The Bible Almanac* (Nashville: Thomas Nelson Publishers, 1980), 445.

170. Ralph Gower, *The New Manners and Customs of Bible Times* (Chicago: Moody Press, 1987), 62; J.A. Thompson, *Handbook of Life in Bible Times* (Downers Grove, IL: Inter-Varsity Press, 1986), 267.

171. P. Maas, *Fruhbyzantinische Kirchenpoesie* (Bonn, 1916), 5. See Constantine D. Kalokyris, *Athos, Themes of Archaeology and Art* [in Greek and English] (Athens: Astir Publishing, Al. & E. Papademetriou, 1963), 18, 321.

172. Kalokyris, *Athos,* p. 322.

173. Ibid.

174. Ibid., p. 324.

175. Ibid.

176. Ouspensky and Lossky, *The Meaning of Icons*, op. cit., p. 159.
177. Matinal Lauds of Nativity, Tone Four.
178. Matinal Lauds of Forefeast (Slav), Tone Plagal Second.
179. *Hymns on the Nativity, Hymn XV,* Nicene and Post-Nicene Fathers of the Christian Church, op. cit., p. 254.
180. *Hom. V de SS. Deip. 1,* in PG 93,1461; *Hom V in SS. Deip.,* in M. Aubineau ed., 158.
181. Saint Gregory Palamas, *Homily 37 on the August Dormition of Our Most Immaculate Lady Theotokos and Ever-Virgin Mary* [in Greek], PG 151, 460-474.
182. Doxastikon of the Nativity Aposticha, Tone Four.
183. Nativity Eve, Third Hour, Tone Three.
184. Nativity Vespers Sticheron, Tone Two, by Anatolios.
185. Saint John of Kronstadt, *My Life in Christ,* trans. by E. E. Goulaeff (Jordanville, NY: Printshop of St. Job of Pochaev, 1984), 255.
186. Third Hour of Nativity, Ideomelon, Tone Plagal Fourth.
187. Matins Canon of Nativity, Ode Seven, Tone One.
188. Matins Canon, Ode Seven, Tone One.
189. Matins Sessional Hymn of Forefeast, Tone Plagal Fourth.
190. Matins Canon of Nativity, Ode Three, Tone One.
191. *Hymns on the Nativity, Hymn V,* Nicene and Post-Nicene Fathers of the Christian Church, op. cit., p. 237.
192. Matins Canon of Nativity, Ode Seven, Tone One.
193. *Hymns on the Nativity, Hymn V,* p. 238.
194. Ibid., p. 237.
195. Ibid.
196. Sessional Hymn of Nativity Matins, Tone Four.
197. *On the Nativity (Mary and the Magi),* Kontakia of Romanos, op. cit., strophe 2, Tone Three, p. 4.
198. Vespers Sticheron, 28 Dec. (Slav), Tone Plagal First.
199. Canon of Forefeast, Ode Seven, Tone Two.
200. Canon of Forefeast, Ode Eight, Tone Two.
201. Ibid.
202. Vespers Sticheron, 28 Dec. (Slav), Tone Plagal First.
203. Matins Ikos 26 Dec.

X. WISE MEN OUT OF THE EAST

1. It is not within the scope of this work to discuss in detail the "times" of Daniel and the difficult interpretation and justification of the years which varies among biblical scholars.
2. *Sermon for the Epiphany,* cited in M.D. Toal, D.D., *The Sunday Sermons of the Great Fathers,* 3rd ed., vol. I, (Chicago: Henry Regnery Co., 1964), pp. 222-223.
3. PG 123, 61.
4. Nativity Dismissal Hymn, Tone Four. Unless otherwise specified, hymns in this section are taken from the Feast on the 25th of September.
5. Matins Canon of Nativity, Ode Nine, Tone One.
6. *Homily 10, On the Gifts of the Magi,* PL 74, 1110.
7. Merrill C. Tenney and Steven Barabas, eds., *Pictorial Encyclopedia of the Bible,* vol. 4 (Grand Rapids: Regency Reference Library & Zondervan Publishing House, 1975), 34.
8. Ibid.
9. Paul A. Underwood, *The Kariye Djami, Vol. 1, Historical Introduction and Description of the Mosaics and Frescoes,* Bollingen Series LXX (NY: Pantheon Books, 1966), 92.

10. Leonid Ouspensky and Vladimir Lossky, *The Meaning of Icons,* trans. by G.E.H. Palmer and E. Kadloubovsky (Crestwood: St. Vladimir's Seminary Press, 1983, repr.), 159-160.

11. Bishop Nikolai Velimirovic, *The Prologue from Ochrid,* Pt. 4, Trans. by Mother Maria (Birmingham: Lazarica Press, 1986), 370.

12. Matins Canon of Nativity, Ode Eight, Tone One.

13. Ibid.

14. *Sermon for the Epiphany,* loc. cit.

15. Saint John Chrysostom, *Homilies on the Gospel of St. Matthew, Homily VI,* The Nicene and Post-Nicene Fathers of the Christian Church, First Series, vol. X, Philip Schaff, D.D., LL.D., ed. (Grand Rapids, MI: Wm. B. Eerdmans Pub. Co., 1975), 37-38.

16. Saint Romanos the Melodist, *On the Nativity (Mary and the Magi),* Kontakia of Romanos, Byzantine Melodist, vol. I, trans. and annot. by Marjorie Carpenter (MO: University of Missouri Press, 1970), strophes 8-9, Tone Three, p. 6.

17. Saint Ignatios of Antioch, *Epistle of St. Ignatios to the Ephesians,* The Ante-Nicene Fathers, The Writings of the Fathers down to A.D. 325, vol. I, Rev. Alexander Roberts, D.D. and James Donaldson, LL.D., eds. (Grand Rapids, MI: Wm. B. Eerdmans Pub. Co., 1987), ch. 19, p. 57.

18. PG 123, 61.

19. Ouspensky and Lossky, *The Meaning of Icons,* 159.

20. *Homily 2 ex Op. Imp.,* op. cit., p. 204.

21. Rev. Alexander Roberts, D.D. and James Donaldson, LL.D., eds., *Apocrypha of the New Testament: The Protoevangelium of James* and *The Gospel of Pseudo-Matthew,* The Ante-Nicene Fathers, The Writings of the Fathers down to A.D. 325, vol. VIII (Grand Rapids, MI: Wm. B. Eerdmans Pub. Co., 1986), pp. 366 and 375-376, respectively.

22. *Serm. 2 ex Op. Imp.,* cited in Toal, *The Sunday Sermons of the Great Fathers,* op. cit., p. 205.

23. Ibid., p. 206.

24. Matins Canon of Nativity, Ode Three, Tone One.

25. *Homily 8 on the Gospels;* cited in Toal, *The Sunday Sermons of the Great Fathers,* op. cit., p. 205.

26. *Hom. 2 ex Op. Imp.,* loc. cit.

27. Ibid.

28. *Homilies on the Gospel of St. Matthew, Homily VII,* The Nicene and Post-Nicene Fathers of the Christian Church, op. cit.

29. Ninth Hour of Nativity, Ideomelon, Grave Tone.

30. Alpha House, *The Protoevangelion,* The Lost Books of the Bible (NY: Meridian Books, 1974), 35.

31. *Hom. 2 ex Op. Imp.,* op. cit., pp. 207-208.

32. Saint Romanos the Melodist, *On the Massacre of the Innocents and the Flight into Egypt,* Kontakia of Romanos, Byzantine Melodist, vol. I, trans. and annot. by Marjorie Carpenter (MO: University of Missouri Press, 1970), strophe 3, Tone Plagal Second, p. 27.

33. *Sermon 4, On the Solemnity of the Epiphany of Our Lord Jesus Christ,* PL 54, 234.

34. *Homily 2 ex Op. Imp.,* loc. cit.

35. Matins Canon of Nativity, Ode Nine, Tone One.

36. *Hom. 2 ex Op. Imp.,* op. cit., pp. 208-209.

37. Vespers Sticheron, 28 Dec. (Slav), Tone Plagal First.

38. Aposticha of Forefeast (Slav), Tone One.

39. Saint Ephraim Syrus, *Hymns on the Nativity, Hymn X,* Nicene and Post-Nicene Fathers of the Christian Church, Second Series, vol. XIII, trans. by Rev. J.B. Morris, M.A. (Grand Rapids, MI: Wm. B. Eerdmans Pub. Co., 1976), p. 244.

40. Saint Ephraim the Syrian, *The Harp of the Spirit,* trans. by Sebastian Brock (England: Fellowship of St. Alban & St. Sergius, 1975), 68.

41. *On the Nativity (Mary and the Magi),* Kontakia of Romanos, op. cit., strophe 4, Tone Three, p. 4.

42. Ibid., strophe 5.

43. Ibid., strophe 6, pp. 5-6.

44. Ibid., strophe 7, p. 6.

45. *On the Nativity (Mary and the Magi),* strophes 8-9, Tone Three, p. 6.

46. Ibid., strophes 9-10, p. 7.

47. Ibid., strophe 13, p. 8.

48. Ibid., strophe 17, p. 9.

49. Ibid., strophe 18, pp. 9-10.

50. Ibid., strophe 19, p. 10.

51. Saint Gregory of Nyssa, *The Life of Moses,* trans. by Abraham J. Malherbe and Everett Ferguson (NY: Paulist Press, 1978), 88.

52. *Sermon 4 on the Solemnity of the Epiphany of Our Lord Jesus Christ,* PL 54, 234.

53. Matins Canon of the Nativity, Ode One, Tone One.

54. *Hom. 2 ex Op. Imp.,* op. cit., p. 210.

55. *Sermon 8, The Epiphany and the Flight into Egypt,* PG 57, 81.

56. Aposticha of Forefeast (Slav) Tone One.

57. *On the Nativity (Mary and the Magi),* strophe 21, p. 10.

58. Nativity Aposticha, Tone Three by Anatolios.

59. Canon of Forefeast, Ode Five, Tone Plagal Second.

60. Ibid., Ode Eight.

61. *On the Nativity (Mary and the Magi),* strophes 22-24, p. 11.

62. *Hom. 2 ex Op. Imp.,* loc. cit.

63. *Homilies on the Gospel of St. Matthew, Homily VIII,* The Nicene and Post-Nicene Fathers of the Christian Church, op. cit., p. 50.

64. *Homily 10, On the Gifts of the Magi,* PL 74, 1110.

At the present time, portions of the gifts of the magi are to be found in the Holy Monastery of St. Paul on the Holy Mountain. They were donated to the monastery by the Empress Kyra-Maro or Mara, the daughter of Serbian Prince George Brankovic. History records that she was the wife of Sultan Murat II and the mother of Mohammed II. It was her desire to present the gifts personally to the monastery, albeit, no woman was allowed to step foot on the Holy Mountain. Nevertheless, the monks received her on the shore and, out of respect and deference to her rank, did not protest when she proceeded up the path to deposit the gifts within the monastery. When she was half-way up the path, however, the Mother of God intervened. Straightway, there was an earthquake, and a feminine voice from heaven was heard, saying, "Do thou not proceed any further, for another Queen rules this place." In other words, the "other Queen" was Mary Theotokos. Mara immediately halted and gave the magi's gifts to the monks and withdrew to the ship. To this day, a chapel may be seen that was built on this site, commemorating the event. By this little narrative, we learn that the Virgin-Mother wisely did not wish to have a precedent set by allowing females to tread on that parcel. As a solicitous Mother over her struggling sons, the monks, she wished to prevent any temptations that might ensue with female visitors.

65. *Hymns on the Nativity, Hymn IV,* Nicene and Post-Nicene Fathers of the Christian Church, Second Series, op. cit., p. 236.

66. *Hom. 2 ex Op. Imp.,* op. cit., p. 212.

67. Ibid.

68. *Homily 10, On the Gifts of the Magi,* loc. cit.

69. Aposticha of Forefeast, Tone One.

70. *Hymns on the Nativity, Hymn IV,* p. 236.

71. Ibid., p. 235.

72. "Saint Joseph the Betrothed," *Orthodox Life* 28, No. 6 (Nov.-Dec., 1978): 6. [Translated from *Lives of the Saints* 8, Munich: St. Job of Pochaev Monastery, 1956, 110-113].

73. Eusebius, *The History of the Church,* trans. by G.A. Williamson (NY: Dorset Press, 1984), pp. 123, 124, 181; Bishop Nikolai Velimirovic, *The Prologue from Ochrid,* Pt. 2, op. cit., p. 106; and *Eccl. History* of Nicephoros Callistos, ch. 3.

74. *St. Symeon,* The Great Synaxaristes of the Orthodox Church [in Greek], 5th ed., vol. IV (Athens, 1979), 559-562.

75. *On the Nativity (Mary and the Magi),* strophes 11-12, p. 7.

76. *Homily on the Nativity,* PG 31, 1464B.

77. *Hom. 3 in Advent.,* in *Corpus Christianorum, Series Latina,* Turnhout (1953), 122, 15. (Hereinafter referred to as CCSL).

78. *In Lucan 1,* in CCSL, 120, 30-31.

79. *Epistle of St. Ignatios to the Ephesians,* The Ante-Nicene Fathers, op. cit., ch. 19.

XI. THE CIRCUMCISION

1. Eusebius, *Evangeliki Apodexis,* 4:17, PG 22, 332; Alfred Edersheim, M.A. Oxon., D.D., Ph.D., *The Life and Times of Jesus the Messiah* (McLean, VA: MacDonald Publishing Co.), 193.

2. Vespers Sticheron, Tone Plagal Fourth. Unless otherwise specified, hymns in this section are taken from the Feast on the 1st of January.

3. *Hom. 17, Catena GP,* cited in M.D. Toal, D.D., *The Sunday Sermons of the Great Fathers,* 3rd ed., vol. I, (Chicago: Henry Regnery Co., 1964), 187.

4. Constantine Callinicos, *Our Lady the Theotokos,* trans. and rev. by Rev. George Dimopoulos (Upper Darby, PA: Christian Orthodox Ed., 1987), p. 56.

5. See Josephus, *Contra Apionem* 2.133; *Kelim Tractate* of the *Mishnah,* i.8. Cited in Joachim Jeremias, *Jerusalem in the Time of Jesus* (Philadelphia: Fortress Press, 1969), p. 373.

6. Toal, op. cit., p. 188.

7. Matins Canon, Ode Seven, Tone Two by Stephen.

8. Ibid., Ode Five.

9. Ibid., Ode One.

10. Dismissal Hymn, Tone One.

11. Matins Canon, Ode Three, Tone Two by Stephen.

12. Sermon *Omnia mihi tradita sunt.*

13. *Homily 5, On the Feast of the Circumcision,* cited in *Commentary on the Gospel of Saint Luke,* trans. by R. Payne Smith (NY: Studion Publishers, Inc., 1983), 57.

14. Matins Canon, Ode Six, Tone Two by Stephen.

15. Ibid.

XII. THE MEETING IN THE TEMPLE

1. *Meeting in the Temple,* The Great Synaxaristes of the Orthodox Church [in Greek], 5th ed., vol. II (Athens, 1978), 58.
2. A cento from Ex. 12::51-13:16, Lev. 12 and Num. 8, read at Vespers.
3. *Meeting in the Temple,* Great Synaxaristes [in Greek], op. cit., 64.
4. Saint Ambrose, *Letter 76, Ambrose to Irenaeus* (c. 387), The Fathers of the Church, vol. 26, trans. by Sister Mary Melchior Beyenka, O.P. (Washington, D.C.: The Catholic University Press, 1987; repr.), 429-431.
5. *Meeting in the Temple,* Great Synaxaristes, op. cit., p. 64, f.n. 1; *Holy Bible from the Ancient Eastern Text (from the Aramaic of the Peshitta),* translated by George M. Lamsa (NY: Harper & Row, Pub., n.d.), 1015.
6. Book IV, ch. 26.
7. D. Cummings, trans., "Canons of the Holy Fathers: St. Dionysios the Alexandrian" in *The Rudder (Pedalion),* (Chicago: The Orthodox Christian Educational Society, 1957), 719.
8. James I. Packer, A.M., D. Phil., Merrill C. Tenney, A.M., Ph.D., William White, Jr., Th.M., Ph.D., eds., *The Bible Almanac* (Nashville: Thomas Nelson Publishers, 1980), 399.
9. Alfred Edersheim, M.A. Oxon., D.D., Ph.D., *The Life and Times of Jesus the Messiah* (McLean, VA: MacDonald Publishing Co.), 194.
10. Packer, Tenney, White, *The Bible Almanac,* p. 403.
11. Saint Ambrose, *Hexaemeron,* The Fathers of the Church, vol. 42, trans. by John J. Savage (Washington, D.C.: The Catholic University Press, 1985; repr.), ch. 19, p. 210.
12. Canon of the Akathist Hymn, Ode Nine, Tone Four.
13. Matins Canon, Ode Nine, Tone Three. Unless otherwise specified, hymns in this section are taken from the Feast on the 2nd of February.
14. Packer, Tenney and White, op. cit., 402; Merrill C. Tenney and Steven Barabas, eds., *Pictorial Encyclopedia of the Bible,* vol. 5 (Grand Rapids: Regency Reference Library & Zondervan Publishing House, 1975), 205.
15. Doxastikon of Vespers, Tone Plagal Second.
16. Sessional Hymn of Matins, Tone Four.
17. Matins Sedalen, 3 Feb., Tone One.
18. Doxastikon of Vespers Lity, Tone Plagal First.
19. Tenney and Barabas, *Pictorial Encyclopedia of the Bible,* vol. 5, p. 343.
20. Ibid.
21. Bishop Nikolai Velimirovic, *The Prologue from Ochrid,* Pt. 3, Trans. by Mother Maria (Birmingham: Lazarica Press, 1986), 141.
22. *Meeting in the Temple,* Great Synaxaristes, op. cit., pp. 62-63.
23. Ibid., p. 63.
24. Vespers Sticheron, 3 Feb., Tone Four.
25. Ibid., pp. 63-64.
26. Saint Irenaeus, *Against Heresies,* Book III, Ante-Nicene Fathers, The Writings of the Fathers down to A.D. 326, vol. I, Rev. Alexander Roberts, D.D. and James Donaldson, eds. (Grand Rapids, MI: Wm. B. Eerdmans Pub. Co., 1987; repr.), ch. 21(2), pp. 451-452.
27. *De vita Moysis.*
28. *The Antiquities of the Jews,* The Works of Josephus, trans. by William Whiston, A.M. (Peabody, MA: Hendrickson Pub., 1988), 12.2.
29. Saint Justin Martyr, *Exhortation to the Greeks,* The Fathers of the Church, vol. 6, 3d ed., trans. by Thomas B. Falls, D.D., Ph.D. (Washington, D.C.: The Catholic University of America Press, 1977), ch. 13, pp. 389-390.
30. Tenney and Barabas, op. cit., p. 344.
31. Ibid., pp. 345-346.

32. Matins Canon, Ode Nine, Tone Three by St. Cosmas.

33. Aposticha of Vespers, Grave Tone.

34. *In Luke, Book 1*, cited in M.D. Toal, D.D., *The Sunday Sermons of the Great Fathers*, 3rd ed., vol. I (Chicago: Henry Regnery Co., 1964), 164.

35. Vespers Lity, Tone One by Anatolios.

36. Matins Canon, 5 Sept., Ode 8, Tone Plagal Fourth.

37. *Prophet Zacharias*, The Great Synaxaristes of the Orthodox Church [in Greek], 5th ed., vol. IX (Athens, 1978), p. 143.

38. Sedalion, 5 Sept., Tone Plagal Fourth.

39. Kathisma of Sunday Matins, Tone Four (actually a "borrowed" melody from Tone Plagal Second).

40. Saint Ephraim Syrus, *Hymns on the Nativity, Hymn IV*, Nicene and Post-Nicene Fathers of the Christian Church, Second Series, vol. XIII, trans. by Rev. J.B. Morris, M.A. (Grand Rapids, MI: Wm. B. Eerdmans Pub. Co., 1976), p. 237.

41. Bishop Nikolai Velimirovic, *The Prologue from Ochrid*, Pt. 4, 386.

42. St. Basil, PG 31, 1468A.

43. Glory of Vespers Aposticha, Tone Plagal Fourth.

44. Glory of the Aposticha of Small Vespers, Tone Two.

45. Matins Canon, Ode Four, Tone Three.

46. Aposticha of Small Vespers, Tone Two.

47. Matins Canon, 27 Jan., Ode Seven, Tone Three.

48. Matins Canon, Ode Five, Tone Three.

49. *The Prologue from Ochrid*, Pt. 1, op. cit., p. 134.

50. Rev. Alexander Roberts, D.D. and James Donaldson, LL.D., eds., *Apocrypha of the New Testament: The Infancy of the Saviour*, The Ante-Nicene Fathers, The Writings of the Fathers down to A.D. 325, vol. VIII (Grand Rapids, MI: Wm. B. Eerdmans Pub. Co., 1986), 406.

51. *On the Presentation in the Temple*, Kontakia of Romanos, op. cit., strophe 3, p. 40.

52. Ibid., strophe 5, p. 40.

53. Matins Canon, Ode Five, Tone Three.

54. Saint Ephraim Syrus, *Homily on Our Lord*, Nicene and Post-Nicene Fathers of the Christian Church, Second Series, vol. VIII, trans. by Rev. Edward A. Johnston, B.D. (Grand Rapids, MI: Wm. B. Eerdmans Pub. Co., 1976), p. 327.

55. Irmos of Matins Canon, Ode Six, Tone Three.

56. Matins Canon, Ode Nine, Tone Three.

57. Ikos of Matins Canon.

58. *On the Presentation in the Temple*, Kontakia of Romanos, strophe 2, p. 40.

59. Ibid., strophe 7, pp. 41-42.

60. Vespers Sticheron, Tone One.

61. Leonid Ouspensky and Vladimir Lossky, *The Meaning of Icons*, trans. by G.E.H. Palmer and E. Kadloubovsky (Crestwood: St. Vladimir's Seminary Press, 1983, repr.), 168.

62. Vespers Lity, Tone Two by Anatolios or St. Andrew of Jerusalem.

63. *Homily on Our Lord*, Nicene and Post-Nicene, op. cit., p. 327.

64. Ibid., p. 328.

65. *On the Presentation in the Temple*, op. cit., strophe 6, p. 40.

66. Small Vespers Sticheron, Tone One.

67. Vespers Lity, Tone One by Anatolios.

68. Vespers Sticheron, Tone One.

69. Vespers Lity, Tone Two.

70. Matinal Lauds, Tone Four.

71. Vespers Aposticha, Grave Tone by St. Cosmas.

72. Matins Canon, 3 Feb., Ode Seven, Tone Four.

73. Matins Canon, Ode Nine, Tone Three.

74. Aposticha of Small Vespers, Tone Two.

75. Matinal Lauds, Tone Four.

76. *On the Presentation in the Temple*, strophes 14-16, pp. 44-45.

77. Ibid., strophe 17, p. 45.

78. Matins Canon, Ode Seven, Tone Three.

79. *Hymns on the Nativity, Hymn IV*, op. cit., p. 236.

80. *On the Presentation in the Temple*, strophe 9, p. 42.

81. Toal, *The Sunday Sermons of the Great Fathers*, op. cit., p. 164.

82. *On the Presentation in the Temple*, strophe 10, pp. 42-43.

83. *On the Presentation in the Temple*, strophes 11-12, pp. 43.

84. Matins Canon. Ode Six, Tone Three.

85. *Oratio in Occursu Domini* or *On the Presentation of Christ in the Temple*, cited in Toal, *The Sunday Sermons of the Great Fathers*, 164-165.

86. Toal, *The Sunday Sermons of the Great Fathers*, p. 166.

87. Ibid., p. 180.

88. Ibid.

89. "The Genealogy of Christ," *Orthodox Life* 24, no. 6 (Nov-Dec. 1974): 10-14. (Trans. from *The Russian Pilgrim*, 1895, Nos. 51, 51).

90. Matins Canon, Ode Seven, Tone Three.

91. *In Luc. Hom. XVII*, cited in *Sources Chretiennes* (Lyons), 87, 257-259.

92. Saint Cyril of Alexandria, *Commentary on the Gospel of Saint Luke, Homily 4*, trans. by R. Payne Smith (NY: Studion Publishers, Inc., 1983), 84.

93. *On the Presentation in the Temple*, strophe 13, p. 44.

94. Saint Paulinus of Nola, *Letter 50, To Augustine*, Ancient Christian Writers, vol. 36, trans. and annot. by P.G. Walsh (NY: Paulist Press, 1967), pp. 17-18.

95. Toal, *The Sunday Sermons of the Great Fathers*, p. 167.

96. *Meeting in the Temple*, Great Synaxaristes, op. cit., pp. 71-72.

97. Ibid., p. 72.

98. Toal, D.D., *The Sunday Sermons of the Great Fathers*, p. 180.

99. Ibid., p. 181.

100. *The Prologue from Ochrid*, Pt. 4, op. cit., p. 387.

101. Toal, *The Sunday Sermons of the Great Fathers*, p. 167.

102. Vespers Lity, Tone Two by Anatolios or St. Andrew of Jerusalem.

103. Matins Canon, Ode Nine, Tone Three.

104. Toal, loc. cit.

105. *Hymns on the Nativity, Hymn IV*, op. cit., p. 237.

106. Ibid.

107. *Meeting in the Temple*, Great Synaxaristes, pp. 76-77; St. Amphilochios, *In Praise of Virginity*, PG 39, 44.

108. PG 39, 44.

109. Matins Canon, Ode Nine, Tone Three.

110. Ibid.

111. Toal, D.D., *The Sunday Sermons of the Great Fathers*, p. 168.

112. PL 92, 347.

113. John Baggley, *Doors of Perception* (Crestwood, NY: St. Vladimir's Seminary Press, 1988), 126.

XIII. MASSACRE OF 14,000 INFANTS

1. Canon of Forefeast, Ode Nine, Tone Plagal Second.
2. Eusebius, *Church History,* The Nicene and Post-Nicene Fathers of the Christian Church, First Series, vol. I, trans. by Rev. Arthur Cushman McGiffert (Grand Rapids, MI: Wm. B. Eerdmans Pub. Co., 1961), 6:6.
3. Matins Resurrection Canon to the Theotokos, Tone Plagal Second.
4. Rev. Alexander Roberts, D.D. and James Donaldson, LL.D., eds., *Apocrypha of the New Testament: The Gospel of Pseudo-Matthew,* The Ante-Nicene Fathers, The Writings of the Fathers down to A.D. 325, vol. VIII (Grand Rapids, MI: Wm. B. Eerdmans Pub. Co., 1986), 376.
5. Alpha House, *The Protoevangelion,* The Lost Books of the Bible (NY: Meridian Books, 1974), 35.
6. Saint Ephraim Syrus, *Hymns on the Nativity, Hymn IV,* Nicene and Post-Nicene Fathers of the Christian Church, Second Series, vol. XIII, trans. by Rev. J.B. Morris, M.A. (Grand Rapids, MI: Wm. B. Eerdmans Pub. Co., 1976), p. 237.
7. Saint Romanos the Melodist, *On the Massacre of the Innocents and the Flight into Egypt,* Kontakia of Romanos, Byzantine Melodist, vol. I, trans. and annot. by Marjorie Carpenter (MO: University of Missouri Press, 1970), Tone Plagal Second, strophe 7, p. 29.
8. Matins Canon of Nativity, Ode Nine, Tone One.
9. *On the Massacre of the Innocents and the Flight into Egypt,* Kontakia of Romanos, op. cit., strophe 7, p. 29.
10. Ibid., strophe 4, pp. 27-28.
11. Ibid., strophe 8, p. 28.
12. Ibid., strophes 5-6, p. 28.
13. Matins Canon Oikos, 29 Dec.
14. *On the Massacre of the Innocents and the Flight into Egypt,* op. cit., strophe 8, p. 29.
15. Canon of Forefeast, Ode Six, Tone Plagal Second.
16. Dismissal Hymn, 29 Dec., Tone One.
17. Vespers Sticheron, 29 Dec., Tone Four.
18. Paul A. Underwood, *The Kariye Djami, Vol. 1, Historical Introduction and Description of the Mosaics and Frescoes,* Bollingen Series LXX (NY: Pantheon Books, 1966), 99-100.
19. *On the Massacre of the Innocents and the Flight into Egypt,* op. cit., strophes 10-12, pp. 30-31.
20. Ibid., strophe 14, p. 32.
21. Ninth Hour of Nativity, Ideomelon, Grave Tone.
22. Saint Ambrose, *Letter 45, Ambrose to the Priest Horontianus,* (dated c.387), The Fathers of the Church, vol. 26, trans. by Sister Mary Melchior Beyenka, O.P. (Washington, D.C.: The Catholic University Press, 1987; repr.), p. 235.
23. Ibid., *Letter 50,* p. 269.
24. Vespers Sticheron, 29 Dec., Tone Four.
25. *Hymns on the Nativity, Hymn IV,* op. cit., p. 237.
26. Rev. Alexander Roberts, D.D. and James Donaldson, LL.D., eds., *Apocrypha of the New Testament: The Protoevangelium of James,* The Ante-Nicene Fathers, The Writings of the Fathers down to A.D. 325, vol. VIII (Grand Rapids, MI: Wm. B. Eerdmans Pub. Co., 1986), 366.
27. Vespers Doxastikon, 29 Dec., Tone Plagal Fourth.
28. Bishop Nikolai Velimirovic, *The Prologue from Ochrid,* Pt. 3, Trans. by Mother Maria (Birmingham: Lazarica Press, 1986), 291.
29. Synaxis, 7 Jan., Matins Doxastikon, Tone Plagal Second.

30. Alpha House, *The Protoevangelion*, op. cit., p. 36.

The other complaint being that their High Priest had placed a married woman in that area designated for virgins.

31. Ibid.; see, also Roberts and Donaldson, *The Protoevangelium of James*, The Ante-Nicene Fathers, loc. cit.

Bishop Nikolai Velimirovic (+1956) also makes mention in his *Prologue* that the Elder Symeon the God-Receiver was also slain and translated to God. [*The Prologue from Ochrid*, Pt. 4, 384]. This statement of Bishop Nikolai, unfortunately, cannot be substantiated with present sources, including the Church service for St. Symeon. Although it may be pious to think that the Elder Symeon crowned all his labors with martyrdom, it seems contrary to his request of the Christ child, "Now let Thy servant depart in peace."

32. Vespers, 5 Sept., Doxastikon of Aposticha, Tone Two by Anatolios.

33. Vespers Sticheron, 5 Sept., Tone Four.

34. *The Prologue from Ochrid*, Pt. 2, p. 353.

35. Ibid., Pt. 3, p. 291.

36. Taken from Eusebius, *Church History*, The Nicene and Post-Nicene Fathers of the Christian Church, First Series, vol. I, trans. by Rev. Arthur Cushman McGiffert (Grand Rapids, MI: Wm. B. Eerdmans Pub. Co., 1961), ch. viii, pp. 94-95.

37. Ibid., p. 95.

XIV. THE FLIGHT INTO EGYPT

1. Bishop Nikolai Velimirovic, *The Prologue from Ochrid*, Pt. 4, Trans. by Mother Maria (Birmingham: Lazarica Press, 1986), 372.

2. Saint Cyril of Alexandria, *Letter 86*, The Fathers of the Church, vol. 77, trans. by John I. McEnerney (Washington, D.C.: The Catholic University of America Press, 1987), 120.

3. Dr. Otto F.A. Meinardus, *The Holy Family in Egypt* (Cairo, Egypt: The American University In Cairo Press, 1986), cited in preface.

4. *Hymns on Mary* cited in *The Harp of the Spirit*, trans. by Sebastian Brock (England: Fellowship of St. Alban & St. Sergius, 1975), 60-61.

5. *Serm. 8* in PG 57, 81.

6. Saint John Chrysostom, *Homilies on the Gospel of St. Matthew, Homily VIII*, The Nicene and Post-Nicene Fathers of the Christian Church, First Series, vol. X, Philip Schaff, D.D., LL.D., ed. (Grand Rapids, MI: Wm. B. Eerdmans Pub. Co., 1975), 52.

7. Dr. Raouf Habib, *The Holy Family in Egypt* (Cairo, Egypt: Mahabba Bookshop), 3; Prof. Murad Kamel, *The Flight of the Holy Family to Egypt*, Coptic Egypt (Cairo, Egypt: American University Press, 1968), 9-10.

8. Kamel, *The Flight of the Holy Family to Egypt*, Coptic Egypt, op. cit., 10.

9. Ibid., pp. 10-11.

10. Ibid., p. 11.

11. Paul A. Underwood, *The Kariye Djami, Vol. 1, Historical Introduction and Description of the Mosaics and Frescoes*, Bollingen Series LXX (NY: Pantheon Books, 1966), 97.

12. PG 56, 385.

13. *Homilies on the Gospel of St. Matthew, Homily VIII*, The Nicene and Post-Nicene Fathers, op. cit., p. 52.

14. Saint John Chrysostom, *Homilies on the Gospel of St. John, Homily XXI*, The Nicene and Post-Nicene Fathers of the Christian Church, First Series, vol. XIV, Philip Schaff, D.D., LL.D., ed. (Grand Rapids, MI: Wm. B. Eerdmans Pub. Co., 1975), 73-74.

15. *On the Incarnation of the Word, 36*, PG 25, 157.

16. Habib, *The Holy Family in Egypt*, op. cit., p. 31.

17. Meinardus, *The Holy Family in Egypt*, p. 31; Alpha House, *Infancy of Jesus Christ*, The Lost Books of the Bible (NY: Meridian Books, 1974), pp. 45-46.

18. Alpha House, *Infancy of Jesus Christ*, op. cit., p. 47.

19. Ibid., p. 46; Bishop Nikolai Velimirovic, *The Prologue from Ochrid*, Pt. 4, Trans. by Mother Maria (Birmingham: Lazarica Press, 1986), 374.

20. Habib, *The Holy Family in Egypt*, p. 3.

21. Ibid., p. 4. This tree has ever since acquired the respect of both Christians and Moslems. Many of them have buried their dead near this tree and, thus, the place is regarded as holy ground. It has also been stated that when Napoleon's soldiers were passing near that town, they wanted to cut the tree down to use it for fueling. However, with the first ax stroke, the tree began to bleed. The soldiers were filled with dread and dared touch it no more. The mosque of Osman Ibn El-Amary, lying in the middle of the town, has been built there as a tribute to the divine travelers' visitation. The tree was eventually cut down in 1850.

22. Kamel, *The Flight of the Holy Family to Egypt*, loc. cit.

23. Habib, *The Holy Family in Egypt*, loc. cit.

24. Kamel, *The Flight of the Holy Family to Egypt*, pp. 11-12.

25. Kamel, p. 12; Habib, loc. cit.

26. Kamel, loc. cit.

27. Meinardus, *The Holy Family in Egypt*, pp. 34-35.

28. Ibid., p. 35.

29. Bishop Nikolai Velimirovic, *The Prologue from Ochrid*, Pt. 4, p. 382; *The Encyclopedia Americana*, 1957 ed., s.v. "Sycamore."

30. Habib, *The Holy Family in Egypt*, loc. cit.

31. The balsam plant was watered by the miraculous spring. Many Christians have come to wash from this water and received healing. The aromatic ointment that was extracted from the plant became a valuable export to Christians kings of Ethiopia, Greece and the Franks, being essential to them in the performance of baptisms, consecrating cathedrals and churches.

Although the gardens of that site have now ceased to produce this perfume for a long time and the blessed tree has been relocated, the same spot is still glorified and revered.

The original tree of the Virgin, where they all rested, became so weakened and worn that it fell down in 1656. Another tree grew in its place, which might be from the stem of the original tree. Due to old age, this tree fell in 1906, but a living shoot from it remains to this day. The water from that place, however, is distributed by a machine to several fountains to irrigate the gardens around the site. The Mataria garden has been famous for centuries and is considered one of the sacred centers. [Cited in Dr. Raouf Habib, "Mataria and the Virgin Tree," *St. Xenia's Monthly Bulletin* 5, No. 3 (Dec.-Jan., 1987) and Habib's, *The Holy Family in Egypt*, op. cit.].

From On, the family went to that area where now stands the Church of the Blessed Virgin in the Harat Zuwaila of Cairo. This is situated in the northeastern district of Cairo. Annexed to the church is a convent. The nuns relate the tradition that, when the holy travelers rested there, Jesus blessed the water of the well and the blessed Virgin drank from it. This well is situated in the floor below the southern sanctuary of the lower church, and the water is stilled used for healing the sick. [Cited in Kamel, pp. 12-13].

32. Alpha House, *Infancy of Jesus Christ*, pp. 41-42.

33. Resurrection Canon to the Theotokos, Tone One, Ode Three.

34. *De Virg., II, 65*, PL 16, 181C.

35. Bishop Nikolai Velimirovic, *The Prologue from Ochrid*, Pt. 3, Trans. by Mother Maria (Birmingham: Lazarica Press, 1986), 216.

36. Saint Romanos the Melodist, *On the Massacre of the Innocents and the Flight into Egypt*, Kontakia of Romanos, Byzantine Melodist, vol. I, trans. and annot. by Marjorie Carpenter (MO: University of Missouri Press, 1970), Tone Plagal Second, strophe 17, p. 33.

37. *The Prologue from Ochrid*, Pt. 2, p. 128.

38. Ibid.

39. The Church of Abu Sarga is the oldest church in Egypt. The church was dedicated to the names of two famous martyrs, Sergios and Bachus, from Al-Rasafah village. They were martyred on October 7, 296 A.D., by Emperor Maximian.

The crypt, according to tradition, was built on the side of the place where the Virgin and child lodged. Actually the church is built over the cave. The cave is to the left upon entering the church, but one must look down into it to see it. [Cited in Rev. Gabriel G. Bestavros, *St. Sargius Church* (Old Cairo, Egypt)].

40. Kamel, p. 13.

41. Meinardus, *The Holy Family in Egypt*, p. 41.

42. Kamel, loc. cit.

43. Ibid., pp. 13-14.

44. Habib, *The Holy Family in Egypt*, p. 5.

45. Kamel, p. 14.

46. Ibid.

47. Habib, *The Holy Family in Egypt*, loc. cit.; Meinardus, p. 48.

48. Kamel, p. 15; Meinardus, loc. cit.

49. Kamel, loc. cit.

50. Meinardus, p. 49.

51. Bishop Nikolai Velimirovic, *The Prologue*, Pt. 4, 381-382.

52. *The Ecclesiastical History of Sozomen, Book V*, The Nicene and Post-Nicene Fathers of the Christian Church, Second Series, vol. II, trans. by Philip Schaff, D.D., LL.D., Henry Wace, D.D., and Chester D. Hartranft (Grand Rapids, MI: Wm. B. Eerdmans Pub. Co., 1983; repr.), ch. 21, p. 343; PG 67, 1281.

53. Canon of Forefeast of Christ's Nativity, Ode Nine, Tone Plagal Second.

54. Rev. Alexander Roberts, D.D. and James Donaldson, LL.D., eds., *Apocrypha of the New Testament: The Gospel of Pseudo-Matthew*, The Ante-Nicene Fathers, The Writings of the Fathers down to A.D. 325, vol. VIII (Grand Rapids, MI: Wm. B. Eerdmans Pub. Co., 1986), 377.

55. Kamel, loc. cit.

56. Ibid.; Habib, *The Holy Family in Egypt*, pp. 5-6.

57. Meinardus, p. 52.

58. Alpha House, *Infancy of Jesus Christ*, pp. 42-43; Rev. Alexander Roberts, D.D. and James Donaldson, LL.D., eds., *Apocrypha of the New Testament: The Infancy of the Saviour*, The Ante-Nicene Fathers, The Writings of the Fathers down to A.D. 325, vol. VIII (Grand Rapids, MI: Wm. B. Eerdmans Pub. Co., 1986), 407.

59. Alpha House, p. 43.

60. Ibid., pp. 43-44.

61. Kamel, loc. cit.; Habib, *The Holy Family in Egypt*, p. 6.

62. Meinardus, loc. cit.

63. Kamel, pp. 15-16; Habib, *The Holy Family in Egypt*, pp. 6-7.

64. The Al-Muharraq Monastery stands at the foot of the western mountain known as Mount Qousqam, after a town demolished long ago. It is twelve kilometers to the west of Al-Qoussieh, in the Asyut Governorate, 48 kilometers north of Asyut and 377 kilometers south of Cairo. To the west of the monastery stretches the western desert. To the north and east of the monastery there exists spacious areas of green land, as a result of the flooding of the Nile (which, in times of inundation, reach the outskirts of the monastery), converting the desert there into one of the most fertile areas of the whole region.

The Church of the Holy Virgin is to the west of the monastery. The main altar of the church stands in the same cave where the holy travelers lived a little more than six months. Patriarch Theophilos (376-403 A.D.) relates that the Virgin appeared in a vision and related the events of their flight into Egypt. In his manuscript, he notes that the church was small and simple, though very famous. It was his desire to erect a great cathedral, becoming the sacredness of the place. The holy Virgin, in a vision, said that the will of her Son was that the church should be kept as it was, to bear testimony to all generations of Christ's humility. Therefore, the patriarch carried out the Virgin's request and, thus, the church has remained unchanged. [Cited in Habib, *The Holy Family in Egypt*, loc. cit.

65. Kamel, p. 16.
66. Habib, *The Holy Family in Egypt*, p. 8.
67. Meinardus, p. 59.
68. *Homilies on the Gospel of St. Matthew, Homily VIII*, op. cit., p. 51.
69. Meinardus, pp. 15-16.
70. Meinardus, p. 61.
71. Ibid., p. 52.
72. Ibid., pp. 62-63.
73. Kamel, pp. 16-17.
74. Meinardus, p. 65.
75. Ibid., pp. 65-66.
76. Kamel, p. 17.
77. Ibid., p. 18.
78. Underwood, *The Kariye Djami*, op. cit., p. 105.

XV. DAILY LIFE

1. Alfred Edersheim, M.A. Oxon., D.D., Ph.D., *The Life and Times of Jesus the Messiah* (McLean, VA: MacDonald Publishing Co.), 225; Merrill C. Tenney and Steven Barabas, eds., *Pictorial Encyclopedia of the Bible*, vol. 2 (Grand Rapids: Regency Reference Library & Zondervan Publishing House, 1975), 642.
2. Tenney and Barabas, *Pictorial Encyclopedia*, op. cit., 642, 644.
3. Ibid., vol. 3, p. 686.
4. Edersheim, *The Life and Times*, p. 225.
5. James I. Packer, A.M., D. Phil., Merrill C. Tenney, A.M., Ph.D., William White, Jr., Th.M., Ph.D., eds., *The Bible Almanac* (Nashville: Thomas Nelson Publishers, 1980), 267.
6. Tenney and Barabas, *Pictorial Encyclopedia*, vol. 2, p. 642.
7. Josephus, *The Wars of the Jews*, The Works of Josephus, trans. by William Whiston, A.M. (Peabody, MA: Hendrickson Pub., 1988), III.iii2.
8. Ibid.
9. James Hastings, M.A., D.D., *A Dictionary of the Bible*, vol. 2 (Peabody: Hendrickson Pub., 1988), 102.
10. Edersheim, *The Life and Times*, pp. 147-148.

11. Vaselin and Lydia Kesich, *Treasures of the Holy Land* (Crestwood, NY: St. Vladimir's Seminary Press, 1985) 29.

12. Edersheim, *The Life and Times*, p. 223.

13. Packer, Tenney, and White, *The Bible Almanac*, p. 513.

14. J.A. Thompson, *Handbook of Life in Bible Times* (Downers Grove, IL: Inter-Varsity Press, 1986), p. 98.

15. Edersheim, *The Life and Times*, p. 225.

16. Tenney and Barabas, *Pictorial Encyclopedia,* vol. 4, p. 387.

17. Edersheim, *The Life and Times*, p. 148.

18. Thompson, *Handbook of Life in Bible Times*, 189.

19. Ralph Gower, *The New Manners and Customs of Bible Times* (Chicago: Moody Press, 1987), 153-155.

20. Packer, Tenney and White, *The Bible Almanac*, 272-274.

21. Gower, *The New Manners and Customs of Bible Times*, 155.

22. Packer, Tenney and White, *The Bible Almanac*, p. 413.

23. *BT Kiddushin 99a 2:2*, literally *Chapters of the Fathers.*

24. Tenney and Barabas, *Pictorial Encyclopedia,* vol. 4, p. 625.

25. Edersheim, *The Life and Times*, p. 252.

26. II.18.

27. Tenney and Barabas, *Pictorial Encyclopedia,* vol. 4, loc. cit.

28. Edersheim, *The Life and Times*, pp. 227-230.

29. M. Haddad-Nolan, *The New Eve*, p. 34.

30. Gower, *The New Manners and Customs*, p. 79.

31. Packer, Tenney and White, *The Bible Almanac*, pp. 452-454; Tenney and Barabas, *Pictorial Encyclopedia,* vol. 4, p. 101.

32. The word *Torah* is usually translated as law or *nomos* in the New Testament. It refers to the Pentateuch, that is, the five Books of Moses. In the Old Testament and in rabbinic usage, however, *torah* is more than a legal code. In rabbinic tradition it connotes the written code, plus interpretation as codified into the 613 precepts. At no time is *torah* purely law in a legal sense. It is rather the Jewish way of life requiring total dedication by reason of the Covenant. [Cited in Tenney and Barabas, *Pictorial Encyclopedia,* vol. 5, pp. 780-781.

33. Packer, Tenney and White, *The Bible Almanac*, pp. 455.

34. Gower, *The New Manners and Customs,* p. 80.

35. Ibid., p. 83.

36. Tenney and Barabas, *Pictorial Encyclopedia,* vol. 3, p. 501.

37. Ibid., p. 502.

38. Edersheim, *The Life and Times*, p. 250.

39. Packer, Tenney and White, *The Bible Almanac*, pp. 466.

40. Ibid., p. 482.

41. Thompson, *Handbook of Life in Bible Times*, p. 60.

42. Gower, *The New Manners and Customs*, pp. 22-30, 32; Packer, Tenney and White, *The Bible Almanac*, p. 387.

43. Gower, *The New Manners and Customs*, p. 32.

44. Thompson, *Handbook of Life in Bible Times*, loc. cit.

45. Gower, *The New Manners and Customs*, pp. 22, 32-33, 46.

46. Thompson, *Handbook of Life in Bible Times*, p. 59.

47. Ibid., p. 67.

48. Gower, *The New Manners and Customs*, pp. 36, 40.

49. Edersheim, *The Life and Times*, loc. cit.; Packer, Tenney and White, *The Bible Almanac*, p. 466.

50. Packer, Tenney and White, p. 465; Thompson, *Handbook of Life in Bible Times*, p. 158.

51. Packer, Tenney and White, p. 471.

52. Gower, *The New Manners and Customs*, pp. 51-53.

53. Packer, Tenney and White, pp. 468, 471.

54. Tenney and Barabas, *Pictorial Encyclopedia*, vol. 1, p. 59.

55. Edersheim, *The Life and Times*, pp. 250-251.

56. Packer, Tenney and White, *The Bible Almanac*, pp. 457.

57. Gower, *The New Manners and Customs*, p. 48.

58. Ibid., pp. 42-44.

59. Thompson, *Handbook of Life in Bible Times*, p. 154.

60. Packer, Tenney and White, *The Bible Almanac*, p. 469.

61. Gower, *The New Manners and Customs*, pp. 46-47.

62. Packer, Tenney and White, *The Bible Almanac*, pp. 469-470.

63. Thompson, *Handbook of Life in Bible Times*, p. 160.

64. Gower, *The New Manners and Customs*, p. 45.

65. Packer, Tenney and White, *The Bible Almanac*, p. 426.

66. Gower, *The New Manners and Customs*, pp. 54-55.

67. Ibid., p. 45.

68. Ibid., pp. 180-181.

69. Ibid., p. 196.

70. Packer, Tenney and White, *The Bible Almanac*, p. 478.

71. Gower, *The New Manners and Customs*, p. 15.

72. Ibid.

73. Packer, Tenney and White, *The Bible Almanac*, p. 480; Gower, *The New Manners and Customs*, p. 250.

74. Packer, Tenney and White, pp. 482-483.

75. Ibid., p. 484.

76. Gower, *The New Manners and Customs*, p. 17.

77. Ibid., p. 48.

78. Thompson, *Handbook of Life in Bible Times*, p. 275.

79. Gower, *The New Manners and Customs*, pp. 235-236.

80. Tenney and Barabas, *Pictorial Encyclopedia*, vol. 3, p. 499; James Hastings, M.A., D.D., *A Dictionary of the Bible*, vol. 2 (Peabody: Hendrickson Pub., 1988), p. 99.

81. Tenney and Barabas, vol. 3, p. 499.

82. Ibid., p. 500.

83. *The Wisdom of the Saints*, compiled by Jill Haak Adels (NY: Oxford University Press, 1987), p. 20.

84. Saint John of Kronstadt, *Spiritual Counsels of Father John of Kronstadt*. Select passages from *My Life in Christ*, edited and introduced by W. Jardine Grisbrooke (London: James Clarke & Co. Ltd., 1967), 60.

XVI. CHRIST AT TWELVE YEARS OLD

1. Alfred Edersheim, M.A. Oxon., D.D., Ph.D., *The Life and Times of Jesus the Messiah* (McLean, VA: MacDonald Publishing Co.), 235-236.

2. See end note 34 of Ch. XVIII of this book for a definition of *Mishnah*.

3. See end note 32 of Ch. XV, of this book, for a definition of *Torah*.

4. Merrill C. Tenney and Steven Barabas, eds., *Pictorial Encyclopedia of the Bible*, vol. 4 (Grand Rapids: Regency Reference Library & Zondervan Publishing House, 1975), 625.

5. Ralph Gower, *The New Manners and Customs of Bible Times* (Chicago: Moody Press, 1987), 63.

6. *On the Gospel of St. Luke*, PL 15, 63.

7. Saint Ambrose, *Concerning Virgins, Book II,* The Nicene and Post-Nicene Fathers of the Christian Church, Second Series, vol. X, Philip Schaff, D.D., LL.D. and Henry Wace, D.D., eds. (Grand Rapids, MI: Wm. B. Eerdmans Pub. Co., 1979), ch. 2, p. 375.

8. Saint Ambrose, *Concerning Widows,* The Nicene and Post-Nicene Fathers of the Christian Church, Second Series, vol. X, Philip Schaff, D.D., LL.D. and Henry Wace, D.D., eds. (Grand Rapids, MI: Wm. B. Eerdmans Pub. Co., 1979), ch. iv., p. 395.

9. *Concerning Virgins, Book II,* The Nicene and Post-Nicene Fathers, loc. cit.

10. Bede in *Hom. Dom. infra oct. Epiph.,* cited in M.D. Toal, D.D., *The Sunday Sermons of the Great Fathers,* 3rd ed., vol. I (Chicago: Henry Regnery Co., 1964), 236.

11. Vaselin and Lydia Kesich, *Treasures of the Holy Land* (Crestwood, NY: St. Vladimir's Seminary Press, 1985) 40-41.

12. Edersheim, *The Life and Times of Jesus the Messiah,* op. cit., p. 246.

13. Rev. Alexander Roberts, D.D. and James Donaldson, LL.D., eds., *Apocrypha of the New Testament: The Infancy of the Saviour,* The Ante-Nicene Fathers, The Writings of the Fathers down to A.D. 325, vol. VIII (Grand Rapids, MI: Wm. B. Eerdmans Pub. Co., 1986), 414-415.

14. Toal, D.D., *The Sunday Sermons of the Great Fathers,* op. cit., 237.

15. Ibid., p. 238.

16. *Bede on Luke,* cited in Toal, p. 236.

17. Saint Ephraim Syrus, *Hymns on the Nativity, Hymn XIII,* Nicene and Post-Nicene Fathers of the Christian Church, Second Series, vol. XIII, trans. by Rev. J.B. Morris, M.A. (Grand Rapids, MI: Wm. B. Eerdmans Pub. Co., 1976), p. 248.

18. Saint John Chrysostom, *Homilies on the Gospel of St. John, Homily XX,* The Nicene and Post-Nicene Fathers of the Christian Church, First Series, vol. XIV, Philip Schaff, D.D., LL.D., ed. (Grand Rapids, MI: Wm. B. Eerdmans Pub. Co., 1975).

19. *On the Gospel of St. Luke,* loc. cit.

20. Saint Cyril of Alexandria, *Commentary on the Gospel of Saint Luke, Homily 5,* trans. by R. Payne Smith (NY: Studion Publishers, Inc., 1983), 64.

21. *Hymns on the Nativity, Hymn IV,* Nicene and Post-Nicene Fathers, op. cit., p. 236.

22. Alpha House, *Infancy of Jesus Christ,* The Lost Books of the Bible (NY: Meridian Books, 1974), p. 58; Roberts and Donaldson, *The Infancy of the Saviour,* op. cit., p. 415.

23. Toal, *The Sunday Sermons of the Great Fathers,* vol. I, p. 238.

24. Ibid., p. 239.

25. *Commentary on the Gospel of Saint Luke, Homily 5,* op. cit., pp. 64-65.

26. Toal, op. cit., p. 240.

27. Ibid.

28. *On the Gospel of St. Luke,* loc. cit.

29. *Hom. in Nativ., Dni.,* cited in *Corpus Christianorum, Series Latina,* Turnhout (1953), 122, 49.

30. *Treasury on the Holy Trinity,* Ass. 28, cited in Toal, p. 241.

31. Ibid.

32. Ibid.

33. PG 123, 732.

34. Toal, pp. 241-242.

XVII. THE REPOSE OF THE RIGHTEOUS ELDER JOSEPH

1. St. Clement of Alexandria (c.150-215), *Books VI and VIII Hypotyposes.*
2. Isaac E. Lambertsen and Holy Apostles Convent, trans., *The Life of the Apostle Jude,* The Lives of the Holy Apostles (Buena Vista, CO: Holy Apostles Convent Publications, 1988), 223.
3. Ibid., pp. 223-224.
4. Rev. Alexander Roberts, D.D. and James Donaldson, LL.D., eds., *Apocrypha of the New Testament: The History of Joseph the Carpenter,* The Ante-Nicene Fathers, The Writings of the Fathers down to A.D. 325, vol. VIII (Grand Rapids, MI: Wm. B. Eerdmans Pub. Co., 1986), 389.
5. Ibid., p. 390.
6. Ibid., p. 391.
7. Ibid., p. 392.

XVIII. THE MARRIAGE AT CANA

1. According to the Russian Typicon, in the Schedule of Gospel Readings for the year, the "Marriage at Cana" is commemorated on the second Monday after Pascha.
2. Saint Romanos the Melodist, *On the Marriage at Cana,* Kontakia of Romanos, Byzantine Melodist, vol. I, trans. and annot. by Marjorie Carpenter (MO: University of Missouri Press, 1970), Tone Plagal Second, strophe 1, 68.
3. *Hom. 14, Post Epiph.,* cited in *Corpus Christianorum, Series Latina,* Turnhout (1953), 122, 96.
4. PG 73, 228B.
5. Saint Cyril of Alexandria, *Letter 17, To Bishop Nestorius,* The Fathers of the Church, vol. 76, trans. by John I. McEnerney (Washington, D.C.: The Catholic University of America Press, 1987), 90.
6. PG 73, 223 seq.
7. *On the Marriage at Cana,* op. cit., strophe 2, p. 68.
8. Saint John Chrysostom, *Homilies on the Gospel of St. John, Homily XX,* The Nicene and Post-Nicene Fathers of the Christian Church, First Series, vol. XIV, Philip Schaff, D.D., LL.D., ed. (Grand Rapids, MI: Wm. B. Eerdmans Pub. Co., 1975).
9. *Homily on the Nativity of Christ,* cited in Michael O'Carroll, C.S.Sp., comp. and ed., *Theotokos* 3rd ed. (Wilmington, DE: Michael Glazier, Inc., 1988), p. 71.
10. *On the Marriage at Cana,* strophe 3, p. 69.
11. Ibid., strophe 5, p. 69.
12. Ibid.
13. Ibid., strophe, p. 70.
14. Ibid., strophes 7-9, pp. 70-71.
15. PG 73, 223 seq.
16. O'Carroll, *Theotokos,* p. 313.
17. Canon of the Akathist, Ode Three, Tone Four.
18. Saint Justin Martyr, *Dialogue with Trypho, Chapter 100,* The Fathers of the Church Series, vol. 6, trans. and ed. by Thomas B. Falls, D.D., Ph.D. (Washington, D.C.: Catholic University Press, 1977), pp. 304-305.
19. Saint John of Kronstadt, *My Life in Christ,* trans. by E. E. Goulaeff (Jordanville, NY: Printshop of St. Job of Pochaev, 1984), 253.
20. *On the Marriage at Cana,* strophe 10, p. 71.
21. Ibid., strophe 12, p. 72.
22. Ibid., strophe 13, p. 72.
23. Ibid., strophe 14, p. 72.
24. Ibid., strophe 16, p. 73.

25. *Homilies on the Gospel of St. John, Homilies XXI and XXII*, The Nicene and Post-Nicene Fathers, op. cit.

26. *On the Marriage at Cana*, strophe 17, p. 73.

27. *Homilies on the Gospel of St. John, Homily XXI*, p. 74.

28. PG 73, 223 seq.

29. *Serm. 22*, PG 59.

30. Saint Ephraim Syrus, *Hymns on the Nativity, Hymn VI*, Nicene and Post-Nicene Fathers of the Christian Church, Second Series, vol. XIII, trans. by Rev. J.B. Morris, M.A. (Grand Rapids, MI: Wm. B. Eerdmans Pub. Co., 1976), p. 239.

31. PG 73, 225C.

32. John Baggley, *Doors of Perception* (Crestwood, NY: St. Vladimir's Seminary Press, 1988), pp. 140-148.

33. *Pictorial Bible Dictionary*, Merrill C. Tenney, ed., (Grand Rapids, MI: Zondervan Publishing House, 1973), 891.

34. The *Mishnah* was the oral conversation of the rabbis as they discussed the proper interpretation and course of action requisite upon Jews in regard to the Mosaic law. It is a complex, verbal and continuous commentary, explaining but objective to the *Torah* of Moses.

   The collection of rabbinical laws, law decisions and comments on the laws of Moses were called the *Talmud*. The major and minor divisions of the *Talmud* or, more strictly speaking, the *Mishnah* and *Talmud*, is divided into six major divisions or Orders which are subdivided into Tractates, sixty-three in number, each of which is divided in turn into chapters. [Taken from Merrill C. Tenney and Steven Barabas, eds., *Pictorial Encyclopedia of the Bible*, vol. 5 (Grand Rapids: Regency Reference Library & Zondervan Publishing House, 1975), 589-591].

35. Alfred Edersheim, M.A. Oxon., D.D., Ph.D., *The Life and Times of Jesus the Messiah* (McLean, VA: MacDonald Publishing Co.), 357.

36. *Serm. 22*, op. cit.

37. Akathist to the Theotokos, Tone Four.

38. Canon of the Akathist, Ode Seven, Tone Four.

39. *On the Marriage at Cana*, strophe 4, p. 69.

40. *Serm. 22*, op. cit.

41. *On the Marriage at Cana*, strophe 19, p. 74.

42. Ibid., strophe 20, p. 74.

43. *Paracletike*, Wednesday Matins, Ode Two, Canon to the Theotokos, Tone One.

44. Isaac E. Lambertsen and Holy Apostles Convent, trans. "The Life of the Apostle Simon the Zealot, *The Lives of the Holy Apostles* (Buena Vista, CO: Holy Apostles Convent Publications, 1988), 229.

45. Ibid., p. 228 (Kontakion of St. Romanos).

46. *Hymns on Virginity* cited in *The Harp of the Spirit*, trans. by Sebastian Brock (England: Fellowship of St. Alban & St. Sergius, 1975), pp. 53-54.

47. Ibid., p. 53.

48. *Homilies on the Gospel of St. John, Homily XXII*.

XIX. CHRIST SHOWS WHO IS HIS MOTHER

1. Archpriest Sergei Shukin, "On Spiritual Kinship," *St. Xenia's Bi-Monthly Bulletin* 6, No. 1 (August-September 1988): 1.

2. See end note 34 of Chapter XVIII, in this book, for a definition of *Mishnah*.

3. Merrill C. Tenney and Steven Barabas, eds., *Pictorial Encyclopedia of the Bible*, vol. 2 (Grand Rapids: Regency Reference Library & Zondervan Publishing House, 1975), 210.

4. Shukin, "On Spiritual Kinship," loc. cit.

5. Ibid., pp. 2-3.

6. Blessed Archbishop John Maximovitch, *The Orthodox Veneration of the Mother of God*, trans. by Fr. Seraphim Rose, (Platina, CA: St. Herman of Alaska Brotherhood, 1987), 52.

7. Ibid.

8. Shukin, p. 2.

9. Saint Cyril of Alexandria, *Commentary on the Gospel of Saint Luke, Homily 42*, trans. by R. Payne Smith (NY: Studion Publishers, Inc., 1983), pp. 182-184.

10. In *Lc 10, 25*, in *Corpus Scriptorum Ecclesiasticorum Latinorum* (Vienna, 1866), 32, 4, 412; PL 15, 1810C.

11. Saint Basil, *Ascetical Works: The Morals*, The Fathers of the Church, vol. 9, trans. by Sister M. Monica Wagner, C.S.C. (Washington, D.C.: The Catholic University Press, 1970; repr.), Rule Twenty-Two, Caps. 1, p. 104.

12. PL 9, 12, 24, 933B.

13. *Panarion*, 78.

14. Henry George Liddell and Robert Scott, compilers, *Greek-English Lexicon*, revised and augmented by Sir Henry Stuart Jones and Roderick McKenzie (Oxford at the Clarendon Press, 1968), 137; William F. Arndt and F. Wilbur Gingrich, *A Greek-English Lexicon of the New Testament and Other Early Christian Literature*, revised and augmented by F. Wilbur Gingrich and Frederick W. Danker from Walter Bauer's Greek-German version and his 5th ed., 1958 (Chicago: The University of Chicago Press, 1979), 66.

15. *Holy Bible from the Ancient Eastern Text (from the Aramaic of the Peshitta)*, translated by George M. Lamsa (NY: Harper & Row, Pub., n.d.), p. 1180.

16. *Ascetical Works: The Morals*, The Fathers of the Church, op. cit., Rule Sixty-Two, Caps. 2, 1, pp. 148-149.

17. Saint John Chrysostom, *Homilies on the Gospel of St. John, Homily XLVIII*, The Nicene and Post-Nicene Fathers of the Christian Church, First Series, vol. XIV, Philip Schaff, D.D., LL.D., ed. (Grand Rapids, MI: Wm. B. Eerdmans Pub. Co., 1975), pp. 173-174.

XX. CHRIST SHOWS WHO IS BLESSED

1. William F. Arndt and F. Wilbur Gingrich, *A Greek-English Lexicon of the New Testament and Other Early Christian Literature*, revised and augmented by F. Wilbur Gingrich and Frederick W. Danker from Walter Bauer's Greek-German version and his 5th ed., 1958 (Chicago: The University of Chicago Press, 1979), 503.

2. *Holy Bible from the Ancient Eastern Text (from the Aramaic of the Peshitta)*, translated by George M. Lamsa (NY: Harper & Row, Pub., n.d.), 1130.

3. Ibid., p. 1131.

4. Saint John Chrysostom, *Homilies on the Gospel of St. Matthew, Homily XXIV*, The Nicene and Post-Nicene Fathers of the Christian Church, First Series, vol. X, Philip Schaff, D.D., LL.D., ed. (Grand Rapids, MI: Wm. B. Eerdmans Pub. Co., 1975), pp. 278, 280.

5. *Exo. in Luc. VI, 38*, cited in *Corpus Scriptorum Ecclesiasticorum Latinorum* (Vienna, 1866), 32(iv), 247, 248.

6. M.D. Toal, D.D., *The Sunday Sermons of the Great Fathers*, 3rd ed., vol. II (Chicago: Henry Regnery Co., 1964), p. 82.

XXI. THE PASSION OF OUR LORD JESUS CHRIST

1. "The Synaxarion of Holy and Great Friday", *Holy Week-Easter (Megalee Ebdomas Pascha)*, Compiled by Fr. George L. Papadeas (New York, 1971), 251.
2. Great Thursday Evening (Matins), Lauds, Tone Three.
3. *Hom. in Purif.*, 18, in *Corpus Christianorum, Series Latina*, Turnhout (1953), 122, 132.
4. Tuesday Vespers, Theotokion from the *Paracletike* in the First Tone.
5. Saint John of Damascus, *Exposition of the Orthodox Faith, Book IV*, The Nicene and Post-Nicene Fathers of the Christian Church, Second Series, vol. IX, trans. by Rev. S.F.D. Dalmond, D.D., F.E.I.S. (Grand Rapids, MI: Wm. B. Eerdmans Pub. Co., 1976), ch. 14, p. 86.
6. Second Canon of Matins on Monday in the Third Week of Lent, Stavro-theotokion of Ode Eight, Tone Plagal Fourth.
7. Second Stasis, Tone Plagal First cited in *The Lamentations of Matins of Holy and Great Saturday*, trans. by Holy Transfiguration Monastery (Boston, 1981), 17.
8. *The Lamentations*, Second Stasis, Tone Plagal First.
9. *Octoechos*, Ode Four, Tone Two.
10. *The Lamentations*, Second Stasis, Tone Plagal First.
11. "The Tale of the Five Prayers" cited in the *Prayer Book*, Holy Trinity Monastery (Jordanville, NY, 1960), 359-361.
12. Daily *Octoechos*, Matins Canon for Friday, Tone Two (Slav).
13. Great Friday Morning, Third Hour, Tone Plagal Fourth.
14. Great Friday Morning, Sixth Hour, Ideomela, Tone Plagal Fourth.
15. Great Friday Morning, Ninth Hour, Tone Two.
16. Apokatheelosis, Great Friday Vespers, Tone Plagal Second.
17. Oikos of Holy and Great Thursday Evening (Friday Matins), cited in Saint Romanos the Melodist, *On Mary at the Cross*, Kontakia of Romanos, Byzantine Melodist, vol. I, trans. and annot. by Marjorie Carpenter (MO: University of Missouri Press, 1970), Tone Plagal Second, strophe 1, p. 196.
18. *On Mary at the Cross*, Kontakia of Romanos, Byzantine Melodist, op. cit., strophe 2, pp. 196-197.
19. Ibid., strophe 3, p. 197.
20. Saint Jerome, *The Perpetual Virginity of Blessed Mary*, The Nicene and Post-Nicene Fathers of the Christian Church, Second Series, vol. VI, Philip Schaff, D.D., LL.D. and Henry Wace, D.D., eds. (Grand Rapids, MI: Wm. B. Eerdmans Pub. Co., 1983), p. 340.
21. *De Resurrectione 2*, in PG 46, 648A.
22. Saint John Chrysostom, *Homilies on the Gospel of St. Matthew, Homily LXXXVIII*, The Nicene and Post-Nicene Fathers of the Christian Church, First Series, vol. X, Philip Schaff, D.D., LL.D., ed. (Grand Rapids, MI: Wm. B. Eerdmans Pub. Co., 1975), p. 522.
23. *Great Friday of the Triodion*, The Great Synaxaristes of the Orthodox Church [in Greek], 4th ed., vol. XIII (Athens, 1977), pp. 606-607; *Sunday of Pascha in the Pentecostarion*, The Great Synaxaristes of the Orthodox Church [in Greek], 5th ed., vol. XIV (Athens, 1979), p. 21.
24. *Homilies on the Gospel of St. Matthew, Homily LXXXVIII*, The Nicene and Post-Nicene Fathers of the Christian Church, loc. cit.
25. Saint John Chrysostom, *Homilies on the Gospel of St. John, Homily LXXXV*, The Nicene and Post-Nicene Fathers of the Christian Church, First Series, vol. XIV, Philip Schaff, D.D., LL.D., ed. (Grand Rapids, MI: Wm. B. Eerdmans Pub. Co., 1975), p. 318.
26. Kontakion of 22 July, (Slav usage), Tone Three.
27. Matins Canon, 22 July, Ode Eight, Tone Plagal Four.

28. Theotokion from the *Paracletike* in Tone One.

29. Eusebius, *Ecc. Hist., Book 3*, 11; see also St. Epiphanios, *Against Her.*, 3, 2, 78, PG 42, 708.

30. Blessed Archbishop John Maximovitch, *The Orthodox Veneration of the Mother of God,* trans. by Fr. Seraphim Rose, (Platina, CA: St. Herman of Alaska Brotherhood, 1987), p. 24.

31. *Sunday of Pascha in the Pentecostarion*, The Great Synaxaristes [in Greek], op. cit., p. 39.

32. *In Luc. II, 61*, cited in *Corpus Scriptorum Ecclesiasticorum Latinorum* (Vienna, 1866), 32(iv), 41. (Hereinafter referred to as CSEL.

33. Saint Ambrose, *Letters 59, To the Church at Vercelli,* (dated 396), The Fathers of the Church, vol. 26, trans. by Sister Mary Melchior Beyenka, O.P. (Washington, D.C.: The Catholic University Press, 1987; repr.), p. 362; *De Inst. Virg., 49*, PL 16, 318C.

34. *In Luc. X, 132*, cited in *CSEL*, op. cit., 505; cp. *De Inst. Virg. VI*, PL 16, 319; *Ep. 63, 110*, PL 16, 1218; *Ep. 49*, PL 16, 1155.

35. *Exp. in Luc. X, 132*, cited in *CSEL*, 32(iv), 506.

36. Saint Ambrose, *Funeral Orations; On the Death of Valentinian*, The Fathers of the Church, vol. 22, trans. by Roy J. Deferrari (Washington, D.C.: The Catholic University Press, 1968, repr.), p. 283.

37. Kontakion of Great and Holy Friday; also, a kontakion of St. Romanos, cited in, *On Mary at the Cross*, p. 196.

38. Holy and Great Thursday Evening (Friday Matins), Lauds, Third Tone.

39. *The Lamentations*, Second Stasis, Tone Plagal First.

40. *On Mary at the Cross, strophe 5, p. 198.*

41. *Mary at the Cross*, strophe 6, cited in *Sources Chretiennes* (Lyons), 128, 168. (Hereinafter referred to as SC).

42. *The Lamentations*, Second Stasis, Tone Plagal First.

43. Saint John Chrysostom. *Homilies on the Epistle of St. Paul the Apostle to the Galatians,* The Nicene and Post-Nicene Fathers of the Christian Church, First Series, vol. XIII, Philip Schaff, D.D., LL.D., ed. Grand Rapids, MI: Wm. B. Eerdmans Pub. Co., 1976, rep., ch. 3(13).

44. *On Mary at the Cross*, strophe 6(2), p. 196.

45. Stavrotheotokion, Tone Plagal Fourth.

46. Stavrotheotokion of Matins Aposticha, Wednesday in the Sixth Week of Great Lent, Tone One.

47. *On Mary at the Cross*, strophe 7, p. 196; Saint Romanos the Melodist, *The Passion of the Lord and the Lamentations of the Theotokos,* Romanos the Melodist, Kontakia [in Greek], ed. by P.A. Sinopoulos (Athens: Apostolikes Diakonias, 1974), strophe 8, p. 112.

48. *On Mary at the Cross,* strophe 9, p. 200; Sinopoulos, strophe 10, p. 113.

49. Ibid., strophe 10, p. 200; Sinopoulos, strophe 11, p. 114.

50. Ibid., strophe 11, p. 201; Sinopoulos, strophe 12, pp. 114-115.

51. *The Lamentations*, First Stasis, Tone Plagal First.

52. Theotokion from the *Paracletike* in Tone One.

53. *On Mary at the Cross*, strophe 12, p. 201.

54. Ibid., strophe 13, pp. 201-202.

55. Ibid., strophe 14, p. 196; Sinopoulos, strophe 15, pp. 116-117.

56. Ibid., strophe 15, p. 202; Sinopoulos, strophe 16, p. 117.

57. Saint Photios, *Homily VII: The Annunciation*, The Homilies of Photius, Patriarch of Constantinople, trans. by Cyril Mango (Cambridge, MA: Harvard University Press, Dumbarton Oaks Studies Three, 1958), p. 143.

58. *On Mary at the Cross*, strophe 16, p. 203; Sinopoulos, strophe 17, pp. 117-118.

59. *The Lamentations*, First Stasis, Tone Plagal First.

60. *On Mary at the Cross*, strophe 17, p. 203.

61. Saint Cyril of Alexandria, *Letter 55*, The Fathers of the Church, vol. 77, trans. by John I. McEnerney (Washington, D.C.: The Catholic University of America Press, 1987), pp. 30-31.

62. *Great Friday of the Triodion*, The Great Synaxaristes, pp. 596-597.

63. *Homilies on the Gospel of St. John, Homily LXXXV*, p. 318.

64. *Hymn on the Crucifixion, 4, 17*, cited in *Corpus Scriptorum Christianorum Orientalium* (Louvain, 1903), 249, 43. (Hereinafter referred to as CSCO).

65. *SC*, 121, 12, 5, p. 216; *Commentary on the Gospel of St. John*, vol. 2, trans. from the Armenian by L. Leboir (Paris, 1954), 117.

66. *Homily 8*, PG 100, 1477B.

67. *Panarion haer, 78*, cited in *Die griechischen christlichen Srif tsteller der ersten drei Jahrhunderte* (Leipzig-Berlin, 1897), 37, 468-470.

68. PG 79, 179D.

69. PL 23, 254AB.

70. *Serm. in SS. Deiparam*, ed. by M. Jugie, A.A., (Rome, 1935), in PG 108, 64.

71. Saint Gregory Palamas, *Homily 37 on the August Dormition of Our Most Immaculate Lady Theotokos and Ever-Virgin Mary* [in Greek], PG 151, 465A; *Hom. 53*, ed. Oikonomos (1861), p. 136, cited in John Meyendorff, *A Study of Gregory Palamas*, trans. from French by George Lawrence (London: Faith Press, 1964), p. 233.

72. Georgios L. Mantzaridis, *The Deification of Man: St. Gregory Palamas and the Orthodox Tradition*, trans. by Liadain Sherrard (Crestwood, NY: St. Vladimir's Seminary Press, 1984), 32.

73. *Exposition of the Gospel of St. Luke, X, 134;* PL 15, 1838.

74. Ibid., VIII, 5; PL 15, 1700C.

75. Saint John of Kronstadt, *My Life in Christ*, trans. by E. E. Goulaeff (Jordanville, NY: Printshop of St. Job of Pochaev, 1984), p. 305.

76. Blessed Archbishop John Maximovitch, *The Orthodox Veneration of the Mother of God*, loc. cit.

77. *CSCO*.

78. *In Mt. 1, 4*, in PL 9, 922B.

79. *Against Her., 3, 2, 78*, PG 42, 713-716.

80. Saint Paulinus of Nola, *Letter 50, To Augustine, Vol. 2*, Ancient Christian Writers, vol. 36, trans. and annot. by P.G. Walsh (NY: Paulist Press, 1967), pp. 289-290.

81. *Funeral Orations; On the Death of Valentinian*, The Fathers of the Church, loc. cit.

82. *The Lamentations*, Second Stasis, Tone Plagal First.

83. *Homilies on the Gospel of St. John, Homily LXXXV*, p. 318.

84. *Adv. Her. 46, 5*.

85. *The Lamentations*, First Stasis, Tone Plagal First.

86. From the 15th Antiphon of the Matins of Holy and Great Friday, Tone Plagal Second.

87. *Hom. 40*, PG 151, 513C, cited in Meyendorff, *A Study of Gregory Palamas*, p. 236. Georgios L. Mantzaridis, *The Deification of Man: St. Gregory Palamas and the Orthodox Tradition*, p. 28.

88. *Homilies on the Gospel of St. John, Homily LXXXV*, p. 319.

89. *Exposition of the Orthodox Faith, Book IV*, The Nicene and Post-Nicene Fathers of the Christian Church, op. cit., ch. ix, p. 78.

90. Saint Ambrose, *The Holy Spirit, Book I, Theological and Dogmatic Works*, The Fathers of the Church, vol. 44, trans. by Roy J. Deferrari, Ph.D. (Washington, D.C.: The Catholic University Press, 1987; repr.), ch. 9(107-

108), p. 74.
91. *My Life in Christ*, op. cit., p. 300.
92. Matins Canon, 21 Nov., Ode One, Tone Two by Basil the monk.
93. Resurrection Matins Kathisma, Tone Two.
94. *Homilies on the Gospel of St. Matthew, Homily LXXXVIII*, p. 522.
95. *SC*, 121, 1, 26, p. 26; and 21, 20, p. 385.
96. *The Lamentations*, Third Stasis, Tone Three.
97. Saint Romanos the Melodist, *Resurrection I*, Kontakia of Romanos, Byzantine Melodist, vol. I, trans. and annot. by Marjorie Carpenter (MO: University of Missouri Press, 1970), Tone One, strophe 2, p. 253.
98. Doxastikon of the Aposticha from Great Friday Vespers, Tone Plagal First.
99. Another famous prophet, who was not from Judea, is Prophet Elias the Tishbite. He was from Gilead [1 Kings 17:1], which borders Galilee to the east.
100. Saint Basil, *Exegetic Homily on Psalm 44 (LXX)*, Homily 17, The Fathers of the Church, vol. 46, trans. by Sister Agnes Clare Way. C.D.P. (Washington, D.C.: The Catholic University Press, 1981; repr.), p. 290.
101. Ralph Gower, *The New Manners and Customs of Bible Times* (Chicago: Moody Press, 1987), pp. 73-74.
102. *The Lamentations*, Third Stasis, Tone Three.
103. *The Lamentations*, Second Stasis, Tone Plagal First.
104. Ibid.
105. *Homilies on the Gospel of St. Matthew, Homily LXXXVIII*, loc. cit.
106. PG 114, 208.
107. Holy and Great Thursday Evening (Friday Matins), Lauds, Tone Three.
108. Bishop Nikolai Velimirovic, *The Prologue from Ochrid*, Pt. 3, p. 132.
109. Aposticha of Great Friday Vespers, Tone Two.
110. Great Saturday Vespers, Tone Plagal Fourth.
111. Aposticha of Great Friday Vespers, Tone Two.

XXII. THE THEOTOKOS AND THE MYRRH-BEARERS

1. PG 151, 244AB.
2. PG 151, 244D.
3. PG 151, 237.
4. Doxastikon of the Lity, Tone Plagal Second. Unless otherwise specified, hymns in this section are taken from the Feast of the Myrrh-Bearing Women, the Third Sunday of Pascha.
5. Matins Ikos of 22 July.
6. PG 151, 240A.
7. Saint John Chrysostom, *Homilies on the Gospel of St. Matthew, Homily LXXXVIII*, The Nicene and Post-Nicene Fathers of the Christian Church, First Series, vol. X, Philip Schaff, D.D., LL.D., ed. (Grand Rapids, MI: Wm. B. Eerdmans Pub. Co., 1975), p. 522.
8. *De Resurrectione, 2*, in PG 46, 633B.
9. PG 151, 240A.
10. *Eccl. His.*, Vol. 1, 23; PG 145, 732-733.
11. Saint Jerome, *The Perpetual Virginity of Blessed Mary*, The Nicene and Post-Nicene Fathers of the Christian Church, Second Series, vol. VI, Philip Schaff, D.D., LL.D. and Henry Wace, D.D., eds. (Grand Rapids, MI: Wm. B. Eerdmans Pub. Co., 1983), p. 340.
12. *The Lamentations*, First Stasis, Tone Plagal First, cited in *The Lamentations of Matins of Holy and Great Saturday*, trans. by Holy Transfiguration Monastery (Boston, 1981).
13. *On Luke*, 24, 12, PG 123, 1112.
14. Stichera of Pascha, Tone Plagal First.

15. *Homilies on the Gospel of St. Matthew, Homily LXXXVIII,* The Nicene and Post-Nicene Fathers of the Christian Church, loc. cit.

16. PG 151, 242.

17. PG 151, 244.

18. *The Lamentations,* First Stasis, Tone Plagal First.

19. *The Lamentations,* Third Stasis, Tone Three.

20. *The Lamentations,* Second Stasis, Tone Plagal First.

21. Saint Romanos the Melodist, *Resurrection VI,* Kontakia of Romanos, Byzantine Melodist, vol. I, trans. and annot. by Marjorie Carpenter (MO: University of Missouri Press, 1970), Tone Plagal Fourth, strophe 1, p. 314.

22. Friday Vespers of the Third Week after Pascha, Tone Two.

23. Resurrection Matins Kathisma, Tone Four.

24. PG 151, 241.

25. Matins Kathisma of the Resurrection, Tone Plagal Second.

26. Saint Romanos the Melodist, *Resurrection I,* Kontakia of Romanos, Byzantine Melodist, vol. I, trans. and annot. by Marjorie Carpenter (MO: University of Missouri Press, 1970), Tone One, strophe 13, p. 257.

27. Ibid., strophe 19, p. 259.

28. Saint Romanos the Melodist, *Resurrection II,* Kontakia of Romanos, Byzantine Melodist, vol. I, trans. and annot. by Marjorie Carpenter (MO: University of Missouri Press, 1970), Tone Plagal Second, strophes 16-17, pp. 268-269.

29. Ibid., strophe 18, p. 269; Saint Romanos the Melodist, *The Passion of the Lord and the Lamentations of the Theotokos,* Romanos the Melodist, Kontakia [in Greek], ed. by P.A. Sinopoulos (Athens: Apostolike Diakonias, 1974), 129-130.

30. PG 151, 241.

31. *Resurrection II,* strophe 19, pp. 269-270.

32. *Homilies on the Gospel of St. Matthew, Homily LXXXIX,* p. 527.

33. *Saint Romanos the Melodist, Resurrection VI,* Kontakia of Romanos, Byzantine Melodist, vol. I, trans. and annot. by Marjorie Carpenter (MO: University of Missouri Press, 1970), Tone Plagal Fourth, strophe 19, p. 322.

34. Ibid., strophe 20, pp. 322-323.

35. Ibid., strophe 21, p. 323.

36. Vespers Doxastikon of the Feast, Tone Plagal Second, by St. Cosmas.

37. Saint Cyril of Alexandria, *Commentary on the Gospel of Saint Luke, Homily 24,* trans. by R. Payne Smith (NY: Studion Publishers, Inc., 1983), p. 615.

38. Stichera of Pascha, Tone Plagal First.

39. PG 151, 240BC.

40. Matins Canon of Wednesday of Mid-Pentecost, Ode One, Tone Four.

41. Dismissal Hymn (Both now...) of the Feast, Tone Two.

42. After Second Matinal Kathisma, Sessional Hymn, Tone Two.

43. PG 151, 240C.

44. Vespers on Wednesday of the Third Week after Pascha, Tone Two.

45. *Resurrection VI,* strophe 22, p. 323.

46. *Homilies on the Gospel of St. Matthew, Homily LXXXIX,* loc. cit.

47. PG 151, 244AB.

48. PG 151, 241, 244C.

49. Resurrection Troparion of Tone Four.

50. *Homilies on the Gospel of St. Matthew, Homily LXXXVIII,* loc. cit.

51. *Homilies on the Gospel of St. Matthew, Homily LXXXIX,* loc., cit.

52. Saint Cyril of Alexandria, *Commentary on the Gospel of Saint Luke, Homily 24,* loc. cit.

53. Theotokion of Second Matinal Sessional Hymn, Tone Two.

54. *Sunday of Pascha in the Pentecostarion*, The Great Synaxaristes of the Orthodox Church [in Greek], 5th ed., vol. XIV (Athens, 1979), pp. 34-36; *Thursday of the Ascension of the Lord in the Pentecostarion*, The Great Synaxaristes of the Orthodox Church [in Greek], 5th ed., vol. XIV (Athens, 1979), p. 270.

55. *Sunday of Pascha in the Pentecostarion*, Great Synaxaristes, pp. 21-22.

56. Resurrection Dismissal Hymn, Tone Plagal Second.

57. *Presentation*, 12, cited in *Sources Chretiennes* (Lyons), 128, 176.

58. Canon of the Theotokos for the Sunday of the Myrrh-bearers, Ode One, Tone One.

59. *Hom. 1, in Praesent.*, 2, in M. Aubindeau ed., Cf. M. Aubineau, S.J., *Les Homelies festales d'Hesychius de Jerusalem* (Brussels, 1979), 13-15.

60. *In SS. Mariam assistentem in sepulchro*, in PG 100, 1497A.

61. PG 151, 237AB-241BC; also *In Dorm.*, in PG 151, 468A; *Hom. 20*, col. 269C, cited in John Meyendorff, *A Study of Gregory Palamas*, trans. from French by George Lawrence (London: Faith Press, 1964), p. 233.

62. PG 151, 236-237.

63. "A Day of Paradisiacal Joy," *Orthodox Life* 39, no. 2 (March-April, 1989): 2. Translated by Rassaphor-monk Michael from *Pribavlenia k Tserkovnim Vedomostic (Supplement to Church Reports)*, Nos. 12-13, 22 Mar. 1915, pp. 395-397.

64. *Resurrection VI*, strophe 3, p. 315.

65. PG 151, 244CD, 245.

66. *Resurrection VI*, loc. cit.

67. Ibid., strophe 4, p. 316.

68. *Homilies on the Gospel of St. John, Homily LXXXV*, p. 321.

69. Matinal Doxastikon of the Resurrection, Grave Tone.

70. *Resurrection VI*, *Prof-Joimion*, p. 314.

71. Ibid., strophe 7, p. 317.

72. *Homilies on the Gospel of St. John, Homily LXXXVI*, p. 323.

73. First Kathisma, Matins Resurrection of Tone Plagal Second.

74. *Resurrection VI*, strophe 9, p. 318.

75. Ibid., strophe 10, p. 318.

76. PG 151, 244D, 245.

77. Nicephoros Kallistos Xanthopoulos (+1335), *The Life of St. Mary Magdalene* [in Greek], Mother Magdalene, ed. (Athens [Kozanes]: Holy Convent of the Ascension, 1974), pp. 9-11.

    Note: The famous melodist, Nicephoros Callistos Xanthopoulos, also composed the service of the Life-Giving Fountain of the Theotokos, chanted Friday of Bright Week.

78. *Resurrection VI*, strophe 11, p. 319.

79. Saint Leo the Great, *Sermon 84*, The Nicene and Post-Nicene Fathers of the Christian Church, Second Series, vol. XII, Philip Schaff, D.D., LL.D. and Henry Wace, D.D., eds. (Grand Rapids, MI: Wm. B. Eerdmans Pub. Co., 1979), p. 189.

80. *Resurrection VI*, strophe 13, p. 319.

81. First Kathisma, Matins Resurrection of Tone Plagal Second.

82. *Resurrection I*, strophe 20, p. 259.

83. Saint Ephraim Syrus, *Hymns on the Nativity, Hymn VIII*, Nicene and Post-Nicene Fathers of the Christian Church, Second Series, vol. XIII, trans. by Rev. J.B. Morris, M.A. (Grand Rapids, MI: Wm. B. Eerdmans Pub. Co., 1976), p. 242.

84. *Paschal Sermon 45*, PG 36, 624.

85. Ode Five, Tone One.
86. Ode Six, Tone One.
87. Resurrection Lauds, Tone Two.

XXIII. THE ASCENSION

1. Ps. 17:10.
2. *Thursday of the Ascension of the Lord in the Pentecostarion*, The Great Synaxaristes of the Orthodox Church [in Greek], 5th ed., vol. XIV (Athens, 1979), pp. 262, 271.
3. Vespers Sticheron, Tone Plagal Second. Unless otherwise specified, hymns in this section are taken from the Feast of the Ascension.
4. Ibid.
5. Aposticha of Feast of the Ascension, Tone Two.
6. Saint John Chrysostom, *Homilies on the Acts of the Apostles, Homily II*, The Nicene and Post-Nicene Fathers of the Christian Church, First Series, vol. XI, Philip Schaff, D.D., LL.D., ed. (Grand Rapids, MI: Wm. B. Eerdmans Pub. Co., 1975), p. 13.
7. Zach. 14:4.
8. Matins Canon, Theotokion, Ode Nine, Tone Plagal First.
9. Leonid Ouspensky and Vladimir Lossky, *The Meaning of Icons*, trans. by G.E.H. Palmer and E. Kadloubovsky (Crestwood: St. Vladimir's Seminary Press, 1983, repr.), p. 196.
10. Saint Leo the Great, *Sermon 73*, The Nicene and Post-Nicene Fathers of the Christian Church, Second Series, vol. XII, Philip Schaff, D.D., LL.D. and Henry Wace, D.D., eds. (Grand Rapids, MI: Wm. B. Eerdmans Pub. Co., 1979), p. 187.

XXIV. THE DESCENT OF THE HOLY SPIRIT

1. "The Dormition of Our Most Holy Lady," *The Orthodox Teachings of the Mother of God*, translated from the Menology of St. Dimitry of Rostov (Moundsville, WV: Fr. Demetrios Serfes Publications), pp. 32-33.
2. Saint John Chrysostom, *Homilies on the Acts of the Apostles, Homily IV*, The Nicene and Post-Nicene Fathers of the Christian Church, First Series, vol. XI, Philip Schaff, D.D., LL.D., ed. (Grand Rapids, MI: Wm. B. Eerdmans Pub. Co., 1975), p. 25.
3. *Discourse 41*, PG 36, 436.
4. *Homilies on the Acts of the Apostles, Homily IV*, The Nicene and Post-Nicene Fathers of the Christian Church, op. cit., pp. 25-26.
5. *Annunciation*, The Great Synaxaristes of the Orthodox Church [in Greek], 5th ed., vol. III (Athens, 1979), pp. 500-501.
6. Matins Canon, 21 Nov., Ode Nine, Tone Four.
7. Matins Canon, 27 Jan., Ode One, Tone Plagal Fourth.
8. Matins Canon of the Resurrection, Ode One, Tone Two.
9. *In Annunt.*, PG 151, PG 177B.
10. Saint Gregory Palamas, *Homilies of St. Gregory Palamas*, comp. by S. Oikonomos (Athens, 1861), Note: This rare edition may be found in Migne, *PG* 151, 472A.
11. Matins Canon of Pentecost, Ode Nine, Tone Four by Sir John of Arcla.
12. *In Dorm.*, PG 151, 468A.
13. Ibid., p. 35.
14. Lavriotiki (Great Lavra) Library, L66, L31 codes; "The Dormition of Our Most Holy Lady," *The Orthodox Teachings of the Mother of God*, op. cit., pp. 35-36.
15. *The Life of St. Nina*, (Jordanville, NY: Holy Trinity Monastery, 1977), 5.
16. Matins Canon, 14 Jan., Ode One, Tone One.
17. Matins Canon, 22 July, Ode Nine, Tone Plagal Fourth.

18. Nicephoros Kallistos Xanthopoulos (+1335), *The Life of St. Mary Magdalene* [in Greek], Mother Magdalene, ed. (Athens [Kozanes]: Holy Convent of the Ascension, 1974), pp. 38-42.

19. Matins Canon, 22 July, Ode Nine, Tone Plagal Fourth.

20. Eusebius, *Church History*, The Nicene and Post-Nicene Fathers of the Christian Church, First Series, vol. I, trans. by Rev. Arthur Cushman McGiffert (Grand Rapids, MI: Wm. B. Eerdmans Pub. Co., 1961), Book 2, ch. 7, p. 110.

XXV. THE EARLY YEARS OF THE CHURCH

1. "The Dormition of Our Most Holy Lady," *The Orthodox Teachings of the Mother of God*, translated from the Menology of St. Dimitry of Rostov (Moundsville, WV: Fr. Demetrios Serfes Publications), p. 34.

2. Ibid., p. 33.

3. "The Dormition of the Most Holy Mother of God," *Orthodox Word* 2, No. 3(9), (July-August 1966): 102.

4. PG 120, 22, 212A.

5. Saint John Chrysostom, *Homilies on the Acts of the Apostles, Homily 17*, The Nicene and Post-Nicene Fathers of the Christian Church, First Series, vol. XI, Philip Schaff, D.D., LL.D., ed. (Grand Rapids, MI: Wm. B. Eerdmans Pub. Co., 1975), pp. 112-113.

6. Saint Cyril of Alexandria, *Letter 50, To Bishop Valerian of Iconium*, The Fathers of the Church, vol. 76, trans. by John I. McEnerney (Washington, D.C.: The Catholic University of America Press, 1987), p. 220.

7. Josephus, *The Antiquities of the Jews*, The Works of Josephus, trans. by William Whiston, A.M. (Peabody, MA: Hendrickson Pub., 1988), XX, 9, 1.

8. Merrill C. Tenney and Steven Barabas, eds., *Pictorial Encyclopedia of the Bible*, vol. 5 (Grand Rapids: Regency Reference Library & Zondervan Publishing House, 1975), p. 272.

9. "The Dormition of Our Most Holy Lady," *The Orthodox Teachings of the Mother of God*, op. cit., p. 34.

10. Isaac E. Lambertsen and Holy Apostles Convent, trans., *The Life of the Pre-Eminent Apostle Paul*, The Lives of the Holy Apostles (Buena Vista, CO: Holy Apostles Convent Publications, 1988), pp. 25-26.

11. "The Dormition of Our Most Holy Lady," *The Orthodox Teachings of the Mother of God*, loc. cit.

12. Saint Basil, *Ascetical Works: The Morals*, The Fathers of the Church, vol. 9, trans. by Sister M. Monica Wagner, C.S.C. (Washington, D.C.: The Catholic University Press, 1970; repr.), Rule Sixty-Five, pp. 152-53.

13. Matins Canon of 27 Dec., Ode Three, Tone Plagal First, by St. John of Damascus.

14. Bishop Nikolai Velimirovic, *The Prologue from Ochrid*, Trans. by Mother Maria (Birmingham: Lazarica Press, 1986), Pt. 3, p. 145; Pt. 4, p. 376.

15. The Holy Church celebrates the memory of St. Nicanor on the 28th of July, together with the three other deacons mentioned in Scriptures, Saint Prochoros, Timon and Parmenas [Acts. 6:5]. Saint Nicanor does not celebrate on the same day as St. Stephen (27th of December) and has no separate day of commemoration other than that date mentioned above.

16. *St. Nicanor*, The Great Synaxaristes of the Orthodox Church [in Greek], 5th ed., vol. VII (Athens, 1977), 541; Bishop Nikolai Velimirovic, *The Prologue from Ochrid*, Pt. 3, op. cit., p. 119.

17. "Benjamin, as a ravening wolf, shall eat still in the morning, and at evening he gives food."

18. "The Dormition of Our Most Holy Lady," *The Orthodox Teachings of the Mother of God*, loc. cit.

19. Michael O'Carroll, C.S.Sp., comp. and ed., *Theotokos* 3rd ed. (Wilmington, DE: Michael Glazier, Inc., 1988), p. 62.

20. Isaac E. Lambertsen and Holy Apostles Convent, trans., *The Life of the Holy Apostle James, Son of Zebedee*, The Lives of the Holy Apostles (Buena Vista, CO: Holy Apostles Convent Publications, 1988), 73.

21. "The Dormition of Our Most Holy Lady," *The Orthodox Teachings of the Mother of God*, p. 33.

22. Ibid., pp. 33-34.

23. Saint Ignatios of Antioch, *The Epistles of St. Ignatios to St. John the Apostle*, The Ante-Nicene Fathers, The Writings of the Fathers down to A.D. 325, vol. I, Rev. Alexander Roberts, D.D. and James Donaldson, LL.D., eds. (Grand Rapids, MI: Wm. B. Eerdmans Pub. Co., 1987), p. 124; *The Assumption of Our Most Holy Lady, The Mother of God and Ever-Virgin Mary*, translated from the Menology of St. Dimitri of Rostov (Jordanville, NY: Holy Trinity Monastery, 1976), p. 21.

24. *The Epistles of St. Ignatios to St. John the Apostle*, Ibid., p. 125.

25. *The Assumption of Our Most Holy Lady, The Mother of God and Ever-Virgin Mary*, loc. cit.

26. *The Wisdom of the Saints*, compiled by Jill Haak Adels (NY: Oxford University Press, 1987), p. 21.

27. Second Matins Canon of 8 July, Feast of the Icon of the Mother of God of Kazan, Ode Four, Tone Four.

28. Dionysius of Fourna, *The Painter's Manual*, trans. by Paul Hetherington (London: Sagittarius Press, 1974), p. 4.

29. Blessed Archbishop John Maximovitch, *The Orthodox Veneration of the Mother of God*, trans. by Fr. Seraphim Rose, (Platina, CA: St. Herman of Alaska Brotherhood, 1987), pp. 15-16.

30. "The Dormition of Our Most Holy Lady," *The Orthodox Teachings of the Mother of God*, p. 35.

31. *Ephesus*, Compiled by Naci Keskin and translated by Ertugrul Uckun (Turkey: Keskin Color Ltd. Co. Printing House), n.d.

32. Ibid.

33. "The Dormition of Our Most Holy Lady," *The Orthodox Teachings of the Mother of God*, loc. cit.

34. Saint Ignatios of Antioch, *The Epistle of St. Ignatios to the Virgin Mary and the Reply*, The Ante-Nicene Fathers, The Writings of the Fathers down to A.D. 325, vol. I, Rev. Alexander Roberts, D.D. and James Donaldson, LL.D., eds. (Grand Rapids, MI: Wm. B. Eerdmans Pub. Co., 1987), p. 126.

35. 1 Cor. 16:13.

36. Lk. 1:47.

37. Saint Ignatios of Antioch, *The Epistle of St. Ignatios to the Virgin Mary and the Reply*, The Ante-Nicene Fathers, loc. cit.

38. Bishop Nikolai Velimirovic, *The Prologue from Ochrid*, Pt. 4, pp. 349-351.

XXVI. THE THEOTOKOS ON MOUNT ATHOS

1. As stated by Stephen of the Holy Mountain. Cited in "The Dormition of Our Most Holy Lady," *The Orthodox Teachings of the Mother of God*, translated from the Menology of St. Dimitry of Rostov (Moundsville, WV: Fr. Demetrios Serfes Publications), p. 36.

2. *Saturday of Lazarus in the Triodion*, The Great Synaxaristes of the Orthodox Church [in Greek], 4th ed., vol. XIII (Athens, 1977), 416.

3. Sotiris Kadas, Archaeologist, *Mount Athos*, trans. by Louise Turner (Athens: Ekdotike Athenon S.A., 1980), 9.

4. Trygonis Lavriotis, Macarios, *Pilgrimage Book of Lavra* (Venice, 1772).

5. Agapios the Cretan, Monk, *Amartolon Sotiria* [in Greek], (Athens: St. Nicodemos, pub., 1899).

6. Andrew Simonopetritis Aghioritis, Monk (Haralampos Teophilopoulos), *Bulwark of Orthodoxy and of the Greek Nation*, trans. by John-Electros Boumis (Thessalonica, GR: Basil Regopoulos Bookstore), pp. 30, 38.

7. Kadas, *Mount Athos*, op. cit., p. 10.

8. *Sunday of All the Saints of Mt. Athos*, Matins Canon, Theotokion of Sedalion, Tone Four.   Unless otherwise specified, hymns in this section are taken from the Feast of the Sunday of All the Saints of Mt. Athos, celebrated on the 2nd Sunday after Pentecost.

9. Matins Canon, Ode One, Tone Plagal Fourth.

10. Matins Canon, Theotokion of Ode One, Tone One.

11. Andrew Simonopetritis Aghioritis, *Bulwark of Orthodoxy and of the Greek Nation*, op. cit., p. 39; "The Dormition of Our Most Holy Lady," *The Orthodox Teachings of the Mother of God*, op. cit., p. 37.

12. Matins Canon, Theotokion of Ode Three, Tone Plagal Fourth.

13. Matins Canon, Ode Five, Tone Plagal Fourth.

14. Andrew Simonopetritis Aghioritis, *Bulwark of Orthodoxy and of the Greek Nation*, pp. 34-35; Agapios the Cretan, *Amartolon Sotiria*, op. cit., p. 314; *St. Peter the Athonite*, The Great Synaxaristes of the Orthodox Church [in Greek], 5th ed., vol. VI (Athens, 1979), 151. [in Greek], (Athens: St. Nicodemos, pub., 1899), p. 151.

15. Matins Canon, Theotokion of Ode Three, Tone One.

16. Andrew Simonopetritis, *Bulwark of Orthodoxy*, loc. cit.; Agapios the Cretan, *Amartolon Sotiria*, loc. cit.

17. Matins Canon, Theotokion of Ode Four, Tone Plagal Fourth.

18. Andrew Simonopetritis, *Bulwark of Orthodoxy*, pp. 34-35; Agapios the Cretan, *Amartolon Sotiria*, loc. cit., *St. Peter the Athonite*, The Great Synaxaristes, loc. cit.

19. Matins Canon, Theotokion of Ode Four, Tone Plagal Fourth.

20. Matins Canon, Theotokion of Ode Seven, Tone One.

21. "The Dormition of Our Most Holy Lady," *The Orthodox Teachings of the Mother of God*, loc. cit.

22. Ibid., (Stephen of the Holy Mountain).

XXVII. THE THEOTOKOS RETURNS TO JERUSALEM

1. Nicephoros Kallistos Xanthopoulos (+1335), *The Life of St. Mary Magdalene* [in Greek], Mother Magdalene, ed. (Athens [Kozanes]:   Holy Convent of the Ascension, 1974), p. 141.

2. Ibid., p. 142.

3. *Sunday of Pascha in the Pentecostarion*, The Great Synaxaristes of the Orthodox Church [in Greek], 5th ed., vol. XIV (Athens, 1979), 38.

4. "The Dormition of Our Most Holy Lady," *The Orthodox Teachings of the Mother of God*, translated from the Menology of St. Dimitry of Rostov (Moundsville, WV: Fr. Demetrios Serfes Publications), 38.

5. Saint Gregory Palamas, *Homilies of St. Gregory Palamas*, comp. by S. Oikonomos (Athens, 1861, copy in Bollandist Library), 6, 214. Note: This rare edition may be found in Migne, *PG* 151.

6. Minas Charitos, *The Repose of Our Most Holy and Glorious Lady the Theotokos*, trans. by J. Vlesmas (W. Brookfield, MA: Orthodox Christian Center and Mission), 18.

7. *Hom. III in Dorm., 1*, in PG 96, 753C.

8. *Hom. 1 in Dorm., 14*, in PG 96, 720CD.

9. "The Dormition of Our Most Holy Lady," *The Orthodox Teachings of the Mother of God*, loc. cit.

10. Ibid., p. 39.

11. Ibid.

12. Saint Ephraim Syrus, *Hymns on the Nativity, Homily X*, Nicene and Post-Nicene Fathers of the Christian Church, Second Series, vol. XIII, trans. by Rev. J.B. Morris, M.A. (Grand Rapids, MI: Wm. B. Eerdmans Pub. Co., 1976), p. 244.

13. "The Dormition of Our Most Holy Lady," *The Orthodox Teachings of the Mother of God*, loc. cit.

14. Blessed Archbishop John Maximovitch, *The Orthodox Veneration of the Mother of God,* trans. by Fr. Seraphim Rose, (Platina, CA: St. Herman of Alaska Brotherhood, 1987), 19.

15. *Hymns on the Nativity, Hymn IV*, Nicene and Post-Nicene Fathers of the Christian Church, op. cit., p. 236.

16. Blessed Archbishop John Maximovitch, *The Orthodox Veneration of the Mother of God,* loc. cit.

17. "The Dormition of Our Most Holy Lady," *The Orthodox Teachings of the Mother of God*, loc. cit.

18. Ibid.

XXVIII. THE DORMITION OF THE THEOTOKOS

1. Matins Canon, Ode Four, Tone Four. Unless otherwise specified, hymns in this section are taken from the Feast on the 15th of August.

2. "The Dormition of the Most Holy Mother of God," *Orthodox Word* 2, No. 3(9), (July-August 1966): 102.

3. Matins Canon, Ode Three, Tone Four, by St. John of Damascus.

4. Matins Canon, Ode Four, Tone One.

5. Minas Charitos, *The Repose of Our Most Holy and Glorious Lady the Theotokos*, trans. by J. Vlesmas (W. Brookfield, MA: Orthodox Christian Center and Mission), 6.

6. Ibid., p. 7.

7. *The Assumption of Our Most Holy Lady, The Mother of God and Ever-Virgin Mary*, translated from the Menology of St. Dimitri of Rostov (Jordanville, NY: Holy Trinity Monastery, 1976), pp. 3-4.

8. Archbishop Nathanael of Vienna and Austria, "The Holy Righteous Abraham, Moses and Elias as Preparers of Man's Salvation," *Orthodox Life* 28, no. 6 (November-December, 1978): 45. Translated by Seraphim F. Englehardt from *Orthodox Observer* (Montreal), No. 27, July, 1959.

9. Rev. Alexander Roberts, D.D. and James Donaldson, LL.D., eds., *Apocrypha of the New Testament: The Passing of Mary*, The Ante-Nicene Fathers, The Writings of the Fathers down to A.D. 325, vol. VIII (Grand Rapids, MI: Wm. B. Eerdmans Pub. Co., 1986), 592.

10. *Dormition of the Theotokos*, The Great Synaxaristes of the Orthodox Church [in Greek], 5th ed., vol. VIII (Athens, 1977), 224; Charitos, *The Repose of Our Most Holy and Glorious Lady the Theotokos*, loc. cit.

11. *The Assumption of Our Most Holy Lady, The Mother of God and Ever-Virgin Mary*, Holy Trinity Monastery, op. cit., pp. 4-5.

12. Ibid., p. 5.

13. *Sermon 3, On the Dormition*, PG 98, 364.

14. *The Assumption of Our Most Holy Lady*, Holy Trinity Monastery, pp. 5-6.

15. Ibid., p. 6.

16. Ibid.; *Dormition of the Theotokos*, The Great Synaxaristes of the Orthodox Church, op. cit., p. 226.

17. *The Assumption*, Holy Trinity Monastery, loc. cit.
18. Ibid.
19. Lity of Feast for St. John the Theologian, 8 May, Tone One by Andrew Pyros.
20. *The Assumption*, Holy Trinity Monastery, pp. 31-32.
21. Ibid., pp. 6-7; *Dormition of the Theotokos*, The Great Synaxaristes, pp. 226, 237; see also St. Germanos, *Sermon 3, On the Dormition*, PG 98, 364.
22. *The Assumption*, Holy Trinity Monastery, p. 6.
23. Ibid., p. 7.
24. Ibid.
25. *The Assumption of Our Most Holy Lady*, Holy Trinity Monastery, loc. cit.; *Dormition of the Theotokos*, The Great Synaxaristes, p. 227.
26. *The Assumption*, Holy Trinity Monastery, p. 32.
    Some, for example, Bishop Meliton of Sardis, affirm that the beloved disciple John had been in Ephesus just prior to the Theotokos' Dormition. Hence, he, like the other Apostles, was caught up on a cloud and brought to his home on Sion. [Ibid., p. 32].
27. Matins Canon, Ode Five, Tone One.
28. Matins Canon, Ode Three, Tone Four.
29. Lity, Tone One.
30. *The Assumption*, Holy Trinity Monastery, pp. 7-8.
31. Vespers Doxastikon, Tone Plagal First.
32. *The Assumption*, Holy Trinity Monastery, p. 8.
33. Ibid., p. 9; *Dormition of the Theotokos*, The Great Synaxaristes, loc. cit.
34. *Dormition of the Theotokos*, The Great Synaxaristes, pp. 237-238.
35. *The Assumption*, Holy Trinity Monastery, p. 8; *Dormition of the Theotokos*, The Great Synaxaristes, p. 227.
36. Roberts and Donaldson, *The Passing of Mary*, The Ante-Nicene Fathers, op. cit., p. 593.
37. *Dormition of the Theotokos*, The Great Synaxaristes, pp. 237-238.
38. Ibid., p. 238.
39. *The Assumption*, Holy Trinity Monastery, loc. cit.
40. *Dormition of the Theotokos*, The Great Synaxaristes, loc. cit.
41. Matins Hymn sung after Psalm 50, Tone Plagal Second by Byzas.
42. *Dormition of the Theotokos*, The Great Synaxaristes, loc. cit.
43. Ibid.
44. Ibid., pp. 238-239.
45. Saint Gregory Palamas, *Homily 37, On the August Dormition of Our Most Immaculate Lady Theotokos and Ever-Virgin Mary* [in Greek], PG 151, 464C; see, also, "Homily on the Dormition," *Orthodox Life* 32, No. 4 (July-August 1982): 3-9.
46. Akathist to the Theotokos.
47. Saint Cyril of Jerusalem, *Catechesis X, On One Lord, Jesus Christ, Vol. I*, The Fathers of the Church, vol. 61, trans. by Leo P. McCauley, S.J. and Anthony A. Stephenson (Washington, D.C.: The Catholic University of America Press, 1969), p. 208.
48. *Dormition of the Theotokos*, The Great Synaxaristes, pp. 239.
49. Ibid.
50. Ibid., pp. 239-240.
51. *The Assumption*, Holy Trinity Monastery, p. 9.
52. Nicephoros Callistos, *Eccl. Hist.* 2, 21, PG 145, 812.

53. Rev. Alexander Roberts, D.D. and James Donaldson, LL.D., eds., *Apocrypha of the New Testament: The Book of John Concerning the Falling Asleep of Mary*, The Ante-Nicene Fathers, The Writings of the Fathers down to A.D. 325, vol. VIII (Grand Rapids, MI: Wm. B. Eerdmans Pub. Co., 1986), pp. 589-590.

54. *The Assumption*, Holy Trinity Monastery, loc. cit.

55. *Sermon 2, On the Dormition*, 3. PG 99, 724.

56. Paul A. Underwood, *The Kariye Djami, Vol. 1, Historical Introduction and Description of the Mosaics and Frescoes*, Bollingen Series LXX (NY: Pantheon Books, 1966), p. 167.

57. *Hom. IV in Dorm.*, PG 97, 865A.

58. PG 151, 469D.

59. Akathist to the Theotokos on Her Dormition, Ikoi 5, 7, 9.

60. Canon of the Akathist, Ode Six, Tone Four.

61. *The Assumption*, Holy Trinity Monastery, loc. cit.

62. Roberts and Donaldson, *The Book of John Concerning the Falling Asleep of Mary*, The Ante-Nicene Fathers, op. cit., p. 590.

63. Charitos, *The Repose of Our Most Holy and Glorious Lady the Theotokos*, loc. cit.

64. *The Assumption of Our Most Holy Lady*, Holy Trinity Monastery, pp. 9-10.

65. Ibid., p. 10.

66. *Homily 37*, PG 151, 472C.

67. Roberts and Donaldson, *The Book of John Concerning the Falling Asleep of Mary*, loc. cit.

68. Ibid.

69. Ibid., p. 591.

70. Ibid.

71. Matins Canon, Ode Eight, Tone One.

72. Roberts and Donaldson, *The Book of John*, loc. cit.

73. Exapostilarion, Tone Three.

74. *The Assumption*, Holy Trinity Monastery, p. 10.

75. Ibid.

76. Matins Canon, Ode Eight, Tone Four.

77. *The Assumption*, Holy Trinity Monastery, loc. cit.

78. Matins Canon, Ode Nine, Tone One.

79. *The Assumption*, Holy Trinity Monastery, loc. cit.

80. Matinal Lauds, Tone Four.

81. *The Assumption*, Holy Trinity Monastery, loc. cit.

82. Matins Canon, Ode Three, Tone One.

83. *The Assumption*, Holy Trinity Monastery, pp. 9-10.

84. Doxastikon of Aposticha, Tone Four.

85. Matins Canon, Ode Nine, Tone One.

86. Ibid., Ode Five.

87. *Dormition of the Theotokos*, The Great Synaxaristes, p. 240.

88. *The Assumption*, Holy Trinity Monastery, p. 11.

89. Ibid.

90. Doxastikon of Lity, Tone Plagal First.

91. Ps. 131:8.

92. *De S. Maria Deip.*, in PG 93, 1464.

93. *Hymns, in Sources Chretiennes* (Lyons), 110, 122-3.

94. *Homilies*, in PG, 97, 869C.

95. *Homilies*, in PG, 96, 724.

96. *Homily 2, On the Dormition*, 18, PG 96,749.

591

97. *The Assumption,* Holy Trinity Monastery, loc. cit.; "The Dormition of the Most Holy Mother of God," *Orthodox Word,* op. cit., p. 104.

98. *The Assumption,* Holy Trinity Monastery, loc. cit.; *Dormition of the Theotokos,* The Great Synaxaristes, loc cit.

99. *The Assumption,* pp. 12-13.

100. Ibid., p. 113.

101. Roberts and Donaldson, *The Book of John,* loc. cit.; *Dormition of the Theotokos,* The Great Synaxaristes, loc. cit.

102. Matins Canon of Annunciation, 23 Mar., Ode Nine, Tone Four by St. John of Damascus.

103. Compare 2 Samuel 6:6-7.
    Matins Canon, Ode Three, Tone One by St. Cosmas.

104. Great Canon, Ode Seven, Tone Plagal Second, taken from Saint Andrew of Crete, *The Great Canon,* trans. by Holy Trinity Monastery (Jordanville, 1976).

105. *The Assumption,* Holy Trinity Monastery, p. 13.

106. Ibid.

107. Ibid., pp. 13-14.

108. *Dormition of the Theotokos,* The Great Synaxaristes, loc. cit.

109. *The Assumption,* Holy Trinity Monastery, p. 14.

110. Akathist to the Theotokos on her Dormition, Ikos 4.

111. PG 151, 464CD, 465A.

112. Matins Canon, Ode One, Tone One.

113. Vespers Doxastikon, Tone Two.

114. Vespers Sticheron, Tone One.

115. Matinal Lauds, Tone Four.

116. Matins Sessional Hymn, Tone Four.

117. PG 96, 741B.

118. PG 151, 461AB.

119. Vespers Doxastikon, Tone Three.

120. Matins Canon, Ode Four, Tone One.

121. Lity, Tone Two.

122. Matins Canon, Ode One, Tone Four.

123. Doxastikon of Lity, Tone Plagal First.

124. PG 151, 469BC.

125. Vespers Doxastikon, Tone Four.

126. Vespers Doxastikon, Grave Tone.

127. PG 151, 472AB.

128. Charitos, *The Repose,* pp. 9-10.

129. Saint John of Kronstadt, *My Life in Christ,* trans. by E. E. Goulaeff (Jordanville, NY: Printshop of St. Job of Pochaev, 1984), 232.

130. Akathist to the Theotokos on Her Dormition, Ikos 6.

131. *The Assumption,* Holy Trinity Monastery, loc. cit.

132. *Dormition of the Theotokos,* The Great Synaxaristes, loc. cit.

133. Matins Canon, Ode Five, Tone Four.

134. *Dormition of the Theotokos,* The Great Synaxaristes, pp. 241; *St. Hierotheos,* The Great Synaxaristes of the Orthodox Church [in Greek], 5th ed., vol. X (Athens, 1978), 120; see, St. Dionysios, *The Divine Names,* iii, 2.

135. *Dormition of the Theotokos,* The Great Synaxaristes, loc. cit.

136. Ibid., pp. 240-241.

137. *Homily 3, On the Dormition,* PG 369-372.

138. Charitos, *The Repose,* pp. 8-9.

139. *The Assumption,* Holy Trinity Monastery, loc. cit.

140. *Dormition of the Theotokos,* The Great Synaxaristes, p. 240.

141. Matins Canon, Ode Four, Tone Four.

142. Akathist to the Theotokos on Her Dormition, Ikoi 10, 12.

143. Underwood, *The Kariye Djami*, op. cit. p. 164.

144. Matins Sessional Hymn, Tone Three.

145. Charitos, *The Repose*, Preface; "The Dormition of the Most Holy Mother of God," *Orthodox Word*, p. 105.

146. *The Life and Struggles of Our Holy Father Among the Saints, Juvenal, Patriarch of Jerusalem (2nd of July)* in The Lives of the Saints of the Holy Land and the Sinai Desert, trans. by Holy Apostles Convent (Buena Vista, CO: Holy Apostles Convent Publications, 1988), 286.

147. Leonid Ouspensky and Vladimir Lossky, *The Meaning of Icons*, trans. by G.E.H. Palmer and E. Kadloubovsky (Crestwood: St. Vladimir's Seminary Press, 1983, repr.), 213.

148. Vespers Sticheron, Tone One.

XXIX. THE THEOTOKOS IS BODILY TRANSLATED

1. Isaac E. Lambertsen and Holy Apostles Convent, trans., *The Life of the Apostle Thomas*, The Lives of the Holy Apostles (Buena Vista, CO: Holy Apostles Convent Publications, 1988), 196.

2. Ibid.; *Dormition of the Theotokos*, The Great Synaxaristes of the Orthodox Church [in Greek], 5th ed., vol. VIII (Athens, 1978), 242-243.

   Note: The Holy Monastery of Vatopedi, the second largest on the Holy Mountain, possesses a gem-encausted jewel box containing the precious treasure of the Virgin's holy cincture.

3. Lambertsen and Holy Apostles Convent, *The Life of the Apostle Thomas*, loc. cit.

4. *Dormition of the Theotokos*, The Great Synaxaristes, loc. cit.; *The Assumption of Our Most Holy Lady, The Mother of God and Ever-Virgin Mary*, translated from the Menology of St. Dimitri of Rostov (Jordanville, NY: Holy Trinity Monastery, 1976), 15.

5. Matins Canon, 31 August, Ode Nine, Tone Four.

6. Matins Canon, 31 August, Ode Three, Tone Plagal Fourth.

7. N. F. Robinson, *Monasticism in the Orthodox Churches*, (NY: American Review of Eastern Orthodoxy, 1964), pp. 136, 168.

8. Matins Canon, Ode Seven, Tone Four by St. John of Damascus. Unless otherwise specified, hymns in this section are taken from the Feast on the 15th of August.

9. *Libri Miraculorum*, in PL 71, 708.

10. *De gloria beatorum martyrum, 4*, in PL 71, 70B.

11. St. Joseph the Hymnographer, *In perviglio obdormitionis...*, in PG 105, 1001A.

12. Matins Canon, Ode Six, Tone One.

13. PG 96, 716B.

14. PG 96, 741B.

15. Matins Canon, Ode Nine, Tone Four.

16. Saint Gregory Palamas, *Homily 37, On the August Dormition of Our Most Immaculate Lady Theotokos and Ever-Virgin Mary* [in Greek], PG 151, 465D. See, also, "Homily on the Dormition," *Orthodox Life* 32, No. 4 (July-August 1982): 3-9.

17. *Encomium in Dormitionem SS. Deiparae*, PG 86bis, 3277-3312.

18. *Marianum* 36 (Rome, 1974), 282.

19. Rev. Michael Azkoul, *The Teachings of the Holy Orthodox Church*, (Buena Vista, CO: Dormition Skete Publications, 1986), f.n. 35.

20. Small Vespers Sticheron, Tone Two.

21. Matins Canon, Ode Four, Tone Four.

22. Vespers Doxastikon, Tone Plagal Second.

23. *Can. 4, 5, apud* E. Follieri, 109.

24. Saint Ambrose, *Concerning Virgins, Book II,* The Nicene and Post-Nicene Fathers of the Christian Church, Second Series, vol. X, Philip Schaff, D.D., LL.D. and Henry Wace, D.D., eds. (Grand Rapids, MI: Wm. B. Eerdmans Pub. Co., 1979), ch. 2, p. 376.

25. Kontakion of Feast, Tone Two.

26. PG 96, 744C.

27. PG 96, 716C.

28. Matins Hypakoe, Tone Plagal First.

29. *Hom. III in Dorm.,* PG 97, 1100.

30. *Dormition of the Theotokos,* The Great Synaxaristes, p. 243.

31. *The Assumption,* Holy Trinity Monastery, loc. cit.

32. Ibid., p. 16.

33. *Dormition of the Theotokos,* The Great Synaxaristes, pp. 243.

34. *The Assumption,* Holy Trinity Monastery, p. 16.

35. "Akathist to the Most Holy Theotokos in Honor of Her Dormition," *Orthodox Life* 34, No. 4 (July-August 1984): 19-27 (Ikos 2).

36. Ibid., Ikos 3.

37. Lity, Tone One.

38. *The Assumption,* Holy Trinity Monastery, loc. cit.

39. Minas Charitos, *The Repose of Our Most Holy and Glorious Lady the Theotokos,* trans. by J. Vlesmas (W. Brookfield, MA: Orthodox Christian Center and Mission), 9.

40. Ibid., p. 14.

41. Charitos, *The Repose of Our Most Holy and Glorious Lady the Theotokos,* loc. cit.

42. Ibid., p. 15.

43. Ibid., p. 16.

44. Ibid.

45. PG 151, 468A.

46. John Meyendorff, *A Study of Gregory Palamas,* trans. from French by George Lawrence (London: Faith Press, 1964), 236.

47. PG 151, 465C.

48. PG 151, 468D.

49. PG 151, 465D.

50. Grave Tone.

51. PG 151, 468A-B.

52. PG 151, 464B.

53. PG 151, 464D-465.

54. Blessed Archbishop John Maximovitch, *The Orthodox Veneration of the Mother of God,* trans. by Fr. Seraphim Rose, (Platina, CA: St. Herman of Alaska Brotherhood, 1987), 53.

55. PG 77, 992BC; E. Schwartz, ed., *Acta Conciliorum Oecumenicorum* (Strasburg, 1914), 1, 1, 2, 102-103.

56. PG 151, 472D.

57. PG 151, 472D-473.

58. Doxastikon of Lity, Tone Plagal First.

APPENDIX: MARY THEOTOKOS AND THE CHURCH

1. Saint John of Damascus, *Exposition of the Orthodox Faith, Book III,* The Nicene and Post-Nicene Fathers of the Christian Church, Second Series, vol. IX, trans. by Rev. S.F.D. Dalmond, D.D., F.E.I.S. (Grand Rapids, MI: Wm. B. Eerdmans Pub. Co., 1976), ch. xii.

2. Matinal Laud of the Nativity of Christ, Tone Four.

3. PG 77, 996C.

4. *Paedag. I, 6, 21,* in *Die griechischen christlichen Sriftsteller der ersten drei Jahrhunderte* (Leipzig-Berlin, 1897), 12, 115; PG, 8, 300-301.

5. *In Praise of the Blessed Virgin Mary* VIII, PL 96, 269D.

6. *In Lucan II,* in *Corpus Christianorum, Series Latina,* Turnhout (1953), 120, 48-49.

7. *In Luc. II,* 7, PL 15, 1555; *Corpus Scriptorum Ecclesiasticorum Latinorum* (Vienna, 1866), 32-IV, p. 45.

8. *On the Institution of Virginity,* XIV, 89, PL 16, 326A.

9. Saint Paulinus of Nola, *Poem 25,* Ancient Christian Writers, vol. 40, trans. and annot. by P.G. Walsh (NY: Paulist Press, 1975), pp. 250-251.

10. Saint Hippolytus, *Christ and Antichrist,* The Ante-Nicene Fathers, The Writings of the Fathers down to A.D. 325, vol. V (American reprint of Edinburgh ed.). Rev. Alexander Roberts, D.D. and James Donaldson, LL.D., eds. (Grand Rapids, MI: Wm. B. Eerdmans Pub. Co., 1986), 217.

11. Saint Methodius, *The Symposium, A Treatise on Chastity,* Ancient Christian Writers, vol. 27, trans. and annot. by Herbert Musurillo, S.J.,D. Phil. (Oxon), (NY: Paulist Press, 1958), pp. 110-112.

12. Ibid., pp. 113, 118.

13. Ch. 33 of St. Andrew's works, cited in Archbishop Averky, *Apocalypse,* trans. and ed. by Fr. Seraphim Rose (Valaam Society of America, 1985), p. 136.

14. Saint Ambrose, *Hexaemeron,* The Fathers of the Church, vol. 42, trans. by John J. Savage (Washington, D.C.: The Catholic University Press, 1985; repr.), ch. 2, p. 130.

15. Charitos, *The Repose of Our Most Holy and Glorious Lady the Theotokos,* op. cit., p. 10.

16. Ibid., pp. 10-11.

17. *On the Revelation,* PG 106, 660.

18. Dionysius of Fourna, *The Painter's Manual,* trans. by Paul Hetherington (London: Sagittarius Press, 1974), 47.

19. "Akathist to the Most Holy Theotokos in Honor of Her Dormition" *Orthodox Life* 34, No. 4 (July-August, 1984): 19-29 (Ikos 12).

APPENDIX B: THE GOSPEL READING

1. The last two verse of this reading during Divine Liturgy may be found in the Gospel according to St. Luke 11:27,28, which is fully discussed in Chapter XX, entitled *Christ Shows Who is Blessed.*

2. Saint Jerome, *Letter XXII: To Eustochium,* The Nicene and Post-Nicene Fathers of the Christian Church, Second Series, vol. VI, trans. by the Hon. W.H. Fremantle, M.A., Rev. G. Lewis, M.A., and Rev. W.G. Martley, M.A., with the editorial supervision of Philip Schaff, D.D., LL.D. and Henry Wace, D.D., eds. (Grand Rapids, MI: Wm. B. Eerdmans Pub. Co., 1983), p. 32.

3. Saint Basil, *Ascetical Works: The Long Rules,* The Fathers of the Church, vol. 9, trans. by Sister M. Monica Wagner, C.S.C. (Washington, D.C.: The Catholic University Press, 1970; repr.), Q.20, pp. 279-280.

4. Saint Clement of Alexandria, *Salvation of the Rich Man,* The Ante-Nicene Fathers, The Writings of the Fathers down to A.D. 325, vol. II, trans. by Rev. William Wilson, M.A.   Under the editorial supervision of Rev.

Alexander Roberts, D.D. and James Donaldson, LL.D. (Grand Rapids, MI: Wm. B. Eerdmans Pub. Co., 1986), repr., p. 594.

5. Saint John Cassian, *The Conferences of John Cassian: First Conference of Abbot Moses*, The Nicene and Post-Nicene Fathers of the Christian Church, Second Series, vol. XI, trans. by Edgar C.S. Gibson, M.A., under the editorial supervision of Philip Schaff, D.D., LL.D. and Henry Wace, D.D. (Grand Rapids, MI: Wm. B. Eerdmans Pub. Co., 1978, repr.), ch. viii, p. 298.

EPILOGUE: THE THEOTOKOS AS MEDIATRESS

1. *The Wisdom of the Saints*, compiled by Jill Haak Adels (NY: Oxford University Press, 1987), p. 20.

2. Thursday Vespers Sticheron, Tone One.

3. Saint John Chrysostom, *Homily VII, The Epistle of St. Paul the Apostle to the Galatians*, Vol. XIII of The Nicene and Post-Nicene Fathers of the Christian Church, First Series. Philip Schaff, D.D., LL.D., ed. (Grand Rapids, MI: Wm. B. Eerdmans Pub. Co., 1976, repr.), p. 430.

4. Ibid., p. 430.

5. Resurrection Theotokion, Tone Three.

6. Saint Irenaeus, *Against Heresies*, Book VI, Ante-Nicene Fathers, The Writings of the Fathers down to A.D. 326, vol. I, Rev. Alexander Roberts, D.D. and James Donaldson, eds. (Grand Rapids, MI: Wm. B. Eerdmans Pub. Co., 1987; repr.), ch. 19(1), 547.

7. Ibid., Book III, ch. 22(4), p. 455.

8. *Ep. 49, 2*, PL 16, 1154.

9. *Ep. 63, 33*, PL, 16, 1198.

10. *De Obitu Theo., 44*, PL, 16, 1400.

11. *Epist. 22, 21*, in PL 22, 408.

12. *Hom. IV Ephesi in Nestorium habita...*, in PG 77, 992BC; E. Schwartz, ed., *Acta Conciliorum Oecumenicorum* (Strasburg, 1914), 1, 1, 8, 104.

13. *Hom. in Deiparam*, in PG 65, 681.

14. *The Wisdom of the Saints*, op. cit., p. 21.

15. Minas Charitos, *The Repose of Our Most Holy and Glorious Lady the Theotokos*, trans. by J. Vlesmas (W. Brookfield, MA: Orthodox Christian Center and Mission), 18; Michael O'Carroll, C.S.Sp., comp. and ed., *Theotokos* 3rd ed. (Wilmington, DE: Michael Glazier, Inc., 1988), 240.

16. *Hymn for the Nativity*, cited in *Sources Chretiennes* (Lyons), 110, 103; Saint Romanos the Melodist, *On the Nativity (Mary and the Magi)*, Kontakia of Romanos, Byzantine Melodist, vol. I, trans. and annot. by Marjorie Carpenter (MO: University of Missouri Press, 1970), Tone Plagal Second, Strophe 10, p. 18.

17. Evlogitaria of the Resurrection, Tone Plagal First.

18. *On the Nativity (Mary and the Magi)*, Kontakia of Romanos, op. cit., Tone Three, strophe 23, p. 11.

19. Codex of Paris, no. 212; Codex of the Library of St. Mark in Venice, no. 14; Savas J. Savas, *Hymnology of the Eastern Orthodox Church*, (MA: Byzantine Melodies, 1983), 67.

20. *In Nativ. Mariae, Serm. I* and *Serm. IV*, in PG 97, 808, 865.

21. Prosomion after Canon for Sunday, Tone Plagal First by St. Andrew of Crete, taken from the *Theotokarion of St. Nikodemos* [in Greek] (Volos, GR: Sot. Schoina, 1979), p. 107.

22. *Hom. in Dorm.*, in PG 96, 713A.

23. *The Wisdom of the Saints*, loc. cit.

24. PG 98, 381B.

25. *Oratio V in Annuntiationem SS. Deiparae*, PG 98, 320-340.

26. PG 98, 321, 352-353.

27. PG 96, 685A-D.

28. PG 99, 725C.

29. PG 98, 1495.

30. PG 98, 1499.

31. Matins Canon for the Sunday of the Publican and the Pharisee, Theotokion of Ode One, Tone Plagal Second.

32. Ibid., Theotokion of Ode Four.

33. Matins Canon for the Sunday of the Prodigal Son, Theotokion of Ode Seven, Tone Two.

34. Monday in the First Week of Great Lent, Matins Ode Eight, Tone Two.

35. Saint Photios, *Homily VII: The Annunciation*, The Homilies of Photius, Patriarch of Constantinople, trans. by Cyril Mango (Cambridge, MA: Harvard University Press, Dumbarton Oaks Studies Three, 1958), 143.

36. Saint Photios, *Homily IX: The Birth of the Virgin*, The Homilies of Photius, Patriarch of Constantinople, trans. by Cyril Mango (Cambridge, MA: Harvard University Press, Dumbarton Oaks Studies Three, 1958), 175.

37. Saint Photios, *Homily III: The Russian Attack*, The Homilies of Photios, Patriarch of Constantinople, trans. by Cyril Mango (Cambridge, MA: Harvard University Press, Dumbarton Oaks Studies Three, 1958), 95.

38. "The Life of Saint Andrew, Fool for Christ of Constantinople," *Orthodox Word* 15, no. 3(86) (May-June, 1979): 128-129.

39. Theotokion after the Polyeleos, Tone Plagal Fourth, 1 Oct.

40. Leonid Ouspensky and Vladimir Lossky, *The Meaning of Icons*, trans. by G.E.H. Palmer and E. Kadloubovsky (Crestwood: St. Vladimir's Seminary Press, 1983, repr.), 15; "The Life of Saint Andrew, Fool for Christ of Constantinople," *Orthodox Word*, loc. cit.

41. Ouspensky and Lossky, *The Meaning of Icons*, loc. cit.

42. *Hom. 14*, PG 151, 169C.

43. *Homily 37, On the August Dormition of Our Most Immaculate Lady Theotokos and Ever-Virgin Mary* [in Greek], PG 151, 464D.

44. *Hom. 14*, PG 151, 177A; cf. *Hom. 53*, cited in *Homilies of St. Gregory Palamas*, comp. by S. Oikonomos (Athens, 1861), 156, 162.

45. *Serm. in Deiparam*, cited in *Marianum* (Rome, 1964) 5, p. 55.

46. Ibid., 10, p. 133.

47. Ibid., 4, 55; 15;205.

48. Ibid., 14, p. 195.

49. Ibid., 15, p. 205.

50. Saint John of Kronstadt, *My Life in Christ*, trans. by E. E. Goulaeff (Jordanville, NY: Printshop of St. Job of Pochaev, 1984), 90.

51. Saint John of Kronstadt, *Spiritual Counsels of Father John of Kronstadt*. Select passages from *My Life in Christ*, edited and introduced by W. Jardine Grisbrooke (London: James Clarke & Co. Ltd., 1967), 59.

52. *My Life in Christ*, trans. by E. E. Goulaeff, p. 179.

53. Ibid., p. 59.

54. Theotokion Troparion of the Sixth Hour.

55. Kontakion of the Resurrection, Grave Tone.

56. Tone Plagal Fourth.

57. Saint John of Damascus, *Exposition of the Orthodox Faith, Book IV*, The Nicene and Post-Nicene Fathers of the Christian Church, Second Series, vol. IX, trans. by Rev. S.F.D. Dalmond, D.D., F.E.I.S. (Grand Rapids, MI: Wm. B. Eerdmans Pub. Co., 1976), ch. xv, pp. 86-87.

58. Constantine Cavarnos, "Iconographic Decoration of Churches" in *Orthodox Iconography* 2d ed. (Belmont, MA: Institute for Byzantine and Modern Greek Studies, 1980): 26-27.

597

59. The Great Supplicatory Canon to the Theotokos. Hiermos of Ode Nine, Tone Plagal Fourth.

60. Ibid., p. 27.

61. Constantine D. Kalokyris, "The Content of Orthodox Iconography: Art of High Theology," *The Essence of Orthodox Iconography,* trans. by Peter A. Chamberas (Brookline: Holy Cross School of Theology, 1971), 23.

62. *Homily 65, On the Gospel of St. Matthew*, PG 58, 617.

63. Resurrection Canon to the Mother of God, Ode Nine, Tone Plagal First.

64. Constantine Callinicos, *Our Lady the Theotokos,* trans. and rev. by Rev. George Dimopoulos (Upper Darby, PA: Christian Orthodox Editions, 1987), pp. 129-130.

65. John Baggley, *Doors of Perception* (Crestwood, NY: St. Vladimir's Seminary Press, 1988), 106.

BIBLIOGRAPHY

Note: The following abbreviations are used in the bibliography and in the footnotes to the text:

ACO: *Acta Conciliorum Oecumenicorum.* E. Schwartz, ed. Strasburg, 1914.

CCSL: *Corpus Christianorum, Series Latina.* Turnhout, 1953.

CSCO: *Corpus Scriptorum Christianorum Orientalium.* Louvain, 1903.

CSEL: *Corpus Scriptorum Ecclesiasticorum Latinorum.* Vienna, 1866.

ES: Schonmetzer, S.J., A. *Enchiridion Symbolorum.* Denziger-Bannwart, ed. 33.

GCS: *Die griechischen christlichen Sriftsteller der ersten drei Jahrhunderte.* Leipzig-Berlin, 1897.

MM: *Marianum* (MM). Rome, 1974.

PG: Migne, J., ed. *Patrologia Graeca.* 161 vols. Paris, 1844-1866.

PL: Migne, J., ed. *Patrologia Latina.* 221 vols. Paris, 1844-1864.

PO: *Patrologia Orientalia.*

PS: *Patrologia Syriaca.*

SC: *Sources Chretiennes.* Lyons.

SOURCES
Acta Conciliorum Oecumenicorum (ACO). E. Schwartz, ed. Strasburg, 1914.

"A Day of Paradisiacal Joy." *Orthodox Life* 39, no. 2 (March-April, 1989): 2. Translated by Rassaphor-monk Michael from *Pribavlenia k Tserkovnim Vedomostic (Supplement to Church Reports)*, Nos. 12-13, 22 Mar. 1915, pp. 395-397.

Agapios the Cretan, Monk. *Amartolon Sotiria* [in Greek]. Athens: St. Nicodemos, pub., 1899.

"Akathist to the Most Holy Theotokos in Honor of Her Dormition." *Orthodox Life* 34, No. 4 (July-August, 1984): 19-29.

Alpha House. "The Gospel of the Birth of Mary;" "The Protoevangelion;" and "Infancy of Jesus Christ." *The Lost Books of the Bible.* NY: Meridian Books, 1974.

599

Andrew Simonopetritis Aghioritis, Monk (Haralampos Teophilopoulos). *Bulwark of Orthodoxy and of the Greek Nation.* Trans. by John-Electros Boumis. Thessalonica, GR: Basil Regopoulos Bookstore.

Arndt, William F. and F. Wilbur Gingrich. *A Greek-English Lexicon of the New Testament and Other Early Christian Literature.* Revised and augmented by F. Wilbur Gingrich and Frederick W. Danker from Walter Bauer's Greek-German version and his 5th ed., 1958. Chicago: The University of Chicago Press, 1979.

Averky, Archbishop. *Apocalypse.* Trans. and ed. by Fr. Seraphim Rose. Valaam Society of America, 1985.

Azkoul, Rev. Michael. *The Teachings of the Holy Orthodox Church.* Buena Vista, CO: Dormition Skete Publications, 1986.

Baggley, John. *Doors of Perception.* Crestwood, NY: St. Vladimir's Seminary Press, 1988.

Bestavros, Rev. Gabriel G. *St. Sargius Church.* Old Cairo, Egypt.

Brianchaninov, Bishop Ignatius. *Exposition of the Teaching of the Orthodox Church on the Mother of God.*

Callinicos, Fr. Constantine. *Our Lady the Theotokos.* Trans. and rev. by Rev. George Dimopoulos. Upper Darby, PA: Christian Orthodox Editions, 1987,

Cavarnos, Constantine. "Iconography of the Holy Virgin" in *Byzantine Sacred Art* 2d ed. Belmont, MA: Institute for Byzantine and Modern Greek Studies, 1985): 107, 110.

Cavarnos, Constantine. "Iconographic Decoration of Churches" in *Orthodox Iconography* 2d ed. Belmont, MA: Institute for Byzantine and Modern Greek Studies, 1980): 26-27.

Charitos, Minas. *The Repose of Our Most Holy and Glorious Lady the Theotokos.* Trans. by J. Vlesmas. W. Brookfield, MA: Orthodox Christian Center and Mission.

Corpus Christianorum, Series Latina (CCSL), Turnhout (1953),

Corpus Scriptorum Christianorum Orientalium (CSCO). Louvain, 1903.

Corpus Scriptorum Ecclesiasticorum Latinorum (CSEL). Vienna, 1866.

Cummings, D., trans. "Concerning the Holy and Third Ecumenical Council." *The Rudder (Pedalion).* Chicago: The Orthodox Christian Educational Society, 1957.

de Strycker, E. *La forme la plus ancienne du Protoevangile de Jacques.* Brussels, 1961.

Die griechischen christlichen Sriftsteller der ersten drei Jahrhunderte (GCS). Leipzig-Berlin, 1897.

Dionysius of Fourna. *The Painter's Manual.* Trans. by Paul Hetherington. London: Sagittarius Press, 1974.

Edersheim, Alfred, M.A. Oxon., D.D., Ph.D. *The Life and Times of Jesus the Messiah.* McLean, VA: MacDonald Publishing Co.

Ephesus. Compiled by Naci Keskin and translated by Ertugrul Uckun. Turkey: Keskin Color Ltd. Co. Printing House, n.d.

Eusebius. *Church History.* Vol. I of The Nicene and Post-Nicene Fathers of the Christian Church, First Series. Trans. by Rev. Arthur Cushman McGiffert. Grand Rapids, MI: Wm. B. Eerdmans Pub. Co., 1961.

Eusebius. *The History of the Church.* Trans. by G.A. Williamson. NY: Dorset Press, 1984.

Gower, Ralph. *The New Manners and Customs of Bible Times.* Chicago: Moody Press, 1987.

Grabar, Andre. *Byzantine Painting.* Trans. by Stuart Gilbert. NY: Rizzoli International Publications, Inc., 1979.

Green, Jay P., Sr., ed. and trans. *The Interlinear Hebrew-Aramaic Old Testament.* Vols. 1-III, 2nd ed. Peabody, MA: Hendrickson Pub., 1985.

Habib, Dr. Raouf. *The Holy Family in Egypt.* Cairo, Egypt: Mahabba Bookshop.

Habib, Dr. Raouf. "Mataria and the Virgin Tree." *St. Xenia's Monthly Bulletin* 5, No. 3 (Dec.-Jan., 1987).

Haddad-Nolan, M. *The New Eve.*

Hastings, James, M.A., D.D. *A Dictionary of the Bible.* Vols. 1-4 and Supplement. Peabody: Hendrickson Pub., 1988.

Holy Bible from the Ancient Eastern Text (from the Aramaic of the Peshitta). Translated by George M. Lamsa. NY: Harper & Row, Pub., n.d.

Holy Bible with Apocrypha. King James Version, 1611 A.D. NY: American Bible Society, 1973.

Holy Week-Easter (Megalee Ebdomas Pascha). Compiled by Fr. George L. Papadeas. New York, 1971.

Josephus. "The Antiquities of the Jews"; "The Wars of the Jews". *The Works of Josephus.* William Whiston, A.M., trans. Peabody, MA: Hendrickson Pub., 1988.

601

Kadas, Sotiris, Archaeologist. *Mount Athos.* Trans. by Louise Turner. Athens: Ekdotike Athenon S.A., 1980.

Kalokyris, Constantine D. *Athos, Themes of Archaeology and Art.* Athens: Astir Publishing, Al. & E. Papademetriou, 1963.

Kalokyris, Constantine D. "The Content of Orthodox Iconography: Art of High Theology" in *The Essence of Orthodox Iconography.* Trans. by Peter A. Chamberas. Brookline: Holy Cross School of Theology, 1971.

Kamel, Murad, Prof. *The Flight of the Holy Family to Egypt.* Coptic Egypt. Cairo, Egypt: American University Press, 1968

Kesich, Vaselin and Lydia. *Treasures of the Holy Land.* Crestwood, NY: St. Vladimir's Seminary Press, 1985.

Lambertsen, Isaac E. and Holy Apostles Convent, trans. "The Life of the Apostle Thomas"; "The Life of the Apostle Jude"; The Life of the Apostle Simon the Zealot". *The Lives of the Holy Apostles.* Buena Vista, CO: Holy Apostles Convent Publications, 1988.

Lamsa, George M. *Idioms in the Bible Explained and A Key to the Original Gospel.* San Francisco: Harper & Roe, Pub., 1985.

Liddell, Henry George, and Robert Scott, compilers. *Greek-English Lexicon.* Revised and augmented by Sir Henry Stuart Jones and Roderick McKenzie. Oxford at the Clarendon Press, 1968.

Mantzaridis, Georgios L. *The Deification of Man: St. Gregory Palamas and the Orthodox Tradition.* Trans. by Liadain Sherrard. Crestwood, NY: St. Vladimir's Seminary Press, 1984.

Marianum (MM). Rome, 1974.

Maximovitch, Blessed Archbishop John. *The Orthodox Veneration of the Mother of God.* Trans. by Fr. Seraphim Rose. Platina, CA: St. Herman of Alaska Brotherhood, 1987.

Meinardus, Otto F.A., Dr. *The Holy Family in Egypt.* Cairo, Egypt: The American University In Cairo Press, 1986.

Menaia [in Greek]. Athens, GR: Apostolikes Diakonias, 1974.

Meyendorff, John. *A Study of Gregory Palamas.* Trans. from French by George Lawrence. London: Faith Press, 1964.

Migne, J. ed. *Patrologia Graeca* (PG). 161 vols. Paris, 1844-1866.

Migne, J. ed. *Patrologia Latina* (PL). 221 vols. Paris, 1844-1864.

Nathanael, Archbishop of Vienna and Austria. "The Holy Righteous Abraham, Moses and Elias as Preparers of Man's Salvation." *Orthodox Life* 28, no. 6 (November-December, 1978): 14, 45. Translated by Seraphim F. Englehardt from *Orthodox Observer* (Montreal), No. 27, July, 1959.

O'Carroll, Michael, C.S.Sp., comp. and ed. *Theotokos* 3rd ed. Wilmington, DE: Michael Glazier, Inc., 1988.

Ouspensky, Leonid and Vladimir Lossky. *The Meaning of Icons.* Trans. by G.E.H. Palmer and E. Kadloubovsky. Crestwood: St. Vladimir's Seminary Press, 1983, repr.

Packer, James I., A.M., D. Phil., Merrill C. Tenney, A.M., Ph.D., William White, Jr., Th.M., Ph.D., eds. *The Bible Almanac.* Nashville: Thomas Nelson Publishers, 1980.

Patrologia Orientalia (PO).

Patrologia Syriaca (PS).

Philaret, Metropolitan of Moscow. "Homily on the Feast of the Annunciation." *Orthodox Life* 28, No. 2 (March-April 1978): 9.

Pictorial Bible Dictionary. Merrill C. Tenney, ed. Grand Rapids, MI: Zondervan Publishing House, 1973.

Roberts, Rev. Alexander, D.D., and James Donaldson, LL.D., eds. *Apocrypha of the New Testament: The Protoevangelium of James; The Gospel of Pseudo-Matthew; The Gospel of the Nativity of Mary; The Infancy of the Saviour; The History of Joseph the Carpenter; The Book of John Concerning the Falling Asleep of Mary; The Passing of Mary.* Vol. VIII of The Ante-Nicene Fathers, The Writings of the Fathers down to A.D. 325. Grand Rapids, MI: Wm. B. Eerdmans Pub. Co., 1986.

Robinson, N.F. *Monasticism in the Orthodox Churches.* NY: American Review of Eastern Orthodoxy, 1964.

Saint Ambrose. *Concerning Virginity.* Vol. X in The Nicene and Post-Nicene Fathers of the Christian Church, Second Series. Philip Schaff, D.D., LL.D. and Henry Wace, D.D., eds. Grand Rapids, MI: Wm. B. Eerdmans Pub. Co., 1979.

Saint Ambrose. *Concerning Widows.* Vol. X in The Nicene and Post-Nicene Fathers of the Christian Church, Second Series. Philip Schaff, D.D., LL.D. and Henry Wace, D.D., eds. Grand Rapids, MI: Wm. B. Eerdmans Pub. Co., 1979.

Saint Ambrose. *Funeral Orations; On the Death of Valentinian.* Vol. 22 of The Fathers of the Church. Trans. by Roy J. Deferrari. Washington, D.C.: The Catholic University Press, 1968, repr.

Saint Ambrose. *Hexaemeron*. Vol. 42 of The Fathers of the Church. Trans. by John J. Savage. Washington, D.C.: The Catholic University Press, 1985, repr.

Saint Ambrose. *Letters 1-91*. Vol. 26 of The Fathers of the Church. Trans. by Sister Mary Melchior Beyenka, O.P. Washington, D.C.: The Catholic University Press, 1987, repr.

Saint Ambrose. *Of the Christian Faith*. Vol. X in The Nicene and Post-Nicene Fathers of the Christian Church, Second Series. Philip Schaff, D.D., LL.D. and Henry Wace, D.D., eds. Grand Rapids, MI: Wm. B. Eerdmans Pub. Co., 1979.

Saint Ambrose. *The Holy Spirit, Book I, II, III, Theological and Dogmatic Works*. Vol. 44 of The Fathers of the Church. Trans. by Roy J. Deferrari, Ph.D. Washington, D.C.: The Catholic University Press, 1987, repr.
Saint Ambrose. *The Incarnation, Theological and Dogmatic Works*. Vol. 44 of The Fathers of the Church. Trans. by Roy J. Deferrari, Ph.D. Washington, D.C.: The Catholic University Press, 1987, repr.

Saint Ambrose. *The Mysteries, Theological and Dogmatic Works*. Vol. 44 of The Fathers of the Church. Trans. by Roy J. Deferrari, Ph.D. Washington, D.C.: The Catholic University Press, 1987, repr.

Saint Ambrose. *The Patriarchs, Exegetical Work*. Vol. 65 of The Fathers of the Church. Trans. by Michael P. McHugh. Washington, D.C.: The Catholic University Press, 1985; repr.

Saint Andrew of Crete. *The Great Canon. Trans.* by Holy Trinity Monastery. Jordanville, 1976, 29.

Saint Athanasios. *Letter 59*. Vol. IV of the Nicene and Post-Nicene Fathers, Second Series. Trans. by Philip Schaff, D.D., LLD. and Henry Wace, D.D. Grand Rapids, MI: Wm. B. Eerdmans Pub. Co., 1975; repr.

Saint Athanasios. *Incarnation of the Word*. Vol. IV of the Nicene and Post-Nicene Fathers, Second Series. Trans. by Philip Schaff, D.D., LLD. and Henry Wace, D.D. Grand Rapids, MI: Wm. B. Eerdmans Pub. Co., 1975; repr.

Saint Basil. *Ascetical Works: The Long Rules*. Vol. 9 of The Fathers of the Church. Trans. by Sister M. Monica Wagner, C.S.C. Washington, D.C.: The Catholic University Press, 1970; repr.

Saint Basil. *Ascetical Works: The Morals*. Vol. 9 of The Fathers of the Church. Trans. by Sister M. Monica Wagner, C.S.C. Washington, D.C.: The Catholic University Press, 1970; repr.

Saint Basil. *Exegetic Homily on Psalm 44 (LXX)*. Vol. 46 of The Fathers of the Church. Trans. by Sister Agnes Clare Way. C.D.P. Washington, D.C.: The Catholic University Press, 1981; repr.

Saint Basil. *Prolegomena.* Vol. VIII of the Nicene and Post-Nicene Fathers of the Christian Church, Second Series. Trans. by Philip Schaff, D.D., LLD. and Henry Wace, D.D. Grand Rapids, MI: Wm. B. Eerdmans Pub. Co., 1975; repr.

Saint Clement of Alexandria. *Salvation of the Rich Man.* Vol. II of The Ante-Nicene Fathers, The Writings of the Fathers down to A.D. 325. Trans. by Rev. William Wilson, M.A. Under the editorial supervision of Rev. Alexander Roberts, D.D. and James Donaldson, LL.D. Grand Rapids, MI: Wm. B. Eerdmans Pub. Co., 1986, repr.

Saint Cyril of Alexandria. *Commentary on the Gospel of Saint Luke.* Trans. by R. Payne Smith. NY: Studion Publishers, Inc., 1983.

Saint Cyril of Alexandria. *Letters 1-50.* Vol. 76 of The Fathers of the Church. Trans. by John I. McEnerney. Washington, D.C.: The Catholic University of America Press, 1987.

Saint Cyril of Alexandria. *Letters 51-110.* Vol. 77 of The Fathers of the Church. Trans. by John I. McEnerney. Washington, D.C.: The Catholic University of America Press, 1987.

Saint Cyril of Jerusalem. *Catechesis I-XII, Vol. 1.* Vol. 61 of The Fathers of the Church. Trans. by Leo P. McCauley, S.J. and Anthony A. Stephenson. Washington, D.C.: The Catholic University of America Press, 1969.

Saint Cyril of Jerusalem. *The Catechetical Lectures.* Vol. VII of the Nicene and Post-Nicene Fathers of the Christian Church, Second Series. Trans. by Edwin Hamilton Gifford, D.D. Grand Rapids, MI: Wm. B. Eerdmans Pub. Co., 1974; repr.

Saint Ephraim Syrus. *Homily on Our Lord.* Vol. XIII of the Nicene and Post-Nicene Fathers of the Christian Church, Second Series. Trans. by Rev. Edward A. Johnston, B.D. Grand Rapids, MI: Wm. B. Eerdmans Pub. Co., 1976.

Saint Ephraim Syrus. *Hymns on the Nativity.* Vol. XIII of the Nicene and Post-Nicene Fathers of the Christian Church, Second Series. Trans. by Rev. J.B. Morris, M.A. Grand Rapids, MI: Wm. B. Eerdmans Pub. Co., 1976.

Saint Ephraim the Syrian. *The Harp of the Spirit.* Trans. by Sebastian Brock. England: Fellowship of St. Alban & St. Sergius, 1975.

Saint Germanos, Patriarch of Constantinople. *Sermon on the Annunciation of the Most Holy Theotokos* [in Greek]. PG 98, 320-340.

Saint Gregory of Nyssa. *On Virginity.* Vol. V of the Nicene and Post-Nicene Fathers of the Christian Church, Second Series. Trans by William M.A. Moore and Henry Austin Wilson, M.A. Grand Rapids, MI: Wm. B. Eerdmans Pub. Co.

Saint Gregory of Nyssa. *The Life of Moses.* Trans. by Abraham J. Malherbe and Everett Ferguson. NY: Paulist Press, 1978.

Saint Gregory the Great. *The Book of Pastoral Rule.* Vol. XII of The Nicene and Post-Nicene Fathers of the Christian Church, Second Series. Philip Schaff, D.D., LL.D., Henry Wace, D.D., Rev. James Barmby, D.D., trans. and eds. Grand Rapids, MI: Wm. B. Eerdmans Pub. Co., 1979; repr.

Saint Gregory Palamas. *Homilies of St. Gregory Palamas.* Comp. by S. Oikonomos. Athens, 1861. Note: This rare edition may be found in Migne, *PG* 151.

Saint Gregory Palamas. *Homily 18, On the Sunday of the Myrrh-bearers* [in Greek]. *PG* 151, 236-243C.

Saint Gregory Palamas. *Homily 37, On the August Dormition of Our Most Immaculate Lady Theotokos and Ever-Virgin Mary* [in Greek]. *PG* 151, 460-474.

Saint Gregory Palamas. "Homily on the Dormition of Our Supremely Pure Lady Theotokos and Ever-Virgin Mary." *Orthodox Life* 32, No. 4 (July-August 1982): 3-9.

Saint Hippolytus. *Christ and Antichrist.* Vol. V of The Ante-Nicene Fathers, The Writings of the Fathers down to A.D. 325. (American reprint of Edinburgh ed.). Rev. Alexander Roberts, D.D. and James Donaldson, LL.D., eds. Grand Rapids, MI: Wm. B. Eerdmans Pub. Co., 1986.

Saint Ignatios of Antioch. *Epistle of St. Ignatios to the Ephesians; The Epistles of St. Ignatios to St. John the Apostle; The Epistle of St. Ignatios to the Virgin Mary and the Reply.* Vol. I of The Ante-Nicene Fathers, The Writings of the Fathers down to A.D. 325. Rev. Alexander Roberts, D.D. and James Donaldson, LL.D., eds. Grand Rapids, MI: Wm. B. Eerdmans Pub. Co., 1987.

Saint Irenaeus. *Against Heresies.* Vol. I of the Ante-Nicene Fathers, The Writings of the Fathers down to A.D. 326. Rev. Alexander Roberts, D.D. and James Donaldson, eds. Grand Rapids, MI: Wm. B. Eerdmans Pub. Co., 1987; repr.

Saint Irenaeus. *Proof of the Apostolic Preaching.* Vol. 16 of Ancient Christian Writers. Trans. and annot. by Joseph P. Smith, S.J. NY: Newman Press, n.d.

Saint Jerome. *Against Jovianus, Book I.* Vol. VI of The Nicene and Post-Nicene Fathers of the Christian Church, Second Series. Philip Schaff, D.D., LL.D. and Henry Wace, D.D., eds. (Grand Rapids, MI: Wm. B. Eerdmans Pub. Co., 1983).

Saint Jerome. *Against the Pelagians, Book I.* Vol. VI of The Nicene and Post-Nicene Fathers of the Christian Church, Second Series. Philip Schaff, D.D., LL.D. and Henry Wace, D.D., eds. Grand Rapids, MI: Wm. B. Eerdmans Pub. Co., 1983.

Saint Jerome. *Letters.* Vol. VI of The Nicene and Post-Nicene Fathers of the Christian Church, Second Series. Trans. by the Hon. W.H. Fremantle, M.A., Rev. G. Lewis, M.A., and Rev. W.G. Martley, M.A., with the editorial supervision of Philip Schaff, D.D., LL.D. and Henry Wace, D.D., eds. Grand Rapids, MI: Wm. B. Eerdmans Pub. Co., 1983.

Saint Jerome. *The Perpetual Virginity of Blessed Mary.* Vol. VI of The Nicene and Post-Nicene Fathers of the Christian Church, Second Series. Philip Schaff, D.D., LL.D. and Henry Wace, D.D., eds. Grand Rapids, MI: Wm. B. Eerdmans Pub. Co., 1983.

Saint John Cassian. *The Conferences of John Cassian: First Conference of Abbot Moses.* Vol. XI of The Nicene and Post-Nicene Fathers of the Christian Church, Second Series. Trans. by Edgar C.S. Gibson, M.A., under the editorial supervision of Philip Schaff, D.D., LL.D. and Henry Wace, D.D. Grand Rapids, MI: Wm. B. Eerdmans Pub. Co., 1978, repr.

Saint John Chrysostom. *Homilies on the Epistle of St. Paul the Apostle to the Galatians.* Vol. XIII of The Nicene and Post-Nicene Fathers of the Christian Church, First Series. Philip Schaff, D.D., LL.D., ed. Grand Rapids, MI: Wm. B. Eerdmans Pub. Co., 1976, repr.

Saint John Chrysostom. *Homilies on the Epistle of St. Paul the Apostle to Timothy.* Vol. XIII of The Nicene and Post-Nicene Fathers of the Christian Church, First Series. Philip Schaff, D.D., LL.D., ed. Grand Rapids, MI: Wm. B. Eerdmans Pub. Co., 1976, rep.

Saint John Chrysostom. *Homilies on the Gospel of St. Matthew.* Vol. X of The Nicene and Post-Nicene Fathers of the Christian Church, First Series. Philip Schaff, D.D., LL.D., ed. Grand Rapids, MI: Wm. B. Eerdmans Pub. Co., 1975.

Saint John Chrysostom. *Homilies on the Acts of the Apostles.* Vol. XI of The Nicene and Post-Nicene Fathers of the Christian Church, First Series. Philip Schaff, D.D., LL.D., ed. Grand Rapids, MI: Wm. B. Eerdmans Pub. Co., 1975.

Saint John Chrysostom. *Homilies on the Gospel of St. John.* Vol. XIV of The Nicene and Post-Nicene Fathers of the Christian Church, First Series. Philip Schaff, D.D., LL.D., ed. Grand Rapids, MI: Wm. B. Eerdmans Pub. Co., 1975.

Saint John of Damascus. *Exposition of the Orthodox Faith.* Vol. IX of The Nicene and Post-Nicene Fathers of the Christian Church, Second Series. Trans. by Rev. S.F.D. Dalmond, D.D., F.E.I.S. Grand Rapids, MI: Wm. B. Eerdmans Pub. Co., 1976.

Saint John of Kronstadt. *My Life in Christ.* Trans. by E. E. Goulaeff. Jordanville, NY: Printshop of St. Job of Pochaev, 1984.

Saint John of Kronstadt. *Spiritual Counsels of Father John of Kronstadt.* Select passages from *My Life in Christ*, edited and introduced by W. Jardine Grisbrooke. London: James Clarke & Co. Ltd., 1967.

Saint Justin Martyr. *Dialogue with Trypho.* Vol. 6 of The Fathers of the Church Series. Trans. and ed. by Thomas B. Falls, D.D., Ph.D. Washington, D.C.: Catholic University Press, 1977.

Saint Justin Martyr. *Exhortation to the Greeks.* Vol. 6 of The Fathers of the Church, 3d ed. Trans. by Thomas B. Falls, D.D., Ph.D. Washington, D.C.: The Catholic University of America Press, 1977.

"Saint Joseph the Betrothed." *Orthodox Life* 28, No. 6 (Nov.-Dec., 1978): 2-5. [Translated from *Lives of the Saints* 8, Munich: St. Job of Pochaev Monastery, 1956, 110-113].

Saint Leo the Great. *Sermons.* Vol. XII of The Nicene and Post-Nicene Fathers of the Christian Church, Second Series. Philip Schaff, D.D., LL.D. and Henry Wace, D.D., eds. Grand Rapids, MI: Wm. B. Eerdmans Pub. Co., 1979.

Saint Methodius. *The Symposium, A Treatise on Chastity.* Vol. 27 of Ancient Christian Writers. Trans. and annot. by Herbert Musurillo, S.J.,D. Phil. (Oxon). NY: Paulist Press, 1958.

Saint Paisios the Great. Jordanville, NY: Holy Trinity Monastery, 1983.

Saint Paulinus of Nola. Letters, Vol. 2. Vol. 36 of Ancient Christian Writers. Trans. and annot. by P.G. Walsh. NY: Paulist Press, 1967.

Saint Paulinus of Nola. *Poems.* Vol. 40 of Ancient Christian Writers. Trans. and annot. by P.G. Walsh. NY: Paulist Press, 1975.

Saint Photios. "Homilies III, V, VII and IX." *The Homilies of Photius, Patriarch of Constantinople.* Trans. by Cyril Mango. Cambridge, MA: Harvard University Press, Dumbarton Oaks Studies Three, 1958.

Saint Romanos the Melodist. "On the Nativity (Mary and the Magi)"; "On the Massacre of the Innocents and the Flight into Egypt"; "On the Presentation in the Temple"; "On the Marriage at Cana"; "On Mary at the Cross"; "On the Victory of the Cross"; "Resurrection I, II, VI." *Kontakia of Romanos, Byzantine Melodist.* Vol. I. Trans. and annot. by Marjorie Carpenter. MO: University of Missouri Press, 1970.

Saint Romanos the Melodist. "On the Nativity of the Virgin Mary"; "On the Annunciation I, II." *Kontakia of Romanos, Byzantine Melodist.* Vol. II. Trans. and annot. by Marjorie Carpenter. MO: University of Missouri Press, 1970.

Saint Romanos the Melodist. "The Passion of the Lord and the Lamentations of the Theotokos." *Romanos the Melodist, Kontakia* [in Greek]. Ed. by P.A. Sinopoulos. Athens: Apostolikes Diakonias, 1974: 107-119.

Saint Vincent of Lerins. *Commonitories.* Vol. 7 of The Fathers of the Church. Trans. by Rudolph E. Morris. Washington, D.C.: The Catholic University Press, 1970, repr.

Savas, Savas J. *Hymnology of the Eastern Orthodox Church.* MA: Byzantine Melodies, 1983.

Schonmetzer, S.J. A. *Enchiridion Symbolorum* (ES). Denziger-Bannwart, ed. 33.

Service to the Venerable and God-Bearing Fathers Who Have Shone Forth in Fasting on Mount Athos. Trans. by Isaac E. Lambertsen. Liberty, TN: St. John of Kronstadt Press, 1989.

Shukin, Archpriest Sergei. "On Spiritual Kinship." *St. Xenia's Bi-Monthly Bulletin* 6, No. 1 (August-September 1988): 1-3.

Smolin, Fr. Deacon J. "Henceforth All Generations Shall Call Me Blessed." *The Orthodox Teachings of the Mother of God.* Moundsville, WV: Fr. Demetrios Serfes Publications.

Sources Chretiennes (SC). Lyons.

Sozomen. *The Ecclesiastical History of Sozomen.* Vol. II of The Nicene and Post-Nicene Fathers of the Christian Church, Second Series. Trans. and ed. by Philip Schaff, D.D., LL.D., Henry Wace, D.D., and Chester D. Hartranft. Grand Rapids, MI: Wm. B. Eerdmans Pub. Co., 1983; repr.

Swete, Henry Barclay, D.D., F.B.A. *An Introduction to The Old Testament in Greek.* Rev. by R.R. Ottley, M.A. Peabody, MA: Hendrickson Pub., 1989.

Tenney, Merrill C., and Steven Barabas, eds. *Pictorial Encyclopedia of the Bible.* Vols. 1-5. Grand Rapids: Regency Reference Library & Zondervan Publishing House, 1975.

The Assumption of Our Most Holy Lady, The Mother of God and Ever-Virgin Mary. Translated from the Menology of St. Dimitri of Rostov. Jordanville, NY: Holy Trinity Monastery, 1976.

"The Dormition of Our Most Holy Lady." *The Orthodox Teachings of the Mother of God.* Translated from the Menology of St. Dimitry of Rostov. Moundsville, WV: Fr. Demetrios Serfes Publications.

"The Dormition of the Most Holy Mother of God." *Orthodox Word* 2, No. 3(9), July-August 1966.

The Encyclopedia Americana, 1957 ed., s.v. "Sycamore."

The Extant Works of Saint Symeon the New Theologian, Part I, pp. 60, 102, 145. As seen in: Cavarnos, Constantine Cavarnos. *Byzantine Thought and Art*, 3rd ed. Belmont: The Institute for Byzantine and Modern Greek Studies, Inc., 1980, 99.

The Festal Menaion. Trans. by Mother Mary and Archimandrite Kallistos Ware. London: Faber & Faber, 1969.

"The Genealogy of Christ". *Orthodox Life* 24, no. 6 (Nov-Dec. 1974): 10-14. (Trans. from *The Russian Pilgrim*, 1895, Nos. 51, 51).

The Gospel of Jesus. MIMEP [Pessano] Milano. Vincenza, Italy: Edizioni Istituto S. Gaetano, 1969.

The Great Synaxaristes of the Orthodox Church [in Greek]. Athens: Matthew Langes, publisher.
February (Vol. II, 1978, 5th ed.): Meeting in Temple; Entrance of Virgin;
March (Vol. III, 1979, 5th ed.): Annunciation; Archangel Gabriel;
April (Vol. IV), 1979, 5th ed.): St. Symeon
June (Vol. VI, 1979, 5th ed.): St. Peter the Athonite;
July (Vol. VII, 1977, 5th ed.): St. Anna; St. Nicanor;
August (Vol. VIII, 1977, 5th ed.): Dormition;
September (Vol. IX, 1978, 5th ed.): Prophet Zacharias; Nativity of the Virgin; SS Joachim & Anna;
October (Vol. X, 1978, 5th ed.): St. Hierotheos;
November (Vol. XI, 1979, 5th ed.): Entrance;
December (Vol. XII, 1974, 5th ed.): Nativity of Christ; Synaxis; Sunday After Nativity;
Triodion (Vol. XIII, 1977, 4th ed.): Saturday of Lazarus; Great Friday;
Pentecostarion (Vol. XIV, 1979, 5th ed.): Pascha; Ascension.

The Lamentations of Matins of Holy and Great Saturday. Trans. by Holy Transfiguration Monastery. Boston, 1981.

The Lenten Triodion. Trans. by Mother Mary and Archimandrite Kallistos Ware. London: Faber & Faber, 1977.

The Lenten Triodion, Supplementary Texts. Trans. by Mother Mary and Archimandrite Kallistos Ware. Bussy-en-Othe, FR: Orthodox Monastery of the Veil of Our Lady, 1979.

"The Life of Saint Andrew, Fool for Christ of Constantinople." *Orthodox Word* 15, No. 3(86) (May-June, 1979): 128-129.

The Life of St. Nina. Jordanville, NY: Holy Trinity Monastery, 1977.

The Lives of the Saints of the Holy Land and the Sinai Desert. Trans. by Holy Apostles Convent and L. Papadopoulos. Buena Vista, CO: Holy Apostles Convent Publications, 1988.

Theotokarion of St. Nikodemos [in Greek]. Volos, GR: Sot. Schoina, 1979.

610

"The Presentation of the Most Holy Theotokos in the Temple." *Orthodox Life*, no. 5 (Sept-Oct. 1971): 22.

The Septuagint with Apocrypha. London: Samuel Bagster & Sons, Ltd.

"The Tale of the Five Prayers" cited in the *Prayer Book.* Jordanville, NY: Holy Trinity Monastery, 1960, 359-361.

The Wisdom of the Saints. Jill Haak Adels, compiler. NY: Oxford University Press, 1987.

Thompson, J.A. *Handbook of Life in Bible Times.* Downers Grove, IL: Inter-Varsity Press, 1986.

Toal, M.D., D.D. *The Sunday Sermons of the Great Fathers.* 3rd ed. Vols. I, IV. Chicago: Henry Regnery Co., 1964.

Underwood, Paul A. *The Kariye Djami, Vol. 1, Historical Introduction and Description of the Mosaics and Frescoes.* Bollingen Series LXX. NY: Pantheon Books, 1966.

Velimirovic, Bishop Nikolai. *The Prologue from Ochrid.* Parts 1-4. Trans. by Mother Maria. Birmingham: Lazarica Press, 1986.

Wigram, George V. *The New Englishman's Hebrew Concordance.* Jay P. Green, Sr., ed. Peabody, MA: Hendrickson Pub., 1984.

Xanthopoulos, Nicephoros Kallistos. *The Life of St. Mary Magdalene* [in Greek]. Mother Magdalene, ed. Athens (Kozanes): Holy Convent of the Ascension, 1974.

Publications
By The Same Publishers

+ + +

Our Hardbound Series:

Vol. 1: The Lives of the Three Hierarchs
Saint Basil the Great,
Saint Gregory the Theologian,
and Saint John Chrysostom

Vol. 2: The Lives of the Holy Apostles
Saints Peter, Paul, Andrew
James the son of Zebedee,
John the Theologian, Philip
Bartholomew, Thomas, Matthew,
James the son of Alphæus,
Jude, Simon the Zealot,
Matthias, Mark, Luke and
James, the brother of the Lord

Vol. 3: The Lives of the Saints of the Holy Land and the Sinai Desert
A collection of over one hundred lives
of holy hierarchs, martyrs, confessors,
ascetics and hymnographers.

Vol. 4: The Life of the Virgin Mary, the Theotokos

The most complete text on the life of the
Theotokos from her Conception to her Dormition
and bodily translation, including her role
in the Church, treated within the framework
of Sacred Scriptures, Holy Tradition,
Patristics and other ancient writings,
together with the Liturgical and Iconographic
Traditions of the Holy Orthodox Church.

Vol. 5: The Lives of the Pillars of Orthodoxy

The lives, struggles, works and miracles of
Saint Photios, Patriarch of Constantinople,
Saint Gregory Palamas, Archbishop of Thessalonica
and Saint Mark Evgenikos, Metropolitan of Ephesus.
Includes chapters on the history of the
Filioque, Causes for Anti-Union Feelings
Among the Byzantines,
Events Leading to the Schism of 1054,
the Fall of Constantinople in 1453,
and Brief Orthodox Replies to the
Innovations of the Papacy.

+ + +

Our Pamphlet Series:

No. 1: The Monastery Builders

The lives and struggles of
Saint Dionysios of Mt. Olympus,
Saint Nicanor of Mt. Callistratos
and St. Paul of Mt. Latros.

Nos. 2 and 3: Spiritual Mothers

The lives and struggles of women monastics.

The universal glory born of men,
who hath given birth unto the Master,
the heavenly gate, let us praise--
Mary the Virgin,
the song of the bodiless hosts
and the adornment of the faithful.
For she was shown to be a heaven
and a temple of the Godhead.
She broke down the dividing-wall of enmity,
ushered in peace, and opened the Kingdom.
Possessing, therefore, this anchor of faith,
we have as champion the Lord Who was born of her.
Take courage, therefore, take courage,
O ye people of God;
for He shall fight thine enemies,
since He is the Almighty One.
[Dogmatic Theotokion of the *Octoechos*, Tone One].

Great is the Name of the Holy Trinity!
Glory to our Triune God!

615